THE PAPERS OF

WOODROW WILSON

VOLUME 6

1888-1890

SPONSORED BY THE WOODROW WILSON
FOUNDATION
AND PRINCETON UNIVERSITY

THE PAPERS OF
WOODROW WILSON

ARTHUR S. LINK, *EDITOR*

JOHN WELLS DAVIDSON AND DAVID W. HIRST

ASSOCIATE EDITORS

JOHN E. LITTLE, *ASSISTANT EDITOR*

JEAN MACLACHLAN, *CONTRIBUTING EDITOR*

M. HALSEY THOMAS, *CONSULTING EDITOR*

Volume 6 · 1888-1890

PRINCETON, NEW JERSEY

PRINCETON UNIVERSITY PRESS

1969

L.C. Card 66-10880

Printed in the United States of America
by Princeton University Press
Princeton, New Jersey

INTRODUCTION

This sixth volume of *The Papers of Woodrow Wilson* might well be called the "Wesleyan volume," since it covers the two years, 1888-90, of Wilson's professorship at Wesleyan University.

That this was a happy interlude between the difficult years at Bryn Mawr and Wilson's tenure as a professor at Princeton is abundantly revealed by the documents printed herein. The Wilsons were taken at once into the hearts of the people of Middletown, Connecticut, and they in turn reciprocated the friendship extended to them by this New England community.

At Bryn Mawr College, Wilson had been "hungry for a class of *men*." The documents in this volume show how that hunger was satisfied at Wesleyan and give ample evidence of Wilson's development as a teacher of history, political science, and economics, as well as of his participation in extracurricular life and athletics at Wesleyan.

This was the time when Wilson came to himself—to use one of his well-known phrases—as a teacher, scholar, and lecturer. Suppressing yearnings for a political career, he accepted the role that Fate seemed to have predestined for him. With something like relentless determination, he completed his first major scholarly book, *The State*, and began his first important historical work, *Division and Reunion*. He compiled a massive working bibliography of the subjects of his primary interest. It is printed in this volume for the first time. He not only continued to lecture annually on administration at the Johns Hopkins but also, as evidenced by his lecture notes printed herein, came to a new understanding and definition of the field. Increasing success and acclaim as a teacher and scholar led in 1890 to the fulfillment of Wilson's old dream—a call to a professorship at his *alma mater*, Princeton.

Beginning during this period what was to be a long and successful career as a popular lecturer, Wilson found a substitute for politics in playing the role of an interpreter of his age. All the while, old friendships were ripening and important new ones—with Frederick Jackson Turner and Albert Bushnell Hart, for example—were germinating. Finally, as the letters also disclose vividly, Wilson's relationship with Ellen Axson Wilson was maturing and deepening.

There have been no significant editorial innovations in this volume. The Editors have continued their practice of printing texts *verbatim et literatim*, including misspellings, repairing words and phrases in brackets only when necessary for clarity. However, in reproducing typed *copies* of letters—for example, Wilson's letters to Albert Shaw and Albert Bushnell Hart—they have silently corrected what seemed to be obvious errors made by the typist who copied them.

The Editors continue to be indebted to librarians and archivists across the country for generous assistance. They are under particularly heavy obligation to John W. Spaeth, Jr., Dean of the Faculty *Emeritus* and Archivist of Wesleyan University, and his assistant, Grace W. Bacon, Reference Librarian, *Emerita*, of the Olin Library at Wesleyan. They not only cheerfully answered numerous questions but also furnished the Editors with voluminous contemporary documents relating to Wilson's career at Wesleyan and ransacked files and attics for letters and photographs of the period. Acknowledgment is due the Librarian of the Huntington Library, San Marino, California, for permission to reproduce letters from Frederick Jackson Turner, as well as to the Librarian of Yale University for permission to print a portion of a letter from Charles McLean Andrews to Elizabeth Williams Andrews.

The Editors are grateful to T. H. Vail Motter, former Consulting Editor, for preparing a draft of the Editorial Note, " 'Leaders of Men,' " and to Mrs. Bryant Putney of Princeton University Press for copyediting and other assistance. Miss Marjorie Sirlouis and Colonel James B. Rothnie, U.S.A., Ret., have continued expertly to decipher Wilson's shorthand. Finally, the Editors here express their wishes for success in his teaching career to the former Assistant Editor, William M. Leary, Jr., and extend a warm welcome to the new Consulting Editor, M. Halsey Thomas.

THE EDITORS

Princeton, New Jersey
October 16, 1968

CONTENTS

ILLUSTRATIONS

Following page 360

ABBREVIATIONS

ALI	autograph letter initialed
ALS	autograph letter(s) signed
API	autograph postal initialed
APS	autograph postal signed
EAW	Ellen Axson Wilson
EAWhw	Ellen Axson Wilson handwriting or handwritten
enc(s).	enclosed, enclosure(s)
env.	envelope
hw	handwriting or handwritten
JRW	Joseph Ruggles Wilson
L	letter
sh	shorthand
TCL	typed copy of letter
tel.	telegram
TL	typed letter
TLS	typed letter signed
WW	Woodrow Wilson
WWhw	Woodrow Wilson handwriting or handwritten
WWsh	Woodrow Wilson shorthand
WWT	Woodrow Wilson typed

ABBREVIATIONS FOR COLLECTIONS AND LIBRARIES

Following the National Union Catalogue of the Library of Congress

CSmH	Henry E. Huntington Library
CtW	Wesleyan University Library
CtY	Yale University Library
DLC	Library of Congress
MdBJ	The Johns Hopkins University Library
NjP	Princeton University Library
NNC	Columbia University Library
RSB Coll., DLC	Ray Stannard Baker Collection of Wilsoniana, Library of Congress
ViU	University of Virginia Library
WC, NjP	Woodrow Wilson Collection, Princeton University Library
WP, DLC	Woodrow Wilson Papers, Library of Congress

SYMBOLS

[– – – –]	undecipherable words in text, each dash representing one word
[Sept. 8, 1889]	publication date of a published writing; also date of document when date is not part of text
[*Sept. 8, 1889*]	latest composition date of a published writing

THE PAPERS OF

WOODROW WILSON

VOLUME 6

1888-1890

THE PAPERS OF
WOODROW WILSON

To the Secretary of the New-York Historical Society

Dear Sir, Grand Union Hotel, New York. 3rd Sept. 1888

I write to ask if permission to see the collections of the Historical Library can be accorded me and my party (of three). Lately Prof. of History and Political Science at Bryn Mawr College, as you may know, I am now Prof. of His'ty and Political Economy in Wesleyan Univ., Middletown, Conn. Cards of introduction to the officers of the Library would be highly appreciated.

Very truly Yours, Woodrow Wilson

ALS (NHi).

From Samuel Rea[1]

My dear Sir: Bryn Mawr, Pa. September—12th 1888

Your letter of Aug. 29 enclosing check for your pew rent in Bryn Mawr Pres. Church duly rec'd—and I herewith return you receipt.

I note what you say about your pew and have declared the same vacant.

Thanking you for your note and regretting your departure,

I am Very truly Saml. Rea Treas.

ALS (WP, DLC). Enc.: receipt dated Sept. 8, 1888, for pew rent of $12 in Bryn Mawr Presbyterian Church from July 1 to Oct. 1, 1888.

1 At this time assistant to the second vice president of the Pennsylvania Railroad.

EDITORIAL NOTE

WILSON'S TEACHING AT WESLEYAN AND THE JOHNS HOPKINS, 1888-89

The document "Wilson's Copy for the Wesleyan University Catalogue," printed at December 1, 1888, is Wilson's own full description of his courses at Wesleyan University during the academic year 1888-89.

Wilson gave sixty-one lectures in the year course that he called "Histories of England and France." The description of his main body of notes for this course, which follows this Editorial Note, reveals that it was in fact a course in the history of western Europe since the fall of Rome. The notes just referred to are in part transcripts, often in expanded and more sophisticated form, of the shorthand notes for Wilson's courses at Bryn Mawr College in the histories of France and of the Renaissance and Reformation.[1] However, Wilson prepared notes for many new lectures on English history for his course at Wesleyan, and he also probably used some of the shorthand notes for his Bryn Mawr course in English history[2] for the last lectures in his Wesleyan course.

The mid-year examination in the English-French history course at Wesleyan, printed at February 16, 1889, gives a good indication of the subjects that Wilson had emphasized to that point, while the reading list printed at February 7, 1889, shows what he required his students to read while he was lecturing at the Johns Hopkins during the following six weeks.

For the few lectures that he gave in his first-semester course in political economy, Wilson used the notes for his Bryn Mawr political economy course covering the history of economic thought through Adam Smith.[3] The final examination printed at February 7, 1889, gives a good view of the subjects that Wilson covered in his course at Wesleyan.

It seems fairly certain that Wilson did not prepare new notes for his senior course at Wesleyan in the history of institutions. At least, no such notes have survived. A news item in the campus periodical reported that he was using various chapters in his forthcoming *The State* as the basis of his lectures in this course.[4] Moreover, it is probable that Wilson also used some of the shorthand notes for his Bryn Mawr undergraduate course in politics[5] for the Wesleyan course in institutions. As the reading list printed at February 7, 1889, and the examination printed at April 2, 1889, reveal, Wilson had his seniors read Bryce's *American Commonwealth* during his stay in Baltimore.

No lecture notes for Wilson's second-semester junior course entitled "Constitution of the United States" have survived, and it is a reasonable assumption that he never prepared any. This course, like the one in political economy, relied heavily upon a textbook, and lectures were, as Wilson put it in the description printed at December 1, 1888, supplementary to classroom recitation and drill. For his lectures, he probably used parts of *The State* or some of the notes for his Bryn Mawr course on politics. The reading list printed at February 7, 1889, and the examination printed at April 2, 1889, reveal that Wilson had his juniors read the *Federalist Papers* and *Congressional Government* while he was in Baltimore.

Wilson began his second series of twenty-five lectures on administration at The Johns Hopkins University on February 11 and completed the series on March 23, 1889. He had laid out a plan for a three-year cycle in the lecture inaugurating the first series on about Feb-

[1] Described at Feb. 1, 1887, Vol. 5.

[2] Described at Oct. 4, 1886, Vol. 5.

[3] See the body of notes described at Oct. 3, 1887, Vol. 5, with Wilson's notations about using them in 1889 and subsequent years.

[4] Middletown, Conn., *Wesleyan Argus*, XXII (Oct. 12, 1888), 17.

[5] These notes are described at Oct. 3, 1887, Vol. 5.

ruary 17, 1888.[6] Having concentrated on central government in his first series,[7] Wilson focused on local government in his lectures at the Hopkins in 1889. His report printed at June 27, 1889, is a brief review of these lectures. His letters to Ellen Axson Wilson—for example, those of February 11, 13, 15, 18, and 28 and of March 1, 9, 14, and 20, 1889—give a more elaborate and intimate picture of Wilson at work at his desk and in the classroom. During these six weeks, he was preparing the notes for his lectures and, at the same time, drafting the outlines of the sections on local government for *The State*. Notes for only three of these lectures have survived. Two sets of notes on local government in pre-revolutionary France are printed at February 13 and 14, 1889. The other set, not printed, is a two-page handwritten manuscript entitled "Lect. XVIII/*Local Government in the U.S.* 3/14/89," Wilson Papers, Library of Congress.

[6] See the announcement printed at this date in Vol. 5.

[7] See the Editorial Note, "Wilson's Teaching at Bryn Mawr and the Johns Hopkins, 1887-88," Vol. 5.

Lecture Notes for a Course in English-French History

[c. Sept. 13, 1888–c. June 1, 1889]

Contents:

(a) A WWhw incomplete list of lecture topics.

(b) A WWhw and WWT complete list of sixty-one lecture topics.

(c) WWhw and WWT notes with the following titles or subtitles: *"Geography &c. of the British Empire"*; *"Geography, Races, etc.* [*of France*]"; *"Course of English History: Roman Occupation of Britain"*; *"Course of French History: Roman Dominion in Gaul"*; *"The Saxon Conquest of Britain"*; *"The Roman Empire and the Barbarian Invasions"*; *"The Frankish Supremacy"*; *"The Northmen in Europe"*; *"The Norman Conquest"*; *"Feudalization and the Capets"*; *"The English in France"*; *"Henry II"*; *"Influence of the Crusades"*; *"Louis IX (1226-1270)"*; *"Edward I: the Parliament"*; *"The States-General (1302-1614)"*; *"The Hundred Years War (1)"*; *"Hundred Years War (2)"*; *"Hundred Years War (3)"*; *"Wars of the Roses (1455-1485)"*; *"Louis XI"*; *"Charles VIII (1483-1498)"*; *"Renaissance*[:] *Beforehand: The Europe of 1453"*; *"The Political Preparation of Italy"*; *"Renaissance: Machiavelli (1469-1527)"*; *"Renaissance: The Intellectual Preparation of Italy"*; *"Renaissance: The Revival of Learning"*; *"Renaissance: Dante, Petrarch, Boccaccio"*; *"Renaissance: Lorenzo de Medici, Poliziano"*; *"Renaissance: Ariosto; Tasso"*; *"Renaissance: Painting and Sculpture: Giotto"*; *"Renaissance: Lionardo da Vinci; Michael Angelo"*; *"Portugal and Spain,—Discovery"*; *"Renaissance—Reformation"*; *"Luther, Zwingli, Calvin"*; *"The English Reformation: Colet, Erasmus, Thos. Cromwell"*; *"The Huguenot Wars (1562-1610)"*; *"French Foreign Policy, 1498-1559"*; *"The Thirty Years' War. 1618-1648"*; *"Résumé: Renaissance—Reformation"*; *"The Tudors:—The Age of Elizabeth"*; *"Richelieu—Louis XIV"*; *"The First Stuarts: James I., 1603-1625*[;] *Charles I., 1625-1649"*; *"The Civil Wars and The Commonwealth. (1642-1649*[;] *1649-1660"*; *"Restoration and Revolution.*

1660[-]1688"; "Louis XV and Louis XVI. 1715-1774; 1774- 1792"; "Causes of the French Revolution"; "The French Revolution"; "Napoleon and the Napoleonic Constitution"; "From Napoleon I to Napoleon III."

Item (b) above shows that Wilson's final lectures were on Ireland, the peerage, the Church of England, British foreign relations, parliamentary reform, British home government, and British colonial government.

Loose pages (WP, DLC).

Marginal Notes[1]

Thomas M. Cooley, *General Principles of Constitutional Law in the United States of America* (Boston, 1880).

Transcripts of WW Shorthand Comments
[c. Sept. 13, 1888]

P. 23:

In America the leading principle of constitutional liberty has from the first been, that the sovereignty reposed in the people; and as the people could not in their collective capacity exercise the powers of government, a written constitution was by general consent agreed upon in each of the States. These constitutions create departments for the exercise of sovereign powers; prescribe the extent of the exercise, and the methods, and in some particulars forbid that certain powers which would be within the compass of sovereignty shall be exercised at all.

? Is this the reason "rationalists therefore misunderstood"

P. 24:

A law is sometimes said to be unconstitutional, by which is meant that it is opposed to the principles or rules of the constitution of the state. . . . According to the theory of British constitutional law the Parliament possesses and wields supreme power, and if therefore its enactments *conflict with the Constitution*, they are nevertheless valid, and must operate as modifications or amendments of it. [WW's italics]

They cannot conflict with the Constitution of what!

P. 98:

Every legislative body is to make laws for the public good, and *not for the benefit of individuals*; and it is to make them aided by the light of those general principles which lie at the foundation

Could this restriction be made effective?

of representative institutions. Here, however, we touch the *province of legislative discretion.* What is for the public good, and what is required by the principles underlying representative government, the legislature must decide under the responsibility of its members to their constituents. [All italics WW's]

P. 207:

Blasphemy, &c.—But the courts of the Union and of the States, *in administering the common law* [WW's italics], find it necessary to take notice that the prevailing religion of the country is Christian, and that because of that fact certain conduct may constitute a breach of public decorum, and therefore be illegal, though it might not be where a different religion prevailed. The law of blasphemy depends largely for its definition and application upon the generally accepted religious belief of the people; and in the law of contracts many provisions might be found to be illegal in a Christian country which would be enforced where the Mohammedan or some other form of religion prevailed.

The federal courts of course administer the common law only in state cases; not in federal cases.

P. 219:

Enforcement Laws.—The same amendment [the Thirteenth] also provides that "Congress shall have power to enforce this article by appropriate legislation." Whether this provision has any importance must depend upon whether the prohibitory clause itself falls short of furnishing a complete and sufficient protection. A constitutional provision is sometimes, of itself, a complete law for the accomplishment of the purpose for which it was established, and sometimes it merely declares a principle which will be dormant until legislation is had to give it effect. When the former is the case, the provision is sometimes spoken of as self-executing.

The enforcement be directed to meet the efforts of the states to infringe the principle, not to carry out the principles directly. Civil rights cases, 109 U. S., 3.

Francis A. Walker, *Political Economy* (2nd edn., New York, 1887).

P. 1:

Political Economy has to do with no other subject, whatsoever, than wealth. Especially should the student of economics take care not to allow any purely political, ethical or social considerations to influence him in his investigations. All that he has, as an economist, to do is to find out how wealth *is* produced, exchanged, distributed and consumed. It will remain for the social philosopher, the moralist, or the statesman, to decide how far the pursuit of wealth, according to the laws discovered by the economist, *should* be subordinated to other, let us say, higher, considerations. The more strictly the several branches of inquiry are kept apart, the better it will be for each and for all. [WW's italics]

Except in so far as they influence others in the pursuit of wealth.

The economist may also be a social philosopher, a moralist, or a statesman, just as the mathematician may also be a chemist or a mechanician; but not, on that account, should the several subjects be confounded.

No not confounded, but made to give much light.

P. 19:

Before proceeding to inquire whether Political Economy should be dealt with as a science or as an art, it seems desirable strongly to emphasize the distinction between a science and an art. This is the more needed because of the strangely persistent habit of economic writers in confusing these two things, which should be kept clearly distinct.

A science, whether the science of mathematics, or physics, or mechanics, or chemistry, or geology, or physiology, or economics, deals only with the relations of cause and effect within its own field. It *assumes nothing to be a good and nothing to be an evil.* It does not start with the notion that something is desirable or undesirable; nor does it arrive at any such conclusion as its result. It has no business to offer precepts or prescriptions. Its sole single concern is to trace effects back to their causes; to project causes forward to their effects.

Laveleye's definition of political economy: "The science which determines what laws men ought to adopt in order that they may, with the least possible exertion, procure the greatest abundance of the things useful for the satisfaction of their wants; may distribute them most justly, and consume them rationally" ["]Les Éléments de l'Économie Politique," trans. by A. W. Pollard. (Am. ed.) p. 3.

Has character nothing to do with economic activity?

P. 429:

In contradiction, then, of Mr. George's proposition that the entire effect of an increase of production is expended in raising rents, neither wages nor the interest of capital deriving any gain whatsoever therefrom, rent indeed absorbing the entire gain, "and more than the gain," we have seen,—. . . .

2. That, in fact, in those forms of

production which especially characterize modern society[2] the rate of enhancement of the demand for labor tends to far exceed the rate of enhancement of the demand for land.

and which are most affected by inventions and improvements

[1] The reader is reminded that, unless otherwise noted, all books from which marginal notes are printed are in the Wilson Library, DLC.

[2] Wilson placed a caret here, indicating that his marginal comment should be inserted at this point.

From Robert Bridges

Dear Classmate: New York, Sept. 20, 1888.

Your committee are glad to report that the Class Memorial is progressing finely, and promises to be all that we expected.[1] St. Gaudens has been at work on it since August 1, and has had a number of sittings from Dr. McCosh. We paid him $2000. on the signing of the contract, and must now make monthly payments of $800. cash. We should, therefore, be glad to receive all or part of your subscription as soon as possible, in order that we may meet the obligation. Please draw checks to the order of C. C. Cuyler, Treasurer '79, and enclose to my address in order that I may keep my share of the account square.

You will be glad to know that the class have subscribed generously, and we feel sure of their financial support.

Faithfully yours, Robert Bridges

Prof. Woodrow Wilson, $25. subscribed.

Dear Tommy: I called twice for you at the Grand Union and missed you both times. RB

TLS with hw postscript (WP, DLC).

[1] See R. Bridges to WW, March 12, 1888, Vol. 5.

From John Franklin Jameson

My dear Wilson: Providence, R. I., Sept. 21, 1888.

Count me among the number of those who welcome you to New England, though I am in one sense myself a newcomer. As I remember Middletown, you are in very attractive surroundings physically speaking; I hope the mental environment may prove equally favorable.

I wrote to you at Bryn Mawr in July or early in August,[1] but don't know whether you received it; but I had no other address.

I wrote to ask what the prospects were as to your contribution to our volume; but still more to speak of a plan for a composite course of public lectures here. I don't know yet whether the plan can be carried out, and among other things whether I can get money enough to pay lecturers moderately. But if I can, I think of utilizing the studies men have been making for the proposed volume, and having, in some sort of centennial commemoration, this winter, a course of lectures on the formation of the Constitution and its installation. Most of the men are in New England. An intelligent audience and adequate hall can be assured.

If the project should be resolved on, can I count on you for one lecture? Though it is proposed that the men shall lecture on the topics which they handle in the volume, as being easiest for them to work up into a public lecture, yet if you can't write up "Chisholm v. Georgia and the Eleventh Amendment" for the volume, or if you have some appropriate subject worked up or lecture already written which you can more easily use, I should be glad under any circumstances to have you take a part in the proposed course. I am, I ought to add, not sanguine as to its being carried out.

With the best wishes for your happiness and success at Middletown, I am, Very truly yours, J. F. Jameson.

ALS (WP, DLC) with WWhw figures and notation on env.: "Ans. 28/Sept/88."
[1] J. F. Jameson to WW, Aug. 4, 1888, Vol. 5.

To John Franklin Jameson

Middletown, Conn.,
My dear Jameson, 106 High Street, 28th Sept., '88.

Assuredly the fates are against me! I have been delaying my answer to your two last letters, not only because moving and all its legion attendant cares of packing, preparing, unpacking, settling have robbed me both of all leisure and of all opportunity to write, but also out of sheer reluctance to tell the truth and say 'I can't write the essay, and I can't lecture in Providence—though I would give my head to be able to.' And yet such is the stern truth. Just look at the case: a topic exactly suited to my tastes and my training, to be written up for a volume I should esteem it a genuine honor and privilege to be allowed to contribute to—and the editor a fellow whose friendship I value as highly as I esteem his scholarship: and yet I'm absolutely barred! It's confoundedly hard luck—that's the whole of it. It's the single unfortunate feature of my move to Middletown—by which, otherwise, I am greatly profiting. If I had had the amount and the quietness of vacation I anticipated this summer, and had *not* had a new field and new lectures this term, I *might* have managed the work for you. But now there's absolutely no hope of its being done. My summer is gone, and my whole energy is absorbed by my new courses here—and the sooner I make acknowledgment of the facts the better for my peace of mind and conscience.

But I can, and do most heartily, congratulate you on having a congenial chair all to yourself. I feel sure that you must be enjoying yourself where you are: I'm sure, at any rate, that I hope so. As for myself, I am enjoying my work with *male* classes, hard as it is, with much zest, and shall, I believe, be not a little benefited by it.

We must certainly try to see something of each other: you are the bachelor,∴, the more movable party—*do* come over and see me and get as hearty a welcome as ever you got. If I had any lecture that would do, I would deliver it for you, pay or no pay.

As ever, Your sincere friend, Woodrow Wilson.

ALS (J. F. Jameson Papers, DLC).

From Thomas Alexander Hoyt

My Dear Woodrow— Phila Oct. 12"[2], 1888

Your favor of yesterday is this moment recd. It is a pleasure to hear from you, although it would have been enhanced by a fuller account of Ellie & the children: I hope she will soon supply your "lack of service" in this respect.

Mr. Wanamaker has unfortunately become involved in Politics: he is straining every nerve for the election of Harrison: he has no time now for academic plans: we must wait until after the election: I hope Mr. W— will be so badly defeated politically, that, like Cicero, he will turn to literature for consolation, & that if he cannot write books that he will "endow" those who can. . . .

I will see Mr W—& arrange for your visit, as soon as possible. It will be very pleasant to have you with us.

With love to all, Sincerely yours, T. A. H.

ALI (WP, DLC). Postmarked Oct. 2, 1888.

From John Franklin Jameson

My dear Wilson: Providence, Oct. 6, 1888.

If so it must be, so it must; but I am mighty sorry. If an extension of time would do you any good, please say so; for if the other essays are in my hands on January 1st, I can wait a month for a single one, I think.

Few things would give me greater pleasure than to come over and see you. I hope to bring this about, by and by, if trains will serve. Meantime, I'm glad you are finding your work so pleasant.

As I feared, the lecture scheme is not likely to be carried out. With sincere regards, Very truly yours, J. F. Jameson.

ALS (WP, DLC).

From Robert Bridges

Dear Tommy: New York Oct 8 1888

Can you tell me where I can find the tax-rate of the principal cities of Europe? I can't put my hands on it.

I had a short talk with Sam Alexander[1] at the Club the other day about *Patton's* idea for a chair of "Political Science." Sam said that he believed it would be forthcoming, and I immediately pointed out to him the man for the place. He thoroughly agreed with me. When you next come to New York he wants to have his brother Archie (who is one of the chief men in the Columbia Coll. School of Pol. Sci)[2] meet you and will have a little dinner at the Club for the purpose. Sam says that the Columbia School is going to be one of the best in the country, and you could possibly have two very musical strings to your bow.

Of course Sam may forget all about this (he generally does), but he is certainly very much in earnest now, and will put a bee in the ear of Henry M.[3]

Faithfully Yours Robert Bridges

ALS (WP, DLC) with WWhw notation on env.: "Ans. Oct. 9/88."

[1] Identified in Volume 5 as a classmate of Wilson's and Bridges', Alexander was at this time a surgeon and professor at the Bellevue Medical College in New York.

[2] Archibald Alexander, Professor of Philosophy, Ethics, and Psychology at Columbia.

[3] Henry Martyn Alexander, New York lawyer, trustee of the College of New Jersey and Princeton University, 1863-99, and father of Samuel and Archibald.

To Robert Bridges

My dear Bobby, Middletown, Conn., 9th Oct., 1888

My own library and the library of the college are both so scant that I cannot say with assurance where any one item of information could be found; but I should expect to find the tax-rates of the principal European cities in each of the following books:

Whittaker's Almanac

Mulhall's Dictionary of Statistics.

Almanach de Gotha

"Statistique Internationale des Villes" (pub. by Guillaumin, & Cie., Paris) The last-named, which must, of course, be accessible in New York, must, I should say, certainly contain what you want. The only drawback is, that it is eleven years old (1877). I wish I could myself supply the tables you wish.

I hope that you have been able to imagine the explanation of my sudden disappearance from N.Y. and my subsequent silence. We ran away from the city, on a sudden resolution, because we found hotel rooms,[1] to which they had, for a great part of the day to be confined, sadly disagreeing with our little Margaret, who was in the last stages of teething. It was a sore disappointment to me to have to leave without seeing you again. Somehow, at that single interview I had not been able to *speak* any of the sympathy I feel for you in your bereavement, though my mind and heart were full of it. I seemed unable to talk about anything not indifferent!

Since coming here, as you may readily imagine, I have been head over ears in house-fixing and lecture-writing. I can hardly count myself my own yet, so constant are the demands upon my time of my new work. But I am coming out of the woods I trust.

So soon as I get out I shall go down to Phila. (for an interview with Mr. Wanamaker) and on my way back I will try to take time to stop over in N.Y.—if only for a few hours.

You certainly know how to lay trains of influence for your friends, my dear fellow: I shall have to work hard to be worthy of all the help you give me so generously. I will certainly try to see Sam. soon and jog his memory. The Columbia *school* I know a good deal about—when their rents are renewed a year or two hence[2] they'll have more money than anybody else in the country for expansion. The idea of a connexion with them is very attractive to a fellow who is on the lookout for institutions which can afford to indulge in specialists.

I shall hope to send my subscription to the Memorial very soon.

With warmest regards from Mrs. W., as ever

Yours affectionately, Woodrow Wilson

ALS (WC, NjP).

[1] At the Grand Union Hotel.

[2] On the leaseholds in the tract of approximately twenty acres known as the Botanic Garden when it was given to Columbia College by the New York legislature in 1814. The tract was developed as a residential area by Columbia in the 1850's and is now the site of Rockefeller Center.

From Joseph Ruggles Wilson

My precious son: Clarksville, Oct. 10, '88.

For the past two or three weeks my mind has been in something of a ferment. Friends in Georgia wrote—one after another—asking if I would consent to have my name come before the Board of Trustees to be voted for the office of Chancellor. I replied that I must by no means be regarded as seeking the position, but thought I could see my way clear to accept if cordially offered to me. I enclose a full account of the proceedings which have just come to hand, in which you will see that my chances were small indeed. But to be defeated by *Boggs*(!)[1] does begruntle me I confess. Perhaps it is a happy escape from a most burdensome charge. Love from us both to you all,

Your affectionate Father

ALS (WP, DLC). Encs.: undated clippings from the Atlanta *Constitution* relating to the election of a Chancellor of the University of Georgia.

[1] The Rev. Dr. William Ellison Boggs, pastor of the Second Presbyterian Church of Memphis, formerly professor at the Columbia Theological Seminary, who served as Chancellor of the University of Georgia from 1889 to 1899.

Two News Items

[Oct. 12, 1888]

Professor, contemplating the number of autographs[1] which greet his arrival at the first weekly recitation in Political Economy: "Gentlemen, I had hoped that you might emulate your Saxon forefathers, who thought it not creditable to be unprepared for anything."[2]

◇

Professor Wilson, who graduated from Princeton in '79, was for some years editor in chief of the *Princetonian* and referee and one of the directors of the Princeton Foot-ball team at the time of its greatest success, and when the championship of the game resided with Princeton College. At one time he was hindered from playing in the victorious team only by a prolonged sickness.[3] He is an admirer of the game and will be an enthusiastic supporter of the Wesleyan team.

Printed in the Middletown, Conn., *Wesleyan Argus*, XXII (Oct. 12, 1888), 17.

1 That is, the names of students who signified that they were unprepared for recitation or examination. There is such a list on the verso of a one-page MS. (WP, DLC) with the WWhw heading "Written Recitation, Oct. 25/89"—a weekly examination in Wilson's senior course on the history of institutions.

2 For the only good article about Wilson at Wesleyan, one rich in anecdotal materials, see Carl F. Price, "When Woodrow Wilson Was at Wesleyan," New York *Christian Advocate*, XCIV (Aug. 7 and 14, 1919), 998-1000, 1030-1031.

3 One can only wonder where the author of this item obtained his misinformation!

Stockton Axson to Ellen Axson Wilson

My dear Sister Athens Ga Oct [c. 19] 1888

I have been intending to answer your letter for days but have been quite busy. An increased number of studies, a stricter method of examination, and an additional amount of society and fraternity work gives me about all that I can handle this year.

How I should like to see little Jess trotting about alone! I know she must be as cute as a kitten. Now if Madge will only begin to talk you will have quite an accomplished family.

I am glad that the pleasant features of Middletown hold out as well as they started. I think the change from Bryn Mawr or rather the people of BM must be truly delightful to you all.

I suppose Bro Woodrow did not accept the Sunday School offer of the South Church,[1] for had he done so I suppose of course that you would have attended that church.[2] I think that it is a great pity he did not especially if he was to teach boys or young men, for I think that his plain practical religious views will do more good for young men than the preaching of half the ministers in the Southern General Assembly.

Our trustees have at last elected Dr Boggs as Chancellor of the University. Possibly you have heard that the two most prominent names before the Board were those of Dr [J. L. M.] Curry and *Dr Wilson*. After the adjournment of the first days meeting it was thought that Dr Wilson would be elected without a doubt. The Atlanta Constitution stated that at nine oclock on the following morning Dr J R Wilson would be elected Chancellor, but for some reason which I never heard Dr Boggs was run in as a dark horse.

Do you suppose Dr Wilson could have been persuaded to leave Clarksville and come here? If he would have accepted I certainly wish that he could have been elected. . . .

With a great deal of love for all

Aff'ly your's Stockton Axson

ALS (WP, DLC).

[1] The South, or Second, Congregational Church, the Rev. Peter M. Snyder, pastor.

[2] The Wilsons joined the North, or First, Congregational Church, the Rev. Dr. Azel Washburn Hazen, pastor, on November 4, 1888, by letter of transfer from the Bryn Mawr Presbyterian Church dated October 26, 1888.

From the Minutes of the Wesleyan University Faculty

Oct. 23, 1888.

Faculty met at 5.35 P.M. . . .

Prof. Wilson was appointed a delegate to the annual Convention of College Officers to be held at Trinity College. . . .[1]

Bound ledger book (CtW).

[1] "At a meeting of the Association of New England College Presidents held November 1, at Trinity in Hartford, the following colleges were represented by the President and one Professor: Yale, Harvard, Boston, Williams, Amherst, Dartmouth, Vermont University, Tufts, Brown and Wesleyan. Professors Van Vleck and Wilson were the representatives from Wesleyan. Among the subjects discussed were the following:

"The advisability of allowing a substitution of American and English history for Roman and Greek history for entrance; the advisability of forbidding intercollegiate athletic contests; improvements in the college catalogue; some methods of college government organization; the feasibility of getting better results from certificates of good character of students entering college." Middletown, Conn., *Wesleyan Argus*, XXII (Nov. 9, 1888), 39.

From Munroe Smith

My dear Prof. Wilson: New York, Oct. 30 1888

I consider your request a great compliment; and I shall be glad to read your chapters on legal evolution in general and the influence of Roman Law in particular.[1]

I am over ears in work just now, bringing the December [Political Science] Quarterly to bed (bed of the press is referred to),—but if you will send your MS. about the tenth of next month, I shall have time to read it.

Yours very truly Munroe Smith

ALS (WP, DLC).

[1] Wilson's letter to Professor Smith, requesting him to read certain sections and chapters of *The State,* is missing, but see WW to M. Smith, Nov. 12, 1888.

From John Franklin Jameson

My dear Wilson: Providence, Nov. 2, 1888.

If I had more time I might use more circumlocution; but having very little I may as well proceed to state directly that I propose soon to accept your kind invitation to visit you. My classes are so arranged that the longest time of absence I can secure for going to Middletown will be got by leaving here on Thursday at 4.30, arriving at 8.30 or 9.00, and returning the next afternoon at 5.00. If not inconvenient, I should like to come over next Thursday; but any later Thursday that suits you better will suit me as well, save Thanksgiving Day. Thanking you for the kindness of which I am thus availing myself, I am, with the kindest regards to Mrs. Wilson,

Very sincerely yours, J. F. Jameson.

ALS (WP, DLC) with WWhw notation on env.: "Ans. 5/11/88."

To John Franklin Jameson

My dear Jameson, Middletown, Conn., 5 Nov., 1888.

Your letter of the 2nd, rec'd this morning, has given me as genuine a sense of sincere pleasure as I've had this long time. I shall be simply delighted to have you come: but let us, if possible, have our lucid intervals (which is, being translated, our periods of professional leisure) coincide. This is "star week" with me–a dark saying which I need not explain further than to say that it means, for one thing, that Friday next will be one of my busiest days–a day of three lectures. Next week on the contrary, such is the interesting dispensation at this institution, will be "dagger week" and its Friday will be one of my free days, with but a single class exercise then falling to my chair.[1] What I propose, therefore, as you doubtless already divine, is that, if perfectly convenient, you come on "dagger week," so that I may see as much of you as possible. Any other 'dagger week' would suit just as well, of course, (dagger weeks alternate with star weeks) but the sooner you come the better pleased I shall be–for I want to see you as soon as may be.

Have you a class on Saturday, that you cannot finish a week with us: to have you stay over Saturday and Sunday would be the ideal plan. But I sha'nt quarrel with Providence–come when you can and stay just as long as you can:–so say we both of us most cordially.

I saw two of your colleagues in Hartford. Did you get the 'regards' I sent you by Prof. Bancroft?[2]

With Mrs. Wilson's regards, and wishes for your speedy coming, joined to my own,

Yours most sincerely, Woodrow Wilson

ALS (J. F. Jameson Papers, DLC).

[1] The *Annual Catalogue of Wesleyan University. 1888-89* (Middletown, Conn., 1888), pp. 44-45, gives the following explanation: "The order of lectures and recitations is set forth in the table given on page 46. In that table each study is assigned to that year to which it belongs in the Classical Course. Exercises which occur on alternate days are denoted by the signs * and †. Of these half-studies, those which are marked with the same sign occur on the same days; those marked with different signs occur on alternate days. It will be observed that recitations in half-studies assigned to the same hour will interfere with each other only when they are marked with the same sign. Letters following the names of studies indicate the days of the week on which certain exercises occur. Letters in connection with the sign * or † indicate that an exercise occurs on the day mentioned in those weeks only in which other exercises marked with the same sign occur on that day."

[2] Frederic Bancroft, then a lecturer at Amherst as well as Librarian of the State Department in Washington.

From Marion Wilson Kennedy

My dearest brother: Batesville [Ark.], Nov. 6th 1888.

I am growing weary of this long silence, and though not in an epistolary mood tonight, still feel I must say something to break the fearful silence between this point and Middletown, Conn. I am not complaining, my brother, but only longing for a letter from you or Ellie. Are you both too busy to write occasionally? My hands are pretty full just now, *for me,* and I am very anxious, too, about Ross. His health is not improving rapidly at all, and he is so sure he will never be well again, that the effect is not as encouraging on either of us as it might be. I am so anxious that he should get well and strong, both for our sakes, and the "work's sake." . . .

Our children are all at school—even Jessie attending a small private school—and so I am much more quiet, most of the time, than of late years. We enjoyed your "Old Master" greatly, for its style, and thought you made a strong case. Do let us know when you publish articles, as our one thousand a year will not allow us to take many magazines. We could always afford special copies, of course.

Do let us hear from you very soon—and do not let's get too careless about keeping up our correspondence, dear. With any amount of love for both brother and sister, and the children, from Ross and Marion.

ALS (WP, DLC) with WWhw notation on env.: "Ans. Nov. 11/88."

From Thomas Dixon, Jr.

My dear Wilson: Boston. Nov. 8th 1888.

Your kind letter[1] came some week or so ago and, it has been a physical impossibility for me to answer it before this which may strike you as a preposterous statement—but if you are ever pastor of a church the size of mine in such a town as Boston you will find that there will come times when a fellow hardly has time to eat. But enough apology. I was rejoiced to hear from you. I have often told my better half of you, and we likewise covet the pleasure of a visit from you. Now, the proper wrinkle is for you and Mrs. Wilson to pack your grips and come down to the HUB and do it up and make your home at the parsonage which has open doors for all our old f[r]iends and we are not over run either for not many of them penetrate so far North as this. I am glad you have drawn so much nearer. You say you know what an anchor a baby is. Well, did you ever allow your mind to relax sufficiently to take in the conception of what two would be? Then, you have not grasped our situation at this time. Miss Lottie Louise, our second, put in her appearance the eighth of September, and she constitutes a whole family in herself on many occasions—so I don't know just when my sweetheart can come down to Conn., but I mean to try to put in an appearance there before a great [while] and will let you know before I get there. I have another very dear f[r]iend in Conn. now—Ed Poteat,[2] pastor of the Calvary Bap. Church at New Haven. I was invited there same time as here, but I recommended my friend Poteat to them and they got him—you see him some time when you go to New Haven—he's a John's Hopkins man—a scholar, a native tar-heel, and an all round tip top fellow.

I know you must enjoy your classes of boys now after your seige with girls only. Dewey (D. R.), and Levermore are here at the Tech.—I see them occasionally. How has you[r] book sold? Has it ever reached second edition? When are you going to bring out another?

Wife joins me in kindest regards to all. *Write.*

Truly, [Thomas Dixon, Jr.]

TL (WP, DLC) with WWhw notation on env.: "94. The Govt. of Solon:—the Crisis." Enc.: printed announcement of Dixon's lecture topics.

[1] It was WW's reply to T. Dixon, Jr., to WW, June 21, 1888, Vol. 5.

[2] Edwin McNeill Poteat.

From Edward Ireland Renick

My dear Wilson, Washington, D. C., Nov 9, 1888.

In your letter of Sept 21st you held out the hope that I was soon to have a full account of your change of base; I know you have been busy, but I mention this to explain my own silence. I am exceedingly anxious to hear from you. . . .

I am sorry to say that owing to certain changes whereby I lost the aid of some friends who rented part of my house, I was obliged to bear the whole rent of $45.00 per month from Aug 1st to October 25th. This has crippled me so that I have not been able to reduce the indebtedness which I had hoped to cancel wholly by this time. . . . We have been thinking of borrowing & sending you the remainder of the money ($60 00) out of which you have been kept too long, but I thought I would first write & ask you frankly to say whether it will inconvenience you to indulge me a little while—say about two months. Please be perfectly candid. I am very sorry that circumstances prevented me from displaying that promptness which I promised & of which I felt so certain when I secured the loan. Please let me hear soon of your family & your work—& give me as much detail as possible.

With kind regards to Mrs Wilson & best wishes for you all from us

I am, As ever yours, E. I. Renick

ALS (WP, DLC) with WWhw notation on env.: "Ans. 12 Nov./88."

To Munroe Smith

My dear Prof. Smith, Middletown, Conn., 12th Novr. 1888

I am sincerely obliged to you for your cordial consent to read my *mss.*—I wonder at your generosity all the more because it is the *mss.* of a text-book, in which topics must from the necessity of the case be spread thin, and not of a work claiming any of the consideration usually vouchsafed to special research.

I shall have to write you a sort of preface-letter, to acquaint you with the general plan and character of the book and with the special place and function in that general plan of the portions I send you.

The book is to be called 'The State: Elements of Historical and Practical Politics.' It is to have seventeen chapters, bearing the following titles:

I. The Probable Origin of Govt.—Its historical origin, i. e., in the family, with a brief indication of the points of controversy bet. the McLennan and Maine schools[1] touching the early history of the family.

II The Probable Early Development of Govt.—From the family in its primitive forms to the antique 'city.'

III. The Govts. of Greece and Rome—Outlining the constitutional histories of Athens, Sparta, and Rome.

IV Roman Dominion and Roman Law—one of the chapters I send you.

V. Teutonic Polity and Govt. during the Middle Ages.—a discussion, of course, of the fusion of Germanic with Roman institutions, of the towns, of the influence for unity of the Church, &c &c. The closing sections of this chapter also I send to you. They concern the entrance of Roman law into modern legal systems.

VI-XII. The Govts. of France, Germany (with special sections on Prussia), Switzerland, Russia, Austria-Hungary and Sweden-Norway, England, and the U. S. The chapter on the U. S. is, naturally, the fullest by far. In it I devote more space to the states than to the general govt. I introduce my sketch of each govt. with an historical outline full enough to give the student his bearings. Sometimes about one third, sometimes quite one half of the chapter is historical.

XIII Summary of some main points of constitutional and administrative development.

XIV. The Nature and Forms of Govt.—from an historical (fact) point of view, not from a theoretical.

XV. The Functions of Govt.—from the same point of view, of course.

XVI. Law: Its Nature and Development. a chapter which I send you.

XVII. The Ends of Govt.

Chapters VI-XII make up, of course, the body of the book: it is for their sake, so to say, that the other chapters were written. These central chapters are of course built, so far as the European govts. are concerned, on Marquardsen's great *Handbuch.* Without that, I would have been very much longer in working out my scheme.

The chapter on Roman law, therefore, is, you will perceive, simply part of a somewhat elaborate historical introduction to those expositions (or rather descriptions) of the govts. of to-day which constitute the main body of the work. A setting forth of the principles, of the contents, of Roman law could, of course, form no part of my plan. I want only a sufficient exhibition of its external history, so to say, and a suggestive indication of its influence. But in proportion as it is generalized is the accuracy and sufficiency of any statement of the history and significance of so great a thing as Roman law imperiled. Detail is your only safe road. I have necessarily had much to say incidentally of Roman law in other chapters, but the sections I send you contain all that I have written systematically; and the question in my mind is, do these sections suffice as parts of a general foundation for the 'Elements of Historical and Practical Politics'?

Chapters XIV-XVII constitute a sort of supplement and commentary to the fact portions of the book. In them I try to collect the ideas—the general conceptions which ought to arise out of a survey of actual govts. past and present. In the chapter on Law, which I send you I fear that I have rather made hotchpotch of the ideas proper to the historical school of jurisprudence, on the one hand, and those belonging to the analytical school on the other. Perhaps there is here another illustration of the dangers of the *via media*. But I thought that way a necessary way for the feet of the expositor—the text-book writer.

Of course the book is for colleges, not for schools. It will probably contain about five hundred and fifty pages.

I have only to add that I am not sensitive to serious criticism. I regard it as a means of grace; and I hope that you will take leave to speak plainly your opinion of my *ms.*

With renewed thanks and warmest regards,

Yours most sincerely, Woodrow Wilson

ALS (*Political Science Quarterly* Papers, NNC).

[1] That is, the schools of thought headed by John F. McLennan and Sir Henry Maine.

From John Franklin Jameson

My dear Wilson: Providence, Nov. 14, 1888.

This is to do you to wit that I arrive in Middletown at 7.18 tomorrow night, after a very slow ride, very cross. Before returning, I shall succeed in prevailing on you to come over and give us two lectures on municipal government in January.[1]

Very sincerely yours, J. F. Jameson.

ALS (WP, DLC).

[1] Wilson did give lectures on municipal government for Jameson on January 11 and 18, 1889. See WW to JRW, Jan. 13, 1889, n. 1, and the newspaper report printed at Jan. 19, 1889.

From Robert Bridges

My dear Classmate: New York, Nov 14–88

Will you permit me to again call your attention to the urgent necessity of remitting to us very soon the whole or part of your subscription to the Class Memorial? We are paying St. Gaudens at the rate of $800.00 per month, and the cash in the treasury is exhausted. In fact we are indebted to Cuyler for an advance of several thousand dollars. This should not be, and we hope that you will respond at your earliest convenience. Please draw your check to the order of C. C. Cuyler, Treasurer, and forward to me. Cuyler will return your receipt.

Sincerely your classmate, Robert Bridges

TLS (WP, DLC) with WWhw notation on env.: "Ans. Nov. 27/88," and WWhw and WWsh bibliographical citations.

From John Franklin Jameson

My dear Wilson: Providence, Nov. 20, 1888.

I have this morning sent you the desired copy of Vom Fels zum Meer, in which you may or may not find something that will interest you.[1] I have enclosed with it my copy of Mr. Cable's pamphlet on the Negro Question,[2] which Mrs. Wilson may like to read. The book for which I referred you to the Academy is entitled "France as it is," and is written by André Lebon and Paul Pelet and translated into English under their supervision. As it is published by Cassell & Co., and they have a house at Philadelphia, you may be able to get a copy in less time than it takes to import one. After I had left you, it occurred to me that your wish for books which might make real and living the political institutions of European countries might to some extent be met, for France, by a little book I saw at Harvard in September, by Jules Simon, entitled Le Livre du petit Citoyen, Hachette, 1880. It was a well-written book, of course. As I remember it, it had a division on the commune, one on the arrondissement, one on the department; or perhaps they were on local, departmental, and central institutions. At all events it was an attempt to describe vividly, from the *petit citoyen's* point of view, the workings of the parts of government with which he might come in contact.

I take it colonial federation comes into your scheme for Great Britain. Have you happened to see about the South African customs union arranged for by a conference last February? It is badly treated of by our consul at Cape Town in pp. 209-219 of Consular Report no. 93, May, 1888; but he gives the essential details.

I don't know when I've had so pleasant a twenty-four-hours as that I spent at Middletown. I am greatly obliged to you for making so delightful an addition to the number of my friends as Mrs. Woodrow Wilson, though it was doubtless done more for other reasons than for my benefit, and has already received other rewards than my gratitude. Commend me to her, please; also to the two infants,–the one with the oval face and the one with the spherical body. I wish you were all nearer. With the pleasantest remembrance and the kindest regards,

Sincerely yours, J. F. Jameson

ALS (WP, DLC).

[1] *Vom Fels zum Meer* was a general magazine published in Stuttgart. J. F. Jameson to WW, Nov. 18, 1889, intimates that Jameson had sent the issue containing an article entitled "Der Mechanismus des Reichstags." However, no such title is listed in the tables of contents of any volumes of the magazine published through 1888.

[2] George Washington Cable, *The Negro Question* (New York, 1888).

From Annie Wilson Howe

My dearest Brother, Columbia, Nov. 26th, 1888

I was so glad after your long silence to receive your letter a couple of weeks ago. I intended to answer it at once and do not see how I have let so many days slip by without writing. . . .

I am so glad you and Ellie are pleased with your new home. I am delighted to know that you will not have to work so hard as you did last winter, although I do not think I ever saw you looking better than when you were in Clarksville.[1]

Doesn't your heart ache for poor Father? He seems to feel his loneliness now more than ever. I cannot bear to think of the long lonely winter evenings before them. Has Father spoken to you of resigning his professorship? I am afraid he will regret it when it is too late.

I suppose you have heard of Mrs. [Benjamin M.] Palmer's death. It was a great shock to us, we had not heard that she was ill. . . . I had a letter from Hattie [Woodrow] Wells today. Her husband is in very delicate health. They have had to move out to Colorado on that account.

You cannot think how I long to see you in your own home. I know it is lovely, because the woman who reigns over it is so lovely. I do not suppose I will ever be able to visit you while you are so far away. Ask Ellie to write to me sometimes. She need not wait until she has time to write long letters.

Mr. Flinn[2] told me the other day that he supposed of course you had sent me your last published article[3] and would I please let him see it as he could not find the "[Princeton] Review" in town. I had to tell him that I had not seen it and did not even know you had written any such article until I saw a notice of it in the Southern Presbyterian. Whenever you have the opportunity dear please send me a copy of any article you may write. Don't you always have several copies? If you cannot send a copy please let me know where I can find it. I will not feel quite so completely cut off from you if you will do this. If it is an unreasonable request please just forget it. . . .

Write as often as you can, dear brother. I will promise to answer every letter promptly. George unites with me in warmest love to you both. Kiss the little girls for me.

Your devoted sister, Annie.

ALS (WP, DLC) with WWhw notation on env.: "Ans. 27 Jany '89."

1 After Mrs. Wilson's death, from about April 17 to April 23, 1888.

2 The Rev. John William Flinn, chaplain of the University of South Carolina.

3 "An Old Master," printed at Feb. 1, 1887, Vol. 5.

To Robert Bridges

My dear Bobby, Middletown, Conn., 27 November, '88

Just a line or two to accompany the enclosed check for my contribution to Jimmie's statue. As you know, I had planned, without promising, to chip in twice as much; but the expense of moving here from Bryn Mawr proved very great indeed, and put me back instead of ahead in my bank account. I wish that the good-will with which the money is given could avail to double its paying capacity.

I have not the energy to-night for a letter: this has been one of my 'three-lecture days' and I am using the few remaining scraps of 'go' in despatching some necessary matters of business—for some time denied attention.

I hope that you are to have the leisure to plan your Thanksgiving in a way to suit your own pleasure. We have been taken possession of by these good New Eng. folks and are, instead of making, to be given our 'Thanksgiving.'

Those two goals from the field,[1] coming right on top of the huge disappointment of the election, have been too much for me!

As ever,

Yours affectionately, Woodrow Wilson

ALS (WC, NjP).

[1] Yale defeated Princeton by two field goals and a score of 10 to 0 in the "great and deciding game of the foot ball season" at the Polo Grounds in New York on November 24, 1888. *The Princetonian*, XIII (Nov. 26, 1888), 1.

Wilson's Copy for the Wesleyan Catalogue for 1888-1889[1]

[c. *Dec. 1, 1888*]

HISTORY AND POLITICAL ECONOMY.

Professor Wilson.

I. *Histories of England and France.* A course of topical lectures in which English and French topics are made to run, as nearly as possible, parallel to each other chronologically, with the double object of affording clues to general European history and of setting the history of the English race in its European connections. Fifteen or sixteen lectures on the Renaissance and Reformation are also included in this course, being introduced when the topics in English and French history have been advanced to the fifteenth century. Required parallel reading is assigned, and frequent recitations are held upon the subject matter of the lectures. *Five times a fortnight.*

Course I. is elective for Juniors.

II. *History of Institutions.* The central aim of this course is to put the development of the political institutions and of the politics of the United States in its true historical setting. It covers such topics as the following: The origin and development of government; ancient political systems; mediæval political organization; the constitutional growth of the leading European states, and the chief features of their constitutions; the governments of England and the United States; the functions and aims of government; the nature and development of law, etc. Parallel readings are assigned and frequent oral examinations are held. *Five times a fortnight.*

Course II. is elective for Seniors.

III. *Constitution of the United States.* Cooley's Principles of Constitutional Law is used as a text-book in the legal aspects of the fundamental law of the Union; but the object of the instruction is to familiarize the class with all the main aspects of our constitution, both state and federal, unwritten developments, practical questions, legislative machinery, etc. For this purpose various commentaries of different grades are more or less used, and supplementary lectures are given. *Five times a fortnight during second half-year.*

Course III. is required of Juniors.

IV. *Political Economy and Statistics.* F. A. Walker's Advanced Political Economy is used as a text-book, and lectures are given on the history of economic thought. The work in political economy is supplemented by a brief course in the general principles of statistics. *Four times a week during first half-year.*

Course IV. is required of Seniors.

V. *Roman History.* A required course in Roman history is given by the Tutor in Latin[2] to Classical and Latin-Scientific Freshmen. Ihne's Early Rome is used as a text-book, and required collateral reading in carefully selected general topics is assigned. *Once a week.*

VI. *Greek History.* A brief course of instruction in Greek history is given the Classical Freshmen by the Tutor in Greek.[3]

Printed in *Catalogue of Wesleyan University,* 1888-89 (Middletown, Conn., 1888 [1889]), pp. 31-32.

1 This catalogue was not published until about February 1, 1889. An announcement of Wilson's courses for the first semester had appeared in the Middletown, Conn., *Wesleyan Argus,* XXII (Sept. 29, 1888), 9.

2 Robert Henry Williams.

3 Franklin Henry Taylor.

To Wilbur Olin Atwater[1]

My dear Prof. Atwater, Middletown, 3 Dec. '88.

I wish I could thank you in person for your kind note touching my Adam Smith. I am the sort of chap that needs such encouragement as your note so cordially conveys, and I thank you most heartily for it.

I am sincerely sorry that I am to see so little of you here.[2]

Very cordially yours, Woodrow Wilson

ALS (CtW).

1 Beach Professor of Chemistry at Wesleyan, 1874-1907.

2 Atwater was away from Middletown a great deal on account of his new duties as director of the Office of Experiment Stations in the Department of Agriculture in Washington.

From Cornelius Cuyler Cuyler

My dear Wilson New York, Dec. 3, 1888

I beg to acknowledge your check for $20.00 the full amount of your subscription to the McCosh fund.

Yours very truly C C Cuyler

P.S. Received the above from Bridges.

ALS (WP, DLC) with WWhw notation on env.: "Receipt McCosh fund."

From John Franklin Jameson

My dear Wilson: Providence, Dec. 7, 1888.

All progresses well with our association and lecture-course. Ex Mayor Low[1] opens the latter on Friday evening, January 4th. Will it suit you to be set down for January 11th and 18th, (and to receive the meagre honorarium of ten dollars each time)? And how are we, in our circular, etc., to state your subjects?—I expect there will be an audience of about two hundred, in a hall somewhat larger than Hopkins Hall. Gardner[2] and I will eat and sleep you. Please reply at once.

My kindest regards to the admirable Madame and Mesdemoiselles Wilson. At Boston, Dewey and Levermore inquired kindly for you. Believe me

Very sincerely yours, J. F. Jameson.

ALS (WP, DLC) with WWhw notation on env.: "Ans 8/12/88."

[1] Seth Low, Mayor of Brooklyn, 1881-85, and President of Columbia University, 1890-1901.

[2] Henry Brayton Gardner, then an instructor in political economy at Brown and completing work on his Ph.D. at the Johns Hopkins.

To Munroe Smith

My dear Prof. Smith, Middletown, Conn., 10 Dec., 1888.

I have experienced no inconvenience at all from not getting my *mss.* back—I had not planned to send them to the printer before Feby. 1st.—but I am sincerely sorry that the cause of their retention has been what it has. I heartily hope that you can now speak of your illness in the past tense. You have my sympathy all the more vividly because I am just now going through a rather sharp spell of indisposition myself. Having been spendthrift of my strength for a great many months past, I had little with which to resist the influences of the villanous weather we have been having, and I have temporarily succumbed.

Don't try your nerves with the *mss.*—they can wait awhile.

Very sincerely Yours, Woodrow Wilson.

ALS (*Political Science Quarterly* Papers, NNC).

From Munroe Smith

My dear Wilson: New York, Dec. 14 1888

I have been suffering from *insomnia*, but am all right again, & shall be able to give you my suggestions, such as they may be, long before the ultimate date you mention.

I am sorry to hear that you are not well. It makes me hesitate to ask what I had meant to ask—whether you would be willing to review Bryce's new book on the United States?[1] But I will leave it to you to decide whether you will undertake it.

The book is not yet out in New York; but from what Bryce told me last summer I imagine it is popular rather than technical, and more sociological than strictly political or legal. I am sure it will be a great book, and my colleagues have warmly endorsed my suggestion that I should ask you to review it.

It should certainly be reviewed in the March number, and we cannot give you more than four weeks—or, at the outside, until Jan. 15.

We will give you *carte blanche* as to space. If your review runs over 2000 words (*and we should be glad to have* 5-6000) we shall print it as a leading article.

P.S. We are now, I am glad to say, able to pay regularly for contributions: not much, but anything is better than nothing. We pay $2.00 a page.

Yours very truly Munroe Smith

The book *must* be out in New York next week: and if you will undertake to read it, I will forward it to you at once.

ALS (WP, DLC) with WWhw notation on env.: "Ans. 12/17/88."

1 Wilson's review is printed at Jan. 31, 1889.

From John Franklin Jameson

My dear Wilson: Providence, Dec. 16, 1888.

If in a day or two you get a circular of our Association,[1] and find therein, in an informal announcement of our course, your own subject stated in a way slightly different from that which you suggested, be not wroth. I was induced to write "Modern Systems of City Government" instead of ". . . Town Government" by an apprehension which may or may not have occurred to you,—an apprehension, namely, lest it should be misunderstood by the Rhode Island public, among whom the word "town" has only the meaning which in most states outside of New England is given to the word "township." As I presume your lecture like the rest will treat of municipalities only, (or of dense aggregations of population organized under whatever name) I provisionally took the liberty of making this change in an informal statement. In the formal announcement a few days later, it shall be changed back if you desire.

Very sincerely yours, J. F. Jameson.

P.S. Over.

P.S.—Are you going to Washington?[2] If so, what doth hinder us to take the 8.00 A.M. from New York down on the 26th, together? Pray recover from your cold; it destroys the tissues here in New

England. In the matter of our book,—suppose its publication should have to be delayed a little, till summer or September 1st, could you do us an essay in season? My best regards to Mrs. Wilson and the Wilsonidae.

ALS (WP, DLC).

[1] The Historical and Economic Association of Brown University.

[2] For the annual meeting of the American Historical Association.

To Joseph Ruggles Wilson

My precious father, Middletown, Ct., 16 December, 1888

My thoughts are full of you and dear 'Dode' all the time. Tennessee seems *so* far away for a chap as hungry as I am for a sight of the two men whom I love. As the Christmas recess approaches I realize, as I have so often before, the *pain* there is in a season of holiday and rejoicing away from you. As you know, one of the chief things about which I feel most warranted in rejoicing is that I am your son. I realize the benefit of being your son more and more as my talents and experience grow: I recognize the strength growing in me as of the nature of your strength: I become more and more conscious of the hereditary wealth I possess, the capital of principle, of literary force and skill, of capacity for first-hand thought; and I feel daily more and more bent toward creating in my own children that combined respect and tender devotion for their father that you gave your children for you. Oh, how happy I should be, if I could make them think of me as I think of you! You have given me a love that grows, that is stronger in me now that I am a man than it was when I was a boy, and which will be stronger in me when I am an old man than it is now—a love, in brief, that is rooted and grounded in *reason*, and not in filial instinct merely—a love resting upon abiding foundations of *service*, recognizing you as in a certain very real sense the author of all I have to be grateful for. I bless God for my noble, strong, and saintly mother and for my incomparable father. Ask 'Dode' if he does not subscribe? And tell him that I love my brother passionately.

We have had about three months of continuously bad weather here and are proportionately 'under the weather' with various forms and degrees of cold; but fine cold days have come at last and we are one and all getting on our feet again. We'll get used to this villanous climate by-and-by, doubtless.

I have been wondering whether the Burney house[1] is snug and dry in winter. I sincerely hope the rigours of the Clarksville weather may not get at you in it.

We are expecting Ellie's cousin, Mary Hoyt, to come up from Bryn Mawr to spend the holidays with us.

Ellie joins me in unbounded love to you both.

Your devoted son, Woodrow

ALS (de Coppet Coll., NjP).

1 Dr. Wilson had sold his house in Clarksville and moved with Joseph R. Wilson, Jr., to the Burney house, a small cottage in that town.

To Munroe Smith

My dear Smith, Middletown, Conn., 17 Decr., '88

I shall be obliged to examine Bryce's book so soon as it comes out in any event, for the sake of being up to date in the literature of subjects upon which I am lecturing, and I think my health is now sufficiently improved to warrant my undertaking a review for the Quarterly. I ought to add, however, provided the book really does come out in N.Y. next week. Otherwise how would it be possible to do anything like justice to a two volume work of so great importance by January 15th? The review would have to be so hastily written that it would certainly be inadequate for its purpose. I saw the proof-sheets of the chapters on Local Government last winter, and know that there will be too much detail in the two volumes to admit of a hasty perusal. Besides some chapters of the book are to be written by other hands than Bryce's, and so the work will probably not be all of a piece (By-the-way, Bryce wanted me—because I was at Bryn Mawr?—to write a chapter for him on woman suffrage! What had I done to deserve that?)[1] In any case, of course, I would do my best to get the review up in season for the March number; but if I don't get the volumes next week, I very much doubt my ability to finish the job by the date you name.

I am sincerely glad that your *insomnia* is cured, and hope you'll never have another visit from the fiend.

Very sincerely Yours, Woodrow Wilson

ALS (*Political Science Quarterly* Papers, NNC).

1 See J. Bryce to WW, Feb. 25, 1888, printed as an enclosure in E. L. Godkin to WW, March 5, 1888, and WW to J. Bryce, March 6, 1888, all in Vol. 5.

From Joseph Ruggles Wilson

My dearly beloved son and friend— [New York, c. Dec. 26, 1888]

I will most assuredly visit you in Middletown—unless the obstacles prove insuperable. I am compelled to be at home early next week, not later if possible than the 2nd of Jany—and during my stay here my hands will be full of public business:[1]—yet a few hours *must* present themselves for a run to your home. It will not be wise for you to come down here—for we might cross each other in transitu.

Should we *not* meet at this time I shall be sorrier than yourself—& then we will come together in the summer for awhile.

Your letters: that which Dode forwarded to me at Columbia—and the one I received here—have afforded me infinite pleasure. Your great love for me gives me both joy & pride—and when you think that it was I who achieved such a son as you are, you attribute to me a work which ought to satisfy ambition itself.

Love to sweet Ellie & to yourself boundless affection

In great haste Your devoted Father

ALS (WP, DLC).

[1] The *New York Times*, December 29, 1888, reported (as did other New York papers) that a joint committee of the northern and southern Presbyterian Churches was then meeting in New York "to ascertain through reciprocal statements and inquiries the possible basis of a reunion of the Northern and Southern branches of the church that separated on the war issues."

This report was somewhat wide of the mark. The General Assemblies of the two Churches, following their joint meeting in Philadelphia on May 24, 1888 (see JRW to WW, May 11, 1888, n. 2, Vol. 5), had appointed committees to discuss ways and means of promoting closer cooperation and fellowship in the work of the two bodies. The joint conference met in New York from December 28, 1888, to January 1, 1889. Dr. Wilson served as chairman of the conference, and the Rev. William E. Moore, of the Presbyterian Church in the United States of America, was secretary. Unable to complete its work, the conference adjourned and met again in Atlanta from April 17 to 19, 1889.

The conference's report, adopted by both General Assemblies in May 1889 with only one significant change in wording, recommended various measures to avoid duplication of effort and friction between the two Churches both in the United States and abroad. On the highly sensitive question of the evangelization of Negroes and their position within the two Churches, the conference was able to agree only that "the relations of the colored people in the two Churches be allowed to remain *in statu quo*, the work among them to proceed on the same lines as heretofore." For the report of the joint conference, see *Minutes of the General Assembly of the Presbyterian Church in the United States. . . . Vol. VII, A.D. 1889* (Richmond, 1889), pp. 650-55. For the report as finally approved by the two General Assemblies, see *Minutes of the General Assembly of the Presbyterian Church in the United States of America . . . , New Series, Vol. XII, A.D. 1889* (Philadelphia, 1889), pp. 69-74.

From Edward Ireland Renick

My dear Wilson, Washington, D. C., Dec. 26, 1888.

I have not time just now to reply properly to your last letter, dated Nov. 12, 1888, which was thoroughly enjoyed.

I only purpose at present to assure you that during the next month I shall close the money matter which has been pending between us, and to regret that circumstances, which I have struggled hard to control, have prevented me for so many months from remitting. I feel that your kindness can never be repaid. I do hope that in some way I can be, in turn, of service to you. Your indulgence only urges me to hurry matters, believe me. Wishing for all of you a Merry Christmas & a very happy & prosperous New Year—I am with love in which all join,

Sincerely yours, Renick.

ALS (WP, DLC).

Marginal Notes

James Bryce, *The American Commonwealth* (3 vols., London and New York, 1888).

Transcripts of WW Shorthand Comments [Dec. 29, 1888-Jan. 2, 1889][1]

Vol. I, 292n.:

In Switzerland the Federal Council of seven are elected by the two Chambers, and then elect one of their own number to be their President, and therewith also President of the Confederation (Constit. of 1874, art. 98). In some British colonies it has been provided that, in case of the absence or death or incapacity of the Governor, the Chief Justice shall act as Governor. In India the senior member of Council acts in similar cases for the Viceroy.

The President is elected, not by Council, but by the Assembly

P. 293:

The Vice-President's office is ill-conceived. . . . The place being in itself unimportant, the choice of a candidate for it excites little interest, and is chiefly used by the party managers as a means of conciliating a section of their party. It becomes what is called "a complimentary nomination." The man elected Vice-President is therefore *never* [WW's italics] a man in the front rank. But when the President dies during his term of office, which has happened to four out of the seventeen Presidents, this second-class man steps into a great place for which he was never intended.

He once was—as witness Calhoun

1 WW's reading dates at the end of the first and second volumes.

P. 341:

It may be answered not merely that the National government has survived this struggle and emerged from it stronger than before, but also that Federalism did not produce the struggle, but only gave to it the particular form of a series of legal controversies over the Federal pact followed by a war of States against the Union. Where such vast economic interests were involved, and such hot passions roused, there must anyhow have been a conflict, and it may well be that a conflict raging within the vitals of a centralized government would have proved no less terrible and would have left as many noxious *sequelae* behind.

Under a unified government, however[,] slavery would hardly have been allowed to be the "peculiar institution" of one part of the country. It would have stood or fallen in both: just so, in the case in question, it would have fallen for the whole country, before it became of such practical importance as it had attained by '61.

P. 366:

But at one time the Presidents claimed the much wider right of being, except in questions of pure private law, generally and *prima facie* entitled to interpret the Constitution for themselves, and to act on their own interpretation, even when it ran counter to that delivered by the Supreme court. Thus Jefferson denounced the doctrine laid down in the famous judgment of Chief-Justice Marshall in the case of *Marbury v. Madison*; thus Jackson insisted that the Supreme court was mistaken in holding that Congress had power to charter the United States bank, and that he, knowing better than the court did what the Constitution meant to permit, was entitled to attack the bank as an illegal institution, and to veto a bill proposing to re-charter it.

This remark hardly applies except in the case of Jackson. Jefferson would not have claimed such a power in any such terms.

P. 407:

The power of a State over all communities within its limits is absolute. It may grant or refuse local government as it pleases. The population of the city of Providence is more than one-third of that of the State of Rhode Island, the population of New York city more than one-fifth that of the State of New York. But the State might in either case extinguish the municipality, and govern the city by a single State commissioner appointed for the purpose, or leave it without any government whatever. The city would have no right of complaint to the Federal President or Congress against such a measure. Massachusetts has lately remodelled the city government of Boston just as the British Parliament might remodel that of Birmingham. Let an Englishman imagine a county council for Warwickshire suppressing the municipality of Birmingham, or a Frenchman imagine the department of the Rhone extinguishing the municipality of Lyons, with no possibility of intervention by the central authority, and he will measure the difference between the American States and the local governments of Western Europe.

Hardly a parallel case; particulars of a unitary government cannot safely be compared with particulars of a federal state.

P. 412:

Thus every American citizen lives in a duality of which Europeans, always excepting the Swiss, and to some extent the Germans, have no experience. He lives under two governments and two sets of laws; he is animated by two patriotisms and owes two allegiances. That these should both be strong and rarely be in conflict is must [most] fortunate. It is the result of skilful adjustment and long habit, of the fact that those whose votes control the two sets of governments are the same persons, but above all of that harmony of each set of institutions with the other set, a harmony due to the identity of the principles whereon both are founded, which makes each appear necessary to the stability of the other, the States to the nation as its basis, the National Government to the States as their protector.

2 sets of authorities rather than 2 governments: it is a single system, if not in law then certainly by historical circumstance.

P. 466:

Thus there might exist great differences between one State and another in the free bestowal of the Federal franchise. That such differences are at present insignificant is due, partly to the prevalence of democratic theories of equality over the whole Union, partly to the provision of the fourteenth amendment to the Federal Constitution, which reduces the representation of a State in the Federal House of Representatives, and therewith also its weight in a presidential election, in proportion to the number of adult male citizens disqualified in that State. As a State desires to

This amendment can hardly be said to be in this respect practically operative.

have its full weight in national politics, it has a strong motive for the widest possible enlargement of its Federal franchise, and this implies a corresponding width in its domestic franchise.

Vol. II, 39:

Politics are less interesting than in Europe. The two kinds of questions which most attract eager or ambitious minds, questions of foreign policy and of domestic constitutional change, are generally absent, happily absent. Currency and tariff questions and financial affairs generally, internal improvements, the regulation of railways and so forth, are important, no doubt, but to some minds not fascinating. How few people in the English or French legislatures have mastered them, or would relish political life if it dealt with little else! There are no class privileges or religious inequalities to be abolished. Religion, so powerful a political force in Europe, is outside politics altogether.

I doubt the validity of this reason as regards America.

P. 41:

None of these causes is discreditable to America, yet, taken together, they go far to account for the large development of the professional element among politicians. Putting the thing broadly, one may say that in America, while politics are relatively less interesting than in Europe and lead to less, other careers are relatively more interesting and lead to more.

The most important cause of all is omitted, namely that there [are] no considerable prizes of leadership to be won.

P. 97:

An illustration of the familiar dictum regarding the wisdom with which the world is governed may be found in the fact that the greatest changes are often those introduced with the least notion of their consequence, and the most fatal those which encounter least resistance. So the system of removals from Federal office which began some sixty years ago, though disapproved of by some of the leading statesmen of the time, including Clay, Webster, and Calhoun, excited comparatively little attention in the country, nor did its advocates foresee a tithe of its far-reaching results.

And disapproved of by these men with full foresight of its results.

Pp. 213-14n.:

During the American Civil War the working class of England stood for the North, a majority of the so-called educated class for the South. And the abolitionist movement in America itself was stronger among the less-educated than in the best-educated classes. In the two former cases the love of freedom which the humbler classes had been led, by their position in their own country, to form may no doubt be thought to have attracted them to the cause which seemed to be that of freedom or of human rights in another country: still it must be remembered that they had no personal interest in these foreign causes—their sympathy with freedom was unselfish. Indeed, in the case of the American Civil War the English work-people had some interest the other way.

Because of the question of cotton, however; scarcely because of the question of liberty.

P. 405:

Two men are wiser than one, one hundred than ninety-nine, thirty millions than twenty-nine millions. Whether they are wiser or not, the will of the larger number must prevail against the will of the smaller. But the majority is not wiser because it is called the Nation, or because it controls the government, but only because it is more numerous. The nation is nothing but so many individuals. The government is nothing but certain representatives and officials, agents who are here to-day and gone to-morrow.

I am inclined to be profoundly skeptical as to the truth of this statement.

P. 449:

This inquiry has shown us that of the faults traditionally attributed to democracy one only is fairly chargeable on the United States; that is to say, is manifested there more conspicuously than in the constitutional monarchies of Europe. This is the disposition to be lax in enforcing laws disliked by any large part of the population, and to be too indulgent to offenders and lawbreakers generally. The Americans themselves admit this to be one of their weak points. How far it is due to that deficient reverence for law which is supposed to arise in popular governments from the fact that the people

Or how far to mere temporary social conditions of newness; of the absence have nothing higher than themselves to look up to, how far rather to the national easy-goingness and good-nature, I do not attempt to determine. It has produced no general disposition to lawlessness, but on the contrary diminishes it in the older parts of the country. And it is counter-balanced or replaced, in a serious crisis, by a firmness in repressing disorders which some European governments may envy.

of that necessity for order which must be so keenly felt in the nice mechanism of the old and complex European unit.

Two Letters from Joseph Ruggles Wilson

Darling Son— [New York] Tuesday, Jan 1, 89.

At the last moment I am compelled to forego the pleasure I had promised myself of running up to see the dear household at Middletown. By no possibility could I spare the time from my public duty—or you may be sure that you would have had more than enough of me before this. I had expected to go up on Saturday evening & spend the Sabbath at your home—but the Committees (of which (jointed) I am Chairman) were in session until late Saturday night—& I was under promise to preach, besides on Sabbath[1]

All therefore that I can now do is to say "a happy new year" and God bless you and yours! I am to be off to the Committee

Your affc Father.

[Postscript on env.:] I leave for home Jan 2nd morning

[1] The major New York dailies give no clue as to where Dr. Wilson may have preached on December 30, 1888.

My precious son— Clarksville, Jany 5, '89.

I never cease thinking of you—but since my return I seem to miss you more than ever. For, was there not an opportunity to achieve a sight of you last week? And this being lost, you appear to be farther off than before. Sometimes my heart cries out for your presence to an extent that can hardly be endured—and this is the case now. At the moment I am writing I would certainly feel far happier had we met during my trip to N. York—for then a new memory would brighten my mind. But why weep over the inevitable? Things were such as utterly to forbid my going to you, and you were not encouraged to come to me. I am sure that you will understand *why* it was not possible for me to get off from my Committee long enough to make a flying visit.

Had I not been Chairman of the joint body I might have stolen away—but as it was there was no chance whatsoever. I would have remained a day for the purpose, after the Committees adjourned: but I was already several days beyond the time at which I must re-appear in my class room, and my conscience would not suffer a further delay. We were treated with great courtesy by the New Yorkers;—wined, dined, fussed over almost ad nauseam indeed. But we accomplished nothing, or nearly nothing; and are to meet again, on the 17th of April at Atlanta, in order to emphasize the non-doing[.] What I had to say in public was said in a manner that you would not, I think, have been ashamed of. Yet, to have had *you* there, to reinforce my thoughts —how much stronger I would have felt and would have been!

Good-bye now, my darling son and truest friend. Please write soon, and relieve my solitude with the bright smiles I know so well. Love to dear Ellie: from us both

Your affc Father

ALS (WP, DLC).

Marginal Note

Carl Schurz, *Life of Henry Clay* (2 vols., 3rd edn., Boston and New York, 1887).

Transcript of WW Shorthand Comment

[Jan. 5, 1889][1]

Vol. II, p. 160:

Calhoun was exasperated. "The difference between me and the Senator from Kentucky," he said, "is as wide as the poles." No doubt it was. Calhoun would have preserved the Union if slavery could have been made secure in it. But he would willingly have sacrificed the Union to save slavery.

No, not willingly.

1 WW's reading date at the end of the book, on p. 414.

A Constitution for the Wesleyan House of Commons[1]

[*c. Jan. 5, 1889*]

CONSTITUTION.

ARTICLE I.

NAME.

The name of this society shall be the "WESLEYAN HOUSE OF COMMONS."

ARTICLE II.

OBJECT.

The object of this society shall be the promotion of the art of debate.

ARTICLE III.

MEMBERSHIP.

SECTION 1. All in regular attendance at Wesleyan University, who are not members of any other similar organization in that institution, shall be eligible as regular members of this society, when nominated by the Executive Ministry.

SEC. 2. The duties and privileges of regular membership in this society, once assumed, can be renounced only by resignation under the conditions and in accordance with the rules hereinafter set forth, or by the final termination of the member's connection with Wesleyan University.

SEC. 3. For the election of regular members of this society, a vote of a majority of the members present at any regular meeting shall be required.

SEC. 4. A willful absence from two successive meetings of the society shall be considered equivalent to an accepted resignation, and shall exclude a member from all privileges as such. Excuses for absence may be offered to the Executive Ministry, who shall be constituted judges of their validity.

SEC. 5. Honorary members of the House, with the privilege of debating, may be elected by a two-thirds vote of the members present at any regular meeting of the House, on the nomination of the Executive Ministry.

ARTICLE IV.

OUTLINE OF GOVERNMENT.

SECTION 1. The executive government of this society shall be vested in an Executive Ministry, a Speaker, and a Sergeant-at-Arms.

SEC. 2. The Executive Ministry shall consist of a Prime Minister, a Secretary for Foreign Affairs, and a Home Secretary.

The Prime Minister shall be appointed by the Speaker, in accordance with rules hereinafter set forth; the Secretary for Foreign Affairs and the Home Secretary by the Prime Minister.

SEC. 3. The Speaker shall be elected by a majority of the votes cast by ballot of the members present at the first regular meeting in February, and the last regular meeting in June, and shall hold office until his successor shall have been installed.

SEC. 4. The Sergeant-at-Arms shall be appointed by the Speaker, to serve during the Speaker's term of office.

SEC. 5. The Speaker shall also appoint a Clerk to serve during the Speaker's term of office.

ARTICLE V.

DUTIES OF OFFICERS.

SECTION 1. It shall be the duty of the Executive Ministry to propose bills for discussion by the House; to direct the order of proceedings of the House, and to act as its Executive Committee in carrying out all business not entrusted to any other committee.

SEC. 2. It shall be the duty of the Prime Minister to appoint the Secretary for Foreign Affairs and the Home Secretary; to act as chairman of the Ministry; and to draft for presentation to the House all questions decided upon by the Ministry.

SEC. 3. It shall be the duty of the Secretary for Foreign Affairs to conduct the correspondence of the House, and to act as its representative or agent in all dealings with outside bodies or individuals.

SEC. 4. It shall be the duty of the Home Secretary to see that the rooms of the society are prepared for its use, and to supervise the Clerk of the House in keeping the minutes and records of the society, and in preparing the business docket.

SEC. 5. The Speaker shall preside over all meetings of the society; shall construe and enforce the constitution and by-laws of the society, and the rules of practice, subject always to an appeal to the House; shall appoint the Prime Minister, Sergeant-at-Arms, the Clerk, all special committees ordered by the House, and all officers *pro tempore*; and shall perform all other duties usually pertaining to presiding officers.

SEC. 6. It shall be the duty of the Sergeant-at-Arms to act as the ministerial agent of the Speaker in enforcing order.

SEC. 7. The Clerk shall keep a record of the proceedings of the society, and an alphabetical roll of its members; shall carefully preserve all its records and all documents that may be entrusted to his keeping; shall transcribe in a book kept for that purpose, all additions and amendments to the constitution and by-laws of the society; and shall keep and announce in order a full business docket. He shall be subject in everything to the supervising authority of the Home Secretary.

It shall be the duty of the Clerk to post on at least one of the college bulletin-boards, three days previous to every regular meeting of the House, a notice stating the heading of the next two bills on the docket.

All persons on being elected members of the Wesleyan House of Commons shall be informed of the fact within forty-eight hours by the Clerk in writing. If the initiation does not take place after two successive meetings, such election shall be deemed null and void.

ARTICLE VI.

REGULAR BUSINESS.

SECTION 1. It shall be the duty of the Executive Ministry, and the privilege of any member, to propose questions for discussion by the House.

SEC. 2. Every question must be introduced in the form of a written bill, and must pass through the regular course of three readings and consideration, either by a special committee or a committee of the whole.

SEC. 3. No bill shall pass through more than two readings at the same meeting of the House.

SEC. 4. Bills proposed shall be put upon the docket by the Clerk in the order of their presentation, which shall be the order of their consideration, unless otherwise ordered by a vote of two-thirds of those present at a regular meeting of the House.

SEC. 5. Bills may be introduced by private members only by leave of the Executive Ministry, after at least one week's notice given of intention to introduce a bill, and of the character of the measure to be proposed.

Similar notice must be given by the Ministry of the introduction of bills to be proposed by themselves.

SEC. 6. The Home Secretary shall keep the Ministry advised of the state of the docket; the Ministry shall see that the discussion of pending bills is facilitated; and shall refuse leave to introduce a bill only when its introduction would inconveniently crowd the docket, unless the bill proposed be of a sort which they think out of keeping with the purposes of the society.

SEC. 7. All motions concerning the appointment of special committees, or expressing the opinions of the House as to the course of the Ministry, or as to any other matter not proper for the form of a bill, must be submitted in writing and signed by the mover.

ARTICLE VII.

RESPONSIBILITY OF THE MINISTRY.

SECTION 1. The Executive Ministry shall be responsible to the House for their opinion on all bills concerning political and collegiate questions. If, at any time in a vote upon such a question, they shall be left in a minority, they shall place their resignations in the hands of the Speaker before the next regular meeting of the society.

SEC. 2. It shall be the duty of the Speaker to accept such resignations, and to appoint a new Prime Minister from the majority represented in such a vote, and the Prime Minister so appointed shall choose his colleagues from the majority which he represents.

SEC. 4. The House may at any time pass a direct vote of want of confidence in the Ministry under the form of a resolution, and upon the passage of such a resolution, the Ministry shall resign and be replaced as directed in Sections 1 and 2 of this Article.

ARTICLE VIII.

RESIGNATION OF MEMBERSHIP.

SECTION 1. Whenever any member wishes to resign, he shall signify his desire in writing to the Executive Ministry, stating fully his reasons, and, upon obtaining their acquiescence, may withdraw.

SEC. 2. The Ministry shall be responsible to the House for the exercise of this, as for the exercise of all of their other prerogatives.

ARTICLE IX.

CHANGES IN THE CONSTITUTION AND BY-LAWS.

SECTION. 1. All motions and resolutions affecting the constitution and by-laws of this society shall be submitted in writing and pass through three readings and a committee of the whole; and not more than two readings shall be taken at one sitting of the House.

SEC. 2. A two-thirds vote of the members present at a regular meeting of the society shall be necessary to amend this constitution; but a vote of a majority of the members present at any regular meeting shall be sufficient to amend the by-laws. The by-laws may be suspended for a single session of the House by a vote of two-thirds of the members present.

BY-LAWS.

ARTICLE I.

MEETINGS.

SECTION 1. The House shall meet every daggar Tuesday[2] in the evening, at 7 o'clock, during the session of the University, with the power of adjournment for any period by a two-thirds vote.

SEC. 2. The Speaker shall call special meetings of the House at the request of the Executive Ministry, or of ten members of the society. Twenty-four hours notice of the meeting and of the business to be considered, being given on one of the college bulletin-boards.

SEC. 3. If, after having been properly requested to do so, the Speaker fail to call a meeting of the House, the Executive Ministry or a quorum of members may convene it, after having given twenty-four hours' notice of the time and object of the meeting. Notice posted twenty-four hours beforehand upon at least one of the bulletin-boards shall be sufficient, if signed by the members of the Ministry, or by a quorum of the members of the society.

ARTICLE II.

QUORUM.

One-third of the members of the society shall constitute a quorum for the transaction of business.

ARTICLE III.

DEBATE.

Any member of the society shall, without limitation of time, be entitled to only one speech at each reading of any bill.

ARTICLE IV.

ORDER OF BUSINESS.

1. Roll Call.
2. Installation of Officers.
3. Reading of Minutes.
4. Nomination, Election, and Initiation of New Members.
5. Election of Officers.
6. Regular Order of Docket Business.
7. Motions and Resolutions.
8. Notice by the Ministry of the Introduction of Measures.
9. Notice by Private Members (after leave asked and obtained of the Ministry) of Introduction of Bills.
10. Notice of Election of Officers.
11. Adjournment.

ARTICLE V.

MISCELLANEOUS BUSINESS.

SECTION 1. The Speaker shall give notice of every election of officers at least two weeks before it is to take place.

SEC. 2. To adjourn before the regular order of business has been completed shall require a vote of two-thirds of the members present. The motion to adjourn shall be debatable.

SEC. 3. At the request of two members a rising vote shall be taken; at the request of one-fifth of the members present the vote shall be taken by yeas and nays.

SEC. 4. The rules of parliamentary practice as set forth in "Robert's Rules of Order" shall govern the proceedings of this society in so far as they are not inconsistent with any provision of its constitution or by-laws.

ARTICLE VI.

FORM OF INITIATION.

The Speaker shall request the newly elected member (or members) to come forward and sign the constitution, and shall then address him (or them) in the following words:

"Sir (or Sirs),—You have voluntarily become a member (or members) of this society, and I have therefore, in its name, to lay you under the most solemn injunctions to obey and uphold its constitution, to observe all propriety as a member and a gentleman (or as members and gentlemen), and to advance by a strict adherence to duty the object of its organization."

ARTICLE VII.

SPEAKER'S DECISION.

SECTION 1. The House may at any time, by a majority vote, require within two weeks a written decision from its Speaker on any point with reference to the government of the House, or on the interpretation of its constitution. Said decisions, when presented to the House by the Speaker, shall lie over for two weeks, when the House shall adopt, amend, or reject the same, as it sees fit.

Constitution and By-Laws of the Wesleyan House of Commons. Adopted Jan. 15th, 1889 (Middletown, Conn., 1889).

[1] For accounts of the formation of the Wesleyan House of Commons, see the news items printed at Jan. 8, 1889.

[2] For the meaning of this phrase, see WW to J. F. Jameson, Nov. 5, 1888, n. 1.

To Munroe Smith

My dear Prof. Smith, Middletown, Conn., 7 Jan'y, 1889.

I have completed my review of Bryce,[1] a little ahead of schedule time, and very much to my own surprise it comes up to the size you, parenthetically, said you would like to have it: it is between five and six thousand words long. I began with the idea of making it brief but sugary; but I must acknowledge to having been very much disappointed by the work's lack of suitable historical background. It seems to me to be done too much in the manner of the early Renaissance, too flat against its background. It is not the book my thought seemed to need—a book rich with historical explanation of more than a formal sort. But perhaps it's just as well, since I myself have privately pre-empted a claim in that territory—the historical explanation—analysis—philosophy of democracy, and am diligently preparing to work it so soon as I can get an appointment to a chair in which my special appetites can be legitimately indulged![2]

How remorselessly "Congressional Government" (a small volume by myself) is swallowed up in Part I of Bryce! Was I not 'nice' not to say anything about it?

Can you tell me whether or no E. J. James, of Pennsylvania has returned home well?

Very sincerely Yours, Woodrow Wilson

ALS (*Political Science Quarterly* Papers, NNC).

1 It was further revised and is printed at Jan. 31, 1889.

2 See the Editorial Note, "Wilson's First Treatise on Democratic Government," Vol. 5.

Two News Items

[*c. Jan. 8, 1889*]

On Tuesday evening, Jan. 8th, the college was present in a body in the lower chapel for the final organization of the Wesleyan House of Commons. Prof. Wilson was chosen temporary chairman, and Davenport, '89,[1] clerk *pro tem.* The constitution was then read through and adopted, section by section, with such amendments as were approved. A committee of five was appointed to draw up and present by-laws. On the third ballot, without nominations, A. W. Partch, '89,[2] was elected speaker. The speaker appoints the ministry, and himself serves until February, when his successor is elected. The House adjourned until Tuesday evening, January 15th. The ministry are S. G. Landon, '89, Jenkins, '91, and Henderson, '92.[3]

◊

THE WESLEYAN HOUSE OF COMMONS.

Prof. Woodrow Wilson is the father of the House of Commons in Johns Hopkins University[4] and in Bryn Mawr College. After consulting with the undergraduates throughout this college, and finding a favorable opinion predominating, he called a college meeting at 9 o'clock Saturday morning, Jan. 5th, and addressed those gathered as follows: In proposing to establish a Wesleyan House of Commons it is necessary to discuss the old style of literary societies. They are uniformly of the same class and style; a galvanic movement simulating life, but not life. The effect of the ordinary debating society is unfortunate. To argue any case on any side, without the basis of a conviction of any sort, is mental suicide. In the ordinary debating society some financial spur to effect attendance and interest is administered, while the generation of interest is the best spur.

The function of our new organization is the function of debate, which is the basis for the special art of oratory. Highest oratory is arrived at through the cultivation of the art of debate. To imitate the House of Representatives would be patriotic, but not interesting. The House of Representatives does not do its own debating, but refers most of its business to standing committees, and if the committees recommend, the House is apt to pass the resolution as a matter of course. So we shall imitate the British House of Commons, thereby introducing a dramatic element in that a body of ministers resigns when defeated. The ministers will support the questions they believe in, and the natural party line will arise without any arbitrary divisions. When this scheme was first introduced at Baltimore, it seemed that a ministry among 200 students would have a precarious existence indeed, but only three ministries were made in four years. Several colleges have already taken up this method of establishing interest in debate. It is this which we seek, and we do not copy the House of Commons of England because it is English, you know.

Prof. Wilson's remarks were received with great applause, and the spirit was a unanimous one to adopt the new plan for developing the interest in debate. The meeting was opened for remarks of an adverse nature, but none forthcoming, the meeting closed with the announcement that on the following Tuesday evening another meeting would be held for the election of speaker and for the adoption of constitution and by-laws. The meeting adjourned, leaving the college impressed with the idea that at last a way had opened for cultivation in a normal way of debate, and that all that tends to divide the college into groups should be forgotten in the new effort of training a wholesome college spirit.

Printed in the Middletown, Conn., *Wesleyan Argus*, XXII (Jan. 18, 1889), 79-80.

1 Frederick Morgan Davenport.

2 Arthur W. Partch.

[3] Samuel Gail Landon, John Evan Jenkins, and Theodore Sommers Henderson.

[4] For a note on the Hopkins House of Commons, see WW to ELA, Dec. 15, 1884, n. 3, Vol. 3. There is no evidence that Wilson had organized a Bryn Mawr House of Commons.

From John Franklin Jameson

My dear Wilson: Providence, Jan. 8, 1889.

This is a doubtless unneeded reminder that we are expecting to have the pleasure of hearing a lecture from you on Friday evening. I'm sure you'll give us a much better lecture than Low did. Yet he took well; and we feel that we have made a very successful start.

I will meet you at the train on Friday afternoon. Leaving Middletown at 2.15 you will arrive here at 5.50, and aid in consuming a frugal supper at my boarding-house. As to leaving in the morning, the trains are all right; my only anxiety is, lest you should do it. With the kindest regards to Mrs. Wilson and the young ladies, Truly yours, J. F. Jameson

I will tell you orally of the American Historical Association; also of a project I have; and you shall answer orally the letters unanswered by pen.

ALS (WP, DLC).

From Joseph Ruggles Wilson

My precious son— Clarksville Jany 10th 89.

Were I in better health you should for once see what a *long* letter I am capable of writing, and how "compact of love" I could make it. For yours, just received, seems to call both for many words and for much affection: the words, in order to remove from your mind an impression that I *might* have visited you (when on my trip to N. York) if I had only willed it: the affection, to further open to you the fact that my heart is altogether yours and that therefore I suffered quite as sorely ("savagely" is your mild term) as yourself in my act of deprivation. But, indeed I do now regret that after all I had not stolen a day from duties here for the purpose of holding my darling boy in my arms once more, and Ellie to boot—for literally as well as metaphorically my arms are extensive enough for such an achievement. I the more regret the non-commission of such an act of theft for the reason that my health seems about to fail me in the shape of a lung-complaint which is beginning with bronchitis—to end who knows when or where? And oh if I should not be permitted to see you again in this world, how bitterly would I mourn the failure to go to Middletown! Yet, do not be needlessly alarmed. You know that I am not accustomed to physical suffering, and am therefore apt to exaggerate every ailment and each symptom. But I contracted a deep "cold" during my return journey which refuses to quit its grip, and renders me somewhat anxious. The doctor however does not look grave over the matter, which heartens me a good deal—and besides I attend to my class duties as usual. Pneumonia is my present dread—but it may be nothing *more* than a dread. Be sure of this, that should I get seriously worse you shall be informed at once. Therefore if you hear nothing, rest satisfied that I am merely scared. And I tell you thus much only to account for a short note instead of a many-paged letter.

Send me a copy of yr. Review article when published—please.

Love unbounded to you all. Your household is in the deepest deep of my inmost heart. Your affc Father.

ALS (WP, DLC).

To Joseph Ruggles Wilson

My precious father, Middletown, Ct., Jan'y 13, '89.

Your account of your cold, caught on your way home, has distressed me infinitely. I hope with all my heart that you are mistaken as to the hold it has or the mischief it means: and your splendid constitution cannot succumb to such influences, if you are as careful as you ought to be for love of us; but the mere fact that you are sick goes far towards keeping my spirits weighted down. Please, Sir, make haste and get well!

It wasn't necessary to say that you would have come to see us if you could: I did not for a moment grieve because you *would* not; I only mourned because you *could* not. I know and love you too well to misjudge anything you do; but it was *so* hard to have you so near and yet not see you!

Your letter came while I was away—on a thirty-hour trip to Providence, R. I. whither I went to deliver a lecture ('under the auspices of the Historical and Economic Association of Brown University') on "Systems of City Organization."[1] I send you the best newspaper report.[2] The first part (about a column) is all right—that I had written out and the reporter copied most of the sentences. Much of the rest is wrong, some of it absurdly wrong. But you can get an idea of what I talked about in general. I was extremely well rec'd and think that I can say that I made a decided hit. After the lecture Col. Goddard,[3] who introduced me, and who is one of the richest men in an extremely rich town, as well as a man of sense and of cultivated tastes, took me to his house and entertained me most handsomely. He tried to make me believe, by almost every turn of his conversation, that I was quite a distinguished man. I came home so puffed up that I could hardly condescend to speak even to my own family! I lecture there again next Friday on the government of Berlin—a model govt. in its kind.

All this keeps me rather too busy on the eve of my departure for Baltimore—for which place I shall set out about the first week in February, (D. V.) I ought to find *some* time for preparation for my work there. I shall stay there fully six weeks, I suppose. It will be a sadly dreary business being separated so long from Ellie and the babies: but Ellie and the babies must be supported—so,∴, must the separation.

I am in excellent health—indeed we are all of us ship-shape now that the weather is behaving itself.

Tell dear 'Dode' that I rec'd and enjoyed his letter.[4] I am so glad that he likes the present I sent him—the "Outing" subscription. I will write to him next.

With love unbounded from us both to you both and a prayer from the bottom of our hearts for your health,

Your devoted son Woodrow.

ALS (de Coppet Coll., NjP).

1 For his lecture at Brown on January 11, 1889, Wilson used a WWhw MS. (WP, DLC) entitled "Modern Systems of City Government." This outline is not printed because it is virtually a verbatim copy of the outline for the public lecture at the Johns Hopkins printed at March 2, 1888, Vol. 5.

2 From the *Providence Journal*, Jan. 12, 1889, or the Providence *Evening Bulletin*, Jan. 12, 1889. The report in the latter was an identical copy of the report in the former.

3 William Goddard, Providence banker and merchant, former colonel in the Union army.

4 J. R. Wilson, Jr., to WW, Jan. 6, 1889, ALS (WP, DLC).

A News Item

[*c. Jan. 15, 1889*]

THE WESLEYAN HOUSE OF COMMONS.

At the meeting of the House of Commons on the evening of January 15, Speaker Partch, on taking the chair, appointed W.

W. Thompson clerk, and L. L. Norton[1] sergeant at arms. The minutes of the preceding meeting were read and accepted with one or two slight corrections. Mr. Miles[2] then reported for the committee on by-laws, submitting a set of laws with the recommendation that they be adopted. Mr. Gascoigne[3] moved that the report be adopted. This motion was seconded and, after some debate, passed. The by-laws were then considered one by one. On the article concerning the time of meeting there was considerable debate. As recommended by the committee, the time of meeting was to be every dagger Tuesday. Mr. Hughes[4] moved to amend by substituting "every alternate Saturday." He said that fewer fellows would be necessarily absent on Saturday evening than on any other, and that as we had no recitations for the next day it would be much easier for the majority of the college to attend. Mr. Glenn[5] opposed the amendment on the ground that there was often as much to do on Saturday evening as on Tuesday and that, later in the year, it would be apt to interfere with the athletic interests. Mr. C. F. Eggleston[6] was opposed to Tuesday evening because it interfered with the meetings both of the Scientific Association and of the Methodist Church League. After some further debate the question was put and the amendment lost. The next amendment of importance offered was at the reading of the article concerning the time each speaker might occupy and the number of times he might speak. As the article read, each speaker had the right to speak without limit. Mr. Miles moved to amend by limiting each speaker to one speech. An amendment to his amendment was moved, limiting each speaker to ten minutes. This was lost. Professor Wilson was called on to give his opinion on the amendment. He said that he favored giving each speaker unlimited time. The house was a body which could defend itself against anyone who was trying to impose on it. It had lungs and the door was open. Slow men often had very good things to say and they were worth waiting for. The amendment was carried. Section 3 was amended by making the wish of one-fifth of those present necessary for a call of the yeas and nays. No more amendments were carried. When the by-laws as a whole came up for adoption, it was moved to amend by inserting "star Wednesday" for "dagger Tuesday" in article I., section I. This amendment was lost and the by-laws, as a whole, were adopted. It was moved and carried that the committee on by-laws be continued to provide for printing the constitution and by-laws, and also that the clerk be ordered to purchase a gavel and sounding block. The ministry gave notice that two bills would be considered at the next meeting; one regarding the changing the name of Wesleyan University, the other on the annexation of Canada. The meeting then adjourned.

Printed in the Middletown, Conn., *Wesleyan Argus*, XXII (Feb. 1, 1889), 90-91.

1 Wilson Wallace Thompson, '90, and Lyon Levi Norton, '90.

2 Rowland Miles, '89.

3 Frederick Augustus Gascoigne, '90.

4 George Mead Hughes, '89.

5 George W. Meek Glenn, '89.

6 Charles Fellows Eggleston, '90.

An Editorial from the *Wesleyan Argus*

[Jan. 18, 1889]

The recently organized House of Commons is, we believe, destined to become one of the most interesting and valuable features of Wesleyan life. The main facts concerning the formation of this new institution are given in the local column. Suffice it to say here that the primary object of the organization is to furnish a channel for the most effective training in the art of debate. Bills are to be introduced and discussed, and ministries are to be formed and dissolved after the manner of the English system. The House of Commons is chosen in preference to our own House of Representatives, because the work of the latter body is accomplished so largely through committees that the function of debate on most questions is a very limited one. And then it is thought that the dramatic element of turning out a ministry will give more than an ordinary interest to the proceedings. The meetings will be held in the chapel on alternate Tuesday evenings, and Administration and Opposition party lines will be drawn very tight. Prof. Woodrow Wilson is the originator of the idea.

We welcome this organization most heartily, because we believe it has in it the germ of great promise. We venture to say that no man has passed through Wesleyan of late years without feeling the lack of a center of corporate, college interest. Fraternity life, though very pleasant and profitable in its way, has been too exclusive; and the consequence has been the considerable development of a narrow, unhealthy, partisan spirit, which has been harmful to the college. The new House of Commons, bringing, as it will, the men of all stripes and creeds into friendly friction and association, ought to destroy the present intense partisan bias and exert a most helpful, broadening influence. Aside from the splendid drill in open discussion and Parliamentary practice, the House will furnish a means which has not hitherto been afforded of getting at the general, intelligent sentiment on all college questions. The result must, we think, be a training in college spirit of the truest and worthiest kind. For all these reasons we are in hearty sympathy with the project.

Printed in the Middletown, Conn., *Wesleyan Argus*, XXII (Jan. 18, 1889), 73.

A Newspaper Report of a Lecture on Municipal Government[1]

[Jan. 19, 1889]

Further Discussion of City Government by Prof. Woodrow Wilson.

Berlin was the foreign example of city organization that Professor Wilson discussed in Manning Hall last evening in the Economic Society's course on City Governments. He reminded his hearers that there are certain principles that obtain as general in cities of the present age. A large city is only a part of a system, a part of the organization of local self-government. The modern city has a different reason for existence than a medieval city had; and that is not a political reason. The township serves the purposes of local self-government better than the city. The city exists because of industrial and commercial reasons. In this relation the city is the creation of the present century, dating from a time well within the memory of a generation still living. The chief characteristic of a city, therefore, is that of a business corporation. But it is by no means so simple as if it were only a business corporation. It is also an organ of government, a political body, and its complexity arises from this fact. The Nineteenth Century has yet to shows [show] its ability to unite a business and a political purpose successfully in one corporation. In so far as it perfects its own means to attain its ends, the city contributes to its own success. All must be done, however, within the larger circle of the State. A city is then a business corporation whose hands are in large part hampered and its existence as a body politic is entirely controlled by outside affairs. It has a double life and a double limitation of its political and industrial activity.

The speaker said he would not dwell upon plans for the improvement of city government, on the power of Mayors and

[1] In this, his second, lecture at Brown University, Wilson followed the outline prepared for a public lecture at the Johns Hopkins, printed at March 16, 1888, Vol. 5. No outline or notes prepared especially for the Brown lecture seem to have survived, and it is probable that Wilson simply used the outline already in hand.

Boards and the responsibility of administrations. These matters do not go to the centre of the question, but they seek after new devices, new methods of improvement from the outside. It will be of interest to try the subject from a different point of view. The way is this, in finding an answer to the question: Who shall participate in the city government? Not what power this or that official or board shall have.

Perhaps what we need is a new analysis of self-government; new principles, instead of new mechanism. There is success under all systems in different cities: one succeeds without concentration of power in the Mayor's hands; another with it. All depends upon the capacity of the men in office. Voting is not self-government. It has been rather wittily said that the modern political man is a new kind of marsupian with a pouch full of voting papers, who goes about trying to drop them. Wherever he does drop them self-government is established. But does the man who votes for another not delegate to that other man his own rights? Self-government consists in taking part in the government and having a hand in it. If we could give, say, to the better middle class the whole power of government, then we should have discovered self-government. It is needless to say that this was formerly the custom, and we find it is so if we go back to the old Germanic system. In some great cities of modern times a curious spectacle is presented. Small private clubs are formed, of four or five, who hire an attorney to watch the City Council, to see that they don't exceed their powers or go beneath the surface in manipulating affairs. When he finds they are doing so, he calls immediate attention in the public prints, or if that does not succeed, he institutes legal proceedings. This singular custom constitutes the people spies, instead of really putting the government into their hands. By voting they abrogate their own powers, and stand off to see government done by somebody else, instead of doing it themselves. What we should seek is a way to harness the people to the great wagon of state and make them pull it: to make their intermittent interest a permanent duty. If we can do that, no argument as to its advisability is necessary, if the way can be shown.

In selecting the example of Berlin, the speaker said it was not a foreign example, strictly speaking: it was just as truly an English example. It is a pan-Teutonic example of processes that seemed to inhere in the ancient policy of the people to which we belong. This is not a fanciful illustration because that has been made the deliberate purpose. Baron von Stein, the originator of the Prussian system, was thoroughly imbued with English precedents, as founded on old Germanic types. Later Gneist has worked in this field, whose reputation rests on English institutions, and whose precedents all go back to England. So we shall not find ourselves on unfamiliar ground by going back to Berlin.

Berlin does not stand by itself, but is closely connected with the other Prussian cities of the system it is a part of. There are three leading principles in its government. There is a Board of Aldermen, composed of certain paid officials with a civil service training, who are elected constantly, so that their term of office is practically permanent. But they constitute a minority of the Board. Alongside of them are other members, chosen from the general body of citizens, who go in with them on perfect [e]quality.

The system of voting is characteristic of the Prussian system. The voters are divided into three classes, according to their contribution to the taxes, chiefly to the income taxes. The division could be made so that each class should include an equal number of citizens; but this is not the case. All who pay the highest amount in taxes, a certain small number, are in the first class; then in the second a few more and in the third the great body of the people. In Berlin the first class has a few over 3000, the second about 16,000, and the third about 166,000. Each one of these classes elects an equal number to the Board of Aldermen; in Berlin 42, there being 126 members in all.

In every department of executive activity there is a coöperation of three classes. First of the Aldermen, second by the Councillors, from the City Council, and third by certain selected and prominent people, associated with these, so to speak, professional people. Whenever the business separates into matters pertaining to the separate wards, additional numbers from the people are chosen to join them. In Berlin there are in this way over 10,000 people associated in the Government, besides the paid officers of the civil service. They serve not only without pay, but without choice to decline. Further, it is the law that a man must serve, or else lose his franchise and have his taxes raised from a sixth to a third. And the law is carried out with an iron determination worthy of the Iron Chancellor.

There is a Mayor who presides over the city government; he is not the chief magistrate but he simply presides over the Board of Aldermen. He has the general oversight of the business, and of the distribution of business through the various branches of administration. Over such branches preside fifteen paid officials and seventeen unpaid, and all the Councillors without salary. The fifteen are elected for twelve years and are generally reëlected. The seventeen are elected for six years, and one-third go out periodically, as in our Federal Senate. The citizen part of the Board of Aldermen is constantly changing, and is sensitive to public opinion; the "professional" part is practically permanent. An Alderman presides over each branch of administration; if a special or technical branch, one of the trained ones.

Take the matter of poor relief. One of the Board of Aldermen presides; associated with him are eight Aldermen, one lawyer, the City Treasurer, one of the two professional School Commissioners, eighteen Councillors and ten selected citizens. In each ward there is a ward committee, including the Councilmen from that ward and twelve to fourteen selected citizens. They have a salary for the payment of a secretary, and office hours, at least one hour a day, to receive application. Altogether there are 3300 people daily engaged in poor relief. When an orphan or an illegitimate child needs to be educated, there is a committee of local magistrates to determine what shall be done with him. Some ladies also serve on the Board, thus giving a proper motherly interest.

If there is to be a summary trial, or a trial in which summary punishment is involved, two citizens are always associated with the magistrate, not as perfunctory advisers, but with as much voice as he, and being two to one they can outvote him. In every ward there is a citizen arbitrator with Deputy to hear cases such as slander. Such an officer generally kills slander before it gets to the Courts. The citizen magistrate knows the circumstances generally and can placate the parties. So in paving the streets, controlling buildings and such matters, there are always citizens associated with the magistrates.

What about the Board of Council? This is an unpaid body with but one function, the preparation and oversight of the budget. History proves, if it proves anything, that large representative bodies have one special excellence, and that is the oversight of expenditures. The speaker acknowledged all the corruption and jobbery that they have perpetrated, but said it never has proved safe to intrust this matter to any other than large representative bodies. This Board of Councillors meet with the City Chamberlain and other officers in open session, and their proceedings must be public and published in the newspapers, so that they shall have as wide publicity as possible. The expenditure of money belongs not to the special officers who may manipulate the funds, but to the Citizen Boards. The good results are manifest. For example, a crying evil of poor relief has always been that the demand for it always increases till it seems as if half the population would be depending upon the other half. Under these citizen committees who know the circumstances of applicants, and how far to go and when to stop, expenditures for poor relief have diminished from 19¾ per cent to 9¾ per cent of the total expenditure. On the other hand, in the branch of education, the expenditures have increased. In other words, [in] those lines of expenditure where an increase is naturally demanded, it has occurred, while where a decrease is necessary for the healthy life of the community, it also has taken place.

The speaker did not claim that the Berlin Government was without defects. But do we want a government without defects? If no one is ever hurt by the application of the system, there will be no growls, and no one will ever start up new reforms. It is obvious that the Berlin plan is cumbrous; it is a most complex machinery, difficult to understand, and also to run. But the principal thing in which we differ from savages is that we want to deliberate, while the savage wishes to act at once. So far as we take time to deliberate, do we take time to succeed. As you increase effectiveness, and speed in government, must you decrease the number of persons concerned; but you also increase the liability to mistake. If in Berlin the central committee did the business, it would make mistakes; as a matter of fact it has only oversight of local boards. This is tedious, the necessity of getting many people to make up their minds; but the test is that the net result is very efficient. And even suppose we admit the loss of efficiency, would it not be worth the price of losing efficiency to educate so many people? Socialism is an infinitely easy thing for the voters and an infinitely difficult one for the administrators; and people who constantly handle affairs will see that Socialism is an extreme difficulty or an impossibility. Competent administrators are exceedingly rare. It is safer to trust the major weight of judgment to many people than to trust a few who may deceive themselves.

If I have made a single impression, said Professor Wilson in conclusion, I have meant it to be this, that there are other ways of reforming a city than by changing the disposition of power. The imperious demand is to get citizens to become stirred up and interested. In the greatest centres of corruption one single day of public indignation sweeps all away and leaves the atmosphere purified for months or years afterwards.

Without inviting assistance from foreign systems, it is worth while to study a system which brings 10,000 people daily and unofficially into public business.

The next lecture will be Friday, Januray 25, by Professor A. B. Hart, of Harvard University, on The People of American Cities.

Printed in the *Providence Journal,* Jan. 19, 1889; one editorial heading omitted.

From Munroe Smith

My dear Wilson: New York City. Jan. 19 '89.

I send proof of your review-article. I hope you will not mind my saying that some of the sentences are not as lucid as your sentences regularly are. You generally have the knack of saying the thing so that it is understood at first glance—but in reading some of the sentences in this article, I found myself running back to see just what you meant. Of course I could always find out, but it was a surprise to me to be obliged to look back at all.

Did you omit reference to Lowe's preface[1] and Goodnow's[2] chapter because you thought them too slight for mention—or because you did not wish to say ill, and could not conscientiously say well of them? The reader who knows the book would, I think, draw the former inference from your silence—in so full a notice.

Take your time about revision. There is an English article going in ahead of yours, of which the revise is not yet back from London. Yours very truly Munroe Smith

P.S. ad p. 10 Surely a generalization from a quantity of facts is an *in*duction, not a deduction—is it not?

P.S. ad p. 14 I should query your theory that the law at any time is what the people suppose it to be. I think this is true only of primitive society. In the most advanced stages of society the popular sense of right still produces law—but only indirectly. The conversion of the vague sense of right into legal rule is accomplished through the medium of a juristic class (as Savigny long ago pointed out); and the people, by and large, neither make the law nor know what it is. *What they think ought to be law* is very likely to become law in a generation or two; but their supposition *what is law* seems rather immaterial, unless it be an expression of their sense of *what ought to be.*

ALS (WP, DLC).

[1] Smith referred to Seth Low, "An American View of Municipal Government in the United States," in James Bryce, *The American Commonwealth* (3 vols., London and New York, 1888), II, 296-317. Low's chapter was actually a postscript to Part II, which dealt with state and local governments.

[2] Frank J. Goodnow, "The Tweed Ring in New York," in *ibid.*, III, 173-98.

Frederick Jackson Turner[1] to Caroline Mae Sherwood[2]

Dear little girl, Baltimore Md. Jan 21, 89

. . . This house[3] has been the home of the brightest men that J.H.U. ever sent out in history and literature. Dr Wilson who is to give a course of lectures in February is to be here when he returns—for he used to board here, and is a great friend of Miss A. I shall enjoy meeting him. He is one of the best historical men in this country. Miss Ashton was telling how he and Dr [C. H.] Shinn (now editor of the Overland Monthly) used to be chums, and how Wilson got a letter from the girl to whom he was engaged, saying that her father had gone insane and that she thought it best that the engagement be broken.[4] "What shall I do?" asked Wilson of Dr Shinn[.] "Go to her at once, sir," was his answer. "But I have not the money." "I will lend it to you." And so he packed his valise and took the next train, while Dr Shinn came down and told Miss Ashton all about the matter. "And now," said Miss A, "he is married to this girl and they are the happiest people in the world"—and I thought there was a touch of pathos in her voice, for she, I suspect, was much impressed by Dr W. herself. . . .

Good by, good by, good by Fred

ALS (F. J. Turner Coll., CSmH).

[1] Born at Portage, Wis., Nov. 14, 1861. A.B., University of Wisconsin, 1884; A.M., same institution, 1888. Ph.D., the Johns Hopkins, 1890. Assistant Professor of History, University of Wisconsin, 1889-91; Professor of History, same institution, 1891-1910; Professor of History, Harvard University, 1910-24. President, American Historical Association, 1909. Noted historian of the American frontier and sectionalism in the antebellum period. Died March 14, 1932. Turner discussed his long friendship with Wilson and Wilson's influence on his own thought in a retrospective letter to William E. Dodd, Oct. 7, 1919 (W. E. Dodd Papers, DLC), printed in Wendell H. Stephenson, "The Influence of Woodrow Wilson on Frederick Jackson Turner," *Agricultural History*, XIX (Oct. 1945), 249-53.

[2] Turner's fiancée, whom he married on November 25, 1889.

[3] Miss Ashton's boardinghouse, where Turner also roomed.

[4] This sheds further light on the reason for Wilson's sudden trip to Savannah, about which see C. H. Shinn to WW, Jan. 21, 1884, n. 3, Vol. 2, p. 662.

From John Franklin Jameson

My dear Wilson: Providence, January 22d, 1889.

Another set of "Cockrell's Report,"[1] on the management of government business, has come to me, though unbound. Would you like it? If so, I'll send it. If you have one, I'll give this to Gardner.

It is my fixed habit, when friends are here and there is little time, never to finish a sentence. I remember that I spoke of the Athenian Empire, and the Leagues, and did not go on to speak of the other two matters which you will see I have, in the same note, mentioned as omitted.[2] This might create the impression that I regarded that as of much more importance than the other two. So I take this opportunity to say that I regard as equally important the Expansion of Hellas, so to call it, in centt. VIII, VII, and cent. III.

I take it $28 will cover your fares and leave $20; so we send a check to that amount, and remain greatly your debtors for two, admirable lectures. With the kindest regards, and to Mrs. Wilson

Truly yours J. F. Jameson.

ALS (WP, DLC) with WWhw notation on env.: "Ans. 26/1/89."

1 Senator Francis M. Cockrell of Missouri was chairman of a special Senate committee appointed in 1887 to "inquire into and examine the methods of business and work in the Executive Departments, etc." The first report of his committee appeared in 1888 in two large volumes (50th Cong., 1st sess., Senate Report No. 507); a second report appeared the following year.

2 Jameson was referring to the section of the manuscript of *The State* dealing with the governments of Greece and Rome, which Wilson had left with Jameson on January 11. Jameson had gone through this section on January 16 and 17, making notes on Wilson's manuscript and observing in his diary: "Went through Wilson's chapter on the governments of Greece and Rome, which he left with me for that purpose. It disappoints me greatly by its insufficiency and want of perspective and entire grasp. Of course it is very clear and well-presented" (January 16, 1889). "Spent the day, outside of classwork, mostly . . . on Wilson's book, this part of which is better, though still inadequate in respect to many points of detail" (January 17, 1889). From Elizabeth Donnan and Leo F. Stock (eds.), *An Historian's World*, p. 48. Jameson returned the manuscript to Wilson, and the two men had talked further about it, when Wilson went back to Providence for his second lecture at Brown University on January 18.

From John Martin Vincent[1]

Dear Friend, Baltimore, Jan 24 18[8]9

For my own benefit I enclose a conundrum for you to ruminate upon ("trusting to make my peace with you when I see you next month")

What kind of a scheme would [it] be, in my treatment of Swiss institutions,[2] to begin, not with the Federal Government, but with the lowest unit, the citizen and his local sphere of action the community. That is, after an introductory historical sketch, begin with the individual and by the cumulative method, so to speak, treat of the various widening spheres of action demanded by larger bodies of society, the community, the district, the canton and finally the most general of all, the Federal government.

I have often thought of this as a desirable way to teach the theory of State by modern instances (as it always is used in tracing the origin of government) but see some difficulties in the way of clearness in descriptive writing.

Let me have your opinion on this point when you come down to Baltimore.

I suppose you expect me to hold your MS till that time.[3]

Very truly your friend J M Vincent.

ALS (WP, DLC) with WWhw notation on env.: "Ans. Jan'y 29/89."

[1] Born Elyria, Ohio, Oct. 11, 1857. A.B., Oberlin College, 1883; A.M., same institution, 1888. Student in Berlin and Leipzig, 1881-83, and at the Johns Hopkins, 1886-90, where he presumably first became acquainted with Wilson while attending Wilson's lectures on administration in 1888. Received the Ph.D. at the Johns Hopkins in 1890 and spent his entire teaching career at that institution as Instructor in History, 1890-91; Associate in History, 1892-95; Associate Professor of History, 1895-1905; and Professor of European History, 1905-25. Died Sept. 22, 1939.

[2] Vincent was referring to his doctoral dissertation, which appeared in published form as *State and Federal Government in Switzerland* (Baltimore, 1891).

[3] Wilson had obviously asked Vincent to read part of the manuscript of *The State*, probably Chapter VIII, "The Governments of Switzerland." No earlier letters between Wilson and Vincent seem to have survived.

To John Martin Vincent

My dear Vincent, Middletown, Conn., 29th., Jan'y, 1889.

I will do my best pondering on your "conundrum," and I feel already that I shall have something to say upon it when I see you. Method is one of the things most difficult to fix upon with any satisfaction to oneself, I find, in every branch of this perplexing and yet fascinating field of comparative politics. Every method has something to be said both for and against it; perhaps we can eliminate each other's difficulties.

Very sincerely Yours, Woodrow Wilson

WWTLS (CSmH).

To Munroe Smith

My dear Smith, Middletown, Conn., 31 Jan'y, '89.

Please pardon my very long retention of the revise of my review of Bryce. Your assurance that I need be in no hurry lulled me into a perilous ease of mind touching it: and I allowed other work to push it aside; it got into a pigeon-hole of my desk—and was overlooked.

I have made some emendations, suggested for the most part by the difficulty you report (with so neatly complimentary an apology) of understanding some part of my utterance upon the first reading; but I am afraid that the very obtuseness which made me write obscurely has prevented my seeing the obscurities. If so, please clarify me, if you can.

I am more than willing to remedy my omission of mention of Prof. Goodnow's chapter. I did not pass it over for either of the reasons you suggest, but simply because, my purpose being, not to outline the contents of the book systematically, but only to indicate its main lines and then strike for certain major points of criticism, I did not at first see how I could at once incidentally and *naturally* characterize a separate chapter contained, not in the systematic, but in the illustrative part of the work. I think that I have mentioned it naturally now; and I am sure that I am heartily glad to mention it with appreciation. As for Mr. Lowe's chapter, though it is good, very good in its way, I don't think that it's good enough to delay a paragraph,–good enough to stop the train for. And how mention Mr. Lowe without mentioning Mr. Bradford?

I have given a fuller expression of my thought in the sentence which imports into the substance of Eng. law contemporary opinion. By opinion I mean *publicist* opinion: and I think that judges are mouth-pieces of such opinion. I do not mean to govern law by the detailed legal views of the masses; but by the general legal views of those who may be said to lead and form (or, rather, formulate) thought,–the constituent thought of politics.

Thank you for the correction of the careless (foolish) writing of *de*ductive for *in*ductive, &c.

Hoping that the delay has not caused you serious inconvenience, Very sincerely Yours, Woodrow Wilson

ALS (*Political Science Quarterly* Papers, NNC).

A Book Review

[*c. Jan. 31, 1889*]

BRYCE'S AMERICAN COMMONWEALTH.

This is a great work, worthy of heartiest praise. Its strength does not lie in its style, although that, while lacking distinction, is eminently straightforward and clear; nor yet altogether in its broad scope of weighty topics,—a scope wide almost beyond precedent in such subjects, and rich in suggestion,—but chiefly in its method and in its point of view. Mr. Bryce does not treat the institutions of the United States as experiments in the application of theory, but as quite normal historical phenomena to be looked at, whether for purposes of criticism or merely for purposes of description, in the practical, every-day light of comparative politics. He seeks to put American institutions in their only instructive setting—that, namely, of comparative institutional history and life.

It is of course inevitable to compare and contrast what Mr. Bryce has given us in these admirable volumes with de Tocqueville's great *Democracy in America.* The relations which the two works bear the one to the other are almost altogether relations of contrast, and the contrast serves to make conspicuous the peculiar significance of what Mr. Bryce has written. De Tocqueville came to America to observe the operation of a principle of government, to seek a well-founded answer to the question: How does democracy work? Mr. Bryce, on the other hand, came, and came not once but several times, to observe the concrete phenomena of an institutional development, into which, as he early perceived, abstract political theory can scarcely be said to have entered as a formative force. The question for which he sought an answer was this: What sort of institutions have the English developed in America? In satisfaction of his curiosity, his keen and elevated philosophical desire, de Tocqueville saw the crude and impatient democracy of Andrew Jackson's time. Mr. Bryce has seen the almost full grown, the measurably sobered America of to-day, and has seen, therefore, with a fairer chance of just proportion.

It will hardly be accounted a disparagement of Mr. Bryce's style to say that it is inferior to de Tocqueville's; the thoughts it has to convey, the meanings it has to suggest belong to quite another class than that to which de Tocqueville's judgments must be assigned: it is not meant to carry the illumination of philosophical conceptions into the regions of fact which it explores; its task is rather exposition than judgment. Mr. Bryce does not feel called upon to compete with de Tocqueville in the field in which de Tocqueville is possibly beyond rivalry. Something very different was needed, and that he has done to admiration: he has written a book invaluable to students of comparative politics,—invaluable because of its fulness, its accuracy, its candor, its sane, perhaps I ought rather to say its sage, balance of practical judgment.

Mr. Bryce's qualifications for the great task he has thus worthily performed were probably equal to those of any other man of our generation. First of all, he is a Roman lawyer steeped in the legal and political conceptions of that race whose originative strength in the field of law and practical sagacity in the field of politics were as conspicuous and as potent in the ancient world as the legal capacity and political virility of the English race are in the modern world. His knowledge of Roman institutions constantly serves to remind him of the oldness and persistency of certain features of institutional development, to warn him against perceiving novelty where it does not exist. In the second place, he is a member of Parliament and an English constitutional statesman, knowing the parent stock from which our institutions sprang, not only through study, but also through having himself tasted of its present fruits. Perhaps no one can so readily understand our institutions as an English public man sufficiently read in our history and our constitutional law not to expect to find bishops in our Senate or prime ministers in the presidency. He has breathed the air of practical politics in the country from which we get our habits of political action; and he is so familiar with the machinery of government at home as to be able to perceive at once the most characteristic differences, as well as the real resemblances, between political arrangements in England and in the United States. He is prepared to see clearly, almost instinctively, the derivation of our institutions, at the same time that he is sure to be struck by even our minor divergences from English practice. But Mr. Bryce brought to the task of judging us a wider and more adequate preparation than even a schooling in Roman law and English practice could by itself have supplied. He is sufficiently acquainted with the history and practical operation of the present constitutions of the leading states of Europe to be able readily to discern what, in American practice, is peculiar to America, or to America and England, what common to modern political experience the world over. In brief, he has a comprehensive mastery of the materials of comparative politics, and great practical sagacity in interpreting them.

Mr. Bryce divides his work into six parts. In Part I he discusses "The National Government," going carefully over the ground made almost tediously familiar to American constitutional students by commentaries without number. But he gives to his treatment a freshness of touch and a comprehensiveness which impart to it a new and first-rate interest. This he does by combining in a single view both the legal theory and interpretation and the practical aspects and operation of the federal machinery. More than that, he brings that machinery and the whole federal arrangement into constant comparison with federal experiments and constitutional machinery elsewhere. There is a scope and an outlook here such as render his critical expositions throughout both impressive and stimulating. Congress, the presidency, and the federal courts are discussed in every point of view that can yield instruction. The forms and principles of the federal system are explained both historically and practically and are estimated with dispassionate candor. Perhaps the most emphasized point made in this part is one which is derived from comparative politics. It is the separation of the executive from Congress, a separation which deprives the executive of all voice in the formation of administrative and financial policy, and which deprives Congress of such leadership as would give its plans coherency and make available for its use that special and intimate knowledge of administrative possibilities without which much well-meant legislation must utterly miscarry. This is of course the particular in which our government differs most conspicuously from all the other governments of the world. Everywhere else there is one form or another of ministerial leadership in the legislature. A body of ministers constitutes, as it were, a nerve centre, or rather a sensitive presiding brain, in the body politic, taking from the nation such broad suggestions as public opinion can unmistakably convey touching the main ends to be sought by legislation and policy, but themselves suggesting in turn, in the light of their own special knowledge and intimate experience of affairs, the best means by which those ends may be attained. Because we are without such legislative leadership we remain for long periods of embarrassment without any solution of some of the simplest problems that await legislation.[1] To this absence of cabinet government in America, and the consequent absence of party government in the European sense of the term, Mr. Bryce again and again returns as to a salient feature, full of significance both for much evil and for some good.[2] The evil

[1] See especially vol. ii, pp. 316, 317. [Eds.' note: WW's footnotes have been renumbered consecutively.]

[2] See particularly vol. i, chap. xxv: Comparison of the American and European Systems.

consists in slipshod, haphazard, unskilled and hasty legislation; the good, so far as it may be stated in a single sentence, consists in delaying the triumphs of public opinion and thereby, perhaps, rendering them safer triumphs.

One chapter of this first part possesses conspicuous merit, namely, chapter xxiii, on "The Courts and the Constitution."[3] It brings out with admirable clearness the wholly normal character of the function of constitutional interpretation, as a function familiar from of old to English judicial practice in the maintenance of charter provisions, and of course necessary, according to English precedents and ideas, to the maintenance and application of charter-like written constitutions. In exposition of this view, now universally held but not always lucidly explained, he gives a prominence such as it has never before had to the very instructive fact that the constitution does not grant the power of constitutional interpretation to the federal courts in explicit terms, but that that power, so marvelled at by Europeans, is simply a necessary inference (at least a necessary *English* inference) from its general provisions touching the functions of a federal judiciary. One point touching the action of the courts is, however, left perhaps a little too much to this same English inference. It is stated that cases involving questions of constitutionality must wait to be made up in the ordinary manner at the initiative of private parties suing in their own interest and are often, most often, decided at the instance and in behalf of such private litigants; but it is left too much to inference—an inference easy of course to an American, but doubtless far from obvious to a foreigner—that a decision, when against the constitutionality of a law, is, not that the law is null and void, but is that the law *will not be enforced in that case.* Therefore other cases involving the same points will not be made up, litigants knowing what to expect, and it is *thus,* indirectly, that the desired annulment is effected. This is not a matter of form merely or only of curious interest. For Mr. Bryce's purpose it is a point of importance. It illustrates the thesis he is trying to establish, namely, the normality of the whole principle and procedure: the entire absence from our system of any idea of a veto exercised by the courts upon legislation or of any element of direct antagonism between Congress and the judiciary, and the matter-of-course interpretation of the supreme law by those who interpret all law.

[3] Vol. i, pp. 237-255.

The appendix to Volume I adds to this first part, besides much other illustrative matter, a statement of the main features of the federal structure of the two great English universities and the federal constitution of Canada.

Part II is devoted to "The State Governments." Here for the first time in any comprehensive treatise the states are given the prominence and the careful examination which they have always deserved at the hands of students of our institutions but have never before gotten. Under some seventeen heads, occupying as many close-packed chapters full of matter, the state governments (including of course local government and the virtually distinct subject of the government of cities), state politics, the territories, and the general topics in comparative politics suggested by state constitutions and state practice are discussed, so far as reliable materials serve, with the same interest and thoroughness that were in the first part bestowed upon the federal government. Mr. Bryce more than once urges upon European students of comparative politics the almost incomparable richness of this well-nigh unexplored region of state law. If he can wonder that Mr. Mill "in his *Representative Government* scarcely refers to" our states, and that "Mr. Freeman in his learned essays, Sir H. Maine in his ingenious book on *Popular Government*, pass by phenomena which would have admirably illustrated some of their reasonings," finding, as he does, in M. Boutmy and Dr. von Holst the only European discoverers in this field, it may profit American students to reflect in what light their own hitherto almost complete neglect of the constitutional history of the states ought to be viewed. This second part of Mr. Bryce's book ought to mark a turning point in our constitutional and political studies. In several of our greater universities some attention is already paid to state law and history; but it is safe to say that in no one of them are these subjects given the prominence they deserve; and it is safe to predict that our state history will some day be acknowledged a chief source of instruction touching the development of modern institutions. The states have been laboratories in which English habits, English law, English political principles have been put to the most varied, and sometimes to the most curious, tests; and it is by the variations of institutions under differing circumstances that the nature and laws of institutional growth are to be learned. While European nations have been timidly looking askance at the various puzzling problems now pressing alike in the field of economics and in the field of politics, our states have been trying experiments with a boldness and a persistency which, if generated by ignorance in many cases and in many fraught with disaster, have at any rate been surpassingly rich in instruction.

Part III, on "The Party System," is the crowning achievement of the author's method. Here in a learned systematic treatise which will certainly for a long time be a standard authority on our institutions, a much used hand-book for the most serious students of politics, we have a careful, dispassionate, scientific description of the "machine," an accurately drawn picture of "bosses," a clear exposition of the way in which the machine works, an analysis of all the most practical methods of "practical politics," as well as what we should have expected, namely, a sketch of party history, an explanation of the main characteristics of the parties of to-day, a discussion of the conditions of public life in the United States, those conditions which help to keep the best men out of politics and produce certain distinctively American types of politicians, and a complete study of the nominating convention. One can well believe that that not super-sensitive person, the practical politician, much as he pretends to scorn the indignant attacks made upon him by "pious" reformers, would be betrayed into open emotion should he read this exact and passionless, this discriminating and scientific digest of the methods by which he lives, of the motives by which he is moved. And certainly those who are farthest removed from the practical politician's point of view will gain from these chapters a new and vital conception of what it is to study constitutions in the life. The wholesome light of Mr. Bryce's method shines with equal ray alike upon the just and upon the unjust.

Mr. Bryce very happily describes our system of nomination by convention as

> an effort of nature to fill the void left in America by the absence of the European parliamentary or cabinet system, under which an executive is called into being out of the legislature by the majority of the legislature. In the European system no single act of nomination is necessary, because the leader of the majority comes gradually to the top in virtue of his own strength.[4]

But what, in view of this, are we to say of his judgment[5] that "a system for selecting candidates is not a mere contrivance for preventing party dissensions, but an essential feature of matured

[4] Vol. ii. p. 187.
[5] Vol. ii, p. 47.

democracy"? Clearly no system for nominating candidates can touch the leading places in a democracy, however matured that democracy may be, if those places be filled under the parliamentary or cabinet system, as they are in England and France. Mr. Bryce is able to show that the selection of candidates by local representative party associations has been coming more and more into vogue in England *pari passu* with the widening of the franchise, having in 1885 been behind almost every new Liberal candidate for the Commons;[6] but is it quite safe to argue *cum hoc ergo propter hoc*? Of course it needs no nominating convention in Midlothian to select Mr. Gladstone, and no caucus in any other constituency to choose for the voters a man who has made himself necessary because of mastery in Parliament, because of proof given there of a dominant mind in statesmanship. But, leaving parliamentary leaders apart, is not all nominating machinery a "separable accident" rather than an essential feature of democracy? Has it failed of construction in Switzerland merely because of the smallness of the Swiss constituencies? Have not the exceeding multiplicity of elective officers and that pernicious principle that no one may be chosen state or national representative except from the district in which he lives—a principle whose history runs back to insignificant Governor Phips of colonial Massachusetts—been more to blame than anything that can be regarded as essential to democracy? Above all is not that complete obscuration of individual responsibility which results from the operation of the "checks and balances" of our system chiefly chargeable? It prevents any man from selecting himself for leadership by conspicuous service and makes the active part of politics turn upon selecting men rather than upon selecting measures. Men are not identified with measures; there must, consequently, be some artificial way of picking them out.

In enumerating the causes why the best men do not enter politics,[7] Mr. Bryce seems to me to omit one of the most important, although he elsewhere repeatedly gives evidence that he is in full view of it, namely, the absence of all great prizes of legislative leadership to be won by sheer strength of persuasive mind and constructive skill. He sums up the reasons he does give with admirable point, however, by saying that "in America, while politics are relatively less interesting than in Europe, and lead to less, other careers are relatively more interesting and lead to more";[8] but he omits to state, in this connection, one of the most

[6] Vol. ii, p. 48, note.

[7] Vol. ii, chap. lviii, pp. 37-43.

[8] Vol. ii, p. 41.

patent reasons why politics are relatively less interesting, why they lead to less, here than elsewhere.[9]

Part IV, on "Public Opinion," its American organs, its American characteristics, its American successes and failures, contains some of the author's best analytical work, but is less characteristic of his method than the preceding parts.

Part V contains "Illustrations and Reflections." It opens with an excellent chapter on the Tweed ring by one of the most lucid of our own writers, Professor Goodnow; treats of other special phases of local ring government; of "Kearneyism in California," of *laissez faire*, of woman's suffrage, and of the supposed and true faults of democracy as it appears in America.

Part VI concerns "Social Institutions"—railroads, Wall street, the bench, the bar, the universities, the influence of religion, the position of women, the influence of democracy on thought and on creative intellectual power, American oratory, *etc.*,—and contains the author's cautious forecast of the political, social, and economic future of the United States.

All through, the work is pervaded with the air of practical sense, the air of having been written by an experienced man of affairs, accustomed to handle institutions as well as to observe them. Besides, this observer is an Englishman without English insularity, with views given elasticity by wide studies of institutions and extensive travel. He understands us with the facility of one who belongs to the same race; but he understands us also in our relations with the politics of the wider world of Europe.

The work, however, has the faults of its good qualities. If it is full of acute and sage observation and satisfying in its wonderfully complete practical analysis, it gains its advantage at a certain sacrifice. The movement of the treatment is irregular, and even hesitating at times, like the varied conversation of a full, reiterative talker; and the internal plan of each part is lacking in executive directness and consistency, is even sometimes a little confused, reminding one now and again of the political system the author is describing. So judicious and balanced is the tone, too, that it is also a little colorless. It is a matter-of-fact book in which, because of the prominence and multiplicity of

9 For Mr. Bryce's recognition of the readiness of the people to receive and follow leaders whenever circumstances produce them, spite of institutions—an acknowledgment apparently not perfectly consistent with some other judgments of the book (*e.g.*, that any arrogation of a right to consideration, greater than that accorded to the ordinary, the average man, is resented)—see vol. ii, pp. 333, 334.

the details, it is often difficult to discern the large proportions of the thought. It is full of thoughts, thoughts singularly purged of prejudice, notably rich in suggestion; but these thoughts do not converge towards any common conceptions. It is rather, one may imagine, like that lost book of Aristotle's which contained his materials of observation than like the *Politics*. It carries one over immense distances characteristic of its great subject; but this it does by carrying one in many directions, in order to do which, from substantially the same point of departure in each case, it repeatedly traverses the same ground. In brief, it is an invaluable store-house of observations in comparative politics rather than of guiding principles of government inductively obtained. The facts, not the principles derivable from them, are prominent.

These underlying principles could not, indeed, have been made prominent without a much freer use, a much fuller use, of the historical method than Mr. Bryce has allowed himself; and it is in his sparing use of history that Mr. Bryce seems to me principally at fault. The other drawbacks to his treatment which I have mentioned are, no doubt, for the most part directly due to his purpose, clearly and consistently kept in view, to explore this rich field of politics in search of the facts only, not in search of generalizations. His method is that of thorough, exact, exhaustive analysis. But history belongs to the very essence of such a method: facts in comparative politics possess little value in the absence of clues to their development; and one cannot but wonder at the apologies which preface Mr. Bryce's occasional introduction of historical matter. Without more history than he gives there must be at least a partial failure to meet the demands of his own method. His work satisfies all who are in search of information, whether as to the existing facts or as to the formal historical derivation of our institutions. But its historical portions do not go beyond the formal history of measures and of methods to make evident the forces of national development and material circumstances which have lain behind measures and methods, and which, when once the nation gets past the youth of its continent, must work deep modification in its institutions and in its practical politics.

I can best illustrate what I mean by taking as points of departure Mr. Bryce's own clear statements of the views with which he approached our institutions. "America," he says, "is made all of a piece; its institutions are the product of its economic and social conditions and the expression of its character."[10] More pointedly and forcibly still does he express the same thing at page 404 of the same volume, in his chapter on *laissez faire*. He there reports himself as having said, to an English friend who bade him devote a chapter to the American theory of the state, "that the Americans had no theory of the state, and felt no need for one, being content, like the English, to base their constitutional ideas upon law and history." "No one doubts," he says, in another place, "that fifty years hence it [America] will differ at least as much from what it is now, as it differs now from the America which de Tocqueville described";[11] and this difference, he is evidently ready to believe, may very possibly be a difference of institutions as well as a difference in material and social condition. Once again, in the chapters in which he discusses the influence of democracy on thought and on creative intellectual power, Mr. Bryce insists, assuredly with perfect justice, that political institutions have comparatively little to do with intellectual product and quality, certainly in the case of the United States. There is really, when American institutions are compared with English, nothing essentially novel in our political arrangements: they are simply the normal institutions of the Englishman in America. They are, in other words, English institutions as modified by the conditions surrounding settlements effected under corporate charters, in separate but neighbor colonies; above all as dominated by the material, economic, and social conditions attending the advance of the race in America. These conditions it is, not political principles, that have controlled our intellectual as well as our political development. Mr. Bryce has frequently to say of propositions of de Tocqueville's that, although possibly or even probably true when advanced, they are now no longer true; for example, certain "supposed faults of democracy." Many things supposed to be due to democracy, to political ideas, have turned out, under the test of time, to be due to circumstances. So disconnected with institutions, indeed, are actual national methods and characteristics that even what Mr. Bryce says of American public opinion in his very suggestive and valuable fourth part will doubtless be true only so long as our country is new. Americans, he says, are sympathetic, but they are unsettled and changeful. This cannot remain true of the people of an old and fully settled country, where sympathy will lead to cohesiveness and to the development of local types of

10 Vol. ii, p. 473.
11 Vol. ii, p. 691.

opinion, where variety, consequently, will take the place of that uniformity of life and opinion which now leads to a too rapid transmission of impressions and impulses throughout the whole body of the nation,—the quick contagion of even transient impressions and emotions. America is now sauntering through her resources and through the mazes of her politics with easy nonchalance; but presently there will come a time when she will be surprised to find herself grown old,—a country crowded, strained, perplexed,—when she will be obliged to fall back upon her conservatism, obliged to pull herself together, adopt a new regimen of life, husband her resources, concentrate her strength, steady her methods, sober her views, restrict her vagaries, trust her best, not her average, members. That will be the time of change.

All this Mr. Bryce sees; his conspicuous merit consists, indeed, in perceiving that democracy is not a cause but an effect, in seeing that our politics are no explanation of our character, but that our character, rather, is the explanation of our politics. Throughout his work you feel that he is generally conscious of the operation of historical causes and always guided by a quick appreciation of the degree to which circumstances enter into our institutions to mould and modify them. A reader who is himself conscious of our historical make-up and tendencies can see that Mr. Bryce is also. But it is one thing for a writer to be conscious of such things himself and quite another thing for him to convey to readers not possessed of his knowledge adequate conceptions of historical development. If our politics are the expression of our character and if that character is the result of the operation of forces permanent in the history of the English race, modified in our case by peculiar influences, subtle or obvious, operative in our separate experience, the influences, namely, of a peculiar legal status and of unexampled physical surroundings, then it is to the explanation of these forces and influences that every means of exposition ought to be bent in order to discover the bases of our law and our constitutions, of our constructive statesmanship and our practical politics. A description of our institutions, even though it be so full and accurate as to call for little either of criticism or addition, like this of Mr. Bryce's, will not suffice unless backed by something that goes deeper than mere legal or phenomenal history. In legal history Mr. Bryce leaves little to be desired: nothing could be more satisfying than his natural history of our courts with their powers of constitutional interpretation. The course of constitutional amendment, too, he traces, and all such concrete phenomena as the growth and operation of nominating conventions, the genesis and expansion of the spoils system, or of municipal rings and "bossdom," *etc.* But outside of legal and phenomenal history he seldom essays to go. If his method were that which de Tocqueville too often followed, there would be little reason why he should look further than visible institutions; if a nation can be understood by the single light of its institutions, its institutions may be made to stand forth as itself. But if institutions be the expression of the national life, as Mr. Bryce rightly conceives, that national life must be brought constantly forward, even in its most hidden aspects, to explain them.

Some passages of Mr. Bryce's work, indeed, afford ground for suspecting that he does not himself always make sufficient private analysis even of the forces operative outside of our laws and acting in support and vivification of them. Thus he permits himself the old expression that we are "trying an experiment" in government. This is not true except in the same sense that it is true that the English are trying an experiment in their extensions of the franchise and in their extreme development of ministerial responsibility to the Commons. We are in fact but living an old life under new conditions. Where there is conservative continuity there can hardly be said to be experiment. Again, Mr. Bryce's statement,—the old statement,—that 1789 witnessed the birth of a national government could be made only by one who had not analyzed the growth of the national idea, which is coincident with the conscious development of the national experience and life. Its truth in juristic theory may be cogently maintained; but from the lay historian's point of view, and particularly from the point of view proper to English institutional and legal history, it is scarcely true at all. In the first place, no people can be a nation before its time, and its time has not come until the national thought and feeling have been developed and have become prevalent. Until a people thinks its government national it is not national. In the second place, the whole history—indeed the very theory—of judge-made law such as ours, whether it be equity or common law, bears witness to the fact that for a body of English people *the fundamental principles of the law are at any given time substantially what they are then thought to be*. The saving fact is that English (and American) thought is, particularly in the sphere of law, cautiously conservative, coherently continuous, not carelessly or irresponsibly spreading abroad, but slowly "broadening down from precedent to precedent" within a well-defined course. It is not a flood, but a river. The complete nationality of our law, therefore, had to await the slowly developed nationality of our thought and habit. To leave out in any account of our development the growth of the national idea and habit, consequently, is to omit the best possible example of one of the most instructive facts of our politics, the development, namely, of constitutional principles outside the constitution, the thoroughly English accumulation of unwritten law. That there has been such an accumulation Mr. Bryce of course points out and illustrates; but because of his shyness touching the use of history, which he fears will be tedious or uninteresting, he leaves the matter, after all, without adequate analysis. For such an analysis is not supplied by his chapter (xxxiv) on "The Development of the Constitution by Usage." That chapter contains a history of measures, of certain concrete practices, but no account of the national sentiment which has so steadily grown into a controlling, disposing, governing force, and which has really become a most tremendous sort of "usage." It is a sketch of the development of the government rather than of the influences which have made the government and altered the conceptions upon which it rests.

This must be taken to explain also the author's somewhat inadequate view of the constitutional effects of the war of secession. He seems to judge the effects of the war by the contents of the thirteenth, fourteenth, and fifteenth amendments.[12] A European reader, I believe, would get the impression that our civil war, which was a final contest between nationalism and sectionalism, simply confirmed the Union in its old strength, whereas it in reality, of course, confirmed it in a new character and strength which it had not at first possessed, but which the steady advance of the national development, and of the national idea thereby begotten, had in effect at length bestowed upon it.

If Mr. Bryce was obliged to exclude such historical analysis from his volumes, whose whole spirit and method nevertheless suggest such an analysis, and seem to await it, if not to take it for granted, why then much remains to be done in elucidation of the lessons of government to be learned in America. Those lessons can be fully learned only from history. There still remains to be accomplished the work of explaining democracy *by* America, in supplement of Mr. Bryce's admirable explanation of democracy *in* America. Comparative politics must yet be made

[12] Thus he expresses surprise at the slightness of the changes wrought by the war in the constitution—meaning, of course, the *formal* changes.

to yield an answer to the broad and all-important question: What is democracy that it should be possible, nay natural, to some nations, impossible as yet to others? Why has it been a cordial and a tonic to little Switzerland and to big America, while it has been as yet only a quick intoxicant or a slow poison to France and Spain, a mere maddening draught to the South American states? Why has England approached democratic institutions by slow and steady stages of deliberate and peaceful development, while so many other states have panted towards democracy through constant revolution? Why has democracy existed in America and in Australia virtually from the first, while other states have utterly failed in every effort to establish it? Answers to such questions as these would serve to show the most truly significant thing now to be discovered concerning democracy: its place and office, namely, in the process of political development. What is its relative function, its characteristic position and power, in politics viewed as a whole?

Democracy is of course wrongly conceived when treated as merely a body of doctrine, or as simply a form of government. It is a stage of development. It is not created by aspirations or by new faith: it is built up by slow habit. Its process is experience, its basis old wont, its meaning national organic unity and effectual life. It comes, like manhood, as the fruit of youth: immature peoples cannot have it, and the maturity to which it is vouchsafed is the maturity of freedom and self-control, and no other. It is conduct, and its only stable foundation is character. America has democracy because she is free; she is not free because she has democracy. A particular form of government may no more be adopted than a particular type of character may be adopted: both institutions and character must be developed by conscious effort and through transmitted aptitudes. The variety of effects produced by democratic principles, therefore, upon different nations and systems, and even upon the same nation at different periods, is susceptible of instructive explanation. It is not the result of accident merely, nor of good fortune, manifestly, that the English race has been the only race, outside of quiet, closeted Switzerland, the only race, that is, standing forward amidst the fierce contests of national rivalries, that has succeeded in establishing and maintaining the most liberal forms of government. It is, on the contrary, a perfectly natural outcome of organic development. The English alone have approached popular institutions *through habit.* All other races have rushed prematurely into them through mere impatience with habit: have adopted democracy, instead of cultivating it. An expansion of this contrast would leave standing very little of the reasoning from experience which constitutes so large a part of Sir Henry Maine's plausible *Popular Government*, and would add to Mr. Bryce's luminous exposition of the existing conditions of life and the operative machinery of politics in the greatest of republics something which might serve as a natural history of republicanism.*

Mr. Bryce has given us a noble work possessing in high perfection almost every element that should make students of comparative politics esteem it invaluable. If I have regretted that it does not contain more, it has been because of the feeling that the author of *The American Commonwealth*, who has given us a vast deal, might have given us everything.†

WOODROW WILSON.

Printed in the *Political Science Quarterly*, IV (March 1889), 153-69.

* Wilson copied most of this paragraph and the one preceding it from "The Modern Democratic State," printed at Dec. 1, 1885, Vol. 5.

† For Bryce's comments on this review, see J. Bryce to WW, Dec. 2, 1891, Vol. 7.

From Edward Ireland Renick

My dear Wilson: Washington, D. C., January 31, 1889.

I take great pleasure in remitting by check the balance of $60 due to you. This cancels the debt in one sense, but a very great obligation remains. You do not, I know, wish me to feel this, and I don't, in the sense of a burden. But I *am* obliged to you, to be sure. I have been very busy lately stirring up public opinion here concerning a Washington University as outlined by Prest. White in the Feb. *Forum*.[1] My part was to interview and Page's to find room in the newspapers for my material. I wish we had the school & you as part of it. Has, I wish to know, Brice stepped on your territory? Have you read his books—will you not undertake to review them—when will yours be forthcoming?—all these things & many more in which you are involved I wish to know. Please try to visit Washington this Spring, you & your good little wife & give us a week.

As ever yours, E. I. Renick

ALS (WP, DLC) with WWhw notation on env.: "*Ans.* Feby 2/89."

[1] Andrew D. White, "A University at Washington," New York *Forum*, VI (Feb. 1889), 622-33.

A News Item

[*c. Feb. 4, 1889*]

THE OVERTHROW OF THE FIRST MINISTRY.

The third meeting of the House of Commons was a most interesting one, witnessing, as it did, the downfall of the first ministry. The meeting opened with a good attendance and much enthusiasm. After the roll call, it was moved and carried that another opportunity be given the college of signing the constitution and that the privileges of the house be given those who had been unable to sign it. The time appointed by the speaker was from 9 to 12 on the following Saturday. The election of speaker was next in order and A. W. Partch was unanimously re-elected. The bill requesting the changing of the name of Wesleyan University was then taken up, as was supposed, for a second reading. The first speaker was Secretary Henderson, who plead forcibly against the name of Wesleyan on the ground that it was denominational and misleading. Following him, Mr. Miles[1] spoke against the bill. The name, he said, made no difference in the character of the college. What we need is not a change of name, but more money. At this point it was moved and carried that the privileges of the house be extended to the members of the faculty and the ladies present. A brisk debate on the bill followed, Messrs. Glenn, Kettell, Murdock, Burke and Landon speaking in favor of its passage, and Messrs. Hart, Davis, Rogers, Bawden, Rollins, and MacMahon opposing it.[2] The chief point made by the ministerial party was the fact that Wesleyan is not strictly a university, many of the speakers on that side expressing themselves in favor of the name Wesleyan. The opposition claimed that there is no true university in this country and that Wesleyan has as much right to the name as many of the other so called universities, and moreover, it was not certain that, in the future, Wesleyan might not become a true university. A motion was then made and carried for the third reading of the bill. The house resolved itself into a committee of the whole; with Mr. Goodrich[3] in the chair, and reported adversely on the bill by a vote of 53 to 34. At this point several rose to a point of order. Although made in various ways the real point was as to whether the bill had really passed through the three readings. After Professor Wilson had explained what the reading of a bill implied, the house decided that its proceedings had been unparliamentary and that the bill had passed through no readings. A motion was then made that the bill pass its first reading, but the opposition was too strong and the bill was killed. Prime Minister Landon and Secretaries Jenkins and Henderson then handed in their resignations and the house adjourned. R. Miles, '89, has been appointed as the second prime minister.

Printed in the Middletown, Conn., *Wesleyan Argus*, XXII (Feb. 15, 1889), 100-101.

[1] Rowland Miles, '89.

[2] These undergraduates were George W. Meek Glenn, '89; George Frederic Kettell, '89; Leonard Colburn Murdock, '90; Arthur Newell Burke, '89; Archibald Clinton Harte, '92; Bernard Marcus Davis, '89; George Henry Rogers, '91; Edward Arthur Bawden, '90; Frank Rollins, '89; and Henry Isaiah McMahon, '91.

[3] Frederic Samuel Goodrich, '90.

To Robert Bridges

[Middletown, c. Feb. 6, 1889]

Spend friday night with you if convenient arrive four afternoon[1] [Woodrow Wilson]

WWhw tel. (draft) on env. of J. R. Wilson, Jr., to WW, Jan. 27, 1889, ALS (WP, DLC).

[1] As the letters will soon reveal, Wilson was making plans for his trip to Baltimore to give his second series of lectures on administration at the Johns Hopkins.

An Examination

[c. Feb. 7, 1889]

Mid-year '88-'89 *Political Economy and Statistics* (Feby)

1. Enumerate the banking functions. Outline the history and the chief features of the present national banking system. Just what is the present bank problem in the United States?
2. Describe the processes of foreign exchange. Explain the causes which make exchange *par*, above *par*, or below *par*.
3. Discuss fully the Errors to be expected in Commercial Statistics.
4. Explain both (a) the significance and (b) the limitations of statistics touching Race and Nationality in Population; the foreign-born in the U. S.; deaths and the death rate; and Crime.
5. Explain the method of constructing mortality tables.
6. Do statistics furnish a method simply, or do they constitute a distinct Science?

WWhw MS. (WP, DLC).

Reading Lists[1]

[c. Feb. 7, 1889]

Required Reading,
1889.
Juniors (Constitution).

The Federalist
"Congressional Government"

Juniors (History).

Lectures on the History of France (Sir James Stephen) Lects. II-XIII incl. (in two vol. ed.) or I-XII incl. (in Harper ed., one vol.)
"Age of the Despots" (J. A. Symonds).

Seniors (History).

"The American Commonwealth" (Jas. Bryce) Parts I-III inclusive.

Woodrow Wilson.

WWT MS. (WP, DLC).

[1] See the Editorial Note, "Wilson's Teaching at Wesleyan and the Johns Hopkins, 1888-89," and the news item printed at Feb. 15, 1889.

A Bibliography[1]

[c. Feb. 7, 1889]

Some Authorities on the period of *Jackson's Administration*
(for Mr. R. Miles, '89)

1. American Authorities:
"The American Annual Register," 1825 to 1833.
Benton, T. H., "Thirty Years' View." 2 vols. 1854.
Benton's *Abridgement*
? *Cobbett*, Wm., "Life of Andrew Jackson" N. Y. 1834.
Curtis, G. T. "Life of Daniel Webster" 2 vols. 1870.
"Documents Relating to New England Federalism" ed. by Henry Adams. Boston, 1877.
Duane, W. J. "Narrative and Correspondence Concerning the Removal of the Deposits," &c., Phila., 1838.
Kendall, Amos "Autobiography," Boston, 1872.
Kendall, Amos, "Life of Andrew Jackson," N. Y., 1843.
"Niles's Register," 1811-1848.
Parton, Jas., "Life of Andrew Jackson," 3 vols., N. Y., 1861.
Sargent, Nathan, "Public Men and Events from the Commencement of Mr. Monroe's Administration in 1817 to the Close of Mr. Filmore's Administration in 1853." 2 vols., Phila., 1875.
Schurz, H. Clay.
"Statesman's Manual," 3 vols., N. Y., 1854.
Sumner, Prof. W. G. "Andrew Jackson," with Bibl.
Tyler, Sam'l., "Memoirs of R. B. Taney," Balto., 1872.
Webster's Works, 6 vols., Boston, 1851.

2. Foreign Authorities:
Chevalier, Michael, "Society, Manners, and Politics in the U. S." Trans., Bost. 1839.

Guigot [Gigot], A., "La Democratie Autoritaire," N. Y. (Christern) 1885.

Martineau, Harriet, "Society in America," 2 vols., N. Y. & Lond., 1837.

Martineau, Harriet, "Retrospect of Western Travel," 2 vols., N. Y. 1838.

Tocqueville, de, A., "Democracy in America," 1st. vol. (References direct and indirect to circumstances of Jackson's Admin.)

Von Holst, Dr. H. "The Const. and Pol. Histy of the U. S." 5 vols. Chicago 1878-1885.

Von Holst, "Life of Calhoun" Bost. '82.

WWhw MS. (WP, DLC).

[1] This was perhaps prepared for special honors work in history. However, Miles did not receive special honors when he graduated.

To Ellen Axson Wilson

My D. W., New York, Sat. morning [Feb. 9, 1889]

Have has [had] as delightful a time here as was possible under the circumstances. Dined with B[ridges]. at University Club last evening, meeting various college friends old and new. Am just about to be off for Phila., having escorted B. down to his desk. Have been thinking the things that cannot be put on a postal card with all my nature. My address in Balto. will be 909 McColloh St.[1]

W. W.

API (WC, NjP).

[1] The new address of Miss Jane Ashton's boarding house. When Wilson had lived there as a graduate student, the number was 8 McCulloh Street. "McColloh" is a misspelling here on Wilson's part.

From Ellen Axson Wilson

My own Darling, Middletown Feb. 9/89

It is too bad that I should have put off writing until nearly night,—still the letter will start tonight I suppose & will probably reach Balt. as soon as you. I intended writing this morning, but first I went with Eddie [Axson], as soon as I could get off, to the freight station, & when I came back I was not very well so I lay down to rest, fell asleep & slept 'till lunch; & after lunch I had to hurry off to the sewing society at Miss Mansfield's[1] which, you know, I promised to attend;—have but just returned from it. Had a very pleasant time at it, and felt almost well.[2] I am really getting on *quite* nicely, darling, and you must not worry about me *at all*. Now that the wrench is over, and you are actually gone I am contradictory enough to be quite cheerful!—

havn't shed a tear since yesterday! And as to the nausea I am if anything better. I enjoyed my walks yesterday & today & felt perfectly well while in the air. The weather is delicious today. There was quite a fall of snow last night—the sort that clings to every twig,—and today it is warm & sunshiny—truly a *beautiful* day in every sense.

I went,—as I threatened!—to consult Dr. Taft[3] yesterday. She seems quite confident that she can help me, and I really feel a a [*sic*] gleam of hope myself from today's experience that she may, not *cure* me of course, but keep the trouble within some sort of bounds. She asked me about a thousand questions and wrote down all the answers! I was never put through such a catagory. Her first impression as to the cause of the trouble was that I had married *too young* & begun to have children before I was properly developed! But I succeeded in convincing her to the contrary! If I am not "cured" (!) at the end of a week I am to go to her again. En passant I like her—her manner &c—extremely. But I have something pleasant to tell & I must make haste & come to it. I went to the freight office, stated my case & told the man I came to pay for the box & enquire as to its chances. He merely asked to whom it was addressed, then went on for some time about his business & finally went off without saying anything, leaving me standing there in some perplexity. But in a moment he returns *with the box*!—imagine my relief. He said they hadn't received the information as to rates & so hadn't forwarded it. There was already quite a hole punched in the box so that I shall have to repack it before it goes. One can imagine from that what its condition would have been at the *other* end. But all's well that ends well.

I have just come up from dinner,—wish you had been there, we had a *delicious* puree of green peas & *very* nice "boeuf braisé." My appetite has revived astonishingly tonight. We are going to have dinner in the middle of the day while you are away; I think it will be better for me at present,—but we couldn't change today because the meat didn't come in time.

There has been no mail for you except an advertising circular, but I received this afternoon from Uncle R.[4] the balance of what was due me on the house in Rome,—this being the end of the year and the other half of the purchase money having been paid. It is $415.50. There is also another $100.00 for Eddie. Do I simply take this check to the bank & deposit it as if it were so many banknotes or is there any formality to be gone through with?[5]

But I must make haste to close since I am anxious for this to get off tonight. Do you know I don't know Miss Ashton's new number—nor her old one either, 'till I go up stairs & hunt it up. How thoughtless in me not to get it. I am half inclined to send this to the J.H.U. But then you might not think to look for it there. Many thanks for the telegram which was promptly received.[6]

And now goodnight, my darling, I love you, I love, *love, love* you more than I could possibly tell you if I wrote all night. And I am *so happy* dearest,—honour bright!—happy in the thought of your sweet, noble, wonderful, perfect love for me. How can I ever love and honour you enough, darling, for all your goodness & thoughtfulness & tenderness to me. Yes dear, you spoke truth when you said that you would not be far from me. I *feel* that you are near me! How can I ever feel lonely while that love is round about me to sustain and bless me. Oh, love, you are all my joy,—my very *life*,—& I am always & altogether

Your own little wife

ALS (WC, NjP).

[1] Katharine M. Mansfield, 75 Main St.

[2] Ellen was again having trouble during a pregnancy.

[3] M. Florence Taft, M.D.

[4] Randolph Axson, whose letter is missing.

[5] See the account book with the WWhw title "Eddie's Account" and WWhw entries between Feb. 15, 1889, and Oct. 1, 1889, in WP, DLC.

[6] It is missing.

To Ellen Axson Wilson

M. S-H. Phila. Sunday morning [Feb. 10, 1889].

Arrived all right; found Prof. James[1] absent in Italy (!); uncle T. and Aunt S.[2] at home—rest away. Spent night with them, and am now (10:35 a.m.) at Broad St. Station about to go out to Bryn Mawr. I am well and am full of thoughts of other people. W.W.

API (WC, NjP).

[1] Edmund J. James, professor at the Wharton School of Finance and Economy, University of Pennsylvania.

[2] The Rev. and Mrs. Thomas A. Hoyt.

To Ellen Axson Wilson

My precious darling, Baltimore, Feby 11th, 1889

I have just returned from the delivery of my first lecture exceedingly fatigued—the strain of meeting a new class and getting re-fitted to an environment added to the strain of my travels.[1] But I am quite well: fatigue will not injure me. And oh, I love you with a love that commands and shapes my whole life.

In Phila. I found Cousin Lillie and Cousin Allie both away, in Nashville.[2] Cousin Allie, it seems, has been dangerously ill—with neuralgia of the heart, but is now better.

At Bryn Mawr I found *vacation*, the first semester examinations over and the half-week vacation 'on.' Most of the old men, ∴, were away; I saw only Shorey and Collitz. But [Gidd]ings and Walker,[3] I found—and I like them both very much—Giddings especially—Walker is harder to know—more formal, but very agreeable indeed. I took dinner at Radnor with Cousin Mary,[4] after having attended church and heard Mr. Miller once more. Saw Miss Hellen Cole, Miss Goff, the Anthonys, Miss Chamberlain, who sent much love to you, and Miss Riegel(!).[5]

Arrived here last night at 10 o'clock.

My heart is simply full of you, my sweet, sweet pet. Oh, how I long for and yearn after my poor little wife, going so bravely about in spite of her trouble. I know she will be brave, and that helps me to be brave also—otherwise I feel as if I might break down. Kiss the babies for me all the time—whenever you kiss them for yourself and give Ed. a great deal of love from me. With a heart fu[ll of] tenderest, most passionate love

Your own Woodro[w]

ALS (WC, NjP). Letter damaged.

1 See the Editorial Note, "Wilson's Teaching at Wesleyan and the Johns Hopkins, 1888-89."

2 Lillian T. Hoyt and Alice Hoyt Truehart, daughters of the Rev. Thomas A. Hoyt, who were visiting their sister, Harriet Hoyt Ewing, in Nashville.

3 Paul Shorey, Hermann Collitz, Franklin H. Giddings, and Williston Walker, all on the Bryn Mawr College faculty.

4 Mary Eloise Hoyt, who had remained at Bryn Mawr after the Wilsons moved to Middletown.

5 Leah Goff, Alice Eliza Anthony, Emily Frances Anthony, and Ella Reigel, Wilson's former students at Bryn Mawr; probably Helen Cecilia Coale, a student at the college; and Rose Chamberlain, who taught French and German at the college.

From Ellen Axson Wilson

My own darling Middletown Feb 11/89

Your two postals came to hand this morning & were most welcome. Am so glad, dear, that you had such a pleasant visit in New York. I did not get my letter written yesterday for the not very good reason that I spent most of the day *sleeping*! I went to church in the morning then lay around "resting" 'till dinner. After dinner I craved the air so that I took a long walk, came back & lay down to "rest" again, fell asleep & slept with only a brief interruption at the children's bedtime until *ten* at night! If I could keep it up at that rate the four months would not be so very long after all! eh? I am still getting on very well; when I am out of doors I feel *quite* well and bright. I took a long walk just after breakfast this morning—up Washington St. as far as the cemetary hill, and though the ther. was nearly at zero and there was no sun in the sky I enjoyed it so much that I was very loathe to turn back. Isn't that a new development for me?

I had a puzzling experience yesterday. I was to all appearances "unwell" for about an hour! Of course in view of the nausea, which was keeping up steadily & quite severely I could not for a moment imagine it to be the 'genuine article.' Suppose, to quote Dr. Chevasse[1] it was "rupture of some small blood-vessels about the mouth of the womb"

There is no news to tell. Mr. Snyder preached for us yesterday —a very good sermon. The children are quite well & as sweet as can be—& I am in *very good spirits*, and I love *love love* you darling, oh *how* I love you! How I wish I could tell you the depth & strength & passion of my love! Alas that is impossible, but try at least to believe & *feel*, dearest, that I love you *just as much as you would have me love.* With all my heart

Your little wife.

I sent you a letter Saturday to the *J. H. U.*

ALS (WP, DLC).

[1] Pye Henry Chavasse or Chevasse, 1810-79, author of numerous popular books on female medical problems and child-rearing.

From Edward Ireland Renick

My dear Wilson: Washington, D. C., Feb 11, 1889.

You must know that we not only have for you a most cordial welcome, but that your coming at any hour will not in the slightest incommode us. Though I should be pleased to have you select Saturday evening & all day Sunday, because I could see more of you—yet choose your own time, but do make an effort to give us many days. Is Mrs. Wilson with you? Of course, if she is, she is embraced in this appeal. Hoping that you will not be stingy to us in this matter

I am most sincerely yours, E. I. Renick

ALS (WP, DLC) with WWhw notation on env.: "Ans."

To Ellen Axson Wilson

My own darling, Balto., 12th Feb'y, '89.

Bless your heart for the sweet, sweet letter, the first one, received this morning. It was handed to me by the small boy in the Bluntschli library this morning just as I was about to begin my lecture: and I had to wait ever so long before I could open it and read it. But it elated and warmed me simply to have the precious document in my pocket; and when I read its sweet, sunny contents I was almost intoxicated, I was so happy. Bless your heart, my matchless little darling, for taking our separation so sweetly, and for loving me so perfectly after the fashion in which I would have you love me—bless you for being a woman after my own heart! The news about your nausea is, I hope, *not* too good to be true; but it is so good that I can hardly realize it. If Dr. Taft can give you relief either wholly or in part, I will be her fast friend for the rest of my life: she could make no more perfect contribution to my happiness. And surely a little woman who can give so evidently genuine a tone of enthusiasm to her description of what she had for dinner cannot have much the matter with her stomach! If you are well that means for me the lifting of one of the heaviest weights—the only heavy weight—that lies on my heart not only, but also a *letter every day*—and your letters are the food upon which my heart lives. Tell me *everything*, darling, that occurs in your day, even the smallest detail is dear to me—for I live with you with my whole imagination. I am at home only with you.

Take the money to the bank, dear, with my bank-book, and the bank officers will show you the very simple process of deposit. The checks are made out in your name, I suppose. Endorse them before giving them in. If they are in my name, you may send them to me for endorsement.

How sweet it is, Eileen, to be married to you: to feel held so close, even if by invisible bonds, to so lovely, so charming a little woman. It gives me such a queer, *properly-related* feeling, as if somehow I were rightly arranged. I could no more help loving you than I could stop existing—because you fit into my nature and have become a part of my existence. Think, little lady, only 23 lectures now, and only five weeks and a half, unless our celebration holiday here on the 22nd is to throw my reckoning out a little. I am coming home *soon*—and then what a quiet, restful summer we will have, if only you keep well! Ah, my pet, how grateful I am for my home, and for the precious little woman that constitutes it! Ditto to yesterday for the sweet babies & Eddie. Your own Woodrow.

ALS (WC, NjP).

From Ellen Axson Wilson

My own darling Middletown, Feb. 12 [1889].

I think I must content myself with a few lines today so as to hurry out & try to get some of these twenty-eight visits that I owe, paid,—it being very bright and pleasant this afternoon. Quite a contrast to this morning when I took my walk to cemetary hill! Then it was blowing a gale & *snowing* hard.

Am glad you got out to Bryn Mawr & had a pleasant visit. It must have been interesting to meet your successors.

Am very sorry to hear of Cousin A's illness; neuralgia of the heart certainly sounds dangerous. What do you hear from Cousin Hattie [Ewing] & the new baby? What is her name?

There is no news whatever. I am still getting on very well and the babies are quite well. Not a particle of mail for you, oddly enough. Good-bye darling, with a heart full, full to overflowing with the truest love, I am as ever

Your own, Eileen

Is it a "*new*" class that you have there? I thought most of them would have been the same that you had last year. How did your lecture 'take'?

ALS (WC, NjP).

Fragmentary Notes for a Classroom Lecture

[Lecture II] [c. Feb. 13, 1889]

Popular character of the administration of justice in the Middle Ages in France. Every man tried by his *peers*—persons of his own region & station. In the courts of the feudal barons the vassals were present to act as judges, much as freemen were present in the Eng. County Courts.

Corps de ville: administrative functions:
Administration of the communal property.
Maintenance of streets and roads
Construction of public edifices
Maintenance of the school.
Assessment and collection of taxes, both municipal and royal. (Ferron, p. 8)[1]

Parliament of Paris denied the exemption from municipal charges claimed by the noblesse.

The Provinces:

Their assemblies not general, but by representation of the several orders

The Estates divided taxes among the generalities or departments. The generalities divided into districts. The districts act thr. assemblies but these nominated by and subordinate to the estates. Assemblies of the districts apportioned taxes among parishes, the officers of these latter among the inhabitants. No royal fiscal agent admitted in the Pays d'États.

The Intendent mere supervisor in the Pays d'États. The king represented in the estates by a commissioner.

Centralization: (1) Louis IX Baillifs and seneschals, who, under the commission to see that the king's authority was recognized and obeyed, gradually absorbed all power.

(2) Treasurers-general and receivers of domains, and captain-generals in the *baillages*.

(3) The Intendants instituted by Richelieu. "From that moment the provincial Estates assembled only upon the order of the king; the duration of their sessions was fixed at 40 days. All their important deliberations, the whole of their receipts and expenses, were subject to approval by decree of the council of the king." (p. 14).

History of the Municipalities (Sir Jas. Stephen,[2] vol. I, Sect. VI).

The organization left the municipalities by Rome was oligarchical, aristocratic. (co-optative *curiae*). Towns become seats of bishops. Bishops and Commons *vs.* Counts and Oligarchy. Former win and establish *democracy*. Example of Italian towns: Consuls, etc.

The (non-Roman) cities north of the Loire agitate for and get charters—all parties aggreeing or confirming.

But gradually Prévotal towns were the predominant type: towns, i.e., in wh. the relative (customary) rights of seigneur and bourgeois were ascertained by charters from the seigneur, and in which the seigneural authority was exercised, by delegation, by a Prévot.

To end of 15th century.

This, the most secure form of municipal govt., and the most naturally connected with the supreme seigneural authority, that of the king, became the most common and the most helpful to the royal power.

Grants of bourgeosie by the king to disaffected vassals of the barons. (*Bourgeoisie du Roi*)

WWhw MS. (WP, DLC).

[1] Henri de Ferron, *Institutions municipales & provinciales comparées* (Paris, 1884). [Eds.' note]

[2] James Stephen, *Lectures on the History of France*, 3rd edn. (2 vols., London, 1857). [Eds.' note]

Frederick Jackson Turner to Caroline Mae Sherwood

Dear little girl– [Baltimore] Feb. 13, 1889

. . . Dr Wilson is here. Homely, solemn, young, glum, but with that fire in his face and eye that means that its possessor is not of the common crowd. He talks but little, Miss Lovell's chatter bores him–but I had a little time with him the other evening. Miss Ashton has some cider and she made up a little company consisting of her niece, Dr Wilson and myself, and we had a pleasant conversation on all sorts of subjects–that is Dr W. and I did, for Miss A. and the school girl kept discretely silent and let us do the talking–and we kept it up until Miss Ashton said "Well, gentlemen, you have drunk all the cider, eaten all the cake, and it is after eleven o'clock–I confess to being very sleepy." Upon that hint we went!

I am enjoying his suggestive lectures very much. They are scholarly and well delivered. . . .

Time to study. Goodnight Mae. Fred

P.S. omitted. ALS (F. J. Turner Coll., CSmH).

To Ellen Axson Wilson

My precious darling, Balto., 13th February, 1889.

I drink in the particulars contained in your letters as if my life depended on them–as indeed it does. It *is* odd, in view of your past bad habits, that you should have so suddenly developed a passion for walking; and yet it is not strange either, if the open air relieves your nausea. I approve of these walks most heartily–I rejoice in them–as you know without the telling; and yet they have to my imagination a strong element of pathos: to think of my lovely little wife taking her walks *alone* is touching in view of the great love borne her by one whom she loves tenderly, delightfully and of the fact that his presence is as indispensable to her as hers is to him. There is something tragic in these separations, sweetheart: and yet they have their side of compensation: they prove the quality of our love for each other–its commanding spiritual, formative nature–as it could be proved no otherwise.

Had you not better see Dr. Taft about that strange affair, your apparent menstruation? It makes me uneasy to have so decided a symptom left unexplained. Wont you, darling, just for my peace of mind? What does Chevasse say the "bursting of blood vessels" of which you speak is indicative of? Does he regard it as serious? or give you any clue to treatment? I advise physician's advice anyhow, darling.

There are no particulars about myself. I saw Hiram Woods at his office; and I have met [Charles W.] Mitchell and one or two other friends on the street. I am just away from an interview with [William P.] Trent—find he has been here for two months, but is to leave for Richmond to-morrow: a capital, most intelligent fellow—wish I could have his companionship. He likes Sewanee very much, barring the superstitions of high-churchism.

I have gotten the impression, somehow (perhaps through my imagination), that my two lectures, so far delivered, have fallen rather flat, and I feel a whit discouraged: but the attention of the class must, shall, be conquered before I get through with them. It's my sensibilities, rather than my courage, that are wounded. To tell the truth, my second lecture was poor,—thrown together, undigested, ill-arranged, inorganic: I can do better.

Your letters give me the impression, darling, that you are a brave, splendid little woman, but that you were not so hopeful about the nausea when you wrote Nos. 2 and 3 as when you wrote No. 1.[1] Please give me exact bulletins and please tell me just what Dr. Taft is doing for you.

I *adore* you, sweetheart; my thoughts are yours, my hopes, my ambitions, my self—and, as for the babies, both through you and for their own precious selves, I love them infinitely. Give ever so much love to dear Ed. In happiness, hope, and love,

Your own Woodrow.

ALS (WP, DLC).

1 Woodrow and Ellen usually numbered the letters in this series. The numbers have been omitted.

From Ellen Axson Wilson

My own darling Middletown Feb. 12[13]/89

I will write but a line today for I havn't been feeling quite so well & have been husbanding my strength in order if possible to call on the Parks[1] & Johnstons,[2]—as they are important visits & I may not be able to go another Wednesday. All well & in good spirits;—still no mail for you—nor for me either,—but I dare say my letter will come this afternoon. I called on the Prentices, Rices,[3] & some others yesterday.

Can you tell me, dear, if your little silver watch is where I can lay my hands on it? I would like to make use of it as I find it so *exceedingly* inconvenient to have no means of telling the time, especially through the night and in the early morning. I hope, dearest, that you are now rested from your journey and enjoying your work & your class[.] I am waiting eagerly for a "real letter" that will tell me "all about everything." I think about you all the time, dearest, trying to follow you in your various comings and goings—to feel that our lives are not entirely apart, even temporarily. Good-bye, my darling, I love, *love* you with every heart-throb. As ever Your own Eileen.

ALS (WC, NjP).

[1] Probably the Rev. and Mrs. J. Lewis Parks. Parks was minister of the Church of the Holy Trinity, the rectory of which was at 60 Broad Street in Middletown.

[2] Probably the Misses Ellen R. and Janette Johnson, who lived at 44 Union Street.

[3] The Rev. Dr. and Mrs. George Prentice and the Rev. Dr. and Mrs. William North Rice. Prentice was the M. L. Taft Professor of Modern Languages at Wesleyan; Rice, the G. I. Seney Professor of Geology and Secretary of the Faculty.

Notes for a Classroom Lecture

Lecture III Feby 14th, '89

The Pays d'États.—The 'provinces with estates' represent one sort of self-government, the towns and other urban communes quite another.

The provinces of old France were 36 in number and represented separate feudal entities—much as the Eng. shires once did.

The towns, on the other hand, in the central and northern portions of France represented nothing but grants of privilege—were communities which had been given a special place in the feudal order.

The assemblies of the provinces, accordingly, were not primary or democratic like those of the towns, but were made up *by estates*, like the assembly of all France wh. appeared in 1302. *Rather*, the States-General was *like them*.

Functions of the Provincial Estates in Finance.—The Estates divided taxes among the sub-divisions of the Province. These districts act thr. assemblies nominated by and subordinate to the prov. Estates. These district assemblies apportion taxes among the parishes, the officers of the latter among the inhabitants.

The king represented in the Estates by a commissioner, but the authority of the chief royal agent in the Province was one of supervision, not one of command.

Centralization.—It is not in the period of their greatest independence, but in the later period of centralization, that we get our clearest view of the Pays d'États.

The steps towards centralization were

(1) The systematization, by Louis IX, not only of the plan of

itinerant judges who brought cases great and small within the royal jurisdiction, but also of the plan of resident *bailiffs* and *prévots*, who, acting under commission to see that the king's authority was recognized and obeyed, the king's taxes collected, etc. gradually absorbed all administrative authority. (See *A*)[1]
(2) There appeared Treasurer's-general and Receivers of Domains; besides captains-general in each of the baillages.
(3) Finally, came the system of *Intendants*, instituted by *Richelieu*. The office of Intendant is said to have originated in that of *master of accounts*. Masters of accounts had been appointed to ride circuit thr. France as fiscal agents of the crown. In later times their functions fell to resident officers known as *Intendants*. The Intendants were properly, .˙., subordinates of the Comptroller General of the Finances; but the Compt. General of the F. became to all intents and purposes Minister of the Interior, fully charged with the oversight of almost all affairs of internal administration,–and the Intendant, his agent in the Provinces, became, by consequence, quite absolute ruler in local affairs. (See B.)

Final Local Division of France under the Ancien Régime.–
As centralization advanced, the significance of the Province changed.
Provinces became units of military organization chiefly.
For purposes of civil administration France was divided into 32 *Generalities*, and it was over a generality that each Intendant ruled.
Ecclesiastical administration was served by still another distinct division into dioceses.

Effects of Centralization.–
Interference in local affairs, more and more systematized, more and more minute and inquisitive, results in the strangulation of local govt. All vitality runs to the veins of the central organism, and, except for the lingering and treasured privileges of the Pays d'États and for here and there a lingering form of town life, France lives in the pigeon-holes of a Bureau. *Tabla rasa* is made of the historical elements of local govt.
The Revolution, changed the central authority, not the local organization of this centralized system. The instrument of the Revolution was Napoleon.

General Remarks (closing)
French Local Govt.

Development *from complex to simple*
Parts not so difficult of assimilation, not so distinctly and separately vital, as in Germany.
Absence of historical elements and groundwork, presence of systematic elements and bureaucratic groundwork.
Permitting free course to the impulses of modern politics–consequently *approaching* confirmed democracy and complete self-government, but approaching them, not upon *old* habit rooted

in wont and prejudice, *running with the grain*, but upon new habit out of line with old wont, depending upon new developments of character—a-making, instead of resting upon something already made.

(B) *Intendants*

Originated in the *Maîtres des requêtes* "who were charged in the 16th century, with making, in the provinces, the inspections called chevauchées" (rides, circuits)

In Richelieu's time, first, there emerge *Intendants de justice et de police* (et finance). These fellows "acted in all those affairs, civil and criminal, which the king wished to take away from the ordinary judges."

Guizot's Summary.—

Intendants were "magistrates whom the king sent into different parts of the kingdom to look to all that concerned the administration of justice, of police, and of the finances; to maintain good order and to execute such commissions as the king or his council laid upon them." (Chéruel,[2] art. 'Intendant des Prov.')

Prevot (*praepositus*) a civil and judicial officer.

From the moment when the system of Intendants is fixed upon the country, says Ferron, (p. 14) "the provincial Estates assembled only upon the order of the king; the duration of their sessions was fixed at 40 days. All their important deliberations, the whole of their receipts and expenditures, were subject to approval by decree of the council of the king."

WWhw MS. (WP, DLC).

[1] Note "A" seems to be missing. [Eds.' note]

[2] Pierre Adolphe Chéruel, *Dictionnaire historique des institutions, moeurs et coutumes de la France* (2 parts, Paris, 1855). [Eds.' note]

To Ellen Axson Wilson

My own darling, Balto., 14th Feby., 1889.

This, you observe, is St. Valentine's day; and, since we are sweethearts, I may, I suppose, if I can, write you a valentine? You have so uniformly expressed your decided disapproval of my poetical muse, that I may not venture upon a poem addressed to my lady: I must say what I have to say in prose, after as plain and straightforward a manner as possible. And, indeed, that serves my needs admirably—for I want to say as plainly as may be that I love you. I am peculiarly susceptible to feminine beauty, as you know, and to all feminine attractions. A pretty girl is my chief pleasure, a winsome girl my chief delight: girls of all degrees of beauty and grace have a charm for me which almost amounts to a spell. If a jealous woman had married me, I am sure she would have found in the catholicity of my admiration for women a source of exquisite torture. But what a goose she would have been (would she not, sweetheart?) and how little she would have known of my real character—the real make-up of the heart you hold in trust! For only one woman is or could be the pivot of my life. I know a little woman whose beauty has somehow lodged itself in my ideal of womanly charm; whose image has somehow fixed itself in the habits of my thought; whose self, with all its subtle charms, all its harmonies of tone, all its fine adjustments of tenderness to strength, all its suggestions of womanly fidelity and trustfulness, all its graces of love and helpfulness, has somehow entered into my character, become part of my way of life, as if it were an atmosphere out of which my mind and heart could not live as they now live, in health, and strength, and hope. *She* knows—for she knows me—that other women may play upon the surface of my susceptibilities, but that she is part of me and that I look at them, as it were, *through her*. If their forms please me, I wish them to say nothing, for they cannot speak as she does; if they are witty and quick to understand, as she is, I want them to look away from me, for they cannot look their thoughts as she can.

I wish I could write the marriage song that my heart sings. I could add to the beautiful things that have been written in anticipation of marriage more beautiful things still in realization of it. To enjoy my sweet one proved to be to enjoy my own full powers: living with her and for her, I have lived life at its best, finding its sorrows only a means of chastening, its joys a source of enlargement, its routine experiences a means for steadying and increasing strength—and *her* a source of perpetual gladness. Ah, I do not *send* my love to my lady, I simply acknowledge it; I thankfully glory in it; I pronounce it the foundation of what is best and fullest of promise in

Woodrow Wilson

The silver watch is in the big drawer of my small desk, darling, away back in the right-hand rear corner. But I am afraid it wont run without repair—and that there's no key with it. Of course it is intolerable to be without a time piece. If the repair of the watch is expensive, get a small clock, unless you want the watch anyhow. We have needed a clock upstairs for a long time.

Oh, I am *so* sorry, pet, to hear that your sickness increases. After the hope generated by your first report from Dr. Taft, I can hardly bear the news. It makes me heartsick beyond endurance, nearly. Your own Woodrow.

ALS (WC, NjP).

From Ellen Axson Wilson

My own darling Middletown Feb. 14 [1889]

Your sweet letter came to hand yesterday afternoon & made me very happy. If my good spirits improve yours and yours improve mine again we should act & react on each other until we are both in quite high spirits. For my part I really am getting on very nicely both as regards health and spirits. I made seven visits yesterday–found five at home–one must be tolerably well to accomplish that, especially with the thermometer nearly at zero. This is the coldest spell we have had; but it is fine weather too–very bright and clear.

Who do you suppose suddenly put in an appearance yesterday afternoon without a word of warning? *Mary*! Maggie[1] herself was as much surprised as anyone. She tells me today that she has come to take Maggie home & that they will start tomorrow! It seems that "Dr. Lindsay," whoever he may be, has made the family believe that Maggie will never be well until "her foot has been 'pulled' & then cut and a bone taken out of it." "I tell the tale as it was told to me,"–don't ask for explanations. So she is to be put in a hospital to submit to this operation. I tried to persuade them to first have Dr. Edgerton[2] give it a careful examination, but without success, she would only repeat again & again what "Dr. Lindsay at Bryn Mawr" said! So now I am sadly puzzled to know what to do. Jennie apparently isnt strong enough to keep the place permanently, & besides is I fear too young and flighty for me to trust the children to her when I am laid up. And I may be left in the lurch at any time, for I told Miss Woodward that I would let her go whenever she found a suitable place for her, as I did not think it right to stand in her way in getting a permanent home. So I don't know what is to be done. It is certainly unfortunate that it happens now, if it were three months hence I shouldn't mind. It is too bad though to trouble you with these things when you are so far away. It is I am afraid *too* natural to me to turn to you in all my troubles, great and small.

The babies are very well and as sweet as can be,–bless their little hearts! Margaret seemed to know Mary—she put her arms around her neck immediately.

But I am a little tired, darling, and must close rather abruptly. I love you sweet-heart, oh *how* I love you! I think of you all the day and dream of you by night. My darling! my love, my life I am always & altogether, Your own Eileen

ALS (WC, NjP).

1 Mary Freeman of Rosemont, Pa., was one of the Wilsons' servants in Bryn Mawr and the mother of "Maggie," who had gone to Middletown with the Wilsons.

2 Francis D. Edgerton, M.D., of Middletown.

To Ellen Axson Wilson

My own darling, Balto., 15th Feby, 1889.

No letter for me as yet to-day: I hope from the bottom of my heart that that don't mean that my precious little wife was too unwell to write. But I will not give up to my loneliness and anxiety. With four lectures off my hands, it is demonstrable that one-sixth of my work is done, is it not? What is telling on me just at this juncture *is the time*. The active movements and friend-seeing of my journey down here and the excitement of getting launched in my course and settled in my bachelor quarters was all very well: it kept off the blues admirably. But now I've come down to 'hard pan,' to the *routine* of living without you, my queen and delight, and of knowing that you are sick & need me—nothing in my room here to help me forget, everything to make me remember. I work (not only on my lectures, but on Hellas, too), I make calls, I go to the minstrels,—but no use: my darling needs me—I need her—and yet I cannot go to her. Don't think, my pet, that I have the 'blues' sure enough: I haven't—I am not going to be faithless to my little wife that way. But the pathos of the situation does lie heavy on my heart, does bring tears to my eyes. And it is a luxury I cannot deny myself (though, if it makes you unhappy I will) to tell you my whole feeling, if only to let you know how infinitely, how passionately you are loved. My love for you gives me the deepest happiness conceivable; but that happiness is not a happiness of smiles always. It seems often to go deep down where smiles cannot go, where all the serious purposes of my life are. There it forms that basis of sober strength which we call peace of mind. It is that sort of happiness that possesses me to-day: a happiness not incompatible with tears—tears of tenderness and longing & hope, meaning that my life is consecrated to you. I wonder, love, if the true note of my love ever reaches your ear in the words I speak and write? I wonder whether you will ever hear the veritable speech of my heart uttered in words? You don't need spoken or written words to make you realize my love, I am sure: but if I can speak them you shall hear them. Nothing comforts me more when I am away from you (or makes me happier when I am with you) than trying to put my love into words—except hearing you try to give the measure of your love for me.

God grant that you are measurably well, my darling—you must tell me the whole fact about your condition: even the torture of knowing that you are sick is exceeded by the torture of not knowing how to [you] are!

I am quite well—and quite sure that never man loved woman more than I love you.

With a heartful of love for the babies and not a little for dear Ed., Your own Woodrow.

ALS (WP, DLC).

From Ellen Axson Wilson

My own darling, Middletown Feb 15/89

It seems impossible for me to get a letter written today because of visitors[.] There has been a constant stream of them this afternoon & now it is so late I shall have to content myself with a short hurried one instead of the long one I had hoped to write in answer to your sweet, precious ones received yesterday & today. I must wait 'till tomorrow for that.

I have just had a letter from Stockton. He says he has been "laying up" with a bad cold for several days—but is about getting out again—says nothing as to his health in the long interval since he last wrote. Says the Cal. plan will be excellent to keep for a *last resort* but he hopes to get well where he is.[1]

I have just been to see Dr. Taft again—it being a week since the last time. She has given me some more powders and "pellets" to take every four hours. I told her about that "symptom," as you desired. Neither she nor Dr. Chevasse attach any importance to it. As you ask for a "more exact" account of my health I will proceed to give it while I am on the subject. I suffer a good deal in the morning from the time I get up until I get out to walk—have great difficulty with my breakfast though I manage to force down a little oatmeal, but the rest of the day until six o'clock

I am pretty comfortable especially if I get out again in the afternoon. I eat a very good dinner. Supper is hard work again, but I take a little bread & milk & go to bed quite soon. I have been practicing a sort of "system" consisting of a judicious mixture of "bracing up" & surrendering, & which I rather think has effected more than Dr. Tafts infinitesimal pellets—though the object of the system is not to cure the nausea but to avoid if possible the nervous breakdown which I dread unspeakably for its *permanent* ill effects on me. My "system" consisted merely in taking a long walk soon after breakfast & then when I returned "going to bed" more or less literally & if possible to sleep; at any rate remaining perfectly quiet & passive 'till one o'clock. In the afternoon I make believe I am well and go about my usual avocations. So as I am on a 'strain' as it were but little more than half the [day] my nerves seem so far to be faring very well. Now that Maggie is gone however I shall have to modify my scheme very materially in order to take care of the children 'till eleven, for unfortunately I can't rest in the afternoon because of visitors.

I have been interrupted *four* times by them while trying to write this unsatisfactory scrawl. The first came at 3½ o'clock when I had just written "my dear Woodrow" & now I am just finishing by lamplight in a desperate hurry because it is time to go to the children. Please excuse *everything*, both pen and ink seem to be bewitched.

But whether I have time to tell you about it or not *I love you*, my darling, from the very depths of my heart & am forever

Your own Eileen.

ALS (WP, DLC).

1 Stockton Axson to EAW, Feb. 11, 1889, ALS (WP, DLC). Stockton Axson was suffering from asthma, and Ellen had suggested that he move to California, perhaps to attend the University of California.

From George Riggs Gaither, Jr.[1]

Dear Sir: Baltimore, February 15th 1889

At the request of Dr. Hiram Woods I enclose you the tickets and bill for dues for the Princeton Alumni Association. The amount charged for the same is $6. I will be at the Hotel Rennert on the evening of the dinner, and payment can be made at that time if you should so desire.

Yours Sincerely George R. Gaither Jr. Treasurer

ALS (WP, DLC). Enc.: tickets for Fourth Annual Dinner of the Princeton Alumni Association, Hotel Rennert, Baltimore, Feb. 19, 1889.

[1] Princeton, '78.

A News Item

[Feb. 15, 1889]

Professor Wilson has given his classes a large amount of reading to do while he is away, with the promise of an examination at the end of the term.[1] One junior, who has made the calculation, says that in both History and Constitution it amounts to 40 pages for every omitted recitation.

Printed in the Middletown, Conn., *Wesleyan Argus*, XXII (Feb. 15, 1889), 99.

[1] See the examinations printed at April 2, 1889.

A Course Examination

[c. Feb. 16] 1889.

Examination: English-French History.

1. Origins and early history of Christianity in England?
2. Causes and processes of feudalism in France; the feudal idea of sovereignty; and the feudal 'incidents.'
3. History of English territorial possessions in France: their acquisition, influence on England, and loss.
4. Influence of the Crusades on Europe?
5. Contrast the English Parliament and the French States-General in origin, composition, and functions.
6. Indicate the geographical, political, and ecclesiastical situation of Europe at the beginning of the Renaissance.
7. Define 'Humanism,' point out the stages of the Renaissance, and enumerate its external and internal characteristics.
8. Differentiate Dante, Petrarch, and Boccaccio; indicate the distinctive contributions of Ariosto and Tasso to the literature of the Renaissance; contrast the work of Lionardo da Vinci and Michael Angelo with that of the Venetian painters.
9. Indicate and explain the relative places of sculpture and painting in the Renaissance.
10. European results of the discoveries which followed upon the heels of the Renaissance?

WWT MS. (WP, DLC).

To Ellen Axson Wilson

My own darling, Balto., 16th February, '89.

Your letter chronicling Mary's arrival has just reached me. Do you suppose you *could* keep these important happenings of the household from me, dear—without breaking our compact and rendering me very wretched? I would look upon each of your letters with suspicion and dissatisfaction if I thought there were anything touching your comfort & welfare, though never so remotely, that they did *not* contain. As for Mary's supremely foolish act, I acknowledge it fills me with a certain consternation. Mary is probably in the hands of a quack in the matter of Maggie's cure: but evidently there's no separating her from her idols. The thing *we* have to work at is *your* rescue from a servantless condition—and that is indeed a serious problem, in view of your condition. Instead of making any more visits, precious, bestir yourself to get a permanent nurse: that is, set all your friends and their servants to looking out for one for you—for that, you know, is the only Middletown method. Get Mrs. Hazen[1] interested, and the Van Vlecks, and any one else who shows any movement of sympathy. Oh, what a misfortune that I should be away! May God help and protect you, my darling! You promised to tell Mrs. Hazen your condition, you know, and that will certainly greatly quicken her interest in the matter of getting you a servant—and all the social and 'domestic' influences of the North Church congregation are at her service in such a matter. To work, little lady—so much depends upon it for you—and therefore for us both!

There's no news with me: we are having a dreary Saturday of rain here—with a bleak, blighting air both outside and inside of the house; but I work hard, and keep the loneliness in the background. My lecture material needs no end of reshaping and adding to, and I do not lack for something to do—and shall not. Next week will be full of 'events' connected with our anniversary —and will contain, for me at any rate among the Univ. men, another 'Event' in the shape of a Princeton dinner. Patriotism bids me go, though a slight disinclination and a decided aversion to paying a big sum for the privilege bid me stay away. My absence would not be understood, I suppose—so go I shall, probably.

Had the pleasure of seeing Trent here—did I tell you?

Oh, my pet, how I long for you, how I love you! You play so big a role in my life that sometimes I lose sight of myself altogether. You dear, precious, lovely, delightful little woman! You and your little babies have made me the happiest husband and father in the world. Give dear Ed. lots of love (how goes the furnace?) and love me as Your own Woodrow.

ALS (WC, NjP).

[1] Mary Butler Thompson Hazen, wife of the pastor of the North (First) Congregational Church of Middletown.

From Ellen Axson Wilson

My own darling, Middletown Feb. 16 [1889]

It is too bad that I should be hurried in writing again today. I meant to write before dinner but could not manage it, and now I am sorry to say I *must* hurry off to enquire about a nurse whom Miss Russell told me about, and who has just left the Alsops who live down by Dr. Edgerton. She is a coloured girl but is said to be a good servant. Dr. Taft says quite decidedly that she does'nt think Jennie has the health for the place, that for my own sake I ought to make a change. So I must lose no time in looking about.

Your sweet letter written yesterday came this morning—earlier than usual. How good you are, precious one, to write me such sweet letters every day! Oh they are *such* a comfort and blessing to me! My darling, my darling, I *live* upon your love. Yet I feel that I *must* emulate your unselfishness & beg you not to feel *obliged* to write me every day the full four pages. I know how much you have to do in the preparation of your lectures and I also know that the writing of these letters is "as much an expenditure of mental energy as the former." So, darling, don't feel obliged to write me long letters because I am sick. I can be brave if I *am* sick & take your love for granted sometimes, or read over the old letters.

Have been interrupted by a long visit from Mrs. Conn,[1] & now must indeed make haste as it is already getting rather late for my errand.

Be sure to tell me how you are enjoying your lectures now, dearest. I was *so* distressed to hear of your discouragement. You don't report on the next two. The babies are well & good, & I *love love love* you my husband, oh what would I not give to be able to tell you *how* I love you! Your own Eileen

ALS (WC, NjP).

[1] Wife of Herbert William Conn, Professor of Biology at Wesleyan.

To Ellen Axson Wilson

My own darling, Balto., 17th Feby., 1889.

I had to promise Dr. Ely to dine with him to-day, so that, instead of having a day of leisure in which to make love to you, I have time before starting (for he lives on the outskirts) for only a brief love-note. Why is it that I *must* always, when I sit down to write to you, write chiefly of my love for you? Why wouldn't my letters of the past six days suffice me in that matter? The true explanation, I suppose, is that when I speak to you I necessarily open my *self* to you—and that self is made up predominantly of love for you. Besides my love for you seems a new love every day: certainly it is a renewed love—every day brings it fresh access of strength and tenderness. Every day, ∴, it must receive fresh expression. Even if I use the same words to express it that I have used scores of times before, those words have a fresh content—new life, added to the old, breathes in the accustomed phrases. In brief, love making, when I speak to you, is self-expression merely. Ah, darling, how I do love you: how close you are to me: how warm it keeps my heart—how fresh my life,—that I have won your complete love, have made you wholly my sweetheart and wife! You bewitch me, my pet—making all my thoughts revolve about you. You are so sweet, darling—you are so charming—you know all the 'short cuts' to my inmost affections and preferences—you wonderful, precious, delightful, incomparable little woman! I am altogether yours and altogether and supremely happy *because* I am Your own Woodrow

ALS (WC, NjP).

From Ellen Axson Wilson

My own darling Middletown, Feb. 17/89

I did not do my errand yesterday after all, for just as I began to get ready it commenced to rain quite hard; so I am still all at sea about a nurse. Mrs. Conn's girl doesn't seem to think there is any Swede I can get at present. I begin to be afraid, dear,—though we are ill able to bear the expense of bringing her here, and the thought of it—the additional expense is most distressing to me—that I will be obliged to try and get Mary back. There is no use trying to blind myself to the fact that I am getting steadily—for the last day or so—rapidly worse. It is only by a tremendous effort that I keep up at all. It is evidently to be the same old story over again. And I suppose it is very weak but it puts me into a sort of fever of nervousness and apprehension to think of having a stranger about me at this time and especially to have her in charge of the children when I am so little able to take the proper oversight. If you were here I wouldn't mind it. And I am getting almost too weak to exert myself very much in the way of looking up some one. I can't imagine why, but yesterday afternoon I seemed to grow suddenly and decidedly worse, and so far I havn't succeeded in regaining the lost ground. I took my walk though as usual this morning. Oh my darling, what a poor weak creature you are tied to! How can you,—how can you write all the sweet things that you do to such an one as I? I have done *so* little to make you happy. When I look back over my married life I am oppressed with a sense of failure so great that it seems to me my heart must break. How much of the time I have been a mere dead weight upon you,—perfectly broken down with sickness.

Of course you will say that was my misfortune & not my fault,—but how much better was it when I was well? Oh this last year! What a shameful record it has been! I have been your *tormentor* instead of your helpmeet. Not the smallest thing has gone wrong but *you* have been teased and worried with seeing me "go all to pieces" over it. I have had no more self-control than a baby. If you were selfish and indifferent like so many men it wouldn't make so much difference for you would not have noticed or cared[.] But that *you* who are so sensitive should have your mind distracted from your work for such unworthy causes! Oh I am not fit to live! What *has* happened to me? What curse has fallen on me? And to think that before I married my most striking characteristic as every one said was my singular *serenity* of disposition! Scarcely anything disturbed it,—small things—never. I remember once when I had a handsome dress stolen before I had ever worn it, yet neither showed nor *felt* the slightest purturbation over it, Mama declared with much feeling that I was altogether "*too* calm and serene." I was "positively exasperating"!

I was so fond of quoting—"hast thy purse been stolen?—let not thy peace of mind go with it, for in so doing thou dost but double thy loss." Alas! how easy it is for young girls—and men—to be philosophical—for *anybody*, indeed, whose nerves have not been racked and tortured by long weary months of *steady* suffering! If it could only be crowded into any reasonable length of time it would not bring such absolute nervous ruin with it. And oh how I would rejoice to have it so though it were a full hundred times more severe while it lasted!

It seems to me the very irony of fate that my failure in my married life should be of just the sort it is; for before we married I was, as you know, filled with many misgivings as to my ability to make you happy. How could *I* in my littleness and ignorance & general mental incapacity satisfy *you*—be anything of a companion or helpmeet to one so much greater and wiser and nobler? And then as one little crumb of comfort I use[d] to tell myself that you would at least have with me a peaceful, serene home-life,—you would not be driven half mad by the ever-varying "humours" of your wife! Oh my love, my love what shipwreck I have made of your happiness! How can I ever forgive myself! What shall I do? What *shall* I do! I can and *do* resolve that with God's help I will strain every nerve to do better in the future. But against what tremendous odds do I work! for here is the whole deplorable cause of the trouble to be passed through again, and what will be the state of my nerves at the end of the ordeal. Already I feel as if every particle in my body were a separate living organism,—and every one in convulsions! It is a *horrible* feeling; no one who has not felt it can form the slightest conception of it. Oh my darling pray for me—pray *hard*. And pardon, this once, my pouring out upon you the bitterness of my spirit. I will never do so again. And I love *love* you—God only knows how I love you my darling. Your own Eileen.

ALS (WP, DLC).

To Ellen Axson Wilson

My own darling, Balto., 18th Feby., 1889.

I have just finished my fifth lecture: there remain only twenty more (five weeks' worth) to deliver—and then home—to take care of my precious little invalid—to devote my *whole* time to actively loving her! Ah, how I delight to dwell upon going back to her! That is what I live on. I have, I think, gotten on my feet again in my lectures: the first discouragement is wearing off, with the first coolness of the class—and I am beginning to feel a certain mastery over the class—a very healthful symptom, you perceive.

I have just been reading your description of your 'system' of taking care of yourself—and have been blessing you for it, my darling, from the bottom of my heart. *That's* the way, my splendid brave little wife! How happy you make me by taking care of yourself so wisely! Doubtless the best part of the plan is the out-of-door exercise: moping in the close air of the house could not but result in making the trouble morbid, and so inducing nervousness. Can't you organize the taking care of the children after breakfast in such a way as to make it work to your own benefit? Can't you take them out—if only on the back veranda? By all means do so if you can. Are not the dear little pets a comfort and diversion to you, sweetheart? I love to think that they help you.

By-the-way, my pet, wont you *number* your letters consecutively as I am doing? The dates inside don't always correspond with those on the post-mark—and I want to be sure wh. is the latest news.

I sincerely hope that you secured the nurse Miss Russell told you of.

In pursuance of a systematic plan of self-amusement which I am following (for purposes which you can imagine), I am going to the Hopkins House of Commons to-day. It meets every Monday night—but last week I was too busy to attend. How goes the Miles ministry—do you hear?[1]

Bless your heart, you sweet thing, I wont write you the 'regular four pages' when I *must* not (as yesterday); but writing to you is my chief indulgence. It *is* an expenditure of nervous energy: but then it is also, & chiefly, an expenditure of *heart* energy such as in my present condition is absolutely essential to me. My heart would break if I were often prevented from spending this hour with you. For you perceive, madame, I have no children to take care of, next to no visits to receive, no cooking or housekeeping to superintend—I am not keeping your house and your little ones for you while you are away (I am determined that you shall realize and appreciate your advantages!)—I am simply a bachelor in a boarding house all my time my own—in wh. to play tricks with my content! Oh, you lovely little woman, what business had you to step in and take such complete possession of a young gentleman who did nothing more than say the truth in telling you that he loved you? He has played you some sad tricks in return, but he glories in your victory over him—he loves to think of himself as

Your own Woodrow.

Kisses for the precious babies and much love for Ed.—W.

ALS (WC, NjP).

[1] See the news item printed at Feb. 4, 1889.

From Ellen Axson Wilson

My own darling, Middletown Feb. 18 [1889]

Your letter treating of the servant question is at hand. I have spoken to Mrs. Crawford[1] & Conn about it;—havn't been able as yet to see about the negro girl before-mentioned because it has stormed all day. I am still divided against myself as to what I should do. When I am most nervous I think I *must* have Mary, come what may, and when I am a little better I think that the additional expense, especially now when there is so much cause to worry about expense anyhow, would be harder to bear than the stranger. I will be sick at the shortest calculation eleven weeks more–most probably thirteen–so that I would have to ask Mary to come for four months, & pay her $14.00 a month,– I could get her for that from what Carry tells me. That would be in the four months $16.00 extra, the ticket here $5.00 & if I had to also pay her way back $5.00 more–a heavy tax to pay for the comfort of having her. If I could only *get* a good white one I would take her in a hurry, but the horizon is quite blank as yet,–and now Jennie has heard of another place and wants to go! Since I began to write this a negro girl whom Carrie has fished up has been in to see me. She has never lived with anyone here–is quite a stranger. I must confess I don't like I [her] looks much, she appears sullen. She refers me to a Mrs. Saxton at Norwich to whom I will write.

I am so sorry, dear, to *fill* my letter again with this subject, for now I am afraid I *must* stop, though surely against my will.

Do you know you are a very naughty boy not to report on your later lectures? You havn't said a word about them since the first two. Don't you *know* I will be distressing myself over your discouragement and letting my mind dwell on it and worry over it until I get a more cheering report? I open every letter and look eagerly over it first of all for that, before I even stop to enjoy your sweet words of love. I can't help feeling a little blue about it this afternoon–thinking you must be still discouraged and unappreciated or you would surely not avoid mentioning the subject so. For now your Sunday's letter has just arrived & it is the same with it.

Such a sweet sweet letter as it is, darling! Oh how can I be grateful enough for your precious love! When I think of it and of *you*,–of all your goodness and tenderness and nobleness my whole nature is caught up into a sort of white passion of almost adoring love and reverence. Oh my darling, my love, my life, surely no one was ever loved before as you are by

Your little wife.

ALS (WC, NjP).

[1] Wife of Morris Barker Crawford, Foss Professor of Physics at Wesleyan.

To Ellen Axson Wilson

Balto., 19th Feby, 1889

My darling, my darling! my poor, poor little girl: if necessary, my pet, I will throw up my engagement here and come to you—in spite of everything. By a kind Providence your letter was brought early this morning and I snatch this moment before going to my lecture, to say that I will run over to Phila (to Rosemont) and see Mary—send her to you if it be possible. My precious one—you are and always have been my delight—if every word in your letter were literally true, my love for you would still cure it all—for my love for you is supreme—hallows everything that I suffer for your sake—I should be ashamed and incapable of a *holiday* love. My *life* is yours—nothing that I can do for you *can* in the nature of the case be a sacrifice—for I love you, I love you, I love you—oh that I could help you. May God bless you, my pet, may God bless & help you. Indeed I do pray for you—constantly, fervently—with a heart unspeakably full of a passionate desire for blessings and help from on high. My pet, let my love sustain you—above all let your trust in God sustain you: he will be with you, I am sure, if you will be [but] lean upon him! And now, good-bye in haste, precious—my lecture hour is at hand—and after that to see Mary.

Your own Woodrow

ALS (WC, NjP).

From Ellen Axson Wilson

My own darling Middletown, Feb. 19 [1889]

I seem fated never to get to Mrs. Alsops[1] to see about that girl. Just as I was about starting Mrs. Armstrong[2] called & made a long visit, so that I could not go this morning, & now I am scarcely equal to it;—walking on level ground is all very well, but that hill "sorter gets me." I have to 'save up' for it. I have been rather more nauseated than usual today, and yet I have been all day in really *high* spirits in spite of it! partly I suppose because I have scarcely been nervous at all. As I lay awake very early this morning my idle fancy began to picture all this over, the baby arrived, the Dr. announcing that it was a "fine boy," & my telling you the news; and I became so delighted and excited over my own dreams that I caught myself laughing aloud! And I have been smiling to myself all day long as the fancy reccurs. My! if I only could know now that it would be a "fine boy" *wouldn't* I be exultant in spite of nausea & nervousness! I am more than willing to undergo it for the mere chance. I thought I was sorry to be pregnant, but the other day when I told the Dr. about that little "flow" she said I must be perfectly quiet after a symptom of that sort or it might lead to a miscarriage,—then I found that I was'nt so sorry after all, for I wouldn't have a miscarriage for *anything.* Yet it would end in short order the nausea & nervousness. My children cost me very dear,—there is no denying that—but I pay the price *most gladly*—only provided that price doesn't include my being a nervous wreck for life.

I am *so* glad & relieved, dear, to learn from your letter this morning that you are encouraged about your lectures now. That is real good news and I humbly thank your highness for communicating it.

You still have no mail at all except printed matter!—isn't that odd! Surely everyone must know that you are in Balt. & is directing letters there.

Your telegram has just come, darling.[3] You dear, sweet thing! I just *love* you for it! Yet I am sorry you went off "half cocked" like that!—bless your heart! If I decided to have Mary at all[,] I wanted to write to her myself[,] bargain with her as to wages, and tell her expressly that I wanted her for *four months.* I wouldn't for *anything* pay her her high rates for a longer time than that. But I am afraid you won't think of those things. And if she should happen to want to stay, as I imagine she may from what Carrie says, she would feel hardly treated if we turned her off like that, unless it was the express arrangement from the first. I find that after college closes I can get a very desirable girl indeed. One who is at the Alpha Delta house. I think,—as the best thing I can do now,—I will write at once to Mary myself, exactly as if I were ignorant of your mission, asking her to come for four months & telling her I will pay $14.00 per month.

So, I must hurry and close this if I am going to do that; for writing is rather slow work with me now;—I have to lie down every few minutes to let a "wave" pass over me & to collect my forces! The babies are well and dear little comforts indeed. Goodbye, dear heart; I love you, darling more than tongue can tell, as much as *your* heart could wish—and oh I am so very *very* happy in your precious love for me. Your own Eileen.

ALS (WC, NjP).

[1] Mary O. Alsop, widow of Joseph W. Alsop, who lived at 151 High Street.

[2] Wife of the Rev. Andrew Campbell Armstrong, Jr., Professor of Philosophy at Wesleyan.

[3] In this telegram, which is missing, Wilson told Ellen that he was rushing to Rosemont to persuade Mary to come to Middletown.

From Elmer Truesdell Merrill[1]

My dear Wilson; Middletown, Conn. 19 Feb. 1889.

'Tis done! The horrid deed is accomplished![2] And the remains, including the weapon with which I slew 'em (a curiously curved blade which the orientals use when they want to do 'emselves up in haru-gari,—shaped something like this ?) await your inspection. They are at present bestowed in secret in my big desk, & will keep without offence till your return, if you say so.

I haven't yet heard from Harrington,[3] & shall wait only till after next Tuesday's steamer. If no reply comes by that time I'll take him at his word & go ahead to look up another fellow.

That man Hatfield[4] who is this year Fellow in Latin at J. H. U. rather takes my eye, especially by his combination of Latin & Sanskrit. Any information about him would be thankfully received,—& if you can set eyes upon him & get a personal impression about his general force & adaptability, so much the better.

I didn't see you much when you were here, but somehow I miss you now that you are away (non quaero modo sed desidero).

The new plan of mid-year examinations in an uninterrupted week was a decided success. No particular news save an unpleasant bit of scandal; a young woman employed as domestic last year in the Alpha Delta Phi club-house gave birth some weeks ago to a (stillborn) illegitimate child, & the father is said by her to be a student.

Auf widersehen! Elmer T. Merrill.

ALS (WP, DLC).

[1] Robert Rich Professor of the Latin Language and Literature at Wesleyan.

[2] Merrill had just given the examination for Wilson printed at February 16, 1889.

[3] Karl Pomeroy Harrington, to whom Merrill had offered the tutorship in Latin for the coming academic year. Harrington accepted the position.

[4] James Taft Hatfield.

From Edward Ireland Renick

Dear Wilson, Washington, D. C., Feb 20, 1889.

Did you get my letter sent to Johns Hopkins, begging you to come over at any time & spend as many days as possible with us? Can't you come on the 22d or next Sunday? Don't disappoint us. I should in goodness to you say that on March 3d 4th & 5th we will be crowded—you would have to sleep on the floor then—but if you can stand it—come even then.[1] At all other times we will have plenty of room. By the way, unless you object I may try to prepare a small "note" for the Nation about the book soon to appear.

With love & a pressing invitation from all of us–& kind regards to Mrs. W–who is included in the invitation if she is with you

Yours as ever Renick

ALS (WP, DLC) with WWhw notation on env.: "*Ans.* Feby 25."

[1] That is, to attend the inauguration of Benjamin Harrison on March 4.

Frederick Jackson Turner to Caroline Mae Sherwood

Dear Maizie: Balto. Md. Feb. 22, 1889

. . . Dr Wilson is away this week–called home by the illness of his wife. I have enjoyed him very much. Went with him to hear Bishop [Henry Codman] Potter (N. Y.) preach the other night. Didn't like Potter, but had a charming walk and chat with W. He is a man [of] fine thought and character, but perfectly familiar and companionable with the graduate students. I like him greatly. . . .

Goodbye, Maizie Fred

ALS (F. J. Turner Coll., CSmH).

From Wilbur Olin Atwater

My dear Wilson Washington, D. C. Feb. 22, 1889

Aren't you coming down here during your stay in Baltimore? Of course the 4th of March is the great day, but perhaps you will find it easier to get off another time, possibly over Sunday. If you will come Mch 4th or any other time before Mch 18th–when I now expect to go to Middletown,–I think we can find a place for you either at our boarding place 813 Vt. Ave or at a hotel or boarding house near by. And we–Mrs Atwater and I–would be most happy to have you as our guest. Personally I should much like the opportunity to talk college matters over with you, a little, and I trust you would find things here to interest you.

Anytime after the 4th of March I feel sure there will be plenty of room at our place, but before then we should want to know in advance so as to be sure to have time to engage room. We had a pleasant visit from Conn. Come if you can, wont you, even if it is only for a few days or even a day?

Address me at either 813 Vt. Avenue or Department of Agriculture Sincerely Yours W. O. Atwater

ALS (WP, DLC) with WWhw notation on env.: "Ans. Feby 25."

To Ellen Axson Wilson

My precious, precious darling, Balto., 24th Feby., '89.

I arrived quite safe and sound this morning, my train about two hours behind hand and an extremely cold, comfortless night behind me, but well and by no means overwhelmed with fatigue. I have washed and dressed, have had a satisfying breakfast, and am now ready, so soon as this letter shall have been written and dispatched, to fulfil my engagement to dine with Charlie Mitchell! What amount of wits I retain for dinner conversation remains to be seen.

Of course my thoughts have continued full of but one thing, my darling's welfare. I am impatient to hear that Mary arrived; that you find solid comfort in her presence and management; that your spirits keep up—in brief that you find it easy to be your own dear, brave self. You don't know what a comfort the two letters that came from you after my departure have been to me this morning. They are such delightfully sweet, brave, cheerful letters—their whole tone an echo of the loveliest traits of your character. Oh, how I love and admire you, Eileen, my peerless little wife! And that waking dream about the coming of your little son, and your mother-happiness—your happy laugh at the thought—is something to be treasured in my memory always—another picture of my sweet one. It is *so* sweet, so natural, so like you. Ah, how I hope that dream may be realized! And yet when I think of our precious, our delightful little daughters, I can't help being as glad at thought of having another little girl—almost—as at the thought of having a boy. Their sweetness and goodness came over me like a great wave again after my brief separation from them. They are lights to the house—treasures of amusement, as well as everything that ought to make a parent's heart glad,—charming in nothing more than in their individuality. My sweetheart it delights me so to see you a mother—to see the traits I love brought out by your children—and to be myself participator in this perfecting of your womanhood—that I am ashamed of myself, in view of the terrible preliminary suffering that child-bearing brings to you, to find myself persistently wishing to see you surrounded by little ones. My resolution is not altered a whit;[1] but my imagination will run to pictures quite incompatible with that resolution!

Ah, darling, this trip did me good—how it has increased—who

would have thought that possible—my admiration of you and my trust in you as the best possible companion for me. You don't know what intercourse with you does for me: it strengthens, expands, renews me. There could be no more conclusive proof of the wisdom of a certain choice declared in Asheville[2] and consummated to the blessing, the exaltation of

Much love to Ed. Your own Woodrow

ALS (WC, NjP).

[1] Woodrow and Ellen had discussed the advisability of Ellen's having no more children.

[2] He refers to their engagement in Asheville, N. C., on September 16, 1883.

Two Letters from Ellen Axson Wilson

My own darling [Middletown] Feb 24 [1889].

I have put off writing—from pure laziness—until it is now almost night and I will just drop a line to say how I am getting on. I have had a much more comfortable day than yesterday, have scarcely been nervous at all, and as to temper have felt very calm and philosophical—in fact am doing quite nicely. Mary arrived safely and is at her post. The children seem to recognize her and are well & happy. I let her bathe them this morning, greatly to my physical benefit though much to my mental dissatisfaction—for of course it is one of the chief pleasures of my day.

But it is so very cold in this room that I must close even more hastily than I expected. I *hope* your journey was not very hard, dear, but I fear it must have been, the weather is so cold. Trust you are having a pleasant time now at the Mitchells. I find some satisfaction in knowing your movements so that I can follow you with my mind's eye. Oh my darling, I am with you in spirit *always*, & I have such a sweet sense too of having you with me. I *love* you, dearest, perfectly, & thank God, I *know* that you love me,—& in the thought of that surely there is no happier woman in the world than Your little wife

My own darling [Middletown] Feb. 25 [1889]

Your sweet letter is at hand and has been I cannot tell you how much enjoyed. If that trip did *you* good, dearest, think what worlds of good it did me. I thank you for it every hour & minute. Oh, love, you are my strength & comfort & helper all the time, *wherever* you are! whatever you are doing!

I feel so shaky this afternoon that I won't try to write a letter.

Don't think I am worse though, I am doing very nicely, & and am quite cheerful. The children are playing about me & are the sweetest dearest little darlings in the world. I love you, my precious one from the bottom of my heart & am always & altogether Your own Eileen.

ALS (WC, NjP).

To Ellen Axson Wilson

My own darling, Balto., 25 Feby., 1889.

After a night's sleep of almost twelve hours, I feel much more like myself, and have taken up my work where I dropped it with renewed vigor. I not only lectured without fatigue this morning but have just completed the last paragraph, and made a topical analysis, of 'Hellas,' my additions to the Greek chapter of the text-book. You see I have gone into my resumed tasks with a swing, which means that I feel strong both in body and in spirit. That visit to you, darling, built me up wonderfully—I did not know how much yesterday, when I was quite too tired to realize anything normally, but I do know to-day. Sick as I found, and left, you, I was reassured by seeing you: I can now know how well you will stand the ordeal in my absence,—how much your mother-gladness and your love for me will sustain you,—how much your pluck and sweet disposition will accomplish. I was never before away from you during *this* trial and I had no means of reckoning your forces separated from mine. But now, somehow, I feel profoundly reassured—as if I had *seen* your strength & endurance for the future as well as in the sweet present when I was close to you. All this, you, doubtless, do not realize—and will fail, perhaps, to understand; but it is as real to me as the whole of my knowledge of you. It by no means reconciles me for so much as as [a] single moment to our separation, but it makes me feel that my visit to you was wholly and only a blessing to me. Darling, how little you know yourself! You call and think yourself weak and yet you give out strength—which I absorb—a feminine strength, of course, but none the less a strength capable of the greatest things.

I enjoyed the dinner and afternoon at Mitchell's very much indeed—a great deal more than I had thought my fatigue would allow. My talking apparatus worked all right—too easily, indeed, for I did most of the talking. Mitchell is thoroughly worth knowing and conversing with. He has opinions, and, what is very rare, is entitled to them.

I stopped at the Hazen's[1] and made, hastily but clearly enough, the explanation you wished me to make. He understood very easily.

I wish I could send my love to sweet Margaret and Jessie—I wish they could understand how I love them—and that they made a reconquest of my affections this time.

As for you, my queen, you know—do you not?—that *you* make reconquest of me every time I come into your presence either in fact or in imagination. Your power over me (for it is nothing else) is a continuously increasing power—and there never was a more willing or delighted subject of power. I love you, I admire you, I honour you, I depend upon you, I live in you and for you, I rejoice in you, and I am in all things

Your own Woodrow.

Much love to dear Ed.

ALS (WC, NjP).

[1] That is, on his way to the station on leaving Middletown.

To Wilbur Olin Atwater

My dear Prof. Atwater, Baltimore, Md., 25th Feby., 1889

I am touched very near the heart by the cordiality of your kind invitation to visit you in Washington, and I need hardly say that my wish and preferences are very strongly engaged on the side of acceptance. But my engagements here are of so engrossing a sort (my lectures having to be put in shape from day to day) that I see no chance of getting off for a run to Washington more than once during my stay here—and for that once I am promised, to an old friend, my one-time law-partner, who is in the Treasury Dept. I shall, however, make every endeavour to see you when I come, even if for only a short time—for it would be a pleasure missed if I should neglect any opportunity to see you and Mrs. Atwater, and I shall not easily deny myself.

If I find it possible to plan ahead, I will let you know the day on which I shall try to look you up, that the chances of missing you or Mrs. Atwater may be reduced to a minimum.

With warmest regards to Mrs. Atwater,

Very cordially Yours, Woodrow Wilson

ALS (CtW).

From Ellen Axson Wilson

My own darling, Middletown Feb. 26 [1889]

What sweet letters you do write! I am perfectly sure that no one else in the whole world ever equalled you in that respect. How I wish I could tell you what a wonderful comfort–what a perfect delight they are to me. If I could only give you by means of mine a small fraction of the happiness that yours bring me! But alas! you know I never knew how to coin my heart into words, & *now* I am absolutely powerless. I sit up & try to write but find I cannot even think,–can do nothing, my head swims & I turn so deadly sick. I am getting on very well though & am in *very* good spirits. As long as I lie down I don't feel so badly, but I try to sit up during the afternoon so as to avoid weakness. And I walk every day in the piazza. I am doing bravely with regard to eating. The dear little ones are well & the sweetest little blessings in the world. Please excuse this dim writing. I am forced to write with an extra hard drawing pencil because no other has a point & I have no knife. Good [God] bless you darling! I love you *devotedly* & am always & altogether Your own Eileen

ALS (WC, NjP).

To Ellen Axson Wilson

My own darling, Balto., 26 Feby., 1889.

I have been using the pen so much to-day that you must overlook the fault if my writing degenerates in the course of this letter into a scribble.

Lecture No. 8 was delivered this morning: the end of this week will see at least ten off my hands–and I shall feel almost half way to my deliverance–my return to you.

Two of your letters have reached me: I now know that Mary arrived, that you have been wise enough to turn the bathing of the children over to her, that your courage continues unabated, and that, judged by the tone of these letters, even if I had no other criterion, you are the most charming little girl in the world. How wonderfully *everything* serves to knit us together, my precious little sweetheart! Bless your heart for saying that you *know* that I love you. If you did not know it you would indeed be hopelessly blind. My love for you sings me songs all day long. It makes me everything that I am in the way of serene strength. Love you! indeed I do, my sweet, sweet wife. Your sickness has this time, in some way, impressed me more than ever before with the beauty of your *motherhood.* I find myself adding more and more to my adoration of you as my sweetheart and wife a yearning tenderness for you as the mother of my children. God bless you, darling, and help you know the love of

Your own Woodrow.

ALS (WC, NjP).

From Ellen Axson Wilson

My own darling, Middletown Feb. 27 [1889]

Let me ask while I think of it,—for I have intended asking for several days & always forget,—at what jewelry store is that watch?—& what too is the sum that is due for it? I had a funny experience the other night. I waked up in the dead of night, as I supposed, looked at the fire, saw that it needed attention, "fixed" it carefully & went back to bed. About ten minutes after comes Mary with the baby's *ten o'clock* bottle! I had a much more doleful time though the night you left,—was waked up by the cold to find the fire *entirely out*, & the room bitterly cold. I worked with it for an hour or more in vain; it wouldn't blow up with mere paper for kindling. At last in utter despair I sacrificed a few *clothespins* that I found among the children's toys & also one of their oldest *blocks*! & so finally succeeded. But the last two nights I have done nothing to it & it has kept very well. I had a note from Mrs. Crawford today saying they had heard of a Swede who wanted a place but they knew nothing about her, except that she speaks very little English. Sounds promising! eh?

I have been having rather a good day & my spirits are *as usual very* good. The butcher brought me some sweetbreads which made a pleasant change, so that eating has not been so much of a task as usual.

I have just finished Turgénieff's "On the Eve," a beautiful & pathetic tale of true and passionate love. Oh, so sad though!

But I must stop for today. Am *so* glad, dearest, that you are getting on so well with the lectures. Are you *enjoying* their delivery now? Goodbye, darling, I love you!—love you *perfectly*[.] I fairly live upon that love & yours for me, & I am altogether

Your own Eileen

ALS (WP, DLC).

Two Letters to Ellen Axson Wilson

My precious darling, Balto., 27th Feby., 1889.

No letter from home as yet to-day, and so I am driven to fall back for agreeable thoughts upon the good news from London—since you don't see the papers I shall assume that you have not heard it, and give myself the satisfaction of repeating it. Pigott, the fellow who supplied the *Times* with the Parnell letters upon which that enterprising journal has been basing its charges of crime against the Irish Nationalist party (the charge which the Commission has been trying) has confessed that he forged them (at least the most important and damaging of them) and the *Times* is thoroughly discredited in the whole matter. Parnell is virtually cleared, and, what is more, it now looks as if the Nationalist cause had received an important impulse forward.[1] Even the *Standard* (the London N.Y. *Tribune*) concedes these points and advises the *Times* to surrender at discretion rather than make a still worse impression on the public mind. I know that you will agree with me that this is good news. The next elections promise to give the Gladstonians a signal triumph. The news has positively excited me.

This is my no-lecture day and I have been spending the morning copying 'Hellas,' having determined not to wait for my Caligraph in preparing for the press. I am giving all the working hours not needed for preparing my lectures to work on the text-book, for I am impatiently longing for emancipation from it. I don't mean to carry the tiresome thing another summer.

I wonder if it is snowing in Middletown as it is here: I wonder how the day is going with my precious little wife, whether she is thinking of me and of the love for her that governs all my life? I dare not dwell in my thoughts on her sickness[:] to do that relaxes every stout resolve in my heart, fills me with a sickening discouragement which I cannot afford long to indulge. I dwell, rather, upon her splendid endurance under the affliction, upon her love for me, and her delight in our sweet babies, upon her wonderful happiness, sweetest proof of my success where success is life to me—my success in demonstrating my love for her, making it tell upon her life. Ah, my darling, you afford me so many delightful things to think about that it is always possible for me to be happy so long as you are mine, so long as you find happiness in my being Your own Woodrow.

[1] The London *Times*, in early 1887, published a series of articles entitled "Parnellism and Crime," accusing Charles Stewart Parnell and other Irish

home-rule advocates in Parliament of conniving in crimes committed by extremists in Ireland. The accusation was based upon a series of letters allegedly written by Parnell and his associates. A special judicial commission, appointed to investigate the *Times*'s charges, sat from October 1888 through November 1889. Richard Pigott, a disreputable Irish journalist and nationalist agitator, who testified in late February 1889, broke down under cross-examination and confessed that he had forged the letters that incriminated Parnell and others. Pigott then fled to Madrid, where he committed suicide on March 1.

My own darling, Balto., 28th Feby., 1889.

I am this morning tearing my hair over the English "Local Government Act, 1888," lately enacted to the upsetting of my so carefully formulated description of local administrative arrangements in the mother country. I have finished my lectures on local government in France and Prussia, and now only a sketch of local govt. in Switzerland and a few notes on Austria, Hungary, Sweden, and Norway stand between me and the necessity to say something coherent and even detailed about local government in England (lectures 11-15 inclusive?) If I could in good conscience devote the rest of the course to England the thing would be easy enough: there's little difficulty in describing complicated affairs in detail—the rub is to describe them compactly, in sum.

Everything is conspiring this year to delay me in my course. Advised—nay, urged—to do so by Dr. Adams, the students of politics are, almost all of them, going over to Washington on Monday next to witness the inauguration of Harrison—an object-lesson in govt. I shall probably, therefore, have no class at 10 o'clock—and Dr. Adams advises me not to lecture. He himself is not going to—no classes are to be held after the hour 9-10. The arrangement is very unpalateable to me, as you may imagine: for I *want to get through*—that is the goal I am most anxious to speed towards—the opportunity to go to you. To see the time *lengthening* ahead of me is appalling. But I still have hopes of making up at least one or two of the dropped lectures—though the fates are certainly against me. You may depend upon it that, with such a reward for haste ahead of me, I will not spare myself in pressing my opportunities.

Do my letters make you happy, darling—oh, I am so glad: they are true outpourings of my heart, I strive in every one of them to give you some faint idea of how much I love you and to succeed is an exceeding great reward for the striving. It *is* a striving—you hit exactly the right expression when you call it "Coining the heart into words": it hurts as if it were a veritable coining—words are so unlike the heart in shape and material. When I try to write as I feel *about you* I suffer a real agony—tho.' a very sweet one, bringing its own immediate reward—for I am trying to speak out *my life*, the principle of action that is in me—to pluck out the heart of my existence, which, next to my dependence upon God, is my love for you, my darling, darling wife, my precious companion and comfort, my queen and my love.

Your own Woodrow

Kisses for the lovely babies—how I love them!—and much love for dear Ed.

ALS (WC, NjP).

Frederick Jackson Turner to Caroline Mae Sherwood

My dear little girl— [Baltimore] Feb. 28, 1889.

. . . Dr Wilson is back. He is a happy father. If you had seen him seated on the footboard of my bed this afternoon talking the most delightful stream of annecdote and epigram to Haskins,[1] Broughall,[2] and myself, while we fairly shook the room with laughter, you would never have recognized him as the grave author of a book that has called out the admiration of the ablest statesmen and historians of the world. Mary Jane (Miss Ashton) is treating us to all sorts of new dishes in honor of his advent. . . .

Goodbye, dear. Fred

ALS (F. J. Turner Coll., CSmH).

[1] Charles Homer Haskins, born in Meadville, Pa., Dec. 21, 1870. A.B., the Johns Hopkins, 1887; Ph.D., same institution, 1890. Instructor in History, the Johns Hopkins, 1889-90. Assistant Professor of European History, 1891-92, and Professor of European History, University of Wisconsin, 1892-1902. Served the remainder of his academic career at Harvard as Professor of History, 1902-1912; Gurney Professor of History, 1912-28; Henry Charles Lea Professor of Medieval History, 1928-31; and Dean of the Graduate School of Arts and Sciences, 1908-24. One of the leading medievalists of his time, he was as famous as a teacher as he was as a scholar. Died May 14, 1937.

[2] James Samuel Broughall.

A News Item

[*c. Feb. 28, 1889*]

THE WASHINGTON'S BIRTHDAY DISASTER.

Of course, the main features of the sad affair which ushered in the 22d of February this year have become sufficiently well known to the alumni and undergraduates through the columns of the daily press. Our purpose in this account is simply to give an authentic statement of the main facts in the case. If anything is erroneous, the fault is that of our authorities, and not of the *Argus.* Any opinions we may have concerning the matter will be reserved for the department of editorial discussion.

It will be noticed that some of the men indirectly connected with the affair are not mentioned. It is our intention, for the present, to give only such names as are directly necessary to explain the carrying out of the scheme. When the part of others is fully known, and the faculty have given their decision on all the cases, we shall have no hesitation in mentioning them also.

Contrary to general expectation and hope, certain members of the class of '92 decided to perpetuate the custom of "firing the cannon" at twelve o'clock on the night of the 21st. To add to the general luridness of the whole thing, they determined to set off certain harmless explosives in the college halls. After a failure on the part of F. H. Tackaberry and H. P. Queal[1] to get the explosives in any other way, there was an agreement among three or four gentlemen by which, a telegram was sent to his father, John A. Tackaberry, of New York city, requesting that six Chinese bombs be sent on the three o'clock express to Middletown. He sent a messenger from his office down to get the bombs, writing on the back of the despatch the address, "IXLD Fireworks Co.," 21 and 23 Park Place, and added as a further indication of the articles wanted "bombs such as students use." The firm he had in mind was the "UNXLD Fireworks Co.," 9 and 11 Park Place. The bombs he meant to get were the kind furnished by this company to give a loud report, but not especially dangerous. The messenger, not finding the firm indicated by Mr. Tackaberry, went to Stern and Lyon, 20 Park Place, and was supplied by them with six so-called "cannon salute bombs." The exact nature of these bombs has not yet been determined, but they are manifestly of too dangerous a nature to be sold without special precautions. The messenger took them as done up, without examining them, carried them to Mr. Tackaberry, who likewise without examining them, sent them to the baggage-master of the three o'clock train. Hall and Gordon carried them from the station to Tackaberry's room. Between ten and eleven that night, C. H. Pierce and H. S. Rooksby went to the room; the package was opened; Pierce took two, Rooksby two, and two were retained in the room. Pierce gave one to E. J. Tamblyn, with the request that he give it to R. E. Smith; another to J. W. Naramore, to be given to N. C. Hubbard, to be fired by him. Rooksby fired one in Observatory Hall, Smith fired one on the fourth floor of

North College. Naramore gave the other to Hubbard, and all that we know absolutely about it after that was the accident which so seriously injured Hubbard.

The other bomb in possession of Rooksby has been recovered and is in possession of the college authorities. The two left in Tackaberry's room are reported to have been thrown in a neighboring creek. Mr. Tackaberry had previously sent to his son, for some celebration at his preparatory school, bombs of the same sort as those, which in this case he meant to send; and he supposed that the bombs were to be discharged out of doors, and under circumstances involving no breach of college order. Thus, manifestly it was by a series of fatal blunders and misunderstandings that a college prank, seriously disorderly, but manifestly not malicious, resulted in what at first sight seemed to have been a fiendish crime. At this writing Hubbard is slowly improving at the New Haven hospital and will probably recover.

The damage to the buildings has been greatly exaggerated. Ten or fifteen dollars will pay for all repairs which it is necessary to make. The result of the action of the faculty is not yet known.

Printed in the Middletown, Conn., *Wesleyan Argus*, XXII (March 1, 1889), 109.

[1] The full names of the members of the Class of 1892 mentioned in this article were Frederic Halsted Tackaberry, Herbert Paul Queal, William Henry Hall, Howard David Gordon, Charles Herbert Pierce, Herbert Spencer Rooksby, Egbert James Tamblyn, Robert Eberle Smith, Joseph White Naramore, and Nelson Chamberlin Hubbard.

From Ellen Axson Wilson

My own darling, Middletown Feb. 28 [1889]

Your letter has just arrived, by the afternoon's mail this time. That is indeed good news from London! No wonder you are excited. If it could only, in *some* way, hasten the "new election"!

I saw Mrs. Conn this morning & for the first time since you left, have been hearing some local news. Perhaps however you have kept up through the papers with the great college sensation. Mrs. C. says the committee have been busy with the matter the *whole* time since; going from committee meeting to faculty meeting & back again;—Dr. Van V[leck]. spent two days in New York investigating. The poor boys seem to have been victimized themselves, since they had no idea of getting such dangerous things,—indeed never saw or heard of anything of the sort 'till they arrived. But they are to be expelled all the same—nine of them. Hubbard *was* one of them. He is doing very well now,—has lost but two fingers,—not the thumb. They say he was a fine pianist

& had intended to make it his profession. It seems one of the boys wrote to his *father* in N.Y. for "crackers." He refused at first but the boys sent an urgent telegram, so he wrote on the back of the telegram: "send such things as college boys use," & sent it by a messenger to what he supposed was the proper place; but at this place they said they did not deal in such things,–referred the messenger, at his request, to some other place where they might be had. There they took the order &–since they can't be kept in stock–made specially six of these things & sent them down by special messenger,–they were too dangerous to travel in the ordinary way. The boys were puzzled by their appearance but thought they must be all right since the boy's *father* had sent them. The latter is of course dreadfully distressed–says it will ruin him. He is a man of standing and a "Sunday-school superintendent"! The authorities have one of the things now, the other two were thrown in the river.

Mrs. Conn told me another sad piece of news, viz. the sudden death of Mrs. Hazen's father.[1] That will be a great blow to her, she was devoted to him.

But I must stop hastily to give Margaret an enema–gave her medecine last night but it hasn't acted. What *shall* I do with her? she *never* has a natural action now. Neither do I, & I have no idea what to take, enemas have no effect on me lately.

I am doing very nicely otherwise & am cheerful & not nervous, but very very happy always in the thought of my darling's love. With a heart full for him in exchange I am as ever

Your little wife

ALS (WP, DLC).

1 William Thompson, D.D., a professor at the Hartford Theological Seminary.

To Ellen Axson Wilson

My own darling, Balto., 1 March, 1889.

It makes me so happy to get one of your 'good day' letters: your sweet spirit brightens up so the moment that dreadful nausea gives you the least respite! You are truly a lovely, noble woman, my pet, to bear up so sweetly under the weight you are carrying. I love to think that it is *for my sake* that you bear yourself so bravely–and for the sake of your womanhood, your motherhood. Does not the thought of the little one that is coming–re-enforced by the reality of the lovely ones that have already come–add sweetness and strength to your love for me and ease to your present trials? Somehow I have a different feeling this time from that which I had either when Margaret or when Jessie was coming. They were *impersonal* to me, even when they were much nearer being persons than the present youngster is: and yet I already love the said youngster. No child of ours shall be unwelcome, darling, that's certain!—and this one shall be, ah, *how* welcome—if only it were not a torture to you to bear him! How many weeks is it now, precious, that you have behind you of the nausea? Four, isn't it? That's almost half—when I get back full half—and more—of the time will be passed—and the rest will be easier to stand, won't it, Eileen, when I am by to help you?

I can't say that I am *enjoying* my lectures—though I feel quite sure that most of the class value them as highly as I could wish—for local government, at any rate *descriptive* local govt.—is dull matter to lecture on—a mere matter of exact phraseology, no space for the (constructive) imagination to turn in. I have to go so slowly in giving the numerous details of the various systems, that the men may get satisfactory notes, that there's no chance for me to take fire as I go: I'm cold—and therefore not comfortable—throughout. Next year (I reflect, with satisfaction and hope) I can deliver matter of a different sort—can bring in more discussion, less description—"penetrate beyond the forms to the spirit that makes them workable."

Do you know, Eileen, that I love you and think you incomparably the sweetest, most loveable woman in the world? I *do*—and you *do* know it. I have been thinking this morning—with a tenderness and gratitude too deep to be uttered—how entirely your life, with all the inestimable treasures of love which it contains, has, since our marriage, been given up to me—and the thought has made me so much the more devotedly

Your own Woodrow

Kisses and love to the babies and to Ed.

ALS (WC, NjP).

From Ellen Axson Wilson

My own darling, Middletown Mar 1 [1889]

It is indeed hard luck that another holiday should interpose to delay your return! However the time *is* shortening in spite of everything. I am so glad to get out of Feb. into March, that seems to mark positive progress. Such a perfect spring day as it is! bright and balmy! March has surely "come in like a lamb."

The children were out a long time this morning & again this afternoon. While Jennie was here they were independent of "housework" & could go whenever the weather suited! But Jennie has gotten a place at last & left an hour or two ago. She goes to a very nice looking young mother to nurse her one baby.

Did you know that Mrs. Harrington's[1] son is coming to be Latin tutor in place of Mr. Williams? He is married & so Mrs. Harrington wants her house for them, & the Conns have to move. I believe next month is moving time, so they are on a desperate & almost hopeless house hunt. Mr. H. was very anxious to get Mr. Merrill's place, but failed.[2]

But there are some little things I must try to get done this afternoon so I won't begin by tiring myself with writing. I am feeling rather more comfortable this afternoon, & am very happy. Goodbye, my darling, darling husband! my treasure of treasures, my own dear love! I love you, dearest, with every heart-throb and I am altogether & always, Your own little wife.

ALS (WC, NjP).

1 Mrs. Calvin Sears Harrington, who boarded at 93 High Street.

2 That is, the Robert Rich professorship to which Merrill had been appointed in 1888.

To Ellen Axson Wilson

My own darling, Balto., 2 March, 1889.

The news items contained in your letter received this morning were most welcome to me: for I knew nothing of the latest doings in Middletown. Prof. Van Vleck went to New York with me, the Saturday night I left, and told me the whole story to date; but since then I have known nothing. Altogether, it is one of the most remarkable college stories I know of. It ought to be a memorable lesson to all parties concerned.

The only items of news I have to give in return are, that Pigott, the forger of the Parnell letters (or, at any rate, a man arrested as Pigott) committed suicide in in [*sic*] Madrid upon being discovered there by the police. That's item No. 1. Item No. 2 is of a very different kind: it is, that in my absence in Middletown last week, at the 22nd Feb'y meeting, the Johns Hopkins Alumni Association elected me President for the ensuing year![1] The election has not been made known to me officially yet: I discovered it quite accidentally in conversation with a friend on the street. The only duty devolving upon me is to be here next 22nd Feby and preside over the meeting and over the lunch (with toast,) given later in the day. Queer trick to play on a quiet, unoffensive fellow!

The news of Dr. Thompson's death is indeed sad. He was so extremely old that, had his last sickness come slowly upon him, it could hardly, I suppose, have been a very great shock to his family. But coming suddenly, as it did, it must have been a terrible blow. I am sincerely sorry for Mrs. Hazen: she is such a sweet, affectionate woman that such a bereavement must cut very deep indeed into her heart. I wish there were some way in which we could express our sympathy.

To-night I go to a reception given by Mrs. [Mr.] & Mrs. Gilman at their hotel. It's hard luck that they chose this particular time; for the Princeton Glee Club gives a concert to-night which I *very much* wanted to attend. I am not quite sure that I will not try to hear *some* of it anyhow.

It looks as if the Hopkins current towards Washington would run so strongly on Monday that I may be swept into it. I suppose I ought to see an inauguration, but it will be a very bitter pill to see this one—embodying, as it does, the beginning of the reign of almost every idea and influence with which I do not sympathize. I can work off the ill humor that may result, however, by resort to the Eng. Local Govt. Act.

Ah, my sweet one, what wonderfully sweet letters you do manage to write despite your trouble! Yours is the most wonderful case I know of, of the triumph of spirit over matter, of love over pain—and that the love that triumphs is love *for me* is the *making* of me, the sweetest fact in all the world. It makes me more passionately than ever Your own Woodrow

Do. [ditto], do., to the babies and Ed.

ALS (WC, NjP).

[1] The only contemporary reference afterwards to the subject was a news item in the Baltimore *Sun*, February 24, 1890, reporting that the Alumni Association had held a banquet in Hopkins Hall on February 22, 1890, and that Wilson had served as toastmaster.

From Ellen Axson Wilson

My own darling, Middletown Feb [March] 2 [1889]

I am afraid I can't write anything of a letter today, for Ed is sick & I have been fussing around over him 'till now I am rather exhausted and can scarcely hold my pencil—my hand shakes so. But as regards the nausea I have had a more comfortable day than usual until a short time ago, and am in good spirits, though of course somewhat worried about Eddie. He waked this morning with his face a little swollen,—something like mumps, & with quite a headache. Since then he has had a chill and fever, so I have thought best to send for the Dr. to see him. Am afraid it is mumps. After all it is an ill wind that blows *no* good, for I shall be able to ask him about Margaret's & my constipations without having him come for the purpose! Isn't that a coldly calculating speech!

I wish you could see the *lovely* violets that Mrs. Armstrong brought me yesterday,—a great bunch of big double ones and *so* fragrant! Wasn't it sweet of her? Goodbye, love, her[e]'s company—& I want to mail this. *I love you.* Your little wife

ALS (WP, DLC).

Frederick Jackson Turner to Caroline Mae Sherwood

My dear little one: Balto. Midnight March 2/3, 1889.

I am just back from Miss Ashton's dining room where Haskins, Miss A.[,] Dr Wilson and I have been eating apples, drinking home-made wine, and listening to Wilson's delightful fund of stories. We talked until the clock struck twelve, then W. started to put the light nearer him to read a paragraph in my concert program, when suddenly it went out. "Ah," he calmly remarked "that's a *girl lamp*—it doesn't like to be touched!" Whereupon we all laughed & came upstairs. . . .

Good night, little Maizie girl. Fred

P.S. omitted. ALS (F. J. Turner Coll., CSmH).

To Ellen Axson Wilson

My own darling, Balto., 3 March, 1889.

Sunday is a dreary day with me in one respect: I get no letter from you and so feel as if our separation were increased in *distance* as well as in *time*. Cut off, for the time, from communication, I seem cut off from comfort too, and therefore from a feeling of security about you. I am more anxious about you on Sunday than on any other day. And yet that is wholly unreasonable, I acknowledge—and thoroughly ungrateful to boot. For what a wealth of comforting thought I have to dwell upon! What sweet pictures of a brave little wife and precious little children there are for my imagination to dwell upon: a wonderful little woman suffering from a deathly nausea and yet keeping in her eyes, her sweet speaking eyes, a depth of courage and of love such as only a woman could bless others by displaying; glad with the joy of motherhood, not only because of the charming little sunbeams at her knee, but also because of thought of the other little one that is coming to claim a welcome; happy because of the love of one who is far away, her husband, living for her, in thought and heart living with her, in all things dependent upon her love. Ah, that is a picture that makes me almost wild with gladness. Sometimes, sweetheart—*sometimes*—my knowledge of myself inclines me to think that in some respects you are better off without me than with me—or, rather, *away* from me than *with* me—for in my absence you can idealize me, can forget my moods, my irritable moments, my occasional discontents and morbid discouragements, and remember only my abiding and controlling love for you, can indulge your fancies as to my greatness and sweetness and those various other matchless qualities which you so abash and humble me by ascribing to me to my own face. But when I do have such thoughts I upbraid myself for harbouring them—for my love does not think thus: she pines for me as passionately as I pine for her: my presence as much enhances her happiness as her presence enhances mine: she waits for me as I wait to go to her, as one might wait for returning life after illness, for liberty after long imprisonment, for sight after being blind. I am not disloyal: I believe in your faith in me as I believe in nothing else except the existence of God and the way of salvation. I only distrust myself—I only know how little I am like what I ought to be to deserve your love, my sweet trustful little wife—whose love only makes me the more devotedly and passionately

Your own Woodrow.

Kisses to the babies[.] Love to dear Ed

ALS (WC, NjP).

From Ellen Axson Wilson

My own darling Middletown Feb [March] 3 [1889]

It is as I suspected, Eddie is in bed with mumps & quite a hot fever. The Dr. says he must have caught cold to have so much fever with it. But there is nothing to be at all alarmed about—nor for you, my darling, to be worried about. The servants are doing splendidly and are just as willing and kind as they can be. Carrie takes the principal care of Eddie, since I prefer Mary shouldn't go back and forth between him & the children—though as I do it myself it is rather a foolish precaution. Of course I am anxious about them, but the Dr. says they may escape,—young children not seeming as susceptible to it as some others. If I had only known about his sickness early yesterday morning so as to separate them promptly! But I was upstairs & knew nothing of it 'till the middle of the day; in the meantime he played with them until eleven o'clock. It also complicates matters somewhat that *I* have'nt had it! But we will hope for the best. Ed will probably be well before anyone else gets down, since it runs its course in a week & also takes more than a week to develop after exposure. Fortunately both servants have had it.

I have had quite a good day as to the nausea. Is'nt it absurd! I have had now two unusually good days & it is evident that I owe them simply to a *broiled spring chicken*, which touched a tender spot in my palate & managed to get itself properly appreciated by my stomach! The children are quite well & *so* sweet & affectionate—dear little souls! They are the greatest comforts in the world. They do all they can to make up for their dear Papa's absence. Several times after a paroxysm I have thrown myself down giving a sort of groan, when Margaret invariably runs up & kisses me and Jessie always follows. Doesn't that look like genuine sympathy? My darling! I think of you and long for you all the time,—but all the same, sir, I am getting on beautifully without you! Though the simple fact is, sweetheart, that I am *not* without you. I feel your presence here—close, close beside me all the time. Your strength supports me, your love blesses me every moment. Oh I am happy; happy because "I love my love & my love loves me"!—because best of all, that love is *true* and *tried*—has proved itself no holiday-love but something that can be depended upon under all circumstances,—always! Are not thoughts like these enough to make any woman happy—and most of all *Your* little wife?

ALS (WC, NjP).

To Ellen Axson Wilson

My own darling, Baltimore, 4 March, 1889

No inauguration for me to-day: it is raining steadily here—as it has been doing for the last thirty-six hours, and promises to be doing for as many hours more. We have had very bad, very trying and depressing weather here almost ever since I got back—you know how dark, damp weather affects your unreasonable husband. I am longing for bright days to return. It's fit enough weather, however, to mark the incoming of the Blaine Republicans to the control of the government.

So Harrington is going to take the Latin tutorship, is he? I knew it had been, informally, offered him; but he was hesitating so about coming when I last heard Merrill speak about the matter that I was about to examine the Latin supply here to see what we could get in his stead. I got the impression from Merrill that he (Merrill) rather hoped Harrington would decline. I never thought of the effect upon the Conns of Harrington's accepting—though it's obvious enough—for I knew he was married. Well, well, that is certainly very hard luck indeed! I am sincerely sorry for anybody who has to go house-hunting in Middletown—and I shall be particularly sorry to lose the Conns from the neighborhood—especially because Mrs. C. has proved so acceptible a companion to you. Please convey to them my profound sympathy.

Your letter of Friday, March 1, is the latest I have received as yet—so that I dont feel as if I knew much about you *at present*—but there's an indefinable charm about this sweet letter of Friday that makes me very happy. It could not have been written by any one in low spirits. It represents you in your *natural* state: its charm is your charm—the charm of the loveliest woman's nature in all the world. It brings with it a sweet fresh air of love without repining, of hope without doubt, of courage without self-consciousness. Though its *words* of love are few, it is full of the atmosphere of love,—and seems entitled to be carried near my heart, where you are. Ah, dear little, darling little lady, may God bless you for your sweet, sweet love, for all the sweet influences that you have brought and are constantly bringing into my life! That life grows steadily brighter and brighter because of you. I'm glad I did not know how much I needed you, how much I could get from you of strength and joy, before we were married: I might have done something desperately indiscreet, if I had, in the way of hastening our marriage. Being married to you, it is possible for me to live a bachelor's life (for six weeks or so) with serenity but, if I were not married to you, it would not be possible for me to be *anything* serenely. For, whether with you or away from you, I am always and altogether your own

Woodrow

Kisses as many as you can give to the dear babies, and to dear Ed. much love

ALS (WC, NjP).

From Ellen Axson Wilson

My own darling Middletown Feb [March] 4, 1889

I enclose a letter from Sister Annie which you will be glad to have,—also a bill from D. C. Heath. This is the only mail except a bill for gas & Camp's,[1] but they can wait I suppose until your return. Camp's is only $17.89 for Feb.—quite a[n] improvement, eh?

Eddie keeps the same,—the fever has not abated yet; it keeps at 103. The mumps have now developed on the other side—which is fortunate I think, as one would prefer to be through with it once for all. The children keep very well and happy. I am doing nicely and am quite bright. I get on beautifully so long as I lie down, but the weather perhaps,—it is close & heavy & pouring rain,—makes me feel today quite sick & exhausted as soon as I sit up. So I will try & content myself with a short & hasty letter.

Am *so* pleased, dear, that they have elected you Pres. of the Ass. though of course it is a very natural selection. Too bad about the concert! I hope you managed to hear some of it. I hope you *will* go to Washington,—it will be quite worth while I should think, but a sorry pleasure of course.

But I will keep my word & write a short letter today, though if I wrote volumes, my darling, I should be just as far from fitly expressing how much you are loved by

Your little wife

ALS (WC, NjP). Encs.: Annie W. Howe to WW, Feb. 27, 1889, ALS (WP, DLC); D. C. Heath & Co. to WW, statement dated Feb. 28, 1889 (WP, DLC).

1 S. T. Camp, grocer, 136 Main St., Middletown.

To Ellen Axson Wilson

My poor, poor darling, Baltimore, 5 March, 1889.

It never rains but it pours! Eddie has the mumps and you and the children are exposed to them! Dear, dear, how *am* I to stay away from my troubled little household! May God sustain and bless and guard you, my precious one. I probably could not *help* you were I there; but oh, how fervently I pray for you!

I hope you told the Dr. your condition—so that he understood the special cause of your constipation?

And so broiled chicken made you better and happier for two days? There's just the point, my darling, of the whole matter—and you *must* keep your promise to me in *spirit*—in the spirit in which I intended it—as well as in the letter. At whatever cost to our pockets you must avoid cost to your health and strength and that of the little one who is coming—you must buy *any*thing that tempts your palate.

This is an extremely busy morning with me—because of the complexities of the Eng. Local Govt. Act., which must be simplicities before my next lecture—and I must cut my letter short in order to get to the bank before it closes; but you know that the love I send and feel is not proportioned to the length of my letters—and to-day there is a special passion of sympathy and love in my heart because of your additional trial. Cannot special precautions be taken to guard *you*? Oh, for freedom to come to you: as it is I have only freedom to love you with all the power of my nature—to yearn over you—to live with my darling every moment in spirit and with the whole love of

Your own Woodrow.

Loving sympathy to dear Ed.

ALS (WC, NjP).

Two Letters from Ellen Axson Wilson

My own darling, [Middletown] Mar. 5 [1889]

I have felt quite unwell today so that I have put off writing until now it is five o'clock & I can only write a hasty line, so that Carrie, who must go out at once on an errand, may mail it.

I think it is the medecine which the Dr. gave me for constipation which has made me feel badly,—& it did not act either. Do you remember what it was that Dr. Savery gave me?—something like *cascara* (?) pills? Wish I knew, for I remember they served nicely.

Eddie seems better today though I don't know positively as the Dr. has not seen him, it being his day in Hartford. The children are well & sweet, & *I am happy*, darling even if I can't hold my head up very long.

Am so sorry you missed the inauguration. We are having wretched weather here too. But C. is waiting & I must stop. I love you, my dear husband, love you with all my heart & soul. Forever Your little wife.

ALS (WP, DLC).

My own darling, Middletown Mar. 6 [1889]

I learn from Mrs. Conn that, as I supposed, it *did* pour rain all day at Washington & that everybody even Harrison was soaked! I can't restrain some malicious pleasure in imagining the scene. I hope the rain put a stop to the students trip & that you were able to lecture. It *is* rather appalling to think that you have now a whole week of lectures—four—*after* the six weeks are over. I really think they *ought* to make room for them since it is their fault & they should not keep you from your work here so much longer than the time stipulated! Speaking of lectures—Mrs. Scott Siddons[1] was here last night—delivered the last of the course from which we have derived so much enjoyment! They have a rather good joke on Dr. Van B.[2] It seems it is a harmless foible of the dear old man's to try to entertain as many "distinguished" people as possible, & to introduce them in public. So they requested the honour of entertaining Mrs. S. S. She graciously consented but made her own terms,—as follows: she was to be met at two o'clock & left undisturbed in her room until four when *dinner* was to be served to her alone in her room; then she was to be undisturbed again until time for the lecture. After it *another dinner* was to be served her again in her room! So they think the good Dr. had rather an empty honour. But what a crank she must be!

By the way you never told me at what jewelry store *that watch* is to be found. Perhaps that letter did not reach you. They seem to have been going irregularly. I have written every day. Eddie is a good deal better though he still has some fever. The Dr. says no one else has been as sick with it as he. I am *much* more comfortable today. The children still perfectly well. Goodbye my darling. I hope the Local Govt. bill isn't worrying you *very* much.

Oh my precious one I love you, *I love you*! I think of you all day long! Ah how happy, happy I shall be when these long weeks are over! Yet don't think, love, that I am at all *un*happy now, for I am *not*. As ever Your little wife

ALS (WC, NjP).

1 Mary Frances Siddons, identified in Vol. 1, p. 457, n. 1.

2 James Cooke Van Benschoten, Jane A. Seney Professor of the Greek Language and Literature.

To Ellen Axson Wilson

My own darling, Balto., 6 March, 1889.

I feel like blessing you anew every morning for your wonderful letters,—wonderful because of their sweet cheerfulness and hope, for their content and courage. I know that you are not deceiving your husband, by making your letters an exception to your humor, and so I can give myself leave to be elated by them. And I do! They make me strangely happy, considering the fact that they do not bring you to me in person. They prove, in other words, how real and potent a transfer of spirit may be made between those who fervently love each other. These letters are gifts of your spirit to me—of your love—your womanliness—your pervading sweetness—all that I love most in my precious little wife and companion. Separation cannot *kill* us, love, anyhow, so long as we live thus together in heart and sympathy and all that makes for our real union. The atmosphere of my *home* comes with these letters of yours: they make me feel comforted not only, but even *snug.* They reanimate me. Just after they come—except when they bring overwhelming news like that of the *mumps*,—I do my best work. I acknowledge the mump news greatly upset me—filled me with a species of despair as to the situation. To-day, however, I have recovered my equilibrium and can look upon the whole matter with a firmer capacity for endurance.

Instead of being relieved, darling, I am somewhat alarmed at the smallness of Camp's bill. Are you stinting yourself, you incorrigible little economist? If you are, you distress me beyond measure—and neglect your promises! Reform, reform!

Have you heard the Cabinet? Blaine, Secretary of State; Windom (a very respectable man), Treasury; Wanamaker Postmaster General; the rest men never heard of till nominated, outside of their own immediate neighborhood—local lawyers of no significance—except Rusk of Minnesota (?)[1] who has been governor, without distinction, and is now in the newly created Department as Secretary of Agriculture. Rather a poor beginning, I take it. What is to be the *policy* of such an administration? I don't know whether to laugh or to rage.

This is absolutely the only news—though these fellows ought to make a good deal speedily.

Glorious weather has succeeded the rain and penetrative dampness of the first of the week and my spirits have risen accordingly. There's plenty of snap and invigoration in the air now to supply the most expansive and exacting lungs.

My chief resource, however, is not the atmosphere but love—

love for a blessed little lady far away, my frequent letters to whom I always sign, Your own Woodrow

Kisses to the sweet ones—love and sympathy to dear Ed.

ALS (WC, NjP).

1 Wilson was close. Jeremiah McClain Rusk was from Wisconsin.

Frederick Jackson Turner to Caroline Mae Sherwood

[My dear little one,] [Baltimore, c. March 6, 1889]

. . . One grows very weary of boarding—even at the best hotels. As Dr Wilson said to me this evening—"I used to have dyspepsia when I boarded—but now that I have a home and have what I prefer to eat and can talk with those I like at my table I am *happy* and have an excellent *digestion*." It is wonderful how close a connection there is between those two very diverse conditions!

We have sat at Miss Ashton's table tonight and gossipped from 7 until 9! Dr W. was in excellent talking trim and I kept him stirred up. I like to talk with him. One is always sure that he must keep his wits about himself or be voted commonplace, and besides he knows that if he does find an idea it will be readily seized by Wilson. But I prefer to be a good listener when in his company. . . .

Now it is late enough to stop and get to reading. I shall not say "goodbye" if that makes you feel bad, dear little girl. . . .

Fred.

ALS (F. J. Turner Coll., CSmH).

To Ellen Axson Wilson

My own darling, Balto., 7th March, 1889.

I sincerely mourn over your letter of this morning with its news of your being made worse by ineffective medicine. Alas, alas, my darling, *some* remedy must be found for that trouble! I remember the name of the pills as you do, 'cascara'—the doctor ought certainly to know about them; for, as I remember the matter, they were ready-made pills kept by the druggist constantly in stock—not 'patent,' but simply standard in their constituents. Do you mean to say that your constipation is absolute—that you get no relief at all—and have gotten none all this time? My poor, poor little girl! Sometimes I feel selfish in being myself so well when you are so sick.

But your letters, darling, are evidently written—*so* evidently written—*to me*: they contain so little of what you suffer, so much of what you enjoy, so many smiles to so few repinings! I wonder if I could write such letters to you if I were sick(?) I'm afraid more than one groan would creep into my sentences. But you need never imagine, my lovely one, that because you do not speak of your sickness (perhaps you do not mention it as much as you are in conscience bound to do?) I do not *feel* it all the time to the bottom of my heart—realize it with a pain that is proportioned to my love for you—sympathize with you with a keenness which does not always fall short of absolute suffering. I rejoice in your ability to emancipate yourself from the dominion of your sickness when you write—I wonder at and delight in your courage and happiness under pain and the trials of separation: but oh, how I pity and yearn over the sweet sufferer with whom my imagination lingers all day—how infinitely would I delight to suffer in her place—but that my suffering would bring to her the same torture that hers brings to me. Which is better: to suffer pain and enjoy the perfect sympathy of one who loves you without stint or drawback or to be the lover and *suffer the sympathy* only? I leave you to answer the question—for I have never suffered as you have.

May God bless Mrs. Armstrong for her kind attentions to you—for the violets & the thoughtfulness they speak! Do you see her when she comes to the house?

I have been omitting to chronicle what we here (heartlessly) call a piece of good luck. I came back to find one of the old maids—much the more objectionable of the two—confined to her room—and she seldom gets out yet!

There's no news but the old news, that I love you always and altogether and am in all things, except my sins,

Yours own Woodrow

Wholesale kisses to Madge and Jessie, bless them! and to dear Ed. love and much sympathy (Give it!)

ALS (WC, NjP).

From the Minutes of the Johns Hopkins Seminary of Historical and Political Science

Historical Library, March 8, 1889.

The Seminary was called to order by Dr. Ely, in the absence of Dr. Adams. . . .

The leading paper of the evening was presented by Prof. Small,[1] on the "Relations of the Continental Congress to the Colonies." The thesis was maintained that at the time of the first meeting of the Continental Congress, the Colonies were thirteen separate corporations, without thought of common interest. The delegates to that first Congress of '74 were extra-legal and irregular. The terms "union" and "national sovereignty" could not properly be applied to the status of the colonies at this time. The study was based upon a careful study of the Journals of Congress and of the credentials to the delegates from the different colonies.

Dr. Wilson spoke in commendation of the paper. He deprecated the study of our institutions from the European standpoint.

Unsigned new entry, bound minute book (MdBJ).

[1] Albion Woodbury Small, who received the Ph.D. from the Johns Hopkins in 1889. He had been Professor of History and Political Economy at Colby College from 1881 to 1888.

From Ellen Axson Wilson

My own darling [Middletown] Friday [March 8, 1889].

Is it "No. 19" or not? I have such an outrageously poor memory for figures that I can't even remember the No. of my letters from day to day:—nor have I the faintest idea what day of the month it is!

We are doing nicely. I am having a comfortable day, & Eddie is nearly well. The swelling hasn't gone down but the fever has entirely left him & to his delight he is no longer on "milk diet." But he is still in bed. The Dr. says "its the safest place for him." The children are still quite well, and *so* sweet and good—dear little souls! By the way, dear, don't worry about my constipation, the enema works now every other day, & I think that is sufficient when I am on low diet. I suffer no inconvenience.

I need you to get me some more books to read! Have finished all those—all except two which were uninteresting so I merely looked them over. I feel inclined after this dose of Balzac to equal or exceed you in your contempt for the French. One of them particularly is a revelation in the singular & total inability shown by both the author & his characters to even form the *conception* of morality! However that is evidently only true of Parisian life. It was consoling to read in Hamerton that the smaller communities are in this respect exactly like the same in England. "There is no question as to the morality of the women,—

it is a matter of course." Even Balzac recognizes conjugal fidelity as a "bourgeoise virtue"!

But having had something to see to I was late in beginning to write & now I must hurry & get this mailed or I fear it won't "go" tonight. Good bye, my precious one. With a heart *full*, full & running over with love for my darling I am as ever

Your own Eileen.

ALS (WP, DLC).

To Ellen Axson Wilson, with Enclosure

My own darling, Balto., 8th March, 1889.

I am ashamed of myself for having been so forgetful of your convenience as to neglect to tell you about the watch. I am chagrined to find that I don't know the name of the shop where I left it—never did—but its whereabouts is of course very clear in my recollection. It is the narrow little jeweller's shop on the College St. side of Camp's store. The charge for the reparing was to be $2.75.

I am feeling particularly happy over your letter to-day, darling, with its bright talk about Harrison's wet induction into office and about Dr. Van B's adventures with Mrs. Scott Siddons, and its assurance that you are feeling *much* easier. Ah, how happy every lifting of the cloud makes me! I get the impression from the general run of your letters, sweetheart, that you are not having *quite* so hard a time of it this time as you had before. Is that true, or is my impression the result of an unconscious, loving deceit on your part?

I could have told good Dr. Van B. that Mrs. S. S. was an intolerable fool—insuferable to all people of good breeding![1] How can people stand such creatures?

I delivered my thirteenth lecture this morning, my precious one—think of that—that's more than half! The graduate class seems so full of engagements that to put in extra lectures seems well nigh impracticable but *something* must be done to shorten, if not to eliminate, that additional week.

I received just now—much to my delight, as you may imagine—a four-page letter from dear father: four pages of his best letter-writing, his best both for love-matter and for expression—and you know how delightful an epistle that means. By-the-way, you may as well enjoy it now: I enclose it. It is in answer to one I wrote at the beginning of the week.

Sweetheart, I love you more than tongue can tell—more than you *yet* know—more than you could realize if you did know. I am in every pulse and hope Your own Woodrow

So glad to hear that dear Ed is better.

ALS (WC, NjP).

[1] See Wilson's rather cool criticism of one of Mrs. Siddons' performances in Vol. 1, pp. 460-61.

ENCLOSURE

From Joseph Ruggles Wilson

My precious son— Clarksville, Tenn., Mar 6, '89.

Your most welcome letter came to hand on yesterday. I would have written you, as a break to the long silence, had I been sure of your address, but it was not known in this part of earth whether you were in M. or in B. There is one thing always sure, however, and this is that you are hour by hour in my thoughts and upon my heart:—and what is just as certain is, that you deserve the place which you occupy within the house of my soul, and even a bigger place were it a bigger soul. How, in my solitude, have I longed for the presence of that dear son in whose large love I trust so implicitly and in the wealth of whose gem-furnished mind I take such delight: him in whom my affections centre as my child, and my confidences as my friend.

I can readily sympathize with you in the satisfaction you experience in getting back to Johns Hopkins once more, where intellectual life rolls its highest waves:—a satisfaction which is augmented by the fact that you are, yourself, a sort of magna pars where there is so much that is great. What would I not give to be in a position for hearing your lectures!—and to talk with you thereanent afterwards, perhaps, too, beforewards. I do not doubt as touching the impression they are making—and as you perceive this it must be very pleasing to your thoughts everyway. You are preaching a gospel of order, and thus of safety, in the department of political morals and conduct, such as has not heretofore been heralded, and success is therefore a personal gratification whilst it is also a public benefit. I feel *very* proud of you when I think of what you are doing and doing so well.

Please do not *forget* to send me that no. of the Political Science Quarterly which is to contain yr. review of Mr. Bryce's book. Somehow I feel jealous of this foreigner who steps in to occupy territory that belongs more especially to you—and all the more because his work is spoken of in terms of such high praise;

whether deservedly or not you best know. One of Tennessee's first men, in law and oratory, Col. House[1]—a resident of this town—to whom I loaned your "Con. Govt.," read it with prolonged care, and then pronounced it the most complete and instructive treatise—and interesting—that he had ever read. He was formerly an M. C., and is astonished at your perfectly life-like depictions of the procedures of that body.

I hope that you went over to see that fourth rate politician inaugurated, on Monday last. It must, though, have been a sad sight to every true lover of his country: the induction into so high an office of a man most of whose principles are prejudices and all of whose prejudices are obstanacies—a little man whose vision is not that of the patriot but the partisan.

We are getting through the days here, in a dragging sort of mode. Josie studies a little, goes about a great deal, and is a member of every possible company—even is a "drum-major." I see not a great deal of him, really—and have grave apprehensions as to his future—he is so easily led by others who are not so good as himself. He does nothing wrong—only he will not apply himself to duty when duty is a little hard. He must go into business at the end of this session—and I have no idea what or where. Advise. He sends lots of love—but no love can equal mine for you. Your affc Father

ALS (WP, DLC).

[1] John Ford House, Member of Congress, 1875-83.

From Munroe Smith

My dear Wilson: [New York] '89. III. 9

I had to cut a few lines out of your article to save a page. It ran a few lines over 17 pages, and we had scant room for book reviews. So I cut out a longish citation from Bryce's book—preferring to sacrifice that rather than any part of your text.

I have the pleasure of sending check for the article.

I feel very guilty about your MS.—but shall get through with it, I hope, very soon.

I had ordered two copies of the Quarterly sent to Middletown, before receiving your letter. If you would like additional copies, I will have them sent you at Baltimore

Very sincerely yours Munroe Smith

ALS (WP, DLC).

To Ellen Axson Wilson

My own darling, Balto., 9 March, 1889.

I have just completed my revision of the 'Local Govt.' part of my chapter (and lectures) on England; and now, so far as I see, there remains nothing (aside from a paragraph to be added or revised here and there) to be done for the completion of the volume except a description of the imperial (Roman) forms of govt. and of the English colonial system. Neither of those will take time or labor commensurable with what either Hellas or this English local govt. required—and then I shall be free from this tedious burden—this text-book! What a job it has been! I am thoroughly tired of it and disgusted with it. I hope nothing with reference to it now except that it may some day be off my mind. Catch me undertaking another fact book! Hereafter (the small book struck off)[1] I mean to be an *author*—never more a book-maker. The discipline has been very serviceable—but now that I am coming to the maturity of my powers I can't afford time for any more discipline of *that* kind.

Have I told you that latterly—since I have been here, a distinct *feeling* of maturity—or rather of maturing—has come over me? The *boyish* feeling that I have so long had and cherished is giving place, consciously, to another feeling—the feeling that I am no longer young (though not old quite!) and that I need no longer hesitate (as I have so long and sensitively done) to assert myself and my opinions in the presence of and against the selves and opinions of old men, "my elders." It may be all imagination, but these are the facts of consciousness at the present moment in one Woodrow Wilson—always a slow fellow in mental development—long a child, longer a difident youth, now at last, perhaps, becoming a self-confident (mayhap a self-assertive) man. I find I look older, my former (Princeton) college friends here being the witnesses.

But, sweetheart, there's one thing in which my nature at one and the same time (my mind and heart) both matures and stays young—and that's *love*. You are, and always will be, to me at once sweetheart, bride, wife, life-companion—my childrens' mother—everything in one,—remaining your old self and retaining the love I felt for you then, constantly becoming a new self, and winning new love in your new characters, bound to me at every turn and in every character—mine and becoming mine—possessing me and acquiring me—safe in the victory which makes you supreme in my heart, and yet daily renewing the sweet conquests that make me Your own Woodrow

The kisses to the babies and the message to Ed.

ALS (WC, NjP).

[1] His projected high school textbook. See the Editorial Note, "Wilson's Elementary Textbook in American Government."

From Ellen Axson Wilson, with Enclosure

My own darling Middletown Mar 9 [1889]

Your letter with the delightful one from Father has just been received. Thank you for forwarding the latter. I enjoyed it *exceedingly.* He certainly does write lovely letters. I enclose one from Dr. Jameson,—have just replyed but of course could give no *definite* answer. I told him you would write as soon as you received this. It certainly is hard if they are going to detain the [you] there another whole week. It almost gives me the blues to think of it—though I *have* foresworn "the blues" altogether.

We are doing well. I am as usual,—Ed almost well. I am a little anxious about Margaret, she seems out of sorts in some way,—don't know whether the mumps are "forming" or not. Her breath is bad so it may be a slight stomach derangement. She has done nothing all day but cry and whine and bulldose Jessie. The Dr. cauterized Jessie's lip this morning so she isn't very happy either,—poor little soul. Both of the dear little bodies insist upon hanging upon me every moment. You should see the reckless scrawl I have just written to Dr. Jameson in consequence of that fact. But I have finally decided a surrender to be inevitable,—writing is out of the question—even to you. But I *love you*, darling if I can't write to you & I think of you *all day long,* whatever else I am doing. Your own Eileen.

ALS (WC, NjP).

ENCLOSURE

John Franklin Jameson to Ellen Axson Wilson

My dear Mrs. Wilson: Providence, March 8, 1889.

I am much disturbed in mind that I have not earlier succeeded in replying to a letter of Mr. Wilson's and returning to him the plan[1] I enclose, which seems to me excellent. Not knowing whether he is in Baltimore or in Middletown, I write to the latter place in order, if you please, to find out, sooner than I can by writing to Baltimore, (with a chance of forwarding thence to Middletown), whether Mr. Wilson will be in the lands of the Yankee again on Friday, March 29th. If you or he will be so kind as to inform me, I shall be much obliged. With love to the Misses Wilson,—lovely beings,—I am

Very sincerely yours, J. F. Jameson.

ALS (WP, DLC). Enc. missing.

[1] It was a plan for a meeting of the history professors of southern New England at the Narragansett Hotel in Providence on March 29, 1889. See J. F. Jameson to WW, March 13, 1889; WW to J. F. Jameson, March 14, 1889; and J. F. Jameson to WW, March 16, 1889.

To Ellen Axson Wilson

My own darling, Balto., 10 March, 1889.

I am going to write my Sunday letter to-night (Saturday), leaving it open till to-morrow, in case there should be anything to add before I mail it. For Sundays turn out to be the days when I have least leisure—least time, i.e., to myself. My friends invite me out to dinner for Sundays, and, since Sunday dinners are invariably mid-day dinners, there is no time till well into the afternoon (too late for a speedy mail to you) when I can write, if I go to church—our breakfast here being almost at church time. To-morrow I am going to run the risk of getting up before breakfast to go to the P. O.—after breakfast would be too late (the P. O. closing at 10 o'clock), and I *must* seek a letter from you. None came to-day and I *can't* go *two* days without hearing from my darling.

The friend with whom I dine to-morrow is "Fred." Warren,[1] an old glee club chum—the other first tenor—who is now teaching here—the Romance languages. A very clever fellow, indeed, but secretive in the most *secretivest* New England style, and just a bit cynical—a man whom you would know little better at the end of a life-time than at the end of a first conversation; whose wife, if he had one, would probably have in reality little more than a speaking acquaintance with him. I feel like a fish out of water—a lung away from air—with him; and yet I like the fellow & shall get through the dinner, probably, without catastrophe to my digestion.

I suppose that it is for the best that I should be dragged out thus from my den to see people: my tendency is too much towards shutting myself up. I love to talk, but only when I can keep the floor much in sympathetic company—isn't that true?

I never talked out my whole thought except in your company—

I never discovered my whole self till you brought your sweet love and sympathy into my life. You have 'drawn me out,' as I have so often told you, as I never would have been drawn out had you not been so daring as to love and marry me. Your love has brought to me self-revelation of the most remarkable kind.

It would be hard to say, sweetheart, in what part of my life and character you have *not* been a supreme and beneficent influence. You are all-powerful in my development. I suppose any wife must play such a part in some degree in the life of any husband who lives the day long with her and is alive intellectually—but *this* wife, this lovely, clinging, tender wife, quick in her sympathies and as quick in her intelligence, capable of sharing my thoughts as well as my other experiencies—*this* wife is the sweetest and most *powerful* of all wives!

Your own Woodrow

ALS (WC, NjP).

[1] Frederick Morris Warren, a fellow-graduate student at the Johns Hopkins in 1883-84. Warren, who received his Ph.D. in 1887, was an instructor in Romance languages at the Hopkins in 1889.

From Ellen Axson Wilson

My own darling, [Middletown] Monday [March 11, 1889]

Both your sweet *sweet* letters came to hand this morning and I wish I could tell you, my darling, just how happy they made me,—what a warm sweet heart-glow I felt when reading those precious words of love and confidence. And it is needless to say how intensely interested and sympathetic I was in reading what you say about yourself—your change of feeling with regard to yourself! My darling, how I *love* to have you feel like that! And I am *so* glad that the text book is coming on so well. Truly it will be a joyful day when that burden is entirely and finally rolled off. You are right—emphatically—in your determination never to undertake another job of the sort.

I have had quite a comfortable day. Margaret seems quite well and bright again & Ed is nearly well. By-the way, I remember you asked a question which I did not answer, for want of time, viz. whether I was not on the whole having an easier time than heretofore? I think I am, *certainly* easier than the *first* time. Indeed often when I am lying quiet I am surprised to find how comfortable I am, and I say to myself "what a lazy thing you are to be lying here idle! get up and bestir yourself! you are not sick." Though when I do bestir myself I find that I am not by any means 'well' after all! It is astonishing what a difference keeping quiet makes.

But I have had so much company today that it is now almost five o'clock & I must hurry & get this mailed. I love you, my darling, love you earnestly, tenderly, passionately, & I am always

Your own Eileen

ALS (WC, NjP).

To Ellen Axson Wilson

My own darling, Balto., 11th March, 1889

I have some jolly good news for you: I have arranged for extra hours of lecturing this week and next, so that (D.V.) I shall finish my course here a week from next Saturday (the 23rd.) at 10 o'clock, within the six weeks, and be free to return home immediately! Think of that, sweetheart, I finish *next week*! How is that for good news? I am exceedingly exalted by it. The program is this: the usual four lectures in the mornings of Monday, Tuesday, Thursday, and Friday *plus* two afternoon lectures this week (Monday and Wednesday at 5 o'clock) and two extra lectures next week—one at 5 P.M. Monday, the other at 9 A.M. Saturday, the 23rd. Thus six lectures a week, this week and next, bring me to the end.

It is most engaging work, and this is a most stimulating atmosphere in which to do it: I shall leave both the work and the atmosphere with great regret—but with greater joy—the atmosphere of my *home*, the stimulation of your love and presence are what is *most* indispensable to me. I can't live a full life away from you, darling: your love and presence *are* my life. They take worry out of my mental processes and wear and tear out of all experiences. With you I can, I feel, grow old: without you, I would wear out. Ah, my love, how sweet you are! How blessed is the thought that I am to be with you once more so soon! The good news of this letter, my pet, must attone for its brevity: for my first extra lecture, you observe, is to come *this* (Monday) afternoon. Besides, on Friday evening I am to read a paper (the chapter, of my text-book, on Law)[1] at the meeting of the Seminary—and that is in the midst of revision, is at present in a quite chaotic condition. So good-bye, precious! I love you, I *love* you! I *love* you! ! Your own Woodrow

ALS (WC, NjP).

[1] See the Seminary minutes printed at March 15, 1889.

From Ellen Axson Wilson

My own darling, [Middletown] Tuesday [March 12, 1889]

Your note announcing the good news has just arrived. Oh, I am so, *so* glad! I had given up all hope of your accomplishing it—didn't expect to see you 'till the 30th. How good it is to be able to say—"he is coming *next* week!" My darling! my darling! I love you so [—] I want you so! I am *so* happy in the thought that soon, soon you will be near me again. And yet—inconsistent mortal that I am—I have also a very keen regret in that very thought, for surely, in spite of all the sweet things you say, it is better for *you* to be there in that pleasant, stimulating atmosphere than here,—in this atmosphere of *nausea*! I have taken infinite comfort in that thought,—constant comfort ever since you went away. It has done more than anything else to keep my spirits up. I have from that point of view positively *enjoyed* your absence!

We are doing well today—except poor Carrie who last night broke off half a large needle in her wrist, which is now very painful & badly swollen. She wanted the Dr. to cut it out but he said it would be like "looking for a needle in a haystack." He might cut for an hour and never find it. It would probably work out somewhere or other in course of time, & after the present swelling goes down may give her no further trouble. Ed *feels* quite well but the swelling *will not* go down so we still keep him in the one room—the down stairs one. The babies are quite well and happy.

Goodbye, my precious one. I love you,—oh *how* I love you! Do you think you can guess how? *I* don't believe it

Your own Eileen.

ALS (WC, NjP).

To Ellen Axson Wilson

My own darling, Balto., 12th March, 1889

Two lectures delivered since I wrote to you yesterday! The score is now sixteen—which, you will observe, leaves but nine, three more of which will be out of the way before the end of this week. What a delight it is to watch the time drawing near which is to take me to you!

I don't like this news about dear little Margaret: I sincerely hope that she is all right by this time. Keep her well, if possible, at least until I get home.

I am so glad, darling, that my letters give your pleasure: they give me a painful sort of pleasure—the pleasureful pain of trying to speak my heart's secrets and not being able to; but often I think that the failure must be quite evident to you—that you must perceive how profoundly I have failed, how remote from my complete thought my incomplete expression is. It must be because I have been able to convince you in other ways of my love that these letters suffice to renew your sense of its reality.

I have worked myself into a rather headachy condition to-day in a struggle to make plain the nature of *Sovereignty* in the chapter on Law which I am to read to the Seminary on Friday night.[1] I wont grudge the headache if I have succeeded in doing the thing that brought it on: but have I?

What a singular agony it is for me to write—what life-blood is drawn every time I try to compose *any*thing! I suppose that expression will never get easy till I cease to have anything to say. Agony is the inseparable incident of birth, and so long as the process is vital so will the pain be.

I shall be impatient to learn, my sweet one, that Mrs. Hazen has succeeded in securing that single efficient 'monthly nurse' for you. If she cannot be had, we must e'en import one from New Haven or New York or Hartford, for a capable one I mean to have.

How goes your thought, my little queen? Do you think much about the little stranger who is coming? I do, as I said before, very constantly. How I wish that the nine mos. could be hastened, for the sake of seeing the baby, as well as for the sake of relieving you! I wonder, my pet, if you feel as quick an accession of warmth in your love for me when you think of me as the father of your children as I experience when I think of you as the mother of mine? All the *poetry* of the situation seems somehow realized for me and I feel a sort of ecstacy of devotion for you.

The letter from Jameson rec'd. Will answer promptly.

So glad to hear that dear Ed. has come thr. so well. Kisses for the precious ones and for *my own darling* the whole love of

Your own Woodrow

ALS (WC, NjP).

[1] This reference seems to mark the first focusing of Wilson's interest on the problem of the nature of sovereignty. As his letter to Ellen of March 15, 1889, indicates, Wilson at this time was reading in the major work of the English jurist, John Austin, *Lectures on Jurisprudence, or the Philosophy of Positive Law*, probably the fifth edition, revised and edited by Robert Campbell (2 vols., London, 1885).

This appears to have been Wilson's first reading of Austin. There is a copy of Robert Campbell's abridgement of Austin's *Lectures on Jurisprudence* (New

York, 1875) in the Wilson Library in the Library of Congress; but there is no evidence that Wilson had read this volume before March 1889. He had apparently first encountered Austin's views on sovereignty in January 1886, when he read Sir Henry Maine's diffuse presentation of them in Maine's famous work, *Popular Government.* (See WW to H. E. Scudder, May 12, 1886, n. 2, Vol. 5.) Wilson's second exposure to Austin's views apparently came with his reading, in July 1886, of Maine's more elaborate summary of Austin in Maine's *Lectures on the Early History of Institutions* (New York, 1875). The copy of this book in the Wilson Library bears the reading date of July 23, 1886.

It seems likely that Wilson, faced with the necessity of preparing the paper on the development of law and the problem of sovereignty for the Seminary and for the chapter on the same subjects for *The State*, concluded that it would be well for him to read Austin's great work in its full form, although, as later documents will reveal, he profoundly disagreed with Austin on the very nature of sovereignty.

From John Franklin Jameson

Dear Wilson: Providence, March 13, 1889.

Mrs. Wilson intimates a doubt whether you will be back by the 29th. I had been think'g to have the gather'g of historical professors that evening, and wish you would please tell me *ιος τάγιςτα* whether you can be present then. If you can't, a later date can be chosen, though with somewhat less convenience. Regards to Adams & Ely Truly yours, J. F. Jameson.

ALS (WP, DLC).

To Ellen Axson Wilson

My own darling, Balto., 13 March, 1889.

A letter like this of yours received to-day would go far to make any hardship easy—even the hardship of separation from you. In the first place, it contains so many words of love; in the second place, it is so full of cheer; in the third place, it is so full of good news, about Margaret, about Ed., above all, about yourself—your ease when lying still, your comfort as compared with previous periods of the same kind. Ah, it is a precious, *precious* letter: all its words are golden—rather, they are unequalled notes of music to my heart. How truly I live in you, darling, these daily messages from you affect me like the atmosphere, more than the weather, more than my own bodily condition: I seem to live or merely to exist according as they are full or empty of good cheer from my home—which is, being translated, my wife.

And so you love to have me feel mature, do you—or at least maturing? You are not afraid of losing the boy in me? You have so often called me 'your boy,' with accents that seemed to contain love enough to make me happy for the rest of my life, that

I supposed you loved the boy in me, maybe more than the man. Are you not afraid to have me grow sedately middle-aged on your hands? Don't you acknowledge a weakness for the frolic that is in me? Or do you think that you can gain more of the man and still have no less of the boy?

I know. You think that we can keep each other young by keeping the love we first had for each other as well as that which we now have and that which is daily being added. And I believe it. Nay, I *know* we can. It's curious what a *young* delight, so to say, I have in loving you and being loved by you. I have an odd consciousness of recognizing in myself the very sort of boyish pleasure in my bride that I used long ago to *expect* to have should I ever find a woman after my own heart. Oh, you precious, precious possession—what a crown you are to my life!

You 'have had so much company'? Do you receive company as usual—or do you mean your specially privileged friends, like Mrs. Conn? If you are receiving friends as usual, you must be uncommonly well, or unspeakably brave, or very foolish!

This afternoon an extra lecture, Mrs. Wilson,—and you know what an *extra* lecture means—that I am coming *soon*—that our separation is hastening toward its close—that every prospect that delights me, that delights us, is approaching reality. My course here almost over—and your period of nausea *half* over. Ah, my darling, we will have a happy, happy summer together. I will try to prove how completely I am Your own Woodrow.

ALS (WC, NjP).

To John Franklin Jameson

My dear Jameson, Balto., (Old Stand) 14 March, 1889

I received your letter, forwarded by Mrs. Wilson, yesterday, but was so pressed for time as to be obliged to put off answering until to-day.

I hope to finish my work here on the 23rd, and to reach home on the 25th. I have hurried my work here a day or two because Mrs. Wilson is very far from well and I am all the more impatient on that account to be with her.

Is it in connection with your history-men-meeting (!) scheme that you want to know my whereabouts on the 29th? I don't know how possible it will be for me to make up my mind to leave Mrs. W. again so soon; but I would make a considerable sacrifice for you.

Had the pleasure of dining at Mrs. Carey's[1] last Sunday—and a genuine pleasure it was. She is charming.

Thanks for the word about the plan I submitted to you. I have worked up the 'Hellas' since coming here.

In haste and affection,

Sincerely yours, Woodrow Wilson

ALS (J. F. Jameson Papers, DLC).

1 Martha Ward Carey, widow of James Carey, whose home at 1217 Bolton Street in Baltimore was a center of hospitality for Hopkins students. Mrs. Carey and her daughter, Estelle, were close friends of Jameson.

To Ellen Axson Wilson

Balto., 14th March, 1889.

I received a document this morning, my darling, which contained ammunition that may be exploded to its own destruction. It is your letter of Tuesday. A wonderfully sweet letter, but not one that will bear logical analysis. In it you protest that you have been happy in our separation in so far as it has secured to me immunity from an "atmosphere of nausea"—in other words, that you have been happy on my account. Now, my precious little logician, does it not strike you as highly probable that you will be still better able to be happy on my account when I have what I most want and need, your companionship? And wont there be added another argument for happiness in this, that my content is measured, when I am with you, by your frame of mind? When I am away from you, I can know nothing of your state of mind save only the mood in which you were when you wrote your letter—that is always perfectly plain to me—and I am anxious, *suspended* in my own moods, as a consequence. When I am with you, I live on seeing you in good spirits. I want nothing more delighting than to see you happy despite all hindrances of disease or discomfort.

Ah, how *much* happier I shall be *with you* again, my loved one! Bachelorhood, which for a week or two was without any morbid features, is now beginning to *tell* on me. I can't bear so long a *separation from sympathy*, from your so perfect sympathy. My heart stagnates, and my life with it, if I must *contain* my moods and my life with it, if I must contain my moods and my thoughts and have not leave to utter myself without breaking confidence with my ideas of self-respectful reserve. You are the *only* person in all the world to whom I can be perfectly unreserved without loss of dignity, of legitimate, necessary dignity—and yet I chafe under the necessity for reserve. If it were not for these letters daily scribbled to you, I should be without safety-valve. In brief, as I have so often said, you are *necessary* to me, darling! You are not only my comfort and delight, but my *safety* also—against all the morbid tendencies which gather in me when I am compelled to live alone.

And now only seven lectures stand between me and my sweet one: I have delivered 18. I got out of English local govt. yesterday afternoon and into American local govt. this morning—to stay in the latter, probably, for five more lectures. The end will be a lecture or two on city govt.

I am *very* sorry to hear of poor Carie's accident, tell her. Hope the wrist's all right by this time.

Kisses for the sweet little misses, love for dear Ed.

My darling, my darling, I love you, *I love you.*

Your own Woodrow.

ALS (WC, NjP).

From Ellen Axson Wilson

My own darling, [Middletown] Thursday [March 14, 1889]

I have just had a visit from Mrs. Hazen who brought me a box of ice-cream & plenty of good cheer. She certainly is one of the sweetest, kindest women I ever saw! She fairly racks her brain to think of kind things to do or kind offers to make. I mean *particular* offers & kindnesses. All the others say in a general way of course "now is there anything I can do for you?" and I answer "You are *very* kind but I believe not," and there's an end, but she *won't* be put off.

I may as well tell you, now it is over, that we have been passing through a sort of domestic crisis. A week ago Tuesday night Mary was taken very ill and was sick for a week,—six days of the time in bed. It began with a most violent colic—intense pain & vomiting all night. The Dr. came to see her twice on Wed., got her relieved of the colic by night & thought she would be well in two or three days. But she turned out to have some inflammation somewhere and had to be blistered severely before she got over it. She seems all right again now. The faithful thing didn't waste much time on convalescence but went to work again yesterday morning, even helping Carrie some, she being rather disabled with her arm.

Of course for a week though I had to do everything for the

children, take entire charge of them day and night, and of course under the circumstances it wasn't so very easy, though I stood it much better than you would have expected. I staid in bed all yesterday and took a good rest—was such a lazy, good-for-nothing thing that I couldn't even make up my mind to write to you. But I feel *quite* bright today,—have had a *very* comfortable day. I mustn't forget to say how nicely Carrie behaved while M. was sick, doing her own work & some of Mary's—that is the fire, washing &c.,—nursing Ed & Mary & even saving me most of the running up and down stairs. Both Mrs. Hazen & Mrs. Van Vleck tried in vain to find some one to help us out. Now don't say I have broken faith in not mentioning this! It wasn't as if any of us were sick. I shall *never* keep that from you. But it would only have worried you to know this without doing a particle of good.

We are all well—except for Margaret's strangely obstinate constipation. Jessie tried to take her turn at being sick but rather broke down at it. She had *quite* a hot fever night before last,—I don't know how much, of course—oh for a fever therm.! It drives me half wild to be obliged to trust entirely to my own inexperience! She scarcely slept all night, would doze off only to wake up screaming every half hour or so. I gave her a laxative & the febrifuge we used before, every three hours during the night and day, & kept her in the one room, & she seems quite well again; indeed I could detect no fever after the one night. But enough and more than enough of sickness. I wish you could see the *lovely* flowers I have just before me,—pansies & violets & heliotrope & geranium!—perfect beauties! Mrs. Winchester brought them yesterday. Wasn't it sweet in her? Was sorry not [to] see her, but had given orders yesterday to be excused to everyone. But I had no idea I was writing so much, & now I am afraid I am tired and must stop,—and I have filled my letter with disagreeable things—too bad!

Goodbye for today, my precious one. Oh how I wish, darling, that I knew how to write down the thoughts of you that fill my heart almost to bursting—the love, the tenderness, the admiration, the devotion. It is my meat & drink, day & night, to think of you & to remember that you love Your little wife.

ALS (WP, DLC) with WWhw notation on env.: "Conn. Boroughs (Calvin H. Carter) New Haven Hist. Soc'y Vol. IV."

From Edward Ireland Renick

My dear Wilson, [Washington] Mar 14 1889 (7 P.M.)

Your telegram just to hand. We are all overjoyed because of it. Come right to the house if you choose. You will be heartily welcomed. But if convenient, drop in at the Treasury & lunch down town with me, & let me put you on the car afterwards & join you again at dinner. Going from B. & P. or B. & O. Depot to 1717 Corcoran take Washt & Georgetown cars which transfer you at the Treasury to 14th Street line. This latter carries you to Corcoran, there alight turn to your left & walk three blocks.

My dear fellow, come prepared to give us a visit what is a visit. We are impatient for Saturday

As ever yours E. I. Renick

ALS (WP, DLC) with WWhw research notes on env.

To Ellen Axson Wilson

My own darling, Balto., 15 March, 1889

It's always a hard day for me which brings no letter from you. I spend it in a state of *suspended animation*, not knowing what mood to be in, and consequently hovering on the verge of several, ready to go into any one of them on slight provocation. I'm not blue—I promised not to be that—but I am in a sort of minor region of anxiety and accentuated loneliness. Because, sweetheart, I do love you so, and do so constantly depend upon you, bless your heart!

I have determined to go over to Washington to-morrow (Saturday) morning, for a visit to Renick, returning Sunday evening, for my 10 o'clock Monday morning lecture. I have made Renick so many promises about coming to see him that I feel that not to go at all now would be to be false. I can see nothing *in my line* in Washington on Saturday and Sunday: but it will be pleasant to see Renick, and I acknowledge a rather acute curiosity to see his home—his household.

I don't see yet just how I am going to get in my letters to you to-morrow and next day, but of course I will manage to write somehow—something. I shall, I think, send you one letter to-morrow morning before leaving, and then one from Washington.

It's singular, considering the judicial frame of mind I *try* to cultivate, what a partisan I am in politics. Somehow, since this reactionary Administration came in, my interest in Washington and governmental affairs there has suffered a decided collapse—temporary, I hope, but none the less real. I feel hostile, instead of helpful as I ought to feel. I'm rather glad to go over for a Saturday and a Sunday, instead of any other days, and spend the time exactly as if I were in any other town, *not* the capital of the country. Are you ashamed of me? Not, I am afraid, as much as you ought to be! For you are more of a partisan, Miss, than I am.

I've been reading this morning a very touching account of the relations of John Austin,[1] the great jurist, and his wife—touching on account of its beauty as well as its pathos. The story's too long for a letter, but I'll not need to be reminded to tell it to you when I come—for it's an infinitely sweet story as told to me and will be seen deeply to concern the life of any intellectual worker perfectly understood and devotedly loved by his wife as John Austin was,—and as I am. Ah, my queen, you are the main part of me! I love you, I live and can work because I am

Your own Woodrow

Kisses to my darlings, much love to dear Ed.

ALS (WC, NjP).

[1] Wilson was probably referring to Sarah Taylor Austin's preface to the edition of her husband's *Lectures on Jurisprudence*, cited in WW to EAW, March 12, 1889, n. 1.

From the Minutes of the Johns Hopkins Seminary of Historical and Political Science

Historical Seminary March 15, 1889

The principal paper of the evening was by Dr. W. Wilson on "The Development of Law." This is to form one of the chapters of the text book[1] on government, which he is now preparing.

Law bespeaks the development, character, & will of the community, whose expression it is. The nature of each state is reflected in its law, & in it we can read the history of the nation.

Law develops through

1. Custom.

This is the earliest expression of law, & ultimately becomes its central part.

2. Religion.

Custom & Religion are at first indistinguishable, & even in the later stage of their growth they can be hardly separated. Priests & magistrates had at first the same functions. This is shown by the history of Early Institutions.

3. Judicature.

Judge is the authoritative voice of the community; he is the minister as well as, in one sense, a maker, of law.

4. Equity—this supplemented what common law did not provide.

5. Scientific Discussion

6. Legislation

This has in our day become almost exclusive source of law.

7. Custom again.

It now enters in new way & with new method. It maintains the forces of will & opinion of the community. Custom is habit in disguise, & hence never ceases to build up practices. Habit may be said to be as great as law; law proper may help to form new habits, but can never originate a new institution, when not sustained by habit. This Dr. Wilson illustrated by the history of France.

Next Dr. Wilson dwelt on the forces that are operative in developing law.

Law is the creation of special need, perils, & misfortunes of the community. The law of some particular state may be the will of a single despot or of a few, but can never become effective unless backed by the public opinion of the community. Legislators can only effect the change of law by & through the habit of the people.

Then the lecturer inquired about the nature & seat of Sovereignity. In England Sov. apparently resides in the Parliament. Whatever it enacts is inviolable. But this is only theoretical. For in practice the Parliament is only the utterer of the wish of the British nation; it cannot enact laws which are against the will of the people. In Russia Sovty. seems to reside in the person of Czar, but even here there is de facto limitation; that is the Czar is limited by the habit of the Russians. Sov., therefore, actually exists nowhere; it is the will of the organized individual country.[2]

The lecturer then spoke about the nature of International law, & laws of nature & of state, about two divisions of law—Public & Private—& about Jurisprudence, & concluded with the summary of the nature & functions of law.

Mr Vincent made a remark on the importance of tracing the history of the development of law. Dr Ely, after expressing his appreciation of the paper, & after commenting upon the necessity of the close union between Political Economy & History, between Pol. Eco. & Jurisprudence, expressed his doubts whether the public opinion is so all-powerful, whether the law-making power is being absorbed by the legislature, whether the course of development of law is so methodical, whether the relation between ethics & law is becoming so loose, as Dr. Wilson states. Dr Adams remarked upon the importance of grasping the truth that law is the product of history, & not a sudden growth, & asked Iyenaga whether Japan is prepared to adapt herself to her new constitution, to which he replied that, because Japan had been preparing for many years for the acceptance of such constitution, & because of the extreme adaptability of her nature to new circumstances, he has good faith on the good working of the new Constitution.

Mr Vincent then explained about the method of voting prevalent among the Romans, & humorously remarked that the so-called Austrian system of voting is after all not so new as supposed to be, but as old as Rome.

The Seminary adjourned at 10 P. M.

Sec. T. Iyenaga[3]

Hw and typed entry (MdBJ).

[1] Wilson was summarizing what would be Chapter XIV of *The State* (1889 edn.), pp. 610-35.

[2] This analysis, the embryo of Wilson's later theories about the limited nature of sovereignty, seems to have been derived largely from Johann Kaspar Bluntschli. Wilson was introduced to Bluntschli by Professor Herbert Baxter Adams, who presented Bluntschli's views on sovereignty in his course, "History of Politics," at the Johns Hopkins. Adams adverted to Bluntschli's interpretation in a lecture in this course on November 20, 1884, and described Bluntschli's views in detail in another lecture on February 18, 1885. (See the first body of lecture notes described at Oct. 8, 1884, Vol. 3.) Wilson, in the autumn of 1885, read for himself Bluntschli's *Allgemeine Statslehre*, in which the author devoted an entire section to sovereignty. (See the Editorial Note, "Wilson's First Treatise on Democratic Government," Vol. 5.)

[3] Toyokichi Iyenaga, graduate student in history at the Johns Hopkins, 1887-90.

From Ellen Axson Wilson

My own darling, [Middletown] Friday [Mar. 15, 1889]

Mrs. Hazen has just written to say that she has seen the nurse and engaged her,—so that is comfortably settled. I was to have gone driving with the Hazens this afternoon but the weather is quite bad, so of course we don't go. I had some more flowers sent me today—a splendid bunch of roses,—Jacks & pure white ones—by Miss Johnson.[1] A pleasure all the greater from being so entirely unexpected from that quarter.

We are all quite well. I have to thank Mrs. Hazen for something else which promises to take a great weight of anxiety off my mind. She brought me yesterday a box of the "Gluten Suppositories" prepared by the "Health Food Co."—for constipation, you know. I gave both Margaret & myself one last night & they worked in both cases most thoroughly & easily this morning. If they will only continue to relieve her I will be *so* delighted, for it has been *dreadful* to see her coming to depend altogether on medecine, requiring larger & larger doses of it & even with that suffering so much.

You ask me, sir, if I don't acknowledge to a weakness for "the frolic" in you. Indeed I do acknowledge it, and I should be sad indeed to think you were outgrowing it. But I am glad to hope there is little danger of that—unless family cares grow *too* overwhelming! You are not writing, sir, of growing sedate & middle-aged; you were speaking of maturity of *intellect*, & what I "love" is for you to feel that *self-confidence*, that sense of *power* in intercourse with other men—other thinkers; for I think it good for you to feel so and I am sure no one has a greater right.

But I have just been interrupted by a call from Mrs. Conn, & now it grows late & I must close in haste. With a heart full to overflowing with love, believe me, darling

Your own Eileen.

ALS (WP, DLC).
[1] See EAW to WW, Feb. 13, 1889, n. 2.

To Ellen Axson Wilson

My own darling Balto., 16 March, 1889

Just a note before starting for Washington. Have just rec'd your note about Mary's sickness—oh, my poor, poor darling! What a time you have had! I can't make up my mind whether to be made wretched by the retrospect or to be delighted that the experience is over! And I can't determine either, whether you have been a faithless little woman in concealing so much from me or only a noble little heroine in bearing it all and writing such sweet, brave letters meantime. If it was faithlessness it was also and principally nobility at the same time. I can't help blaming you a *little* for holding me off from you, even for a time only, in anything—it is the prerogative of my great love for you to be allowed to suffer with you in all things. But ah, how infinitely I admire and delight in you too, my precious little heroine—my perfect little woman—my matchless little wife! What with pride in you and a boundless love for you my heart seems likely to burst this morning! *What* a time you did have, my darling—with *Jessie* sick too into the bargain. Oh, how I love you, how I sympathize with you, how I admire you, how proud I am of you, how infinite a delight it is to be

Your own Woodrow

ALS (WC, NjP).

From Ellen Axson Wilson

My own darling, [Middletown] Saturday [March 16, 1889]

I am very glad you are having a little trip to Washington, hope you will enjoy it and that you are not having such weather as ours here. We are having a regular windstorm; it has been howling and the house shaking all day, and it is almost too dark to read or write.

I enclose a bill for you,—though I don't know that you care for it before your return. There is also a circular from the "Boston Teacher's Agency" for you to fill out for Mr. Dudley Abbott. But it I suppose can wait until you return? The curious "no mail" phenomenon still continues, you percieve.

I am quite tolerable today,—the rest all well. The suppositories still work as desired. The babies have been very sweet and good and winsome today in spite of the dreary weather and their mother has been enjoying them,—and is *very* happy. Shall I tell you why? Because all day long her heart has been fairly singing to itself the magical words "in one week—only one week,—one week from this very hour perhaps!" Oh my darling, my darling, how my heart leaps in anticipation, it will almost break for joy when the times comes. My precious one you are loved infinitely more than life itself by Your little wife.

ALS (WP, DLC). Enc. missing.

From John Franklin Jameson

My dear Wilson: Providence, March 16, 1889.

I am very sorry indeed to hear that Mrs. Wilson is not well, and wish you would express my regret to her. I shall be sorry to draw you away from home if you will be uneasy. But you get home Monday and the 29th is Friday, so very likely by that time you will feel able to be absent a day without anxiety, as well as if it were a week later. You know you can leave here earlier on

Saturday than you did when here before, and get home a little after noon. I enclose a time-table.

It remains to say, what logically belonged at the beginning, that the meeting of the history-professors of southern New England occurs here on the 29th, that the Narragansett Hotel, (not far from depot) is the headquarters; and that you are invited to dine with me there at 6.30.

Truly yours, J. F. Jameson.

ALS (WP, DLC) with WWhw notations on env.

From Ellen Axson Wilson

My own darling [Middletown] Sunday Mar 17 [1889]

I have just been reading with deep interest and admiration a very fine review of Bryce's book by one Woodrow Wilson. It strikes me as a particularly fine piece of work. Have you seen it?

And *have* you read the extraordinarily venomous, outrageous article on "Irish Secession,"[1] in the same magazine? I don't think I ever read a[n] article in which argument was so entirely superseded by abuse,—varied occasionally by excited remarks which strongly suggest the exclamation with which Mr. Puck makes our protectionists answer the arguments of their opponents, "That's nothing to do with the case." I wonder the "Quarterly" would publish such an article.

We are doing well. I am better than I was yesterday,—had an unusually good night's sleep which brightened me up considerably. The children are perfectly well—in spite of the wretched weather—which I do hope you are not sharing. But we had such beautiful weather during the early part of the month that we have no right to complain now. I hope you enjoyed your trip to Washington. I shall be curious to hear your account of the Renick ménage, *poor* fellow! But after all there are compensations in every thing!—he, for instance, is in no danger of suffering (indirectly) from nausea! Have you seen much of Mr. & Mrs. [Thomas K.] Worthington, and have you made the acquaintance of their youngster?

And that reminds me,—by some association of ideas,—that you have never said anything as to what you have learned of the state of affairs at the J.H.U.—whether they grow more or less hopeful; and what measures for relief are being taken. What is thought of the new president of the B. & O.?[2] Is much expected of him? But since you are coming home so soon why should I tease you with such questions now? By the way, have they done anything about the Latin chair, and did you use your influence for Dr. Shorey[3] as you intended? But enough of this! It will not be worth your while to answer any of these questions on paper. What *bliss* there is in that simple thought! He is coming—coming *this week*, only five more days—"and days are short this time of year." What *hour* do you arrive darling? I must know that as soon as possible for—happy thought—the calculation which has passed from weeks to days will soon drop down to hours. How true it is that "as thy day is so shall thy strength be" for when at the end of one of these long separations I look back over it, it seems almost incredible that it has been borne at all. It seems as though it *could* not have been & could not be. I wonder what would happen to me now if I should suddenly learn that you were to stay six weeks more! But farewell for today. I love you, I love you, my darling, with a depth and strength of which you have no idea and I am forever Your own Eileen

ALS (WC, NjP).

[1] Hugh O. Arnold-Forster, "An English View of Irish Secession," *Political Science Quarterly*, IV (March 1889), 66-103.

[2] Charles F. Mayer, Baltimore merchant.

[3] That is, Paul Shorey at Bryn Mawr.

To Ellen Axson Wilson

My own darling, Balto., 18 March, 1889

It turned out as I ought, I suppose, to have foreseen, that I could find no time at all yesterday in Washington for writing a letter, so constantly was I occupied seeing friends. In the first place, Renick's own home is full of friends; in the second place, there were other friends to go to see; in the third place, I suddenly and quite to my astonishment discovered a relative. Two couples board with the Renicks: one the Battens from Georgia; the other the [Walter E.] Faisons of North Carolina. Mrs. Batten was Miss Minnie Alston (daughter of the Col. Alston who was shot in Atlanta)[.] Mrs. Faison, you remember, was Miss Kate Sprunt, your schoolmate,—Faison himself being an old Univ. of Va. friend of mine. Mrs. Faison sent all sorts of messages, evidently of genuine cordiality, to you; and gave me, at my request, a picture of her children to take to you. Her children are with their grandmother in N. C. Of course I heard a great deal of news about N. C. friends.

The relative I found was (is) a Mrs. Flemming, who was a

Miss Ralston,[1] her mother a Larramore,[2] the Larramores cousins of fathers. Mrs. F. was from Norristown, Pa., but her husband is a Confederate major from Raleigh, N. C. She is homely, he is odd, &c. &c.

As for the Renicks, *they* are odd, very. I must reserve my description of them until I see you. Suffice it to say for the present that it seems to be a love marriage, now at any rate, whatever may have been true at first. They are evidently very fond of each other—I even suspected from one or two indications—nay from several—that he is proud of her! Certainly she is proud of him. This is a queer world! It is 'for a fact'! I did not see the daughter, she was sick. The son has taken Renick's name and has developed, apparently, into a manly, fine fellow.[3]

The good news in this morning's letter—about the nurse having been secured and about the Suppositories has put me in thoroughly good spirits. Besides, *this is the week.* This morning No. 20 was delivered; this afternoon No. 21 will be—and so it goes: the home-stretch has been reached: home is fairly in sight. I expect my spirits to mount steadily higher and higher as the week advances. You will find me the happiest man in the United States—when once I have my darling in my arms again. Ah, Eileen, I love you passionately. I am altogether and always, and always increasingly, Your own Woodrow

ALS (WC, NjP).

1 Ella Ralston Flemming of Washington.

2 One of the daughters of Mary Jane Wilson, sister of Joseph Ruggles Wilson, who married Joseph C. Larimore of Steubenville, Ohio, in 1831.

3 See WW to ELA, Sept. 6, 1884, Vol. 3.

From Ellen Axson Wilson

My own darling, [Middletown] Monday [March 18, 1889]

I have just come from rather a long drive with the Hazen's and am a little tired so will try and content myself with a brief note. I had a very pleasant drive though the day isn't very good,—damp and overclouded. While I think of it—Mr. Hazen has just told me a piece of news, viz. that Mr. Walker[1] is going to leave Bryn Mawr next year, is coming to Hartford to be assistant Prof. in church history.[2] And what of *his* contract! I wonder if it is *very* naughty to be just a little pleased to hear of people leaving B. M.—because it gives those trustees and others trouble of just the sort they most deserve to have!

We are all well and happy, & I *love you love you*, darling, more than tongue can tell and am now and always

Your own Eileen.

Am so sorry I did not write this morning so that I could have written more, but I didn't know the Hazens were coming for me in time for that. Shall I write on Thursday or will Wed's letter be the last that would reach you.

ALS (WC, NjP).

[1] Williston Walker, who, as Associate in History, had succeeded Wilson at Bryn Mawr in 1888.

[2] At the Hartford Theological Seminary.

To Ellen Axson Wilson

My own darling, Balto., 19 March, 1889

I have misplaced my schedules of the trains between here and New York, so that I can't be perfectly certain about the exact hour of my arrival at home, but I can come near it: I shall reach Middletown (Providence permitting) Saturday evening (the 23rd) either at 5.40 or at 7.24. I ought to reach the house, therefore, either about six or about a quarter to eight. Of course I will get another schedule and tell you definitely what train I shall take. I shall write to you only twice more before going in person, your perceive—and there are now only three lectures ahead of me. Ah, how infinitely sweet it is to see your spirits rising with the prospect of seeing me! All your letters (except the one that took me home) have breathed a wonder of sweet contentment and gentle happiness, but these last two show a marked change in your mood: before, you were happy without joy, now you are joyous. Oh, my precious, how can I ever repay you for this inestimable blessing of your love. It is the light of my way. I glory in it; I revel in it; it has entered into my life as an inseparable, indispensable part of it. Bless your heart, you delightful little woman! I shall have to devise some means of reclaiming when I come all the hours of companionship I have lost these dreary weeks. Will you help me to regain the time? Now that you ought not to run about much you can stay all the while close by me and let the delight of your actual presence soak into and thoroughly pervade my consciousness, so that all the wounds inflicted here may be cured and forgotten—all the cruel wounds of lonely, restless hours. Do you realize, darling, *what* a boon and solace the presence of our precious little girls is to you? Sometimes I wish I had brought one of them with me! If Margaret gets enough of a big girl's habits by next February, I believe I *will* bring her with me! You will then have two left for yourself and can spare me. And how I love the precious little bodies for being so sweet to you, and such a comfort. That's what they are for!

Yes, pet, I am coming this week,—I am coming in a few days,—I am already making sundry minor preparations for leaving; and I am going to bring you more love than you can contain. I am coming back more than ever Your own Woodrow.
Much love to dear Ed.

ALS (WC, NjP).

From Ellen Axson Wilson

My own darling, [Middletown] Tuesday [March 19, 1889]

No letter from you today! It is doubtless owing to your trip to Washington and the longer time it takes mail to reach me from there. Odd, isnt it? that the want of a letter which may be read in a few moments should make the day seem so long and blank! However I have been sufficiently amused for I have been reading one of Emile Gaboriau's detective stories lent me by Mrs. Conn. You should see the odd stack of trash which she has sent me over! (at my request.) She felt called on to apologize for her husbands taste! "in summer when he is resting he is a very indiscriminate reader[.]" I have had an unusually good day—a pleasant change, for the last two or three were rather painful. The children are quite well—those blessed suppositories still serving us both. Ed is in a great state of excitement[.] He has sold some four or five Confederate postage stamps for a quarter and his chum says he can sell another—an unusual one—to someone for $4.00(!) "So mote it be!" as Artemus [Ward] says.

I have been trying all day to remember if your trunk was full or not when you left. I am seized with a "longing" for some southern corn bread, which I can't get rid of. If you have room for two lbs. of the meal it would doubtless satisfy me, for I get tired of everything after two or three trials. But it seems to me now that nothing would taste so good; of course it is no use trying the sawdust they sell here for corn meal.

But Carrie is impatient to go down town so I must close in haste. I love you my precious one more than I could ever tell you if I wrote all day, & oh I am *so happy*, love, that I am so soon to be again in my darling's arms. With all my heart

Your own Eileen

Your letter just received. Am very glad you enjoyed your visit & that you saw Katie Sprunt[.] It will be quite a pleasure to me to hear about her & hers.

ALS (WC, NjP).

To Ellen Axson Wilson

My own darling, Balto., 20th March, 1889

No more lectures added to my score yet, for this is Wednesday and I have no class till the afternoon, at 5 o'clock; but a *day* is added to our reckoning: the time has grown shorter though the work has not. I am in an odd fix about these last lectures, by the way. My special field this year, you remember, was to be local government with special reference to the govt. of cities: i. e. I expected to describe the various systems of local govt. in about fifteen or sixteen lectures and to have some nine or ten hours left in which to discourse upon city govt. in particular. But, as it has turned out, it has taken (or will this afternoon have taken) me twenty-three lectures to finish local govt.,—and now the question is, what to do with the two lonely hours left over? It's a very unsatisfactory state of affairs: like the turkey which is of inconvenient size because 'too large for one and yet not large enough for two,' this small remainder of two hours is too short for anything but generalizations, and yet not long enough to make generalizations substantial. I shall probably make out to give the men *some*thing not altogether nonsensical.

Do you know, young lady, that I find it hard to write to you now that the time for seeing you is drawing so near? I can think of nothing that I want to say that I do not also want to *save*. It will be so sweet to sit by you and talk to you again; it is so intolerable to have to write now that the other privilege is close at hand, that I find my letter-writing power gone: I can't write when I am about to hold you in my arms and make kisses serve for punctuation marks! All my energy seems to have gone into my eagerness and impatience to see you. What a wonder it is, darling, this love of ours: how it dominates me at every turn and in every*thing*. I believe, for instance, that if I were not in love with you, sedateness and loss of frolic *would* go along with the sense of maturity in intellectual matters of which I wrote you the other day. It is *you* who keeps me young, not myself. How *can* I grow middle-aged or old so long as you love me and so command my spirits to laugh and take holiday? Old age of heart will never touch me so long as I am

Your own Woodrow.

So Walker leaves Bryn Mawr next year? Indeed!
According to the shedules I have just examined I shall be able to reach Middletown at 5.40, the house at 6

ALS (WP, DLC).

From Ellen Axson Wilson

My own darling, [Middletown] Wed. Mar 20 [1889]

It is storming so terribly that I scarcely know whether I shall be able to get this mailed after I have written it, as of course I am afraid to send Eddie out. However I will write and then see what I can do. I have had a pretty comfortable day and the rest are well and we are all happy. I am as happy as a bird as I pursue my occupation of checking off the hours and find them becoming "small by degrees and beautifully less!" Ed too is happy, for—will you believe it—his friend Fred Washburne actually sold that stamp for $5.00 and gave Eddie four of them! I don't know what idiot bought it. And then he sent back offering to pay a quarter extra for the envelope it was on. The stamp had on it simply the words "Athens Ga" & someone's name as postmaster. Was it the custom to issue local stamps during the war?

Your account of the Renick couple certainly fills one with wonder. I am curious to hear all about them.

And now good-bye for today, love. Oh I wish I could write the thoughts of which my heart is so full—so full today and all the days. But I can't—I can't! and now I hav'nt strength enough to tease myself with trying, but must try & content myself with the simple words *I love you* Your own Eileen.

ALS (WP, DLC).

To Ellen Axson Wilson

My own darling, Balto., 21st March, 1889

I delivered the twenty-*fourth* lecture this morning, and this is the last letter I shall write you before leaving for home! Ah, my love, my blessed little wife, when I hold you once more close to my heart, all the aches it has suffered because of this separation will be cured—will be remembered only to intensify the joy of our reunion. I am so impatient for the time of my going to come that I can hardly keep my mind on what remains of my work. And what can I *say* to you when my lips are so near yours—in time—when I am just on the eve of discarding pen and ink to look straight into the depths of these beautiful eyes that gladden me with their precious love-light more than the sun gladdens me—when I am just about to have my love in my arms by the hour, telling her my *whole* thought with every succession of mood or fancy—when, best of all, she is to reply to me instantly, with look, with gesture, with tone, as well as with her sweet words of sympathy and love and earnest thought? Oh, do you wonder that I hate writing materials when such thoughts surge in my heart? *You* would hate them if you were going to be blest as I am going to be, on Saturday! I feel all my old life coming back into me as I draw near to my darling. I have nothing but as perfect a message of love as possible for her to-day. I am eagerly, passionately, altogether, Your own Woodrow.

ALS (WC, NjP).

Charles McLean Andrews to Elizabeth Williams Andrews

My dear Mama, [Baltimore] March 25, 1889

. . . Dr. Wilson has finished his lectures and there is a lull, till some more extra work. Dr Wilson says that work here reminds him of the sinners in the brimstone lake of Dante's Inferno. No sooner do they reach the surface of the lake, than they find grinning demons with tridents and pikes ready to push them down again; so here no sooner do you emerge from the first load of work with which you have been covered than another pile of books is hurled at you. . . . Your loving son, Charlie

P.S. omitted. (C. M. Andrews Papers, CtY).

From Horace Elisha Scudder

My dear Mr Wilson Boston 25 March 1889

Ever since I heard of your going to Wesleyan I have had it in mind to write to you, for I assume that in making the change from Bryn Mawr you were consulting your own interests and inclinations. Besides I like to think of you as gravitating toward this centre!

I let the chance of your change go by without using it, and

now I am stirred again by the report that your book on *The State* is finished. Is this the monograph which you told me you were preparing for Ginn? It seems from the account given in *The Nation*[1] to be bigger and more comprehensive than that, but I know how books grow! Let me congratulate you, at any rate, on coming to a landing place in your progress up-stairs.

Have you read Bryce's book? I had to read it by lightning and report it in *The Atlantic* by telegraph, so to speak, and neither reading nor writing were the work of a man of leisure. I wonder if I should write any better if I were not under the goad. A goad is all well enough to start one from his slumbers, but it is hard to have one's flank always irritated.

I hope all goes well with you. Do you ever come to Boston or Cambridge? I have a feeling that I am talking to a man who has gone out of the room, so I will stop till I hear you are listening. Cordially yours Horace E. Scudder.

ALS (WP, DLC) with WWhw notation on env.: "Ans. 31 March/89."

[1] "We learn that Dr. Woodrow Wilson, whose 'Congressional Government' met with such a favorable reception, will soon have ready for publication a more extensive and serious study of governmental functions, entitled 'The State: Elements of Historical and Practical Politics.' This work has been in hand for several years, and is now finished. It will contain about 550 pages, 12mo." New York *Nation*, XLVIII (March 21, 1889), 246.

Wilson probably wrote this notice himself when he visited Renick in Washington on March 16, and Renick sent it in to the *Nation* at once, in time for publication in the issue of March 21.

Frederick Jackson Turner to Caroline Mae Sherwood

Dear girl: Baltimore, Md. March 30, 1889

. . . There is to be a vacancy at the celebrated Bryn Mawr University for girls soon—in History. They call this Johanna Hopkins, because it is a Quaker College and gets its professors largely from Johns Hopkins. Woodrow Wilson once taught there —and he says it is a very dangerous place for a young unmarried man to go, so I suppose there will be plenty of applicants from the men here! . . .

Good night, and God bless you little girl! Fred.

ALS (F. J. Turner Coll., CSmH).

To Herbert Baxter Adams

My dear Dr Adams, Middletown, Conn., 31 March, '89

I was sincerely sorry not to see you to tell you good-bye, profoundly sorry that the cause of my not seeing you was what it was.[1] I know how cold expressions of sympathy seem to those who are suffering an irreparable loss; but I also feel that it is the prerogative of those who really feel sympathy to express it.

The time of my coming away took me quite unawares, 'spite the fact that I knew when it was to be. Your office work seemed so interrupted every day without my assistance that I hesitated to intrude—and now I have to regret many things un-talked over. Among the rest I wanted to speak of my enjoyment of your 22nd Feby. address,[2] which, by-the-way, I have just read aloud to Mrs. W., much to her satisfaction. It's a worthy piece of persuasion done to admiration.

With sincerest regard,

Cordially Yours, Woodrow Wilson

ALS (H. B. Adams Papers, MdBJ).

[1] Adams's brother, Charles Dickinson Adams, a New York lawyer, had died on March 20.

[2] This was Adams's Founder's Day Address at the Hopkins. After reviewing the university's accomplishments during its short life and its importance to Baltimore, the State of Maryland, and the nation, Adams urged further private benefactions to strengthen the institution, suggested that it should be exempt from all state and city taxes, and hinted that Maryland should provide direct financial aid. See H. B. Adams, "The Encouragement of Higher Education: An Address . . . February 22, 1889," reprinted in *State Aid to Higher Education: A Series of Addresses Delivered at the Johns Hopkins University* (Baltimore, 1898).

Two Course Examinations

Seniors: Bryce's American Commonwealth.

Examination, 2 April, 1889.

1. Describe the committee organization of Congress and its effects upon legislation.
2. Discuss the relations of Congress & the Executive.
3. Reproduce the main points of the author's chapter on the Courts and the Constitution.
4. What points of comparison does he enumerate between our own and European systems?
5. What does the author say as to the nature of the American State?
6. How has direct legislation by the people been introduced into our state systems? Discuss the effects of such popular legislation upon the state constitutions.
7. Give, with some detail, the several types of local government in the United States.
8. Why, in Mr. Bryce's opinion, do our best men not go into politics?
9. Describe the Machine and how the Machine works.
10. Describe elections and election machinery.

Juniors: Constitution.

Examination, 2 April 1889.

1. What reasons were assigned by the Federalist for the fear that

unless a real union was effected there would be wars between the states?

2. What reasons were assigned for the belief that there was more apt to be independence and even anarchy among the states than tyranny by the central power; and what comparison was made between the means of influence upon the people possessed by the states on the one hand and by the central government on the other?
3. What distinction is drawn in the Federalist between a democracy and a republic, and what definition is given of a republic?
4. What were the nine defects attributed in the Federalist to the Confederation?
5. What are said to have been the difficulaties which surrounded the task of the Convention that framed the present Constitution?
6. Outline the Federalist's discussion of Montesquieu's maxim as to the separation of executive, legislative, and judicial functions.
7. Describe (a) the intended mode of choosing the President as expounded by the Federalist, and (b) the actual mode at present in use.
8. Describe the organization of the House of Representatives and the general course of legislation in Congress. How does the organization of the Senate differ from that of the House?
9. Describe in particular the methods of financial legislation as regards both appropriation and taxation, and the relations of taxation to appropriation under our present system.
10. What are the chief points of difference between our legislative methods and the English?

WWT MSS. (WP, DLC).

From Robert Bridges

Dear Tommy: [New York, c. April 3, 1889]

I do hope you can attend the Reunion. Please write soon that you can.

I had a great and glorious trip to California.

Yours BoBridges

ALS written on W. R. Wilder and C. C. Cuyler to "My dear Classmate," printed form letter dated March 29, 1889 (WP, DLC), soliciting contributions for the Saint-Gaudens statue of President McCosh and announcing plans for the tenth reunion of the Class of 1879. For a brief account of the unveiling of the statue, see JRW to WW, June 22, 1889, n. 1.

To Daniel Coit Gilman

My dear Mr. Gilman, Middletown, Conn., 6 April, 1889

I thank you very much for your kind invitation to be present at the Japanese meeting of April 17th.[1] I should certainly be present did my engagements here not imperatively forbid. They unfortunately concentrate, as it happens, on that particular date. I will be glad to contribute what I can by letter to the occasion, if you can *procure me a copy of the new constitution.*[2] I have not been able to secure one.

With warmest regards,

Very sincerely Yours, Woodrow Wilson

ALS (MdBJ).

[1] See the news item printed at April 20, 1889.

[2] "Sent Apr. 8"—hw notation on this letter.

To Robert Bridges

My dear Bobby, Middletown, Conn., 7th April, 1889

I have received the class circular with your note on it. I shall certainly attend the Reunion unless I am providentially prevented. I have already promised to act as one of the Lynde Prize (no—the *McLean* Prize)[1] judges on the Monday night of Commencement week. That week is the period of our final examinations here: but I shall make special arrangements to be absent Monday, Tuesday, and Wednesday. Is a special answer to the circular necessary, or will you notify Wilder that one of the three houses must be big enough to hold me?

Hurrah for the western trip and the success of it! I was confident you would enjoy it. I shall expect to hear a full account of it.

I fully expected to stop over and see you on my way back from Balto., as you know; but Mrs. Wilson's health was so poor while I was away that anxiety about her made me hasten through New York without stopping. Indeed I ran up for a day or two during my engagement in Balto., to see how she was getting along.

Who is to deliver the memorial in the name of the class? Has it been decided?

As ever, Affectionately Yours, Woodrow Wilson

ALS (WC, NjP).

[1] About the Lynde Prize at Princeton, see Vol. 1, p. 145. The MacLean Prize, established by Henry A. Stinnecke, 1861, is an award of $100 to the "orator who shall pronounce the best oration in the Junior Oratorical Contest" of the American Whig and Cliosophic Societies.

From Edward Wright Sheldon

My dear Wilson: New York. April 11, 1889.

I should not advise you to buy stock of the American Meat

Company. It is all experimental as yet; it will probably pay no dividends for some time, and not being a regularly listed stock, its sale might not be easily accomplished. For your purposes, it would be better, I think, to buy some well known security, that you could dispose of at any time, and in which the element of fluctuation was comparatively small.

You might buy instead, $2,000 Omaha & St. Louis 1st mortgage 4% bonds, interest January and July. They sell at about 75. This whole matter of investment securities, I may add, is not in the direct but only the incidental line of my work. This Omaha Company, however, I happen to be connected with as counsel and Secretary and I believe its bonds to be well secured. At the present price the investment would bring you a little over five per cent. Let me know how this strikes you. I should be glad to make further inquiries on the subject and report the results to you, as well as in any other way possible to assist you in the matter. If you fix upon any stock or bonds as a purchase, I could easily arrange here to complete the transaction.

Can't you manage to lunch with me some day, even if a longer interview is impracticable?

Yours sincerely, Edward W. Sheldon.

ALS (WP, DLC).

To Daniel Coit Gilman

My dear Mr. Gilman, Middletown, Conn., 13 April, 1889

I have read the Japanese constitution, which you were kind enough to send me, with great interest, and have devoted such time as was at my disposal for the purpose to a comparison of its provisions with those of various European constitutions.[1]

The question of derivation is nowadays an extremely difficult one when the mere text of a constitution is the only evidence one has upon which to make up his judgments. All modern constitutions have a close family resemblance to each other, for the well-known reason that they are all of the same family. They all derive a great part of their principles and a very large number of their forms from English precedent. The 'Bill of Rights' embodied in the constitution of Belgium, for instance, evidently derives its provisions from England, as do also the similar *Grundgesetze* of the Prussian constitution. The same is true of the intervention everywhere of ministers between the sovereign and responsibility, whether to the provisions of law merely or to the votes of parliaments. At almost every turn one is reminded by European constitutional provisions of the experiences peculiar to English parliamentary history. And this universal political debt to England is made all the more interesting by the somewhat blind way in which it has been contracted. In borrowing English principles, as Prof. Jellinek[2] of Vienna has very acutely remarked, European constitution-makers have 'rationalized and therefore misunderstood' them; as, for example, most conspicuously, in adopting the practice of having all money bills originate with the popular House of the legislature, after the historical situation which made that practice indispensable to the maintence of popular liberties has passed away. And in this matter, as in all others, the Japanese constitution has followed the prevailing fashion.

The only practicable way, therefore, in which the immediate connection of one constitution with another can be determined from internal evidence is by a likeness, not in principles, but in the formulation of principles, or by the reproduction in one of certain characteristic or exceptional provisions to be found in the other.

Judging by these criteria, I think there can be no doubt that the Japanese have copied, in the main, the constitution of Prussia. The correspondences might be traced in detail, but I shall mention only some half dozen points, beginning with particular, ending in general, features.

1. In formulating the position and powers of the monarch, Prussian doctrine is followed very closely (Articles I-XVI). Article III, "The Emperor is sacred and inviolable" quite exactly reproduces the "Der König ist unverletzlich" of Art. 43 of the Prussian constitution; the legislative power ascribed to the Emperor in Arts. V & XXXVII faithfully reproduces the Prussian principles touching the position and function of the sovereign in legislation (Prussian Const., Art. 63); and Art. VI might serve as a paraphrase of the words ("Er allein befiehlt die Verkündigung der Gesetze") of Art. 45 of the Prussian instrument.

2. Article VIII borrows without modification Art. 63 of Prussia's constitution, which reserves to the King the right to promulgate ordinances, when the maintenance of the public safety or the meeting of an unexpected emergency requires, which shall have the force of law till the next assembling of the Houses. It is interesting to note that the Norwegian Fundamental Law (§17) confers a similar power upon the King, during a recess

of the legislature, with reference to four specified subjects of legislation, viz., commerce, tariffs, trades, and police, and makes mere expediency (of which the King, of course, is the judge) a sufficient ground for his exercise of the prerogative.

3. Again, the composition of the House of Peers, though apparently more simple than that of the corresponding Prussian chamber, suggests the Prussian House of Peers rather than any other upper house I know of as its model. The names, House of Peers and House of Representatives, given to the two Houses of the Japanese legislature, moreover, are translations of *Heerenhaus* and *Abgeordnetenkammer*, the names of the Prussian chambers, rather than of the names of any other European bodies. And Art. XXXIX, which forbids the reintroduction of a bill during the same session during which it has been previously rejected adds to imitation of Prussian organization imitation of a rule of Prussian legislative procedure.

4. The rule with reference to amending the constitution in the fifth paragraph of the enacting clauses is a necessary logical inference from the fact, common to Prussia and Japan, that the constitution proceeds from the sovereign, is his gift to his subjects, and therefore depends for its validity wholly upon his will, for its enlargement or alteration wholly upon his initiative. This principle, however, is no more characteristic of Prussian than of Austrian public law.

5. In the provision for establishing Administrative Courts distinct in organization and jurisdiction from the ordinary courts of law, (Art. LXI) we have the adoption of a system which, though common to Prussia and France, to be found indeed in most European countries, seems to be taken from Prussia, not only because other parts of the instrument are evidently derived thence, but because the ground impliedly ascribed for this separation of jurisdictions in the second line of the Article, seems to be meant to embody Steins doctrine with reference to administrative competency.

6. But the crowning point of resemblance between this constitution and the Prussian is to be seen in the position of the ministers of state in the system. The ministers are responsible to the Emperor, not to the legislature, if I rightly interpret Art. LV., and are given, by Art. LIV, the right to sit and speak in either House. Here the model is not one of "responsible government" in the English, French, Italian sense. The ministers and the legislature stand related to each other in function as do the

Prussian ministers and legislature. This is the central, the test resemblance between the two governments.

I have selected these points from among a score of others that might have been chosen with almost equal propriety. Here and there are Articles which seem to have been imported from some more English constitution than the Prussian; but in the main I think there can be no mistaking the model.

And I think that, considering the stage of development in which Japan now finds herself, the Prussian constitution was an excellent instrument to copy. Her choice of it as a model is but another proof of the singular sagacity, the singular power to see and learn, which is Japan's best constitution and promise of success.

Very sincerely Yours, Woodrow Wilson

ALS (MdBJ).

[1] See the photographic section for a reproduction of the first page of the Japanese Constitution with Wilson's marginal comments.

[2] Georg Jellinek (1851-1911), German jurist, then Professor at the University of Basel. The son of the distinguished German-born rabbi, Adolf Jellinek of Vienna, Georg Jellinek had grown up in the Hapsburg capital and served for two years in the Austrian civil service.

From Edward Wright Sheldon

My dear Wilson: New York. April 17, 1889.

The Omaha and St. Louis bonds are for $1,000 each and sell at about 75. This will dispose of $1,500 of your money, but if you wish to put it all in one security, a stock might be chosen instead of the bonds. If you will let me know how you feel about this, I will act accordingly.

Yours sincerely, Edward W. Sheldon.

ALS (WP, DLC) with WWhw notation on env.: "Ans."

A News Item

A WEST-EASTERLY COMMEMORATION AT JOHNS HOPKINS.

Baltimore, April 20, 1889.

The *Nation* for December 20, 1888, in an editorial which spoke of Johns Hopkins University as "one of the most potent of the intellectual forces of this country," used these significant words: "But the service which Johns Hopkins University has done to the advancement of learning in America cannot be measured by the instruction that has been given within its own walls and the researches which have been carried on by its members." That the Johns Hopkins University epitomizes in its policy and attitude towards every forward intellectual or political movement of the day the most virile spirit of the American mind, has been strikingly shown this week by a notable meeting held in Hopkins Hall on the evening of Wednesday, April 17. The invitation to this gathering read as follows:

"Johns Hopkins University Commemoration of the Promulgation of the Constitution of Japan.

"You are respectfully invited to be present at an assembly of members of this University interested in Political Science, which will be held in Hopkins Hall, Wednesday evening, April 17th, 1889, at eight o'clock, to commemorate the promulgation of the written Constitution of the Empire of Japan.

"D. C. Gilman, President."

The platform was artistically decorated with the flags of Japan and the United States, draped over a large emblazoned shield of the University, with its stirring motto, "The Truth shall make you free!" while in front of this effective background were grouped masses of the pyrus japonica, flowering peach, yellow broom plant, wild cherry, and magnolias—all blossoms with whose decorative value the Japanese have made us familiar. The Chairman of the evening was T. M. Cooley, LL.D., late Chief Justice of Michigan, now an active member of the Inter-State Commerce Commission. On the stage with him were, besides the trustees and leading professors of the University, and the Japanese post-graduate students, the Mayor of Baltimore and members of the Japanese Embassy, who had come from Washington to take part in this first public recognition, by any leading seat of learning, of the importance of the promulgation of a document aptly called the Magna Charta of Japan. . . .

Prof. Adams read portions of a letter from Dr. Woodrow Wilson, author of 'Congressional Government,' explaining that while the constitutional ideas common to all political growth of this century had entered into Japan's new constitutional law, her statesmen had drawn details more largely from the German Constitution than from that of any other people, Germany's organic law being more acceptable to the citizens of a monarchy where the divine ancestry of the Mikado is still an article of faith, or at least of sentiment, with the mass of the people. . . .

Printed in the New York *Nation*, XLVIII (April 25, 1889), 341-42.

From Edward Wright Sheldon

My dear Wilson: New York. April 22, 1889.

The $2,000 Omaha & St. Louis bonds were bought for your account today at 75. If you will send me $1,500 I will complete the transaction and forward the bonds to you.

Yours sincerely, Edward W. Sheldon.

ALS (WP, DLC) with WWhw notation on env.: "Ans. Apr. 23/89."

From Albert Bushnell Hart

My dear Prof. Wilson, Cambridge, Mass. April 23, 1889

It was a matter of great regret to me not to able to attend the meeting in Providence,[1] as I particularly wished to see you about some business which I must now enter upon in this less satisfactory way.

Messrs. Longmans Green & Co, of London, are starting an American house; among the works the[y] propose to put forth from that press is an addendum to their Epochs of Modern History—with which you are doubtless familiar. It is to be known as the Epochs of American History; is to be uniform with the other series, and in fact a part of it, and is to be published on both sides of the water.

They have asked me to edit the series, which is to consist of three volumes; one on the period from discovery to 1750: one on the Revolution and Consolidation (1750-1829); this second I shall undertake myself: the third the United States from 1829 to say 1889, I should like to ask you to undertake.[2]

Your work in Civil Government is, I understand nearly ready; so that I hope you may have leisure for a piece of work which does not make great demands on one so familiar with the run of our politics. The scope of the work is sufficiently shown by the volumes of the Epoch series now issued. It is to be rather a sketch of causes, movements and results than a detailed history. The publishers agree to furnish each volume with a good apparatus of historical maps. It is to be uniform in page with the English series: but the margins are to be more like American books.

There are several reasons which I might urge on you why you may find it pleasant to take part in this work, besides the personal pleasure it would give me to become better acquainted with you. You know the lack of text-books for classes in United

States History. The series would make such a text-book: and your own class-work, as well as that of many other college teachers, would be simplified. It would thus be a real service to the advancing interest in our history. The writers of the English series are men whom one could be glad to be associated with: Morris, McCarthy, Gardiner, Freeman, Stubbs[,] Creighton and others are honorable names. The preparation for the work ought not to require any labor which will not tell directly in our own preparation for lectures. The time allowed is sufficient: I should be satisfied to see the MS. a year hence. The publishers are a house with which any writer might be glad to come into relations—and finally, the payment is five hundred dollars ($500.00) payable on the appearance of the book.

It is expected that the volumes will each run from 200 to 256 pages of 320 words each.

It has long been in my mind to see what is being done at Wesleyan: and I should probably have called upon you, but for an unlucky illness. Should you wish to confer further on the matter, I shall be very glad to do so: but I hope you may be persuaded to undertake the third volume. The writer for the first volume is not yet selected; but it will be a man of established reputation.

Hoping for a favorable answer I am,

Yours very truly, Albert Bushnell Hart

ALS (WP, DLC) with WWhw notation on env.: "Ans. 1 May/89" and WWhw sums.

1 Of southern New England historians on March 29.

2 This letter marks the beginning of letters and documents relating to what would become Wilson's *Division and Reunion*. For a guide to the important documents in this volume and in subsequent ones, see the Editorial Note, "Wilson's *Division and Reunion*," Vol. 8.

From Edward Wright Sheldon

My dear Wilson: New York. April 24, 1889.

I am sending you by express the two Omaha & St. Louis 4% bonds purchased at your request and trust that they will reach you safely. In July when the coupons mature you can of course deposit them in your bank for collection. They are payable at the Office of the U. S. Trust Co.

Yours sincerely, Edward W. Sheldon.

ALS (WP, DLC) with WWhw notation on env.: "Ans. Apr. 25/89."

To Munroe Smith

My dear Smith, Middletown, Conn., 26 April, '89

I am ashamed to ask you to send the *mss.* which I submitted to you, for I am afraid that you will think me either impatient or impolite. I can only assure you that I am neither (!) and trust to your good nature to prompt you to believe me.

The fact is that I have several jobs waiting for me, and if I don't get this one of this text-book off my hands forthwith I shall be caught in all sorts of entanglements. The rest of my *mss.* are now about as ready as I can (at the present stage of my studies) make them for the printer, and, if you think those you have will stand the printing, I should like to get them off with the rest. If you think they will not, I am anxious to know the worst. If you have not had time to examine them, I am sure I can be obliged to you for your friendliness in *wishing* to do so.

I suppose everybody ought to be in New York on the 30th to see the new century of the government properly inaugurated; but the fact is that I am to deliver an address[1] here to the few people of this part of this 'suburban' state who do not make their exodus New Yorkwards. Pray 'celebrate' for me: perhaps you can find other friends of mine to take part of the job off your hands—for there's lots of it: I feel very patriotic!

Most sincerely Yours, Woodrow Wilson

ALS (*Political Science Quarterly* Papers, NNC).

[1] Printed at April 30, 1889.

A News Item

[*April 28, 1889*]

Prof. Woodrow Wilson led the Sunday morning prayer meeting of the College Y. M. C. A. the 28th inst.

Printed in the Middletown, Conn., *Wesleyan Argus*, XXII (May 1, 1889), 146.

A Commemorative Address[1]

Address *April 30, 1889*

Precedence belongs to-day as of right to thoughts of thanksgiving and joy. To have kept our national government from

[1] Wilson delivered this address on the centennial of Washington's inauguration in the North, or First, Congregational Church in Middletown. For an account of the exercises, see the Middletown, Conn., *Wesleyan Argus*, XXII (May 16, 1889), 157-58.

destruction or decay for one hundred years were itself justification for gratification and pride. But we have done more than that. We are more—much more—than a preserved nation: we are a strengthened, elevated, matured nation. We have triumphed over difficulties, not by steadfastness merely but by progress also. We have had that best evidence of health, namely growth. Vastly better, greater, more worthy, whether for strength, for unity, or for achievement are the Re-United States than were the merely *United* States. We have done more than kept faith with the deeds of our Fathers: we have kept faith with their spirit also. We cannot doubt than [that] in building together a compact and confident nation out of the somewhat disagreeing elements which they handled, with courage and in hope but not without doubt and misgiving, we have returned them their own with usury. Their thirteen talents, coined in various mints, bearing no single or standard value have become in our hands thirty-eight talents made up of coins bearing all the same image and superscription, emblem of liberty and nationality.

We may boast, too,—if boasting may have a place—that we have led the modern movement of Politics: that it is at our hands that popular liberty has received its most absolute test and its highest confirmation. Never before we gave them scope of empire had the principles of democratic government received more than a narrow local application. Snug Swiss cantons, buttressed by Nature against the disturbances of European politics; mediaeval cities forcibly holding the feudal world a while at arm's length; Rome straining her city Constitution to the point of breaking by imposing upon it the weight of an Empire's affairs; the republics of Greece ruling territories ridiculously small when compared with the power and the abiding influence of the peoples whom they sustained—none of these afford any precedent for this continental rule of the people, so familiar to us now, but which we have astonished the world by successfully establishing. Our success has been on the scale of our geography: democracies there had been before and confederacies not a few; but never a democracy of sixty millions of people, never a federal state as large and as whole as a continent.

But these great things, which have unquestionably put us at the front of the world's politics, have not been accomplished by those elements of thought and character which make for pride and self-gratulation. It is significant of the forces that have made us what we are that we celebrate to-day not only the establishment of a government but also the inauguration of a man. You know by heart, of course, Mr. Lowell's fine lines, of 1876:

> "Virginia gave us this imperial man
> Cast in the massive mould
> Of those high-statured ages old
> Which into grander forms our mortal metal ran. . . .
> Mother of States & undiminished men
> Thou gavest us a Country giving him."[2]

But Washington, it seems to me, though high-statured even beyond the other giants of his day, bore in his mein and stature the marks of the race to which he belonged. In him we may discern the "brief chronicle and abstract" of a time and a nation. His courageous calmness in seasons of political crises; his solemn sense of public duty; his steady aptitude for affairs; his hold upon men of various and diverse natures; his capacity for persuasive counsel; his boldness without dash, and power without display—do we not see in these things the perfect epitome of what the slow processes of Eng. national history had proved themselves capable of producing in the way of manhood and character? Washington was neither an accident nor a miracle. Neither chance nor a special Providence need be assumed to account for him. It was God, indeed, who gave him to us; but God had been preparing him ever since English constitutional history began. He was of the same breed with Hampden, and Pym and Cromwell. Burke and Chatham both recognized him as a brother so soon as they saw opened before them the credentials of his deeds. He was of such heroic stuff as God had for centuries been so graciously and so lavishly weaving into the character of our race.

Do you recall that striking story of one of the opening incidents of the Const. Convention related by Gouverneur Morris, an eye-witness of scenes? "Of the delegates," he says, "some were for halfway measures, for fear of displeasing the people; others were anxious and doubting. Just before there were enough to form a quorum, Washington, standing self-collected in the midst of them, his countenance more than usually solemn, his eye seeming to look into futurity, said:—'It is too probable that no plan we propose will be adopted. Perhaps another dreadful conflict is to be sustained. If, to please the people, we offer what

[2] From James Russell Lowell's "Under the Old Elm: Poem Read at Cambridge on the Hundredth Anniversary of Washington's Taking Command of the American Army, 3d July, 1775."

we ourselves disapprove, how can we afterwards defend our work? Let us raise a standard to which the wise and honest can repair; the event is in the hands of God.' " That is an utterance, not of statesmanship merely, but of character as well: and do we not understand that character; do we not thrill at its expression? It strikes to the quick of our sensibilities because we are of the same race and derivation that this man was of.

I press this point because it seems to me the point of chief instruction and inspiration, the best point, of to-day's suggestion. There is no strength in mere self-gratulation: there is no hope in being sure. Enlightened endeavour is the law of progress: a stout-hearted dissatisfaction with what has been done, a clear-sighted understanding of what there remains to do, an undaunted spirit to undertake and achieve it. I fear that we are becoming a little prone as a nation to mistake the real nature of our success. It does not lie in the forms but in the essence of our institutions. We are not great in popular govt. because we invented written constitutions: for we did not invent them. We are not successful because we put into our constitutions new devices whereby to moderate the disorders or facilitate the better influences of politics: for we originated no devices. We are great because of what we perfected & fulfilled, not because of anything that we discovered: and it is only by extending such lines of development as can be clearly traced backwards thr. the normal evolutions of politics in the past that we can make further permanent advances. We did not break with the past: we understood and obeyed it, rather. The most thorough way of understanding ourselves lies thr. an intimate acquaintance with the long processes of our breeding. There are no individual discoveries to be made in politics as there are in astronomy or biology or physics; society grows as a whole, and as a whole grows into knowledge of itself. Society is an organism, which does not develop by the cunning leadership of a single member so much [as] by a slow maturing and an all-round adjustment, though led at last into self-consciousness and self-command by those who best divine the laws of its growth.

So long were we compelled to centre our thoughts in national politics upon the interpretation of our written standards—so short is the period during which we have been excused from looking exclusively into our constitutions for the sanction and substance of our national life, that it is open to question whether we have even yet accepted the fact that the real foundations of political life in the U. S. are to be found elsewhere than in our legal documents. Our politics and our character were derived from a

> "land that freemen till
> That sober-suited Freedom chose,
> The land, where girt with friends or foes
> A man may speak the thing he will;
>
> "A land of settled government,
> A land of just and old renown,
> Where freedom broadens slowly down
> From precedent to precedent:
>
> "Where faction seldom gathers head,
> But by degrees to fulness wrought,
> The strength of some diffusive thought
> Hath time and space to work & spread."[3]

We have been strong and successful—and shall be—just in proportion to our fidelity to this so great heritage of political manliness. It is no light thing to have such traditions behind us: liberty is not something that can be laid away in a document, a completed work. It is an organic principle, a principle of life, renewing and being renewed. Democratic institutions are never done—they are, like the living tissue, always a-making. It is a strenuous thing this of living the life of a free people: and we cannot escape the burden of our heritage.[4]

But this burden is light: the only grievous burden is to be held back from liberty by a heritage of subjection. Those of you who have followed the course of events in France and who share with all lovers of liberty the anxiety caused by the present posture of her affairs will know whence my best illustration will be drawn. You know how straight M. Monod has pointed his finger at his country's trouble in what he says in the current (the April) number of the *Contemporary Review*. "France," he says, "is suffering mainly from moral instability and diseases of the imagination, the result of a too sudden rupture with her own traditions." "After every revolution," he adds,—and he is right,—"and in spite of 17 changes of const. in a single century, she always rights herself, and knows no pause in her intellectual and industrial activity, nor any decline in her material force."[5] This is indeed

[3] From Tennyson's "You ask me, why, tho' ill at ease."

[4] Wilson wrote "inheritance" above "heritage" without crossing out the latter.

[5] Gabriel Monod, "The Political Situation in France: 1789-1889," London *Contemporary Review*, LV (April 1889), 477-94.

true. In her habit of being prosperous France is established; in her habit of making her wit tell in literature and in art she is well grounded; but the habit of being free she as yet most imperfectly possesses. That habit instead of having something like a thousand years of steady practice in it with her as with us, has but the uneven exertions of a brief hundred years of feverish change. She is acquiring it: but it would be a miracle could she adopt it, as one would put on a garment. We only make ourselves contemptible when we despise France because she has failed at the miracle: we only make ourselves ridiculous when we pity her; she deserves sympathy and she will achieve success: we cannot do better than learn a lesson from her.

The profitable thing for us to remember is, that, though the saving habit in politics may be acquired by wisdom and sober, steadfast endeavour, which are very rare, it may be lost by folly, which is very common. Evidently wisdom and endeavour have had rare good opportunities in America during the century that is past: wisdom is not difficult where resources are unbounded; endeavour is not arduous where there is exceeding rich reward. But the century which *begins* to-day will doubtless make a very different distribution of its favours among us. It is easier to be new than to be old—far lighter work to be pioneers needing mere muscle and physical courage, than patiently and resolutely to face the problems of a crowded and perplexed civilization. It was easier to drive out an army of Eng. troops than it will be to assimilate a heterogeneous horde of immigrants. It required less self-possession to establish our governments than it will require to maintain them: the principles on which they should be constructed to meet our needs in the beginning were much plainer to see than are the principles upon which they must be modified to meet the needs of the present & future.

For us this is the centennial year of Washington's inauguration; but for Europe it is the centennial year of the French Revolution. One hundred years ago we gained, and Europe lost, self-command, self-possession. But since then we have been steadily receiving into our midst and to full participation in our national life the very people whom their home politics have familiarized with revolution: our own equable blood we have suffered to receive into it the most feverish bloods of the restless old world. We are facing an ever-increasing difficulty of self-possession with ever deteriorating materials: for your only reliable stuff in this strain of politics is Character.

Think! Our task is to be

"A nation yet, the rulers and the ruled—
Some sense of duty, something of a faith,
Some reverence for the laws ourselves have made,
Some patient force to change them when we will,
Some civic manhood firm against the crowd"[6]

And our material? "Minds cast in every mould of race, minds inheriting every bias of environment, warped by the histories of a score of different nations, warmed or chilled, closed or expanded by almost every climate of the globe"!

This is not the place or the occasion for the discussion of policies: we are here only to renew our vows at the altar of Liberty, only to look ourselves in the face, to examine and know ourselves,—to confess ourselves to God and ask of him succour and guidance. It behooves us once and again to stand face to face with our ideals, to renew our enthusiasms, to reckon again our duties, to take fresh views of our aims and fresh courage for their pursuit. To-day we should stand close to the thought and close to the hearts of those who gave our nation life. The tasks of the future are not to be less but greater than the tasks of the past: it is our part to improve even the giant breed of wh. we come—to return to the high-statured ages: to weld our people together in a patriotism as pure, a wisdom as elevated, a virtue as sound as those of the greater generation whom to-day we hold in special and grateful remembrance—a nation knowing

"Its duties,—prompt to move, but firm to wait,—
Knowing, things rashly sought are rarely found:
That, for the functions of an ancient State—
Strong by her charters, free because imbound,
Servant of Providence, not slave of Fate—
Perilous is sweeping change, all chance unsound."[7]

WWhw MS. (WP, DLC).

[6] From Tennyson's "The Princess: A Medley."

[7] From Wordsworth's "Sonnets Dedicated to Liberty and Order," No. IV, "Blest Statesman He, whose Mind's unselfish will. . . ."

To Albert Bushnell Hart

My dear Prof. Hart, Middletown, Conn., 1 May, '89.

I perhaps owe you an apology for delaying so long in answering your letter of a week ago; but I felt that the matter it contained was too important to deal with before looking the ground over,—not the ground of American history, but the ground of my resources and opportunities for work in the line proposed.

The task you suggest has very strong attractions for me indeed: if my hands were quite free, I should not hesitate to undertake it. But as matters stand I must, before accepting, tell you just how I am situated.

The book on Civil Government which I have been writing for college use is indeed finished—at least I hope to have it off my hands within a week; but another book I am still under engagement to write as soon as possible, namely, a school text-book on govt. It is to be brief,—not more than 175 or 200 pages duodecimo—and the *writing* of it is all that remains for me to do, for I have of course material in abundance; but it is just the writing of it that will cost life-blood: for I mean to spend every effort to make it tell on young minds. I believe the school beginning in this subject is the critical period of the study, and I want to do my best. The summer vacation (which with us here is only eleven weeks) will, therefore hardly suffice for the completion of this work.

Next winter there will be twenty-five new lectures to be prepared on Administration for a graduate class in Baltimore.

Our library here affords a reasonable abundance of material for the early period of the Union but is most unreasonably bare of the authorities for the period following 1829.

The sum of the whole matter is, that I do not see how it would be possible for me to write the book you want within a year from now—indeed it would, I am sure, be quite impossible for me to do so. I am bound, therefore, in good conscience, to say that, at the same time that I should be most willing to write the 'Epoch' you propose, I could not do anything like justice to it in the time named—my material here being so scanty that the work would necessarily be much retarded.

How far would it be practicable to extend the time for the preparation of the third and last of the series? Upon the answer to that question must depend my decision.

I share very heartily your regret that we did not meet at Providence—I specially regret that illness was the cause of your not being there. I trust that we shall have an early opportunity of making each others acquaintance and that you are now entirely restored to health. I am very sorry indeed that you could not carry out your plan of visiting Middletown. I am keeping house and should be delighted to have a visit from you.

Very sincerely Yours, Woodrow Wilson

TCL (RSB Coll., DLC).

EDITORIAL NOTE
WILSON'S ELEMENTARY TEXTBOOK IN AMERICAN GOVERNMENT

Wilson worked with such single-minded intensity upon *The State* between the summer of 1887 and the spring of 1889 as to give the impression that he had forgotten his promise to D. C. Heath to write a textbook in American government for secondary schools for that Boston publisher.[1]

Actually, Wilson had the high-school text very much in mind even while he was preoccupied with the more advanced book. "The D. C. Heath books . . . [are] now on the stocks in a somewhat advanced stage of construction," Wilson wrote, for example, to Richard Heath Dabney on January 20, 1888. Wilson was referring to the lectures on American government that he was then writing for his "politics" course at Bryn Mawr. He meant that he would use these lectures for both textbooks. Moreover, he well knew that it would be a simple task, as he put it later in a letter to Ellen Wilson on March 9, 1889, to "strike off" the high-school text once he had completed *The State*.

As Wilson's letter to Albert Bushnell Hart of May 1, 1889, just printed, makes clear, Wilson had virtually completed the manuscript of *The State* by this date and was about to undertake composition of the elementary textbook.

First, however, Wilson wrote out a draft of an outline of the book. He then prepared a more elaborate second draft of this outline envisaging a book of eight chapters divided into sections numbered consecutively throughout the text. The chapter titles, as listed in the second outline, were "The Double Government," "Double Citizenship," "The States and the Nation," "Organization [of the Federal and State Governments]," "Powers [of the Federal and State Governments]," "Action of the Fed. and State Govts. Contrasted," "History of Parties in the U. S.," and "Principles of Govt."[2]

Very soon afterward, Wilson began writing the first draft of the textbook that he called "The American State: Elements of Historical and Practical Politics in the United States,"[3] using as the basis for this draft his shorthand notes for his Bryn Mawr course on politics, beginning with Lecture X.[4] Wilson used large portions of his Bryn

[1] See the Editorial Note, "Wilson's Plan for a Textbook in Civil Government," Vol. 5.

[2] These outlines are WWhw and WWsh MSS. entitled "Elements of Historical and Practical Politics in the United States . . ." and "*The American State: Analysis*" (WP, DLC).

[3] Wilson had long since abandoned the very elementary first chapter printed at Aug. 8, 1886, Vol. 5.

[4] This body of notes is described at Oct. 3, 1887, Vol. 5.

Mawr lectures in edited form, but he made numerous additions (some of them from portions of *The State*) and rearrangements of subject matter. Generally speaking, "The American State" was an expanded version (insofar as it went) of the Bryn Mawr lectures, but one written in simpler language because of the readers for whom it was intended.

Wilson wrote the first draft of "The American State" on fifty-four pages of regular-sized paper, and the handwriting and ink would indicate that he wrote this, as it turned out, incomplete manuscript within a relatively brief period. At some time, perhaps soon after finishing this portion, Wilson cut the pages of his manuscript in two in order, it would appear, to make insertions easier. He did make some insertions and revised the entire manuscript very extensively by emendations.

Wilson had apparently just begun Section 28 in Chapter IV of "The American State," on the federal judiciary (Lecture XXV in the Bryn Mawr course), when he completed the manuscript of *The State* and sent it off to Heath on June 3, 1889. In his letter to Heath of the same date, Wilson seems to have said that he would simply have to lay "The American State" aside for a time—probably because of sheer exhaustion, and also because at this point he had had enough of "fact" books. "We will have to wait for the smaller book," Heath replied on June 4. But the Boston publisher, in this same letter, also suggested the possibility of immediately issuing the chapter on American government in *The State* as a separate book. Wilson's reply is missing, but in it he obviously said that he thought well of the suggestion.

Even though he had postponed further writing on "The American State," Wilson seems to have suggested in his letter to Heath of June 11, 1889,[5] that the publisher send a contract for "The American State" along with one for *The State*. Heath did send two copies of a contract for the elementary textbook on about June 13, 1889, but Wilson did not sign and return one.[6]

Wilson's interest in "The American State" revived briefly a year later, as D. C. Heath's letter to him of July 30, 1890, discloses. This is the last reference in the extant correspondence to the high-school book until 1898. Then a mention of the book in a missing Wilson or Heath letter led the two men to discuss the project again, and Wilson said that he was no longer interested in the book.[7]

The foregoing history of the provenance of "The American State" is based upon what seems to be the plain meaning of the evidence in the documents relating to the manuscript. It is impossible to draw any firm inferences about precise dates of composition from the internal evidence in "The American State" itself, as that evidence is contradictory and not very revealing. However, it should be said that some internal evidence raises the possibility that Wilson composed the main portion of "The American State" in late 1887. If true, this would account, among other things, for Wilson's explicit state-

[5] The draft of this letter printed below is obviously fragmentary.

[6] Both copies remain unsigned in WP, DLC.

[7] D. C. Heath to WW, Feb. 14 and 17, 1898, to be printed in a future volume.

ment at the beginning of Chapter III of "The American State": "There are now (1887) thirty-seven States in the Union." In any event, it seems reasonably certain that the text reproduced below represents the revised version as it stood in late May or early June of 1889.

The following text includes a few penciled changes that Wilson may have made after 1889 and omits only a minimum of superfluous punctuation and a few notations by Wilson to himself concerning further revision.

Chapters of a Textbook

[c. May 1–c. June 5, 1889]

The American State:

Elements of Historical and Practical Politics in the United States.

A Text-book for Grammar and High Schools.

I. THE DOUBLE GOVERNMENT

1. The people of the United States live under a double government. Some of the laws which it is their duty to obey are made by the federal Congress in Washington; the rest are made by the legislatures of the States, or by some local authority, subordinate to the State, which is empowered by the State to make them.

This does not mean that every man in the United States lives under two separate governments, a federal government and a state government. The federal and state governments are not separate governments; they are simply two parts of a single great plan or system[.] Together they make up a *double government.* Each part of this double government has a 'Constitution' of its own, that is, a great law passed by the people on which it is built, and which says what it must or may do and what it must not do. But these Constitutions are closely connected with each other, and are made to suit each other. The Constitution of the United States, wh. is the name given to the Const. of the fed. govt., was adopted by the people of all the States, while the Constitution of each State was adopted only by the people of that State; but the people of the State made their Constitution fit itself into the Constitution of the United States, so that the two might be parts of the same great plan of government. We shall see as we go on what that plan is.

2. *Other Double Governments.* The people of the United States are not the only people who live under such a double government. The people of Switzerland and the people of Germany, as well as some of the people of South America, live under governments which are very much like ours in this respect. We were the

first to bring this peculiar political system to its present perfection; but the Germans and Swiss have copied our plans partly in making their governments what they are now. The German government differs from ours in having an Emperor instead of a President at the head of its national government, and kings and dukes instead of governors at the head of its state governments. It is, besides, a monarchy instead of a republic, and its laws are in many ways very different from our laws. But it has exactly our plan of having some of the laws which govern its citizens passed by national authorities and the rest by state authorities.

The Swiss call their double government a 'Confederation'; we call ours a 'Union'; but their Confederation is not very different from our Union.

3. *Old-time Confederations.* We find from the history of the past, however, that 'confederation' once meant a very different sort of government. The Swiss Confederation is very old, more than three hundred years old, and before the Swiss people changed their system, in 1848 and again in 1874, in such a way as to make it more like ours, it was like certain old-time Confederations. These did not have two sets of laws, one national and the other state, both of which the people had to obey, as we have, and as the S. have now[.] Instead of that they had one set of laws which the people had to obey and another set which the States were bound to obey. The laws which the States were bound to obey, were made by meetings of men appointed by the States to represent them, and were the federal laws of the Confederation. Our federal laws say what each person in the United States must or must not do, and if he does not do what they command he will be punished by the federal courts; but the federal laws of the old-time confederacies said what the States must or must not do, and if a State refused to fulfil its obligation to obey them there was nobody to punish it except the other States. They could punish it only by fighting it and so beginning a civil war. They did not care to do this often; and federal laws were constantly disregarded by such of the federated States as found it inconvenient or unpleasant to obey them. You can put a man in jail, but not a State; laws, ∴, which command each man are much better than laws which command States, because they can be enforced.

One of the first confederations of this old-time sort of which history speaks was the *Achaean League*, which was composed of the principal city-states of the northern Peloponnesus, in Greece, and which took a very prominent part in the great Macedonian wars and afterwards in the wars between Greece and Rome.[1]

4. *The Confe*[*de*]*ration of the United States of America.* We ourselves once had such a confederation in this country. For about eight years before the formation of the present Union (1781-1789), the States which then called themselves the 'United States' lived under a federal constitution which is known as the Articles of Confederation. This confederation made laws as to what the States should do; but it could not compel the States to obey without civil war; and because the States often refused to obey and even seemed about to become hostile to each other if so loose and imperfect a political arrangement continued much longer, our present federal Constitution was made "to secure a more perfect union."

II. DOUBLE CITIZENSHIP.

5. Since every citizen of the United States lives under a double government, he has a double citizenship. He is a citizen of the United States, and he is also a citizen of the State in which he lives. He thus owes duties to the whole country as well as to his neighbours and the other people of his own State. And his double citizenship is of such a sort that he cannot be a citizen of the United States alone, or only of his State: he must be a citizen of both or of neither. The two parts of his citizenship cannot be separated.

Of course he may be a citizen of neither. There are a great many persons in the United States who have no citizenship here at all. No foreigner who comes to this country is a citizen of it until he makes himself one by doing what the laws says shall be done to make a foreigner a citizen. When he does this he is said to '*naturalize*[']' himself, and the laws about it are called *naturalization* laws (§ 8). Every child of citizens is a citizen, however, even though he was not born in this country, but in some other country while his mother was abroad.

It is very common in the United States, more common than in most other countries, for persons to change their place of residence often; and when they move they frequently go from one State to another. In doing this they transfer their state citizenship, without at all changing the other part of their double citizenship, their citizenship of the United States. The laws of the

[1] In his manuscript, Wilson indicated in the margin that this and various other passages to follow should be set in reduced type, and the Editors have observed the practice.

United States and of the States concerning such matters make it very easy to transfer one's citizenship from one State to another. Generally the transfer is considered complete one year after the change of residence was made.

6. *Citizenship under a Confederation.* Under the old-time confederations there was no double citizenship such as exists in the United States. The confederation had no citizens. It had *members*: the States which united to form the confederation were its members. The people were citizens of the several States only, and were connected with the federal government only through the governments of the States, of which they were citizens. The state governments, not their citizens, were bound by federal laws.

7. *Citizenship in Germany and Switzerland.* Something like this is true also in Germany and Switzerland. With us the federal government makes the naturalization law which prescribes how those who are not citizens already may make themselves citizens of a State and of the Union; but in Germany and Switzerland the States alone determine in what way their citizenship shall be acquired, and a German or Swiss is a citizen of the Empire or of the Confederation only by conforming to laws made by a State with ref. to its own citizenship. The federal govt. acts as if it had no citizenship of its own and says nothing about how he shall become a citizen. After he becomes a citizen of a State, however, he has a double citizenship just like that which we possess. He is bound to obey both federal and state govts: the first with reference to all national affairs, the second with reference to all state affairs. He is no less a citizen of the Empire or of the Confederation than he is a citizen of the particular State in which he lives.

8. *Naturalization.* The law of the United States concerning naturalization requires that the person desiring to become a citizen must apply to a court of law in the State or territory in which he wishes to exercise the rights of citizenship for papers declaring him legally a citizen, and that before receiving the papers he must take an oath to be an orderly and loyal citizen. In order to obtain these papers he must have lived in the United States at least five years and in the State or territory in which he makes application at least one year; and at least two years before his application he must have declared in court under oath his intention to become a citizen.

It is not necessary for a person who came to the United States to live three years before coming of age to make such a sworn declaration of his intention to become a citizen.

If a man who has made such a declaration in due form dies before taking out papers of naturalization, his widow and minor children may become citizens by merely taking the necessary oath of citizenship at the proper time.

The children of persons who become naturalized, if they live in the U. S. and are under twenty-one years of age at the time their parents take the oath of citizenship, become citizens by virtue of the naturalization of their parents.

III[.] THE STATES AND THE NATION.

9. *The Colonies*: I. There are now (1887)[2] thirty-seven States in the Union. At first there were only thirteen, namely Virginia, Massachusetts, New Hampshire, Rhode Island, Connecticut, New York, New Jersey, Pennsylvania, Delaware, Maryland, North Carolina, South Carolina, and Georgia, which have ever since been known as "the thirteen original States." When the Union was established, in 1789, it was but seven years since these thirteen States had been thirteen Colonies of Great Britain. They had asserted their independence in 1776, but had not won from England an acknowledgment of their independence till 1782. They had been sending delegates to annual Congresses in Philadelphia (*Continental Congresses*, they were called) since 1774, with a view to agreeing upon means of resisting the oppressive laws which Parliament had been passing concerning them; but before 1774 they had been thirteen Colonies only, loosely bound together by their common duty to obey the government in England, but not connected by any bonds of government on this side the ocean. Each Colony had its own officers, legislature, and courts; but these had no connexion with the officers, legislatures, or courts of the other Colonies.

II. There were many circumstances which made the Colonies sympathize with each other, however, and feel that any injustice done by the royal government to any one of them was a threat made against them all. They were all of them inhabited principally by Englishmen. They had, therefore, besides the same blood and the same language, the same ideas about political justice; they stood in the same general position towards the English authorities, and they were all equally interested in develop-

[2] Wilson transcribed this sentence from his Bryn Mawr shorthand notes. He was writing this manuscript after the adoption (in February 1889) of the so-called Omnibus bill authorizing North Dakota, South Dakota, Montana, and Washington to draft constitutions preliminary to their admission as states. However, none of these territories had yet completed these formalities, and Wilson apparently wrote directly from his shorthand notes with the intention of revising this sentence in his final typed draft once the new western states had been admitted.

ing the new country in which they lived, and in making happy homes for themselves there. It was, therefore, easy for them to make common cause against oppression, easy for them to see the advantage, as well as the necessity, for holding together in the future under a common government of their own, and easy for them to understand and sympathize with each other when they came to discuss the best means of organizing a Union. Their common sympathies, ideas, and necessities led them[,] after they had lived through the revolutionary war in voluntary submission to the guidance of their Congresses in Philadelphia, to set up the Confederation (4 and 12) in 1781, and, when that proved an insufficient government, created the Union in 1789.

10. *Formation of the Colonies*: I. The independent Colonies, then, which called themselves States (that is[,] independent political bodies organized to govern themselves) when they asserted their independence, were the units which constituted the Union. Some of the Colonies had themselves been formed by the union of still smaller units, and all of them had had very small beginnings. A populous colony cannot be made in a year or in many years; and the thirteen American Colonies sprang from small settlements on the Atlantic coast which at first promised to come to nothing at all. On the Southern coast, from Virginia to Georgia, the adventurous colonists from the mother country entered the mouths of the fine rivers, as the Dutch entered the mouth of the Hudson, and, being invited by the rich soil, spread out, as fast as the hostile Indians would suffer them, into scattered farming communities, cultivating large tracts of land, and sending their produce down the river to the sea, thence to be taken to England. They had few towns, therefore, and from the first organized their government on the plan of large counties such as they had left behind them at home. In New England a very different plan was adopted. The soil there was rocky and did not at all invite to much farming. The people who settled on the New England coast, therefore, planted only what was necessary and devoted themselves to trading with the Indians and the colonists to the South and to seafaring for a livelihood. They kept together in towns; and at first each town had its own separate government and was completely independent of the other coast towns, its neighbours. Only by degrees did they come together, first into small, then into wider groups, till at length, all the communities of an extensive territory having at length been united, a Colony such as we see at the time of the Revolu-

tion had come into existence. The middle Colonies of the coast did not have the same development as either the Southern or the New England Colonies had had. Their early history was made unlike that of the others partly because Dutch and Swedes, as well as Englishmen, formed part of their population. They consequently had in the beginning some rural, agricultural communities like those of the South, and some 'townships,' like those of New England.

II. In all the Colonies alike, however, the beginning was a small self-governing group of settlers which ruled itself, whenever let alone by the government in England, very much as the Germans whom Caesar knew, and who were the ancestors of the English, ruled their primitive communities in the forests by the Rhine. The settlers themselves met together in public meeting to decide what rules should govern them in their relations with each other, and the officers whom they elected, or whom the King's Counsellors in England set over them, were expected to heed the common will in what they did. It was from these simple organizations, these 'local governments' as we should call them now, that the Colonies and States of the Confederation and Union had grown. As the Union had its constituent units, its States, so Massachusetts had had her constituent units, her towns; and so it may be said of the South that its counties were older than its Colonies.

11. *The United States of New England: New England Confederation.* So far back as 1643, when it was not fifty years since the establishment of a permanent English settlement in America, the New England Colonies, which were still only small groups of towns, formed a confederation in order that they might stand together to better effect in fighting against the Indians; but so soon as the Indians had been greatly reduced and the danger had ceased to be pressing, the young Colonies fell apart again. They were too scattered and too little developed to do more than gradually draw more towns to themselves and so prepare the way for larger combinations. It is by such slow stages that states have always grown. No states were made to order in America. But this attempt at making a wide Confederation, although it was made too early to succeed, showed a healthy tendency to recognize common interests and combine under some common form of government.

12. *The United States of America: The Confederation.* I. The war for independence gave to the Colonies the necessary impetus

toward Union at just the right time. Had they waited till later to unite, one or more of the Colonies might in the meantime have become so populous and powerful as to have overshadowed the rest and so to have rendered a combination on equal terms impossible. Had it been necessary to unite earlier, the Colonies might have been individually too small and weak to have avoided surrendering completely to the Union and being absorbed by it, as the New England towns had been absorbed by the larger colonial combinations. The colonists had been jealous from the first to guard local privileges; each little local group had been anxious to continue to govern its own affairs in its own way and had fought as long as it could any interference on the part either of the government in England or of their neighbour colonists in America. But the small local governments, the towns in the North and the rural communities in the Carolinas and Georgia, had not been strong enough to live alone. They had gradually been absorbed into large Colonies. The Colonies of 1776, on the other hand, were most of them sufficiently large and strong to live apart to themselves. They had formed successful govts. and were stiffly attached both by pride and interest to their individual independence. Nothing but some tremendous necessity like that which came with the Revolution could have forced them to come together and subordinate the local interests of each to the common interests of all.

II. Even then, however, they did not entirely sacrifice themselves for the sake of union. Unlike the towns and counties, they could avoid being swallowed up. They determined to limit the control of the common government they were making as much as possible. Their own history taught them how to do this effectually. Their own governments as Colonies had been conducted under charters granted them by the sovereign authorities in England: in imitation of this mode of constituting a government, they determined that they would frame a charter, or constitution, for the government of the United States in which they would definitely set forth its rights and their own, as their charters had definitely set forth what powers their colonial govts. might exercise and what the Crown. The result was the *Articles of Confederation*, the constitution of the Confederation. These Articles had hardly gone into operation, however, before it began to be evident that their desire to remain independent so far as possible had made the colonists go too far in limiting the powers of the general government. They had made it too weak to accomplish anything. It represented the Colonies in all dealings with foreign powers; it commanded the common army, and had the oversight of many common interests; but it could raise no money for its own support by taxation, it could only ask the States to raise money for it; and it could command nothing, but only advise the States what ought to be done and helplessly submit when they refused to heed its advice. Without power to raise money by taxation and without power to command obedience from any one except States more powerful than itself, a government is nothing but a makebelieve and must speedily prove worthless. The Colonies had made a mere paper government when they chartered the Confederation. It was necessary to begin over again.

13. *The Making of the Union.* I. In the Constitutional Convention of 1787 the delegates of the thirteen States framed a new constitution, a new charter, for the government of the United States. This new charter, like the first one, was very exact and definite in setting forth what the powers of the federal authorities were to be, and it still reserved to the States the entire control of the vast majority of subjects with which law-making and government have to do. Only those powers were given to the Union which it was necessary that it should have in order that affairs which were of equal interest to all the States, and which ought on that account to be managed according to some single uniform plan, might be properly attended to. But the new Constitution was very different from the Articles of Confederation in this: it made the powers of the Union real powers. The new government was given full right of taxation and it was authorized to command individuals, whom it cd. punish for disobedience, instead of advising States, which it could not punish at all. It was allowed not only to have a will of its own, but to have also all the necessary means of carrying out its will. It was made a complete government, of supreme authority and power with regard to the matters entrusted to its care.

II. Still it was not intended that it should encroach upon the powers of the States and widen its own sphere as it chose. Every means that wisdom and practical experience could suggest were taken to prevent its doing so. In the first place, as I have said, a careful and explicit list of the eighteen matters it was to be privileged to control was put into the Constitution, so that its powers might be clear and so that there might be no pretext or excuse for its assuming any others. In the second place, in order that there might be some authority as high in dignity as Congress itself to prevent the carrying into effect of any law passed by the government of the Union which it was not warranted to pass by the Constitution, a Supreme Court was created by the Constitution itself to pass upon the constitutionality of all federal laws and prevent any one from taking advantage of any that the Constitution did not sanction. And in order that the States, too, might be prevented from forgetting or breaking the constitutional arrangements upon which their Union rests, this court was given the further power of testing in some way the laws of the States by the Constitution of the Union (.).[3] In colonial days the colonists had known a court which did something like this. The Privy Council in England, which was in some cases the highest court in England, had been the supreme court which had tested the laws passed by the Colonial govts. and determined whether or not they were such laws as their charters gave them a legal right to enact. As their charters had been interpreted and their laws tested, so should the charter and laws of the Union be interpreted and tested by a great court from whose decision no appeal could be made.

III. This idea was carried out not only with reference to the charter of the Union but also with reference to the constitutions of the States themselves. The people of the States had replaced the charters which had been granted them by the King in Parliament by charters, or constitutions, of their own making in which they prescribed the sort of government they wished to have and the powers they did *not* wish those governments to exercise without fresh constitutional permission given by themselves, the people, in a particular way. These constitutions did not claim for the state govts. the powers which had been given to the federal govt, and, while they gave to the state authorities almost all other powers which any govt. can exercise, there were some which they withheld and which they commanded should not be exercised at all. Thus the people of each State had chartered a state govt. and the people of all the States together had chartered a federal govt. And, as the great federal court was given the duty of testing the conformity of all laws to the federal charter, so the state courts were given the duty of testing the conformity of state laws to both the state and the federal charters. The federal court was to guard the federal charter not only against federal laws but also against state laws wh. conflicted with its

[3] Wilson obviously left this space for a cross reference.

provisions. The state courts were to guard the state charters from violation by state laws, and were also, subject to correction by the federal court, to determine whether state laws were or were not in conformity with the federal charter. ( )

14. *The Early Character of the Union.* I[.] Most of the men who saw the Union established regarded it with no love at all. They loved first and most their own States, and consented to a strong government for the Union only because they saw no other way of escaping trouble between the States and of keeping together in dealing with foreign States and in managing the affairs which it was necessary to manage in partnership. The Colonies had all had long and eventful histories. Their citizens had had to make a great many sacrifices to maintain their property and lives against the attacks of the Indians and their govts. against the interferances of the English authorities, and in striving to keep their homes and their liberties had become passionately attached to their colonial institutions. They were obstinately opposed to any measures which would lessen the dignity or the power of any Colony any more than was necessary to keep it bound to its neighbours in friendliness and general helpfulness. The people of each Colony or State looked upon the State govt. as their home govt. which they were especially bound to serve and defend. Each man's first duty, it was thought[,] was to his State, only his second to the Union, which was a new, far-off government in which he was not particularly interested. He loved his State, but he only respected the Union.

II. There were not many people in those first days of the new federal government who thought that the Union was more than an experiment. There was for some time a very general feeling that the States had not shut themselves out from a right to withdraw from the federal arrangement and act separately for themselves. The colonists regarded themselves as all alike Americans, but they did not think that by binding the States together in a great federation they had made themselves a homogeneous nation. They acted together as a single people, they said, for the purposes for which the Union was established, but, except in that way, they were not a single people, but a collection of peoples. The Union was not a State, but a bundle of States. And the States were still more important than the Union: they did not exist for the sake of the Union, it had been entered into for their sakes. It remained to be seen whether it would be worth preserving or not.

III. This was the feeling of a majority of the people of the thirteen States so far as we can tell now. Among the leaders of the people there was a great division of opinion. After the Convention of 1787 had framed the federal Constitution, conventions in all the States, elected to consider it, voted for its adoption (1788-'9), and the party which favoured its adoption, and which had carried the day at the elections at which delegates to these conventions were chosen, were called *Federalists.* George Washington was a federalist, and the federalists had charge of the federal government for many years after its establishment. But they held views as to the character of the new government, after it had been established, which a good many of the people who had voted for the adoption of the Constitution did not hold. They thought that the purpose of the new Constitution was to subordinate state interests to the interests of the general government, and they acted accordingly in their management of affairs. But there were so many people who thought them wrong in this that before many years had passed they were deprived of the charge of the government, and others were elected to the federal offices who held the view of the majority of the people, that the general government ought to be confined as closely as possible within the limits marked out so carefully in the Constitution. (See VIII, "History of Parties.")

15. *Growth of the National Idea.* I. This was in the days when there were no railroads and when consequently it was so hard to get from one place to another that the people of one colony saw very little of the people of the other colonies and so felt very little like members of one great State. So long as this continued to be the case, the majority of the people continued to put the States before the nation in their thoughts and to demand that the rights of the States in the management of their own affairs should be carefully guarded against every attempt on the part of the federal government to make its own powers greater than they were intended to be at first. But when railroads began to be built, when seeing each other and trading with each other began to make the people of all the States very much more like one another, when people from all the States began to go out and settle the West together, when new States which had grown up in the West without any of the old conservative colonial traditions began to be admitted to the Union, and when a second war with England and a great war with Mexico had tested the government and strengthened a feeling of patriotism for the whole

country,—then the people began to feel very much more like a single great nation and began to believe that the Federalists had been right after all, that the federal government ought to come first in their consideration, even if they had to sacrifice a little bit of state pride for the purpose of making and keeping the nation strong.

II. What stood most in the way of the universal growth of this sort of opinion was the great difference between the North and the South caused by the existence of slavery in the South. So long as the labourers in the South were slaves and the labourers in the North free men, the North and the South could not become like each other, and so could not have the same national feeling. The North and the great Northwest, the two richest and most populous portions of the country, could sympathize and act together, and could mean the same thing when they talked about the nation; but when the people in the South talked about the nation they meant a nation with institutions like their own. There was one nation for the North and West and another for the South. The two sections, therefore rapidly became more and more dissatisfied with living under the same system, and the great War of Secession came, in which the South tried to break away from the Union and keep her own ways of life and labour and the North and West tried to prevent her.

16. *Present Character of the Union.* I. Secession was prevented; the Union was preserved; and slavery was forever abolished. There was no longer any reason why the South should not become like the rest of the country. Since the war North and South have come to be the same in modes of life and thought, so that now there is nothing to prevent our being in in [*sic*] reality one great nation. The effort made in the war to preserve the Union and the result of the war in making the country at last homogeneous throughout has made the federal government, as the representative of the nation, seem greater in the eyes of all, and has brought about a great many changes in the way in which the old questions about the rights of the States are regarded

II. This does not mean that the States have been swallowed up by the federal government: it means simply this, that the people of the United States, instead of regarding the govt. of the Union and the govt. of a State as two governments, as they once did, now regard them as two parts of one and the same government, two parts of a single system. (1). They look upon themselves as constituting one nation; but they value as much as ever the plan of government which they adopted at the first, the plan, namely, of dividing the functions of government between national and state authorities. The national government still has its charter, somewhat enlarged since the War ( ), and must still confine itself to doing only what that charter says it may do: the States still have their charters and still claim all the powers not specially granted to the national government. But the people are willing that the federal charter should be very liberally construed and that all truly national interests should be taken care of by Congress. It is still essential to their ideas of political right that all local affairs should be left exclusively to the States without any interference by the national authorities; but it is no longer consistent with their ideas that the States should be hostile to the federal authorities as if they were officers of an outside government.

III. The Nation properly comes before the States in honour and importance: not because it has swallowed up the States or is *more* important than they are, but because it is *all-important to them* and to the maintenance of every principle of government which we have established and now cherish. *It is the organic frame of the States: it has enabled and still enables them to exist.*

IV[.] THE ORGANIZATION OF GOVERNMENT.

A. THE FEDERAL GOVERNMENT.

17. *The Federal Government* is the agency through which the people of the United States manage those affairs which they wish to manage as a nation and not as separate States. It is founded upon a great law called the Constitution of the United States which declares what powers it shall have and by what means it shall exercise those powers. When we speak of the organization of a government we mean the persons who, according to its constitution or fundamental law, make its laws; the persons who execute and enforce its laws; and the various ways in which these persons act, together or separately, in performing their parts of the duties of legislating and governing. The Constitution of the United States does not contain all the rules upon which the organization of the federal government rests. It says that there shall be a Congress which shall make the laws which it is proper for the federal government to make, a President who shall have charge of the business of having the laws of Congress carried into effect, and a Supreme Court which shall be the highest court of the land for determining what is lawful to be

done, either by individuals or by the States, under the Constitution and laws. It does not command how Congress shall do its work of law-making, however, or what officers shall help the President, or what officers and what lower courts shall help the Supreme Court. All these details of organization it leaves to be arranged for by the laws passed by Congress. Only the principal and most important things about the organization of the government are to be learned from the Constitution, all the rest,—and the rest is the greater part by far,—is to be found in the federal laws, which are known as the Statutes of the United States.

18. *The Constitution.* The organization of the government rests upon the Constitution as its foundation, and so do also all the laws, or statutes, of the United States. This is the reason why we call the Constitution the *fundamental* law. It is the law upon which both all the laws passed by the federal government and that government itself are founded. It differs from all other laws in not having been passed by ordinary legislation, and in not being changeable by ordinary legislation. It was framed, not by a legislature, but by a special convention, which met for that purpose and no other; and it was adopted, not by the vote of that Convention, but by the votes of the people of the States acting through special state conventions elected for the single purpose of voting upon its adoption. It can be changed only by consent of the people of three-fourths of the States added to the consent of Congress.

Changes, or "amendments," in the Constitution may be proposed in one of two ways: either two-thirds of the members of each house of Congress may agree that certain amendments are necessary, *or* the legislatures of two-thirds of the States may petition Congress to have a general convention called for the consideration of amendments and two-thirds in Congress agree to the calling of the convention proposed. Then, when amendments have been proposed by two-thirds of Congress, or by a convention called in the manner described, they must be submitted to the States to be voted on either by the state legislatures or by state conventions called for the purpose. If three-fourths of the States adopt them, they become parts of the Constitution.

Fourteen[4] amendments to the Constitution have been adopted, but these have added to rather than changed it.

Almost all the greater States of Europe now have written constitutions, which, although not made and adopted exactly as ours was, and in many cases much more easily changed than is ours, in other respects stand very much in the same position of special, fundamental law. England has no written constitution; her laws

[4] Wilson wrote the figure 15 above "Fourteen."

and her constitution are one: her constitution consists of those laws which have regard to the form and functions of her government. Her constitution is not, therefore, separate from her other laws; it is no more fundamental, except in the estimation of the people, than are they; Parliament can alter all alike at its pleasure. It would not, of course, however, think of changing the most important arrangements of the government.

19. *The Capital, or Seat of Government.* The first Congress of the United States met in New York City; there the first President was inaugurated, and the organization of the new government begun. In 1790 it was determined that the federal officers should live and Congress meet in Philadelphia, as the Continental Congresses and the Congress of the Confederation had done, for ten years; after that in a district specially set apart for the use of the federal government. It would of course have been very inconvenient for the federal government to have no territory of its own on which to build its public offices and legislative halls, and where it could be independent of local or other state regulations. The Constitution therefore provided that Congress should have exclusive authority within any district not more than ten miles square which any State might give the federal government for its own uses. Maryland and Virginia, taking the hint, promptly gave territory of the proper amount for that purpose. Other States would have been quite willing to give land, but it was decided to establish the government on the borders of Virginia and Maryland. The gift of these States was, ∴, accepted and the homeland of the federal government laid out under the name of *The District of Columbia.* There the public buildings were erected, and there, after the removal of the government offices thither in 1800, the City of Washington grew up, the capital city of the nation. The District of Columbia, therefore, belongs exclusively to the federal government, and is not under the laws of any State, but only under the laws passed for its government by Congress. It is the centre, the seat or residence, of the federal government.

20. *Federal Property.* 1. *Forts, Arsenals, Dockyards, &c.* The District of Columbia is not the only property owned exclusively by the national government. The Constitution provides that the general government shall have exclusive authority also over all places purchased from any State, by the consent of the legislature of the State "for the erection of forts, magazines, arsenals, dockyards, and other needful buildings"; and the gen. govt. has in fact made many such purchases. It exercises over the places

thus bought all the rights of complete ownership just as it does in the District of Columbia; so that any crime committed in such places must be tried by the federal courts, not by the state courts, and punished according to federal laws.

2. *The Territories.* Forts, arsenals, dockyards, and even the District of Columbia are owned by the United States simply for the purposes of government, only to enable the federal authorities to carry out their functions. There is another sort of federal property which is best described as the property of the nation. This is the Territories of the United States. The first territories of the United States lay in the lands between the western borders of the thirteen States and the great Mississippi river,—lands which had once belonged to the States separately, chiefly to Virginia, but which the States had given up to be the common property of the Union. Until 1803 the United States owned no territory beyond the Mississippi. But in 1803 we bought Louisiana from France: and 'Louisiana' then meant an immense slice of the continent extending North and West from the present State of Louisiana to the Rocky Mountains, possibly even to the Pacific, —nobody in those days knew exactly how far,—a vast triangle of territory larger than the whole area of the United States at that time. Afterwards, in 1848 as a result of war, and in 1852 [*sic*] as a result of negociation, we purchased almost the whole of the present Pacific coast of the country from Mexico[.] These purchases, together with some small additions gained from England by treaty (Oregon, 1842), made up the present splendid domain of the Union and opened the way for an almost boundless extension of the population and institutions of the country. As different parts of this vast territory became settled,—first that part on this side of the Mississippi, and then that on the other side—it was divided, under the direction of Congress, into portions of various sizes, generally about the size of the larger States, but sometimes larger than any State except Texas, the largest. These portions were called, for want of a better name, Territories, and were given governments constituted by federal law. That is to say, they were given governors and judges appointed by the President, and, when their inhabitants became numerous and settled enough in their ways of living, legislatures elected by the people of the Territory themselves and authorised to make laws subject to the approval of Congress. Afterwards when they became still more developed they were given as full power to make their own laws as the States themselves possessed. Finally, one by one,

a great many of them were permitted to form governments of their own and were admitted to the Union as States. Twenty-two ? of the present States of the Union were admitted in this way.

The State of Texas was a foreign State, not a territory, when it was admitted; and West Virginia was a part of Virginia.

That part of the territory which has not yet been made into States is still under territorial governments and is still subject to the laws of Congress.

3. *Post-offices, Custom-houses, &c.* Of course the government of the United States has the same right to buy and own property that private persons have, and so long as it is not forbidden to do so by state laws, it may buy what land it can for the erection of such buildings as it needs, without going through all the formality of asking the consent of the state legislatures and having land set apart for its exclusive control, as it has done before building its forts, dockyards, and arsenals. It owns custom-houses in many of the great cities of the Union, and post- ? offices in almost every considerable town in the country, besides buildings for the use of United States courts in many places. These are built on lots bought from private persons just as any individual would buy them. Where the federal government does not actually own the post-office and federal court buildings, it often rents or leases them. Such property is not taken from under the laws of the State in which it lies just because the general government owns or occupies it. It is subject to state laws exactly as any other property would be. Those laws regard and treat it in just the same way in which they would regard and treat property held by a great corporation, a railroad company, for instance. The United States, moreover, cannot take it out of the reach of the state laws by making special rules of its own concerning it. They can get exclusive control of it only by obtaining the consent of the state legislature and having it set apart as federal territory.

Branches of the Government

21. *Branches of the Government.* Every government must do at least three things: it must make laws for the government of its citizens and for the management of its own affairs; it must judge in disputes between its citizens as to their rights and duties under its laws; and it must carry out, through the necessary officers, all the provisions of its laws which concern the management of its affairs and the fulfilment of its various functions.

In other words, it must exercise legislative, judicial, and executive functions, making laws, executing laws, and passing judgment in law-cases. The earliest government of which we know anything was the government of the *family*: *the family was the the first State*, existing long before the great States we know now-a-days had begun to grow up. In the family the father was king: he made the laws, he executed them, and he acted as judge: one man exercised all of the three great functions of which I have spoken. Larger States grew up presently by the union of several families, and the kings of these new States were given powers like those of the father of a family—for these united families regarded themselves as all of one kin, and their king as standing in place of a father. It was a long time before this plan and idea were outgrown. For century after century of the world's early history the chief man of the State continued to be law-maker, law-executor, and judge, as well as priest. It was only in later days, when States had so grown that they had lost the idea of being great families of kinsmen under a father-king, that men came to feel that it was very much better that these three functions of government should not be in the hands of one person, or even of one set of persons. This person or set of persons might be wicked and unsc[r]upulous; they would have the opportunity to use their great powers for selfish purposes, to first make laws to suit themselves and then put those laws into execution and themselves judge and condemn everybody who disobeyed them. The constitution of every enlightened government of our own day, therefore, separates the legislative, executive, and judicial powers of the government and makes the persons who exercise them independent of each other, so that if one of them does wrong the others may check him by refusing to coöperate with him. The legislator cannot force the judge; the judge cannot interfere with the privileges of the legislator; and judge and legislator can no more compel the executive officer to do as they like than he can compel them to do as he likes. The law controls them all, but forbids them wrongly to control one another.

Thus it has come about that we speak of the legislative, executive, and judicial *branches* of a government. We treat law-making as something separate and distinct from the execution of law, and both of these as separate and distinct from the deciding of cases arising under the laws. The courts constitute one branch of government, the officers who carry the laws into effect constitute another branch, and the law-making assemblies a third branch, and we speak of these as the legislative, executive, and judicial branches of government. We mean that, although these are all functions of the one great agency called a government, they are not exercised by the same persons.

22. *Congress*[.] The law-making or legislative branch of the federal government is called the *Congress of the United States.* It consists of two parts,–two *houses*, we say, because these two parts are really separate bodies, sitting in different rooms quite independently of each other, having each its own way of doing its business, possessing each its own officers, servants, &c. One of these two parts of Congress is called the *House of Representatives*, the other the *Senate.*

23. The law-making branches of all the great modern governments are divided into two parts, just as our Congress is. In England one of these parts is called the House of Commons, the other the House of Lords; in France one is called the Chamber of Deputies, the other the Senate; in Germany one is known as the Imperial Assembly, the other as the Federal Council, &c.

The reasons for having legislatures consist of two houses are not easy to explain. Generally one house is composed of representatives of one class of the people in the country and the other of representatives of another class, as in England and in several of the States of the German Empire; or the members of one house (the Senate) are elected in a different way from that in which the members of the other house are elected, and to represent each a larger number of the people, as in France; or, if the government be a federal government, the members of one house represent the States of the Union, the members of the other the people in general, as in the government of the United States and the imperial Government of the German Empire. The idea upon which these differences between the two houses rest is, that, since they do not represent the same persons or exactly the same principles, and since the members of one house are elected for a longer term than that for which the members of the other house are elected, the two houses will have slightly or altogether different ways of looking at the questions which come up before them; and that, consequently, if one house acts rashly, the other will be more apt to act as a check upon it than if it were exactly the same kind of an assembly.

Probably, however, the example of England, which a little more than a century ago possessed the only great and successful free government in the world, has had more to do with the preference for double legislatures than any general theories about their advantages. Most modern European governments are in large part copied from the English government, and that government has, and has long had, a double legislature. She has such a legislature, however, more by accident than by design. She once had only a great single legislature; but it happened that, in the reign of

Edward I, this great single parliament was made larger and then, for the sake of convenience and not out of any set plan, divided into two parts. It might just as naturally have been divided into three or four.

The statesmen who made the Constitution of the United States also adopted the English fashion of a double legislature. They were Englishmen themselves and it was natural that they should do so. But they were also influenced by more ancient example. The two greatest nations of antiquity had double legislatures, and because such legislatures existed in ancient as well as in modern times, it has come to be very generally believed that they are the only natural kind. Both the Greeks and the Romans, however, had at first, like the English, only a single law-making assembly in their governments—a great Senate, namely, which represented the elders and nobles of the community and was thought fit to act a sort of fatherly part towards the rest of the citizens. But at length, as it happened, the people clamored so loudly for some law-making power to be given to them also, in order that they might check what they considered to be the partiality of the Senate, that it became necessary to grant their demands in order to avoid civil war. And so another assembly sprang up beside the Senate whose consent became as necessary as that of the Senate to the validity of laws. From this ancient manner of legislating, then, which did not spring out of any general plan or abstract reasoning formed beforehand, but only out of the particular circumstances of the history of Greece and of Rome, we derived the same idea that we had derived from English practice, the idea, that is, of the general reasonableness of a double legislature.

24. *The Senate* of the United States is composed of two representatives of each of the States of the Union. It has, therefore, seventy-four[5] members. Each Senator is elected, for a term of six years by the Legislature of the State which he represents; and a state legislature is free to choose any one Senator who has been a citizen of the United States nine years, who has reached the age of thirty, and who is at the time of the election a resident of the State he is chosen to represent. The Constitution directed that, immediately after coming together for its first session, the Senate should divide its members, by lot as exactly as it could into three equal groups; that the members of one of these groups should vacate their seats after the expiration of two years, the members of another after the expiration of four years, and the members of the third after the expiration of six years. As the members of each of these groups vacated their seats, their places

[5] There were still thirty-eight states and seventy-six senators when Wilson was writing this. He probably intended to write "eighty-four," anticipating the addition of eight new senators once the four western states had been admitted into the Union, and "seventy-four" was a slip of the pen.

were filled by Senators elected for six years. It was thus brought about that one-third of the members of the Senate are elected every two years, though the term of each Senator is six years. The result of this way of electing is, that the Senate has a sort of continuous life; the terms of the Senators never expire all at one and the same time and leave an entirely new Senate to be elected,—no one election-year affects the seats of more than one-third of the Senators.

The Senate is the *federal* house of Congress: its members represent the States. They may be said to represent the governments of the States rather than the people of the States, for they are elected, not by the people, but by the legislative branches of the state governments. And in the Senate all the States are upon an equality: large and small States alike have exactly the same representation: Rhode Island has as many Senators as New York has. In voting, however, upon the laws and other matters which come under their consideration, the Senators vote according to their individual opinions. They represent the governments of the States, but those governments have no right to tell them how they shall vote; two Senators from the same State may vote on opposite sides of any question: it is not required that they should vote together and thus represent their States as a single man.

In these respects the position of Senators of the United States differs very greatly from the position of the members of the old Congress of the Confederation. That Congress consisted of but one house, and in that house the States, not the people, were represented, as in our Senate. Each State could send any number of representatives she chose from two to seven, but all votes were cast according to States, and each State had but one vote. No matter whether she sent two representatives, or five, or seven, whatever their number, they were required by the Constitution of the Confederation to vote together, deciding by a majority of their own number how the one vote of their State should be cast.

In the federal house of the German Imperial Legislature, the Federal Council, the States are represented according to their respective size and importance, Prussia having as many as seventeen representatives while the small States of the Union have only one each. In the votes of the Federal Council the vote of each member counts as one, but the representatives of each State which has more than one member in the Council must agree together how they will vote and cast all the votes of their State upon the same side of the question. Prussia's seventeen votes, for instance, must never be divided, but must always go together. In Switzerland, on the other hand, the Council of Estates (the branch of the federal legislature which corresponds to our Senate) is made up of two members from each State and each member has an individual vote of his own, just as in the Senate of the United States.

The Vice-President of the United States (20, iv, (a)) is president of the Senate. He is not a member of the Senate, however; he simply presides over its proceedings, and has a vote only when the votes of the Senators are equally divided and his vote becomes necessary for a decision.

The Senate makes its own rules of procedure, and its president is of course bound by those rules. It is by these rules that the Senate decides in what way it will consider the business brought before it and what its own inside organization shall be,—how many clerks it will have, how [many] official reporters to take down the speeches made by Senators, how many door-keepers and pages, &c. The most important part of the organization of the Senate for which these rules provide is the division of its members into "Standing Committees," that is, into small groups to each of which is entrusted the preparation of a certain part of the Senate's business. The Senate would not have time to look into the history and particulars of every matter brought before it. It therefore divides itself into the committees, whose members the Senators choose by ballot, and when a proposal is made to pass a certain law that proposal is referred to the committee which has questions concerning the making of such as that proposed in charge. The committee takes the proposal and considers it, in connexion with all other proposals relating to the same subject, and reports to the Senate what it thinks ought to be done with reference to it,—whether it is advisable to pass such a law as the one proposed or not.

Thus there is a Committee on Finance to which all questions about taxes and like matters are referred; a Committee on Appropriations which advises the Senate concerning all votes for spending money; a Committee on Railroads which considers all railroad questions; a Committee on the Army which reports upon all military matters; a Committee on Foreign Affairs which takes care of all questions concerning our relations with foreign governments; &c.

These Committees of course have a great deal of influence and constitute a very important part of the Senate's organization. The Senate is always inclined to listen to their advice, because each Committee necessarily knows much more about the subjects committed to its care than the rest of the Senate can know.

One of the chief uses of the Committees is to get information for the Senate concerning the affairs of the government. But since the executive branch of the government is quite separate from Congress, it is often difficult for the Senate and House of Representatives to find out all they wish to know about the condition of affairs in the executive departments. The action of the two houses upon some questions must of course be greatly influenced by what they can know of the experience of the executive in such matters, however, and to make the proper inquiries is therefore one of the duties of the Standing Committees. The Senate has the right to ask what questions it pleases of the officers of the government, either through its Committees or by requiring a written report to be made directly to itself. But it is not always easy, or even possible, to get all of its questions answered fully and correctly, because the officers of the government are in no way responsible to the Senate: they belong to a separate and independent branch of the government. The Committees are frequently prevented from doing their work of inquiry well, consequently, and the Senate sometimes has to act quite in the dark.

25. *The House of Representatives* represents not the States but the people of the United States; and yet it represents them according to States. Congress itself decides by law how many representatives there shall be; it then divides the number among the several States of the Union according to population; after which each State is divided by its own legislature into as many districts as it is to have representatives and the people of each of these districts are entitled to elect a member of the House of Representatives. At present there are three hundred and twenty-five (325) members in the House and the States are given one member for every one hundred and fifty-four thousand three hundred and twenty-five (154,325) of their inhabitants. In case a State has more than an even number of times that many inhabitants, it is given another member. Thus, if it have four times 154,325 inhabitants and a few thousand over, it is given five members, instead of four only, in the House of Representatives. If any State have less than 154,325 inhabitants, it is given one member anyway, because the Constitution itself says that each State shall have at least one.

There are at present four States which have but one representative apiece in the House, namely, Delaware and Nevada [ ];[6]

[6] Wilson, uncertain about the number of states that would be entitled to only one congressman once the new western states had been admitted, wrote the figure 2 over "four" and left a long blank after "Nevada," indicating that he intended to revise this sentence once he knew the names of the rest of the states.

but these States, like the rest, have two Senators each. The reason for allowing a State a representative for the fraction of her people remaining over after division by the standard number, 154,325, is that the apportionment of representatives is made according to States and not by an even allotment of representatives to the people of the country taken as a whole. The election districts,—"Congressional districts," they are called,—are arranged within the limits of each State; no district can cross a state line. Otherwise a very even arrangement of districts might be made, and it would be unnecessary to provide for the representation of fractions of population over the standard number. As it is, the people are represented by States.

The only limitation put by the Constitution itself upon the number of representatives is, that there shall never be more than one for every thirty thousand inhabitants. The first House of Representatives had sixty-five members, upon the proportion of one to every thirty-three thousand inhabitants. The number has of course grown, and the proportion decreased, with the growth of population. A census is taken every ten years, and the rule is to make readjustments and redistributions after every census.

Any one may be chosen a representative who has reached the age of twenty-five years, has been a citizen of the United States for seven years, and is at the time of his election an inhabitant of the State from one of whose districts he is chosen. The term of a representative is two years; and two years is also the term of the whole House: for its members are not chosen a section at a time as the members of the Senate are. On the contrary, the whole membership of the House is renewed every second year. Each biennial election results in the choice of a "new House," as we usually say; for, although many former members may be re-elected, all the members alike are freshly elected; the House is newly made-up by the electors.

The Senate, as we have seen, is never thus entirely renewed at any one time but has a sort of continuous, unbroken life. We speak of the Congress now sitting,[7] however, as the fiftieth Congress, because the present House of Representatives is the fiftieth that has been elected since the government was established, counting Congresses by the number of House of Representatives, although the name "Congress" includes the Senate, which is not the fiftieth Senate.

Congress does not determine who shall vote in the States for members of the House of Representatives. The only federal regulation concerning that matter is the provision of the Constitution which says that all those persons in each State who are allowed by the constitution and laws of their State to vote for members

[7] That is, the Congress that had adjourned on March 4, 1889.

of the larger of the two houses of the state legislature may also vote for members of the House of Representatives of the United States. Any one, therefore, who is qualified to vote for members of the House of Representatives of his own state legislature is qualified also to vote for members of the larger house of Congress.

In the Fourteenth Amendment to the Constitution (passed 1866-1868) a very great pressure is laid upon the States to induce them to exclude no man of mature age from the right to vote in the election of representatives; for that Amendment provides that, should any State deny to any of its male citizens who are twenty-one years of age the right to vote for members of its own legislature, and thus the right to vote for representatives in Congress, for any reason except that they have committed crime, it shall have only so many representatives in Congress as it would have were its population reduced in the same proportion that the number of persons so excluded from the right to vote bears to the whole number of male citizens of twenty-one years of age in the State. This must of course greatly influence the States; for no State wishes the representation of its people in Congress to be reduced.

The House of Representatives is not given a president by the Constitution as the Senate is. It elects its own president, who is called its "Speaker,"—a name which is taken from the English House of Commons, whose president received the name of Speaker because whenever, in the old days, the members of the House of Commons went into the presence of the King for the purpose of laying some matter before him, or of answering a summons from him, their president was their spokesman or "Speaker."

This name is used also in the legislatures of all the English colonies,—wherever, indeed, English legislative practice has been directly inherited.

The House, like the Senate, has its Rules, which regulate the number and the duties of its officers and its ways of doing business; and these Rules, like those of the Senate, provide for the creation of a great number of Standing Committees. The Standing Committees of the House of Representatives are not elected by the ballots of the members of the House, however, as the members of the Senate's Committees are elected; they are appointed by the Speaker; and this power of the Speaker's to appoint the Standing Committees of the House makes him one of the most powerful officers in the whole government. The Committees of the House are even more influential than those of the Senate in deciding what shall be done with reference to the matters referred to them; they, as a matter of fact, have it in their power to determine almost all the acts of the House. It is this fact which makes the Speaker so powerful an officer: he appoints the Committees, and the Committees decide what the House is to do. He often appoints certain members on certain Committees because he knows that they favour certain things which he wants the Committees on which he puts them to favour, in order that the House also may favour them; and in this way he has a very great influence on legislation.

The House has so many Standing Committees that every representative is a member of one or another Committee. But many of the Committees have little or nothing to do,–some of them, though still regularly appointed, have no duties assigned them by the Rules. Other Committees, on the other hand, are of very great importance, as, for instance, the Committee on Ways and Means, which has charge of taxation, and the Committee on Appropriations, which has charge of the general spending of money; and it is to the appointment of such Committees that the Speaker pays most attention. Some members, because of their long service in Congress, are considered entitled to be put on important Committees, and on every Committee there must be some members of both the great political parties represented in Congress; but these customs do not very much limit the choice of the Speaker.

The appointing power of the Speaker makes his election a very exciting part of the business of each new House, and he is always selected with reference to what he will do about the important Committees.

The House has to depend, just as the Senate does, upon its Standing Committees for information about the affairs of the government, and is just as often and as much embarrassed because of its entire exclusion from easy, informal, and regular intercourse with the executive departments. They cannot advise it unless it asks for their advice; and it cannot ask for their advice except indirectly through its Committees or formally through written reports.

26. *Laws.* It is the business of Congress to pass laws concerning the national matters entrusted to its care by the Constitution of the United States. No one can propose a law in either house except a member of that house. Every proposal of a law is carefully written out and in this written form is called a "Bill." In order to become a Law, or Act of Congress, a Bill must be voted for by a majority of the members in each of the houses and must be approved and signed by the President:–so that the President shares with Congress the exercise of the legislative powers of the government. If the President refuses to approve

and sign a Bill passed by the houses, they may make it a Law without his approval, if they can pass it again by a vote of two-thirds of the members of each house. A Law is, therefore, a Bill passed by both Houses and approved by the President, or a Bill passed twice by both houses, the second time, if not the first, by a two-thirds majority in each.

Neither house can do any business unless a majority of its members are present. This number necessary to the transaction of business is called a *quorum*. In some other legislatures the *quorum* is much less than a majority of the members; in the English House of Commons, for instance, it is forty members, although the total number of members of the House of Commons is almost seven hundred. When it is said that under certain circumstances a Bill must be passed by a vote of two-thirds in order to become a Law, it is meant that it must be voted for by two-thirds of the members *present*, not necessarily by two-thirds of all the members of the house.

A Bill may be considered first, that is may "originate," as the technical expression goes, in either house, unless it be a Bill relating to the raising of revenue. In that case it must "originate" in the House of Representatives, though the Senate may propose what amendments, or changes, it pleases in such a Bill as in any other which comes to it from the House. Of course if one of the houses pass a Bill and when that Bill is sent to the other house that other house propose changes in it, those changes must be adopted by the house in which the Bill originated before the Bill can be sent to the President and made a Law. When the two Houses disagree about amendments proposed by one of them to a Bill, they appoint Conference Committees: that is to say, each house appoints a committee to consult with a similar committee appointed by the other house to see what can be done towards bringing about an agreement between the houses.

If the President disapproves a Bill which has been sent to him, he must return it to the house in which it originated with his reasons for not approving it. If he does not return a Bill, either signed or disapproved, within ten days after it is sent to him, it becomes a Law anyway, unless the houses have adjourned in the meantime. In that case the Bill simply disappears without becoming a Law.

27. *Congressmen and Their "Constituents."* The "constituents" of Congressmen are the persons whom they represent. Thus the constituents of a member of the House of Representatives are the people of the district in which he was elected. It is not so easy to say who the constituents of a Senator are,—not the members of the legislature which elected him: they are merely the instruments of the State in cho[o]sing him,—and they may be, probably will be, replaced by others before his term in the Senate

expires, for their terms are not so long as his; he was chosen to represent his State as a political body, a member of the Union, not to represent them. A Senator, therefore, though he represents his State, which is much the same as saying the people of his State, can hardly be said to have any constituents. It is all the more certain, therefore, that he cannot be instructed by any one what to do in the Senate after his election. That would be certain in any case, however, so long as the Constitution and the laws say nothing about the matter. It is as certain in the case of a representative as it is in the case of a Senator. A representative is not chosen to do what he is told to do by the people who elected him, though he will always naturally wish to do what they desire; if he were, he would be merely an agent. He is chosen because his constituents think that they can trust him to do what is best when he sees the whole case with regard to any legislative matter, as he will when it is presented to Congress. He is charged with the duty of judging of public matters in their stead: he acts in their place, representing not their particular but their general views of affairs.

The Judiciary.

28. *The Judiciary*, or judge system, of the United States is composed of the Supreme Court of the United States, the Circuit Courts of the United States, and the District Courts of the United States. The Supreme Court was created by the Constitution, the Circuit and District Courts were created by Acts of Congress, that is by Statutes of the United States.

WWhw MS. (WP, DLC).

A News Item

[May 1, 1889]

THE WESLEYAN HOUSE OF COMMONS.

Early in the winter term a students' House of Commons was organized upon the model of societies already existing at the Johns Hopkins University, in the Columbia Law School, and elsewhere. It was felt by the students and by those who were interested in assisting them in this scheme that the College would be much better off for a society in which all the men alike could meet and compare talents for public speech and for public business upon an equal footing; in which an organic college feeling could be generated and kept at a proper glow; and in which every one who chose could, under the most stimulating conditions, perfect himself in debate and in parliamentary practice.

It was thought best to take the English House of Commons rather than our own House of Representatives as a model of organization, because it would be necessary in order to reproduce the organization and methods of the House of Representatives to have a complete set of standing committees, to commit all measures to them for consideration, and so to divide among sections of its members the debating function which it was desired the whole House should exercise. The organization of the House of Commons, moreover, offered a dramatic and personal element not to be found in our own House of Representatives. The presence and responsibility of a ministry, as has been proved by the experience in Baltimore and New York, stimulates interest in parliamentary tactics and debate as no other way of conducting business could be expected to do.

According to the plan adopted, the "House" discusses modern political questions and questions affecting college matters. Every question comes up in the form of a bill and goes through the regular parliamentary stages of legislation. It is the duty of the ministers, and the privilege of any member, to introduce bills, and the ministers are responsible to the House for their opinions upon every question of importance introduced: that is, like their English prototypes, they must resign if defeated. The Speaker of the House takes the place of the Crown in the appointment of ministers. Upon the resignation of a cabinet, he appoints the leader of the opposition Prime Minister, and the Prime Minister appoints his colleagues, selecting them, of course, from his own side of the House. The ministry consists of three members only (though there is already some agitation for the addition of a fourth), namely, a Prime Minister, a Secretary for Foreign Affairs, and a Home Secretary.

So far, the interest in the House has been very great, not only among the students, but among the townspeople as well. It has manifest advantages over the old-style literary society, in which men were arbitrarily appointed to the side of the question which they were to advocate, and in which they were stimulated, not by ambition to support their views, but by fines; and the success of similar societies in other colleges, after a trial of several years, gives a very reasonable ground for confidence that Wesleyan will be equally persistent and enthusiastic in her activity in this kind of work.

Printed in the *Wesleyan University Bulletin*, May 1, 1889, pp. 10-11.

From Albert Bushnell Hart

My dear Prof Wilson: Cambridge, Mass. May 2, 1889

Your cordial letter of the 1st has been received, and I hasten to say that I think the question of time can be arranged to your satisfaction. I have written to the Longmans on the subject and will write definitely on the subject, as soon as I hear from them.

It will be a great pleasure to be at work on the same series; and I think I can arrange for some use of books from our library which will save you both travel and trouble.

Thank you for your kind suggestion of welcome. I hope we shall meet each other soon.

Hastily yours, Albert Bushnell Hart

ALS (WP, DLC).

To Robert Bridges

My dear Bobby, Middletown, Conn., 4 May, 1889

I am about to send off the *mss.* of the text-book I have so long been at work upon. You remember when I last saw you I was wondering what were the best terms an author could expect from his publisher on a text-book. Can you find out for me soon, through your publishing-house connections? I want to have a basis for negotiation with Heath.

In haste and love, Yrs. as ever, Woodrow Wilson

ALS (WC, NjP).

From Henry Holt & Company

Dear Sir: New York. May 6/89.

Prof. Johnston tells us that you are at work upon an elementary textbook on Government & that your ideas chime in with his. You know we publish two of his books[1] & we expect to publish others as his strength permits. May we suggest that your book might find in them congenial company? If you have not already made your business arrangements for it, are you willing to let us see the MS.?

Very truly yours, Henry Holt & Co., Bristol.

ALS (WP, DLC) with WWhw notation on env.: "Ans May 13/89."

[1] Alexander Johnston, *History of American Politics* (New York, 1877 and later edns.) and *A History of the United States for Schools* (New York, 1885 and later edns.).

From Robert Bridges

Dear Tommy: New York May 8 1889

Arthur Scribner is very well posted on book-publishing terms, and his advice is that you take a royalty, rather than a lump sum for your book. In pushing text-books there is, he says, a constant expenditure of money by the publisher; whereas, a book of standard literature sells on its reputation after a while. You cannot, therefore, get quite so good terms on text-books. He says you will make good terms if you get 10 per cent on the *net* price which in school-books is about 15% less than the *long* or retail price. Of course you would be wise in trying to get 10% on the long price. This would be a very advantageous arrangement.

I am hoping to see you surely at the reunion. Try to get down by Saturday the 15th June.

Chang[1] sends me the enclosed this morning. I am more inclined to believe his California stories since I have been there.

Your Friend BoBridges

ALS (WP, DLC). Enc.: newspaper clipping describing the view from Mount Hamilton in California with the handwritten note: "Comment is unnecessary. W.B.L."

[1] William B. Lee.

From Joseph Ruggles Wilson

My darling son— Clarksville, May 9, '89.

The sight of your dear handwriting has as usual done me "lots" of good. What would I not give to have been present when your Centennial oration was exciting the admiration of so many! I can hardly imagine what line of thought you took, to prevent the piling up of still more straw upon the heap which the threshers of the G. W. theme have for so long been lifting to the astonished sky. No doubt, however, you gave the matter a new turn—for I am beginning to think that there is no limit either to your acquirements or your ability to use them. I am certainly vastly proud of my noble boy, in every way.

I thought I had written you to express my great satisfaction upon reading your article in the March no. of the "Political Sci. Quarterly." First, let me thank you for the copy of this journal which came to hand early in April. Secondly, allow me to say that nothing could be finer than your treatment of Bryce's book. Your style seems to me to be constantly improving. It has lost nearly altogether that gauze-veil which sometimes either suspended or disguised the meaning. Your meanings are now always clear and sharply clear. Or, there is only occasionally a sentence which the pruning-knife of criticism might improve by cutting away a certain impeding redundancy. However, I altogether envy you your facility and your freshness of expression, and your ability to get down to the bottoms of things from which to bring to the surface what you wish your readers to see, and to see moist with a certain rhetorical smile upon it all which is infinitely winning. Perhaps you *praise* Mr. Bryce too much; so it struck me. Was it partly because you wished to show generosity to a rival in the same field of investigation?

I dread to hear of your undertaking still more original work; although it will, in a sense, be a walk through some of the off-meadows of your present studies, to collect materials for the historical volume you have agreed to furnish. What has become of the text-book? I had hoped to see it advertised before this. Please, dearest of my heart, do not overtask your time and surburden your mind. I agree with you, though, that you are the very man who can impartially review the scenes of our American story which lie between '29 and '89—60 years, not all eventful, but some of them in which history is packed like sardines. What will you say, I wonder, as touching the causes that made our prodigious war inevitable. But you know so much more than I do, now, that I feel like sitting at your feet to learn as you once sat at mine.

I am to leave for the Gen. Assembly on the 14th. It will convene at Chattanooga—and remain in session for about ten days I presume:—and then I am to preach the baccalaureate sermon at what is known as the University of Tennessee—at Knoxville—on the 2nd day of June.

Josie and I are reasonably well, and do not allow ourselves to be inconsolable in view of the vacancy which the world presents—your sweet mother being out of it. Love from us both to dear Ellie, & to the babies if they have gumption enough to receive it. And for yourself love & love & love:

Your affc Father

ALS (WP, DLC) with EAWhw notes on env.

From Albert Bushnell Hart

My dear Prof Wilson: Cambridge, Mass. May 10, 1889.

After consultation with the Longmans, they desire me to close the arrangement with you for the third volume of the Epoch series, provided a time not too distant may be set for its completion. There would be a certain advantage in having the volumes follow each other in order. I expect to be ready about a year hence. Could you not, with reasonable assurance, look forward to turning in your MS. at the beginning of the second College year hence, i e September 1890? If that, or somewhere near that time, seems to you probable, the arrangement may be closed at once: and the Longmans will at any time submit an agreement.

I hope now to get Hosmer[1] for the first volume, and then to have it announced

As to the details, they may be settled at a later time. Can you not find it convenient to make me a visit in Cambridge some time before the middle of June? At any rate, we shall find an opportunity to discuss the whole matter

I send you a little circular on books on Civil government, which may interest you. We have quite a collection of these text books—mostly very poor ones,—which is at your service. For the Epoch, I can aid you with some very careful bibliographies prepared by my students, and referring directly by number to all books in the college library.

Sincerely yours Albert Bushnell Hart

ALS (WP, DLC) with WWhw notation on env.: "Ans. May 13/89."

[1] James Kendall Hosmer, Professor of English and German Literature at Washington University in St. Louis, who had recently published a biography of Samuel Adams. Hart did not "get" Hosmer for the first volume in the Epoch Series.

From Stockton Axson

My dear Bro Woodrow, Athens Ga May 10 1889

Your letter, which has set me almost wild with enthusiasm, just received; and I hasten to answer it at once.[1]

It is only too true that journalism, the journalism of the nineteenth century, is only a nearer *approach* to what I really want to do than is the cotton business in which I was engaged.[2] And now in speaking of this other thing, I want to talk very plainly to you. I want to tell you exactly what I think, and feel, and fear, and then I want your honest advice and counsel.

If I have thought once, I have thought a thousand times that I would rather be a college professor of English Literature than to be anything else in the world. One of the principal things which has held me back from this is the fact that I felt unable to persue this course because of the lack of funds.

When, however, the way does seem clear to this end, another difficulty, and a much more serious one confronts me. And it is of this, which I wish to speak plainly. You will understand that I am not robing myself in any false and assumed modesty, for this is no time for that. I really feel that I lack the mental ability to persue this course. This want is due in part to nature, but more especially to a sad lack of training. I have never been to school but four years in my life, one at Fort Mill, one at Davidson, and two here.[3] All the rest has been wasted, utterly wasted. The consequence is that I have been thrown directly into studies which require the trained mind of a man, and I have had to grapple with them with the wild and untutored mind of a child. My mind is therefore utterly incapable of grappling with a knotty subject, and unravelling its mysteries with care and patience.

I have the *desire*, a mad, longing desire to do the work which I mentioned. I am more than willing to work to the best of my ability. I am entirely ready to spend every cent which I have (I suppose I will have about $1400). I am willing to do all this, but the question of *ability* halts me frightened and undecided. It would, of course, be better for me to go quietly on in a course which is not pleasant, possibly not even agreeable, than for me to spend four years more of study, and then be a failure.

Now you see why I hesitate, and you understand my fears. I would like now to have your candid opinion. It would seem that a man should be his own best judge of a thing of this kind, but one's very anxiety hinders his judgement, and an outsider may be better able to give the needed advice.

I know that one doesnt need so logical a mind for literature as he does for some of the sciences; but do you think that it would be *safe* for me to venture on the course proposed knowing what I have told you. I will let the matter rest here until I hear from you. I have never given up all thought of college, for I still hoped in a few years to be able to go to some college, and take just such a course as I now contemplate, but it was only with the end of making of myself a more finished writer, and not of entering Literature as a profession.

It is needless for me to tell you that I am deeply grateful to you for your kind letter, and your generous offer of a year with you at Middletown. I am more grateful than I can say.

Your letter may be the means of changing the whole current

of my life, and if such is the case I hope that current will not "run awry."

With warmest love for all I am

Aff'ly yours Stockton Axson.

ALS (WP, DLC) with WWhw names and addresses on env.

1 Wilson had written suggesting that Stockton Axson attend Wesleyan and live with him and Ellen. Wilson's letter is missing, but Axson, in a memorial address on Professor Caleb Thomas Winchester, recalled Wilson's invitation as follows: "It was from President Wilson that I first heard Professor Winchester's name. I was an undergraduate in the University of Georgia; Dr. Wilson was in the first year of his membership in the Wesleyan faculty, with a high regard for the teaching profession, in general, and for the Wesleyan faculty, in particular; in the subsequent changing years he frequently remarked that there was less 'dead wood' in the Wesleyan faculty than in any other faculty he had known. He wrote me a letter saying that he had an inkling that I could be made into a serviceable teacher of English, and suggested that I come to Wesleyan and study under 'the foremost teacher of English literature in America [Winchester].'" Stockton Axson, "Memorial Address," in *A Memorial to Caleb Thomas Winchester* (Middletown, Conn., 1921), p. 165.

2 With his uncle, Randolph Axson, in the firm of Warren and Axson of Savannah.

3 That is, at the University of Georgia.

An Address[1]

May 10-16, 1889

Nature of Democracy in the United States.

There is one thought which must, I am sure, have been common to all serious minds during the past few weeks, namely, *That it is a long time since 1789*,—if time is to be measured by change. Everything apprises us of the fact that we are not the same nation now that we were then. And I suppose that in looking back to the time in which our government was formed you have gotten the same impression that has for some time been fixing itself upon my mind, and that is, that we started with sundry wrong ideas about ourselves. We thought ourselves rank democrats, whereas we were in fact only progressive Englishmen. Turn the leaves of that sage manual of constitutional interpretation and advocacy, the *Federalist*, and note the perverse tendency of its writers to refer to *Greece and Rome* for prece-

1 In writing this address, delivered before the Owl Club in Hartford on May 17, 1889, Wilson extracted most of its text from "The Modern Democratic State," printed at Dec. 1, 1885, Vol. 5. Small portions, including several passages of poetry, were also drawn from the address on Washington printed at April 30, 1889.

The text printed is that of Wilson's draft typed on half sheets with numerous handwritten emendations. Wilson later made further changes to prepare this text for publication as an essay, "Character of Democracy in the United States," in *Atlantic Monthly*, LXIV (Nov. 1889), 577-88. This essay was published with a few additional changes in Wilson's *An Old Master and Other Political Essays* (New York, 1893), pp. 99-138.

dents,—that Greece and Rome which haunted all our earlier and even some of our more mature years. Recall, too, that familiar story of Daniel Webster which tells of his coming home exhausted from an interview with the first President-elect Harrison, whose Secretary of State he was to be, and explaining that he had been obliged in the course of the conference, which concerned the inaugural address about to be delivered, *to kill nine Roman consuls*, whom it had been the intention of the good conqueror of Tippecanoe publicly to take into office with him. The truth is that we long imagined ourselves related in some unexplained way to all ancient republicans. Strangely enough, too, we at the same time accepted the quite incompatible theory that we were related also to the French philosophical radicals. We claimed kinship with democrats everywhere—with all democrats.

We can now scarcely realize the atmosphere of those thoughts. We do not now often refer to the ancients or to the French for sanction of what we do. We have had abundant experience of our own by which to reckon.

"Hardly any fact in history," says Mr. Bagehot, writing about the middle of the century, "is so incredible as that forty and a few years ago England was ruled by Mr. Percival. It seems almost the same as being ruled by the *Record* newspaper" (Mr Bagehot would now probably say the *Standard* newspaper)[.] "He had the same poorness of thought, the same petty Conservatism, the same dark and narrow superstition." "The mere fact of such a premier being endured shows how deeply the whole national spirit and interest was absorbed in the contest with Napoleon, how little we understood the sort of man who should regulate its conduct,—'in the crisis of Europe,' as Sidney Smith said, 'he safely brought the *Curates' Salaries Improvement Bill* to a hearing'—and it still more shows the horror of all innovation which the recent events of French history had impressed on our wealthy and comfortable classes. They were afraid of catching revolution, as old women of catching cold. Sir Archibald Allison to this day holds that revolution is an infectious disease, beginning no one knows how, and going on no one knows where. There is but one rule of escape, explains the great historian, 'Stay still, don't move; do what you have been accustomed to do, and consult your grandmother on everything.' "

Almost equally incredible to us is the ardour of revolution that then filled the world—the fact that one of the rulers of the world's mind in that generation was *Rousseau*, the apostle of all that is fanciful, unreal, and misleading in politics. To be ruled by him was like taking an account of life from *Mr. Rider Haggard.* And yet there is still much sympathy in this timid world for the dull people who felt safe in the hands of Mr. Percival; and happily much sympathy still among those who can conceive ideals for those also who caught a generous elevation of spirit from the speculative enthusiasm of Rousseau.

Indeed, I think that you will agree with me that for us who stand in the dusty, matter-of-fact world of to-day there is even a touch of pathos in recollections of the ardour for democratic liberty that filled the air of Europe and America a century ago with such quickening influences. We may even catch ourselves regretting that the innoculations of experience have closed our systems against the infections of hopeful revolution.

"Bliss was it in that dawn to be alive,
But to be young was very heaven!—oh times
In which the meagre, stale, forbidding ways
Of custom, law, and statute took at once
The attraction of a country in romance!
When Reason seemed the most to assert her rights,
When most intent on making of herself
A prime Enchantress—to assist the work
Which then was going forward in her name!
Not favoured spots alone, but the whole earth,
The beauty wore of promise, that which sets
(As at some moment might not be unfelt
Among the bowers of paradise itself)
The *budding* rose above the rose *full blown*.["]

Such was the inspiration which, not Wordsworth alone, but Coleridge also and many another generous spirit whom we love caught in that day of hope.

It is common to say, in explanation of our regret that that dawn and youth of democracy's day is past; that our principles are cooler now and more circumspect, with the coolness and circumspection of advanced years. It seems to some that as our sinews have hardened our enthusiasms have become tamer and more decorous: that as experience has grown idealism has declined.

But to speak thus is to speak with old self-deception as to the character of our politics. If we are suffering disappointment, it is the disappointment of an awakening: we were dreaming[.]

For we never had any business harkening to Rousseau or consorting with Europe in revolutionary sentiment. Our Government, founded one hundred years ago, was no type of an experiment in advanced democracy, as we allowed Europe and even ourselves to suppose; it was simply an adaptation of English constitutional government. If we suffered Europe to study our institutions as instances in point touching experimentation in politics *she was the more deceived.* If we began the *first* century of our national existence under a similar impression ourselves, there is the greater reason why we should start out upon a *new* century of national life with accurate conceptions about our place in history. It is my modest purpose to-night to make such contribution as I may to this end. I shall, therefore, ask you to note:

(1) That there are certain influences astir in this century which make for democracy the world over, and that these influences owe their origin in part to the radical thought of the last century; but that it was not such forces that made us democratic, nor are we responsible for them.

(2) That, so far from owing our governments to these general influences, we began, not by carrying out any theory, but by simply carrying out a history, inventing nothing, only establishing a specialized species of English government. That we founded, not Democracy, but Constitutional government, in America.

(3) That the government which we set up thus in a quite normal manner has nevertheless *changed greatly* under our hands by reason both of growth and of the operation of the general democratic forces,—the European or rather world-wide domocratic forces, of which I have spoken; and

(4) That the very *size* to which our governmental organism has attained, and more particularly this new connection of its character and destiny with the character and destiny of the the [*sic*] common democratic forces of the age of steam and electricity have created new *problems of organization* which it behooves us to meet in such spirit and with such measures as I shall briefly indicate before closing. If you will vouchsafe me much kind patience, I will make such expedition as I may in this large undertaking.

First, then, for the forces which are bringing in democratic temper and method the world over. You familiarly know what these forces are, but it will be profitable to our thought to pass them once more in review. They are freedom of thought and the diffusion of enlightenment among the people. Steam and electricity have coöperated with systematic popular education to accomplish this diffusion. The progress of popular education and the progress of democracy have been inseparable. The publication of their great *Encyclopaedia* by Diderot and his associates in France in the last century was the sure sign of the change that was setting in. Learning was turning its face away from the studious few to the curious many. The intellectual movement of the modern time was emerging from the narrow courses of scholastic thought and beginning *to spread itself abroad* over the extended, if shallow, levels of the common mind. The serious forces of democracy will be found, upon analysis, to reside, not in the disturbing doctrines of eloquent revolutionary writers, not in the turbulent discontent of the pauperized and oppressed, but in the educational forces of the last hundred and forty years which have elevated the masses in many countries to a plane of understanding and of orderly, intelligent purpose more nearly on a level with the average man of the hitherto governing classes. The movements towards democracy which have mastered all the other political tendencies of our own day are not older than the middle of the last century: and that is just the age of the now ascendent movement towards systematic popular education.

Organized popular education is, after all, however, only *one* of the quickening influences which have been producing the general enlightenment which is everywhere becoming the promise of general liberty: or, rather, it is only part of a great whole vastly larger than itself. Schools are but separated seedbeds in which only the staple thoughts of the steady and stay-at-home people are prepared and nursed. Not much of the world, after all, goes to school in the school-house. But through the mighty influences of commerce and the press *the world itself has become a school.* The air is alive with the multitudinous voices of information. Steady trade-winds of intercommunication have sprung up which carry the seeds of education and enlightenment, wheresoever planted, to every quarter of the globe. No scrap of new thought can escape being borne away from its place of birth by these all-absorbing currents. No idea can be kept exclusively at home, but is taken up by the trader, the reporter, the traveller, the missionary, the explorer, and is *given to all the world,* in the newspaper, the novel, the memoir, the poem, the treatise, till every community may know, not only itself, but all the world as well for the small price of learning to read and keeping its ears open. All the world, so far as its news and its stronger thought are concerned, is fast being made every man's neighbour.

Carlyle unquestionably touched one of the greater truths concerning modern democracy when he declared it to be the result of *printing*. In the newspaper press a whole population is made critic of all human affairs: democracy is "virtually extant," and "democracy virtually extant will insist on becoming palpably extant." Looked at in the large, the newspaper press is a type of democracy, bringing all men without distinction under comment made by any man without distinction; every topic reduced to a common standard of news; everything noted and argued about be [by] everybody. Nothing could give surer promise of popular power than the activity and alertness of thought which is made through such agencies to accompany the training of the public schools. The activity may often be misdirected or unwholesome, may sometimes be only feverish and mischievous, a grievous product of narrow information and hasty conclusion; but it is none the less a growing and potent activity. It at least marks the initial stages of effective thought[.] It makes men conscious of the existence and interest of affairs lying outside of the dull round of their own daily lives. It gives them nations, instead of neighborhoods, to look upon and think about. They catch glimpses of the international connexions of their trades, of the universal application of law, of the endless variety of life, of diversities of race, of a world teeming with men like themselves and yet full of strange customs, puzzled by dim omens, stained by crime, ringing with voices familiar and unfamiliar.

And all this a man can get nowadays without stirring from home, by merely spelling out the print that covers every piece of paper about him. If men throw themselves from any reason into the swift and easy currents of travel, they find themselves brought daily face to face with persons native of every clime, with practices suggestive of whole histories, with a thousand things which challenge curiosity to satisfy itself, with enquiries which enlarge knowledge of life and shake one imperatively loose from old preconceptions.

These are the forces which have established the drift towards democracy. When all sources of information are accessible to all men alike, when the world's thought and the world's news are scattered broadcast where the poorest may find them, the non-democratic forms of government find life a desperate venture.

Exclusive privilege needs privacy, but cannot have it. Kingship of the elder patterns needs sanctity, but can find it nowhere obtainable in a world of news items and satisfied cur[i]osity. The many will no longer receive submissively the thought of a ruling few, but insist upon having opinions of their own. The reaches of public opinion have been infinitely extended: the number of voices that must be heeded in legislation and in executive policy has been infinitely multiplied. Modern influences have inclined every man to clear his throat for a word in the world's debates. They have popularized everything they have touched.

In the newspapers, it is true, there is but little concerted between the writers; little but piece-meal opinion is created by their comment and argument; there is no common voice amidst their counsellings. But the *aggregate* voice thunders with tremendous volume; and that aggregate voice is 'public opinion.' Popular education and cheap printing and travel vastly thicken the ranks of thinkers everywhere that their influence is felt, and by rousing the multitude to take *knowledge* of the affairs of government directly prepare the time when the multitude will, so far as possible, take *charge* of the affairs of government,–the time when, to repeat Carlyle's phrase, democracy will become palpably extant.

But, mighty as such forces are,–democratic as they are,–no one can fail to see that they are inadequate to *produce of themselves* such a government as ours. There is little in them of *constructive* efficacy. They could not of themselves build any government at all. They are critical, analytical, questioning, quizzing forces;–but not architectural, not powers that devise and build. The influences of popular education, of the press, of travel, of commerce, of the innumerable agencies which nowadays send knowledge and thought in quick pulsations through every part and member of society, do not necessarily mould men for effective endeavour. They may only confuse and and [*sic*] paralyze the mind with their myriad stinging lashes of excitement. They may only strengthen the impression that 'the world's a stage' and that no one need do more than sit and look on through his ready glass, the newspaper. They overwhelm one with impressions, but do they give stalwartness to his manhood; do they make his hand any steadier on the plow, or his purpose any clearer with reference to the duties of the moment? They stream light about him, it may be, but do they clear his vision? Is he better able to see because they give him countless things to look at? Is he better able to judge because they fill him with a delusive sense of knowing everything? Activity of mind is not necessarily strength of mind. It may manifest itself in mere dumb show; it may run into jigs as well as into strenuous work at noble tasks. A man's farm does not yield its fruit the more abundantly in its season because he reads the world's news in the papers. A merchant's shipments do not multiply because he studies history. Banking is none the less hazardous to the banker's capital or taxing to his powers because the best writing of the best essayists is to be bought cheap.

Having thus expanded my first point by exhibiting the general forces of that democracy which we recognize as belonging to the age and to the world at large, rather than exclusively or even characteristically to ourselves, I now ask you to turn to view by contrast our origins in politics.

How different were the forces back of us! Nothing establishes the republican state save trained capacity for self-government, practical aptitude for public affairs, habitual soberness and temperateness of united action. When we look back to the moderate sagacity and steadfast, self-contained habit in self-government of the men to whom we owe the establishment of our institutions in the United States we are at once made aware that there is no communion between their democracy and the radical thought and restless spirit called by that name in Europe. There is almost nothing in common between popular outbreaks such as took place in France at her great Revolution and the establishment of a government like our own. Our memories of the year 1789 are as far as possible removed from the memories which Europe retains of that pregnant year. We *manifested* one hundred years ago what Europe *lost*, namely self-command, self-possession. Democracy in Europe, outside of closeted Switzerland, has acted always *in rebellion* as a *destructive* force: it can scarcely be said to have had, even yet, any period of organic development. It has built such temporary governments as it has had opportunity to erect on the old foundations and out of the discredited materials of centralized rule, elevating the people's representatives for a season to the throne, but securing almost as little as ever of that every-day local self-government which lies so near to the heart of liberty. Democracy in America, on the other hand, and in the English colonies, has had, almost from the first, a truly organic growth. There was nothing revolutionary in its movements: it had not to overthrow other polities; it had only to organize itself. It had, not to create, but only to expand self-government. It did not need to spread propaganda: it needed nothing but to methodize its ways of living.

In brief, we were doing nothing essentially new a century ago. Our politics and our character were derived from a

> "land that freemen till,
> That sober-suited Freedom chose.
> The land, where girt with friends or foes
> A man may speak the thing he will;
>
> "A land of settled government,
> A land of just and old renown,
> Where freedom broadens slowly down
> From precedent to precedent:
>
> "Where faction seldom gathers head,
> But by degrees to fulness wrought,
> The strength of some diffusive thought
> Hath time and space to work and spread."

Our strength and our facility alike inhered in our traditions; those traditions made our character and shaped our institutions[.] Liberty is not something that can be created by a document; neither is it something which, when created, can be laid away in a document, a completed work. It is an *organic* principle, a principle of *life*, renewing and being renewed. Democratic institutions are never done; they are like living tissue, always a-making. It is a strenuous thing, this of living the life of a free people; and our success in it depends upon training, not upon clever invention.

Our democracy, plainly, was not a body of doctrine: it was a stage of development. Our democratic state was not a piece of developed theory, but a piece of developed habit. It was not created by mere aspirations or by new faith; it was built up by slow custom. Its process was experience, its basis old wont, its meaning national organic oneness and effective life. It came, like manhood, as the fruit of youth. An immature people could not have had it, and the maturity to which it was vouchsafed was the maturity of freedom and self-control. Such government as ours is a form of conduct, and its only stable foundation is character. A particular form of government may no more be *adopted* than a particular type of character may be adopted: both institutions and character must be developed by conscious effort and through transmitted aptitudes.

Governments such as ours are founded upon discussion and government by discussion comes as late in political as scientific thought in intellectual development. It is a habit of state life created by long-established circumstance, and possible for a nation only in the adult age of its political life. The people which successfully maintains it must have gone through a period of political training which shall have prepared it by gradual steps of acquired privilege for assuming the entire control of its affairs. Long and slowly widening experience in local self-direction must have prepared them for national self-direction. They must have acquired adult self-reliance, self-knowledge, and self-control, adult soberness and deliberateness of judgment, adult sagacity in self-government, adult vigilance of thought and quickness of insight. When practiced, not by small communities, but by wide nations, democracy, far from being a crude form of government, is possible only amongst peoples of the highest and steadiest political habit. It is the heritage of races purged alike of hasty barbaric passions and of patient servility to rulers, and schooled in temperate common counsel. It is an institution of political noon-day, not of the half light of political dawn. It can never be made to sit easily or safely on *first generations*, but strentghens through long heredity. It is poison to the infant, but tonic to the man. Monarchies may be made, but democracies must grow.

It is a deeply significant fact, .˙. , again and again to be called to mind, that only in the United States, in a few other governments begotten of the English race and in Switzerland where old Teutonic habit has had the same persistency as in England, have examples yet been furnished of successful democracy of the modern type. England herself is close upon democracy. Her backwardness in entering upon its full practice is no less instructive as to the conditions prerequisite to democracy than is the forwardness of her offspring. She sent out to all her colonies which escaped the luckless beginning of being made penal settlements comparatively small, homogeneous populations of pioneers with strong instincts of self-government and with no social materials out of which to build government otherwise than democratically. She herself, meanwhile, retained masses of population never habituated to participation in government, untaught in political principle either by the teachers of the hustings or of the school house. She has had to appraoch democracy, therefore, by slow and cautious extensions of the franchise to those prepared for it: while her better colonies, born into democracy, have had to receive all comers into its pale. She has been paring down exclusive privileges and levelling classes; they have from the first been asylums of civil equality. They have assimilated new, she has prepared old, populations.

Erroneous as it is to represent government as only a commonplace sort of business, little elevated in method above merchandizing, and to be regulated by counting-house principles, the favour easily won for such views among our own people is very significant. It means self-reliance in government. It gives voice to the eminently modern democratic feeling that government is no hidden cult to be left to a few specially prepared individuals, but a common everyday concern of life, even if the biggest such concern. It is this self-confidence, in many cases mistaken, which is gradually spreading among other peoples, less justified in it than are ours.

One cannot help marvelling that facts so obvious as these should have escaped the perception of some of the sagest thinkers and most thorough historical scholars of our day. And yet so it is. Sir Henry Maine even, the great interpreter to Englishmen of the historical forces operative in law and social institutions, has utterly failed, in his plausible work on Popular Government to distinguish the democracy, or rather the popular government, of the English race, which is bred by slow circumstance and founded upon habit, from the democracy of other peoples, which is bred by discontent and founded upon revolution. He has missed that most obvious teaching of events, that successful democracy differs from unsuccessful in being a product of history, a product of forces not suddenly become operative, but slowly working upon whole peoples for generations together. The level of democracy is the level of everyday habit, the level of common national experiences, and lies far below the elevations of ecstasy to which the revolutionist climbs.

So much for my second main point, as to the origins of our institutions in constitutional precedents rather than in democratic precepts. It is my object to consider, in the third place, the changes which have been or may be wrought in our institutions by means of the influences of the age, of our own growth as a political organism, and of our adulterated populations.

While there can be no doubt about the derivation of our government from habit rather than from doctrine, from English experience rather than from European thought; while there can be no doubt that our institutions were originally but products of a long, unbroken, unperverted constitutional history; and while there can be no doubt that we shall preserve our institutions in their integrity and efficiency only so long as we keep true in our practice to the traditions from which our strength is derived; there is as little doubt that the forces peculiar to the new civilization of our day, and not only these but also the restless forces of European democratic thought and anarchic turbulence brought to us in such alarming masses by immigration, have deeply affected and may deeply modify the forms and habits of our politics.

All *vital* governments,—and by vital governments I mean those which have life *in their outlying members*, as well as life in their heads,—all systems in which self-government indeed *lives* and retains its self-possession must be governments *by neighbours*, by peoples homogeneous not only but characterized within by the existence of easy neighbourly knowledge of each other among their members. Not foreseeing steam and electricity or the diffusions of news and knowledge which we have witnessed, our fathers were right in thinking it impossible for the government which they had founded to spread without strain or break over the whole of the continent. Were not California now as near neighbour to the Atlantic states as Massachusetts once was to New York, national self-government on our present scale would assuredly hardly be possible or conceivable even. Modern science, scarcely less than our pliancy and steadiness in political habit, may be said to have created the United States of to-day.

Upon some aspects of this growth it is very pleasant to dwell, and very profitable. It is significant of a strength which it is even inspiring to contemplate. The advantages of bigness accompanied by abounding life are many and invaluable. It is impossible among us to hatch in a corner any plot which will *affect* more than a corner. With life everywhere throughout the continent it is impossible to seize illicit power over the whole people by seizing any central offices. To hold Washington would be as useless to a usurper as to hold Duluth. *Self-government cannot be usurped.*

It has been said by a French writer that the autocratic ascendency of Andrew Jackson illustrated anew the long credited tendency of democracies to give themselves over to one hero. The country is older now than it was when Andrew Jackson delighted in his power, and few can believe that it would again approve or applaud childish arrogance and ignorant arbitrariness like his: but even in his case, singular and ominous as it was, it must not be overlooked that he was suffered only to strain the Constitution, not to break it. He held his office by orderly election; he exercised its functions within the letter of the law; he could silence not one word of hostile criticism; and, his second term expired, he passed into private life as harmlessly as did James Monroe. A nation that can quietly reabsorb a vast victorious army is no more safely free and healthy than is a nation that could reabsorb such a President as Andrew Jackson, sending him into seclusion at the Hermitage to live without power and die almost forgotten.

A huge stalwart organism like our own nation, with quick life in every individual limb and sinew, is apt, too, to have the strength of variety of judgment. Thoughts which in one quarter kindle enthusiasm may in another meet coolness or arouse antagonism. Events which are fuel to the *passions* of one section may be but as a passing wind to the minds of another section. No single *moment* of indiscretion, surely, can easily betray the whole country at once. There will be entire populations still cool, self-reliant, unaffected. Revolutions have to take such nations as ours in detail. Generous emotions sometimes sweep whole peoples, but evil passions, happily, sinister views, base purposes do not and cannot. Sedition cannot surge through the hearts of a wakeful nation as patriotism can. In such organisms poisons diffuse themselves slowly, only healthful life has unbroken course. The sweep of agitations set afoot for purposes unfamiliar or uncongenial to the customary popular thought is broken by a thousand obstacles. It may be easy to re-awaken old enthusiasms, but it must be infinitely hard to create new ones, and impossible to surprise the people into unpremeditated action.

I wish to give full weight to these great advantages of our big and strenuous and yet familiar way of conducting affairs; but I wish at the same time to make very plain the influences which are pointing towards threatening changes in our politics—changes which threaten loss of organic wholeness and soundness in carrying on an efficient and honest government. The union of strength with bigness depends upon the maintenance of *character*, and it is just the character of the nation which is being most deeply affected and modified by the enormous immigration which year after year pours into the country from Europe: our own temperate blood, schooled to self-possession and to the measured conduct of self-government is receiving a constant infusion and yearly experiencing a partial corruption of foreign blood: our own equable habits have been crossed with the feverish habits of the restless old world. We are unquestionably facing an ever-increasing difficulty of self-command with ever-deteriorating materials, possibly with degenerating fibre. We have so far succeeded in remaining

> "A nation yet, the rulers and the ruled—
> Some sense of duty, something of a faith,
> Some reverence for the laws ourselves have made,
> Some patient force to change them when we will,
> Some civic manhood firm against the crowd."

But we must reckon our power to continue to do so with a people made up of minds cast in every mould of race, minds inheriting every bias of environment, warped by the diverse histories of a score of different nations, warmed or chilled, closed or expanded by almost every climate in the globe.

What was true of our early circumstances is not true of our present. We are not now simply carrying out under normal conditions the principles and habits of English constitutional history. Our tasks of construction are not done: we have, not simply to conduct but also to preserve and freshly adjust our government. Europe has sent her habits to us; and she has sent also her political philosophy,—that philosophy which has never been purged by the cold bath of practical politics. The communion which we did not have at first wi[t]h her heated and mistaken ambitions, with her radical speculative habit in politics, with her readiness to experiment in forms of government, we may possibly have to suffer now that we are receiving her populations. Not only printing and steam and electricity have gotten hold of us to expand our English civilization, but also those general, and yet to us alien, forces of democracy of which I have spoken; and these are apt to tell disastrously upon our Saxon habits in government.

It is thus that I am brought to my fourth and last point. I have endeavored (1) to show you the general forces of democracy which have been sapping old forms of government in all parts of the world; (2) to remind you of the error of supposing ourselves indebted to those forces for the creation of our government, or in any way connected with them in our origins; and (3) to point out the effect they have nevertheless had upon us as parts of the general influences of the age as well as by reason of our vast immigration from Europe,—an immigration which brings to us European ideas and European habits. I am now to speak of the *new problems* which have been prepared for our solution by reason of our growth and of the effects of immigration, and which may require as much political capacity for their proper solution as any that faced the architects of our government.

These problems are chiefly problems of organization and leadership. Were the nation homogeneous, were it composed simply of later generations of the same stock by which our institutions were planted, few adjustments of the old machinery of our politics would, perhaps, be necessary to meet the exigencies of growth. But every added element of variety, particularly every added element of foreign variety, complicates even the simpler questions of politics. The dangers attending that variety which is heterogeneity in so vast an organism as ours are of course the dangers of *disintegration*, nothing less: and it is unwise to think these dangers remote and merely contingent because they are not as yet pressing. We are conscious of oneness as a nation, of vitality, of strength, of progress; but are we often conscious of common thought in the concrete things of national policy? Does not our legislation, rather, wear the features of a vast conglomerate? Are we conscious of any national leadership: are we not, rather, dimly conscious of being pulled in a score of directions by a score of crossing influences and contending forces?

This vast and miscellaneous democracy of ours must be led: its giant faculties must be schooled and directed. Leadership cannot belong to the multitude: masses of men cannot be self-directed. Neither can groups of communities[.] We speak of the sovereignty of the people, but that sovereignty, we know very well, is of a peculiar sort, quite unlike the sovereignty of a king or of a small easily concerting group of confident men. It is judicial merely, not creative. It passes judgment or gives sanction, but it connot direct or suggest. It furnishes standards, not policies. Questions of government are infinitely complex questions, and no multitude can of themselves form clear-cut, comprehensive, consistent conclusions touching them. And yet without such conclusions, without single and prompt purposes, government cannot be carried on. Neither legislation nor administration can be done at the ballot-box. The people can only accept the governing act of representatives. But the size of the modern democracy necessitates the exercise of persuasive power by dominant minds in the shaping of popular judgments in a very different way from that in which it was exercised in former times. "It is said by eminent censors of the press," said Mr. Bright on one occasion in the House of Commons, "that this debate will yield about thirty hours of talk, and will end in no result. I have observed that all great questions in this country require thirty hours of talk many times repeated before they are settled. There is much shower and much sunshine between the sowing of the seed and the reaping of the harvest, but the harvest is generally reaped after all." And so it must be in all self-governing nations of to-day. They are not a single audience within sound of an orator's voice; but a thousand audiences. Their actions do not spring from a single thrill of feeling, but from slow conclusions following upon much talk. The talk must slowly percolate through the whole mass. It cannot be sent through them straight like the pulse which is stirred by the call of a trumpet. A score of platforms in every neighbourhood must ring with the insistent voice of controversy; and for a few hundreds who hear what is said by the public speakers, many thousands must read of the matter in the newspapers, discuss it interjectionally at the breakfast table, desultorily in the street-cars, laconically on the streets, dogmatically at dinner. And all this with a certain advantage, of course. Through so many stages of consideration passion cannot possibly hold out. *It gets chilled by over-exposure.* It finds the modern popular state organized for giving and hearing counsel in such a way that those who give it must be careful that it is such counsel as will *wear well*, and those who hear it handle and examine it enough to *test* its wearing qualities to the utmost.

All this, however, when looked at from another point of view, but illustrates an infinite difficulty of achieving *energy and organization.* There is a certain peril almost of disintegration attending such phenomena.

Everyone now knows familiarly enough how we accomplished the wide aggregations of self-government characteristic of the modern time, how we have articulated governments as vast and yet as whole as continents like our own. The instrumentality has been *representation*, of which the ancient world knew nothing, and lacking which it always lacked national integration. Because of representation and the railroads to carry representatives to distant capitals, we have been able to rear colossal structures like the government of the United States as easily as the ancients gave political organization to a city, and our great building is as stout as their little one.

But not until recently have we been able to see the full effects of thus sending men to legislate for us at capitals distant the breadth of a continent. It makes the leaders of our politics many of them mere names to our consciousness instead of real persons, whom we have seen and heard, and whom we know. We have to accept rumours concerning them, we have to know them through the variously coloured accounts of others: we can seldom test our impressions of their sincerity by standing with them face to face. Here certainly the ancient pocket republics had much the advantage of us: in them citizens and leaders were always neighbours; they stood constantly in each other's presence. Every Athenian knew Themistocles' manner and gait and address, and had felt directly the just influence of Aristides. No Athenian of a later period needed to be told of the vanities and fopperies of Alcibiades, any more than the elder generation needed to have described to them the personality of Pericles.

Our separation from our leaders is the greater peril because democratic government more than any other needs organization in order to escape disintegration, and it can have organization only by full knowledge of its leaders and full confidence in them. Just because it is a vast body to be persuaded it must know its persuaders: in order to be effective it must always have choice of men who are *impersonated policies*. Just because none but the finest mental batteries, with pure metals and unadulterated acids, can send a current through so huge and yet so rare a medium as democratic opinion, it is the more necessary to look to the excellence of these instrumentalities. There is no permanent place in democratic leadership except for him who 'hath clean hands and a pure heart'[.] If other men come temporarily into power among us, it is because we cut our leadership up into so many little parts and do not subject any one man to the purifuing influences of centred responsibility. Never before was consistent leadership so necessary; never before was it necessary to concert measures over so vast areas, to adjust laws to so many interests, to make a compact and intelligible unit out of so many fractions, to maintain a central and dominant force where there are so many forces.

It is a noteworthy fact that the admiration for our institutions which has during the past few years so suddenly grown to large proportions among publicists abroad is almost all of it directed to the *restraints* we have effected upon the action of government. Sir Henry Maine thought our federal Constitution an admirable *reservoir* in which the mighty waters of democracy are held at rest, kept back from free destructive course. Lord Rosebery has wondering praise for the *security of our Senate* against usurpation of its functions by the House of Representatives. Mr. Goldwin Smith supposes the saving act of organization for a democracy to be the drafting and adoption of a *written constitution*. Thus it is always the *statical*, never the *dynamic* forces of our government which are praised. The greater part of our foreign admirers find our success to consist in the achievement of stable safeguards against hasty or retrogressive action: we are asked to believe that we have succeeded because we have taken Sir Archibald Allison's advice and have resisted the infection of revolution by staying quite still.

But, after all, progress is motion, government is action. The waters of democracy are useless in their reservoirs unless they may be used to drive the wheels of policy and administration. Though we be the most law-abiding and law-directed nation in the world, law has not yet attained to such efficacy among us as to frame or adjust or administer *itself*. It may restrain but it cannot lead us: and I believe that unless we concentrate legislative leadership, leadership, i.e., in progressive policy, unless we give leave to our nationality and practice to it *by* such concentration, we shall sooner or later suffer something like national paralysis in the face of emergencies. We have no one in Congress who stands for the nation. Each man stands but for his part of the nation,—and so management and combination, which may be effected in the dark, are given the place that should be held by centred and responsible leadership, which would of necessity work in the focus of the national gaze.

What is the valuable element in *monarchy* which causes men constantly to turn to it as to an ideal form of government, could it but be kept pure and wise? It is its *cohesion*, its readiness and power to act, its abounding loyalty to certain concrete things, to certain visible persons, its concerted organization, its perfect model of progressive order. Democracy abounds with vitality; but how shall it combine with its other elements of life and strength this power of the governments that know their own minds and their own aims? We have not yet reached the age when government may be made impersonal.

I believe that the only way in which we can preserve our

nationality in its integrity and its its [*sic*] old-time originative force in the face of growth and imported change is by *concentrating* it, by putting leaders forward vested with abundant authority in the conception and execution of policy. There is plenty of the old vitality in our national character to tell, if you will but give it leave. Give it leave and it will the more impress and mould those who come to us from abroad. I believe that we have not made enough of leadership.

"A people is but the attempt of many
To rise to the completer life of one;
And those who live as models for the mass
Are singly of more value than they all."

We shall not again have a true national life until we compact it by such legislative leadership as other nations have. But, once thus compacted and embodied, our nationality is safe. An accute English historical scholar has said that "the Americans of the United States are a nation because they once obeyed a king": we shall remain a nation only by obeying leaders.

"Keep but the model safe
New men will rise to study it."

Woodrow Wilson

WWT MS. (WP, DLC).

To Henry Holt & Company

Dear Sirs, Middletown, Conn., 13 May, 1889

Allow me to thank you very much for your suggestion concerning the publication of my text-book on Government. I am preparing two, one a large book, of somewhat elaborate plan, for college use, the other an elementary and small book for schools.

I am writing them, however, at the suggestion of Mr. D. C. Heath, though not under any contract with him. To him, therefore, belongs, of course, the first examination of the *MSS.*

You will allow me to say, however, that, were it otherwise, I should be very glad to have you see and, if you pleased, publish my books. Very sincerely yours, Woodrow Wilson

ALS (Henry Holt Archives, NjP).

To Albert Bushnell Hart

My dear Prof. Hart, Middletown, Conn., 13 May, 1889.

I sincerely hope that you will not think me unreasonable when I say that the extension of time suggested by the Longmans is not sufficient to made [make] me feel justified in consenting to do the "Epoch." Were the period to be discussed one which had been frequently worked over, not one two-thirds of which is practically new ground (1850-1889), were the materials for its history collected and thereby made easily accessible, and, above all, were I not already feeling something like the strain of over-work, I might consent to restate its main points in fifteen months, notwithstanding the fact that three of those months were already "mortgaged"[.] But the truth of the matter is, that, with my nervous disposition, if I were to suspend over myself the whip of a contract, to descend upon me in case I should not do something that it would be barely possible for me to do if my health and opportunities kept at their best, my health would, I am afraid, incontenently desert me at the critical moment. In brief I dare not, under the circumstances, undertake to do the work within less than twenty or twenty-four months.

If I have caused you serious delay or embarrassment in your editorship of the series by not saying this at first, I am heartily sorry; but I did not feel, when writing my first letter to you on this subject, that the affair had advanced to a stage at which I could suggest the terms, as to time, etc., that would suit me.

I quite agree with you that it is extremely desirable that the volumes of the series should follow each other in somewhat rapid succession: it is for that reason that I now decline the third volume, instead of asking whether a still further extension of time would not be possible.

I cannot decline, however, without expressing my sincere regret that I am not to have the pleasure of knowing and co-operating with you in work which would itself be so attractive.

Very sincerely Yours, Woodrow Wilson

TCL (RSB Coll., DLC).

A News Item

[May 18, 1889]

Comparative Politics.

A large and cultural audience was present at Good Will Hall last evening, by invitation of the Owl Club, to listen to the very able and scholarly address of Professor Woodrow Wilson, Ph.D., LL.D., of Johns Hopkins university, upon "Comparative Politics."

Printed in the *Hartford Courant*, May 18, 1889.

From Melville R. Hopewell

Dear Sir Tekamah, Nebraska, May 20 1889

I have collected altogether for lease of your mothers lands for season of 1889, for grass & pasture $120.00.

I enclose receipts for taxes, covering all her land I think, in this County for 1888.	91.33.
Com 10% on $120.	12.00.
New York Dft to bal. less Ex	16.77
	$120.00 [*sic*]

The boom, or activity in lands, which I expected to see by this time, has not yet arrived. I have had some inquiries for prices, for a portion of the lands, but no offers, which I considered desirable. Will communicate to you any that I may have.

I presume your P. O. is still at Bryn Mawr, and so direct. If not, it will likely be forwarded to you.

Yours Truly M. R. Hopewell

You will notice 40. acres that was not paid on for 1887, it must have been oversight of Treasurer.

ALS (WP, DLC) with WWhw notation on env.: "Receipt 1888." Encs.: tax receipts dated May 18 and 20, 1889.

From Stockton Axson

Dear Bro Woodrow, Athens Ga May 21/89

I havent answered your last letter not because of a lack of interest, but simply because I have had my hands so full of final examinations that I have had no time for any thing else. However I have just finished my last regular final, and so draw a breath of relief.

I have, of course, thought of little during the past ten days, except the "new scheme." I have been trying to weigh every thing carefully, and see exactly what is the best thing for me to do. . . .

With a great deal of love for yourself, sister and "all" the children I am Aff'ly yours Stockton Axson.

ALS (WP, DLC) with WWhw notation on env.: "Ans. by E. May 25/89."

Stockton Axson to Ellen Axson Wilson

My dear Sister Athens Ga May 27th 1889

Your letter received this afternoon, and I hasten to answer it. The plan of entering Wesleyan College next term suits my idea to a "T." In the first place I am sure that a year there would be infinitely more valuable to me than a year here, and in the second place I would be able to start on my life's work a year earlier, and this is no small item.

Now I will be fully able to keep up with the Senior Class, if I can only get in it. . . .

So if this plan can be carried out it is undoubtedly the best yet considered, and it seems to me that there should be no real good reason why I shouldnt be allowed to do this. They could try me and if I dont prove satisfactory they could turn me out. Bro Woodrow might mention that in nearly all my studies here I have come distinguished, in fact, in all so far as I know except Chemistry. I will be able to get certificates from the professors testifying to the satisfactoriness of my course. I will mail you a catalogue tomorrow. . . .

I will never be able to sufficiently thank you and Bro Woodrow for all your interest and enthusiasm in this matter.

Hoping that you are all well I am, with a great deal of love

Your aff brother Stockton Axson.

ALS (WP, DLC).

From Albert Bushnell Hart

My dear Prof. Wilson: Cambridge, Mass. June 1, 1889.

You will of course understand that I did not mean to let your courteous letter stand so long unanswered. I began an answer the moment I received it, which seemed however somewhat beyond my authority: and I am now able to complete it.

The publishers agree with me that we cannot let a question of time stand between us. In stipulating the fall of 1890, I thought I was suggesting a time which you had yourself believed possible; the publishers are anxious to see the third volume out as early as may be: they are still very anxious to have your coöperation; and I am authorized to say that if you will undertake the volume, you will not be held to any period within the next two years. They strongly desire to see the MS. by Jan'y 1891; and it would be to the interest of the series and of the volume;

but if you need a longer time to satisfy yourself—the public is more easily satisfied,—you need not feel hurried. All I ask of you is to put this next after your brief text-book of civil government; and to look forward to finishing as long before the summer of 1891 as possible.

One special reason, among many others, why I have been anxious to get your consent to this proposition is the feeling that the work ought to be done by a man who can impartially judge the South, and its degree of responsibility and its share in the restoration of the Union

If further argument be necessary, I shall be glad to come down and put the case in oral form. I shall be exceedingly disappointed if we are not able to come to an agreement on this new basis of time.

Sincerely yours, Albert Bushnell Hart

ALS (WP, DLC) with WWhw notation on env.: "Ans. June 3/89."

To Albert Bushnell Hart

My dear Prof. Hart, Middletown, Conn., 3 June, '89

Your letter of June 1st. reached me this morning. Certainly you and the Messrs. Longmans are very generous, and I appreciate very highly indeed your willingness to make some sacrifice of plans to secure my cooperation. Of course I have no more resistance to offer. I accept the task with pleasure.

Let me say that I particularly appreciate your reference to judging the part played by the South during the period of which I am to write. Your confidence in my impartiality I greatly value—and shall hope to deserve. Though born in the South and bred in its sympathies, I am not of Southern-born parents. My father was born in Ohio, my mother in England. Ever since I have had independent judgments of my own I have been a Federalist(!) It is this mixture of elements in me—full identification with the South, non-Southern blood, and Federalist principles—that makes me hope that a detachment of my affectionate, reminiscent sympathies from my historical judgments is not beyond hoping for.

I shall certainly aim to make Jan'y, 1891 my time limit in the completion of the volume; and I believe that I shall be all the better able to realize my purpose because I know that any real necessity for continuing my preparation of it beyond that time will be accepted by you and by the publishers as compatible with our understanding at the first. I will assuredly use all possible diligence, and shall not expect to use all the time given me,—though no man may foresee his opportunities or his strength, or pre-engage his inspiration.

I shall be glad to know, when you have time to write, your ideas about the plan to be followed in the series. I suppose that it will be eminently desirable that a certain uniformity of plan should obtain throughout.

Very sincerely Yours, Woodrow Wilson

TCL (RSB Coll., DLC).

EDITORIAL NOTE

WILSON'S "THE STATE"

The Editorial Note, "Wilson's Plan for a Textbook in Civil Government," Volume 5, has pointed out that as early as the spring of 1886 Wilson had conceived the general structure, scope, and objectives of the book that was to become *The State: Elements of Historical and Practical Politics*. As he made clear in the announcement printed in the Editorial Note just cited, Wilson had in mind a general work in modern comparative government. But he was determined not to write another abstract treatise on political theory, or even a merely descriptive book. He would describe not only the structures of modern governments, but also their organic, historical development and their actual functioning. Finally, he planned to include a statement about the functions and objectives of government based upon what he deemed to be the best modern thought on this subject, as well as upon his own well-considered judgments.

Wilson seems to have done some general background reading for *The State* during the summer of 1886, which he and Ellen spent in Clarksville with the elder Wilsons. We know little about Wilson's reading during these months, so sparse is the documentation for this period. However, a body of notes in his papers indicates that he was doing preliminary reading and research upon various aspects of federal and state constitutional problems.[1] We may be sure that by the end of that summer Wilson at least understood the formidable dimensions of his task—that he had, as he would say later in the Preface to *The State*, conceived nothing less than a unique book, one for which he had no sure guidelines. It was little wonder that he should write to Herbert Baxter Adams on November 27, 1886: "I have not yet gone over, with even a first survey, the whole field; and the habit of my mind is such that until I see my *whole* subject I can't write on a part of it anything that I would like to put forth in public as *results*. I am, therefore, so to say, *waiting on myself*, waiting on the slowness of my thought,—expecting the time when, all the ingredients of the *entire* substance of my studies being mixed in, the several portions of my treatment may crystalize symmetrically."

[1] See the Editorial Note, "Wilson's Plan for a Textbook in Civil Government," Vol. 5.

The very full documentary record for the academic year 1886-87 at Bryn Mawr makes it abundantly clear that Wilson had time for no more than sporadic reading for *The State* between October 1886 and June 1887. Sheer and unrelenting academic necessity forced him to spend most of his time during these months preparing lectures for new courses in English, French, American, and Renaissance and Reformation history.[2] This fact, and knowledge of his deficiency in German, was one of the reasons for Wilson's strong (but unfulfilled) desire to spend the year 1887-88 in Europe. He also wanted to observe first-hand the functioning of European governments.[3]

Wilson set methodically to work on *The State* once final examinations were over at Bryn Mawr and he and Ellen went to Gainesville, Georgia, on about June 15, 1887, so that Ellen could be near her aunt, Mrs. Brown, during the last stage of her second pregnancy. There is a sketchy and obviously very early outline of *The State* in his papers.[4] If, as seems possible, he composed this outline soon after arriving in Gainesville, then it can be said that the book had already taken fairly clear shape in his mind. However, Wilson's main task for the summer of 1887 was to make a good start on the volumes in the collaborative series on government and public law then being edited by Professor Heinrich Marquardsen of the University of Erlangen under the general title, *Handbuch des Oeffentlichen Rechts der Gegenwart.* This series was published in four volumes, each with many parts, at Freiburg im Breisgau and Tübingen between 1883 and 1906. Wilson had acquired all the parts that he would use in writing *The State* at least by the spring of 1887. A complete list of the titles in the Marquardsen series to that date follows:

Volume I, First Half:
- Karl Gareis, *Allgemeines Staatsrecht* (1883).
- Paul Hinschius, *Staat und Kirche* (1883).

Volume I, Second Half:
- Otto von Sarwey, *Allgemeines Verwaltungsrecht* (1884).
- August von Bulmerincq, *Völkerrecht oder Internationales Recht* (1884).
- H. Marquardsen, *Politik* (1884).

Volume II, First Half:
- Paul Laband, *Das Staatsrecht des Deutschen Reiches* (1883).
- A. Leoni, *Das Staatsrecht der Reichslande Elsass-Lothringen* (1883).

Volume II, Second Half:
- H.J.F. Schulze, *Das Staatsrecht des Königreichs Preussen* (1884).
- C. E. Leuthold, *Das Staatsrecht des Königreichs Sachsen* (1884).

Volume III, First Half:
- Wilhelm Vogel, *Das Staatsrecht des Königreichs Bayern* (1884).
- L. Gaupp, *Das Staatsrecht des Königreichs Württemberg* (1884).

2 See the Editorial Note, "Wilson's Teaching at Bryn Mawr, 1886-87," Vol. 5.
3 See, e.g., WW to H. B. Adams, Dec. 5, 1886, Vol. 5.
4 Outline entitled "*Government,*" on loose sheets (WP, DLC).

K. Schenkel, *Das Staatsrecht des Grossherzogth. Baden* (1884).
Karl Gareis, *Das Staatsrecht des Grossherzogth. Hessen* (1884).

Volume III, Second Half:

Otto Büsing *et al.*, *Das Staatsrecht von Mecklenburg-Schwerin* . . . (1884).

Georg Meyer *et al.*, *Das Staatsrecht der Thüringischen Staaten* . . . (1884).

J. Wolffson *et al.*, *Das Staatsrecht der freien und Hanse-Städte Hamburg, Lübeck,* Bremen (1884).

Volume IV, First Half:

J. Ulbrich, *Das Staatsrecht der österreichisch-ungarischen Monarchie* (1884).

Alois von Orelli, *Das Staatsrecht der schweizerischen Eidgenossenschaft* (1885).

Hermann von Holst, *Das Staatsrecht der vereinigten Staaten von Amerika* (1885).

L. de Hartog, *Das Staatsrecht des Königreichs der Niederlands* (1886).

André Lebon, *Das Staatsrecht der französischen Republik* (1886).

T. A. Aschehoug, *Das Staatsrecht der vereinigten Königreiche Schweden und Norwegen* (1886).

Precisely how many of these volumes Wilson took with him to Gainesville and read during the summer of 1887, we do not know, since he wrote only one reading date–that of August 18, 1887, in Schulze–in all the Marquardsen volumes. Wilson's marginal comments on Dicey's *Lectures Introductory to the Study of the Law of the Constitution*, printed at September 19, 1887, reveal that he was doing some reading in addition to the Marquardsen monographs during this period.

An additional outline of *The State* in the Wilson Papers[5] is much more detailed than the one mentioned earlier in this note. It may well be that Wilson prepared this outline before he left Gainesville. In any event, by October 1887 he knew almost precisely the kind of book that he would write. Moreover, he had taken careful pains to guarantee that his course work at Bryn Mawr and the first series of lectures on administration that he was to give at the Hopkins in early 1888 would provide grist for the mill of *The State*. As he put it in his letter to Ellen on October 3, 1887, he simply had to make his lectures serve the purposes of the textbook.

Wilson's major undergraduate course at Bryn Mawr in 1887-88 was one that he called "Politics." For this he prepared about ten lectures on the origins of government and then went into his main subject–federal and state government in the United States–which he of course intended to discuss thoroughly in *The State*. He apparently covered much the same ground in his first-semester graduate course at Bryn Mawr that year; but in the second semester he extended the purview of his graduate lectures to Roman law and comparative

[5] It is a two-page WWhw and WWsh MS. listing forty-two topics and beginning: "1. The Probable Original basis of govt. among Aryan races. . . ."

modern politics.[6] His lectures at the Johns Hopkins in early 1888 on the functions of government and particularly on the structure of certain major central governments were also prepared with *The State* very much in mind.[7]

Wilson completed the notes for his "Politics" lectures on May 31, 1888. Then came final examinations and the end of the academic year at Bryn Mawr on about June 8. Immediately afterward, Wilson began to write *The State*,[8] and he left such a clear trail that we can follow the course and progress of his work without difficulty.

Wilson wrote *The State* in sections, which he numbered consecutively when the book was completed. Perhaps he wrote out preliminary drafts of the sections in longhand or shorthand. No such drafts have survived. However, he did apparently type on his Caligraph his more or less final drafts on half sheets. Only a few pages of this copy—a portion of the chapter on the government of Greece—have survived. These pages are so clean that Wilson must have typed them from an earlier copy, and it does not seem unreasonable to assume that he prepared his entire manuscript in similar form. However that may have been, he did not write the sections in any particular order. For example, the shorthand on the envelope of Joseph R. Wilson, Jr., to Woodrow Wilson, June 8, 1888, is a portion of Chapter XV, "The Functions of Government," and indicates that Wilson may have written this chapter first.

Wilson was able to piece much if not most of *The State* together from lectures and other writings already in hand. Or it would perhaps be better to say that the lectures, lecture notes, and other materials[9] that Wilson had in hand by early June 1888 provided the more or less basic text which he then re-wrote in more polished and sophisticated—and sometimes condensed—form.

The notes for Wilson's first lectures in his "Politics" course were the basis of the first two chapters of *The State*, "The Probable Origin of Government" and "The Probable Early Development of Government." For Chapters III-V, on the governments of Greece and Rome, Roman law and administration, and Teutonic government, Wilson drew very extensively from his Greek-Roman history course at Bryn Mawr in 1885-86,[10] and perhaps also from his graduate lectures on Roman law at the same institution. The reader may see how Wilson assimilated his notes for his Greek-Roman history course into *The State* by comparing his lecture, "*Reforms of Solôn*," printed at October 15, 1885, Volume 5, with Sections 72 and 73, "Solon's Economic Reforms" and "Solon's Political Reforms: the Four Property Classes," in *The State*. Wilson was able in like manner to use portions of his

[6] See the Editorial Note, "Wilson's Teaching at Bryn Mawr and the Johns Hopkins, 1887-88," Vol. 5.

[7] *ibid.*

[8] See E. I. Renick to WW, Aug. 17, 1888, n. 1, Vol. 5, for evidence that Wilson had begun to write *The State* at least by June 19, 1888.

[9] Some of Wilson's outlines, research notes, etc., remain in the Wilson Papers, Library of Congress, grouped together as notes relating to *The State*. These documents are of such a random nature that it would be very hazardous to try to date them.

[10] For a guide, see the Editorial Note, "Wilson's Teaching at Bryn Mawr, 1885-86," Vol. 5.

lectures on English and French history at Bryn Mawr in 1886-87 in Chapters VI and X on the governments of France and Great Britain. Chapter XV, "The Functions of Government," is a reduced version of the two Hopkins lectures with the same title printed at February 17 and 18, 1888, Volume 5.

The longest chapter in *The State*, Chapter XI, "The Government of the United States," was a more or less edited and upgraded transcript of Wilson's shorthand lecture notes for his Bryn Mawr "Politics" course. However, Wilson was able to use portions of these notes for Chapter XI with only minor emendations. A comparison of a transcript of a portion of these notes and its counterpart in *The State* provides a graphic illustration:

Transcript of Wilson's Lecture Notes.

The House, like the Senate, has its own rules regulative of the number and duties of its officers and of its ways of doing business; and these rules, like those of the Senate, are chiefly concerned with the creation and empowering of the great number of standing committees. The committees of the House are not, however, elected by the ballots of the members, as the committees of the Senate are; they are appointed by the Speaker; and this power of the Speaker's to appoint standing committees of the House makes him one of the most powerful officers in the whole government. The committees of the House are even more influential than those of the Senate in determining what shall be done with reference to matters referred to them: they, as a matter of fact, have it in their power to control almost all the acts of the House. The Senate, being a comparatively small body, has time to consider fully the reports of its committees and general[ly] matters [manages] to control its own conclusions; but the House of Representatives is too large to do much debating; it must be guided by its committees or it must do nothing. It is this fact

From *The State*, pp. 552-53.

1071. *Organization of the House*. The House, like the Senate, has its own rules, regulative of the number and duties of its officers and of its methods of doing business; and these rules, like those of the Senate, are chiefly concerned with the creation and empowering of a great number of standing committees. The committees of the House are not, however, elected by ballot, as the committees of the Senate are; they are appointed by the presiding officer of the House, the 'Speaker'; and this power of the Speaker's to appoint the committees of the House makes him one of the most powerful officers in the whole government. For the committees of the House are even more influential than those of the Senate in determining what shall be done with reference to matters referred to them: they as a matter of fact have it in their power to control almost all the acts of the House. The Senate, being a comparatively small body, has time to consider fully the reports of its committees, and generally manages to control its own conclusions. But the House is too large to do much debating: it must be guided by its committees or it must do nothing. It is this

which makes the Speaker's prerogative of appointment so vastly important: he determines who shall be on the committees and the committees determine what the House shall do: he nominates those who shape legislation.	fact which makes the Speaker's power of appointment so vastly important: he determines who shall be on the committees, and the committees determine what the House shall do. He nominates those who shape legislation.
The appointing power of the Speaker often makes his election a very exciting part of the business of the new House: for he is always selected of course with reference to what he will do about the membership of the committees.	1072. The appointing power of the Speaker often makes his election a very exciting part of the business of each new House: for he is always selected, of course, with reference to what he will do in constituting the principal committees.

Wilson drew most of his basic information for his chapters on the governments of Imperial Germany and Prussia, Switzerland, Austria-Hungary, and Sweden-Norway from the Laband, Schulze, Orelli, Ulbrich, and Aschehoug volumes in the Marquardsen series. He relied upon Lebon in the same series to a lesser degree. These chapters in *The State* were in turn undoubtedly based upon Wilson's lectures on modern central governments in his Hopkins series of 1888, most of which are missing. In preparing these lectures and the manuscript draft of *The State,* Wilson seems to have worked from his own detailed digests of large portions of the above-mentioned volumes. There are such digests of the Laband, Schulze, and Orelli volumes in the Wilson Papers. Perhaps Wilson made similar digests of Lebon, Ulbrich, and Aschehoug. Or he may have written directly from these three, for he made only a few marginal notes and numerous linear markings and underscorings on the pages of these monographs.

In his Preface, Wilson candidly acknowledged his heavy indebtedness to the Marquardsen series, and any one interested in doing so can easily perceive this indebtedness by making his own textual comparisons. Generally speaking, Wilson digested the Marquardsen volumes. Occasionally, his own text bore considerable resemblance to the text that he was working from. However, Wilson almost invariably imposed his own interpretation, drew useful comparisons, and ended with what might be called an independent text. The two following examples will illustrate the above generalizations:

From Laband, p. 42.	From *The State*, p. 256.
Die Kompetenz des Bundesraths lässt sich nicht durch eine allgemeine Regel abgränzen. Da der Beschluss des Bundesrathes den Willen der Gesammtheit der Bundesglieder, also des Trägers der Reichssouveränetät, darstellt, so ist die Kompetenz des Bundes-	407. *Functions of the Bundesrath.*–The *Bundesrath* occupies a position in the German system in some respects not unlike that which the Roman Senate held in Rome's government (sec. 149). It is, so to say, the residuary legatee of the constitution; all

rathes eine allgemeine, d. h. alle Bethätigungen und Aeusserungen des staatlichen Willens des Reiches umfassend, welche nicht durch Bestimmungen der Reichsgesetze anderen Organen, insbesondere dem Kaiser und den Reichsbehörden, zugewiesen sind. Keine Thätigkeit des Reiches ist dem Bundesrath grundsätzlich entzogen; er ist Organ der Gesetzgebung, der Verwaltung, der Rechtsprechung.

functions not specifically entrusted to any other constitutional authority remain with it; no power is in principle foreign to its jurisdiction. It has, therefore, a composite character; it is at one and the same time an administrative, a legislative, and a judicial body.

From Laband, pp. 51-52.

Die Verhandlungen des Reichstages sind öffenlich. R.V. Art. 22 Abs. 1. Ein Ausschluss der Oeffentlichkeit durch Beschluss des Reichstages ist unzulässig; eine nicht öffentliche Sitzung hätte nur den Charakter einer Privat-Zusammenkunft von Reichstags-Mitgliedern; ein in einer solchen Sitzung gefasster Beschluss wäre kein "Reichstagsbeschluss" in Sinne der Verfassung, sondern ein Beschluss von Privatpersonen. Wahrheitsgetreue Berichte über Verhandlungen in den öffentlichen Sitzungen des Reichstages bleiben von jeder Verantwortlichkeit frei. R.V. Art. 22 Abs. 2. Strafges. B. 12.

From *The State*, p. 262.

417. *Sessions of the Reichstag.*—The *Reichstag* meets at the call of the Emperor, who must call it together at least once each year; he may convene it oftener. He must summon at the same time the *Bundesrath.* The sessions of the *Reichstag* must be public; it is not within its choice to make them private. A private session is regarded as, legally, only a private conference of the members of the *Reichstag* and can have no public authority whatever.

Wilson's dependence upon the Marquardsen series is additionally and strikingly revealed by the fact that Wilson wrote no chapter on the government of Russia—even though his early outlines of *The State* had envisaged such a chapter—because no monograph on Russia in the Marquardsen series was available in 1888. (In fact, it was never written.) Wilson does not seem ever to have planned a chapter on the government of Italy. Hence the fact that E. Brusa's *Das Staatsrecht des Königreichs Italien*, in the fourth Marquardsen volume, appeared in 1888 and was too late for Wilson's possible use is of no consequence. Wilson himself never added chapters on Russia and Italy in later editions,[11] although he did acquire the Brusa volume in 1892.

Wilson's reading for *The State* of course ranged far beyond the Marquardsen series, even for the chapters based principally upon the

[11] Edward Elliott, in his considerable revision of *The State* published in 1918, included chapters on Russia and Italy.

Handbuch. Since Wilson listed his major sources and authorities at the end of each chapter, it would be redundant to repeat them here, especially since the working bibliography printed at March 27, 1890, gives a more comprehensive view of Wilson's reading than do the end-of-chapter bibliographies in *The State.* It is perhaps enough to point out that *The State*, like all of his earlier major works, was built upon extensive foundations in research and writing that he had been laying since his undergraduate days at Princeton.

Wilson's letter to Robert Bridges of August 26, 1888, indicates that he was far advanced in the composition of the manuscript of *The State* by this date. His letter to Munroe Smith of November 12, 1888, makes it fairly certain that Wilson had completed the manuscript, except for the chapter on the government of Russia, which he still intended to write, and sections of chapters that will be noted later.

At this point, Wilson began to ask friends and other scholars to read portions of his manuscript. To Professor Smith he sent Chapter IV on Roman dominion and law, a part of Chapter V on Teutonic government, and Chapter XIV on the nature and development of law. At about the same time, Wilson sent the chapter on the governments of Switzerland to John Martin Vincent, who was then writing a doctoral dissertation on that subject at the Johns Hopkins. Wilson also left Chapter III on the governments of Greece and Rome for John Franklin Jameson to read when he, Wilson, was in Providence for a lecture at Brown University on January 11, 1889. Jameson returned the chapter when Wilson came back for a second lecture at Brown on January 18; Vincent seems to have handed the chapter on Switzerland to Wilson when the latter arrived in Baltimore for his second series of lectures on administration at the Johns Hopkins on about February 10, 1889.

The documentation for the early months of 1889 is so complete that we are able to follow Wilson closely in the last stages of the revision and completion of his manuscript. Jameson had been very disappointed with the chapter on Greece and Rome and had made numerous suggestions for changes.[12] Wilson worked at revising this chapter off and on until about mid-March.[13] Having devoted his Hopkins lectures of 1889 to local government, Wilson also was busy rewriting these lectures as the sections on local government for his manuscript of *The State.*[14] Wilson's letter to his wife of March 9, 1889, discloses that he had completed the manuscript except for the revision of the section on the imperial Roman system and for writing the section on English colonial administration. These he had finished by April 26, when he wrote to Professor Smith asking him to return the chapters previously sent to him.

Wilson spent most of his spare time during May 1889 writing the

[12] See Jameson's diary entries dated Jan. 16 and 17, 1889, printed in J. F. Jameson to WW, Jan. 22, 1889, n. 2.

[13] Wilson's notes on his additional research for this chapter remain in his papers, along with some of the typed pages which he re-wrote.

[14] The notes for two of these lectures are printed at Feb. 13 and 14, 1889. Wilson wrote "C" (for "copied") across some of the pages of these notes, indicating that he had cannibalized them.

rough draft of the first part of a high school textbook in American government, printed at May 1, 1889. Perhaps he also put the finishing touches on the manuscript of *The State* at the same time. In any event, he sent copy off to D. C. Heath on June 3, 1889. Page proof began to pour in only slightly more than a month later—probably on about July 15—and Wilson spent the next six weeks reading pages and making an index. He also made some slight revisions in the chapters on Roman law and on the nature and development of law on the basis of Munroe Smith's criticisms, which had come after the manuscript had gone to press.[15] The last page proof—that of the index—came while Wilson was on a brief vacation, and Ellen read and returned it to Heath on about September 5.[16] Wilson had bound books in hand at least by September 23, 1889, when he wrote Smith that he was dissatisfied with the cover and would try to persuade Heath to "remedy the worst features of it."

The State went through many reprintings with minor changes and through new editions with major changes in 1898 (revised and rewritten by Wilson), 1911 (with a revised chapter on Sweden and Norway by Charles H. McIlwain), and 1918 (when it was updated and considerably revised by Edward Elliott). *The State* was also published with an introduction by Oscar Browning by Isbister & Company in London in 1899 and was translated into Russian, Italian, Spanish, and German between 1905 and 1922. The chapter on the government of the United States was published by D. C. Heath and Company as a separate book in 1889 and 1899 under the title, *The State and Federal Governments of the United States. A Brief Manual for Schools and Colleges.*

Contemporary reviewers and scholarly analysts have long since pointed out the deficiencies of *The State*, while other commentators have emphasized that it was the first textbook in comparative government in any language and was used by students throughout the world for more than a generation. The progress of scholarship and the political upheavals of the twentieth century have rendered obsolete great portions of *The State*. However, the last four chapters mark such a milestone in Wilson's general thinking about law and government, and are so essential to clear understanding of his future political and scholarly development, that they are printed below. Wilson's footnotes have been numbered consecutively within chapters.

[15] See WW to M. Smith, June 12 and Aug. 5, 1889, and M. Smith to WW, Aug. 26, 1889.

[16] The page proofs in the Wilson Papers consist of a title page in EAWhw, and what seem to be the original set of pages of the Preface, Topical Analysis, and Index and the revised pages of the main body of the book.

Four General Chapters from *The State*

[*c. June 3, 1889*]

XIII.

NATURE AND FORMS OF GOVERNMENT.

1154. *Government Rests upon Authority and Force.*—The essential characteristic of all government, whatever its form, is authority. There must in every instance be, on the one hand, governors, and, on the other, those who are governed. And the authority of governors, directly or indirectly, rests in all cases ultimately on *force*. Government, in its last analysis, is organized force. Not necessarily or invariably organized armed force, but the will of one man, of many men, or of a community prepared by organization to realize its own purposes with reference to the common affairs of the community. Organized, that is, to rule, to dominate. The machinery of government necessary to such an organization consists of instrumentalities fitted to enforce in the conduct of the common affairs of a community the will of the sovereign man, the sovereign minority, or the sovereign majority.

1155. *Not necessarily upon Obvious Force.*—This analysis of government, as consisting of authority resting on force, is not, however, to be interpreted too literally, too narrowly. The force behind authority must not be looked for as if it were always to be seen or were always being exercised. That there is authority lodged with ruler or magistrate is in every case evident enough; but that that authority rests upon force is not always a fact upon the surface, and is therefore in one sense not always practically significant. In the case of any particular government, the force upon which the authority of its officers rests may never once, for generations together, take the shape of armed force. Happily there are in our own day many governments, and those among the most prominent, which seldom coerce their subjects, seeming in their tranquil noiseless operations to run themselves. They in a sense operate without the exercise of force. But there is force behind them none the less because it never shows itself. The strongest birds flap their wings the least. There are just as powerful engines in the screw-propeller, for all she glides so noiselessly, as in the side-wheeler that churns and splashes her way through the water. The better governments of our day—those which rest, not upon the armed strength of governors, but upon the free consent of the governed—are without open demonstration of force in their operations. They are founded upon constitutions and laws whose source and sanction are the will of the majority. The force which they embody is not the force of a dominant dynasty nor of a prevalent minority, but the force of an agreeing majority. And the overwhelming nature of this force is evident in the fact that the minority very seldom challenge its exercise. It is latent just because it is understood to be omnipotent. There is force behind the authority of the elected magistrate, no less than behind that of the usurping despot, a much greater force behind the President of the United States, than behind the Czar of Russia. The difference lies in the *display* of coercive power. Physical force is the prop of both, though in the one it is the last, while in the other it is the first resort.

1156. *The Governing Force in Ancient and in Modern Society.* —These elements of authority and force in government are thus quite plain to be seen in modern society, even when the constitution of that society is democratic; but they are not so easily discoverable upon a first view in primitive society. It is common nowadays when referring to the affairs of the most progressive nations to speak of 'government by public opinion,' 'government by the popular voice'; and such phrases possibly describe sufficiently well all full-grown democratic systems. But no one intends such expressions to conceal the fact that the majority, which utters 'public opinion,' does not prevail because the minority are convinced, but because they are outnumbered and have against them not the 'popular voice' only, but the 'popular power' as well—that it is the potential might rather than the wisdom of the majority which gives it its right to rule. When once majorities have learned to have opinions and to organize themselves for enforcing them, they rule by virtue of power no less than do despots with standing armies or concerting minorities dominating unorganized majorities. But, though it was clearly opinion which ruled in primitive societies, this conception of the might of majorities hardly seems to fit our ideas of primitive systems of government. What shall we say of them in connection with our present analysis of government? They were neither democracies in which the will of majorities chose the ways of government, nor despotisms, in which the will of an individual controlled, nor oligarchies, in which the purposes of a minority prevailed. Where shall we place the force which lay behind the authority exercised under them? Was the power of the father in the patriarchal family power of arm, mere domineering strength of will? What was the force that sustained the authority of the tribal chieftain or of that chief of chiefs, the king? That authority was not independent of the consent of those over whom it was exercised; and yet it was not formulated by that consent. That consent may be said to have been involuntary, *inbred.* It was born of the habit of the race. It was congenital. It consisted of a custom and tradition, moreover, which bound the chief no less than it bound his subjects. He might no more transgress the unwritten law of the race than might the humblest of his fellow-tribesmen. He was governed scarcely less than they were. All were under bondage to strictly prescribed ways of life. Where then lay the force which sanctioned the authority of chief and sub-chief and father in this society? Not in the will of the ruler: that was bound by the prescriptions of custom. Not in the popular choice: over that too the law of custom reigned.

1157. *The Force of the Common Will in Ancient Society.*—The real residence of force in such societies as these can be most easily discovered if we look at them under other circumstances. Nations still under the dominion of customary law have within historical times been conquered by alien conquerors; but in no such case did the will of the conqueror have free scope in regulating the affairs of the conquered. Seldom did it have any scope at all. The alien throne was maintained by force of arms, and taxes were mercilessly wrung from the subject populations; but never did the despot venture to change the customs of the conquered land. Its native laws he no more dared to touch than would a prince of the dynasty which he had displaced. He dared not play with the forces latent in the prejudices, the fanaticism of his subjects. He knew that those forces were volcanic, and that no prop of armed men could save his throne from overthrow and destruction should they once break forth. He really had no authority to govern, but only a power to despoil,—for the idea of government is inseparable from the conception of *legal regulation.* If, therefore, in the light of such cases, we conceive the throne of such a society as occupied by some native prince whose authority rested upon the laws of his country, it is plain to see that the real force upon which authority rests under a government so constituted is after all the force of public opinion, in a sense hardly less vividly real than if we spoke of a modern democracy. The law inheres in the common will: and it is that law upon which the authority of the prince is founded. He rules according to the common will: for that will is, that immemorial custom be inviolably observed. The force latent in that common will both backs and limits his authority.

1158. *Public Opinion, Ancient and Modern.*—The fact that the public opinion of such societies made no choice of laws or constitutions need not confuse for us the analogy between that public opinion and our own. Our own approval of the government under which we live, though doubtless conscious and in a way voluntary, is largely hereditary—is largely an inbred and inculcated approbation. There is a large amount of mere *drift* in it. Conformity to what is established is much the easiest habit in opinion. Our constructive choice even in our own governments, under which there is no divine canon against change, is limited to *modifications.* The generation that saw our federal system established may have imagined themselves out-of-hand creators, originators, of government; but we of this generation have taken what was given us, and are not controlled by laws altogether of our own making. Our constitutional life was made for us long ago. We are like primitive men in the public opinion which preserves, though unlike them in the public opinion which alters our institutions. Their stationary common thought contained the generic forces of government no less than does our own progressive public thought.

1159. *The True Nature of Government.*—What, then, in the last analysis, is the nature of government? If it rests upon authority and force, but upon authority which depends upon the acquiescence of the general will and upon force suppressed, latent, withheld except under extraordinary circumstances, what principle lies behind these phenomena, at the heart of government? The answer is hidden in the nature of Society itself. Society is in no sense artificial; it is as truly natural and organic as the individual man himself. As Aristotle said, man is by nature a social animal; his social function is as normal with him as is his individual function. Since the family was formed, he has not been without politics, without political association. Society, therefore, is compounded of the common habit, an evolution of experience, an interlaced growth of tenacious relationships, a compact, living, organic whole, structural, not mechanical.

1160. *Society an Organism, Government an Organ.*—Government is merely the executive organ of society, the organ through which its habit acts, through which its will becomes operative, through which it adapts itself to its environment and works out for itself a more effective life. There is clear reason, therefore, why the disciplinary action of society upon the individual is exceptional; clear reason also why the power of the despot must recognize certain ultimate limits and bounds; and clear reason why sudden or violent changes of government lead to equally violent and often fatal reaction and revolution. It is only the exceptional individual who is not held fast in his obedience to the common habit of social duty and comity. The despot's power, like the potter's, is limited by the characteristics of the materials in which he works, of the society which he manipulates; and change which roughly breaks with the common thought will lack the sympathy of that thought, will provoke its opposition, and will inevitably be crushed by that opposition. Society, like other organisms, can be changed only by evolution, and revolution is the antipode of evolution. The public order is preserved because order inheres in the character of society.

1161. *The Forms of Government: Their Significance.*—The forms of government do not affect the essence of government: the bayonets of the tyrant, the quick concert and superior force of an organized minority, the latent force of a self-governed majority,—all these depend upon the organic character and development of the community. "The obedience of the subject to the sovereign has its root not in contract but in force,—the force of the sovereign to punish disobedience";[1] but that force must be backed by the general habit (secs. 1200–1206). The forms of government are, however, in every way most important to be observed, for the very reason that they express the character of government, and indicate its history. They exhibit the stages of political development, and make clear the necessary constituents and ordinary purposes of government, historically considered. They illustrate, too, the sanctions upon which it rests.

1162. *Aristotle's Analysis of the Forms of Government.*—It has been common for writers on politics in speaking of the several forms of government to rewrite Aristotle, and it is not easy to depart from the practice. For, although Aristotle's enumeration was not quite exhaustive, and although his descriptions will not quite fit modern types of government, his enumeration still serves as a most excellent frame on which to hang an exposition of the forms of government, and his descriptions at least furnish points of contrast between ancient and modern governments by observing which we can the more clearly understand the latter.

[1] John Morley, *Rousseau*, Vol. II, p. 184.

1163. Aristotle considered Monarchy, Aristocracy, and Democracy (Ochlocracy) the three standard forms of government. The first he defined as the rule of One, the second as the rule of the Few, the third as the rule of the Many.[2] Off against these standard and, so to say, *healthful* forms he set their degenerate shapes. Tyranny he conceived to be the degenerate shape of Monarchy, Oligarchy the degenerate shape of Aristocracy, and Anarchy (or mob-rule) the degenerate shape of Democracy. His observation of the political world about him led him to believe that there was in every case a strong, an inevitable tendency for the pure forms to sink into the degenerate.

1164. *The Cycle of Degeneracy and Revolution.*—He outlined a cycle of degeneracies and revolutions through which, as he conceived, every State of long life was apt to pass. His idea was this. The natural first form of government for every state would be the rule of a monarch, of the single strong man with sovereign power given him because of his strength. This monarch would usually hand on his kingdom to his children. They might confidently be expected to forget those pledges and those views of the public good which had bound and guided him. Their sovereignty would sink into tyranny. At length their tyranny would meet its decisive check at some Runnymede. There would be revolt; and the princely leaders of revolt, taking government into their own hands, would set up an Aristocracy. But aristocracies, though often public-spirited and just in their youth, always decline, in their later years, into a dotage of selfish oligarchy. Oligarchy is even more hateful to civil liberty, is even a graver hindrance to healthful civil life than tyranny. A class bent upon subserving only their own interests can devise injustice in greater variety than can a single despot: and their insolence is always quick to goad the many to hot revolution. To this revolution succeeds Democracy. But Democracy too has its old age of degeneracy—an old age in which it loses its early respect for law, its first amiability of mutual concession. It breaks out into license and Anarchy, and none but a Cæsar can bring it back to reason and order. The cycle is completed. The throne is set up again, and a new series of deteriorations and revolutions begins.

1165. *Modern Contrasts to the Aristotelian Forms of Government.*—The confirmations of this view furnished by the history of Europe since the time of Aristotle have been striking and numer-

[2] Not of the absolute majority, as we shall see presently when contrasting ancient and modern democracy (secs. 1170, 1173).

ous enough to render it still oftentimes convenient as a scheme by which to observe the course of political history even in our own days. But it is still more instructive to contrast the later facts of political development with this ancient exposition of the laws of politics. Observe, then, the differences between modern and ancient types of government, and the likelihood that the historian of the future, if not of the present and the immediate past, will have to record more divergencies from the cycle of Aristotle than correspondences with it.

1166. *The Modern Absolute Monarchy.*—Taking the Russian government of to-day as a type of the vast absolute Monarchies which have grown up in Europe since the death of Aristotle, it is evident that the modern monarch, if he be indeed monarch, has a much deeper and wider reach of power than had the ancient monarch. The monarch of our day is a Legislator; the ancient monarch was not. Ancient society may be said hardly to have known what legislation was. Custom was for it the law of public as well as of private life: and custom could not be enacted. At any rate ancient monarchies were not legislative. The despot issued edicts—imperative commands covering particular cases or affecting particular individuals: the Roman emperors were among the first to promulgate 'constitutions,'—general rules of law to be applied universally. The modern despot can do more even than that. He can regulate by his command public affairs not only but private as well—can even upset local custom and bring all his subjects under uniform legislative control. Nor is he in the least bound to observe his own laws. A word—and that his own word—will set them aside: a word will abolish, a word restore, them. He is absolute over his subjects not only—ancient despots were that—but over all laws also—which no ancient despot was.

1167. Of course these statements are meant to be taken with certain important limitations. The modern despot as well as the ancient is bound by the habit of his people. He may change laws, but he may not change life as easily; and the national traditions and national character, the rural and commercial habit of his kingdom, bind him very absolutely. The limitation is not often felt by the monarch, simply because he has himself been bred in the atmosphere of the national life and unconsciously conforms to it (secs. 1200–1206).

1168. *The Modern Monarchy usually 'Limited.'*—But the present government of Russia is abnormal in the Europe of today, as abnormal as that of the Turk—a belated example of those crude forms of politics which the rest of Europe has outgrown. Turning to the other monarchies of to-day, it is at once plain that they present the strongest contrast possible to any absolute monarchy ancient or modern. Almost without exception in Europe, they are 'limited' by the resolutions of a popular parliament. The people have a distinct and often an imperative voice in the conduct of public affairs.

1169. *Is Monarchy now succeeded by Aristocracy?*—And what is to be said of Aristotle's cycle in connection with modern monarchies? Does any one suppose it possible that when the despotism of the Czar falls it will be succeeded by an aristocracy; or that when the modified authority of the emperors of Austria and Germany or the king of Italy still further exchanges substance for shadow, a limited class will succeed to the reality of power? Is there any longer any place between Monarchy and Democracy for Aristocracy? Has it not been crowded out?

1170. *English and Ancient Aristocracy contrasted.*—Indeed, since the extension of the franchise in England to the working classes, no example of a real Aristocracy is left in the modern world. At the beginning of this century the government of England, called a 'limited monarchy,' was in reality an Aristocracy. Parliament and the entire administration of the kingdom were in the hands of the classes having wealth or nobility. The members of the House of Lords and the crown together controlled a majority of the seats in the House of Commons. England was 'represented' by her upper classes almost exclusively. That Aristocracy has been set aside by the Reform Bills of 1832, 1867, and 1885; but it is worth while looking back to it, in order to contrast a modern type of Aristocracy with those ancient aristocracies which were present to the mind of Aristotle. An ancient Aristocracy *constituted* the state; the English aristocracy merely controlled the state. Under the widest citizenship known even to ancient democracy less than half the adult male subjects of the state shared the franchise. The ancient Democracy itself was a government by a minority. The ancient Aristocracy was a government by a still narrower minority; and this narrow minority monopolized office and power not only, but citizenship as well. There were no citizens but they. They were the State. Every one else existed for the state, only they were part of it. In England the case was very different. There the franchise was not confined to the aristocrats; it was only controlled by them. Nor did the aristocrats of England consider themselves the whole of the State. They were quite conscious—and quite content—that they had the State virtually in their possession; but they looked upon themselves as holding it in trust for the people of Great Britain. Their legislation was, in fact, class legislation, after a very narrow sort; but they did not think that it was. They regarded their rule as eminently advantageous to the kingdom; and they unquestionably had, or tried to have, the real interests of the kingdom at heart. They led the state, but did not constitute it.

1171. *Present and Future Prevalence of Democracy.*—If Aristocracy seems about to disappear, Democracy seems about universally to prevail. Ever since the rise of popular education in the last century and its vast development since have assured a thinking weight to the masses of the people everywhere, the advance of democratic opinion and the spread of democratic institutions have been most marked and most significant. They have destroyed almost all pure forms of Monarchy and Aristocracy by introducing into them imperative forces of popular thought and the concrete institutions of popular representation; and they promise to reduce politics to a single pure form by excluding all other governing forces and institutions but those of a wide suffrage and a democratic representation,—by reducing all forms of government to Democracy.

1172. *Differences of Form between Ancient and Modern Democracies.*—The differences of form to be observed between ancient and modern Democracies are wide and important. Ancient Democracies were 'immediate'; ours are 'mediate,' that is to say, *representative*. Every citizen of the Athenian State—to take that as a type—had a right to appear and vote in proper person in the popular assembly, and in those committees of that assembly which acted as criminal courts; the modern voter votes for a representative who is to sit for him in the popular chamber—he himself has not even the right of entrance there. This idea of representation—even the idea of a vote by proxy—was hardly known to the ancients; among us it is all-pervading. Even the elected magistrate of an ancient Democracy was not looked upon as a representative of his fellow-citizens. *He was the State*, so far as his functions went, and so long as his term of office lasted. He could break through all law or custom, if he dared. It was only when his term had expired and he was again a private citizen that he could be called to account. There was no impeachment while in office. To our thought all elected to office—

whether Presidents, ministers, or legislators—are representatives. The limitations as to the size of the state involved in the absence from ancient conception of the principle of representation is obvious. A State in which all citizens were also legislators must of necessity be small. The modern representative state has no such limitation. It may cover a continent.

1173. *Nature of Democracy, Ancient and Modern.*—The differences of nature to be observed between ancient and modern Democracies are no less wide and important. The ancient Democracy was a class government. As already pointed out, it was only a broader Aristocracy. Its franchise was at widest an exclusive privilege, extending only to a minority. There were slaves under its heel; there were even freedmen who could never hope to enter its citizenship. Class subordination was of the essence of its constitution. From the modern Democratic State, on the other hand, both slavery and class subordination are excluded as inconsistent with its theory, not only, but, more than that, as antagonistic to its very being. Its citizenship is as wide as its native population; its suffrage as wide as its qualified citizenship, —it knows no non-citizen class. And there is still another difference between the Democracy of Aristotle and the Democracy of de Tocqueville and Bentham. The citizens of the former lived for the State; the citizen of the latter lives for himself, and the State is for him. The modern Democratic State exists for the sake of the individual; the individual, in Greek conception, lived for the State. The ancient State recognized no personal rights—all rights were State rights; the modern State recognizes no State rights which are independent of personal rights.

1174. *Growth of the Democratic Idea.*—In making the last statement embrace 'the ancient State' irrespective of kind and 'the modern State,' of whatever form, I have pointed out what I conceive to be the cardinal difference between all the ancient forms of government and all the modern. It is a difference which I have already stated in another way. The *democratic idea* has penetrated more or less deeply all the advanced systems of government, and has penetrated them in consequence of that change of thought which has given to the individual an importance quite independent of his membership of a State. I can here only indicate the historical steps of that change of thought; I cannot go at any length into its causes.

1175. *Subordination of the Individual in the Ancient State.*—We have seen that, in the history of political society, if we have read that history aright, the rights of government—the magistracies and subordinations of kinship—antedate what we now call the rights of the individual. A man was at first nobody to himself; he was only the kinsman of somebody else. The father himself, or the chief, commanded only because of priority in kinship: to that all rights of all men were relative. Society was the unit; the individual the fraction. Man existed for society. He was all his life long in tutelage; only society was old enough to take charge of itself. The state was the only Individual.

1176. *Individualism of Christianity and Teutonic Institutions.*—There was no essential change in this idea for centuries. Through all the developments of government down to the time of the rise of the Roman Empire the State continued, in the conception of the western nations at least, to eclipse the individual. Private rights had no standing as against the State. Subsequently many influences combined to break in upon this immemorial conception. Chief among these influences were Christianity and the institutions of the German conquerors of the fifth century. Christianity gave each man a magistracy over himself by insisting upon his personal, individual responsibility to God. For right living, at any rate, each man was to have only his own conscience as a guide. In these deepest matters there must be for the Christian an individuality which no claim of his State upon him could rightfully be suffered to infringe. The German nations brought into the Romanized and partially Christianized world of the fifth century an individuality of another sort,—the idea of allegiance to individuals (sec. 228). Perhaps their idea that each man had a money-value which must be paid by any one who might slay him also contributed to the process of making men units instead of state-fractions; but their idea of personal allegiance played the more prominent part in the transformation of society which resulted from their western conquests. The Roman knew no allegiance save allegiance to his State. He swore fealty to his *imperator* as to a representative of that State, not as to an individual. The Teuton, on the other hand, bound himself to his leader by a bond of personal service which the Roman either could not understand or understood only to despise. There were, therefore, individuals in the German State: great chiefs or warriors with a following (*comitatus*) of devoted volunteers ready to die for them in frays not directed by the state, but of their own provoking (secs. 226–228). There was with all German tribes freedom of individual movement and combination within the ranks,—a wide play of individual initiative. When the German settled down as master amongst the Romanized populations of western and southern Europe, his thought was led captive by the conceptions of the Roman law, as all subsequent thought that has known it has been, and his habits were much modified by those of his new subjects; but this strong element of individualism was not destroyed by the contact. It lived to constitute one of the chief features of the Feudal System.

1177. *The Transitional Feudal System.*—The Feudal System was made up of elaborate gradations of personal allegiance. The only State possible under that system was a disintegrate state embracing not a unified people, but a nation atomized into its individual elements. A king there might be, but he was lord, not of his people, but of his barons. He was himself baron also, and as such had many a direct subject pledged to serve him; but as king the barons were his only direct subjects; and the barons were heedful of their allegiance to him only when he could make it to their interest to be so, or their peril not to be. They were the kings of the people, who owed direct allegiance to them alone, and to the king only through them. Kingdoms were only greater baronies, baronies lesser kingdoms. One small part of the people served one baron, another part served another baron. As a whole they served no one master. They were not a whole: they were jarring, disconnected segments of a nation. Every man had his own lord, and antagonized every one who had not the same lord as he (secs. 238–243).

1178. *Rise of the Modern State.*—Such a system was, of course, fatal to peace and good government, but it cleared the way for the rise of the modern State by utterly destroying the old conception of the State. The State of the ancients had been an entity in itself—an entity to which the entity of the individual was altogether subordinate. The Feudal State was merely an aggregation of individuals,—a loose bundle of separated series of men knowing no common aim or action. It not only had no actual unity: it had no thought of unity. National unity came at last,—in France, for instance, by the subjugation of the barons by the king (sec. 253); in England by the joint effort of people and barons against the throne,—but when it came it was the ancient unity with a difference. Men were no longer State fractions; they had become State integers. The State *seemed* less like a natural organism and more like a deliberately organized association.

Personal allegiance to kings had everywhere taken the place of native membership of a body politic. Men were now subjects, not citizens.

1179. *Renaissance and Reformation.*—Presently came the thirteenth century with its wonders of personal adventure and individual enterprise in discovery, piracy, and trade. Following hard upon these, the Renaissance woke men to a philosophical study of their surroundings—and above all of their long-time unquestioned systems of thought. Then arose Luther to reiterate the almost forgotten truths of the individuality of men's consciences, the right of individual judgment. Ere long the new thoughts had penetrated to the masses of the people. Reformers had begun to cast aside their scholastic weapons and come down to the common folk about them, talking their own vulgar tongue and craving their acquiescence in the new doctrines of deliverance from mental and spiritual bondage to Pope or Schoolman. National literatures were born. Thought had broken away from its exclusion in cloisters and universities and had gone out to challenge the people to a use of their own minds. By using their minds, the people gradually put away the childish things of their days of ignorance, and began to claim a part in affairs. Finally, systematized popular education has completed the story. Nations are growing up into manhood. Peoples are becoming old enough to govern themselves.

1180. *The Modern Force of Majorities.*—It is thus no accident, but the outcome of great permanent causes, that there is no more to be found among the civilized races of Europe any satisfactory example of Aristotle's Monarchies and Aristocracies. The force of modern governments is not now often the force of minorities. It is getting to be more and more the force of majorities. The sanction of every rule not founded upon sheer military despotism is the consent of a thinking people. Military despotisms are now seen to be necessarily ephemeral. Only monarchs who are revered as seeking to serve their subjects are any longer safe upon their thrones. Monarchies exist only by democratic consent.

1181. *New Character of Society.*—And, more than that, the result has been to give to society a new integration. The common habit is now operative again, not in acquiescence and submission merely, but in initiative and progress as well. Society is not the organism it once was,—its members are given freer play, fuller opportunity for origination; but its organic character is again prominent. It is the Whole which has emerged from the disintegration of feudalism and the specialization of absolute monarchy. The Whole, too, has become self-conscious, and by becoming self-directive has set out upon a new course of development.

XIV.

LAW: ITS NATURE AND DEVELOPMENT

1182. *What Is Law?*—In the nature and development of Law three things stand revealed; namely, the nature, the functions, and the history of government. Law is the will of the State concerning the civic conduct of those under its authority. This will may be more or less formally expressed: it may speak either in custom or in specific enactment. Law may, moreover, be the will either of a primitive family-community such as we see in the earliest periods of history, or of a highly organized, fully self-conscious State such as those of our own day. But for the existence of Law there is needed in all cases alike (1) an organic community capable of having a will of its own, and (2) some clearly recognized body of rules to which that community has, whether by custom or enactment, given life, character, and effectiveness. The nature of each State, therefore, will be reflected in its law; in its law, too, will appear the functions with which it charges itself; and in its law will it be possible to read its history.

1183. *The Development of Law: its Sources.*—Law thus follows in its development, with slow, sometimes with uneven, but generally with quite distinct steps, the evolution of the character, the purposes, and the will of the organized community whose creation it is. The sources whence it springs, therefore, are as various as the means by which an organic community can shape and express its will as a body politic.

1184. 1. *Custom.*[1]—Of course the earliest source of Law is custom, and custom is formed, no one can say definitely how, except that it is shaped by the co-operative action of the whole community, and not by any kingly or legislative command. It is not formed always in the same way; but it always rests upon the same foundation, upon the general acceptance of a certain course of action, that is, as best or most convenient. Whether custom originate in the well-nigh accidental formation of certain habits of action or in a conscious effort on the part of a com-

[1] I adopt here the classification usual in English writings on Jurisprudence. See, *e.g.*, T. E. Holland, *Jurisprudence*, pp. 48 *et seq.*

munity to adjust its practices more perfectly to its social and political objects, it becomes, when once it has been formed and accepted by the public authority, a central part of Law. It is difficult, if not impossible, to discover the exact point at which custom passes from the early inchoate state in which it is merely tending to become the express and determinate purpose of a community into the later stage in which it becomes Law; but we can say with assurance that it becomes Law only when it wins the support of a definite authority within the community. It is not Law if men feel free to depart from it.

1185. Under the reign of customary law that state of things actually did exist which modern law still finds it convenient to take for granted: everybody knew what the law was. The Teutonic hundred-moots, for example (sec. 654), the popular assemblies which tried cases under the early polity of our own ancestors, declared the law by the public voice; the people themselves determined what it was and how it should be applied. Custom grew up in the habits of the people; they consciously or unconsciously originated it; to them it was known and by them it was declared.

1186. 2. *Religion.*–In the earliest times Custom and Religion are almost indistinguishable; a people's customs bear on every lineament the likeness of its religion. And in later stages of development Religion is still a prolific source of Custom. No primitive community contained any critic who could, even in his secret thought, separate Law from Religion. All rules of life bore for the antique mind the same sanction (sec. 30). There were not in its conception rules moral and rules political: morals and religion were indistinguishable parts of one great indivisible Law of Conduct. Religion and Politics soon, indeed, came to have different ministers. In name often, if not always in fact, the priest was distinct from the magistrate. But throughout a very long development, as we have seen (secs. 50, 58, 69, 197), the magistrate either retained priestly functions or was dominated by rules which the priest declared and of which the priest was the custodian.

Thus the early law of Rome was little more than a body of technical religious rules, a system of means for obtaining individual rights through the proper carrying out of certain religious formulæ (sec. 197); and it marked the beginning of the movement of Roman law towards a broad and equitable system of justice when these rules of procedure were changed from sacerdotal secrets into public law by the publication of the Twelve Tables.

1187. 3. *Adjudication.*—One of the busiest and one of the most useful, because watchful, open-minded, and yet conservative, makers of Law under all systems has been the magistrate, the Judge. It is he who in his decisions recognizes and adopts Custom, and so gives it the decisive support of the public power; it is he who shapes written enactments into suitability to individual cases and thus gives them due flexibility and a free development. He is the authoritative voice of the community in giving specific application to its Law: and in doing this he necessarily becomes, because an interpreter, also a maker of Law. Whether deliberately or unconsciously, in expounding and applying he moulds and expands the Law. It is his legitimate function to read Law in the light of his own sober and conscientious judgment as to what is reasonable and just in custom, what practicable, rational, or equitable in legislation.

1188. It is this 'judge-made' law which is to be found, and is therefore so diligently sought for, in the innumerable law Reports cited in our courts. Except under extraordinary circumstances, our courts and those of England will always follow decisions rendered in similar cases by courts of equal jurisdiction in the same state. *A fortiori* do they follow the decisions of the highest courts: by these they are in a sense bound. In the courts of the continent of Europe, on the other hand, decisions are listened to as important expressions of opinion, but not as conclusive authority: are heard much as our own courts or those of England hear the decisions of courts of other states acting under like laws or similar circumstances.

1189. 4. *Equity.*—Equity too is judge-made Law; but it is made, not in interpretation of, but in addition to, the laws which already exist. The most conspicuous types of such Law are the decisions of the Roman Prætor (secs. 201, 202) and those of the English Chancellor (sec. 666). These decisions were meant to give relief where existing law afforded none. The Prætor declared, for instance, that he would allow certain less formal processes than had hitherto been permitted to secure rights of property or of contract, of marriage or of control, etc. The English Chancellor, in like manner, as keeper of the king's judicial conscience, supplied remedies in cases for which the Common Law had no adequate processes, and thus relieved suitors of any hardships they might otherwise suffer from the fixity or excessive formality of the Common Law, and enabled them in many things to obtain their substantial rights without technical difficulty.

1190. After the official decrees of the Prætors had been codified by the Prætor Salvius Iulianus, in the time of the Emperor

Hadrian, and still more after they had been embodied in the Code of Justinian, the *Corpus Juris Civilis*, the Prætor's 'equity' became as rigid and determinate as the law which it had been its function to mend and ameliorate. In the same manner, our own State codes, many of which have fused law and equity in the same courts and under common forms of procedure (sec. 955), have given equity the sanction and consequently the fixity of written law. The English Judicature Act, also, of 1873, merging, as it does, the Common-law and Equity courts into a single homogeneous system (sec. 732), shows at least a strong tendency in the same direction to exist in England. The adjustments of Equity are less needed now that legislation is ever active in mending old and creating new law and, when necessary, new procedure.

In the same case with Equity must be classed the numerous so-called 'fictitious actions' which were the invention of the Common-law courts and which, by means of imaginary suitors or imaginary transactions, duly recorded as if real, enabled things to be done and rights acquired which would have been impossible under any genuine process of the Common Law.

1191. 5. *Scientific Discussion.*—The carefully formed opinions of learned text-writers have often been accepted as decisive of the Law: more often under the Roman system, however, than under our own (secs. 211–213), though even we have our Cokes, our Blackstones, our Storys, and our Kents, whom our courts hear with the greatest possible respect.

1192. 6. *Legislation.*—That deliberate formulation of new Law to which the name Legislation is given is for us of the modern time, of course, the most familiar as well as the most prolific source of Law. For us Legislation is the work of representative bodies almost exclusively; but of course representation is no part of the essential character of the legislative act. Absolute magistrates or kings have in all stages of history been, under one system or another, plenipotent makers of laws. Whether acting under the sanction of Custom or under the more artificial arrangements of highly developed constitutions, father or prætor, king or archon has been a law-giver. So, too, the assemblies of free men which, alike in Greece and in Rome, constituted the legislative authority were not representative, but primary bodies, like the *Landsgemeinden* of the smaller Swiss cantons.

1193. Representation came in with the Germans; and with the critical development of institutions which the modern world has seen many new phases of Legislation have appeared. Modern Law has brought forth those great private corporations whose by-laws are produced by what may very fitly be called private legislative action. We have, too, on the same model, chartered governments, with legislatures acting under special grants of law-making power (secs. 826, 886, 887, 890, 1137).

Legislation has had and is having a notable development, and is now the almost exclusive means of the formulation of new Law. Custom of the older sort, which gave us the great Common Law, has been in large part superseded by acts of legislatures; Religion stands apart, giving law only to the conscience; Adjudication is being more and more restricted by codification; Equity is being merged in the main body of the Law by enactment; Scientific Discussion now does hardly more than collate cases: all means of formulating Law tend to be swallowed up in the one great, deep, and broadening source, Legislation.

1194. *Custom Again.*—Custom now enters with a new aspect and a new method. After judges have become the acknowledged and authoritative mouthpieces of Equity and of the interpretative adaptation of customary or enacted Law; after scientific writers have been admitted to power in the systematic elucidation and development of legal principles; even after the major part of all law-making has fallen to the deliberate action of legislatures, given liberal commission to act for the community, Custom still maintains a presiding and even an imperative part in legal history. It is Custom, the silent and unconcerted but none the less prevalent movement, that is, of the common thought and action of a community, which recognizes changes of circumstance which judges would not, without its sanction, feel, or be, at liberty to regard in the application of old enactments, and which legislators have failed to give effect to, by repeal or new enactments. Laws become obsolete because silent but observant and imperative Custom makes evident the deadness of their letter, the inapplicability of their provisions. Custom, too, never ceases to build up practices legal in their character and yet wholly outside formal Law, constructing even, in its action on Congresses and Parliaments, great parts of great constitutions (secs. 688, 1099, 1107). It constantly maintains the great forces of precedent and opinion which daily work their will, under every form of government, upon both the contents and the administration of Law. Custom is Habit under another name; and Habit in its growth continually adjusts itself, indeed, to the standard fixed in formal Law, but also compels formal Law to conform to its abiding influences. Habit may be said to be the great Law within which laws spring up. Laws can extend but a very little way beyond its limits. They may help it to gradual extensions of its sphere and to slow modifications of its practices, but they cannot force it abruptly or disregard it at all with impunity.

1195. The history of France during the present century affords a noteworthy example of these principles in the field of constitutional law. There we have witnessed this singular and instructive spectacle: a people made democratic in thought by the operation of a speculative political philosophy has adopted constitution after constitution created in the exact image of that thought. But they had, to begin with, absolutely no democratic habit—no democratic custom. Gradually that habit has grown, fostered amidst the developments of local self-direction; and the democratic thought has penetrated, wearing the body of practice, its only vehicle to such minds, to the rural populace. Constitutions and custom have thus advanced to meet one another—constitutions compelled to adopt precedent rather than doctrine as their basis, thought, practical experience rather than the abstract conceptions of philosophy; and habit constrained to receive the suggestions of written law. Now, therefore, in the language of one of her own writers, France has "a constitution the most summary in its text" (leaving most room, that is, for adjustments), "the *most customary in its application*, the most natural outcome of our manners and of the force of circumstances" that she has yet possessed.[2] Institutions too theoretical in their basis to live at first, have nevertheless furnished an *atmosphere* for the French mind and habit: that atmosphere has affected the life of France,—that life the atmosphere. The result some day to be reached will be normal liberty, political vitality and vigor, civil virility.

1196. *Typical Character of Roman and English Law.*—Roman law and English law are peculiar among the legal systems of western Europe for the freedom and individuality of their development. Rome's *jus civile* was, indeed, deeply modified through the influence of the *jus gentium*; it received its philosophy from Greece, and took slight color from a hundred sources; and English law, despite the isolation of its island home, received its jury system and many another suggestion from the continent, and has been much, even if unconsciously, affected in its development by the all-powerful law of Rome. But English and Roman law alike have been much less touched and colored than other systems by outside influences, and have, each in its turn, presented to the world what may be taken as a picture of the natural, the normal, untrammelled evolution of law.

1197. *The Order of Legal Development.*—As tested by the history of these systems, the order in which I have placed the Sources

2 Albert Sorel, *Montesquieu* (Am. trans.), pp. 200, 201.

of Law is seen to be by no means a fixed order of historical sequence. Custom is, indeed, the earliest fountain of Law, but Religion is a contemporary, an equally prolific, and in some stages of national development an almost identical source; Adjudication comes almost as early as authority itself, and from a very antique time goes hand in hand with Equity. Only Legislation, the conscious and deliberate origination of Law, and Scientific Discussion, the reasoned development of its principles, await an advanced stage of growth in the body politic to assert their influence in law-making. In Rome, Custom was hardly separable from Religion, and hid the knowledge of its principles in the breasts of a privileged sacerdotal class; among the English, on the contrary, Custom was declared in folk-moot by the voice of the people,—as possibly it had been among the ancestors of the Romans. In both Rome and England there was added to the influence of the magistrate who adopted and expanded Custom in his judgments the influence of the magistrate (Prætor or Chancellor) who gave to Law the flexible principles and practices of Equity. And in both, Legislation eventually became the only source of Law.

1198. But in Rome Legislation grew up under circumstances entirely Roman, to which English history can afford no parallel. Rome gave a prominence to scientific discussion such as never gladdened the hearts of philosophical lawyers in England. The opinions of distinguished lawyers were given high, almost conclusive, authority in the courts; and when the days of codification came, great texts as well as great statutes and decrees were embodied in the codes of the Empire. The legislation of the popular assemblies, which Englishmen might very easily have recognized, was superseded in the days of the Empire by imperial edicts and imperial codes such as the history of English legislation nowhere shows; and over the formulation of these codes and edicts great jurists presided. The only thing in English legal practice that affords a parallel to the influence of lawyers in Rome is the cumulative authority of judicial opinions. That extraordinary body of precedent, which has become as much a part of the substance of English law as are the statutes of the realm, may be considered the contribution of the legal profession to the law of England.

1199. Savigny would have us seek in the history of every people for a childhood in which law is full of picturesque complexities, a period of form for form's sake and of symbols possessed of mystic significance; a period of adolescence in which a special class of practical jurists make their appearance and law begins to receive a conscious development; a full young manhood in which legislation plays a busy work of legal expansion and improvement; and an old age amusing itself with external and arbitrary changes in legal systems, and finally killed by the letter of the law.[3]

1200. *The Forces Operative in the Development of Law.*—The forces that create and develop law are thus seen to be the same as those which are operative in national and political development. If that development bring forth monarchical forms of government, if the circumstances amidst which a people's life is cast eradicate habits of local self-rule and establish habits of submission to a single central authority set over a compacted state, that central authority alone will formulate and give voice to Law. If, on the other hand, the national development be so favorably cast that habits of self-reliance and self-rule are fostered and confirmed among the people, along with an active jealousy of any too great concentration of only partially responsible power, Law will more naturally proceed, through one instrumentality or another, from out the nation: *vox legis, vox populi.* But in the one case hardly less than in the other Law will express not the arbitrary, self-originative will of the man or body of men by whom it is formulated, but such rules as the body of the nation is prepared by reason of its habits and fixed preferences to accept. The function of the framers of Law is a function of formulation rather than of origination: no step that they can take successfully can lie far apart from the lines along which the national life has run. Law is the creation, not of individuals, but of the special needs, the special opportunities, the special perils or misfortunes of communities. No 'law-maker' may force upon a people Law which has not in some sense been suggested to him by the circumstances or opinions of the nation for whom he acts. Rulers, in all states alike, exercise the sovereignty of the community, but cannot exercise any other. The community may supinely acquiesce in the power arrogated to himself by the magistrate, but it can in no case make him independent of itself.

1201. Here again France furnishes our best illustration. We have a vivid confirmation of the truths stated in such an event as the establishment of the Second Empire. The French people were not duped by Louis Napoleon. The facts were simply these. They were keenly conscious that they were making a failure of the self-government which they were just then attempting; they

[3] Bluntschli, *Geschichte der neueren Staatswissenschaft,* ed. 1881, pp. 627, 628.

wanted order and settled rule in place of fears of revolution and the existing certainty of turbulent politics; and they took the simplest, most straightforward and evident means of getting what they wanted. The laws of Napoleon were in a very real sense their own creation.

1202. *The Power of the Community must be behind Law.*—The law of some particular state may seem to be the command of a minority only of those who compose the state: it may even in form utter only the will of a single despot; but in reality laws which issue from the arbitrary or despotic authority of the few who occupy the central seats of the state can never be given full effect unless in one form or another the power of the community be behind them. Whether it be an active power organized to move and make itself prevalent or a mere inert power lying passive as a vast immovable buttress to the great structure of absolute authority, the power of the community must support law or the law must be without effect. The bayonets of a minority cannot long successfully seek out the persistent disobediences of the majority. The majority must acquiesce or the law must be null.

1203. This principle is strikingly illustrated in the inefficacy of the English repressive laws in Ireland. The consent of the Irish community is not behind them, though the strength of England is, and they fail utterly, as all laws must which lack at least the passive acquiescence of those whom they concern.

1204. There can be no reasonable doubt that the power of Russia's Czar, vast and arbitrary as it seems, derives its strength from the Russian people. It is not the Czar's personal power; it is his power as head of the national church, as semi-sacred representative of the race and its historical development and organization. Its roots run deep into the tenacious, nourishing soil of immemorial habit. The Czar represents a history, not a caprice.

Temporary, fleeting despots, like the first Napoleon, lead nations with them by the ears, playing to their love of glory, to their sense of dignity and honor, to their ardor for achievement and their desire for order.

1205. *Roman Law an Example.*—The law of Rome affords in this respect an admirable example of the normal character of law. It was the fundamental thought of Roman law that it was the will of the Roman people. The political liberty of the Roman consisted in his membership of the state and his consequent participation, either direct or indirect, in the utterance of law. As an individual he was subordinated to the will of the state; but his own will as a free burgess was a part of the state's will: the state spoke his sovereignty. He was an integral part of the organic community, his own power found its realization in the absolute *potestas et majestas populi*. This giant will of the people, speaking through the organs of the state, constituted a very absolute power, by which the individual was completely dominated; but individual rights were recognized in the *equality* of the law, in its purpose to deal equally with high and low, with strong and weak; and this was the Roman recognition of individual liberty.

1206. *The Power of Habit.*—Much of the truth with reference to the character and sanctions of law may be obscured by a failure to make just analysis of the part played by Habit in giving efficacy to enactment. Legislators, those who exercise the sovereignty of a community, build upon the habit of their so-called 'subjects.' If they be of the same race and sharers of the same history as those whom they rule, their accommodation of their acts to the national habit will be in large part unconscious: that habit runs in their veins as in the veins of the people. If they be invaders or usurpers, they avoid crossing the prejudices or the long-abiding practices of the nation out of caution or prudence. In any case their activity skims but the surface, avoids the sullen depths of the popular life. They work arbitrary decrees upon individuals, but they are balked of power to turn about the life of the mass: that they can effect only by slow and insidious measures which almost insensibly deflect the habits of the people into channels which lead away from old into new and different methods and purposes. The habit of the nation is the material on which the legislator works; and its qualities constitute the limitations of his power. It is stubborn material, and dangerous. If he venture to despise it, it forces him to regard and humor it; if he would put it to unaccustomed uses, it balks him; if he seek to force it, it will explode in his hands and destroy him. The sovereignty is not his, but only the leadership.

1207. *Law's Utterance of National Character.*—Law thus normally speaks the character, the historical habit and development of each nation. There is no universal law, but for each nation a law of its own which bears evident marks of having been developed along with the national character, which mirrors the special life of the particular people whose political and social judgments it embodies (sec. 1196). The despot may be grossly arbitrary; he may violate every principle of right in his application of the law to individuals; he may even suspend all justice in individual cases; but the law, the principles which he violates or follows at pleasure, he takes from the people whom he governs, extracts from their habit and history. What he changes is the application merely, not the principles, of justice; and he changes that application only with reference to a comparatively small number of individuals whom he specially picks out for his enmity or displeasure. He cannot violently turn about the normal processes of the national habit.

1208. *Germanic Law.*—We have in Germanic law an example of the influence of national character upon legal systems as conspicuous as that afforded by Roman law itself, and the example is all the more instructive when put alongside of the Roman because of the sharpness of the contrasts between Roman and Germanic legal conceptions. Although so like the Romans in practical political sagacity and common-sense legal capacity, the Germans had quite other conceptions as to the basis and nature of law. Their law spoke no such exaltation of the public power, and consequently no such intense realization of organic unity. The individual German was, so to say, given play outside the law; his rights were not relative, but absolute, self-centred. It was the object of the public polity rather to give effect to individual worth and liberty than to build together a compact, dominant community. German law, therefore, took no thought for systematic equality, but did take careful thought to leave room for the fullest possible assertion of that individuality which must inevitably issue in inequality. It was a flexible framework for the play of individual forces. It lacked the organic energy, the united, triumphant strength of the Roman system; but it contained untold treasures of variety and of individual achievement. It, no less than Roman law, rested broadly upon national character; and it was to supply in general European history what the Roman system could not contribute.

1209. *Sovereignty: Who gives Law?*—If, then, law be a product of national character, if the power of the community must be behind it to give it efficacy, and the habit of the community in it to give it reality, where is the seat of sovereignty? Whereabouts and in whom does sovereignty reside, and what is Sovereignty? These, manifestly, are questions of great scope and complexity, and yet questions central to a right understanding of the nature and genesis of law. It will be best to approach our answers to them by way of illustrations.

In England, sovereignty is said to rest with the legislative power: with Parliament acting with the approval of the Crown, or, not to disuse an honored legal fiction, with the Crown acting with the assent of Parliament. Whatever an Act of Parliament prescribes is law, even though it contravene every principle, constitutional or only of private right, recognized before the passage of the Act as inviolable. Such is the theory. The well-known fact is, that Parliament dare do nothing that will even seem to contravene principles held to be sacred in the sphere either of constitutional privilege or private right. Should Parliament violate such principles, their action would be repudiated by the nation, their will, failing to become indeed law, would pass immediately into the limbo of things repealed; Parliament itself would be purged of its offending members. Parliament, then, is master, is an utterer of valid commands, only so far as it interprets, or at least does not cross, the wishes of the people. Whether or not, therefore, it be possible to say with the approval of those who insist upon maintaining the rules of a strict abstract logic that the sovereignty of Parliament is limited *de jure*, that is, in law, it is manifestly the main significant truth of the case that parliamentary sovereignty is most imperatively limited *de facto*, in fact. Its actual power is not a whit broader for having a free field in law, that is, above the fences, so long as the field in which it really moves is fenced high about by firm facts.

1210. Again, it is said, apparently with a quite close regard for the facts, that in Russia sovereignty is lodged with the Czar, the supreme master "of all the Russias." That his will is law Siberia attests and Nihilism recognizes. But is there no *de facto* limitation to his supremacy? How far could he go in the direction of institutional construction? How far could he succeed in giving Russia at once and out of hand the institutions, and Russians the liberties, of the United States and its people? How far would such a gift be law? Only so far as life answered to its word of command. Only so far as Russian habit, schooled by centuries of obedience to a bureaucracy, could and would respond to its invitation. Only so far, in a word, as the new institutions were accepted. The measure of the Czar's sovereignty is the habit of his people; and not their habit only, but their humor also, and the humor of his officials. His concessions to the restless spirit of his army, to the prejudices of his court, and to the temper of the mass of his subjects, his means of keeping this side assassination or revolution, nicely mark the boundaries of his sovereignty.

1211. Sovereignty, therefore, as ideally conceived in legal theory, nowhere actually exists. The sovereignty which does exist is something much more vital, though, like most living things, much less easily conceived. It is the will of an organized independent community, whether that will speak in acquiescence merely, or in active creation of the forces and conditions of politics. The kings or parliaments who serve as its vehicles utter it, but they do not possess it. Sovereignty resides in the community; but its organs, whether those organs be supreme magistrates, busy legislatures, or subtle privileged classes, are as various as the conditions of historical growth have commanded.

1212. *Certain Legal Conceptions Universal.*—The correspondence of law with national character, its basis in national habit, does not deprive it of all universal characteristics. Many common features it does wear among all civilized peoples. As the Romans found it possible to construct from the diversified systems of law existing among the subject peoples of the Mediterranean basin, a certain number of general maxims of justice out of which to construct the foundation of their *jus gentium*, so may jurists today discover in all systems of law alike certain common moral judgments, a certain evidence of unity of thought regarding the greater principles of equity. There is a common legal conscience in mankind.

Thus, for example, the sacredness of human life; among all Aryan nations at least, the sanctity of the nearer family relationships; in all systems at all developed, the plainer principles of 'mine' and 'thine'; the obligation of promises; many obvious duties of man to man suggested by the universal moral consciousness of the race, receive recognition under all systems alike. Sometimes resemblances between systems the most widely separated in time and space run even into ceremonial details, such as the emblematic transfer of property, and into many details of personal right and obligation.

1213. *Law and Ethics.*—It by no means follows, however, that because law thus embodies moral judgments of the race on many points of personal relation and individual conduct, it is to be considered a sort of positive concrete Ethics,—Ethics crystallized into definite commands towards which the branch of culture which we call 'Ethics' stands related as theory to practice. Ethics concerns the whole walk and conversation of the individual, it touches the rectitude of each man's life, the truth of his dealings with his own conscience, the whole substance of character and conduct, righteousness both of act and of mental habit. Law, on the other hand, concerns only man's life in society. It not only confines itself to controlling the outward acts of men; it limits itself to those particular acts of man to man which can be regulated by the public authority, and which can be regulated in accordance with uniform rules applicable to all alike and in an equal degree. It does not essay to punish untruthfulness as such, it only annuls contracts obtained by fraudulent misrepresentation and makes good such pecuniary damage as the deceit may have entailed; it does not censure ingratitude or any of the subtler forms of faithlessness, it only denounces its penalties against open and tangible acts of dishonesty; it does not assume to be the guardian of men's character, it only stands with a whip for those who give overt proof of bad character in their dealings with their fellow-men. Its limitations are thus limitations both of kind and of degree. It addresses itself to the regulation of outward conduct only: that is its limitation of kind; and it regulates outward conduct only so far as workable and uniform rules can be found for its regulation: that is its limitation of degree.

1214. *Mala Prohibita.*—Law thus plays the rôle neither of conscience nor of Providence. More than this, it follows standards of policy only, not absolute standards of right and wrong. Many things that are wrong, even within the sphere of social conduct, it does not prohibit; many things not wrong in themselves it does prohibit. It thus creates, as it were, a new class of wrongs, relative to itself alone: *mala prohibita*, things wrong because forbidden. In keeping the commands of the state regarding things fairly to be called indifferent in themselves men are guided by their *legal* conscience. Society rests upon obedience to the laws: laws determine the rules of social convenience as well as of social right and wrong; and it is as necessary for the perfecting of social relationships that the rules of convenience be obeyed as it is that obedience be rendered to those which touch more vital matters of conduct.

Thus it cannot be said to be inherently wrong for a man to marry his deceased wife's sister; but if the laws, seeking what is esteemed to be a purer order of family relationships, forbid such a marriage, it becomes *malum prohibitum*: it is wrong because illegal.

It would certainly not be wrong for a trustee to buy the trust estate under his control if he did so in good faith and on terms manifestly advantageous to the persons in whose interest he held it; but it is contrary to wise public policy that such purchases should be allowed, because a trustee would have too many opportunities for unfair dealing in such transactions. The law will under no circumstances hold the sale of a trust estate to the trustee valid. Such purchases, however good the faith in which they are made, are *mala prohibita*.

Or take, as another example, police regulations whose only object is to serve the convenience of society in crowded cities. A street parade, with bands and banners and men in uniform is

> quite harmless and is immensely pleasing to those who love the glitter of epaulettes and brass buttons and the blare of trumpets; but police regulations must see to it that city streets are kept clear for the ordinary daily movements of the busy city population, and to parade without license is *malum prohibitum.*

1215. In all civilized states law has long since abandoned all attempts to regulate conscience or opinion; it would find it, too, both fruitless and unwise to essay any regulation of conduct, however reprehensible in itself, which did not issue in definite and tangible acts of injury to others; but it does seek to command the outward conduct of men in their palpable dealings with each other in society. Law is the mirror of active, organic political life. It may be and is instructed by the ethical judgments of the community, but its own province is not distinctively ethical; it may regard religious principle, but it is not a code of religion. Ethics has been called the science of the well-being of man, law the science of his right civil conduct. Ethics concerns the development of character; religion, the development of man's relations with God; law, the development of men's relations to each other in society. Ethics, says Mr. Sidgwick, "is connected with politics so far as the well-being of any individual man is bound up with the well-being of his society."

1216. *International Law.*–The province of international law may be described as a province half way between the province of morals and the province of positive law. It is law without a forceful sanction. There is no earthly power of which all nations are subjects; there is no power, therefore, to enforce obedience to rules of conduct as between nation and nation. International law is, moreover, a law which rests upon those uncodified, unenacted principles of right action, of justice, and of consideration which have so universally obtained the assent of men's consciences, which have so universal an acceptance in the moral judgments of men everywhere, that they have been styled Laws of Nature (secs. 208–9), but which have a nearer kinship to ethical maxims than to positive law. "The law of nations," says Bluntschli, "is that recognized universal Law of Nature which binds different states together in a humane jural society, and which also secures to the members of different states a common protection of law for their general human and international rights."[4] Its only formal and definite foundations aside from the conclusions of those writers who, like Grotius and Vattel, have given to it distinct statements of what they conceived to be the leading, the

[4] *Das Völkerrecht,* sec. I.

almost self-evident principles of the Law of Nature, are to be found in the treaties by which states, acting in pairs or in groups, have agreed to be bound in their relations with each other, and in such principles of international action as have found their way into the statutes or the established judicial precedents of enlightened individual states. More and more, international conventions come to recognize in their treaties certain elements of right, of equity, and of comity as settled, as always to be accepted in transactions between nations. The very jealousies of European nations have contributed to swell the body of accepted treaty principles. As the practice of concerted action by the states of the continent of Europe concerning all questions of large interest, the practice of holding great Congresses like those of Vienna in 1815, of Paris in 1856, and of Berlin in 1878 has grown into the features of a custom, so has the body of principles which are practically of universal recognition increased. International law, says Dr. Bulmerincq, "is the totality of legal rules and institutions which have developed themselves touching the relations of states to one another."[5]

1217. International law is, therefore, not law at all in the strict sense of the term. It is not, as a whole, the will of any state: there is no authority set above the nations whose command it is. In one aspect, the aspect of Bluntschli's definition, it is simply the body of rules, developed out of the common moral judgments of the race, which *ought* to govern nations in their dealings with each other. Looked at from another, from Dr. Bulmerincq's, point of view, it is nothing more than a generalized statement of the rules which nations have actually recognized in their treaties with one another, made from time to time, and which by reason of such precedents are coming more and more into matter-of-course acceptance.

These rules concern the conduct of war, diplomatic intercourse, the rights of citizens of one country living under the dominion of another, jurisdiction at sea, etc. Extradition principles are settled almost always by specific agreement between country and country, as are also, of course, commercial arrangements, fishing rights, and all similar matters not of universal bearing. But even in such matters example added to example is turning nations in the direction of uniform principles, such, for instance, as this, that political offences shall not be included among extraditable crimes, unless they involve ordinary crimes of a very heinous nature, such as murder.

[5] *Das Völkerrecht* (in Marquardsen's *Handbuch*, Vol. I.), sec. I. of the monograph.

1218. *Laws of Nature and Laws of the State.*—The analogy between political laws, the laws which speak the will of the state, and natural laws, the laws which express the orderly succession of events in nature, has often been dwelt upon, and is not without instructive significance. In the one set of laws as in the other, there is, it would seem, a uniform prescription as to the operation of the forces that make for life. The analogy is most instructive, however, where it fails: it is more instructive, that is, to note the contrasts between the laws of nature and laws of the state than to note such likeness as exists between them. The contrasts rather than the resemblances serve to make evident the real nature of political regulation. "Whenever we have made out by careful and repeated observation," says Professor Huxley, "that something is always the cause of a certain effect, or that certain events always take place in the same order, we speak of the truth thus discovered as a law of nature. Thus it is a law of nature that anything heavy falls to the ground if it is unsupported. . . . But the laws of nature are not the causes of the order of nature, but only our way of stating as much as we have made out of that order. Stones do not fall to the ground in consequence of the law just stated, as people sometimes carelessly say; but the law is a way of asserting that which invariably happens when heavy bodies at the surface of the earth, stones among the rest, are free to move." Whatever analogies may exist between such generalized statements of physical fact and the rules in accordance with which men are constrained to act in organized civil society it may be profitable for the curious carefully to inquire into. What it is most profitable for the student of politics to observe is the wide difference between the two, which Professor Huxley very admirably states as follows: "Human law consists of commands addressed to voluntary agents, which they may obey or disobey; and the law is not rendered null and void by being broken. Natural laws, on the other hand, are not commands, but assertions respecting the invariable order of nature; and they remain law only so long as they can be shown to express that order. To speak of the violation or suspension of a law of nature is an absurdity. All that the phrase can really mean is that, under certain circumstances, the assertion contained in the law is not true; and the just conclusion is, not that the order of nature is interrupted, but that we have made a mistake in stating that order. A true natural law is a universal rule, and, as such, admits of no exception."[6] In brief, human choice enters into the laws of the state, whereas from natural laws that choice is altogether excluded: they are dominated by fixed necessity. Human choice, indeed, enters every part of political law to modify it. It is the element of change; and it has given to the growth of law a variety, a variability, and an irregularity which no other power could have imparted.

1219. *Limitations of Political Law.*—We have thus laid bare to our view some of the most instructive characteristics of political law. The laws of nature state effects invariably produced by forces of course adequate to produce them; but behind political laws there is not always a force adequate to produce the effects which they are designed to produce. The force, the *sanction,* as jurists say, which lies behind the laws of the state is the organized armed power of the community: compulsion raises its arm against the man who refuses to obey (sec. 1154). But the public power may sleep, may be inattentive to breaches of law, may suffer itself to be bribed, may be outwitted or thwarted: laws are not always 'enforced.' This element of weakness it is which opens up to us one aspect at least of the nature of Law: Law is no more efficient than the state whose will it utters. The law of Turkey shares all the imperfections of the Turkish power; the laws of England bespeak in their enforcement the efficacy of English government. Good laws are of no avail under a bad government; a weak, decadent state may speak the highest purposes in its statutes and yet do the worst things in its actual administration. Commonly, however, law embodies the real purposes of the state, and its enforcement is a matter of administrative capacity or of concerted power simply.

1220. *Public Law.*—The two great divisions under which law may best be studied are these: (1) *Public Law,* (2) *Private Law.* Public law is that which immediately concerns the being, the structure, the functions, and the methods of the state. Taken in its full scope, it includes not only what we familiarly know as constitutional law, but also what is known as administrative law, and all that part of criminal law which affects crimes against the state itself, against the community as a whole. In brief, it is that portion of law which determines a state's own character and its relations to its citizens.

1221. *Private Law.*—Private law, on the other hand, is that

[6] These passages are taken from Professor Huxley's *Science Primer. Introductory.*

portion of positive law which secures to the citizen his rights as against the other citizens of the state. It seeks to effect justice between individual and individual; its sphere is the sphere of individual right and duty.

> 1222. It is to the Romans that we are indebted for a first partial recognition of this important division in the province of Law, though later times have given a different basis to this distinction. I say 'indebted['] because the distinction between public and private law has the most immediate connections with individual liberty. Without it, we have the state of affairs that existed in Greece, where there was no sphere which was not the state's (sec. 1236); and where the sphere of the state's relations to the individual was as wide as the sphere of the law itself. Individual liberty can exist only where it is recognized that there are rights which the state does not create, but only secures.

1223. *Jurisprudence.*—Jurisprudence is a term of much latitude, but must be taken strictly to mean the Science of Law. The science of law, of course, is complete only when it has laid bare both the nature and the genesis of law: the nature of law must be obscure until its genesis and the genesis of the conceptions upon which it is based have been explored; and that genesis is a matter, not of logical analysis, but of history. Many writers upon jurisprudence, therefore, have insisted upon the historical method of study as the only proper method. They have sought in the history of society and of institutions the birth and development of jural conceptions, the growths of practice which have expanded into the law of property or of torts, the influences which have contributed to the orderly regulation of man's conduct in society.

1224. In the hands of another school of writers, however, jurisprudence has been narrowed to the dimensions of a science of law in its modern aspects only. They seek to discover, by an analysis of law in its present full development, the rights which habitually receive legal recognition and the methods by which states secure to their citizens their rights, and enforce upon them their duties, by positive rules backed by the abundant sanction of the public power. In their view, not only is the history of law not jurisprudence, but, except to a very limited extent, it is not even the material of jurisprudence. Its material is law as it presently exists: the history of that law is only a convenient light in which the real content and purpose of existing law may be made plainer to the analyst. The conclusions of these writers are subject to an evident limitation, therefore; their analysis of law, being based upon existing legal systems alone and taking the fully developed law for granted, applies to law in the earlier stages of society only by careful modification, only by more or less subtle and ingenious accommodation of the meaning of its terms.

1225. Historical jurisprudence alone,—a science of law, that is, constructed by means of the historical analysis of law and always squaring its conclusions with the history of society,—can serve the student of politics. The processes of analytical jurisprudence, however, having been conducted by minds of the greatest subtlety and acuteness, serve a very useful purpose in supplying a logical structure of thought touching full-grown systems of law.

1226. *The Analytical Account of Law.*—In the thought of the analytical school every law is a command, "an order issued by a superior to an inferior." "Every positive law is 'set by a sovereign person, or sovereign body of persons, to a member or members of the independent political society wherein that person or body of persons is sovereign or superior.'" In its terms, manifestly, such an analysis applies only to times when the will of the state is always spoken by a definite authority; not with the voice of custom, which proceeds no one knows whence; not with the voice of religion, which speaks to the conscience as well as to the outward life, and whose sanctions are derived from the unseen power of a supernatural being; nor yet with the voice of scientific discussion, whose authors have no authority except that of clear thought; but with the distinct accents of command, with the voice of the judge and the legislator.

1227. *The Analytical Account of Sovereignty.*—The analytical account of sovereignty is equally clear-cut and positive. Laws, "being commands, emanate from a determinate source," from a sovereign authority; and analytical jurisprudence is very strict and formal in its definition of sovereignty. A sovereign "is a determinate person, or body of persons, to whom the bulk of the members of an organized community are in the habit of rendering obedience and who are themselves not in the habit of rendering obedience to any human superior."

It follows, of course, that no organic community which is not independent can have a law of its own. The law of the more fully developed English colonies, for example, though it is made by the enactment of their own parliaments, is not law by virtue of such enactment, because those parliaments are in the habit of being obedient to the authorities in London and are not themselves sovereign, therefore. The sovereignty which lies back of all law in the colonies is said to be the sovereignty of the parliament of England.

1228. It would seem to follow that our own federal authorities are sovereign. They are a determinate body of persons to whom the bulk of the nation is habitually obedient and who are themselves obedient to no human superior. But then what of the authority of the states in that great sphere of action which is altogether and beyond dispute their own (sec. 889), which the federal authorities do not and cannot enter, within which their own people are habitually obedient to them, and in which they are not subject to any earthly superior? It has been the habit of all our greater writers and statesmen to say that with us sovereignty is divided; but the abstract sovereignty of which the legal analyst speaks is held to be indivisible: it must be whole. Analysis, therefore, is driven to say that with us sovereignty rests in its entirety with that not very determinate body of persons, the people of the United States, the *powers* of sovereignty resting with the state and federal authorities by delegation from the people.

The difficulty of applying the analytical account of sovereignty to our own law is in large part avoided if law be defined as "the command of an authorized public organ, acting within the sphere of its competence. What organs are authorized, and what is the sphere of their competence, is of course determined by the organic law of the state; and *this* law is the direct command of the sovereign."[7] The only difficulty left by this solution is that of making room in our system for both a sovereign people of the single state and a sovereign people of the Union.

1229. *Summary.*—Law, then, is the determinate will of the state concerning the civic conduct of those under its authority. Spoken first in the slow and general voice of custom, it speaks at last in the clear, the multifarious, the active tongues of legislation. It grows with the growth of the community: it cannot outrun the conscience of the community and be real, it cannot outlast its judgments and retain its force. It mirrors social advance: if it anticipate the development of the public thought, it must wait until the common judgment and conscience grow up to its standards before it can have life; if it lag behind the common judgment and conscience, it must become obsolete, and will come to be more honored in the breach than in the observance.

Several Representative Authorities.

Robertson, E., Article 'Law,' *Encyclopædia Britannica.* 9th ed.
Savigny, "Beruf unserer Zeit für Gesetzgebung und Rechtswissenschaft."
Ihering, v., "Geist des Römischen Rechts."
Holland, T. E., "Elements of Jurisprudence." 4th ed. Oxford, 1888.

[7] This definition I have taken the liberty of extracting from some very valuable notes on this chapter kindly furnished me by a friend who upon this subject speaks authoritatively.

Austin, John, "Lectures on Jurisprudence, the Philosophy of Positive Law." 2 vols.
Maine, Sir H. S., "Ancient Law," and "Early History of Institutions," Lectures XII., XIII.
Heron, D. C., "Introduction to the History of Jurisprudence." London, 1880.
Bluntschli, J. C., "Allegemeines Staatsrecht," 6th ed. Stuttgart, 1885.
Holtzendorff, F. v., "Enzyklopädie der Rechtswissenschaft." Leipzig, 1882.
Jellinek, Georg, "Gesetz und Verordnung," Freiburg in B. 1887.

XV.

THE FUNCTIONS OF GOVERNMENT.

1230. *What are the Functions of Government?*—The question has its own difficulties and complexities: it cannot be answered out of hand and in the lump, as the physiologist might answer the question, What are the functions of the heart? In its *nature* government is one, but in its *life* it is many: there are governments *and* governments. When asked, therefore, What are the functions of government? we must ask in return, Of what government? Different states have different conceptions of their duty, and so undertake different things. They have had their own peculiar origins, their own characteristic histories; circumstance has moulded them; necessity, interest, or caprice has variously guided them. Some have lingered near those primitive institutions which all once knew and upheld together; others have quite forgotten that man ever had a political childhood and are now old in complex practices of national self-government.

1231. *The Nature of the Question.*—It is important to notice at the outset a single general point touching the nature of this question. It is in one aspect obviously a simple *question of fact*; and yet there is another phase of it, in which it becomes as evidently a question of opinion.

The distinction is important because over and over again the question of fact has been confounded with that very widely different question, *What ought the functions of government to be?* The two questions should be kept entirely separate in treatment. Under no circumstances may we instructively or safely begin with the question of opinion: the answer to the question of fact is the indispensable foundation to all sound reasoning concerning government, which is at all points based upon experience rather than upon theory. The facts of government mirror the principles of government, in operation. What government does must arise from what government is: and what government is must determine what government ought to do. The present chapter, therefore, will confine itself to the question of fact: the question of opinion will be broached and partially answered in Chapter XVI.

1232. *Classification.*—It will contribute to clearness of thought to observe the functions of government in two groups, I. *The Constituent* Functions, II. *The Ministrant.* Under the *Constituent* I would place that usual category of governmental function, the protection of life, liberty, and property, together with all other functions that are necessary to the civic organization of society,—functions which are *not optional* with governments, even in the eyes of strictest *laissez faire*,—which are indeed the very bonds of society. Under the *Ministrant* I would range those other functions (such as education, posts and telegraphs, and the care, say, of forests) which are undertaken, not by way of *governing*, but by way of advancing the general interests of society,—functions which *are* optional, being necessary only according to standards of convenience or expediency, and not according to standards of existence; functions which assist without constituting social organization.

> Of course this classification is based primarily upon objective and practical distinctions and cannot claim philosophic completeness. There may be room for question, too, as to whether some of the functions which I class as Ministrant might not quite as properly have been considered Constituent; but I must here, of course, simply act upon my own conclusions without rearguing them, acknowledging by the way that the line of demarcation is not always perfectly clear.
>
> "The admitted functions of government," said Mr. Mill, "embrace a much wider field than can easily be included within the ring-fence of any restrictive definition, and it is hardly possible to find any ground of justification common to them all, except the comprehensive one of general expediency."

1233. *I. The Constituent Functions:*

(1) The keeping of order and providing for the protection of persons and property from violence and robbery.

(2) The fixing of the legal relations between man and wife and between parents and children.

(3) The regulation of the holding, transmission, and interchange of property, and the determination of its liabilities for debt or for crime.

(4) The determination of contract rights between individuals.

(5) The definition and punishment of crime.

(6) The administration of justice in civil causes.
(7) The determination of the political duties, privileges, and relations of citizens.
(8) Dealings of the state with foreign powers: the preservation of the state from external danger or encroachment and the advancement of its international interests.

These will all be recognized as functions which are obnoxious not even to the principles of Mr. Spencer,[1] and which of course persist under every form of government.

1234. *II. The Ministrant Functions.*–It is hardly possible to give a complete list of those functions which I have called Ministrant, so various are they under different systems of government; the following partial list will suffice, however, for the purposes of the present discussion:

(1) The regulation of trade and industry. Under this head I would include the coinage of money and the establishment of standard weights and measures, laws against forestalling, engrossing, the licensing of trades, etc., as well as the great matters of tariffs, navigation laws, and the like.
(2) The regulation of labor.
(3) The maintenance of thoroughfares,–including state management of railways and that great group of undertakings which we embrace within the comprehensive terms 'Internal Improvements' or 'The Development of the Country.'
(4) The maintenance of postal and telegraph systems, which is very similar in principle to (3).
(5) The manufacture and distribution of gas, the maintenance of water-works, etc.
(6) Sanitation, including the regulation of trades for sanitary purposes.
(7) Education.
(8) Care of the poor and incapable.
(9) Care and cultivation of forests and like matters, such as the stocking of rivers with fish.
(10) Sumptuary laws, such as 'prohibition' laws, for example.

These are all functions which, in one shape or another, all governments alike have undertaken. Changed conceptions of the nature and duty of the state have arisen, issuing from changed historical conditions, deeply altered historical circumstance, and part of the change which has thus affected the idea of the state

[1] As set forth in his pamphlet, *Man versus the State.*

has been a change in the method and extent of the exercise of governmental functions; but changed conceptions have left the functions of government *in kind* the same. Diversities of conception are very much more marked than diversities of practice.

1235. The following may be mentioned among ministrant functions not included under any of the foregoing heads, and yet undertaken by more than one modern government: the maintenance of savings-banks, especially for small sums (*e.g.*, the English postal savings-bank), the issuance of loans to farmers, and the maintenance of agricultural institutes (as in France), and the establishment of insurance for workingmen (as in Germany).

1236. *History of Governmental Function: Province of the Ancient State.*—Notable contrasts both of theory and of practice separate governments of the ancient omnipotent from governments of the modern constitutional type. The ancient state, standing very near, as it did, in its thought, to that time, still more remote, when the State was the Kin, knew nothing of individual rights as contrasted with the rights of the state. "The nations of Italy," says Mommsen, "did not merge into that of Rome more completely than the single Roman burgess merged in the Roman community." And Greece was not a whit behind Rome in the absoluteness with which she held the subordination of the individual to the state.

1237. This thought is strikingly visible in the writings of Plato and Aristotle, not only in what they say, but also, and even more, in what they do not say. The ideal Republic of which Plato dreams is to prescribe the whole life of its citizens; but there is no suggestion that it is to be set up under cover of any new conception as to what the state may legitimately do,—it is only to make novel experiments in legislation under the *old* conception. And Aristotle's objection to the utopian projects of his master is not that they would be socialistic (as we should say), but merely that they would be unwise. He does not fear that in such a republic the public power would prove to have been exalted too high; but, speaking to the policy of the thing, he foresees that the citizens would be poor and unhappy. The state may do what it will, but let it be wise in what it does. There is no one among the Greeks to deny that it is the duty of the state to make its citizens happy and prosperous; nay, to *legislate* them happy, if legislation may create fair skies and kind fortune; the only serious quarrel concerns the question, What laws are to be tried to this end?

1238. *Roman Conception of Private Rights.*—Roman principles, though equally extreme, were in some respects differently cast. That superior capacity for the development of law, which made the Romans singular among the nations of antiquity, showed itself in respect of the functions of government in a more distinct division between public and private rights than obtained in the polity of the Greek cities. An examination of the conception of the state held in Rome reveals the singular framework of her society. The Roman family did not suffer that complete absorption into the City which so early overtook the Greek family. Private rights were not individual rights, but family rights: and family rights did not so much curtail as supplement the powers of the community. The family was an indestructible *organ of the state*. The father of a family, or the head of a gens, was in a sense a member of the official hierarchy of the City,—as the king, or his counterpart the consul, was a greater father: there was no distinction of principle between the power of king or consul and the power of a father; it was a mere difference of sphere, a division of functions.

A son was, for instance, in some things exempt from the authority of the City only because he was in those things still subject, because his father still lived, to the dominion of that original state, the family. There was not in Rome that separation of the son from the family at majority which characterizes the Greek polity, as it now characterizes our own. The father continued to be a ruler, an hereditary state officer, within the original sphere of the family life, the large sphere of individual privilege and property.

1239. This essential unity of state and family furnishes us with the theoretic measure of state functions in Rome. The Roman burgess was subordinated, not to the public authority exactly, but rather to the *public order*, to the conservative integrity of the community. He was subject to a law which embodied the steady, unbroken habit of the State-family. He was not dominated, but merged.

1240. *Powers of the Roman Senate*.—The range of state power in ancient times, as a range broken only by limits of habit and convenience, is well illustrated in the elastic functions of the Roman Senate during the period of the Republic. With an unbroken life which kept it conscious of every tradition and familiar with every precedent; with established standards of tested experience and cautious expediency, it was able to direct the movements of the compact society at whose summit it sat, as the brain and consciousness direct the movements of the human body; and it is evident from the freedom of its discussions and the frequency of its actions upon interests of every kind, whether of public or of private import, that the Roman state, as typified

> in its Senate, was in its several branches of family, tribe, and City, a single undivided whole, and that its prerogatives were limited by nothing save religious observance and fixed habit. Of that individual liberty which we cherish it knew nothing.

1241. *Government the Embodiment of Society.*—As little was there in Greek politics any seed of the thought which would limit the sphere of governmental action by principles of inalienable individual rights. Both in Greek and in Roman conception government was as old as society,—was indeed nothing less than the express image and embodiment of society. In government society lived and moved and had its being. Society and government were one, in some such sense as the spirit and body of man are one: it was through government, as through mouth and eyes and limbs, that society realized and gave effect to its life. Society's prejudices, habits, superstitions did indeed command the actions of government; but only because society and government were one and the same, not because they were distinct and the one subordinate to the other. In plain terms, then, the functions of government had no limits of principle, but only certain limits of wont and convenience, and the object of administration was nothing less than to help society on to all its ends: to speed and facilitate all social undertakings. So far as full citizens of the state were concerned, Greek and Roman alike was what we should call a socialist; though he was too much in the world of affairs and had too keen an appreciation of experience, too keen a sense of the sane and possible, to attempt the Utopias of which the modern socialist dreams, and with which the ancient citizen's own writers sometimes amused him. He bounded his politics by common sense, and so dispensed with 'the rights of man.'

1242. *Feudalism: Functions of Government Functions of Proprietorship.*—Individual rights, after having been first heralded in the religious world by the great voice of Christianity, broke into the ancient political world in the person of the Teuton. But the new politics which the invader brought with him was not destined to establish at once democratic equality: that was a work reserved for the transformations of the modern world. Meantime, during the Middle Ages, government, as we conceive government, may be said to have suffered eclipse. In the Feudal System the constituent elements of government fell away from each other. Society was drawn back to something like its original family groups. Conceptions of government narrowed themselves to small territorial connections. Men became sovereigns in their own right by virtue of owning land in their own right. There was no longer any conception of nations or societies as wholes: union there was none, but only interdependence. Allegiance bowed, not to law or to fatherhood, but to ownership. The functions of government under such a system were simply the functions of proprietorship, of command and obedience: "I say unto one, Go, and he goeth; and to another, Come, and he cometh; and to my servant, Do this, and he doeth it." The public function of the baron was to keep peace among his liegemen, to see that their properties were enjoyed according to the custom of the manor (if the manor had been suffered to acquire custom on any point), and to exact fines of them for all privileges, whether of marrying, of coming of age, or of making a will. The baronial conscience, bred in cruel, hardening times was the only standard of justice; the baronial power the only conclusive test of prerogative.

This was between baron and vassal. Between baron and baron the only bond was a nominal common allegiance to a distant king, who was himself only a great baron. For the rest there was no government, but only diplomacy and warfare. Government lived where it could and as it could, and was for the most part divided out piecemeal to a thousand petty holders. Feuds were the usual processes of justice.

1243. *The Feudal Monarchy.*—The monarchy which grew out of the ruins of this disintegrate system concentrated authority without much changing its character. The old idea, born of family origins, that government was but the active authority of society, the magistrate but society's organ, bound by society's immemorial laws, had passed utterly away, and government had become the personal possession of one man. The ruler did not any longer belong to the state; the state belonged to him: he was himself the state, as the rich man may be said to be his possessions. The Greek or Roman official was wielded by the community. Not so the king who had swept together into his own lap the powers once broadcast in the feudal system: he wielded the community. Government breathed with his breath, and it was its function to please him. The state had become, by the processes of the feudal development, his private estate.

1244. *Modern De-socialization of the State.*—The reaction from such conceptions, slow and for the most part orderly in England, sudden and violent, because long forcibly delayed, on the Continent, was of course natural, and indeed inevitable. When it came it was radical; but it did not swing the political world back to its old-time ideas; it turned it aside rather to new. It became the object of the revolutionist and the democrat of the new order of things to live his own life: the ancient man had had no thought but to live loyally the life of society. The antique citizen's virtues were not individual in their point of view, but social; whereas our virtues are almost entirely individual in their motive, social only in some of their results.

In brief, the modern State has been largely *de-socialized.* The modern idea is this: the state no longer absorbs the individual; it only serves him: the state, as it appears in its organ, the government, is the representative of the individual, and not his representative even except within the definite commission of constitutions; while for the rest each man makes his own social relations. 'The individual for the State' has been reversed and made to read, 'The State for the individual.'

1245. *More Changes of Conception than of Practice.*—Such are the divergencies of *conception* separating modern from ancient politics, divergencies at once deep and far-reaching. How far have such changes of thought been accompanied by changes of function? By no means so far as might be expected. Apparently the new ideas given prevalence in politics from time to time have not been able to translate themselves into altered functions but only into somewhat *curtailed* functions, breeding rather a difference of degree than a difference of kind. Even under the most liberal of our modern constitutions we still meet government in every field of social endeavor. Our modern life is so infinitely wide and complex, indeed, that we may go great distances in any field of enterprise without receiving either direct aid or direct check from government; but that is only because every field of enterprise is vastly big nowadays, not because government is not somewhere in it: and we know that the tendency is for governments to make themselves everywhere more and more conspicuously present. We are conscious that we are by no means in the same case with the Greek or Roman: the state is ours, not we the state's. But we know at the same time that the tasks of the state have not been much diminished. Perhaps we may say that the matter stands thus: what is changed is not the activities of government but only the morals, the conscience of government. Government may still be doing substantially the same things as of old; but an altered conception of its responsibility deeply modifies *the way in which it does them.* Social convenience and advancement are still its ultimate standard of conduct, just as if it were still itself the omnipotent impersonation of society, the master of the individual; but it has adopted new ideas as to what constitutes social convenience and advancement. Its aim is to aid the individual to the fullest and best possible realization of his individuality, instead of merely to the full realization of his *sociality*. Its plan is to create the best and fairest opportunities for the individual; and it has discovered that the way to do this is by no means itself to undertake the administration of the individual by old-time futile methods of guardianship.

1246. *Functions of Government much the Same now as always.*—This is indeed a great and profound change; but it is none the less important to emphasize the fact that the functions of government are still, when catalogued, found to be much the same both in number and magnitude that they always were. Government does not stop with the protection of life, liberty, and property, as some have supposed; it goes on to serve every convenience of society. Its sphere is limited only by its own wisdom, alike where republican and where absolutist principles prevail.

1247. *The State's Relation to Property.*—A very brief examination of the facts suffices to confirm this view. Take, for example, the state's relation to property, its performance of one of the chief of those functions which I have called Constituent. It is in connection with this function that one of the most decided contrasts exists between ancient and modern political practice; and yet we shall not find ourselves embarrassed to recognize as natural the practice of most ancient states touching the right of private property. Their theory was extreme, but, outside of Sparta, their practice was moderate.

1248. *In Sparta.*—Consistent, logical Sparta may serve as the point of departure for our observation: she is the standing classical type of exaggerated state functions and furnishes the most extreme example of the antique conception of the relations of the state to property. In the early periods of her history at least, besides being censor, pedagogue, drill sergeant, and housekeeper to her citizens, she was also universal landlord. There was a distinct reminiscence in her practice of the time when the state was the family, and as such the sole owner of property. She was regarded as the original proprietor of all the land in Laconia, and individual tenure was looked upon as rather of the nature of a usufruct held of the state and at the state's pleasure than as resting upon any complete or indefeasible private title.

1249. *Peculiar Situation of the Spartans.*—There were in Sparta special reasons for the persistence of such a system. The Spartans had come into Laconia as conquerors, and the land had first of all been tribal booty. It had been booty of which the Spartan host as a whole, as a State, had had the dividing, and it had been the purpose of the early arrangement to make the division of the land among the Spartan families as equal as possible. Nor did the state resign the right of disposition in making this first distribution. It remained its primary care to keep its citizens, the favored Spartiatæ, upon an equal footing of fortune to the end that they might remain rich in leisure, and so be the better able to live entirely for the service of the state, which was honorable, to the avoidance of that pursuit of wealth which was dishonorable. The state, accordingly, undertook to administer the wealth of the country for the benefit of its citizens. When grave inequalities manifested themselves in the distribution of estates it did not hesitate to resume its proprietary rights and effect a reapportionment: no one dreaming, the while, of calling its action confiscation. It took various means for accomplishing its ends. It compelled rich heiresses to marry men without patrimony; and it grafted the poor citizen upon a good estate by means of prescribed adoption. No landed estate could be alienated either by sale or testament from the family to which the state had assigned it unless express legislative leave were given. In brief, in respect of his property the citizen was both ward and tenant of the state.

1250. *Decay of the System.*—As the Spartan state decayed this whole system was sapped. Estates became grossly unequal, as did also political privileges even among the favored Spartiatæ. But these changes were due to the decadence of Spartan power and to the degeneration of her political fibre in days of waning fortune, not to any conscious or deliberate surrender by the state of her prerogatives as owner, guardian, and trustee. She had grown old and lax simply; she had not changed her mind.

1251. *In Athens.*—When we turn to Athens we experience a marked change in the political atmosphere, though the Athenians hold much the same abstract conception of the state. Here men breathe more freely and enjoy the fruits of their labor, where labor is without reproach, with less restraint. Even in Athens there remain distinct traces, however, of the family duties of the state. She too, like Sparta, felt bound to dispose properly of eligible heiresses. She did not hesitate to punish with heavy forfeiture of right (*atimia*) those who squandered their property in dissolute living. There was as little limit in Athens as in Sparta to the theoretical prerogatives of the public authority. The freedom of the citizen was a freedom of indulgence rather than of right: he was free because the state refrained, as a privileged child, not as a sovereign under Rousseau's Law of Nature.

1252. *In Rome.*—When we shift our view to republican Rome we do not find a simple city omnipotence like that of Greece, in which all private rights are sunk. The primal constituents of the city yet abide in shapes something like their original. Roman society consists of a series of interdependent links: the family, the gens, the city. The aggregate, not the fusion, of these makes up what we should call the state. But the state, so made up, was omnipotent, through one or other of its organs, over the individual. Property was not private in the sense of being individual; it vested in the family, which was, in this as in other respects, an organ of the state. Property was not conceived of as state property, because it had remained the undivided property of the family. The father, as a ruler in the immemorial hierarchy of the government, was all-powerful trustee of the family estates. Individual ownership there was none.

1253. *Under Modern Governments.*—We with some justice felicitate ourselves that to this omnipotence of the ancient state in its relations to property the practice of our own governments offers the most pronounced contrasts. But the point of greatest interest for us in the present connection is this, that these contrasts are contrasts of *policy, not of power.* To what lengths it will go in regulating property rights is for each government a question of principle, which it must put to its own conscience, and which, if it be wise, it will debate in the light of political history: but every government must regulate property in one way or another. If the ancient state was regarded as the ultimate owner, the modern state is regarded as the ultimate heir of all estates. Failing other claimants, property *escheats* to the state. If the modern state does not assume, like the ancient, to administer their property upon occasion for competent adults, it does administer their property upon occasion for lunatics and minors. The ancient state controlled slaves and slavery; the modern state has been quite as absolute: it has abolished slaves and slavery. The modern state, no less than the ancient, sets rules and limitations to inheritance and bequest. Most of the more extreme and hurtful interferences with rights of private ownership government has abandoned, one may suspect, rather because of difficulties of administration than because of difficulties of conscience. It is of the nature of the state to regulate property rights; it is of the policy of the state to regulate them *more* or *less*. Administrators must regard this as one of the Constituent functions of political society.

1254. *The State and Political Rights.*—Similar conclusions may be drawn from a consideration of the contrasts which exist in the field of that other Constituent function which concerns the determination of political rights,—the contrasts between the *status* of the citizen in the ancient state and the *status* of the citizen in the modern state. Here also the contrast, as between state and state, is not one of power, but one of principle and habit rather. Modern states have often limited as narrowly as did the ancient the enjoyment of those political privileges which we group under the word *Franchise*. They too, as well as the ancient states, have admitted slavery into their systems; they too have commanded their subjects without moderation and fleeced them without compunction. But for all they have been so omnipotent, and when they chose so tyrannical, they have seldom insisted upon so complete and unreserved a service of the state by the citizen as was habitual to the political practice of both the Greek and the Roman worlds. The Greek and the Roman belonged each to his state in a quite absolute sense. He was his own in nothing as against the claims of his city upon him: he freely acknowledged all his privileges to be but concessions from his mother, the commonwealth. Those privileges accrued to him through law, as do ours; but law was to him simply the will of the organic community, never, as we know it in our constitutions, a restraint upon the will of the organic community. He knew no principles of liberty save only those which custom had built up: which inhered, not in the nature of things, not in abstract individuality, but in the history of affairs, in concrete practice. His principles were all precedents. Nevertheless, however radically different its doctrines, the ancient state was not a whit more completely master touching laws of citizenship than is the state of to-day.

1255. *As regards the State's Ministrant Functions.*—Of the Ministrant, no less than of these Constituent functions which I have taken merely as examples of their kind, the same statement may be made, that practically the state has been relieved of very little duty by alterations of political theory. In this field of the Ministrant functions one would expect the state to be less active now than formerly: it is natural enough that in the field of the Constituent functions the state should serve society now as always. But there is in fact no such difference: *government does now whatever experience permits or the times demand*; and though it does not do exactly the same things it still does substantially the same kind of things that the ancient state did. It will conduce to clearness if I set forth my illustrations of this in the order of the list of Ministrant functions which I have given (sec. 1234).

1256. *The State in Relation to Trade.*—(1) All nations have habitually regulated trade and commerce. In the most remote periods of which history has retained any recollection the regulation of trade and commerce was necessary to the existence of government. The only way in which communities which were then seeking to build up a dominant power could preserve an independent existence and work out an individual development was to draw apart to an absolutely separate life. Commerce meant contact; contact meant contamination: the only way in which to develop character and achieve cohesion was to avoid intercourse. In the classical states this stage is of course passed and trade and commerce are regulated for much the same reasons that induce modern states to regulate them, in order, that is, to secure commercial advantage as against competitors or in order to serve the fiscal needs of the state. Athens and Sparta and Rome, too, regulated the corn trade for the purpose of securing for their citizens full store of food. In the Middle Ages the feuds and highway brigandage of petty lords loaded commerce with fetters of the most harassing sort, except where the free cities could by militant combination keep open to it an unhindered passage to and fro between the great marts of North and South. As the mediæval states emerge into modern times we find trade and commerce handled by statesmen as freely as ever, but according to the reasoned policy of the mercantilist thinkers; and in our own days according to still other conceptions of national advantage.

1257. *The State in Relation to Labor.*—(2) Labor, too, has always been regulated by the state. By Greek and Roman the labor of the handicrafts and of agriculture, all manual toil indeed, was for the most part given to slaves to do; and of course law regulated the slave. In the Middle Ages the labor which was not agricultural and held in bondage to feudal masters was in the cities, where it was rigidly ordered by the complex rules of the guild system, as was trade also and almost all other like forms of making a livelihood. Where, as in England, labor in part escaped from the hard service of the feudal tenure the state stepped in with its persistent "statutes of laborers" and sought to tie the workman to one habitation and to one rate of wages. 'The rustic must stay where he is and must receive only so much pay,' was its command. Apparently, however, all past regulation of labor was but timid and elementary as compared with the labor legislation about to be tried by the governments of our own day. The birth and development of the modern industrial system has changed every aspect of the matter; and this fact it is which reveals the true character of the part which the state plays in the case. The rule would seem to be that in proportion as the world's industries grow must the state advance in its efforts to assist the industrious to advantageous relations with each other. The tendency to regulate labor rigorously and minutely is as strong in England, where the state is considered the agent of the citizen, as it was in Athens, where the citizen was deemed the child and tool of the state, and where the workman was a slave.

1258. (3) *Regulation of Corporations.*—The regulation of corporations is but one side of the modern regulation of the industrial system, and is a function added to the antique list of governmental tasks.

1259. (4) *The State and Public Works.*—The maintenance of thoroughfares may be said to have begun with permanent empire, that is to say, for Europe, with the Romans. For the Romans, indeed, it was first a matter of moving armies, only secondarily a means of serving commerce; whereas with us the highway is above all things else an artery of trade, and armies use it only when commerce stands still at the sound of drum and trumpet. The building of roads may therefore be said to have begun by being a Constituent function and to have ended by becoming a Ministrant function of government. But the same is not true of other public works, of the Roman aqueducts and theatres and baths, and of modern internal improvements. They, as much as the Roman tax on old bachelors, are parts, not of a scheme of governing, but of plans for the advancement of other social aims, —for the administration of society. Because in her conception the community as a whole was the only individual, Rome thrust out as of course her magnificent roads to every quarter of her vast territory, considered no distances too great to be traversed by her towering aqueducts, deemed it her duty to clear river courses and facilitate by every means both her commerce and her arms. And the modern state, though holding a deeply modified conception of the relations of government to society, still follows no very different practice. If in most instances our great iron highways are left to private management, it is oftener for reasons of convenience than for reasons of conscience.

1260. (5) *Administration of the Conveniences of Society.*—Similar considerations of course apply in the case of that modern instrumentality, the public letter-post, in the case of the still more modern manufacture of gas, and in the case of the most modern telegraph. The modern no less than the ancient government unhesitatingly takes a hand in administering the conveniences of society.

1261. (6) *Sanitation.*—Modern governments, like the government of Rome, maintain sanitation by means of police inspection of baths, taverns, and houses of ill fame, as well as by drainage; and to these they add hospital relief, water supply, quarantine, and a score of other means.

1262. (7) *Public Education.*—Our modern systems of public education are more thorough than the ancient, notwithstanding the fact that we regard the individual as something other than a mere servant of the state, and educate him first of all for himself.

1263. (8) *Sumptuary Laws.*—In sumptuary laws ancient states of course far outran modern practice. Modern states have of course foregone most attempts to make citizens virtuous or frugal by law. But even we have our prohibition enactments; and we have had our fines for swearing.

1264. *Summary.*—Apparently it is safe to say with regard to the functions of government taken as a whole that, even as between ancient and modern states, uniformities of practice far outnumber diversities of practice. One may justly conclude, not indeed that the restraints which modern states put upon themselves are of little consequence, or that altered political conceptions are not of the greatest moment in determining important questions of government and even the whole advance of the race; but that it is rather by gaining practical wisdom, rather by long processes of historical experience, that states modify their practices; new theories are subsequent to new experiences.

XVI.

THE OBJECTS OF GOVERNMENT.

1265. *Character of the Subject.*—Political interest and controversy centre nowhere more acutely than in the question, What are the proper objects of government? This is one of those difficult questions upon which it is possible for many sharply opposed views to be held apparently with almost equal weight of reason. Its central difficulty is this, that it is a question which can be answered, if answered at all, only by the aid of a broad and careful wisdom whose conclusions are based upon the widest possible inductions from the facts of political experience in all its phases. Such wisdom is of course quite beyond the capacity of most thinkers and actors in the field of politics; and the consequence has been that this question, perhaps more than any other in the whole scope of political science, has provoked great wars of doctrine.

1266. *The Extreme Views Held.*—What part shall government play in the affairs of society?—that is the question which has been the gauge of controversial battle. Stated in another way, it is the very question which I postponed when discussing the functions of government (sec. 1231), '*What,*' namely, '*ought the functions of government to be?*' On the one hand there are extremists who cry constantly to government, 'Hands off,' '*laissez faire,*' '*laissez passer*'*!* who look upon every act of government which is not merely an act of police with jealousy, who regard government as necessary, but as a necessary evil, and who would have government hold back from everything which could by any possibility be accomplished by individual initiative and endeavor. On the other hand, there are those who, with equal extremeness of view in the opposite direction, would have society lean fondly upon government for guidance and assistance in every affair of life, who, captivated by some glimpse of public power and beneficence caught in the pages of ancient or mediæval historian or by some dream of cooperative endeavor cunningly imagined by the great fathers of Socialism, believe that the state can be made a wise foster-mother to every member of the family politic. Between these two extremes, again, there are all grades, all shades and colors, all degrees of enmity or of partiality to state action.

1267. *Historical Foundation for Opposite Views.*—Enmity to exaggerated state action, even a keen desire to keep that action down to its lowest possible terms, is easily furnished with impressive justification. It must unreservedly be admitted that history abounds with warnings of no uncertain sound against indulging the state with a too great liberty of interference with the life and work of its citizens. Much as there is that is attractive in the political life of the city states of Greece and Rome, in which the public power was suffered to be omnipotent,—their splendid public spirit, their incomparable organic wholeness, their fine play of rival talents, serving both the common thought and the common action, their variety, their conception of public virtue, there is also much to blame,—their too wanton invasion of that privacy of the individual life in which alone family virtue can dwell secure, their callous tyranny over minorities in matters which might have been left to individual choice, their sacrifice of personal independence for the sake of public solidarity, their hasty average judgments, their too confident trust in the public voice. They, it is true, could not have had the individual liberty which we cherish without breaking violently with their own history, with the necessary order of their development; but neither can we, on the other hand, imitate them without an equally violent departure from our own normal development and a reversion to the now too primitive methods of their pocket republics.

1268. Unquestionable as it is, too, that mediæval history affords many seductive examples of an absence of grinding, heartless competition and a strength of mutual interdependence, confidence, and helpfulness between class and class such as the modern economist may be pardoned for wishing to see revived; and true though it be that the history of Prussia under some of the greater Hohenzollern gives at least colorable justification to the opinion that state interference may under many circumstances be full of benefit for the industrial upbuilding of a state, it must, on the other hand, be remembered that neither the feudal system, nor the mediæval guild system, nor the paternalism of Frederic the Great can be rehabilitated now that the nineteenth century has wrought its revolutions in industry, in church, and in state; and that, even if these great systems of the past could be revived, we would be sorely puzzled to reinstate their blessings without restoring at the same time their acknowledged evils. No student of history can wisely censure those who protest against state paternalism.

1269. *The State a Beneficent and Indispensable Organ of Society.*—It by no means follows, however, that because the state may unwisely interfere in the life of the individual, it must be pronounced in itself and by nature a necessary evil. It is no more an evil than is society itself. It is the organic body of society: without it society would be hardly more than a mere abstraction. If the name had not been restricted to a single, narrow, extreme, and radically mistaken class of thinkers, we ought all to regard ourselves and to act as *socialists*, believers in the wholesomeness and beneficence of the body politic. If the history of society proves anything, it proves the absolute naturalness of government, its rootage in the nature of man, its origin in kinship, and its identification with all that makes man superior to the brute creation. Individually man is but poorly equipped to dominate other animals: his lordship comes by combination, his strength is concerted strength, his sovereignty is the sovereignty of union. Outside of society man's mind can avail him little as an instrument of supremacy, and government is the visible form of society: if society itself be not an evil, neither surely is government an evil, for government is the indispensable organ of society.

1270. Every means, therefore, by which society may be perfected through the instrumentality of government, every means by which individual rights can be fitly adjusted and harmonized with public duties, by which individual self-development may be made at once to serve and to supplement social development, ought certainly to be diligently sought, and, when found, sedulously fostered by every friend of society. Such is the socialism to which every true lover of his kind ought to adhere with the full grip of every noble affection that is in him.

1271. *Socialism and the Modern Industrial Organization.*—It is possible indeed, to understand, and even in a measure to sympathize with, the enthusiasm of those special classes of agitators whom we have dubbed with the too great name of 'Socialists.' The schemes of social reform and regeneration which they support with so much ardor, however mistaken they may be,—and surely most of them are mistaken enough to provoke the laughter of children,—have the right end in view: they seek to bring the individual with his special interests, personal to himself, into complete harmony with society with its general interests, common to all. Their method is always some sort of co-operation, meant to perfect mutual helpfulness. They speak, too, a revolt from selfish, misguided individualism; and certainly modern individualism has much about it that is hateful, too hateful to last. The modern industrial organization has so distorted competition as to put it into the power of some to tyrannize over many, as to enable the rich and the strong to combine against the poor and the weak. It has given a woeful material meaning to that spiritual law that "to him that hath shall be given, and from him that hath not shall be taken away even the little that he seemeth to have."[1] It has magnified that self-interest which is grasping selfishness and has thrust out love and compassion not only, but free competition in part, as well. Surely it would be better, exclaims the Socialist, altogether to stamp out competition by making all men equally subject to the public order, to an imperative law of social co-operation! But the Socialist mistakes: it is not competition that kills, but unfair competition, the pretence and form of it where the substance and reality of it cannot exist.

[1] F. A. Walker's *Political Economy* (Advanced Course), sec. 346.

1272. *A Middle Ground.*—But there is a middle ground. The schemes which Socialists have proposed society assuredly cannot accept, and no scheme which involves the complete control of the individual by government can be devised which differs from theirs very much for the better. A truer doctrine must be found, which gives wide freedom to the individual for his self-development and yet guards that freedom against the competition that kills, and reduces the antagonism between self-development and social development to a minimum. And such a doctrine can be formulated, surely, without too great vagueness.

1273. *The Objects of Society the Objects of Government.*—Government, as I have said, is the organ of society, its only potent and universal instrument: its objects must be the objects of society. What, then, are the objects of society? What *is* society? It is an organic association of individuals for mutual aid. Mutual aid to what? To self-development. The hope of society lies in an infinite individual variety, in the freest possible play of individual forces: only in that can it find that wealth of resource which constitutes civilization, with all its appliances for satisfying human wants and mitigating human sufferings, all its incitements to thought and spurs to action. It should be the end of government *to accomplish the objects of organized society*: there must be constant adjustments of governmental assistance to the needs of a changing social and industrial organization. Not license of interference on the part of government, only strength and adaptation of regulation. The regulation that I mean is not interference: it is the equalization of conditions, so far as possible, in all branches of endeavor; and the equalization of conditions is the very opposite of interference.

1274. Every rule of development is a rule of adaptation, a rule for meeting 'the circumstances of the case'; but the circumstances of the case, it must be remembered, are not, so far as government is concerned, the circumstances of any individual case, but the circumstances of society's case, the general conditions of social organization. The case for society stands thus: the individual must be assured the best means, the best and fullest opportunities, for complete self-development: in no other way can society itself gain variety and strength. But one of the most indispensable conditions of opportunity for self-development government alone, society's controlling organ, can supply. All combination which necessarily creates monopoly, which necessarily puts and keeps indispensable means of industrial or social development in the hands of a few, and those few, not the few selected by society itself but the few selected by arbitrary fortune, must be under either the direct or the indirect control of society. To society alone can the power of dominating combination belong: and society cannot suffer any of its members to enjoy such a power for their own private gain independently of its own strict regulation or oversight.

1275. *Natural Monopolies.*–It is quite possible to distinguish natural monopolies from other classes of undertaking; their distinctive marks are thus enumerated by Mr. T. H. Farrer in his excellent little volume on *The State in its relation to Trade* which forms one of the well-known English Citizen series:[2]

"1. What they supply is a necessary," a necessary, that is, to life, like water, or a necessary to industrial action, like railroad transportation.

"2. They occupy peculiarly favored spots or lines of land." Here again the best illustration is afforded by railroads or by telegraph lines, by water-works, etc.

"3. The article or convenience they supply is used at the place and in connection with the plant or machinery by which it is supplied"; that is to say, at the favored spots or along the favored lines of land.

"4. This article or convenience can in general be largely, if not indefinitely increased, without proportionate increase in plant and capital"; that is to say, the initial outlay having been made, the favored spot or line of land having been occupied, every subsequent increase of business will increase profits because it will not proportionately, or anything like proportionately, increase the outlay for services or machinery needed. Those who are outside of the established business, therefore, are upon an equality of competition neither as regards available spots or lines of land nor as regards opportunities to secure business in a competition of rates.

"5. Certain and harmonious arrangement, which can only be attained by unity, are paramount considerations." Wide and systematic organization is necessary.

1276. Such enterprises invariably give to a limited number of persons the opportunity to command certain necessaries of life, of comfort, or of industrial success against their fellow countrymen and for their own advantage. Once established in any field, there can be no real competition between them and those who would afterwards enter that field. No agency should be suffered

[2] P. 71. Mr. Farrer is Permanent Secretary of the English Board of Trade (sec. 694).

> to have such control except a public agency which may be compelled by public opinion to act without selfish narrowness, upon perfectly equal conditions as towards all, or some agency upon which the government may keep a strong hold of regulation.

1277. *Control not necessarily Administration.*—Society can by no means afford to allow the use for private gain and without regulation of undertakings necessary to its own healthful and efficient operation and yet of a sort to exclude equality in competition. Experience has proved that the self-interest of those who have controlled such undertakings for private gain is not coincident with the public interest: even enlightened self-interest may often discover means of illicit pecuniary advantage in unjust discriminations between individuals in the use of such instrumentalities. But the proposition that the government should control such dominating organizations of capital may by no means be wrested to mean by any necessary implication that the government should itself administer those instrumentalities of economic action which cannot be used except as monopolies. In such cases, as Mr. Farrer says, "there are two great alternatives. (1) Ownership and management by private enterprise and capital under regulation by the state. (2) Ownership and management by Government, central or local." Government regulation may in most cases suffice. Indeed, such are the difficulties in the way of establishing and maintaining careful business management on the part of government, that control ought to be preferred to direct administration in as many cases as possible,—in every case in which control without administration can be made effectual.

1278. *Equalization of Competition.*—There are some things outside the field of natural monopolies in which individual action cannot secure equalization of the conditions of competition; and in these also, as in the regulation of monopolies, the practice of governments, of our own as well as of others, has been decisively on the side of governmental regulation. By forbidding child labor, by supervising the sanitary conditions of factories, by limiting the employment of women in occupations hurtful to their health, by instituting official tests of the purity or the quality of goods sold, by limiting hours of labor in certain trades, by a hundred and one limitations of the power of unscrupulous or heartless men to out-do the scrupulous and merciful in trade or industry, government has assisted equity. Those who would act in moderation and good conscience in cases where moderation and good conscience, to be indulged, require an increased outlay of money, in better ventilated buildings, in greater care as to the quality of goods, etc., cannot act upon their principles so long as more grinding conditions for labor or more unscrupulous use of the opportunities of trade secure to the unconscientious an unquestionable and sometimes even a permanent advantage; they have only the choice of denying their consciences or retiring from business. In scores of such cases government has intervened and will intervene; but by way, not of interference, by way, rather, of making competition equal between those who would rightfully conduct enterprise and those who barely conduct it. It is in this way that society protects itself against permanent injury and deterioration, and secures healthful equality of opportunity for self-development.

1279. *Society greater than Government.*—Society, it must always be remembered, is vastly bigger and more important than its instrument, Government. Government should serve Society, by no means rule or dominate it. Government should not be made an end in itself; it is a means only,—a means to be freely adapted to advance the best interests of the social organism. The State exists for the sake of Society, not Society for the sake of the State.

1280. *Natural Limits to State Action.*—And that there are natural and imperative limits to state action no one who seriously studies the structure of society can doubt. The limit of state functions is the limit of *necessary co-operation* on the part of Society as a whole, the limit beyond which such combination ceases to be imperative for the public good and becomes merely convenient for industrial or social enterprise. Co-operation is necessary in the sense here intended when it is indispensable to the equalization of the conditions of endeavor, indispensable to the maintenance of uniform rules of individual rights and relationships, indispensable because to omit it would inevitably be to hamper or degrade some for the advancement of others in the scale of wealth and social standing.

1281. There are relations in which men invariably have need of each other, in which universal co-operation is the indispensable condition of even tolerable existence. Only some universal authority can make opportunities equal as between man and man. The divisions of labor and the combinations of commerce may for the most part be left to contract, to free individual arrangement, but the equalization of the conditions which affect all alike may no more be left to individual initiative than may the organization of government itself. Churches, clubs, corporations, fraternities, guilds, partnerships, unions have for their ends one or another special enterprise for the development of man's spiritual or material well-being: they are all more or less advisable. But the family and the state have as their end a general enterprise for the betterment and equalization of the conditions of individual development: they are indispensable.

1282. The point at which public combination ceases to be imperative is of course not susceptible of clear indication in general terms; but it is not on that account indistinct. The bounds of family association are not indistinct because they are marked only by the immaturity of the young and by the parental and filial affections,—things not all of which are defined in the law. The rule that the state should do nothing which is equally possible under equitable conditions to optional associations is a sufficiently clear line of distinction between governments and corporations. Those who regard the state as an optional, conventional union simply, a mere partnership, open wide the doors to the worst forms of socialism. Unless the state has a nature which is quite clearly defined by that invariable, universal, immutable mutual interdependence which runs beyond the family relations and cannot be satisfied by family ties, we have absolutely no criterion by which we can limit, except arbitrarily, the activities of the state. The criterion supplied by the native necessity of state relations, on the other hand, banishes such license of state action.

1283. The state, for instance, ought not to supervise private morals because they belong to the sphere of separate individual responsibility, not to the sphere of mutual dependence. Thought and conscience are private. Opinion is optional. The state may intervene only where common action, uniform law are indispensable. Whatever is merely convenient is optional, and therefore not an affair for the state. Churches are spiritually convenient; joint-stock companies are capitalistically convenient; but when the state constitutes itself a church or a mere business association it institutes a monopoly no better than others. It should do nothing which is not in any case both indispensable to social or industrial life and necessarily monopolistic.

1284. *The Family and the State.*—It is the proper object of the family to mould the individual, to form him in the period of immaturity in the practice of morality and obedience. This period of subordination over, he is called out into an independent, self-directive activity. The ties of family affection still bind him, but they bind him with silken, not with iron bonds. He has left his 'minority' and reached his 'majority.' It is the proper object of the state to give leave to his individuality, in order that that individuality may add its quota of variety to the sum of national activity. Family discipline is variable, selective, formative: it must lead the individual. But the state must not lead. It must create conditions, but not mould individuals. Its discipline must be invariable, uniform, impersonal. Family methods rest upon individual inequality, state methods upon individual equality. Family order rests upon tutelage, state order upon franchise, upon privilege.

1285. *The State and Education.*—In one field the state would seem at first sight to usurp the family function, the field, namely, of education. But such is not in reality the case. Education is the proper office of the state for two reasons, both of which come within the principles we have been discussing. Popular education is necessary for the preservation of those conditions of freedom, political and social, which are indispensable to free individual development. And, in the second place, no instrumentality less universal in its power and authority than government can secure popular education. In brief, in order to secure popular education the action of society as a whole is necessary; and popular education is indispensable to that equalization of the conditions of personal development which we have taken to be the proper object of society. Without popular education, moreover, no government that rests upon popular action can long endure: the people must be schooled in the knowledge, and if possible in the virtues, upon which the maintenance and success of free institutions depend. No free government can last in health if it lose hold of the traditions of its history, and in the public schools these traditions may be and should be sedulously preserved, carefully replanted in the thought and consciousness of each successive generation.

1286. *Historical Conditions of Governmental Action.*—Whatever view be taken in each particular case of the rightfulness or advisability of state regulation and control, one rule there is which may not be departed from under any circumstances, and that is the rule of historical continuity. In politics nothing radically novel may safely be attempted. No result of value can ever be reached in politics except through slow and gradual development, the careful adaptations and nice modifications of growth. Nothing may be done by leaps. More than that, each people, each nation, must live upon the lines of its own experience. Nations are no more capable of borrowing experience than individuals are. The histories of other peoples may furnish us with light, but they cannot furnish us with conditions of action.

Every nation must constantly keep in touch with its past: it cannot run towards its ends around sharp corners.

1287. *Summary.*—This, then, is the sum of the whole matter: the end of government is the facilitation of the objects of society. The rule of governmental action is necessary cooperation; the method of political development is conservative adaptation, shaping old habits into new ones, modifying old means to accomplish new ends.

From Daniel Collamore Heath

Dear Prof. Wilson: Boston, Mass. June 4, 1889.

Your favor of the 3rd inst. received. We shall expect the MS. by first express. I had forgotten what our correspondence was with reference to terms. No doubt you recall it, and if you will kindly write me your own wishes in the matter, I have no doubt we can fix the whole matter satisfactorily in a short time. The enclosed slip may be an aid to you.[1]

I am sorry you have worked so hard on it. We will have to wait for the smaller book; but we feel that we can afford to.

By the way, have you seen Thorpe's new book,[2] published by Eldridge? They are making very strong claims for it. You can get a copy at their agency here, 3 Tremont Place.

The MS. has come, and I have looked over the chapter on U. S. Government. It seems to me it would be well to print it in a pamphlet by itself; and as I understand it, it can be done by making a few changes before the type in [is] distributed, and by making an extra set of plates; but we can tell better after the whole is in type, and decide the matter before distributing the type. Yours truly, D. C. Heath.

TL (WP, DLC) with WWhw notation on env.: "Ans. 7 June '89."

[1] The enclosure is missing.

[2] Francis Newton Thorpe, *The Government of the People of the United States* (Philadelphia, 1889).

From Albert Bushnell Hart

My dear Prof Wilson: Cambridge, Mass., June 5, 1889

Yours of the 3d is just at hand and gives me sincere and hearty pleasure: both at counting you in the enterprise, and at the prospect of numerous conferences and many pleasant relations henceforth.

I have forwarded your letter to the publishers, who will make the business arrangements direct

The first question for the contributors to settle is the precise title of the three books. I hope in a very few days to be able to announce to you the accession, for the first volume, of a very able Western man. Pending that, can you give me your opinion as to the best titles, brief, yet suggesting the scope of each volume.

The first (1492-1760) ought plainly to be the Epoch of Colonization; do you think of anything to add?

For the second (1750-1829), I have thought of the Epoch of Revolution and Federation; but you may very likely suggest a more telling phrase.

For your volume (1829-1889), I hardly know what to suggest. Epoch of Union would be striking—but it was not all Union. Epoch of Division and Reunion might express it. It is possible in two words to put the reader in possession of a political theory and to indicate a point of view

This is the most pressing question, as I am anxious to have the announcements made as soon as possible.

Very soon I will write more at length about proportions, general views of the series and kindred points.

I am, Sincerely yours, Albert Bushnell Hart

ALS (WP, DLC) with WWhw notation on env.: "Ans. June 12 1889."

A News Item

[June 7, 1889]

Prof. Wilson has decided to give an alternate course in Junior history next year. The course will be in American history. The English history course of this year will be repeated the following year, so that any one may take both courses.

Printed in the Middletown, Conn., *Wesleyan Argus*, XXII (June 7, 1889), 177.

From Richard Heath Dabney

My dear Friend: Richmond, Va. June 7th, 1889.

From the bottom of my heart I thank you for the warm friendship and deep sympathy for me that appear in every line of your letter.[1] And, what is more, I know you well enough to be certain that your words are not the mere conventional phrases of custom, but are fraught with sincerest feeling. . . .

Time & again did my darling speak to me of the pleasure she

had felt at meeting you & your sweet wife last summer, and I wish now to thank you both most earnestly for your kindness & cordiality towards her.

Most truly your friend R. H. Dabney.

P.S. omitted. ALS (WP, DLC) with WWhw notation on env.: "Ans. 31 Oct./89."

1 Wilson's letter is missing. Dabney's wife, Mary Bentley Dabney, had died of peritonitis on May 18, 1889, after giving birth to a daughter on May 12.

From Robert Bridges

Dear Classmate: New York June 8th, 1889.

The Committee have engaged rooms in Princeton to accomodate all the men who will attend the class reunion from June 15th to June 19th. I have arranged that the Witherspoon Crowd can be quartered, as we were during the Sexennial, at the House of Mrs. Smith, on Railroad Avenue. I shall also arrange to have club board there for the Crowd. We want you all to be on hand by Saturday night, so that we can have as long a time as possible together. Please notify me *immediately* when you expect to arrive in Princeton. Faithfully yours, Robert Bridges

Be sure to come Sat. 15th. BoB

TLS (WP, DLC) with handwritten postscript and WWhw notation on env.: "Ans."

From Daniel Collamore Heath

Dear Prof. Wilson: Boston June 8th, 1889

Your favor of the 7th inst. received. To tell the truth, I looked over only a little of the MS. on U. S. Government. I did not care to look it over. I felt sure you were the man to make the book when I approached you on the subject, and I now feel as sure you have made a good one, even without inspecting it. I know it will be a credit to our list as well as to yourself.

We send with this a contract just signed by Prof. Corson, on his Introduction to Shakespeare.[1] This is the kind of contract we think would be fair all around on your book. If you should insist upon it, we should leave the Contract in its original form, viz., we to pay you royalty as soon as the money put in plates has been returned to us. Prof. Corson's, you will see, is made to mean that we pay royalty as soon as we begin to make any money ourselves on the book. In other words, we shall donate from 500 to 1000 copies, and the whole cost of these, with postage, is to be given back to us in addition to the cost of plates before we pay royalty. We sometimes specify that royalty shall be paid after 1000 copies of the book have been sold. This is the English plan. Perhaps you would prefer it. As to the Chapter Heading, we think you will like those in the proof sent you.

Yours Truly, D. C. Heath & Co.

TL (WP, DLC).

[1] Hiram Corson, *An Introduction to the Study of Shakespeare* (Boston, 1889). Wilson returned the contract.

From Stockton Axson to Ellen Axson Wilson

Dear Sister Athens Ga June 10 [1889]

Bro W's letter and your postscript to hand. To tell you that I am delighted is to speak mildly. There now remains nothing but to persuade Uncle Randolph that I am not stark mad, and then I will come on. I will leave Athens the early part of week after next. (The week beginning with Sunday 17th). I will write you the exact date in a few days. I am now staying with Cousin Ed, Cousin Mayme having gone home.[1] E. H.,[2] who has been spending the week in Athens returned home today, and I am consequently a little broken up—the only cloud on my horizon.

With a heart full of love for all Your's Stockton.

APS (WP, DLC).

[1] The Edward T. Browns.

[2] Stockton's girl friend, Emily Howell, daughter of Evan Park Howell, publisher and later editor of the *Atlanta Constitution*.

Four Bibliographies[1]

[June 10–c. June 12, 1889]

Growth of the English Constitution
Work for Special Honors, Class of '90
Bibliography

MAIN AUTHORITIES:

Creasy, "Rise and Progress of the English Constitution."

Freeman, "Growth of the English Constitution."

Macaulay, "History of England," chap. I.

"Hallam's Constitutional History," in his Miscellaneous Essays, vol. I.

Brougham, "The British Constitution."

De Lolme, "The Constitution of England." Old, but excellent as a picture of the English constitution at the time and as a comparison of the English with foreign systems of government at the period.

Taswell-Langmead, "Constitutional History of England." A scholarly epitome, founded both upon the standard writers (Stubbs, Hallam, and May) and upon independent study.

Sheldon Amos. "Fifty Years of the English Constitution," 1830 to 1880. Traces the institutional changes effected since the first Reform Bill.

Bagehot, "The English Constitution." Incomparably the best description of the present character of the government of England.

Subsidiary:

Todd, "Parliamentary Government in the English Colonies."

FOR REFERENCE:

The standard histories of *Stubbs, Hallam,* and *May,* which together constitute a continuous constitutional history of England from the earliest times down to the present century. Ought constantly to be consulted, and in large part *read.*

◊

Revolution of 1688: Its Political Importance (1660-1704)
Work for Special Honors, Class of '90
Bibliography

I. MAIN AUTHORITIES:

Green, "History of the English People," Book VIII;
"Short History of the English People," Chapter IX.

Burnet, "History of My Own Times."

Macaulay, "History of England," chaps. IV-XX. Relies very largely upon Burnet.

Mackintosh, "History of the Revolution in England, 1688."

Hallam, "Constitutional History of England," chaps. XII-XV. A chief reliance for the constitutional effects of the events and transactions of the period.

Ranke, "History of England, particularly in the Eighteenth Century," vols. IV-VI,–especially the critical matter at the end of the last volume.

II. SUBSIDIARY AND ILLUSTRATIVE:

Gairdner and Spedding, "Studies in English History,["] Essay VII, on "The Divine Right of Kings: The History of a Doctrine."

Echard, "The History of the Revolution and the Establishment of England in the Year 1688."

Christie, "Life of the First Earl of Shaftesbury."

Memoirs of Sir William Temple, in *Temple's Works,* vol. 2.

Dixon, "Life of Penn."

Evelyn's Diary

Saville Correspondence

Letters from the Bodleian.

"Narratives Illustrative of the Contests in Ireland, 1640, 1690." (Camden Society's Publications)

III. FOR REFERENCE:

Somerville, "History of Political Transactions and of Parties."

State Trials, vols. 10, 11.

Cooke, G. W., "History of Party," vol. I.

Woodrow Wilson 11 June, 1889.

◊

Constructive Period of U. S. History (1774-1809)
Work for Special Honors, Class of '90.
Bibliography

I. General Histories:
Pitkin, "History of the United States," (1763-'97)
Hildreth, do. do. First Series, vol. III, Second Series, vol. I.
Bancroft, "History of the United States," vols. VII-X inclusive.
McMaster, "History of the People of the United States," vol. I.
Schouler, "History of the United States under the Constitution," vols. I, II.

II. *With special reference to* the genesis and history of *the Constitution*:
Eliot's Debates
The Federalist
Curtis, "History of the Constitution."
Bancroft, do. do.
von Holst, "Constitutional History of the United States," vol. I.
Winsor (editor), "Narrative and Critical History of America," vol. VI and chaps. I-IV in vol. VII.
Frothingham, "Rise of the Republic of the United States."

III. Biographies:
Jared Sparks, "Life of Gouverneur Morris."
American Statesmen Series, volumes on

Washington	John Quincy Adams
Jefferson	Patrick Henry
Madison	Hamilton
Samuel Adams	Marshall
John Adams	Gouverneur Morris

IV. Books of General Reference:
Collected Works of

Washington	Hamilton (*Lodge's* edition)
Adams	Jay
Jefferson	

Benton, Abridgment of the Debates of Congress, vols. I, II.
The Statesman's Manual, vol. I.
Johnston, "History of American Politics."
Sherman, Henry, "Governmental History of the United States."

Woodrow Wilson 11 June, 1889.

◊

French Revolution
Work for Special Honors, Class of '90
Bibliography

I. Introductory:
Arthur Young, "Travels in France," together with the general summary of same in
Alison, "History of Europe," vol. I.

Sir James Stephen, "Lectures on the History of France," lectures XVII-XXIV.

John Morley, Miscellanies, "France in the Eighteenth Century."

Buckle, "History of Civilization in England," vol. I., chapters 8-14.

Taine, "The Ancient Régime"

Tocqueville, de, "The Ancient Régime and the Revolution."

Gardiner, Mrs. B. M., "The French Revolution" (Epoch Series), a brief epitome of the results of the latest research.

W. O. Morris, "The French Revolution and the First Empire" (Epoch Series), contains in appendix a rather full bibliography.

Lacombe, "The History of a People," a French epitome of national history.

II. Standard General Histories whose accounts are brought down to the Revolutionary period:

Kitchin, "History of France."
Guizot, do. do.
Martin, do. do.

III. Special Histories of the Revolutionary Period:

von Sybel, "History of the French Revolution."
H. A. Taine, "The French Revolution."
Thiers, do. do.
Mignet, do. do.
Necker, J., do. do.
de Stael, Madame, do. do.

Necker's account is, of course, that of a contemporary, and the history of his daughter, Madame de Stael, naturally follows in the same line.

Stephens, "The French Revolution," one volume, a second to be published. *The period of Napoleon and the first Empire* is best treated in the two following works:

Lanfrey, "History of Napoleon I."

Thiers, "The Consulate and the Empire."

IV. Sources of Side Light and Suggestion:

Frederic Harrison, "Choice of Books," Essay on "Histories of the French Revolution."

Memoirs of St. Simon

Memoirs of Lafayette.

Smyth, "Lectures on the French Revolution."

Brougham, "Historical Sketches" of prominent actors in the Revolution.

C. K. Adams, "Democracy and Monarchy in France."

Carlyle, "The French Revolution," an extraordinarily vivid and suggestive prose poem.

Blanqui, "History of Political Economy," vol. II, chap. 37 throws light on the history of the *thought* which was preparing the Revolution.

John Morley, Lives of Voltaire, Diderot, and Rousseau, indicates the influence of the skeptical thought of the eighteenth century in France upon the revolutionary tendencies of the time.

Edward Dowden, "Studies in Literature," Essay on "The French Revolution and Literature."

Edmund Burke, "Reflections on the French Revolution"

Mackintosh, "*Vindiciae Gallicae*," an answer to Burke.

Rosenthal, "America and France: Influence of the United States on France in the Eighteenth Century."

V. Books of General Reference:

Chéruel, "Dictionnaire historique des Institutions, Moeurs, et Coutumes de la France," is excellent for explaining institutions, taxes, offices, etc.

"Comparative Display of the French Revolution," a collection of the views of various writers.

Henry Reeve, "Royal and Republican France."

Gautier, "Précis de l'Histroire [Histoire] du Droit Française," explains the privileges of clergy and noblesse and all other legal points bearing upon the Revolution.

"Paris and Its Historical Scenes."

E. Baines, "Wars of the French Revolution."

Woodrow Wilson 10 June, 1889

WWT MSS. (WP, DLC).

1 Arranged in the order of Wilson's list of topics, printed at June 12, 1889, rather than by date of composition.

From Longmans, Green & Company

Dear Sir, New York June 10 1889

We are much pleased to learn from Professor Hart that you are willing to undertake the preparation of the volume in our proposed series 'Epochs of American History' about which you have been in correspondence with him. We will if you please send you in the course of a few days the formal agreements for your signature & we hope to be able to announce the undertaking in our list very shortly.

We need not, in view of the fact that Professor Hart has arranged the terms of payment, &c. recapitulate them here but we should like to say that we should be perfectly willing to pay half the agreed upon sum on acceptance of your *MS.* & the balance on publication, instead of waiting for the publication of the volume for the full payment, if such an arrangement would be preferable to you.

We think you would like to have a set of the Epochs of Modern & Ancient History to which we propose the new series as a companion set. Probably they would be of use to you as illustrative of the general style of book we want, though of course you will be in communication with Professor Hart on all such details. We therefore send a set of each to your address, by Express, & beg your acceptance of them.

We trust before very long to find an opportunity of making your personal acquaintance. Meanwhile we are, Dear Sir

Faithfully yours Longmans, Green & Co

ALS (WP, DLC) with WWhw notation on env.: "Ans. June 11/89."

To Robert Bridges

Dear Bobby, Middletown, June 10th/89

Just a hasty line to give assurance that I will (D. V.) be in Princeton the evening of Sat., the 15—at just what hour I have not the (schedule) means of saying. Until then, much hard work, but also much joyful anticipation.

As ever,

Affectionately Yours, Woodrow Wilson

ALS (WC, NjP).

To Daniel Collamore Heath

My dear Mr. Heath, Middletown, Conn., 11 June. 1889.

I have examined and herewith return the Corson agreement which you were kind enough to send for my examination. I do not insist upon having the contract in the original printed form of this one,—I do not want to insist unreasonably upon any particular terms,—but I will say frankly that I should feel very much better satisfied to have it so. Indeed, I have had a certain expectation that the terms would be those of the printed form, for it was such terms that you suggested in our original correspondence on the subject as an alternative arrangement should I not care to own the plates.[1]

[Sincerely yours, Woodrow Wilson]

WWTL (draft) (WP, DLC).

[1] Heath undoubtedly sent Wilson a contract for *The State* on June 13, at the same time that he sent contracts for "The American State" referred to in the Editorial Note, "Wilson's Elementary Textbook in American Government." Heath may have sent only one copy of the contract for *The State*, which Wilson at once signed and returned. In any event, there is no copy of this agreement in the Wilson Papers. Heath submitted the printed form contract for "The American State" providing for a royalty of 10 per cent after the publisher's investment had been recovered. It is reasonable to assume that Heath sent the same contract for *The State*.

To Munroe Smith

My dear Prof. Smith, Middletown, Conn., 12 June, '89

Let me thank you very heartily for your kindness in giving to my MS. so thorough a reading, and for your very helpful criticisms and suggestions. As I need not tell you (or, rather, as I *have* told you) I am very far indeed from being a specialist in the history of Roman Law, and just such minute corrections, as well as general, as you have given me were what I needed. I must do myself the justice to say that you were right in supposing that I was not ignorant of most of the points to which you called my attention. But it is one thing to have a fairly accurate knowledge of a subject and quite another to be used to generalizing and summarizing upon it: and I was quite prepared for the discovery that I had both made slips and *seemed*, from my tyro statements, to make still more. I am the more grateful, therefore, for the guidance of your more accurate acquaintance with the subject and of your more experienced perception of how statements stand related towards one another within its domain.

The book has now gone to the printer and I have leisure to think calmly (?) of the rash experiment of publishing a text which deals with a little of everything—with things of which I have only a general knowledge as well as with things of which I have more than a general knowledge!

The table of contents of the last No. of the *Quarterly*[1] commends itself to a reader of my tastes—and doubtless, when the present load of annual examinations is lifted from me, exploration beneath the titles will repay me.

With renewed thanks and sincerest regard,

Very cordially Yours, Woodrow Wilson

ALS (*Political Science Quarterly* Papers, NNC).

[1] Wilson was referring to the June 1889 issue of the *Political Science Quarterly*, which contained the following articles: Albert Shaw, "Municipal Government in Great Britain"; J. Hampden Dougherty, "The Constitutions of the State of New York. II"; Edward P. Cheyney, "Decisions of the Courts in Conspiracy and Boycott Cases"; Frederick W. Whitridge, "Rotation in Office"; and Jeremiah W. Jenks, "The Development of the Whiskey Trust."

An Announcement of Topics for Special Honors Work in History

History
Special Honor Work
Class of '90

12 June 1889.

The candidates for special honors in History may choose their field of study from among the following topics:

1. *Growth of the English Constitution*
2. *The English Revolution of 1688.* (1660-1704)
3. *The Constructive Period of American History.* 1774-1809.
4. *The Old Régime and the Revolution in France* (1774-1815)

The choice should be made after consultation with me. After consultation I will furnish bibliographies.

Woodrow Wilson

WWT MS. (WP, DLC).

To Albert Bushnell Hart

My dear Prof. Hart, Middletown, Conn., 12 June, '89

Much rumination has failed to reveal to me better titles for the 'Epoch' volumes than these you suggest. They are excellent, and, I believe, no more open to criticism than are all simple descriptions of complex things. There were a score of other forces at work in the period 1829–, of course, besides the forces that made for 'Division': the lusty life was accumulating which was to assure Reunion; but a title's means of expression, like our own, are limited.

Does it not seem to you that a new 'Epoch,' in the sense of our series, opened at the close of the reconstruction period, in 1876, and that the beginning of a second century of independence will constitute a natural 'term' for the volume I am to prepare? The nation seems to me to have been a new nation since 1876.

I have had a very courteous note from Messrs. Longmans, Green, & Co., and they have very handsomely presented me with a complete set of the 'Epochs.'

I suppose that you are just now, like myself, laboring under the grievous burden of examinations.

Very sincerely Yours, Woodrow Wilson

TCL (RSB Coll., DLC).

To John Franklin Jameson

My dear Jameson, Middletown, Conn., 12 June, '89

Will you think it taking a base advantage of your friendship if I ask you to do for me some work of the most grievous kind? I have four examination papers, written for a prize,[1] to be read. I may not judge them myself—our rules exclude me; as probably knowing something of the men beforehand (!) I can have a subcommittee appointed to read them from the visiting examiners (ministers, lawyers, doctors, &c.) whom we invite here at our annuals in a quite old fashioned way, and who are really a practical factor in decisions; but I want some one who knows something about the subject! The subject is that (or rather those) covered by my forth-coming text-book (which is really in the hands of the printer). I am allowed to choose a committee (of one or more), if I prefer, outside the college to whom to send the papers, and I very much want you. I know that if I cannot have you, you will say so forthwith, but that, if possible, you will consent. The decision would have to be returned to us by the evening of Saturday, June 22nd.

I seem to have lost you, somehow: many times I have been conscious of our silence since that delightful meeting which was your 'treat,' and all the time I have been, so to say, sub-conscious of it. I have not been half so comfortable as I might have been without such pains and penalties.

You may have heard that Hart of Cambridge is to edit three 'Epochs of American History' for Longmans, Green, & Co., the perpetrators of the other 'Epochs'; but you have doubtless not heard that I am to write the third (1829–?)—the 'Epoch of Division and Reunion' (?) Rash, and intrinsically unlikely, but true!

Mrs. Wilson is not even yet quite well, but she is much better than when I saw you, and still commands sufficient good judgment to wish to be remembered to and by you in the kindest possible way.

With warm regards to Gardiner and for yourself much affection,

Yours as ever, Woodrow Wilson

ALS (J. F. Jameson Papers, DLC).

[1] It was almost certainly the Joseph D. Weeks Prize, awarded to that member of the senior class who wrote the best essay on political economy. The subject for the essay in 1889, set by Wilson, was "The Nature of Wages, and the Relation between Wages and Capital." *Annual Catalogue of Wesleyan University. 1888-89*, p. 59. The prize went to Mary Graham, honorable mention to Dudley Chase Abbott. Middletown, Conn., *Wesleyan Argus*, XXII (July 13, 1889), 186.

From Albert Bushnell Hart

My dear Prof. Wilson: Cambridge, Mass. June 13, 1889

Yours of the 12th is just at hand. I am to spend two or three days at New London holding examinations for the crew, beginning next Monday, and have tried in vain to find a rail connection which would take me over to Middletown and back in an afternoon. Could you run down say to Saybrook some afternoon and talk things over? I can get there at 1.40 P.M. either Monday or Tuesday.

One other thought about titles had come to me. To call 1750-1829, Formation of the Union: and 1829-1889 (76?) Consolidation of the Union, or Confirmation of the Union, or something of that sort. This point must be settled within a very few days, for the announcement.

The writer of Vol I is to be Mr Reuben G. Thwaites, Secy of the State Hist. Soc. of Wisconsin, a Yale graduate. Perhaps you know him[.] I am much pleased at the combination: representatives of Johns Hopkins, Yale and Harvard, which we shall all three agree in considering the three most important universities in America; an exponent of the real spirit of the South, West and East, (which is modest for a man born in Ohio and a willing renegade to New England[)].

Yours sincerely, Albert Bushnell Hart

Please send me or give me a list of your degrees and publications

ALS (WP, DLC) with WWhw notation on env.: "Ans. June 14/89."

From John Franklin Jameson

My dear Wilson: Providence, June 13 [1889].

You're right in thinking I'd do it for you if I could, but I just can't add another hour's work before July 1st, what with the wind-up here, Mrs. Carey's, (forgot you knew her) book,[1] and my own.[2] I write in haste, in order to reply at once to your communication *qua* request. Shall reply to it *qua* letter before long. Kindest regards to Mrs Wilson & yourself.

Yours J. F. Jameson.

ALS (WP, DLC).

1 Victor Duruy, *A History of France*, translated and abridged by Martha Ward Carey, with an introduction by Jameson (New York, 1889).

2 J. F. Jameson (ed.), *Essays in the Constitutional History of the United States in the Formative Period, 1775-1789* (Boston and New York, 1889).

From Joseph Ruggles Wilson

Dearest Son New York June 17 1889.

I have just written to dear Ellie[1] (in reply to her note of 15th) to say that I would not go to Princeton,[2] because (1) I hate a crowd; (2) I cannot consent to interfere with your freedom of movement amongst old friends, & (3) that I would go to Middletown after your commencement there—meanwhile making my annual pilgrimage to Saratoga. I left (carefully) my N. York address with Josie, which it seems he did not communicate to you. It is 33 East 22nd St. where I have rooms.[3]

I would have told you all my plans if I had had any.

Your affc Father in great hurry.

ALS (WP, DLC).

[1] JRW to EAW, June 17, 1889, ALS (WP, DLC).

[2] That is, for commencement and the tenth reunion of Woodrow's class.

[3] The home of Elizabeth Bartlett Grannis, about whom see JRW to WW, July 25, 1889, n. 1.

From Marion Wilson Kennedy

My dearest Woodrow: Batesville [Ark.], June 18th/89.

The invitation came yesterday, and I hasten to obey its instructions. Am so sorry, and doubtless you will be so disappointed that we can't accept. I do hope Ellie has not wearied herself getting ready for us. I do not know why I have started off in this strain, unless it is to keep from taking the very opposite tone. The truth is, I am very unhappy just now; and see no signs of anything in the future,—as far as this life goes—, but increased darkness. Ross has, apparently, lost his health finally. There are, of course, bare chances of his recovery, but no physician has seemed to have any hope of late. About two weeks ago, Ross had a slight hemorrhage, which he thought came from his throat, but the doctor told me came from his lungs. Since then, he has every day spit a little blood at intervals. . . . But oh! Woodrow, I do feel as if I *cannot* stand for long this dreadful suspense. At any moment the fatal hemorrhage may come. . . .

I do so want to see you, my brother. There are matters which look so dreadful when written out in black and white, that I feel I must ask someone about, and Annie and Josie are too easily excited on these subjects to make it desirable to consult them. Is there any chance of seeing you before the summer is over? *Do come*, if possible. We will be more than glad to have a visit from you, Ellie and the dear babies, all. Please try to come. Father told me of your book for that English house. I am glad, only the remuneration seems to me very small for the amount of work necessary, and the limit set to the time. Have you finished those text books yet? I am very busy just now. Studying the science of Music, and doing a good deal of practicing, to fit myself for a position of teacher. They tell me, I am quite competent to teach now, but I want to be able to do more than just ordinarily well. Then, I am brushing up on the two languages I ever studied, and studying some Greek, to help Joe,[1] who is to study that and Algebra with me this summer. I have to keep busy, or I would lose my mind. Please write to me when you can, my brother. I want one of your letters so badly. . . . With much love to you all,

Your loving sister Marion.

ALS (WP, DLC) with WWhw notation on env.: "Ans. June 30."
[1] Her son, Joseph Leland Kennedy.

From Stockton Axson to Ellen Axson Wilson

Dear Sister, Athens Ga June 20/89

Your letter received. It seems that I must have misunderstood Bro Woodrow's letter. I will come on very soon though it is impossible for me as yet to give the exact date. Would it be possible for you to postpone the German lessons until the 10th or 15th of July. I will be on before that date, but this gives a good margin. My plans have been changed so often during the past month that I am afraid to say anything definite just yet as to the exact time of my coming.

My little turn at journalism has been very hard, but very pleasant. With love for all I.S.K.A.

API (WP, DLC).

From Herbert Baxter Adams

Dear Mr. Wilson Amherst, Mass. June 21, 1889.

Will you kindly send me a brief report of your second year's course of lectures for use in our review of the past year, and also a brief statement or outline of your course for 1889-90?[1] The barest skeleton will serve our present purpose. I thank you for your prompt examination of the theses.

Very cordially H. B. Adams

ALS (WP, DLC) with WWhw notation on env.: "Ans. June 27 '89."
[1] It is printed at June 27, 1889.

From Joseph Ruggles Wilson

Dearest Woodrow– N. York, Saturday, 22nd [June 1889]

Your sweet note (duplicate I presume of that which you have sent to Saratoga) was received this morning. This, together with dear Ellie's letter, has made me quite happy. I am detained here longer than I had expected to be; but shall certainly (God willing) make for Saratoga on Monday or Tuesday next. I feel that I *must* have the waters there–and very soon. But how long I shall remain in their enjoyment (?) cannot easily be foreseen–probably though not beyond a couple of weeks:–and then for Middletown if at the Middletown end the way be clear, of which you will advise me I am sure in all that candor which genuine affection implies.

I hope that you will have a delectable vacation, and happy is he who is permitted to find it at *home.*

Had you a good time during the little Princeton visit? As you say nothing about it, I presume that it was somewhat colorless.[1]

Believe me to be Your affectionate Father, with a heart full of love for dear Ellie & the bairns.

ALS (WP, DLC).

[1] The commencement festivities opened on June 15 and ended with the one hundred and forty-second Annual Commencement in the First Presbyterian Church on June 19. A highlight of the affair was the unveiling of Saint-Gaudens' statue of President McCosh, given by the Class of 1879, in Marquand Chapel on June 18. For an account of the ceremony, in which Wilson did not participate, see *The Princetonian,* XIV (June 19, 1889), 1.

The statue stood in Marquand Chapel until all but the head was destroyed when the Chapel burned in 1920. However, a cast of the statue had been made for an exhibition of Saint-Gaudens' works at the Metropolitan Museum of Art in 1907. A bronze statue made from this cast, which was happily preserved, now stands in the Princeton University Chapel. A contemporary picture of the statue appears in the photographic section of Volume 5.

From Longmans, Green & Company

Dear Sir, New York June 25, 1889

We have the pleasure to send you with this two (2) copies of the formal 'Memorandum of Agreement' for your volume in our series *Epochs of American History* duly signed &c on our part & we shall be glad if you will execute them and return one copy to us at your early convenience.[1] We are preparing announcements of the Series and will send you copies as soon as they are ready.

We are Dear Sir

Faithfully yours Longmans, Green & Co

ALS (WP, DLC). Enc.: contract between Longmans, Green & Company and WW, dated June 24, 1889, for publication of *Division and Reunion.*

[1] As Longmans, Green & Company to Wilson of June 28, 1889, reveals, Wilson returned a signed copy of the contract to the publisher on June 27. It is in the possession of the David McKay Company of New York, successor to Longmans, Green. The terms of the contract were those outlined in A. B. Hart to WW, April 23, 1889.

To Herbert Baxter Adams

My dear Dr Adams, Middletown, Conn., 27 June '89

Everybody in this little town has to entertain visitors as well as attend all exercises during the Commencement season, and I have not had a moment's time to answer your note of June 21 until now.

I enclose the outlines you want.[1] Hope they are all right.

We had the pleasure of having Dr Learned[2] with us for a couple of days. I had never met him before and Mrs. Wilson and I enjoyed his stay with us immensely. He's famously good company, and certainly in every way worth knowing.

I have been indiscreet enough to consent to prepare one of the three 'Epochs of American History' which Prof. Hart of Harvard is to edit for Longmans, Green, & Co. I am to have the third, 1829-1889. The rôle of historian will be a new one for me, but I trust that my newness will not stick out in the result. It's a period concerning which I have some ideas of my own—and I shall enjoy the opportunity to work them out.

The year here has been quite prosperous, but I am just now not a little tired.

As ever, Sincerely Yours, Woodrow Wilson

ALS (H. B. Adams Papers, MdBJ).

1 Wilson's enclosure is missing, but the version that appeared in print is given below.

2 Marion Dexter Learned, Associate in German, The Johns Hopkins University.

Wilson Reviews His Lectures at the Johns Hopkins

[*c. June 27, 1889*]

Dr. Woodrow Wilson gave twenty-five lectures upon Administration to twenty-four graduate students.

The lectures comprised a systematic and somewhat detailed account of the methods and machinery of local government in Prussia, France, England, and the United States, together with a brief notice of the organization of local administration in Switzerland, Austria-Hungary, and Sweden-Norway.

Printed in *Fourteenth Annual Report of the President of the Johns Hopkins University, 1889* (Baltimore, 1889), p. 58.

From Longmans, Green & Company

Dear Sir, New York June 28, 1889

We have your letter of yesterday's date together with the signed copy of the Memo. of Agreement—American Epochs—for which we thank you.

With regard to clause 5 we need only say that we accept your conditions & are quite content to know that you will let us have your book as early as you can.

We are announcing the Series in our forthcoming "Monthly List" & we find we are not quite sure as to how we should describe your connection with Wesleyan University. We have no recent catalogue at hand. We announce your volume thus:—

Division and Reunion (1829-1889)

By Woodrow Wilson, Ph.D. LL.D.
Professor of   in
Wesleyan University, Middletown, Conn.
Author of 'Congressional Government' &c. &c.

Will you be so good as to fill in any thing omitted or suggest any change which may seem to you desirable & let us have your criticism by return mail.

We are gratified to learn that you are pleased with the 'Epochs' Series in its new dress.

With compliments We are, Dear Sir

Faithfully yours Longmans, Green & Co

ALS (WP, DLC) with WWhw notation on env.: "Ans. June 29/89."

From Joseph Ruggles Wilson

Dearest Woodrow— Saratoga July 1 89.

I am now planning to be with you by the 4th of July—or the 5th at latest. I have to go down to N. York which is only a little out of my way from here to Middletown—and, if I think it safe to travel on the 4th will be with you then. Should any change in my expectations occur I will promptly advise you.

I preached yesterday to a big congregation, and am said to have filled utmost expectations.

In great haste & greater love to dearest Ellie & yourself

Your affc Father

ALS (WP, DLC).

From Joseph R. Wilson, Jr.

My dearest brother: C'ville. Tenn., 7/7/'89.

Your most welcome letter reached me yesterday and it is needless to say how much I enjoyed it. Thanks for your good advice.[1] I had about reached the same conclusion myself after mentioning the matter to Julia and asking her opinion. There is no formal engagement existing at present, I have no right to ask for one now, so there is no need of going to head quarters.[2] I know well how *I* feel, and know also how much she cares for me. This is as far as it can go now. Dear father and sister Marion sent their love to Julia through me, and she seemed much pleased. Cant you send her some message?

I expect to leave home for Batesville next Tuesday evening reaching B. about noon on Wednesday. I feel so very very sorry for dear sister Marion. She wrote to me some little while ago telling me of her fears as to the possibility or *probability* of Bro. Ross' health failing entirely. What could be done if he were to die, brother? I have thought of this often, and wondered what should be done if such a misfortune should fall upon our dear sister. I am extremely anxious to see sister Marion, for you know it has been about seven years since I last saw her. The last time was when we were all together in Wilmington one Christmas. Dont you remember what a joyful time we all had? The memory of that day should be dear to us, for that was the last time our family was together, the last time our beloved mother had all her children about her.

After spending a few weeks in Arkansas, I will go to Columbia for a short while[,] returning home about the middle of August probably. Brother, it is needless to say how sorry I am that I cannot visit Middletown this summer. You know full well how much joy such a visit would give me, but it seems impossible.

I suppose dear father is with you now. How delightful it must be to welcome him in your own home! May God spare him and me, so that I will have a happy home in which he will always be welcome, *so* welcome. When I get such a home, I believe I will be as happy as a man can be in this world.

I am quite well, I believe. Unbounded love to dear sister Ellie, the little girls, dearest "pop," and your own dear self, from

Your aff. bro. Joseph.

ALS (WP, DLC).

[1] In Wilson's reply to J. R. Wilson, Jr., to WW, June 13, 1889, ALS (WP, DLC) with WWhw notation on env.: "Ans."

[2] In his letter of June 13, Joseph R. Wilson, Jr., had told Woodrow that he and Julia Lupton of Clarksville were in love and had asked whether Wilson thought he should request her parents' permission to become engaged in spite of the fact that his present prospects did not augur well for an early marriage. The romance with Julia did not last much longer, for Josie became engaged to Kate Wilson of Clarksville in 1890—without, however, asking his brother's advice about the best method of pursuing his suit. See J. R. Wilson to WW, Sept. 5, 1890, Vol. 7.

From Robert Bridges

Dear Tommy: [New York] July 15-89.

I met President Patton today, and had a very pleasant talk with him. He spoke of you and your work, and regretted that he had only met you casually, as he is very much interested in that line of study. I told him that it would give me great pleasure to bring you together, and suggested dinner at the [University] Club in the near future. He was very well disposed toward this idea, and modified it by suggesting luncheon on Monday next, July 22, as he will then be in the city (probably the last convenient day this summer.) I am very anxious that you should meet him then, and hope that you will stretch a point, (several if necessary to get here.) Please write me immediately that you can come. We'll have luncheon here at 1 p.m. You can then get a quiet corner in the smoking room and have a good long talk.

Please believe that this will be as much of a pleasure to Dr. Patton as to me, and don't let anything prevent your coming. I should be most happy to have you spend Sunday with me. We have a half holiday Saturday, and we could go off into the country together.

I ask an early reply so that I can write Dr. Patton.

Yours Sincerely Robert Bridges

ALS (WP, DLC) with WWhw notation on env.: "Ans. July 16/89."

From Horace Elisha Scudder

Dear Mr. Wilson Boston. 15 July 1889

I have been considering if it might not be well to have a paper in the Atlantic at this time touching some of the questions which arise out of the erection of territories into states. The work of the four territories will doubtless be over soon, but the public interest will continue to linger over this addition to our collection of states, and I could indeed find room for a paper by you on the subject in the October number if I had the copy within two or three weeks. What do you say? Has your mind been running in that direction? But I like your work so well that I will say frankly I am more desirous of having a paper from you than of indicating the subject too closely.

Perhaps I ought to explain that in the absence of Mr Aldrich in Europe this summer I am in charge of the magazine.

Ever truly your friend H. E. Scudder

ALS (WP, DLC) with WWhw notation on env.: "Ans. 24 July/89."

From Annie Wilson Howe

New Brighton Hotel[,] Sullivan Island [S. C.]
My darling Brother, July 15th, 1889

Your letter came the day before we left home. I think if it had come a few days sooner we would have changed our plans, and accepted your cordial invitation. *Nothing* could give me as much pleasure as a visit to you and dear Ellie. I have longed to see you in your own home, and to see those dear little girls. Maybe, if we all live until next summer, we can make you a visit. I had intended to stay at home this summer, but was taken sick a few weeks ago, and lost my strength altogether. Dr. George then decided that I must come to the seashore for a few weeks, and then go to the mountains. When your letter came we thought we would go from this place to you, instead of going to the mountains, but found that the trip would cost nearly twice as much as the one we had planned, so we had to give it up. . . .

I suppose dear Father is with you now. I had expected Josie to join me here, but he has just gone to Batesville, where he expects to stay for several weeks he says. He will come to us later. . . .

I am glad you are not going to work hard this summer. You certainly ought to rest. Father's visit will refresh you, I am sure. His visits are so short, always, that we hardly have time to realize that he is with us, before he is gone again. His restlessness is pitiful to me. Don't you feel troubled about Ross? I am afraid he will not live much longer. Marion wrote to me not long ago in great distress. Ross was in Little Rock for treatment. Do you know just what his trouble is?

I feel better already, and hope to be quite strong and well when I go home. The sea air always does me good. I fatten on it. . . .

Write to me whenever you can Woodrow, please. I am afraid there is no use asking Ellie to write. The boys send a great deal of love. With a heart *full* for you both and kisses for the little girls, Your devoted sister, Annie.

ALS, (WP, DLC).

To Robert Bridges

My dear Bobby, Middletown, Conn., 16 July, 1889

I go to the New England (Chatauqua) Assembly at Northampton, Mass., to lecture on Saturday next, the 20th.[1] The lecture is to be given at 10 A. M.—and I could probably get to New York late that afternoon (I do not know the schedules up that way). That would give me Sunday with you, but not the trip into the country. I should like ever so much to spend Sunday with with [*sic*] you; but if you would rather go out of town, do so, by all means, and I will come down Monday morning. In any case, I accept with pleasure the invitation to meet Dr Patton at luncheon at your Club at one P. M. on Monday—and unless something unforeseen prevents, you may confidently expect me.

Let me know by a line what you prefer as to Sunday.

In haste and affection

Yours as ever, Woodrow Wilson

ALS (WC, NjP).

[1] See the news item printed at July 22, 1889, and Wilson's lecture, "A Literary Politician," printed at July 20, 1889.

From Robert Bridges

Dear Tommy: New York July 17 1889

I shall be glad to see you Saturday evening, or anytime that suits your convenience. Let me know when you expect to arrive so that I may not keep you waiting for me. We can take a little run into the country on Sunday if it is pleasant.

I am very glad that you can come.

See this week's *Harpers Weekly* for picture of McCosh statue and fine article.[1] Yours Robert Bridges

ALS (WP, DLC).

[1] Robert Bridges, "St. Gaudens's Mural Statue of Dr. McCosh," *Harper's Weekly*, XXXIII (July 20, 1889), 580.

From Marion Wilson Kennedy

My dearest Woodrow: Batesville [Ark.], July 17th, 1889.

I have waited all this while to answer your most welcome and highly appreciated letter, that I might have something definite to say, in reply to your suggestion. In the meantime, I wrote to our Little Rock doctor, and asked him what he thought of such a trip for Ross. The fact was, I was quite certain what he would say, but wanted to be able to give you the opinion of someone who knew what he was talking about. You see, when Ross first got to Little Rock, the doctors examined his lungs, and advised him to go immediately to some higher and drier climate, Minnesota, for instance. But in the two weeks of Ross' stay in Little Rock, his strength failed so rapidly, and the lung trouble increased so fast, that the doctors agreed it was *too late* for any trip to do good. Ross is unable to sit up the fourth part of a day, and as for any work, he can scarcely dress and undress himself, even with my help, for shortness of breath. You know, both lungs are seriously affected. The right lung has quite a cavity in it. The doctors say, he may linger for some months. . . .

He could not begin to stand the trip across the plains at this season, and he can hardly hope to have strength for it in the fall, if indeed, he is spared us until then. It seems terrible even to speak of that, Woodrow, and yet it is only *our* side that even *seems* hard, and I do not feel that it is something to cry out about. "It is the Lord. Let Him do what seemeth Him good." Though I know well enough that all the earthly brightness will go out of my life when my dear husband goes, still I just feel that my only prayers must be for resignation and strength for myself, and grace for my darling, and that the will of the Lord may be done. I know He loves our dear ones and us far better than we can love each other, and so, why should I be afraid of anything He may send to us? Of course, I hardly dare expect to feel this confidence so clearly all the time, but when I don't feel so, it will be altogether my own fault. Your words of sympathy are very sweet to me, my brother, and are a great comfort to me. I did not show your last letter to your brother Ross. He has settled down to try nothing more than we are now trying, and knows all we know as to his condition, and there seemed no need to disturb him afresh. How are you all this summer? Do write me more about yourself and Ellie and the children. Do you know, *I* did not know Ellie had even *one* brother, until since Joe came. We are, of course, enjoying Joe immensely, and hope to keep him with us a good while. He looks strikingly like, and yet quite as strikingly unlike you. There is no reason at all why he should not stay with us at least until the first of August, and probably until the middle of that month. I want him to stay as long as possible, that we may become well acquainted with him again. You know, this is our first sight of him since seven years ago last January. He was then only in his sixteenth year.

But I must not write any more now. Ross cannot read for longer than a few minutes, and then he gets lonely, if I am not there to talk to him, or fan him, or just sit quietly by. As for myself, I count every moment I have to spend away from him as lost time; for how long I may have him, only One knows.

Josie send[s] warmest love—as does also your brother Ross and

Loving sister Marion.

Ask Ellie to write, and tell me all about the two girlies and herself.

ALS (WP, DLC).

From Ellen Axson Wilson

My darling Middletown July 20/89

Lest you should be disturbed at the non-appearance of your proof, I drop a line to say that none arrived this morning. If it turns up this afternoon I will forward at once. I rather hope they *will* "let up" for a bit so that you may have a real holiday in N. Y. It has cleared off quite hot here & I fear you will find it the same there. Please sir, be careful not to run any risk of sun-stroke.

I had a card from little Randolph[1] today. They left N. Y. yesterday for Niagara; from there they go to Boston & will then come here about the 1st of Aug. It is rather a pity that everyone postpones their visits so, since for obvious reasons, I should much prefer to have all the company I am going to 'and be done with it' as soon as possible. By the way, don't forget to invite Mr. *Sheldon*![2]

We are all well & had a good night,—but *ah*! how I miss you, darling! One would think it wouldn't be quite so dreary as usual in your absence now that S.[3] is here, but it doesn't seem to make any difference. I vow that when the children grow up, you shall *never* get away from me, sir,—no not even to a baseball game in the next village! It is only the philosophical reflection that it is absolutely unavoidable which enables me to endure it with equanimity now. If I *could* follow you around it would be intolerable not to. But Ed is "going down town" and is waiting for this so I must stop. If you have time, drop me a line to say how the lecture passed off, what sort of an audience you had, &c. I hope you will have 'a *real* nice time' in N. Y. even at the Luncheon. With a heart full, full to overflowing with love for my darling. Your little Wife.

ALS (WC, NjP).

1 Randolph Axson, Jr.

2 Edward Wright Sheldon, Wilson's classmate at Princeton.

3 Stockton Axson.

Wilson's Critique of Bagehot's *Physics and Politics*

[c. July 20, 1889][1]

The figure and idea of evolution, it would seem, is approaching the misfortune of being overdone. Everybody knows that govt. was never invented and can never be safely altered by invention; but everybody is now grown weary of hearing Sir James Mackintosh,[2] no great authority, after all, quoted to the effect that govts. are not made, but grow. Mr. Mill is at great pains to prove, in his Essay on *Representative Government*, that human choice and originating thought do have some not inconsiderable part in giving to political institutions the impulse of change–wh. is the impulse of progress. The formula of evolution is easy, we know; but it is not wholly safe, we suspect. True Mr. Bagehot was a great thinker upon such topics and an incomparable critic of politics, whether old or new; and Mr. Bagehot, in his quite incomparable *Physics and Politics* deliberately applies the laws of heredity and natural selection to political society. For my part, I acknowledge, I religiously believe most that the book contains. If it be not true, it is a sin to have presented it so charmingly. It is made to appear so irresistably probable that no man of historic imagination can long hold out against believing it. But of course Mr. B. was speaking by analogy. He knew that Politics was *not* Physics: that they proceeded not by laws of nature but laws of character and mind. And that is just the fact that makes the analogy risky. We need a fresh formulation of the principles [of] political change, and a a [*sic*] somewhat shifted point of view.

WWhw MS. (WP, DLC).

1 The Editors ascribe this composition date on the assumption that Wilson might have re-read *Physics and Politics* before writing the lecture on Bagehot, printed below, and because the handwriting of the memorandum on *Physics and Politics* is typical of this period.

2 A prolific British historian and philosopher of the first half of the nineteenth century.

A Lecture on Walter Bagehot[1]

[July 20, 1889]

A Literary Politician

It is to be my pleasant function this evening to introduce to

1 Wilson gave this lecture many times before its final publication in revised form in *Mere Literature and Other Essays* (Boston and New York, 1896). The text printed here includes two new opening paragraphs that Wilson probably added when he gave this lecture at the Methodist Church in Middletown on October 15, 1889, as well as handwritten emendations that he may have made after the first delivery at Northampton.

you a literary politician. I am not sure that he would himself have accepted this summary description. It is not a label much in vogue; and I suspect that it is my first duty to justify it by saying at once what I mean by a 'literary politician.' I do *not* mean a politician who affects literature—one who seems to appreciate the solemn moral purpose of Wordsworth's Happy Warrior and yet is opposed to ballot reform. Neither do I mean a literary man who affects politics, who earns his *victories* through the publishers and his *defeats* at the hands of the men who manage the primaries. I mean the man who has the genius to see deep into affairs and the discretion to keep out of them—a man to whom, by reason of knowledge and imagination and sympathy, governments and policies are as open books, but who, instead of seeking to put haphazard characters of his own into those books, wisely prefers to read their pages aloud to others. A man, this, who knows politics and yet does not handle policies.

I have observed a very wide-spread skepticism as to the *existence* of such a man. Many people would ask me to *prove* him as well as define him; and that, as they assume, upon a very obvious principle:

It is a rule of universal acceptance in *theatrical* circles that no one can write a good play who has no practical acquaintance with the stage. A knowledge of green-room possibilities and of stage machinery, it is held, must go before all successful attempts to put either passion or humour into action on the boards if pit and gallery are to gain a sense of reality from the performance. No wonder that Sheridan's plays were effective: Sheridan was both author and actor; but abundant wonder that simple Goldsmith succeeded with his exquisite 'She Stoops to Conquer,' unless we are to suppose that an Irishman of the last century, like the Irishman of this, had some sixth sense which enabled him to understand other people's business better than his own. For poor Goldsmith could not act (even off the stage) and his only connexion with the theatre seems to have been his acquaintance with Garrick. Lytton, we know, had Macready constantly at his elbow to give, and enforce, suggestions calculated to render plays playable. And in our own days the authors of what we indulgently call 'dramatic literature' find themselves constantly obliged to turn tragedies into comedies, comedies into farces, to satisfy the managers: for managers know the stage and pretend to know all possible audiences also. The writer for the stage must be playwright first, author second.

It is principles of criticism similar to these which are not a little affected by those who play the parts, great and small, on the stage of politics. There is on that stage too, it is said, a complex machinery of action and of scene-shifting, a green-room practice as to costume and make-up, as to entry and exit, necessities of concession to foot-lights and of appeal to the pit quite as rigorous and quite as proper for study as are the concomitants of that other thing which we frankly *call* acting. This is an idea, indeed, accepted in some quarters outside the political play-house as well as within it. The late Mr. Sidney Colvin[2] was rightly of the opinion that "Men of letters and of thought are habitually too much given to declaiming at their ease against the delinquencies of men of action and affairs. The inevitable friction of practical politics," he argued, "generates *heat* enough already, and the office of the thinker and critic should be to supply not heat but light. The difficulties which attend his own unmolested task, the task of seeking after and proclaiming salutary truths, should teach him to make allowance for the far more *urgent* difficulties which beset the politician, the man obliged, amidst the clash of interests and temptations, to practice from hand to mouth, and at his peril, the most uncertain and at the same time the most indispensable of the experimental arts."

Mr. Colvin was himself of the class of men of letters and of thought; he accordingly puts the case against his class rather mildly,—much more mildly than the practical politician would desire to see it put. Practical politicians are wont to regard closeted writers upon politics with a certain condescension, though a condescension dashed with slight traces of apprehension,—or at least of uneasy concern. "Literary men can say strong things of their age," said Mr. Bagehot, "for no one expects that they will go out and act on them. They are a kind of ticket-of-leave lunatics, from whom no harm is for the moment expected; who seem quiet, but on whose vagaries a practical public must have its eye." I suppose that the really serious practical man in politics would see nothing of satirical humour in such a description:—he would have you note that, although traced with a sharp point of wit the picture is nevertheless true. He can cite you a score of instances illustrative of the danger of putting faith in the political judgments of those who are not politicians, bred in the shrewd and moving world of political management.

[2] WW's announcement of Colvin's death was premature, inasmuch as Sir Sidney lived until 1927. The error was corrected in the published version of this essay (*ibid.*, p. 71).

The genuine practical politicians, such as, (even our enemies being the witnesses) we must be acknowledged to produce in great numbers and perfection in this country, reserves his acidest contempt for the literary man who assumes to utter judgements touching public affairs and political institutions. If he be a reading man, he is able to point you, in illustration of what you are to expect in such cases, to the very remarkable essays of the late Mr. Matthew Arnold on parliamentary policy and the Irish question. If he be not a reading man, (as sometimes happens,) he is able to ask, much to your confusion, 'What does a fellow who lives inside a library know about politics, anyhow?' You have to admit, if you are candid, that most fellows who live in libraries know little enough. You remember Macaulay, and acknowledge that, although he made admirable speeches in Parliament, held high political office, and knew all the considerable public men of his time, he *did imagine* the creation to have been made in accordance with Whig notions, and did hope to find the judgments of Lord Somers some day answering mankind as standards for all possible times and circumstances. You recall Gibbon and allow (to you[r] own thought at least) that, had he not remained silent in his seat, a very few of his sentences would probably have sufficed to freeze the House of Commons stiff. The ordinary literary man, even though he be an eminent historian, is ill enough fitted to be a mentor in affairs of government. For, it must be allowed, things are for the most part *very simple in books*, —and in practical life very complex. Not all the bindings of a library enclose the world of circumstance.

But the practical politician should discriminate. Let him but find a man with an imagination which, though it stands aloof, is yet quick to conceive the very things in the thick of which the politician struggles,—to that man he should resort for instruction: —and that there is occasionally such a man we have proof in Bagehot., the man who first clearly distinguished the facts of the English constitution from its theory.

Walter Bagehot is a name known, I suppose, to not a few of those who have a zest for the juiciest things of literature, for wit that illuminates and knowledge that refreshes. I do not speak of him, .·. , because I hope to introduce him to all, but because I would fain obtain the good fortune to introduce him to some. To ask you to know Bagehot is like inviting you to seek pleasure. Now and again a man is born into the world whose mission it evidently is to clarify the thought of his generation, and to vivify it,—to give it speed where it is slow, vision where it is blind, balance where it is out of poise, saving humour where it is dry—and such a man was Bagehot. When he wrote of history he made it seem human and probable; when he wrote of political economy he made it seem credible, entertaining, nay, engaging even; when he wrote criticism hc wrote sense. You have in him a man who can jest to your instruction, who will *beguile* you into being informed beyond your wont and wise beyond your birth-right. Full of manly, straightforward meaning, earnest to find the facts that guide and strengthen conduct, a lover of good men and seers, full of knowledge and a consuming desire for it, he is yet genial withal, with the geniality of a man of wit, and *alive* in every fibre of him, with a life that he can communicate to you. One is constrained to agree, almost, with the verdict of a witty countryman of his, (who happily still lives to cheer us,) that when Bagehot died he "carried away into the next world more originality of thought than is now to be found in the Three Estates of the Realm."

If you would have an epitome of the man's life, I would give it by saying that he was born in Feb'y. 1826 and died in *March* 1877 —the month in which one would prefer to die; that between those two dates he had much quaint experience as a boy and much sober business experience as a man; that he wrote essays on poets, prose-writers, statesmen—whom he would—with abundant insight but without too much respect of persons; also books on banking, on the early development of society, and on English politics, kindling a flame of *interest* with these dry materials such as made men stare who had often *described* the facts of society *themselves*, but who had never dreamed of applying *fire* to them as Bagehot did, to make them give forth light and wholesome heat; that he set the minds of a few fortunate friends aglow with the delights of the very wonderful tongue which Nature had given him, through his mother; and that then he died, while his power was yet young. Not a life of event or adventure; but a life of deep interest, none the less, because a life in which those two things of our modern life, commonly deemed incompatible, business and literature, namely, were combined without detriment to either; and from which, more interesting still, politics gained a profound expounder in the person of one who was no politician, and no party man, but, as he himself said, "between sizes in politics."

Mr. Bagehot was born in the centre of Somersetshire, that south-western county of old England whose coast towns look across Bristol Channel to the high-lands of Wales: a county of small farms, and pastures that keep their promise of fatness to many generous milkers; a county broken into abrupt hills, and sodden moors hardly kept from the inroads of the sea, as well as rural valleys open to the sun: a county visited by mists from the sea, bathed in a fine soft atmosphere all its own—visited also by people of fashion, for it contains Bath,—visited now by those who have read "Lorna Doone," for it contains part of that Exmoor Forest in which stalwart John Ridd lived and wrought his mighty deeds of strength and love: a land that the Celts kept for long against both Saxon and Roman, but which Christianity easily conquered, building Wells cathedral and the monastery at Glastonbury. Nowhere else in days of travel could Bagehot find a land of so great delight save in the north-west corner of Spain, where a golden light lay upon every-thing, where the sea shone with a rare, soft lustre, where there was a like varied coast-line to that he knew and loved at home. He called it "a sort of better Devonshire"—and Devonshire, you know, is Somersetshire,—only more so. The atmospheric effects of his county certainly entered the boy Bagehot, and coloured the nature of the man. He had its glow, its variety, its richness, and its imaginative depth.

But better than a fair county is a good parentage: and that too Bagehot had—just the parentage one would wish to have who desired to be a force in the world's thought. His father, Thomas Watson Bagehot, was for thirty years Managing Director and Vice President of Stuckey's Banking Company, one of the oldest and best of those sturdy joint-stock companies which have for so many years stood stoutly up alongside the Bank of England as managers of the vast English fortune. But he was something more than a banker: he was a man of mind, of sturdy liberal convictions in politics, and of an abundant knowledge of English history wherewith to back up his opinions: he was one of the men who think and who think in straight lines; who see—and see *things*. His mother was a Miss Stuckey, a niece of the founder of the banking Company:—but it was not her connection with bankers that made her a valuable mother. She had, besides beauty, a most lively and stimulating wit—such a mind as we most desire to see in a woman—a mind that stirs without irritating you, that rouses but does not belabour, amuses and yet subtly instructs. She could preside over the young life of her son in such a way as at once to awaken his curiosity and set him in the way of satisfying it. She was brilliant company for a boy, and rewarding for a man. And she had suggestive people among her kinsmen, into whose company she could bring her son. Bagehot had that for which no University can ever offer an equivalent, the constant and intelligent sympathy of both his parents in his studies, and their companionship in his tastes. To his father's strength his mother added vivacity: he would have been wise, perhaps, without her, but he would not have been wise so delightfully.

Bagehot got his schooling in Bristol, his university training in London. In Bristol lived Dr. Prichard, his mother's brother-in-law and author of a notable book on the "Races of Man"; and from him Bagehot unquestionably got his bent towards the study of race origins and development. In London Cobden and Bright were carrying on an important part of their great agitation for the repeal of the Corn Laws—and were making such speeches as it stirred and bettered young men to hear. Bagehot had gone to University Hall, London, rather than to Oxford or Cambridge, because his father was a Unitarian and would not have his son submit to the religious tests then required at the great Universities: but there can be no doubt that there was more to be *had* at University Hall in that day than at either Oxford or Cambridge. Oxford and Cambridge were still dragging the very heavy chains of a hindering tradition; the faculty of University Hall contained many thorough and some eminent scholars,—what was more, University Hall was in London, and London itself was a quickening and inspiring teacher for a lad in love with both books and affairs, as Bagehot was. He could ask penetrating questions of his professors, and he could also ask questions of London,—seek out her secrets of history, and so experience to the full the charm of her great abounding life. In after years, though he loved Somersetshire and clung to it with a strong home-keeping affection, he could never stay for more than six weeks at a time away from London. Eventually he made it his place of permanent residence.

His University career over, Bagehot did what so many thousands of young graduates before him had done; he studied for the Bar, and then, having prepared himself to practice law, followed another large body of young men in deciding to abandon it. He joined his father in his business as shipowner and banker in Somersetshire, and after a time succeeded to the office of Vice Chairman of the Banking Co. For the rest of his life this man, whom the world knows as a man of letters, was first of all a man of business. In his later years, however, he identified himself, with what may be called the literary side of business by becoming editor of that great financial authority, the London *Economist.* He had, so to say, married into this position. His wife was the daughter of the Rt. Hon. James Wilson, who was the mind and manager, as well as the founder of the *Economist.* Wilson's death seemed to leave the great financial weekly by natural *succession* to Bagehot. And certainly natural *selection* never made a wiser choice. It was under Bagehot that the *Economist* became a sort of financial Providence for business men on both sides of the Atlantic. Its sagacious prescience constituted Bagehot himself a sort of supplementary Chancellor of the Exchequer: the Chancellors of both parties resorting to him for advice with equal confidence and solicitude. His constant contact with London and with the leaders of politics and opinion there of course materially assisted him also to those penetrating judgments touching the structure and working of English institutions which have made his volume on the 'English Constitution' and his essays on Bolingbroke and Brougham and Peel, on Mr. Gladstone and Sir George Cornewall Lewis the admiration and despair of all who have read them.

Those who know Bagehot only as the writer of some of the most delightful and suggestive literary criticisms in the language wonder that he should have been an authority on practical politics; those who used to regard the London *Economist* as omniscient and who knew *him* only as the editor of *it*, marvel that he dabbled in literary criticism, and incline to ask themselves, when they learn of his vagaries in that direction, whether he can have been so safe a guide as they deemed him, after all; those who know him through his political writings alone, venture upon the perusal of his miscellaneous writings with not a little surprise that their master should wander so far afield. *And yet the whole Bagehot is the only Bagehot.* Each part of the man is incomplete, not only, but a bit inconceivable also without the other parts. What delights us most in his literary essays is their broad practical sagacity, so uniquely married, as it is, with pure taste and the style of a rapid artist in words. What makes his financial and political writings whole and sound is the scope of his mind *outside* finance and politics, the validity of his observation *all around* the circle of thought and affairs. There is constant balance, there is just perspective everywhere. He was the better critic for being a competent man of business and a trusted financial authority: he was the more sure-footed in his political judgments because of his play of mind in other and supplementary spheres of human activity.

What did he look like, we wonder? I never feel thoroughly at home with a writer until I have seen some adequate likeness of him, or else read some realistic description of his personal appearance: it helps me to run with him in all his thought if he looks what he is, as Bagehot did. A mass of black, wavy hair; a dark eye with depths full of slumbrous, playful fire; a ruddy skin that bespoke active blood quick in its rounds; the lithe figure of an excellent horseman; a nostril full, delicate, quivering, like that of a blooded racer,—such were the fitting outward marks of a man in whom life and thought and fancy abounded. This is the aspect of a man of unflagging vivacity, of wholesome hearty humour, of a ready intellectual sympathy, of wide and penetrative observation. It is no narrow logical shrewdness or cold penetration that looks forth at you through that face, even if a bit of *mockery does* lurk in the privatest corner of the eye. Among the qualities which he seeks out for special praise in Shakespeare is a broad tolerance and sympathy for illogical and common minds. It seems to him an evidence of size in Shakespeare that he was not vexed with smallness, but was patient, nay, even sympathetic, in his portrayal of it. "If every one were logical and literary," he exclaims. "how would there be scavengers, or watchmen, or caulkers, or coopers? A patient sympathy, a kindly fellow-feeling for the narrow intelligence necessarily induced by narrow circumstances,—a narrowness which, in some degrees, seems to be inevitable, and is perhaps more serviceable than most things to the wise conduct of life—this, though quick and half-bred minds may despise it, seems to be a necessary constituent in the composition of manifold genius. 'How shall the world be served?' asks the host in Chaucer. We must have cart-horses as well as race-horses, draymen as well as poets. It is no bad thing, after all, to be a slow man and to have one idea a year. You don't make a figure, perhaps in argumentative society, which requires a quicker species of thought, but is that the worse?"

Indeed one of the things which strikes us most in Bagehot is *his* capacity to understand inferior minds,—and there can be no better test of sound genius. He stood in the midst of affairs and knew the dull duty and humdrum fidelity which make up the equipment of the ordinary mind for business,—for the business which keeps the world steady in its grooves and makes it fit for a habitation. He perceives quite calmly, though with an odd, sober amusement, that the world is under the dominion in most things of the average man, and the average man he knows. He is, he explains, with his characteristic covert humour, "a cool, common person, with a considerate air, with figures in his mind, with his own business to attend to, with a set of ordinary opinions arising from and suited to ordinary life. He can't bear novelty or originalities. He says: 'Sir, I never heard such a thing *before* in my life': and he thinks this a *reductio ad absurdum.* You may see his taste by the reading of which he approves. Is there a more splendid monument of talent and industry than the *Times*? No wonder that the average man—that any one—believes in it. As Carlyle observes: 'Let the highest intellect able to write epics try to write such a leader for the morning newspapers, it cannot do it; the highest intellect will fail.' But did you ever see any-thing there you had never seen before? Out of the million articles that everybody has read, can any one person trace a single marked idea to a single article? Where are the deep theories, and the wise axioms, and the everlasting sentiments which the writers of the most influential publication in the world have been the first to communicate to an ignorant species? Such writers are far too shrewd. The two million, or whatever number of copies it may be, they publish, are not purchased because the buyers wish to know new truth. The purchaser desires an article which he can appreciate at sight; which he can lay down and say: 'An excellent article, very excellent; exactly *my own* sentiments.' Original theories give trouble; besides a grave man on the Coal Exchange does not desire to be an apostle of novelties among the contemporaneous dealers in fuel;—he wants to be provided with remarks he can make on the topics of the day which will not be known *not* to be his; that are not too profound; which he can fancy the paper only reminded him of. And just in the same way," thus he proceeds with the sagacious moral "precisely as the most popular political paper is not that which is abstractedly the best or most instructive, but that which most exactly takes up the minds of men where it finds them, catches the floating sentiment of society, puts it in such a form as society can fancy would convince another society which did not believe,—so the most influential of constitutional statesmen is the one who most felicitously expresses the creed of the moment, who administers it, who embodies it in laws and institutions, who gives it the highest life it is capable of, who induces the average man to think: 'I could not have done it any better, if I had had time myself.' . . . ["]

See how his knowledge of politics proceeds out of his knowledge of men. "You may talk of the tyranny of Nero, and Tiberius"; he exclaims "but the real tyranny is the tyranny of your next door neighbour. What law is so cruel as the law of doing what he does? What yoke is so galling as the necessity of being like him? What espionage of despotism comes to your door so effectually as the eye of the man who lives at your door? Poblic [Public] opinion is a permeating influence, and it exacts obedience to itself; it requires us to think other men's thoughts, to speak other men's words, to follow other men's habits. Of course, if we do not, no formal ban issues, no corporeal pain, the coarse penalty of a barbarous society, is inflicted on the offender; but we are called 'eccentric'; there is a gentle murmur of 'most unfortunate ideas,' 'singular young man,' 'well intentioned, I dare say; but unsafe sir, quite unsafe.' The prudent, of course, conform."

There is, of course, a touch of mockery in all this: but there is unquestionable insight in it, too, and a sane knowledge also that dull common judgments are after all the cement of society. It is Bagehot who says, somewhere, that it is only dull nations, like the Romans and the English, who can be and remain for any length of time self-governing nations, because it is only among them that duty is done through lack of knowledge or imagination sufficient to suggest anything else to do, only among them that the stability of slow habit can be had.

You will have observed by this time that although, at the outset, I introduced Bagehot as a 'literary politician'; I have not been giving you his political opinions, but have, instead, dwelt on his life, his looks, his versatility, his views on common men and on the tyranny of that aggregate common man which we call Public Opinion. The truth is that I think these things the essence of his extraordinary power as a critic and analyst of institutions. In order to know institutions you must know men: you must be able to imagine histories: to appreciate characters radically unlike your own: to see into the heart of society and its thoughts, great and small. Your average critic, it must be acknowledged, would be the worst possible commentator on affairs. He has all the movements of intelligence without any of the reality. But a man who sees authors with a Chaucerian insight into them *as men*, and who knows literature as a realm of vital thought conceived by real men, of actual motive felt by concrete persons, this is a man whose opinion you may confidently ask, if not on current politics, at any rate on all that concerns the permanent relations of men in society.

It is for such reasons that I have preferred to make known the most masterly of the critics of English political institutions as a man of catholic tastes and attainments, shrewdly observant of many kinds of men and of affairs. Know him once in this way, and it seems to me his mastery in political thought is explained.

In making choice, .·. , of a few extracts from his works to read this evening I have had it in view to recommend him as a politician by recommending him as a man of infinite capacity in serving and understanding men of all kinds, past and present. If I can show you in his case the equipment of a mind on all sides open to the life and thought of society, and penetrative of the secrets of minds of many sorts, I can by so doing authenticate his credentials as a writer upon politics, which is nothing else than the public and organic life of society.

First I shall take his essay on the early "Edinburgh Reviewers" and read what he says of Sydney Smith. We have all laughed with that great-hearted clerical wit; but it is questionable whether we have all appreciated him as a man who wrote and wrought wisdom. Indeed I believe you will find Sydney Smith a very delicate test of sound judgment the which to apply to friends of whom you have suspicions. There was a *man* beneath those excellent witticisms—a big, wholesome, thinking man—but none save men of like wholesome natures can see and value his manhood and his mind.

"Sydney Smith was an after-dinner writer. His words have a flow, a vigour, an expression, which is not given to hungry mortals. You seem to read of good wine, of good cheer, of beaming and buoyant enjoyment. There is little trace of labour in his composition; it is poured forth like an unceasing torrent, rejoicing daily to run its course. And what courage there is in it! There is as much variety of pluck in writing across a sheet, as in riding across a country. Cautious men have many adverbs, 'usually,' 'nearly,' 'almost': safe men begin, 'it may be advanced': you never know precisely what there [their] premises are, nor what there conclusion is; they go tremulously like a timid rider; they turn hither and thither; they do not go straight across a subject, like a masterly mind. A few sentences are enough for a master of sentences. A practical topic wants rough vigour and strong exposition. This is the writing of 'Sydney Smith.' It is suited to the broader kind of important questions. For anything requiring fine nicety of speculation, long elaborateness of deduction, evanescent sharpness of distinction, neither his style nor his mind was fit. He had no patience for long argument, no acuteness for delicate precision, no fangs for recondite research. Writers, like teeth, are divided into incisors and grinders. Sydney Smith was a 'molar.' He did not run a long sharp argument into the interior of a question; he did not, in the common phrase, go deeply into it; but he kept it steadily under the contact of a strong, capable, heavy, jawlike understanding, pressing its surface, effacing its intricacies, grinding it down. Yet, as we said, this is done without toil. The play of the 'molar' is instinctive and placid; he could not help it; it would seem that he had an enjoyment in it.

"The story, is that he liked a bright light; that when he was a poor parson in the country, he used, not being able to afford more delicate luminaries, to adorn his drawing-room with a hundred little lamps of tin metal and mutton fat. When you know this, you see it in all his writings. There is the same preference for perspicuity throughout them. Elegance, fine flavour, sweet illustration, are quite secondary. His only question to an argument was, 'Will it tell?' as to an example, 'Will it exemplify?' Like what is called 'push' in a practical man, his style goes straight to its object; it is not restrained by the gentle hindrances, the delicate decorums of refining natures. There is nothing more characteristic of the Scandinavian mythology, than that it had a god with a hammer. You have no better illustration of our English humour, than the great success of this huge and healthy organization."[3]

That is good: he evidently knows and likes Sydney Smith: and heartily appreciates him as an engine of Whig thought. You feel, somehow, as sure as possible, after reading such a passage, that Bagehot himself, knowing thus and enjoying Smith's free-hand method in writing, *could do the like himself*—could himself make English ring to all the old Whig tunes, like an anvil under the hammer. And yet you have only to turn back a page in the same essay to find quite another Bagehot—a Bagehot such as Sydney Smith could not have been. He is speaking of that other militant Edinburgh reviewer Lord Jeffrey and is recalling, as everyone recalls, Jeffrey's review of Wordsworth's *Excursion.* You remember that the first words of that review were 'This will never do,' and there followed upon those words, though not a little praise of the poetical beauties of the poem, a thoroughly meant condemnation of the school of poets of which Wordsworth was the greatest representative. Very celebrated in the world of literature, of course, is the leading case of Jeffrey *vs.* Wordsworth. It is in summing up this case that Bagehot gives us another taste of his quality:

"The world has given judgment. Both Mr. Wordsworth and Lord Jeffrey have received their reward. The one had his own generation; the laughter of men, the applause of drawing-rooms, the concurrence of the crowd: the other a succeeding age, the fond enthusiasm of secret students, the lonely rapture of lonely

[3] Literary Studies [by the late Walter Bagehot, Richard Holt Hutton (ed.), 2 vols., London, 1879], Vol. I, pp. 30-31. 33-34 [This and the following notes by by WW. Wilson had typed these extracts on separate pages and numbered them I through IV.]

minds. And each has received according to his kind. If all cultivated men speak differently because of the existence of Wordsworth and Coleridge; if not a thoughtful English book has appeared for forty years, without some trace for good or evil of their influence; if sermon writers subsist upon their thoughts; if 'sacred poets' thrive by translating their weaker portion into the speech of women; if, when all this is over, some sufficient part of their writing will ever be found fitting food for wild musing and solitary meditation, surely this is because they possessed the inner nature—'an intense and glowing mind,' 'the vision and the faculty divine.' But if, perchance, in their weaker moments, the great authors of the 'Lyrical Ballads' did ever imagine that the world was to pause because of their verses: that Peter Bell would be popular in drawing-rooms; that Christabel would be perused in the City; that people of fashion would make a handbook of the Excursion,—it was well for them to be told at once that this was not so. Nature ingeniously prepared a shrill artificial voice, which spoke in season and out of season, enough and more than enough, what will ever be the idea of the cities of the plain concerning those who live alone among the mountains; of the frivolous concerning the grave; of the gregarious concerning the recluse; of those who laugh concerning those who laugh not; of the common concerning the uncommon; of those who lend on usury concerning those who lend not; the notion of the world of those whom it will not reckon among the righteous—it said, 'This wont do!' And so in all time will the lovers of polished Liberalism speak, concerning the intense and lonely prophet."[4]

This is no longer the Bagehot who could 'ride across a sheet' with Sydney Smith. It is now a Bagehot whose heart is turned away from the cudgelling Whigs to see such things as are hidden from the bearers of cudgels and revealed only to those who can await in the sanctuary of a quiet mind the coming of the vision.

These are but single specimens among an infinite variety of the same and many other kinds,—and *these* lose their wholeness and perspective by being separated from their context. Even they by themselves prepare one, however, for expecting of Bagehot keener, juster estimates of difficult historical and political characters than it is given to the merely exact historian, with his head full of facts and his heart purged of all imagination, to speak. And the expectation is of course justified. Take, for example, this passage touching the Cavalier. It occurs in his essay on Macaulay.

[4] Literary Studies, Vol. I, pp. 28, 29. 31, 32

"What historian has ever estimated the Cavalier character? There is Clarendon, the grave, rhetorical, decorous lawyer, piling words, congealing arguments; very stately, a little grim. There is Hume, the Scotch metaphysician, who has made out the best case for such people as never were, for a Charles who never died, for a Strafford who would never have been attained; a saving, calculating North-countryman, fat, impassive, who lived on eightpence a day. What have these people to do with an enjoying English gentleman? It is easy for a doctrinaire to bear a post-mortem examination—it is much the same whether he be alive or dead; but not so with those who live during their life, whose essence is existence, whose being is in animation. . . . A Cavalier is always young. The buoyant life arises before us, rich in hope, strong in vigour, irregular in action: men young and ardent, "framed in the prodigality of nature"; open to every enjoyment, alive to every passion, eager, impulsive; brave without discipline, noble without principle; prizing luxury, despising danger; capable of high sentiment, but in each of whom the

"Addiction was to courses vain;
His companies unlettered, rude, and shallow,
His hours filled up with riots, banquets, sports,
And never noted in him any study,
Any retirement, any sequestration
From open haunts and popularity."

We see these men setting forth or assembling to defend their king and church, and we see it without surprise: a rich daring loves danger, a deep excitability likes excitement. . . . The political sentiment is part of the character; the essence of Toryism is enjoyment. Talk of the ways of spreading a wholesome Conservatism throughout this country! Give painful lectures, distribute weary tracts (and perhaps this is as well,—you may be able to give an argumentative answer to a few objections, you may diffuse a distinct notion of the dignified dullness of politics); but as far as communicating and establishing your creed are concerned, try a little pleasure. The way to keep up old customs is, to enjoy old customs; the way to be satisfied with the present state of things is, to enjoy the present state of things. Over the 'Cavalier' mind this world passes with a thrill of delight; there is an exultation in a daily event, zest in the 'regular thing,' joy at an old feast."[5]

[5] Literary Studies, Vol. II, pp. 231-3. 69-70

Now it seems to me most natural that the writer of such passages as these should have been a consummate critic of politics, seeming institutions *through men*, the only natural way. It was as necessary that he should be able to enjoy Sydney Smith and recognize the seer in Wordsworth as that he should be able to conceive the Cavalier life and point of view. He is as little at fault in understanding men of his own day. Here is his celebrated analysis of the character of a constitutional statesman (he is speaking of Sir Robert Peel).

His "character itself, its traits, its deficiencies, its merits, are so congenial to the tendencies of our time and government, that to be unjust to him is to be unjust to all probable statesmen. . . . A constitutional statesman is a man of common opinions and uncommon abilities. The reason is obvious. When we speak of a free government, we mean a government in which the sovereign power is divided, in which a single decision is not absolute, where argument has an office. The essence of the 'government of advocates,' as the Emperor Nicolas called it, is that you must persuade so many persons. The appeal is not to the solitary decision of a single statesman; not to Richelieu or Nesselrode alone in his closet; but to the jangled mass of men with a thousand pursuits, a thousand interests, a thousand various habits. Public opinion, as it is said, rules; and public opinion is the opinion of the average man. Fox used to say of Burke: 'Burke is a wise man; but he is wise too soon.' The average man will not bear this." Presently he goes on to this description of Peel's mind (he is contrasting it with Byron's, Peel's school-mate.)

"His opinions resembled the daily accumulating insensible deposits of a rich alluvial soil. The great stream of time flows on with all things on its surface; and slowly, grain by grain, a mould of wise experience is unconsciously left on the still, extended intellect. You scarcely think of such a mind as acting; it seems always acted upon. There is no trace of gushing, overpowering, spontaneous impulse; everything seems acquired. The thoughts are calm. . . . The stealthy accumulating words of Peel seem like the quiet leavings of some outward tendency, which brought these, but might as well have brought others. There is no peculiar stamp, either, in the ideas. They might have been any one's ideas. They belong to the general diffused stock of observations which are to be found in the civilized world. They are not native to the particular mind, nor 'to the manner born.' Like a science, they are credible or incredible by all men equally. This *secondary* character, as we may call it, of intellect, is evidently most useful to a statesman of the constitutional class. He insensibly takes in and imbibes, by means of it, the ideas of those around him. If he were left in a vacuum, he would have no ideas.["][6]

What strikes one most, perhaps, in all these passages is the *realizing imagination* which illuminates them. And it is an imagination with a *practical* character all its own. It is not a creating, but a conceiving imagination. Not the imagination of the fancy, but the imagination of the understanding. Conceiving imaginations, however, are of two kinds: for the one kind the understanding serves as a lamp of guidance; upon the other the understanding acts as an electric excitatant, a keen irritant. Bagehot's was evidently of the first kind, Carlyle's conspicuously of the second. There is something in common between the minds of these two men as they conceive society. Both have a capital grip of the actual; both can conceive without confusion the complex phenomena of society;; [*sic*] both send a humourous glance of searching insight deep into the hearts of men. But it is the *difference* between the men that most arrests our attention. Bagehot has the *scientific* imagination, Carlyle the passionate. Bagehot is the embodiment of witty common-sense—all the movements of his mind illustrate that *vivacious sanity* which he has himself called "animated moderation"; Carlyle, on the other hand, conceives men and their motives too often with a hot intolerance: there is *heat* in his imagination—a heat that often scorches and consumes. Besides, the actual upon which Carlyle gets so sure, so Titanic a hold is the *picturesque* actual—the after-seen actual. Life is for him dramatic, full of fierce, imperative forces: even when the world rings with laughter, it is laughter which, to his ears, is succeeded by an echo of mockery—laughter which is but a defiance of tears. The actual which you touch in Bagehot is the practical, operative actual of a world of workshops and parliaments—a world of which workshops and parliaments are the natural and desirable products. Carlyle flouts at modern legislative assemblies as "talking shops" and yearns for action such as is commanded by masters of action—preaches the gospel of work and silence in some thirty volumes octavo. Bagehot points out that prompt, crude action is the instinct and practice of the savage—that talk, the deliberation of assemblies, the slow concert of masses of men, is the cultivated fruit of civilization, nourishing to all the

[6] "Peel," pp. 437 et seq. Works [of Walter Bagehot, Forrest Morgan (ed.), 5 vols., Hartford, Conn., 1889], Vol. III, p. [17.] [Bagehot's essay on Peel first appeared in the London *National Review*, III (July 1856), 146-74. It is impossible to find the first source cited by Wilson, which was the one from which he copied.]

powers of right action in a society which is not simple and primitive, but advanced and complex. He is no more *imposed on* by parliamentary debates than Carlyle is: he knows that they are stupid and, so far as wise utterance goes, in large part futile also: but he is not irritated, as Carlyle is. For, to say the fact, he sees more than Carlyle sees. He sees the force and value of the stupidity. He is wise, along with Burke, in regarding prejudice as the cement of society. He knows that slow thought is the ballast of a self-governing state. Staunch, knitted timbers, are as necessary to the ship as sails. Unless the hull is conservative in holding stubbornly together in the face of every argument of sea-weather, there'll be lives and furtunes lost. Bagehot can laugh at unreasoning bias; it brings a merry twinkle into his eye to undertake the good sport of dissecting stolid stupidity; but he would not for the world abolish bias and stupidity. He would much rather have a society held together—much rather see it grow than undertake to reconstruct it. "You remember my joke against you about the moon," writes Sydney Smith to Jeffrey, "d—n the solar system—bad light—planets too distant—pestered with comets; feeble contrivance; could make a better with great ease." There was nothing of this in Bagehot. He was inclined to be quite tolerant of the solar system. He understood that society was more quickly bettered by sympathy than by antagonism. He could laugh, but he could not laugh with Carlyle.

Of course you are waiting to hear me speak of Bagehot's limitations; of what he could *not* do. His limitations, though they do not obtrude themselves upon your attention, are, in truth, as sharp-cut and clear as his thought. It would not be just the truth to say that his power is that of *critical analysis* only: for he can and does *construct* thought touching antique and obscure systems of political life and social action; but it is true that he does not construct *for the future*. You receive stimulation from him and a certain feeling of elation. There's a fresh air stirring in all his utterances that is unspeakably refreshing: you open your mind to the fine influence and feel younger for being in such an atmosphere: it is an atmosphere clarified and bracing almost beyond example elsewhere. But you know what you lack in Bagehot if you have read Burke. You miss the deep eloquence which awakens purpose. You are not in contact with systems of thought or with principles that dictate action, but only with *a perfect explanation*. You would go to Burke, not to Bagehot, for inspiration in the infinite tasks of self-government—though you would, if you were wise, go to Bagehot rather than to Burke if you wanted to realize just what were the practical daily conditions under which those tasks were to be worked out.

Moreover, there is a deeper lack in Bagehot. He has no sympathy with the voiceless mass of the people, with the "mass of unknown men." He conceives the work of government as a work possible only to the instructed few. He would have the mass served, and served with devotion–but he would tremble to see them endeavour to serve themselves. He has not the stout fibre and the unquestioning faith in the right and capacity of inorganic majorities, which makes the democrat. He has none of the heroic blindness necessary for faith in wholesale political aptitude and capacity. He takes democracy in detail in his thought–and to take it in detail makes it look very awkward.

And yet I don't believe it would occur to the veriest democrat that ever vociferated the 'sovereignty of the people' to take umbrage at anything Bagehot might chance to say in dissection of democracy: what he says is seldom *provokingly* true: there's something in it all that is better than a 'saving clause'–and that's a saving *humour*. Humour ever keeps the whole of his matter sound: it is an excellent salt, that keeps sweet the sharpest of his sayings. Indeed, Bagehot's wit is so prominent among his gifts that I am tempted here to enter a general plea for wit as fit company even for high thoughts and weighty subjects. Wit does'nt make a subject light; it simply beats it into a shape to be handled readily. For my part, I make free acknowledgement that no man seems to me master of his subject who cannot take liberties with it,–who cannot slap his propositions on the back and be hail fellow well met with them. Suspect a man of shallowness who always takes himself and all that he thinks seriously. For light in a dark subject commend me to a ray of wit. Most of your solemn explanations are mere farthing candles in the great expanse of a difficult question. Wit is not, I admit, a *steady* light: but, ah! its flashes give you sudden glimpses of unsuspected things such as you will never see without it. It is the summer lightning, which will bring more to your startled eye in an instant out of the hiding of the night than you will ever be at the pains to observe in the full blaze of noon.

Wit is movement, is *play* of mind,–and the mind cannot get play without a sufficient play-ground. Without movement outside the world of books, it is impossible a man should see aught but the very neatly arranged phenomena of that world; but it is possible for a man's thought to be instructed by the world of affairs without the man himself being a part of it. Indeed, it is exceedingly hard for one who is in and of it to hold it off at arm's length and observe it. He has no vantage ground. He had better for a while seek the distance of books and get his perspective. The literary politician, let it be distinctly said, is a very fine, a very superior species of the man thoughtful. He reads books as he would listen to men talk. He stands apart and looks on, with humourous, sympathetic smile, at the play of politics: he will tell you what the players are thinking about: he divines at once how the parts are cast: he knows beforehand what each Act is to discover: he could readily guess what the dialogue is to contain: were you short of scene-shifters, he could serve you admirably in an emergency:—and, believe me, he's a better critic of the play than the players.

Had I command of the culture of men, I should wish to raise up for the instruction and stimulation of my nation more than one sane, sagacious, penetrative critic of men and affairs like Walter Bagehot.

But that of course. My main point concerns the make-up of the successful student of politics. Even if I had time I should not put myself to the pains of setting forth Bagehot's political judgments. Everybody who reads them acknowledge's their power just as surely as everyone who takes hold of the handles of a charged battery acknowledges that it has electricity in it. I did not intend at the outset to expound Bagehot's political thought. I have used him to hang a thesis on; and that thesis is this: It is not the constitutional lawyer, nor the student of the mere machinery and legal structure of institutions, nor the politician, a mere handler of that machinery, who is competent to u[n]derstand and expound government; but the man who finds the materials for this thought far and wide, in everything that reveals character and circumstance and motive. It is necessary to stand with the poets, as well as with law-givers; with the fathers of the race, as well as with your neighbour of to-day; with those who toil and are sick at heart, as well as with those who prosper and laugh and take their pleasure; with the merchant and the manufacturer, as well as with the closeted student;—with the schoolmaster and with those whose only school is life, with the orator and with the men who have wrought always in silence, in the midst of thought and also in the midst of affairs, if you would really comprehend those great *wholes* of history and of character which are the vital substance of Politics.

WWT and WWhw MS. (WP, DLC).

To Ellen Axson Wilson

My own darling, 5 E. 17th St., New York 21 July, '89

Dont send any proof on Monday, please ma'am—I'm coming back on Tuesday. I'm lonely and discontented already away from home—from you: it's the only place for me.

The lecture at the "Connecticut Assembly" was a very funny affair. Delivered in a tent on a rainy morning to a few (perhaps 15 or 20) women and about 5 men—almost all of whom—though they listened—were quite insensible to any charms my style of criticism may conceivably have for some possible audience. I pitied my poor little lecture, so earnestly laboured over night and day; and yet there was an infinitely laughable side to its failure which very neatly fitted my sense of the ludicrous. I can't help smiling—even laughing—at the scene, though at the time I was deeply disappointed, too.

Here I find Bridges and dear father as enjoyable as ever: but there can be no rest for me away from you. I am coming, my darling, as soon as possible

With love to all, Your devoted Woodrow

ALS (WC, NjP).

A News Item

[July 22, 1889]

The Northampton Chautauqua.

Laurel Park, Sunday, July 21.

The rain of yesterday kept away the crowd which was expected, but those who did come were well repaid. There were three good lectures during the day, and some well-rendered readings in the evening. . . .

At 10 o'clock yesterday morning Prof. Woodrow Wilson of Wesleyan university lectured on "A Literary Politician." It was an interesting lecture and it is a pity that more people could not have heard it. The lecture was a sketch of Walter Bagehot, the famous English writer on such a variety of subjects, varying from financial articles to literary criticism. . . .

In closing, he [Wilson] spoke of the contempt men active in political life are apt to have for literary men who attempt to deal with politics, and praised the happy combination of literary power and practical wisdom in Bagehot. . . .

Printed in the *Springfield* (Mass.) *Republican*, July 22, 1889; some editorial headings omitted.

To Robert Bridges

My dear Bobby, Middletown, Conn., 23 July, '89

I was sorely tempted to let my five o'clock train go without me yesterday afternoon and stay over to tell you about the interview. There's much to tell—but, fortunately, it may be summed up with some brevity. Our conversation after you left became immediately pertinent in the most natural possible manner by my telling him,[1] in answer to his questions as to the nature of the text-book whose proofs were calling me home, just my views as to the field of that book, the field of my own special studies. We went on easily into talk about Princeton plans, and the net result (a result to which I was able to make a considerable contribution out of my own views) was this: His plan is to replace Johnston[2] with a specialist in Political Economy; that done, he will be ready to add within a year (by means of the income from "Brown Hall," the dormitory immediately to be erected) a professorship of 'Public Law,' to include the history and philosophy of laws and institutions, (the subjects of which I most wish to become and remain a master). These three departments (Sloane's and the two I have mentioned) will complete, at any rate for the present, the 'School of Political Science,' upon which Patton will seek to build, at as early a time as possible, a liberal and in every way worthy 'School of Law.'[3]

As for myself, a tentative idea of his had been that I should at once fill Johnston's place, until, next year being tided over, a specialist in Political Economy could be secured, and I put into the new chair of 'Public Law.' This I discouraged because (1) of my obligations to the people here, who have been much too generous to me to be left in the lurch for next year (2) of my engagement for a portion of next year at the Johns Hopkins, and (3) of my disinclination to teach Political Economy. I have every reason to believe, however, that I am his choice for the chair of Public Law—and he every reason to believe that I would accept it. It will be the very sort of chair I've been waiting for.

That is the gist of a whole conversation, almost two hours long, in which he made me feel perfectly at ease and in which, consequently, we were able to get well acquainted with each other's minds. Your good-will and generous good offices seemed to preside over the whole interview. I feel that I now have still another proof of a friendship such as seems, in point of vigilance and soundness, to have been reserved for your creation.

I reached home *in statu quo*, have read fifty pages more of proof, and am now settling down to be lazy—luxuriating in the recollection of a most enjoyable visit.

I knew that you would want to know about the interview as soon as possible.

Mrs. W. joins me in warmest regards.

As ever Yours affectionately, Woodrow Wilson

ALS (WC, NjP).

[1] President Patton.

[2] Professor Johnston had died on July 20, 1889.

[3] See the Editorial Note, "Wilson's Plans for a School of Law at Princeton," Vol. 7.

To Horace Elisha Scudder

My dear Mr. Scudder, Middletown, Conn., 24 July, 1889

I should have answered your kind letter of the 15th much sooner had I not been called away from home almost immediately upon its receipt.

I am, alas, compelled always to confess, in reply to such suggestions as you make, that I am "a barren rascal." I cannot (creditably) entertain more than one idea at a time, and the one idea at present my guest is *not* an idea about the admission or organization of the new states. Naturally, too, with such a mind, I have no extra, no odd ideas. What am I to do, then, when asked for an article but acknowledge, if the asker be a friend, that I have no ideas to spare, things of that sort being scarce with me.

The only things I have on hand are a character sketch which I sent to Mr. Aldrich under an assumed name and which he promptly returned;[1] and an address on "The Nature of Democracy in the United States."[2] The latter contains between 6,000 and 7,000 words, perhaps, and could easily be prepared, so far as forms of expression are concerned, for publication. If you are not scared off by the title, I can lick it into shape and send it to you with the understanding that it shall be treated as if I had offered it, not as if you had asked for it. It contains some of the best I can do, I judge.

It is refreshing to me to see your handwriting, and strengthening to be made conscious of the friendship that comes with it. You may be sure that you have your own again with usury.

Most sincerely, Yours, Woodrow Wilson

TCL (RSB Coll., DLC).

[1] "The World and John Hart," printed at Sept. 1, 1887, Vol. 5. This sketch was rejected by Edward L. Burlingame, editor of *Scribner's Magazine*, but there

is no evidence that Wilson ever submitted it to the *Atlantic Monthly.* Wilson was probably confusing "The World and John Hart" with "The Eclipse of Individuality," which Thomas Bailey Aldrich had rejected. See the Editorial Note, "Wilson's Desire for a 'Literary Life,'" Vol. 5.

2 Printed at May 10, 1889.

From Joseph Ruggles Wilson

My precious Son— N. York, 25th [July 1889]

Your dear letter was received, and with a welcome which a letter from no one else could have—for never I think has father loved son as I love you. But this [is] a topic upon which I dare not trust myself to dilate. I was pleased to learn that you had reached home, to find all well. I was however especially charmed with your account of the interview with Dr. P. In the first place I was glad to have my opinion of him reversed in at least one important particular. In the second place your courage in resisting the temptation to accept a position at Princeton at once I greatly prize, and particularly for the reasons you assigned. In the third place I have permitted myself to gloat over the prospect, which seems to be so fair, of just such a professorship as shall fulfill your dream. Of course, if Dr. P. be a true man—which he is I dare say—the foundation of the chair you describe and the proffer of its incumbency to yourself will be simultaneous. I do not doubt, dearest of sons, that you on your part managed the interview as a Christian gentleman should, and that you left a deeply favorable impression upon the mind of your interlocutor by reason of the insight he must have gained by your expert knowledge and of your personal character—so that he cannot but be your friend hereafter & always. At any rate my pride in you is complete whatever may betide. . . .

I wish I could help you with the "proof"—but you have "lots" of assistance as things are. Please give my love to dearest Ellie—and also to the boys: the girls have of course forgotten grandpa.

Your Father—in fondest love

Mrs. Grannis[1] is enthusiastic in your praise—and she has not a little perspicacity in the matter of exploring character

ALS (WP, DLC) with WWhw sums on env.

1 Elizabeth Bartlett Grannis, editor of the New York *Church Union.* As the letters in this and the next volume will soon disclose, there is some reason to suspect that the relationship between Dr. Wilson and Mrs. Grannis was more than platonic. Mrs. Grannis, widow of Colonel Fred W. Grannis, was—in addition to being editor of the *Church Union* for twenty-three years—also editor of *Children's Friend and Kindergarten Magazine*, founder and president of the National Christian League for the Preservation of Purity, a lecturer on the sanctity of the home, and active in the movement for the sterilization of habitual criminals and mental defectives.

From Melville R. Hopewell

Dear Sir Tekamah, Nebraska, July 25th 1889

Your letter of July 10th at hand & contents noted—lands have not advanced in price as I had expected, when I advised you a year ago not to sell. Lands are not in demand and consequently cannot be sold for what they should be, considering quality and location. I think however I can dispose of a considerable portion of your land by offering it at a lower price than I have heretofor held it at, and I will make an immediate effort and get the best offer I can, and submit same to you.

Yours Truly M. R. Hopewell

ALS (WP, DLC).

From Horace Elisha Scudder

Dear Mr. Wilson Little Boar's Head, N. H. 26 July 1889

Certainly I cannot refuse to entertain such a visitor as you offer to send me. You know I value your work and I shall be very glad to hear what you have to say, whether I give the readers of the Atlantic the same pleasure or not. I hope you will feel free at any time to send such passages of your magnum opus as may seem to you to have either an episodical character, or so much integrity as not to arouse the reader's suspicion that they are fragments of some bigger whole.

Do you ever want a whiff of salt air? If so, come and make me a little visit. We should be delighted to see you and could give you a glimpse of an exceedingly beautiful bit of the New England coast. We are keeping house and I should very much like to have you and Mrs. Scudder know each other.

Cordially yours H. E. Scudder

ALS (WP, DLC) with WWhw notation on env.: "Ans. 9 Aug '89."

From Robert Bridges

Dear Tommy: New York, July 30–89

Your letter about the Patton interview was very satisfying to me, and I have thought a great deal about it. It seems to me that your decision was a wise one, provided it leads surely to the Law Professorship. That, of course, is the end in view, and I should not like to look at the possibility of your missing it. By accepting Johnston's chair temporarily for this year, you would bind them to giving you the new professorship next year. The thing is now within your grasp as surely as anything temporal. If, however, you stay at Wesleyan this year, then Princeton is under no obligations to you whatever, and the situation may so change that another man may be elected. This is only a possibility (which I do not think at all a probability) and only a certain amount of Scotch "cannyness" leads me to suggest it. Sloane has been doing Johnston's work for a year, and has taken a great burden upon himself which I believe amounted to 70 new lectures last year. Naturally he is anxious to be relieved of it. His influence with the trustees I believe to be very great. Probably the man whom he favors for a chair in the school of Political Science will be elected. Speaking confidentially and with some guile, I believe that he is a good man to conciliate. He would probably thoroughly appreciate your helping him over the difficulties of the coming year at some inconvenience to yourself. When you entered upon the Law Professorship your fields of work, I take it, would not conflict, and you could sail along beautifully together, notwithstanding radical differences in your historical points-of-view. Sloane is a good-fellow who is making many friends among the children of this world. He is also a good diplomat. I believe that his views as to the "New Princeton" which we long for, are practically what you and I hold. He believes in gentlemanly scholars who can be men of affairs; he is opposed to pietism as such; he has a real admiration for scholarship, and is nothing of a prig. You can meet him heartily on that ground, however much you may differ in other things which need not bring you into any conflict.

If then you hope to throw in your lot with the New Princeton, I think you could serve a good point at the start by tiding them over the coming year in the Chair of Economics. Of course this whole argument falls to the ground if they can put their hands *now* on the right man to fill the place permanently.

I admit the force of your arguments against leaving Wesleyan this year, but think that something might be said on the other side:—

1) It would, no doubt, be a serious inconvenience to them for you to leave now, but would they consider it ungrateful if all the circumstances were explained, and you aided them in every way to get a good man for the place? Their plight is not worse than Princeton's now is, and they have, I presume, an

A recently discovered photograph of Wilson as a young man in Columbia, S. C., about 1873

The "brownstone row" on the Wesleyan campus in the 1880's

View of Middletown about 1884, showing Wilson's house in the center

A photograph of Wilson in the spring of 1889
by Pach Bros. of New York

John Monroe Van Vleck, Professor of Mathematics and Astronomy and Acting President of Wesleyan University, 1887-89

Caleb Thomas Winchester,
Professor of Rhetoric and English Literature,
Wesleyan University

The Reverend Azel Washburn Hazen, D.D.,
pastor of the First Congregational
Church of Middletown

The Wesleyan University faculty, 1889-90

(3)

CONSTITUTION.

CHAPTER I.

THE EMPEROR.

ARTICLE I.

The Empire of Japan shall be reigned over and governed by a line of Emperors unbroken for ages eternal.

ARTICLE II.

The Imperial Throne shall be succeeded to by Imperial male descendants, according to the provisions of the Imperial House Law.

ARTICLE III.

The Emperor is sacred and inviolable.

ARTICLE IV.

The Emperor is the head of the Empire, combining in Himself the rights of sovereignty, and exercises them, according to the provisions of the present Constitution.

ARTICLE V.

The Emperor exercises the legislative power with the consent of the Imperial Diet.

ARTICLE VI.

The Emperor gives sanction to laws, and orders them to be promulgated and executed.

ARTICLE VII.

The Emperor convokes the Imperial Diet, opens, closes and prorogues it, and dissolves the House of Representatives.

ARTICLE VIII.

The Emperor, in consequence of an urgent necessity to maintain public safety or to avert public calamities, issues, when the Imperial Diet is not sitting, Imperial Ordinances in the place of law.

Such Imperial Ordinances are to be laid before the Imperial Diet at its next session, and when the Diet does not approve the said Ordinances, the Government shall declare them to be invalid for the future.

III
"Der König ist unverletzlich" (Const. Prussia, Art. 43).

V
Leg. power exercised "gemeinschaftlich durch den König und die Kammern, die Uebereinstimmung des Königs und beider Kammern ist zu jedem Gesetze erforderlich" (Prus. 62) See Art. XXXVII, post.

VI
"Er allein befiehlt die Verkündigung der Gesetze" (Prus. 45)

Prus. Const, 63; Compare Norwegian Grundgesetz § 17: —

Wilson's marginal notes on Articles III, V, VI, and VIII of the Japanese Constitution of 1889. The transcript of Wilson's shorthand reads: "The king has the right to issue ordinances touching trade, tariffs, industries, and police, in cases where he deems it desirable as well as in cases where it seems necessary, when the Storthing is not in session, to be valid only during the recess."

equal opportunity to make temporary provision. (I write this in ignorance of your contract with Wesleyan.)

2) I have little doubt that Princeton would give you the time needed for your Johns Hopkins lectures. Moreover, Princeton is so near Baltimore that you could easily run over for two days a week.

3.) As to teaching Economics for another year—as I understand it you will do this at any rate at Wesleyan, and will not, therefore, be seriously diverted from your work by doing likewise at Princeton.

I have tried to take the other point of view bluntly in this letter, so that we may look at all the possibilities. Personally, I have few doubts that you will ultimately get the new professorship which seems to be falling from the sky as though made for your purposes. I cannot bear to think of the possibility of your missing it. I know that you will accomplish your work under any conditions, but these seem to be the most favorable.

Patton's conversation may have given you light on the whole subject which will upset my whole argument, but as your friend I could not resist putting the other side in its strongest terms.

I do not doubt that your own judgments will be essentially right.

Your friend Robert Bridges

ALS (WP, DLC) with WWhw notation on env.: "Ans. 9 Aug /89."

To Munroe Smith

My dear Prof. Smith, Middletown, Conn., 5 August, 1889

I send you to-day, *via* New York, the proof of my chapter on Law—not to ask you to read it again (!) but to obtain your sanction for a quotation from your *ms.* notes and for the mention of your name in a foot-note. (p. 635)

For fear the proof may not be promptly forwarded to you, I will transcribe here the passage:

I have been speaking of the difficulty of making the analytical account of sovereignty fit our own political system. I add: "The difficulty . . . is in large part avoided if law be defined as 'the command of an authorized public organ, acting within the sphere of its competence. What organs are authorized, and what is the sphere of their competence, is of course determined by the organic law of the State; and *this* law is the direct command of the sovereign.' The only difficulty left by this solution is that of making room in our system for both a sovereign people of the single state and a sovereign people of the Union." I then say in a foot-note, "This definition I have taken the liberty of extracting from some very valuable notes on this chapter kindly furnished me by Prof. Monroe Smith."

Now, if there is anything in this that you object to I trust that you will let me know, that I may change it. The printers are waiting for the 'revise,' and I hope I may hear from you soon.

Trusting that your vacation is bringing you everything it should bring, in haste and with warmest regards,

Yours very sincerely, Woodrow Wilson

ALS (WC, NjP).

To Horace Elisha Scudder

My dear Mr. Scudder, Middletown, Conn., 9th August, 1889

There has been some delay in sending you the paper of which I spoke to you because it much needed to be copied—and that, in a busy household, was a job that consumed some days in the doing. I could not get the address *style* out of the thing without entirely re-writing it. I did the best I could, and now commend the production to your indulgent perusal.

I shan't be altogether sorry if you conclude that it had best remain an address, and send it back to me. For, while it of course speaks my convictions and is not much of it what I have said before, I'm a bit sorry to return *in print* to an old theme, as I do in the closing paragraphs of the paper.

However, I trust your judgment as to what the Monthly's constituents will stand. I believe the central points of the paper thoroughly worth making—and making through all possible *media* of utterance.

I am much tempted by your kind invitation to visit you by the sea and make Mrs. Scudder's acquaintance. I feel that I should be altogether the gainer in such an experience. I am gratified that you should want me, and deeply disappointed that I must bow to home duties and acknowledge their right to keep me back from such indulgences—such profitable indulgences even—as an acceptance of your invitation. But I have more to do than the remaining month of "vacation" will suffice for doing and must postpone all goings off.

With warmest regards,

Most sincerely Yours, Woodrow Wilson

TCL (RSB Coll., DLC).

To Robert Bridges

My dear Bob, Middletown, Conn., 9th Aug., 1889

I need not say how sincerely I appreciated your letter touching the Princeton matter:—or rather appreciate—for the appreciation is certainly vigorously in the present tense. I have thought about it continuously since I received it: it has had its full fruit of pondering—largely, perhaps, because the doubts it urges were present and powerful in my mind already. The fixed point of the case, so to speak, is this: I have fully committed myself to Dr. Patton as to the necessity of my remaining here another year. I could not now recede from that position without serious loss of dignity. Besides, the argument for my remaining is a good deal stronger than I made it either in my interview with Patton or in my letter to you. The teaching in political economy at Princeton would of necessity be by lecture and require constant originative work—so much as to make it impossible for me to push the work on my American 'Epoch' which I have promised to have ready by the spring of 1891. Here I am at liberty to lecture on American history all the year and concentrate my energies on the preparation of the 'Epoch' in such a way as to have my contract touching it well nigh fulfilled in time to set me measurably free for the year '90-'91 and any new openings that it may bring. To do a year of Johnston's work and the 'Epoch' at the same time—with a prospect, not of increased leisure, but of new and still more arduous work for the year following—would be impossible: I would feel obliged to attempt the impossible—and might kill myself as poor Johnston did.

And the argument is not altogether a selfish one. It was a question of good conscience chiefly that I had in mind in my conversation with Dr. Patton. I am under no *contract* obligation to stay here any longer than I choose; but when I came here the department of which I have charge had, in incompetent hands, greatly run down at the time of my election. They wanted it built up; that I have been partially able to do: but, were I to leave it now it would collapse again: for a small college like this has by no means the same chances for obtaining a good or even a tolerable man on short notice that Princeton has. The men here have made me respect and admire them very much. They are earnest and capable teachers and liberal men. The college is changing horses crossing a stream—is getting a new President[1] of unknown tendencies just as it had decisively undertaken a new and liberal policy likely to make the college thoroughly first class of its kind. I believe that another year's work would enable me not only to clear my own docket but also to put a deep stamp on the department; possibly to choose my own successor—certainly to do my full duty by the college—and I am inclined to regard these considerations as conclusive. I know that they would not have called me here had they not felt reasonably assured of keeping me at least two years—and they have treated me not only honorably but generously.

Certainly to lose the new chair at Princeton would seem to me fatal—would dash all my most cherished hopes; and the temptation to seek the temporary place they now wish to fill—to seek it as a "pull" on what is to come later—is truly enormous. But should I take it I would reach the coveted chair vastly overworked and much torn in my conscience as to Wesleyan. Besides, were I one or two degrees more sanguine that [than] I am (I repay fortune for its uniform generous good-will towards me with fears and misgivings) I should feel confident of getting the chair in any event. Dr. Patton, according to all reasonable interpretation in the dealings of one gentleman with another, committed himself in my favour for the appointment. He could not speak for the Trustees, and he was careful not to seem to do so: but for himself he did speak, and that clearly, as it seemed to me. He went back of the present and told me that (on the initiative of Johnston) I was the man thought of for Sloane's place had Sloane gone to Columbia.

As for Sloane, Dr. P. told me that *he* would, he knew, be glad to have me for a colleague. I never feel sure of a thing—so suspicious am I of good fortune—till I get it actually within my grasp; but I came away from the talk with Dr. P. feeling as sure as *I can* feel that the new place was to be offered to me.

None the less, I am deeply thankful to you for your letter—notwithstanding the fact that it has caused me much purturbation of spirit. It's immensely gratifying to me that the longest letter I ever received from you concerned altogether my own affairs. By contrast, this long one from me concerns nothing but *my own affairs*! I believe though that you know how much I *might*, on occasion, write about *yours*.

With warmest regards from Mrs. W.

As ever Yours most affectionately Woodrow Wilson

ALS (WC, NjP).

[1] The Rev. Dr. Bradford Paul Raymond, former President of Lawrence University, Appleton, Wis.

From Horace Elisha Scudder

My dear Wilson Little Boar's Head, N. H. 16 August 1889

I found your paper in town the other day and read it with great pleasure. There *was* something of an audience in front of some of the sentences, and it may be that when we see it in proof we may be able to reduce this effect. I am disposed to think that a judicious pruning of the poetical extracts may do something. The main purpose of the address was, however, too good and too essential, in my judgment, to merit a merely local audience only.

Faithfully yours H. E. Scudder.

ALS (WP, DLC).

From Joseph Ruggles Wilson

My precious son— Buffalo, N. Y. Aug 16 1889

Although I write from a hotel, I am not staying thereat. I am with your cousin Mary (1131 Delaware Avenue)[.] It is probable that I shall go down to Cleveland on Tuesday next, where my address will be 613 Euclid Avenue (your aunt's[1] residence). As a matter of course my welcome here is exceedingly warm—just as it was last summer. We speak often of you, as you may easily guess; and it will require no great stretch of your fancy to reach the terms of said speech[.] Mary would be only too happy to see the beloved one about whom his foolish father has so much to say, and of whom they are, for every reason, proud.

I rather agree with you that the refusal to be engaged for Princeton at once was as wise as it was honorable—and it will, in my judgment, accrue to your benefit if Patton & Co. are what they seem to be. One who holds himself cheap is not likely to be regarded as dear by others. Still,—I should greatly prefer to have you at Princeton, *just now*: could it be possible all things considered.

I am to dine to-day at Rev. Dr. Smith's (T. Ralston) my cousin "Tom." He is a very fine man, and he & I are quite "thick." His family, too, is quite interesting. I am to preach for him on Sunday, which I don't like, because he is himself a much better preacher than am I. Best love to dear Ellie.

Your hurried but most loving Father.

ALS (WP, DLC).

[1] Mrs. Adam J. (A. Elizabeth Wilson) Begges of Cleveland, Dr. Wilson's sister. The identity of "Cousin Mary" in Buffalo and the relationship of the Rev. Dr. T. Ralston Smith to Joseph Ruggles Wilson are unknown.

From Daniel Collamore Heath

Dear Prof. Wilson: Boston August 20th, 1889.

Your favor of the 12th inst. came duly to hand. I have been without a stenographer, hence my late reply. What I mean to say in regard to price was that our wholesale and introduction price would be $1.60, like Compayre's two books, found under the heading of *Education* on the enclosed list,[1] and that we pay royalty on this amount less our discount, which is 20%. In other words, we pay you royalty on $1.28, and not $1.20, as you suggest, or we pay you nearly 13 cts. a copy. The reason we mentioned a retail price was because the book is likely to sell thro' the general book stores and to people outside of the schools. In that event, a retail price is best. The dealer always expects a large discount from that price, and gives to his purchaser often 20% discount, as you know from your experience in book buying. The book will really retail for about $1.75, instead of $2.00.

We have but a few books on our list to which we give a retail price. The last one under the heading of *Education* has such a price, also the last one under the heading of *Reading.*

We will print the separate chapter on the United States by itself.[2] Don't you want to add a prefatory note to it?[3] What had we better entitle it? Can we use a portion of the Index with it? I see on looking the matter up that we can use the Topical Analysis by re-setting a couple of pages, and making plates on purpose for the portion on the U. S. It will be only about two pages, will it not? If you will send us proofs changed for this edition, you will oblige,

Yours Truly, D. C. Heath.

TL (WP, DLC) with WWhw notation on env.: "Ans. 22 Aug/89."

[1] Jules Gabriel Compayré, *The History of Pedagogy*, translated by W. H. Payne (Boston, 1886), and Compayré's *Lectures on Pedagogy, Theoretical and Practical*, translated by Payne (Boston, 1887). Heath's enclosure is missing.

[2] It was Woodrow Wilson, *The State and Federal Governments of the United States. A Brief Manual for Schools and Colleges* (Boston, 1889).

[3] Wilson did enclose a prefatory note dated August 22, 1889, in his letter to Heath of that same date. It is printed in the book cited above.

From Joseph R. Wilson, Jr.

My dearest brother: Clarksville, Tenn., Aug. 21st. '89.

I reached home last evening at about seven o'clock, having left Batesville and the dear folks there at an early hour Monday afternoon. I left them all about as usual. More of my trip another time, however. My mind is so full of another matter, that I *must* find out about.

I have heard from three parties today that it is reported about town as coming from a member of the faculty that *father is to be married this fall.* Is this true? Father would not, or *did* not, tell me the cause of his early departure for the North this summer, saying it would take "too long to explain" &c. This made me suspect something. Then, too, his very frequent letters to that "Church Union" editress of New York City, Mrs. Grannis, opened my eyes somewhat to the possibility of such a step on his part.

Brother how could he marry, and so soon after his precious wife's death? The chief comfort I find in thinking of it is what sister Marion told me—and that is that mother always expected it. My fear is that my respect for father would be so much less than now if he were to marry again. I told him last winter that I could never stay with him if he did marry again, and he told me to have no fear of his ever doing so and that he could not blame me for leaving him were he to marry again. No brother, I cannot and *will* not remain in the same house with a woman who is there in the place our precious mother once occupied and filled so perfectly. Brother, I *write* because I cannot bare anyone to know I credit such a report, else I would telegraph so great is my anxiety. *Please* dear brother, *telegraph* me an answer worded so that no operator need know of what you speak. Telegraph me *at once* for I cannot wait for a letter if I can possibly get word sooner. Telegraph "*collect*," and *at once*, please. Do not think me foolish in my haste. I must know at once, and act according to the knowledge I gain. I feel that God will be with me no matter what I have to bear, and the sooner I know all the better.

I am quite well, and in good spirits, very good spirits, considering. The fact is I wont be surprised at anything, I feel.

With love unbounded to dear sister Ellie, the girls & your dear self, Your devoted bro., Joseph.

ALS (WP, DLC) with WWhw notation on env.: "Ans. Aug. 24/89."

From Daniel Collamore Heath

Dear Prof. Wilson: Boston August 23rd, 1889

After writing you this morning,[1] your letter of the 22nd came. It seems to me if we use the same plates for the U. S. portion, the cross references and portion of the book not included had better remain as they are, without asterisks, as the teacher will be inclined to purchase, at least for his own use, a copy of the large book for reference, and if he has it, the pupil can gain access to it.

If we use the same plates, you will need to write in your special index to this portion your old section references, and we would return the copy to you for that purpose.[2]

We will push the book in southern and western colleges by letter writing, advertisements, and by a circular giving the main points in which your book systematically differs from the usual Manual of our Government. By the way, won't you write such a circular for us.[3] If it is not too long we can make a letter of it and address it to the college professor personally. We can then send a full description of the book to the high schools.

It would be well in the circular or letter to call attention to the O. S. Leaflets as supplying in convenient and cheap form the Constitution, Articles of Confederation, &c. These Leaflets, to which we are adding all the time, will furnish an admirable context of documents for your book; and as Mr. Mead believes thoroughly in you and your book, it might not be amiss for you to suggest to him (or to us and we will tell him) any Leaflets that would go well in his series.[4]

Yours Truly, D. C. Heath.

TL (WP, DLC) with WWhw notation on env.: "Ans. Aug. 24/89."

[1] Heath must have discarded this earlier letter after receiving Wilson's.

[2] The subsequent correspondence does not reveal the fact, but Heath must have had the type re-set for the separate book on American government, as its sections were renumbered to begin with Section 1, and its index referred to the new section numbers, not to those in *The State*.

[3] It is printed at Sept. 16, 1889.

[4] Edwin Doak Mead was the first editor of the *Old South Leaflets*, a series of historical documents. Beginning in 1883, the pamphlets were published first by the Old South Meeting House in Boston and later by the Directors of the Old South Work. Heath published an edition of the leaflets "for schools and the trade."

To Frederick Jackson Turner

My dear Turner, Middletown, Conn., 23 August, 1889.

You will, I believe, be interested to learn that I have undertaken to write, for Longmans, Green, & Co's 'Epochs of American History,' a sketch of our history between the years 1829 and 1889; and you will, I fear, be somewhat dismayed to learn that I very much need your assistance in the work. Don't be unduly alarmed, though: I am a petitioner for materials only, not for written assistance,—for western resources, not for what I would scarcely have the cheek to ask, work by yourself in my behalf.

You remember, I suppose, our talks in Baltimore on the growth of the national idea, and of nationality, in our history, and our agreement that the rôle of the west in this development was a very great, a leading, rôle, though much neglected by our historians? Well, of course I want to bring out this growth as emphatically as possible in what I shall write, and I want especially to form and express a right judgment as to the contribution of the West. And this on a somewhat peculiar line. Enough has been said, perhaps, of the spread of population and of the *material* development of the West (though doubtless even this could be said better, by being given a better perspective); but little or nothing has been said of the *self-consciousness*, so to say, of the West during this period and now,—of its own conception of its relations to the Union and of its own part in national development. My attention was called at one time to very interesting conventions held in the South not long before the war, conventions looking towards the industrial development of the South so that she might be put more upon an equality in wealth and resources with the other sections of the country; and in the debates of these bodies there appeared as clear indications as one could desire of the southern conception of the South's place in the race and mission of the nation. Now, do you know of any similar conventions or of any like expressions of policy in the West, any conventions looking towards the extension and perfection of railroad systems, of water connexions, or of manufactures, and accompanied by debates expressive of sectional ambitions in material development? If so, can you put me in the way of getting at reports of their proceedings? or magazine articles bearing upon their action and critical of their utterances?

Lacking such materials, are there magazines saturated with western ideas of development and of national policy which might yield a similar product? The period in which it would be most helpful to find such matter would be the period 1830-1850,—the period, that is, which just preceded the crisis of the slavery struggles,—the period before the time at which slavery absorbs the whole thought of the country.

It occurs to me also that biographical material, of men active in the development of the West, might serve a similar purpose. But you catch my idea. It is that *self-expression* by the West in some authentic manner touching it[s] material and political ambitions, its attitude of separation or coöperation, as the case might be, towards the rest of the country, its sentiments towards Congress and the national policy,—anything that might furnish a *raison d'être* for fellows like Jackson and Benton, would furnish the best possible interpretative material for a history of the period which is by distinction the period of national development,—of the completion of the Union.

Now, I realize that I am asking much, that I am stretching any claims I may have upon you; but I have learned to have such a faith in your interest in national history and in your personal generosity that I appeal to you with not a little confidence to be put on the scent of rich western material, and in the way of getting the use of it when found.

Can you tell me something of my co[-]laborer in the 'Epoch' series, Mr. Reuben Gold Thwaites? Tell me as much about him as you can.

But more still do I want to know about yourself, your own fortunes. I noted with genuine satisfaction your appointment to the chair of American history:—I trust it is indeed a full and independent chair. But let me ask you a question, at the same time that I repose in you a rather delicate confidence. It may be that, should I like the offer as finally made (I am scarcely at liberty to say as yet by whom) I shall go to another college next year, that is to say 1890-'91; not because of the least dissatisfaction with the chair or the conditions of instruction here, for these are in every way agreeable and advantageous, but because the new place will bring me closer to my specialty, namely, historical and practical politics. Now, would it at all attract your fancy to succeed me here as Professor of History and Political Economy (very little political economy and a good deal of history,—average number of hours per week, eight and a half)? I ask this question in the strictest confidence, both as to yourself and as to the revelation of my own possible plans, and I must hasten to add that I have no means of knowing for how much my advice would count when my predecessor comes to be named: perhaps it would not be decisive as against special Wesleyan ideas. But I do wish to feel at liberty to urge your name in case I think it best to accept a call elsewhere; for you will permit me to confess that during our acquaintance in Baltimore I conceived a very sincere admiration for you, and that I have ever since had a strong desire to serve your best interests.

Hoping to hear from you soon, and wishing that I might hope to hear from you often,

Very sincerely Yours, Woodrow Wilson

WWTLS (F. J. Turner Coll., CSmH).

From George Howe, Jr.

Dear Woodrow Danville, Ky., Aug. 23 1889

The above heading will indicate to you my whereabouts. I stole a week's vacation and ran up here, after being joined by Annie and the boys at Asheville. This is our second day in the blue grass region, and it is quite a novelty to us.

Your letter has just reached me and I hasten to reply. I am one of those who believe that there is one drawback to women doctors, namely that the nervousness which most of them suffer from at their menstrual periods, unfits them for some of the emergencies arising in the practice of medicine. Aside from this, I see no reason why the woman should not be quite as efficient as the man in the medical profession. Some of them have shown themselves equal to any man. This in general. As to your particular case, I am somewhat at a loss how to advise you. Experience, provided it has been profitted by, is of vast importance in the practice of obstetrics. Other things being equal, I would select the rough man of experience rather than the gentle, refined woman who lacks experience. The lady M. D.[1] you allude to however, may have had enough experience to make her efficient. If she has, why by all means employ her, for refinement is of vast importance to the woman suffering the pangs of labor. I have not the least respect for homeopathy, it is a fraud, but a fraud that is very captivating to many. I should think some of Ellie's lady friends in whose judgement she has confidence, and who have had the services of these M. Ds, might help her out. I do not know that I can say more on the subject, and yet I realize the fact that I have not aided you very much.

Annie and the boys are pretty well. A. was very complaining in the spring[,] so much so, that I became very uneasy about her, not knowing what would develope. Her improvement I hope is going to be permanent. We expect to be at home by the 7th Sept. and hope we will then hear good news from Ellie.

Annie is in another part of the house and so I cannot give the message that I am sure she will want to send to you.

With love to Ellie & yourself from us both, I am yrs. affly
Geo Howe

Upon another reference to your letter I see that we cannot expect to hear from Ellie until Oct. Annie received your letter at the Asheville Springs & promises to reply to it very soon

ALS (WP, DLC).
[1] Probably Dr. Taft of Middletown.

From Joseph R. Wilson, Jr.

My dearest Brother: Clarksville, Tenn., Aug. 25th '89.

Your telegram was received yesterday afternoon, and I am grateful for it. You say the matter is as we would wish. *I* wish him *not* to marry, and for this reason he seems to be keeping it all from me. I had felt rather sure, for some reasons, that the report is untrue, but the wording of the telegram did not enable me to find out certainly, as I *wished* to do. It is a comfort to know it is "as we would wish," but you did not say anything about it certainly. I wanted a strictly negative or affirmative answer. Please write *at once* and tell me all you know. I have a right to know, and it should not be kept from me any longer. It is surprising that father has been trying to keep it from me and that the first news of such a thing reaches me when I reach home and that it is given by strangers. All I know is from the common report about town. They say that person Mrs. Winter[1] is the one. Last fall father and I were talking of such things as second marriages and he assured me, of his own free will, that such a thing would never happen with him. I then said that I would never live in the same house with a step mother. He said he would not blame me. No sir, it will be "Good-bye Josie." Do you suppose I would live with a *step*-mother now, after having had such a *mother,* and so soon after her death? Not a bit of it! I am over twenty two, through with college, and am going to work to make a home of my own

Father writes me very seldom now. Where is he? I have to smooth it over as best I can when people ask me. I always say his head-quarters are in New York. That must be a sweet woman, that Mrs. Grannis.

I am in wonderfully good spirits about the whole matter. I am prepared for any news now, and my plans are all made. I have never been out in the world as yet, but I am preparing to do battle with it and am determined to come out conqueror in as short a while as God permits. No, I am not especially blue about it for my mind is pretty well made up that father has taken or is soon to take this step. Brother tell me all, please, for I must know. . . .

I am as well as usual, I believe. Please answer directly, for I am naturally anxious for some family news. It seems hard to find out about this. Why should it be kept from *me*, pray?

With unbounded love to all, Your aff. bro. Joseph.

ALS (WP, DLC).
1 Who lived in Clarksville.

From Munroe Smith

My dear Prof. Wilson: York Harbor, Me., August 26 1889

Your letter of the 5th inst. has only just reached me, and your proof has not been forwarded at all. In the definition which you credit me with there is nothing to criticize: the wording is, I think, exact. But it is not, to my mind, the definition of *law*: it is the definition of *a law*. *Law* I regard as the entire mass of such commands—the '*system of social order, established and enforced by the State*.' To use German phraseology, the definition cited is not a definition of *das Recht* but of *eine Rechtsregel*.

I cannot see where your "difficulty" is left, under this definition, of determining where sovereignty lies in our system. I, for my part, do not recognize any such thing, in our public law, as "a sovereign people of the single state." Sovereignty I consider one & indivisible: it lies with the people of the Union. For the purpose of constructing supreme national law (federal constitutional law) the people of the Union act by districts which we call states. So Jameson, in his Const. Conventions;[1] he says that a state convention is an organ of the people of the U. S. For the purpose of constructing state constitutions, the people of the single states act within the lines left open to them by the people of the United States. They do not act as a sovereign, but as an authorized public organ.

In our system, according to my mind, the only *sovereign* is the people of the U. S., organized under the federal constitution as *amending power*. Under them are law-making organs of all grades; some federal, like Congress and the departmental officers with ordinance power; some local, ranging down in consequence from a state convention to a board of town selectmen.

Much confusion arises from the fact that a state convention

acts or may act in a dual capacity. When it votes an amendment to the federal constitution, it is a part of the sovereign, a part of the federal amending power; when it makes a state constitution, it is simply a territorial organ, acting within its limited territorial competence.

But you do not make *me* responsible for this "difficulty," as the passage reads in your letter; so I have no objection to make.

Please see that my name is spelt with a *u* (not an *o*) in the first syllable. Yours cordially M*u*nroe Smith

P.S. I spent July & a part of August in Montpelier, Vermont. Your letter was not forwarded to Montpelier until I had left; and has since been following me in various directions. Hence the delay.

ALS (WP, DLC).

[1] Smith was referring to John Alexander Jameson, *The Constitutional Convention: Its History, Powers, and Modes of Proceeding* (New York and Chicago, 1867), pp. 17-65.

From Marion Wilson Kennedy

My darling brother: Batesville [Ark.], 8/27/89.

Your letter did me good in many ways. In the first place, your expressions of sympathy made me very happy, even though they were not necessary to assure me of its existence. Then, your letter gave me, what I had not had for months before, a *good cry*—and Ellie,—my dear sister—, can probably tell you how much good that does one. Joe *was* a great comfort to us while here, and seemed to enjoy his quiet stay very much. . . .

Give much love to dear Ellie. I am so glad to know that we think of each other in the same way. How I wish I had some of her intellectual energy! Kiss the girlies for me. Ross joins me in warmest love and grateful recognition of a sympathy which is very sweet to us. Lovingly your sister, Marion.

ALS (WP, DLC) with WWhw notation on env.: "Ans. Sept. 29/89."

To Ellen Axson Wilson

New York

My precious darling, Wednesday morning [Aug. 28, 1889]

I have waited to write till I should have seen a physician. I found a classmate here[1]—about whom I had forgotten—but who is already a distinguished physician and surgeon, whose opinion I can ask and take with confidence—as I *feel* after a conversation with him. He said that Dr. Lusk,[2] the only specialist to whom he would care to send me, was out of town.

I am glad to say that his diagnosis of your case corresponds in all essential points with Dr. Edgerton's. He says that, nothing being the matter with your urine, there is nothing to be uneasy about; that fatigue *plus* a little malaria or a little neuralgia would explain the symptoms; and that if the trouble *decreases* that is further assurance that it has nothing to do with the kidneys. But both he and I want to be sure; your instructions, therefore, are as follows: get a four ounce bottle, fill it with your urine, but [put] it in a small pasteboard box, packed in cotton, and send it by Express to the name and address on the enclosed card. I am greatly relieved, and shall have a lighter heart in my vacation-making—provided you get more comfortable and don't get the *blues*. Ah, how I do love and prize my darling!

As you see from the address at the head of this letter, Bridges has made me come to his room: my address, ∴, is Care Mr. Robt. Bridges, 5 East 17th St. Please, ma'am, use that address as often as you can.

Last night Bridges and I went to hear young Southern in "Lord Chumley" and enjoyed it much. This afternoon—or, rather, as soon as I get through with this letter—I shall go to Coney Island, for the boat-ride etc. So you see I am "going it" already. Weather delightful, I am enjoying myself.

Oh, if my darling were only with me—how sweet that would be! Be a brave, un-blue, well little woman this time, darling, and then we will plan to be companions in this sort of thing as soon as possible! I love you—I love you—I love you! ! !

Love to Stock and Eddie. Your own Woodrow

ALS (WP, DLC).
[1] Jasper J. Garmany, M.D.
[2] William T. Lusk, M.D.

From Ellen Axson Wilson

My own darling, [Middletown] 10 ½ A.M. Aug. 28 [1889].

I write in *desperate* haste, for I am detaining Stock. whom I have just found on the point of going down town,—so please excuse. I am much better this morning,—that is somewhat better than on yesterday and *decidedly* better than on previous days;—the trouble is really quite slight this morning. We had a delightful ride yesterday,—it was such a perfect day; we took the children too & of course they were very happy. This morning it is almost wintry. I have a fire for them. Jessie was delighted with the doll and has shown her appreciation by already breaking it *all to pieces*! She is incorrigible!

I send the proof of your preface; but there isn't a *word* from *Mr*. Heath so of course you can't change it back yet. How very stupid in him not to write!

There is a long letter from Mr. Munroe Smith which seems—though I havn't read it—to be a discussion as to the nature of law! Shall I forward? He didn't object to your using his name;—but of course it is too late for that now.

Someone in Balt. has sent you a marked paper about a Mr. M'Coy's will. He has left a large number of rather small legacies & then made the *J.H.U.* his *residuary legatee*! But it doesn't say how large his fortune was. Have you any idea? I am *wild* to know. The University also has his library, said to be very valuable.[1]

Goodbye darling, I love you *dearly*—but havn't time this morning to even *try* to say how much. As ever,

Your little wife Eileen

Am in *excellent* spirits.

ALS (WC, NjP).

[1] John W. McCoy, a Baltimore businessman, who died on August 20, 1889, had named The Johns Hopkins University as the residuary legatee of his estate. The university received his home, which became the President's house, McCoy's library of some 8,000 volumes, and securities worth about $500,000.

From Joseph R. Wilson, Jr.

My dear Brother: C[larks]ville., Tenn., Aug. 28/89.

Your letter of the 24th inst. reached me on yesterday. If I didn't believe that you mistake the tone of my last letter, I would feel somewhat hurt at the way you write. I dont believe I am the head-strong boy you give me credit for being, nor will I be "betrayed into doing" any-thing "so preposterous," as you seem to fear. My allegiance to father is as firm and unshakeable as yours, I believe, and it is and has been far from my *thoughts*, even, to "in any [way] discipline him."

I never hinted to father that the thought of his second marriage had entered my mind, even, until *he* spoke of it one day saying that such a thing were not possible. I then said I could no longer live with him if he did marry. I heard that Mrs. Winter is his "intended" and I repeat that if she *is*, I will not live in the same house, although the thought of objecting to father's marriage is not in my mind. What do you take me for, any way? No, I am willing for him to marry, although I was not at first. I want him to do anything that can make him more happy. I feel that you have mistaken me, although I dont, of course, resent anything said, knowing it was said altogether in love. I may have been, no doubt *was* somewhat excited over hearing the report for the first time, but I was not in such a fever of excitement as you seem to think. . . .

Good-bye until next time. I can't write and fight mosquitoes at the same time, very well. With love unbounded to dear sister Ellie and your dear self, your devoted but wicked (?) brother

Joseph.

Please write as often as possible, brother.

ALS (WP, DLC).

From Ellen Axson Wilson

My own darling, Middletown Aug 29 [1889]

Your letter is just at hand;—am delighted to get it,—to know that you are with Mr. Bridges and are enjoying yourself. Am especially glad to know that the weather is fine,—was afraid you were having it to match ours. It is *infamous* here, just what it was when we came last fall, except for the heavy rains; we have only a little drizzle now. We are all so cold and wretched and trying so hard to "catch cold" besides that I have just decided to have the furnace fire made.

We are getting on quite nicely. The children are perfectly well and sweet; my eyes have almost returned to their normal condition,—a little weak perhaps, but that is partly due to cold. I am still using them very sparingly. If you see the Dr. again I would be glad if you would ask him whether under the circumstances it will do any harm to use them for reading &c.

There is still nothing from Mr. Heath. You will have to write again on the point; won't you? He has not sent the index either.

No other mail for you except a letter from Josie,—written before the receipt of yours however; it is scarcely worth forwarding. It is rather amusing than otherwise. It seems now that Father is to marry *two* ladies—and that immediately,—Mrs. Gramis & Mrs. Winter! Oh the omniscience of the gossiping tribe! Josie however is much less excited than when he wrote before.

I enclose the article about the Hopkins legacy. Be sure to

write me what you know or can learn on that point. How *splendid* if it should be a million or so!

But I must stop and get this off. You must try and enjoy every moment of your time, dear, & to that end dismiss all care about us, believe me we are doing finely in *all* respects, & I will be so happy to know that you are so. And just think there appears as I write a genuine gleam of *sunshine*. I love you, my darling, from the bottom of my heart & am always & altogether,

Your own Eileen.

ALS (WP, DLC). Enc.: Clipping from the Baltimore *Sun*, Aug. 27, 1889, article entitled "John W. M'Coy's Will."

Two Letters to Ellen Axson Wilson

My own darling, New York, 29 Aug., 1889.

One thing that my doctor here advised I forgot to tell you yesterday. He thinks you had better take five grains of of [*sic*] Hydro Chlorate of Quinia morning and evening. What we call quinine without further description is a *sulphate* of quinia, you know. The hydro chlorate agrees with digestion better. It will relieve you of any difficulty of an atmospheric kind. Try it, please ma'am, for a day or two and report effects. Take it in capsules like the other.

My programme yesterday was Coney Island including Vanity Fair at one end and a capital orchestral concert at the other (Manhattan Beach) end. Coming back in time for the theatre, I went to see "Bootle's Baby"[1] and was much edified. It's really a very good thing.

I fancy when I look around at the theatres that they are full of Southern people.

Bobby wants me to go *outside* to Baltimore with him (on his way home) and then to return thence by steamer to Boston, on *my* way home, and I'm half inclined to do it. What do you think?

No word from you yet, sweetheart, and I am wofully hungry for one, but I know it will come soon. My precious little wife, my love, my darling—I think always of you. I love you all the time and altogether.

To-day to Seabright. Love to the dear chaps.

Your own Woodrow

[1] "Bootle's Baby," a four-act romantic comedy by Hugh Moss, which had opened at the Madison Square Theatre on August 5, 1889.

My own darling, New York, 30 August, 1889

Your letter of yesterday I had for breakfast this morning—and no food could have been sweeter or more invigorating. True it told of blue weather out of doors and did not disavow like weather in-doors; but it also says you are better, and all through it there stirs the sweet breath of the love that keeps me alive and happy.

The inclosure taken from the Balto paper contains capital news; but I'm afraid, in view of the smallness of the specific bequests, that there will be no very big residuum for the University. What I chiefly rejoice at is that the fashion is being set of remembering the University in this way. Other wills may follow suit.

Had a delightful day at quiet Seabright yesterday—came back sunburned and happy. For to-day I have no programme as yet except to see the professional base-ball match this afternoon. To-morrow I shall probably go outside to Longbranch.

I will ask the Dr. about your eyes being used.

I love you with a fervour that keeps me all aglow. I think of you always—and with an increasing love!

Your own Woodrow

Love to the boys and babies
Proof of title-page and prefatory note rec'd

ALS (WC, NjP).

From Ellen Axson Wilson, with Enclosure

My own darling, Middletown Aug 30 [1889].

I will only write a few lines this morning because my eyes are troubling me rather more & it would perhaps be imprudent. They are not *bad* however & I am quite well otherwise. The weather has cleared off *gloriously* & I have quite thrown off the cold which was troubling me yesterday. I did not get the bottle off yesterday as I should but will do so today. I am inclined however to rebel against the quinine; I am sure if the Dr. knew how *miserable* it makes me both as to head & stomach he would not insist on it for so slight cause. The very thought of it sickens me. *Do* let me off!

Am *very* sorry my letters have not reached you; I wrote early the morning after you left & Stockton mailed it at the office immediately. Of course you understand that it was directed, according to orders, simply to "New York City." I enclose you this morning a pleasant one from Mr. Jameson to take the place of the one I cannot write. Still nothing from Mr. Heath. By-the-way, I also sent the *preface* directed to "New York City." I think the programme proposed by Mr. B. delightful;–would follow it *by all means*;–& you can make a short stay in Balt. before you turn back. But I really must not write longer. I love, *love love* you, my darling, with all my heart & am altogether

Your own Eileen.

ALS (WC, NjP).

ENCLOSURE

From John Franklin Jameson

My dear Wilson: Westport, Maine, August 28, 1889.

You perceive that I am not wholly untrue to my statement that I was going to write to you. I can't profess to have been very prompt about it; but the summer is no time for promptness. And now the summer is nearly over, and in three weeks comes the beginning of a new college year. I shall be interested to see how far things go differently with Andrews[1] as president. Old Perry,[2] you remember, thought such things made little difference. At all events, Andrews may be expected to be a valuable promoter of the interests of the historical department. I expect to like him, for I am told he is a genial, whole-souled, and upright man. I fancy he is not perfectly cultivated (I have never met him), and he will not make so imposing a figurehead as old Dr. Robinson. You should have seen the old doctor at Commencement, in his gown, and with the Oxford cap upon his beautiful white hair! But indeed his manners and his sociability lagged much behind his appearance, and Andrews may do as well in impressing people, all thing considered. I doubt if he is as good a thinker in philosophy, which chair he is to take in addition to the presidency. In all the other functions than these two, he will be an incomparably better president.

I haven't wholly made up my mind what to do next year with my spare time. It seems a pity to be consuming one's time with pot-boilers or with minor writings, and yet I don't feel quite at the right point for an *opus majus*, at least for any that at the moment attracts me sufficiently to ensure momentum. The history of the South from 1783 to 1829 or so, a topic of which I have spoken with you, seems hard to work in this latitude; yet I may find it possible to do more toward it than now appears. As for a book on modern historians and historiography, I have a good deal of material ready, but I fear I am not ripe enough and, like the candidates whom the mediæval bishops used to reject, *minus sufficiens in literatura.* In the summer one pauses and reflects; and sees that he knows all too little. In term-time he finds he can't do much about it.

I see that your book, yea even brace of books, is coming out, and therefore hope you are near a point of rest. You have perhaps seen that Houghton is bringing out the volume edited by me; I wish he were doing it faster. I am not very well satisfied with it; it is but a *frustum* of what I planned, you know. I hope it won't be too awfully sat upon. (The second half of the penultimate sentence seems like an ungracious reference to friends who did not contribute, as if the absence of their communications were its one failing; Lord! I wish it were.)

But meanwhile, where are you spending the summer? Beneath the patulous fage,[3] I hope; but in Georgia or elsewhere? Shall you visit Boston before September 14th? If so, write to me at Winchester, Mass., and tell me when you arrive, that I may meet you and take you home with me, and set meat before you, and bid you discourse, θεᾷ εοικώς [*sic*]. And if Mrs. Wilson accompanies you, you will be doubly welcome. Do not come to Boston in those two weeks without letting me know, on pain of Our supreme displeasure. And come to Providence whenever you can. I want to hear you talk about your "Epoch." Hart intimated that he was likely to ask you. He is going to entertain us next; whether in fall or spring I do not know. I hope Mrs. Wilson is much better. Remember me to her and the girls most kindly. Levermore has a daughter. Mrs. Carey and Estelle have been in New England this summer. I was with them two weeks at Monomet, and they made us a visit. Are now somewhere in Maine. A good new year to you. Sincerely yours, J. F. Jameson

ALS (WP, DLC).

1 Elisha Benjamin Andrews had recently succeeded Ezekiel Gilman Robinson as President of Brown University.

2 Jameson probably referred to Amos Perry, of the Rhode Island Historical Society.

3 A Latinism for "spreading beech."

From Frederick Jackson Turner

Department of History, University of Wisconsin.
My dear Dr Wilson: Madison, Wis. August 31, 1889

On my return from a brief absence from the city I am very much pleased to find your kind letter of the 23d. Replying in the order of your queries, I will first say that I shall be glad to help you to the material you mention as far as is in my power. Mr. Thwaites had already told me of your connection with Longmans, Green and Co's new work, and I am especially glad to know that you are to do the important *third period.* So few writers have grasped the historical importance of the West in this period that it is gratifying to know that in the present undertaking it will fall to one who appreciates the matter. There is no lack of *self-consciousness* on the part of the West. The trouble will be rather in *selection* than in th[e] finding of material for the history of its "self-expression." But I fear that I shall not be able to help in the important work you are about to do, as much as I could wish to. You know I have fifteen hours a week here to say nothing of my studies for a degree at JHU, the examination for which occurs in May next. Moreover, just before leaving Balto. I promised Dr Adams to take the Northwest in the proposed text book in American history on the co-operative plan, which he is to edit. You are probably familiar with its scope and purpose (It is not yet to be made public). With a view to working up this field I shall offer a Seminary in Northwest history this fall—to continue through the year. If I can find a few good students to work under my direction I can accomplish more than I could with only myself to work at the unorganized material. If you are content with the arrangement I will put one of my students at work on the collection of the material you wish, and give what attention I am able to spare additionally to the matter. I need not assure you that this will be as large a measure as I can make it. It would be still larger were I not under this prior pledge to Dr Adams, to whose scheme, of course, I owe first allegiance. Of course if I make the arrangement with a student he will first agree that he is merely collecting material as a discipline under my direction, not for purposes of original work.

It is always a pleasure to be able to speak well of a friend. Mr. Thwaites, Secretary of the State Historical Society, is a young man of about thirty-five, I judge. He took special studies at Yale in history and political economy, doing considerable work, he once told me, in the colonial period. Then he became a newspaper reporter and editor, for th[e] most of th[e] time at this city. When he first returned to Wisconsin he wrote a series of sketches of pioneer life, and Oshkosh local history, based on personal interviews and original research. This brought him to th[e] notice of Dr Lyman C Draper then Secretary of the Society, and when he retired some four years ago he secured the election of

Mr Thwaites as his successor. Since then the latter has written a book called Historic Waterways (McClurg & Co), a pleasant account of canoe trips on Wisconsin rivers, in which he finds interesting things in uninteresting places, and weaves in bits of history. His style is lively and attractive. At present he is writing the Story of Wisconsin for the "Story of th[e] States" series. His more strictly historical work thus far published is an account of the Black Hawk War, and a paper on the Boundaries of Wisconsin—both original and careful studies—published in th[e] Magazine of Western History. He has also edited volume xi of th[e] Wis. Hist. Collections, the best of the series, containing matter of more than usual interest, annotated in a careful and judicious manner.[1] As in most of such collections, the antiquarian point of view is somewhat too prominent. His own tastes lead him to write history *ad narrandum*, and where he can safely do it he puts forward the romantic and popular side, for his training and sympathies are rather in this direction than in that of institutional history and "history as past politics."

I believe he does not make use of German and French writers, and his training in general institutional history is not such that he studies local history from that point of view. But his outlook is not narrow, and he is saved at least from hasty philosophising. Personally he is a pleasant companion, genial and generous. I like him thoroughly, and I think you would. He is a friend of Edwin D Mead, who I suspect, may have had some influence in securing him for this work. I think he will get up a good volume. His judgement as to the value of authorities is good, and he has an excellent workshop for his purpose, in the State Hist. Library.

Finally, in regard to myself. I know of no one whose good opinion I would sooner have than your own, and so I am glad indeed if you at all reciprocate the regard I formed for you as a scholar and a friend at Baltimore. I count the weeks that you spent at Miss Ashton's the best of my stay at Johns Hopkins. I appreciate, too, the honor that your suggestion in regard to Wesleyan does me. It is not entirely a surprise to me that you contemplate leaving, for besides th[e] fact that it must have been only a question of time when you would go where you could do your work in Politics to the best advantage, I had made a shrewd guess that that time had come, some weeks ago. Let me tell you frankly of my own situation. I am Assistant-Professor of American History, at a salary of $1500. I teach two classes in this specialty, and I have, besides, classes in General History,

Nineteenth Century, Northwest History, Political Economy, and possibly to fill out my fifteen hours I may be asked to teach some Rhetoric. I am assured, however, that it is th[e] intention of the institution to make American History an independent department as soon as the funds will permit. It is possible also that I may succeed Prof [William Francis] Allen who is now sixty years old, and yet I have so high a regard for him that I hope this may [be] very distant. He is very friendly to me, and ready to do all he can to help me. The fact that the university is in the same city with th[e] Historical Library, which is the best on Western history, and perhaps on local history, in the country, gives my department a peculiar advantage. The institution itself is already one of th[e] best in the West, and bids fair I think to take a still higher rank. This is th[e] favorable side. On th[e] other hand I think that the authorities are disposed to trade on these possibilities, and demand more hours, while giving smaller remuneration, than they should. I think it is advisable for me to stay here, *if* I am not asked to pay too high a price in health and pecuniary sacrifice. Just now I cannot know how this will be. I know how to value the kindness of your suggestion. Until you are willing to have it otherwise I shall hold your confidence in secrecy. Before you urge any name, I should be glad to learn more about the matter.

Whenever you find time to write on any subject I shall be glad to hear from you.

Very cordially yours Frederick J. Turner.

ALS (WP, DLC).

[1] The "sketches of pioneer life, and Oshkosh local history" were probably written for Oshkosh newspapers and for the Madison *Wisconsin State Journal*, of which Thwaites was managing editor from 1876 to 1886. The other writings mentioned in this paragraph are *Historic Waterways* . . . (Chicago, 1888); *The Story of Wisconsin* (Boston, 1890); "The Black Hawk War," *Magazine of Western History*, v (Nov. and Dec. 1886), 32-45, 181-96; "The Boundaries of Wisconsin," *ibid.*, vi (Sept. and Oct. 1887), 489-504, 529-41; and State Historical Society of Wisconsin, *Collections*, xi (Madison, 1888).

To Ellen Axson Wilson

My own darling, New York, 31 Aug. (Sat.), 1889

I found your first letter at the P. O. yesterday. I had asked twice before there, and had rec'd the preface and title-page proof; but had not asked for the letter at the right time.

Yesterday I loafed and went to the Eden Musée[1] (!) in the morning, and in the afternoon went to see my first professional game of base-ball. The latter I enjoyed immensely. It was between the two best nines in the country—Boston and New York.[2]

At night I saw Sol. Smith Russell in "A Poor Relation"—a really capital thing well done.[3]

This morning I find myself tired of gadding about and intend to visit publishers, etc. For the rest of the day I have no programme, except that this evening I shall go out somewhere with Bobby.

You are mistaken, love, about the quinine affecting your stomach—the quinine that Garmany prescribed. The sulphate would, he knew, and accordingly chose the hydro-chlorate, which will not. Try a little of it, please ma'am.

No, I will wait to read Monroe Smith's letter; you need not send it on. Jameson's I enjoyed. I have written to him that I am coming to Boston—for the New York-Balto.-Boston sea trip is virtually decided upon.

Ah, how I love you, sweet one! I had your letter for breakfast again this morning—and oh, it does do me *so* much good to have these words of yours come to me. At best, I'm lonely, dreadfully lonely, without you! Of course you are taking advantage of the return of sunshine to take another of the [*sic*] those rides, my love?

Kiss the babies for me. Give Ed. and Stock my love, and remember that you are all the world—my precious Eileen, my sweet little wife—my darling—to Your own Woodrow.

ALS (WC, NjP).

1 A museum of waxworks at 55 W. 23rd St.

2 New York defeated Boston seven to two.

3 It was Edward E. Kidder's comedy, "A Poor Relative," then playing at Daly's Theatre.

To John Franklin Jameson

My dear Jameson, New York, 31 Aug., 1889.

A hasty line or two in reply to your letter forwarded me from home. I stayed in Middletown until this week, revising proofs, &c. &c., and am now off on a short spree, freshening up for the work of the next college year. I *do* intend to make a very brief visit to Boston. I am going by steamer with a friend to Balto. Thence I expect to take a steamer back to Boston. I shall leave Balto. at 4 P. M. Thursday next, (the 5th) but what time the vessel reaches Boston I don't know and can't find out: on Saturday, I presume. I am afraid that is too indefinite to enable you to meet me as you so kindly suggest. And yet I want very much to see you. Perhaps I can telegraph you more definitely from Balto. But if it should be inconvenient to meet me under the circumstances by all means give it up. I shall be obliged to make for home on Monday, the 9th.

Hurridly but affectionately Yours, Woodrow Wilson

ALS (J. F. Jameson Papers, DLC).

Two Letters to Ellen Axson Wilson

My dear darling, New York, 1 Sept., 1889.

It's Sunday and I shall have to do without a letter from you till to-morrow morning—& to tell the truth that's the hardest thing in the world for me to do. I need constant and direct communication with you to keep my spirits up when I'm away from my precious, home-making little wife. Oh, sweetheart, my love for you *bounds* uncontrolably from height to height when we are separated. Every sweet or pretty face I see, every touching stage-scene, seems to add to the poignancy of my love for you:—for it *is* poignant. It hurts keenly, though with a sweet pain that seems to sweeten and strengthen my manhood. It gives me both elasticity and purity—so far as I can be pure! I dont deserve you, my lovely, pure little wife. You bless me and help me in every way—even towards the sort of manhood that would be worthy of your sweet, unstained womanhood; but, my precious one, will I ever reach that manhood, even with your help? I'm not in the blues, pet,—I'm not in the least dispirited—I'm loving you from the depth of my heart and consciousness—that's all. Whenever I love you in this sober, intense mood (and that's all the time, nearly, when I'm away from you) I compare myself with you—with the natural results. And that reminds me to speak of one thing, darling, that never seemed so clear to me before. I've been thinking (for the ten thousandth time) how I can *best* love and serve you, and (again for the 10,000th time) I've reached the conclusion that I owe you rest, for a long time at any rate, from child-bearing—but that this time the old conclusion is in a new light. I see now another and larger reason for it. You have blessed me continuously—never having done anything to make me unhappy except suffer pain—but you have not *felt* that you you [*sic*] were helping and blessing me—because your ill health has kept you from full and active companionship—has kept you from being wholly your*self* for me. You have been suffered to be at your best for me only one winter: I can make you happiest by restoring you to yourself & suffering you to love and help me as you did that delightful winter. Isn't that true, little lady? Well, my precious one, it remains for me to prove my devotion as it has never yet been proved. I have never yet shown you by any infallible proof *how much* I love you—but, with God's help, I will hereafter!

I have no news of myself: I did nothing yesterday important enough to break the thought of this letter by telling. I am simply your lover this morning—and when I'm that I'm at my best—it's then that I would be most willing to have my whole heart laid bare to the search of the world!

Kisses without stint for the sweet babies, and love most sincere for dear Stock and Ed.

With a full heart, Your own Woodrow

ALS (WC, NjP).

My own darling, New York, 2 Sept., 1889

The specimen you sent to the Dr. was not delivered till this (Monday) morning—and was therefore spoiled, not fit for qualitative analysis. You will have to send more. Send it to the Express office about the middle of the morning and mark it "perishable—deliver at once." Do this at once, please ma'am. He will send the analysis to you (Dr. J. J. Garmany, 20th St., cor 6th Ave.)

He was able to make the general tests for albumen, however, and found some. There was not enough for alarm at all; but enough to make the strict observance of the following directions necessary: (1) *Stop taking cold water baths* (this is imperative) and instead take three warm water baths per week, preferably just before going to bed. The water comfortably warm. (2) Stop eating eggs, heavy meats and, as much as possible, *bread* also—in short albuminous foods, and substitute a green vegetable and fruit diet. Eat *fowl*, potatoes, etc. (3) Take gentle exercises (ride etc.) I have put the items in the order of importance, but they must all be carefully and scrupulously observed. If they are, the Dr. says I can go on my trip with easy mind.

The Dr. says that the sea trip is just the thing to cure a cold I've been fool enough to take. We sail to-morrow afternoon at 3. Write to me in Balto., dear, to the J.H.U. and have the letter reach there Thursday morning pretty early. I sail for Boston at 4 P. M. Thursday, the 5th. Telegraph me that you are all right.

Care "Merchants' and Miners' Transportation Co. (Boston Steamer)" for fear your letter should not arrive in time. I will telegraph you the same day.

Heath's letter rec'd.[1]

I've only been doing business errands to-day, but shall try the Opera to-night.

In haste and unbounded love, Your own Woodrow

Love to all.

ALS (WP, DLC).

[1] D. C. Heath's letter is missing.

From Ellen Axson Wilson

My own darling, [Middletown] Sept. 2/89.

I did not write yesterday morning as of course the letter would not have been "collected";—intended to do so before night however so that the letter might start early this morning, but my sight was much too dim to make it possible. It is rather troublesome this morning again, but I will try and write a few lines to go by an early mail. Am sorry this trouble keeps me under the necessity of writing only short hasty notes! Yet after all, sir, they are as long as yours!

We are all well—the children even more than usually "peart" & *mischievous*! is no word for it! Last night after they went to bed they grew so riotous that I went up to stop it; and found Margaret in Jessie's bed & Jessie running all about the floor; and of course both they and the beds pretty well stripped! The weather is still lovely and we are doing nicely & quite cheerful. We had a sort of Browning symposium last night;—we went so deep in him, read so long and late and grew so enthusiastic.

But I am afraid it is really my duty to cut this short. I hope to learn today something more definite as to your movements. I suppose it will scarcely be worth while writing again to N.Y., will it? With a heart full of overflowing with love I am as ever

Your little wife Eileen.

ALS (WC, NjP).

From George Howe, Jr.

Dear Woodrow Asheville, N. C. Sept. 2d, 1889

Your last letter reached me just as I was leaving Danville, and this is my first opportunity to reply to it. My first thought in reference to Ellie's head trouble would be to refer it to the kidney as a cause. The analysis that has been made excludes that. The next organ to look after would be the liver. The pressure of the gravid uterus upon the vessels backing up the blood might produce some torpor of the liver. I would suggest a gentle laxative, repeated every morning. A heaping teaspoonful of Tarrants Seltzer Apperient would be good. To this add a low diet for a few days, with a plenty of *pure* water, either hot or cold, taken upon an empty stomach. This line of treatment would be efficient either for the kidney or liver. I hope you will find it so.

We expect to be at home on the 7th and will be glad to hear from you there.

Annie joins me in love to you both.

Yrs affly Geo Howe

ALS (WP, DLC).

Two Letters to Ellen Axson Wilson

My own darling, New York, Sept. 3, 1889

Of course I shall write to you on the steamer, if the state of my stomach *permits*; but, unless I can find a chance to mail it at Norfolk before transferring to the Bay Line boat, it will have to wait till Thursday morning to start, and will not reach you till Saturday morning, probably. You must possess your soul in patience, therefore, my precious one, between the time of getting this letter and the time of getting that. The steamer we take here this afternoon does not go all the way to Balto. but transfers us to the Bay boat at Norfolk.

My cold is already breaking up—and breaking *me* up to some extent. It has prepared my liver and stomach for a grand clearance at sea, I suspect! But that will prepare me for my second voyage and I may expect to reach you a new man—not exactly "as fresh as a May morning," but "as clear as a whistle." How provoking it is that I should have caught this cold; but I am not sick, and I imagine that this upsetting plus the sea will purge me of all ill humours and save me my Autumn troubles. That will be jolly, wont it? At any rate going to sea in my present condition is the best thing I could do.

The doctor does not seem to think, darling, that a moderate use of your eyes will injure *them*, but he says that the use of them will aggravate your headache.

I have heard of no more *rides*, though you say the weather is lovely. You better not venture to face me with a broken promise, Miss.

I love to think of you having Browning symposia with such enthusiasm, my sweet one,—I love to hear of anything that makes your heart light during my absence. Nothing in the world so braces and stimulates me as your *joy*. Judging you by myself, I know what a dire hard task it is to be happy in spite of our separation! The gnawing at my heart for lack of you, my pet, sometimes grows all but intolerable. I long for the depths of your eyes, the sweet touch of your hands, the precious sweetness of your lips and your caresses. Life has gotten to seem to me *unreal* without you. Nothing but the conviction that this trip is an indispensable preparation for my winter's work, and that I could not serve you as I would—in perfect health and spirits—when you most need my service keeps me from taking the earliest possible train for Middletown. I love you, I live in you, I live for you! You are my unspeakable treasure, my perfect little wife, and I am wholly and in all things

Your own Woodrow

Kisses to the babies, love to the boys.
I've bought a new satchel, and send Stock's back by express.

Steamship Roanoke

My own darling, Wednesday, 10 A. M. [Sept. 4, 1889]

The sea has been as still as a pond, so far; the swell made Bridges a little squeamish last night, but I have been affected scarcely at all. It is just rough enough to make writing awkward.

There is a most commonplace and uninteresting crowd of people on board, but quite a crowd—more than the state-rooms can accommodate. One pretty (?) girl; one graceful (?),—the rest not worth looking at a moment—at any rate more than a moment. This is not the most lively mode of travelling,—nor the most comfortable—considering the scarcity of water in the state-rooms; but it is the most restful and the most healthful, and I am enjoying it not a little.

I shall have only a few hours in Balto. Shall reach here to-morrow morning (about 7 or 8 o'clock, I suppose) and shall sail for Boston at 4 P.M. the same day. I expect to be rather lonely on that part of the journey, having had Bridges with me on this part.

I find myself constantly thinking of you and your trip from New York to Savannah,[1] sweetheart—of your acquaintance, for the nonce, with young Mitchell, etc. I wonder about it and dwell on it in imagination all the time. I wish I could meet somebody as pretty and charming as you on my way to Boston! But if I *found* her as pretty and charming as you—what would happen? I should have to bring her home with me, if I could! Fortunately there is no great excitement in the speculation since it is impossible that any steamer should carry such a treasure so long as you are on land, my little beauty. Ah, sweetheart, I'm glad that you like to be made love to: for I can't help courting you even now that you are won and are the sweet queen of my home. I am looking forward to next Monday with a consuming longing. I grudge every mile that is added to the distance between us. You are my mainstay, darling. The love that is in your arms gives them strength to sustain me in all things if only they are thrown about me!

I am glad you told me about Margaret's and Jessie's escapade the other night—it does me *so* much good to get these glimpses of my beloved home.

I'll try to find time to write from Balto., if only a card.

Kisses to the babies, love to the boys.

Your own Woodrow

ALS (WC, NjP).

[1] He refers to Ellen's voyage by sea from New York to Savannah in late May and early June 1885, just before their marriage.

From Ellen Axson Wilson

My own darling, Middletown Sept 5/89

I think I will at least begin a letter before breakfast this morning while my eyes are still clear, and while I am as usual waiting on the boys. I sent off the telegram last night as directed,[1] though it seemed useless, as of course the letter will reach you. We are all quite well, and I have just made the pleasant discovery that Jessie has two new *teeth*, large, almost full-grown molars. So that now she has but two more to cut. I am so *very* very sorry, love, about that unfortunate cold. It is too bad to have the pleasure of your trip so marred; I cannot avoid feeling uneasy too because you don't say whether it is simply in your head or deeper. I hope the Dr. is right in thinking the sea-voyage will work a cure, though I fear that under all the circumstances it will be rather a severe remedy. Stockton's "little friend"[2] as he calls her is coming to New York from Sav. for the benefit of the sea voyage;—will arrive next Tuesday. She has been quite sick;—

nearly had typhoid fever. Stock will go to New York to see her. She is with her parents. I suppose I shall have to invite them to come up;–will I not? But I suppose they won't come,–I certainly hope *not* under the circumstances. I *have* kept my promise religiously with regard to the rides;–took the last one day before yesterday and had a particularly charming one, the day was so lovely, the lights so fine, and we hit upon such a beautiful road. The children too have enjoyed their rides immensely.

Mr. Rice has just been here to find out where he can write to you & when you will return. I told him I didn't know;–but you *won't* return 'till Monday,–will you? I hope *not*; and I *hope* you will refuse positively to do what they wish, which is to make a speech somewhere. He is going to write to you about it today however. All the people, nearly, have returned, Van V's, Van B's, Crawford's, Conns &c.; even some of the boys seem to be about. Stockton has finally decided to try for the A. M. even if he has to enter the Sophomore Greek. Mr. Bergstrom[3] is sure that at worst he could accomplish it in that way. He is now busy reviewing his Greek. Eddie is in the higher Latin class, as we wished. Your pictures have come from Pach[4] and I spend most of my time now looking at it,–carry it with me to the table & everywhere else. Am so glad they came to comfort me while you were away! My precious one! my dear, dear husband! To look at it & to think of *you* fairly thrills me, makes me happy down to the very bottom of my heart,–fills me with "thoughts that do often lie too deep for tears." Oh my darling, my darling, how I *do love* you! *You* can't imagine how, because alas! I cannot tell you. I love you 'till it fairly *hurts*! That seems to prove, doesn't it?–that there is something excessive somewhere,–viz., that you are altogether *'too* good & perfect'! But here is barely room & time left to sign myself

Your little wife Ellie

The index came from Heath yesterday. We read it, without changing the numbers of course, & will return at once.

ALS (WC, NjP).

1 See WW to EAW, Sept. 2, 1889. EAW's telegram is missing.

2 Probably Emily Howell.

3 Probably John Andrew Bergström of Middletown, '90.

4 Pach Brothers, photographers, of 841 Broadway, New York, who had a studio in Middletown. A reproduction of this picture appears in the photographic section of this volume.

To Ellen Axson Wilson

[Baltimore] Thursday 1:40, P. M. [Sept. 5, 1889]

As my letter & telegram will have told you, our journey thus far has been as prosperous as possible. I find I shall have all day at Old Point to-morrow and you may expect a letter from that point. Here I find myself unexpectedly rushed. You know how my letter would end, were it not a letter patent. Yrs. W. W.

API (WC, NjP).

From Ellen Axson Wilson

My dear W. [Middletown] Thursday [Sept. 5, 1889]

Isn't it *too* provoking? The letter that I sent you to the J.H.U. they *returned* immediately & it has just arrived. It was very plainly postmarked "Middletown" too. Very stupid! So now you will be disappointed as to hearing from me in Balt. Am glad the telegram went. A satisfactory letter from Bro. George just arrived.[1] Affly E. A. W.

API (WP, DLC).

[1] G. Howe to WW, Sept. 2, 1889.

To Ellen Axson Wilson

My own darling, Norfolk, Va., 6th Aug. [Sept.], '89

The plans I had expected to execute to-day have been spoiled by a fog in the bay which detained us six or seven hours, spent idly at anchor. We are just making fast to the dock here now, 12:15 P.M. Had we reached here about 5:30 A.M., as we should have done, I could have spent the day at Old Point, Virginia Beach —where I pleased. As it is I can go nowhere. It's extremely hot, though, and I dont know that I'm extremely anxious to go anywhere.

May-be this letter will not reach you very many hours before I do—doubtless it will be kept, undigested in the Sunday maw of the *Post Office*—but perhaps you would like to know even a few hours only before my arrival that the steamer I am on, the Chatham is a comparatively new and very comfortable boat, quite large, evidently thoroughly sea-worthy, and apparently well officered. The supper and breakfast we have had were quite good, and promise well for the dinner yet to be served. Probably we shall get off about 5 P.M. in spite of our delay. If so we should reach Boston on Sunday afternoon—not *much* after noon. If kept here longer handling freight, we may not reach B till late Sunday night. I will telegraph immediately upon reaching there, provided it be not too late in the night—in that case early in the morning.

I have an amiable old man in my state-room with me who is something of a nuisance.

In Balto. Bob and I dined with Hiram at his Club, Mrs. Woods being but just up from being confined with a boy. We called on Mrs. Woods, however, and saw her—looking quite well. We also called on Mitchell and cheered him up a bit.

By the way, Mrs. Hiram said she had heard from various quarters that you were the "favorite lady" at Bryn Mawr. Of course you were! you darling. You are the favorite lady of everybody who meets you and if I had not won you and made you safely Mrs. Wilson, I should be the most miserable fellow alive. As it is, I am the very happiest, possessing you and being

Your own Woodrow

ALS (WC, NjP).

From Melville R. Hopewell

Dear Sir Tekamah, Nebraska, Sept. 6th 1889

I hand you herewith deed to Alexander Corbin for E 1/2 SW 1/4 10-21-11- 80. acres, for execution by Jeanie W. Wilson and husband. The sale as you will see by the consideration is at $11.00 per acre. Mr Corbin will pay 1/3 or 1/4 down and bal in one & two years, or if you are anxious to have all cash, he will get the whole amt. for a reasonable discount.

It is desired to have the deed signed by your father & mother, instead of by you, under your Power of Atty. I suppose this will occasion a short delay. Upon receipt of deed I will forwards proceeds, as you may direct, less my com 5% & cost of abstract.

Yours Very Truly M. R. Hopewell

You will note that I have made sale subject to taxes for year 1889. This tax was levied last spring and is a lien on the land, although not yet due. Mr Corbin, who is a close man, may object to this and ask that the amt of tax be deducted, and I presume, rather than miss the sale, you would prefer that we pay it.

Custom would require Mr C to pay the tax.

I am expecting to make a sale in section 4-21-11- have been

offered $2000. for 240 acres, but I do not think it enough. Have said to party, I would send in bid of $10.00 per acre. I think 2 parties want the land, if so I may be able to get more.

ALS (WP, DLC). Enc.: Unexecuted warranty deed for transfer of land from Jeanie W. Wilson and Joseph R. Wilson to Alexander Corbin, dated Sept. 7, 1889.

From Annie Wilson Howe

Dearest Brother, Columbia, S. C. Sept. 13th 1889

I cannot tell you how much obliged I am for the pictures, received this morning. I think yours is very fine, and that of the dear little girls is lovely. They make me long to see you all, more than ever, if possible. I wish you had sent one of dear Ellie too. We got home last Friday. I am ever so much better—feel like another woman, and Dr. George gained several pounds in flesh during his short vacation.

You asked me in your last letter if I was not a little bit ashamed to confess that we had waited for an *invitation* to your home. It was not that we were not sure of a loving welcome, dear, but we could not be certain that it would be convenient for you to have us. You might not have had a vacant room. I would have given anything to have been able to go. I do not think I have ever longed to see you as much as I have this summer. I have not heard a word from Father or Josie for six weeks. Uncle James [Woodrow] told Dr. George, the other day, that he saw Father in New York.

I hope Ellie is feeling better than when you wrote to Dr. George in Danville. Give her much love from me. I am going to try and get a good picture of the boys and send to you. You would hardly recognise Wilson.

I hope that before another year passes, we will be able to meet somewhere. Dr. Geo. unites with me in unbounded love to you, dearest brother, & Ellie. Kiss the little girls for me.

Annie.

ALS (WP, DLC).

A Promotion Letter from D. C. Heath & Company[1]

Dear Sir, Boston, Mass. Sept. 16, 1889.

Prof. Woodrow Wilson, who is well known as a successful student of comparative politics, has prepared a brief manual of our government which we confidently expect to prove especially acceptable to teachers because of its freshness and soundness of method. Departing altogether from the usual plan of making a formal analysis of the federal constitution serve as an explanation of the structure and operation of our gover[n]ment, he describes it as he would any other system, by making plain its historical derivation, detailing its actual structure and methods,—whether these rest upon constitutional provision or only upon statute,—and bringing it into constant comparison with other governments. Viewing our system thus historically and practically, he gives to the state governments the prominence to which their great functions entitle them.

The book, a thin duodecimo of some 125 pages, is entitled "The State and Federal Governments of the United States." It treats of these governments as parts of a single system; of the state governments as the chief, the everyday instrumentalities of law-making and administration; of the federal government as the great unifying and uniting frame-work, as the great crowning structure and enabling force, of the complex whole. The local governments of the states, as well as their central executive and law-making organs, are described, with the result that more space falls to the description of state than of national institutions. At the same time the state governments are never dissociated from the federal government in the thought of the author, and a description of the powers and organization of the states incidentally becomes a partial description of federal institutions as well.

These characteristics [of] the work derives largely from the fact that it is one of a series of descriptive studies of modern governments which make up a much larger work ("The State: Elements of Historical and Practical Politics") which the author has just published with us. Price $1.60.

We would suggest that the Old South Leaflets would furnish an excellent documentary appendix to Prof. Wilson's work. We will send any four of these, (such, e. g., as Magna Charta, the colonial charter of Massachusetts, the Articles of Confederation and the Constitution of the United States) with each copy of the book without extra charge. The Leaflets are Seventeen in number and include a large variety of documents bearing on our constitutional and political history, as may be seen by the enclosed circular. In ordering the book and Leaflets please enclose 75 cents.

Respectfully yours, D. C. Heath & Co.

Printed L (WP, DLC).

[1] Based in large part, no doubt, upon Wilson's draft. See D. C. Heath to WW, Aug. 23, 1889.

EDITORIAL NOTE

WILSON'S TEACHING AT WESLEYAN UNIVERSITY AND THE JOHNS HOPKINS, 1889-90

Wilson described his formal course work at Wesleyan during 1889-90 in his copy for the Wesleyan catalogue for 1889-90 printed at December 1, 1889.

There is no mystery why Wilson decided to introduce a junior year course in American history as an alternate to his course in English-French history. On June 3, 1889, he agreed to contribute a volume on American history between 1829 and 1889 to the Epochs of American History Series being edited by Albert Bushnell Hart of Harvard University. Characteristically, Wilson at once decided to kill two birds with the same stone. He immediately prepared the following announcement, which appeared in the *Wesleyan Argus*, XXII (June 7, 1889), 177: "Prof. Wilson has decided to give an alternate course in Junior history next year. The course will be in American history. The English history course of this year will be repeated the following year, so that any one may take both courses."

As his copy for the Wesleyan catalogue indicates, he devoted the first term of this new course to drill work in American history before 1829 and then, during the second and third terms, lectured on the period to be covered in his book for Hart. For these lectures, Wilson seems to have fallen back upon the notes prepared for his course in special topics in American history at Bryn Mawr in 1886-87.[1] However, it is possible that he filled out the Bryn Mawr lectures to make them chronologically more complete. The examinations printed at May 28 and June 12, 1890, give a clear view of Wilson's coverage in his Wesleyan course and indicate that he got only as far as the secession crisis. It is interesting that he had gone no further in his lectures at Bryn Mawr.

In his other course work at Wesleyan in 1889-90, Wilson seems to have substantially repeated the courses that he had given the year before on the history of institutions, the Constitution of the United States, and political economy. The reader is, therefore, referred to the Editorial Note, "Wilson's Courses at Wesleyan and the Johns Hopkins, 1888-89." However, there is revealing supplementary evidence about the work of the class in political economy in 1889-90 in the news items printed at January 18 and February 15, 1890.

Wilson's announcement of topics for special honors work in history,[2] printed at June 12, 1889, and the bibliographies for these topics, printed at June 10, 1889, give full evidence of the kind of advanced independent work that Wilson offered at Wesleyan in 1889-90. The presence in the Wilson Papers of only one special bibliography prepared in the academic year 1888-90—the one printed at February 7, 1889—and the fact that no history majors were graduated with special honors in 1889 indicate (a) that honors work in history was at a low ebb when Wilson came to Wesleyan, and (b) that Wilson's announcement of a full-fledged program in June 1890 was an obvious effort to stimulate his own students to do the kind of work that students in other departments were already doing.

Having focused on central and local governments in his first and second series of lectures on administration at the Johns Hopkins, Wilson in 1890 concentrated on problems of city government and public law and administrative justice. The following notice in the Baltimore *Sun*, February 4, 1890, signaled the beginning of the third series: "Professor Woodrow Wilson began a course of twenty-five lectures on 'Administration' yesterday morning in the historical library of the Johns Hopkins University." Wilson's letter to Ellen Axson Wilson of March 10, 1890, indicated that he completed this series on that day. His complete notes for these lectures are printed at February 3, 1890, along with an Editorial Note, as is his review of the lectures at June 1, 1890. The final lecture or lectures on administrative justice might well have been added because Wilson had miscalculated and was about to complete his lectures ahead of time.

[1] See the Editorial Note, "Wilson's Teaching at Bryn Mawr, 1886-87," and the body of lecture notes described at Oct. 4, 1886, both in Volume 5.

[2] For a description of special honors work at Wesleyan at this time, see the Wesleyan catalogue for 1888-89, pp. 62-65.

To Munroe Smith

My dear Prof. Smith, Middletown, Conn., 23 Sept., 1889

Your letter came while I was away. Unfortunately it was necessary to send the sheets to press before your answer arrived, so that I did not venture to use your name unsanctioned. I substituted a description of you as "a friend who upon this subject speaks with authority," and had to satisfy myself with a general acknowledgement to you by name in my preface.

The book is afloat, in a cover that ought to lead to its being condemned unread. So soon as I have gotten the publisher to remedy the worst features of it, I shall give myself the pleasure of sending you a copy. Until then I shall go without a bound copy myself.

With sincerest regards,

Yours cordially, Woodrow Wilson

ALS (WC, NjP).

From John Franklin Jameson

My dear Wilson: Providence, Oct. 1, 1889.

I have a scheme for getting you over here, which *must* succeed. We propose to begin, on the evening of Monday, November 11th, a course of about six lectures, on social reforms accomplished by legislation, or legislation for social reform, or government's action in social reform; we haven't fixed our title. But whatever the title, there will be such lectures as one on factory legislation, one by Judge Wayland[1] on prison-reform, one on state charities, one on the relations of the state to education, etc. For the opening lecture, we want one which shall treat, in a scholarly fashion and with impartiality, the opposing theories respecting the functions of government in such matters; a lecture of this sort, on *laissez-faire* and t'other notion, would fitly introduce our course.[2]

I will frankly say that we tried to get [Francis A.] Walker to give us this lecture; because I think that there is more of compliment than of the reverse in saying that, since we can't get him, owing to engagements, we want you to come and deliver a lecture on this subject for us. Terms as last year, I am sorry to say. But pray do come. It is vain to say that that isn't just exactly the subject for you, because it evidently is, exactly. So I assume that you will come. Nevertheless, as M. Jourdain[3] would say, make believe that I do not, and write me that you will; write soon, if you can.

Everything starts well with Andrews. Remember me most kindly to Mrs. Wilson and the olive-plants, and believe me

Very truly yours, J. F. Jameson.

ALS (WP, DLC).

1 Francis Wayland, Jr., Dean of the Yale University Law School, 1873-1903.

2 Wilson did give the lecture on November 11, 1889. See the newspaper report printed at November 12, 1889.

3 The leading character of Molière's *Le Bourgeois Gentilhomme*.

To John Franklin Jameson

My dear Jameson, Middletown, Conn., 5 Oct., 1889

Since I am evidently bound to say 'Yes' to your proposition, I do, with the best grace possible under the circumstances. The circumstances are, first, a very pronounced feeling of inability to do what will be expected of me, and, second, lack of time to *write* what I shall have to say and the consequent necessity of depending upon the digestion and mood of the evening of November 11th.

The line of argument I shall take is indicated in the last chapter of 'The State.' Have you seen that laboured composition? I directed Heath to send you a copy immediately upon publication; but so soon as I *saw* the bound volume I was sorry I had! More barbarous taste than is displayed in the lettering of its title I never had the ill fortune to see. I have directed a change to be made: it is being made now, and, if you have not already been shocked by receiving the vulgar-looking book, I will send you one of the less objectionable when my copies come. I have no bound copy yet myself. I would not have it in that style.

I am very anxious to learn your full and candid judgment of the book as a whole,—and of its serviceableness as a text-book.

I am sincerely glad that I am to have an opportunity to see you so soon again, though I should have preferred to have it without the prospect of doing public talking. I enjoyed deeply the opportunity of meeting your family:[1] I sincerely wish that they were with you in Providence, so that I might renew and extend the acquaintance.

I do esteem it a compliment to be asked to make the first lecture of your course next after Walker; but it's an embarrassing compliment—it's so much too big for me!

I'm glad you like Andrews' start. I shall be curious to meet him. Is he the president of your Ass'n?

If you will clip a R. R. time table (Middletown to Providence) from the paper for me this time as you did last I shall be much obliged. It's not possible to get a complete one at this end!

Mrs. Wilson joins me in warmest regards—in which the babies would also join, we are sure, if they knew how.

As ever, Your sincere friend, Woodrow Wilson

ALS (J. F. Jameson Papers, DLC).

[1] That is, Jameson's parents, in Boston on about September 8.

From Joseph Ruggles Wilson

My precious son: Clarksville, Oct. 5th 1889.

Every day has heard my resolution to write to you—or might have heard it, if due attention had been given by the listening hours. I have no excuse except the singular one of too much love: i.e., I did not relish the thought of boring you with commonplaces, and I had no other stock on hand with which to treat their dear reader. Besides, I could *think* of you without disturbing any one—and this I have done with a plentifulness and a constancy worthy of the object of my affections were these affections ten-fold deeper than they are—if possibility be competent to ascertain for my heart a depth it has not already explored to youward. Ah, my son, this old heart—you fill it, and with a charm that is quite unspeakable:—so that I am made to feel that after all I can never be lonely, were every thing else stricken from my grasp, and you alone were to remain. Of course I am not forgetting—and do always remember—the other children, who are very close to my sympathies. But you were my companion more entirely than they; and are now not merely my child to whom consanguinity attaches by a tie of natural regard, but my *friend* to whom community of thought binds by ligatures which are thicker than blood. I am sure that we are the two who thoroughly —most thoroughly—comprehend each other. You satisfy my intellect as I believe I am able to content yours. You gratify my pride also, and I feel assured that your corresponding emotion has its demands measurably met in me, to whom you have long been accustomed to look up with an eye that perceives in me far more than there really is of goodness and of largeness—(for which I parenthetically take this occasion to thank you.) I did not intend to write in this way when I began the present letter—but you will, I know, pardon an old man's fondness, which, when it enjoys the opportunity for a little airing, can hardly find the place where it ought to stop.

I am looking with expectant interest for a copy of your new book, and hope that you will not wait too long for a suitable *binding* to justify its speedy transmission. I shall want to purchase a number of copies, when I know the price and the right time, for sending to our relatives and others in Buffalo and Cleveland. If, however, you would meanwhile address one to your aunt Lizzie (613 Euclid Avenue, Cleveland) with your compliments written on a fly-leaf, I will pay the bill and be grateful besides. Mrs. Adam J. Begges is her proper address. She, too, would be immensely pleased.

Josie is looking (in vain so far) for a business in which to engage. He is a source of real trouble to me on this account: and I am utterly at a loss as to what to do with him.

Things in the college are moving along at their old dull rate. I don't see how I am to endure much longer the teaching of classes with only four or five men—not of the highest quality—in each.

Present my warmest love to dearest Ellie—& to the little dumb ones. Your affc Father

ALS (WP, DLC) with WWhw notation on env.: "Ans. 31 Oct/89."

An Editorial from the *Wesleyan Argus*

[Oct. 9, 1889]

The closing weeks of the last college year witnessed a flagging of interest in the House of Commons. Though this was a disappointment to many in college who are interested in debate, it was nevertheless to be expected that the pressure of examinations and other work peculiar to the season of the year would bring about such a result. At the end of the term, however, provision was made, by a re-organization of the ministry, for a continuance of its sessions during the current year. When it is called to meet it will doubtless be too much to expect such a universal manifestation of interest as marked its beginning last January. It then had all the charm of novelty and excitement. The House of Commons nevertheless ought to receive a hearty support at the hands of the college, not because it is novel, but because the training which it supplies is a necessity for him who aims at a well-rounded development. The benefits to be obtained from such practice in debate as the House of Commons affords can be secured but meagrely in the regular college work.

Printed in the Middletown, Conn., *Wesleyan Argus*, XXIII (Oct. 9, 1887), 2.

From Marion Wilson Kennedy

My dearest Woodrow: Batesville [Ark.], Oct. 12th/89.

Many thanks for the photographs! I was only disappointed that dear Ellie's was not there, and not greatly surprised, either. You have not improved yourself, in my estimation, by discarding your mustache. What does Ellie think? You are good enough looking anyway, but better looking with a mustache than without, I think. Does that opinion weigh anything so far off as Middletown, Conn.? . . .

Ross has not been so well for the past ten days. He thinks he is losing ground quite decidedly. What the doctor thinks, no one knows. I don't believe *he* has any opinion on the subject. He seems just to be waiting to see what will happen next. Perhaps no one could do any otherwise; I don't know.

We are,—the rest of us—, pretty well, except little Woodrow. He has been quite delicate since last Spring, and does not seem to improve at all, permanently. He gets better for a while, and then worse again. Joe and Will are studying Latin this year, the one in Latin Reader, the other just beginning. So you see, I am still reading somebody's Latin.

Ross joins me in warmest love for yourself, Ellie and the two dear little lassies over whom our larger children all four go wild —"they are such darlings."

Lovingly your sister, Marion.

ALS (WP, DLC).

From the Minutes of the Conversational Club[1]

Oct. 14, 1889.

Club met with Prof Winchester. The records of the last meeting were read and approved. . . .

Prof W. Wilson was chosen President for the ensuing term. . . .[2]

Prof Woodrow Wilson read a paper on "Literary Individuality,"[3] and the general discussion that followed was participated in by several literary individuals. . . .

D. W. Northrop, Sec'y.[4]

Bound minute book (CtW).

[1] The Conversational Club, organized in 1862, was a group of Wesleyan faculty members and townspeople who met informally in members' homes to hear papers and discuss topics of various interest. See [T. M. Russell, Jr.,] *The Conversational Club, Middletown, Connecticut, A Commemorative Pamphlet, 1862-1962* (Middletown, Conn., 1965).

[2] Wilson first attended the Conversational Club on October 8, 1888, and was elected a member on December 31, 1888.

[3] Undoubtedly Wilson's essay, "The Author Himself," printed at Dec. 7, 1887, Vol. 5.

[4] Judge David Ward Northrop of Middletown.

An Essay on the Teaching of Ancient History

[Oct. 15, 1889]

Preparatory Work in Roman History.

Our preparatory schools are already overtaxed by the various and constantly increasing demands made upon them by the colleges. The resources of the colleges are, as a rule, growing faster than the resources of the schools, and the speed of change and improvement possible to the one is not often possible to the other. There are few things more mournful to the listener, or more reproving, if he be a college man, than the discussions of grievances to be heard at conventions of schoolmasters when the theme is preparing boys for college. It is therefore a grateful circumstance that one can once and again make a suggestion to the heads of preparatory schools which they can adopt without either increasing their teaching force or changing their classroom methods.

What is needed in the way of improvement in preparatory instruction in Roman history is, to put it summarily, a recognition of the fact that Roman history is not history simply, but the material of much of the world's literature besides. It is generally assumed by the teacher of ancient history, naturally enough of course, that his chief if not his sole function is to lay the foundation for his pupil's further pursuit of historical studies in college, or, more concretely still, to make him ready for the college entrance examination. As a matter of fact, however, it is not the college professor of history only, but also the college professors of literature to whom it is a matter of vital interest that Freshmen should have been schooled in ancient history; and the trouble is that the professors of history and the professors of literature want, not the same sort, but different sorts of preparatory instruction in this branch. There are, as everybody by this time knows, two histories of Rome, the one traditional and improbable, the other that which has been produced by treating the traditional with the acids of criticism, and which is regarded as probable because indestructible by such treatment. The first is that which is told by Livy; the second, that proposed by Niebuhr, reduced to its coldest outlines by Ihne, expanded to new imaginative proportions by Mommsen.

But it is the legendary history only which has entered literature: Roman history as reconstructed by modern criticism has found entrance nowhere except into scholarship. The Roman writers themselves believed as Livy did, and accounts like his of the origins and early history of the imperial city run like a rich embroidery over the whole of the literary work of his race. They repeat, reform, re-moralize upon the tradition of their city in every manner known to their art. Unless you know the stories as they did, you cannot understand the historical allusions with which Roman prose and Roman poetry alike overflow. And not only so. The stories are told and told again in all modern literatures. The imaginations of neither Italians nor French nor Germans nor English waited to be chastened by the modern criticism. They accepted the fascinating old tales with a faith as ready and as apt at digesting as that of the Roman imagination itself. Modern literatures are saturated with the same colors of legendary history that have taken hold of the canvasses of the old masters of classical literature. Livy's fictions are realities so far as the imaginative, and even the moral and political, writings of subsequent ages are concerned. Niebuhr failed to get in at the death, so far as the matter affects them.

It is indispensable to the teacher of literature, therefore, that his pupils should know the traditional history of Rome; the critical history of the city is of little or no consequence to him; and now that the preparatory schools are buying and using text-books built upon Niebuhr and Mommsen, there is nothing left for the professors of literature, at any rate for the professors of Latin literature, to do but to turn to and teach their pupils what the professors of history inform them is quite unworthy of serious belief. The schools are using Leighton[1] and like text-books, in which all the legendary history that is given at all is relegated to disconnected foot-notes, which the pupil either skips or reads without realizing–reads with a torpid imagination. The school-teacher is at the same time at a very considerable disadvantage in trying to make his pupils realize the history of Rome as it really was, with the aid of such books. They are at the age to accept legends with interest and satisfaction, as they never can accept them afterwards; and they are not at the age to care very much about a history in which so little that is entertaining happened, as appears in the veritable history of the city by the Tiber. They are not prepared to appreciate historical criticism, and they are prepared to miss the things that historical criticism denies them. The facts of Roman history now left standing in the early periods are fragments–the wholes of which they formed parts are largely conjectural; and when the pupil reaches the periods of greater certainty, touching which the Latin historians are to be credited, he finds himself on an arid plain of constitutional, agrarian, social struggles and factional contests. His sole entertainment is afforded by foreign wars. The attempt to get the scientific history of Rome into his mind to remain a part of it is largely futile.

The legendary history of Rome, on the other hand, is a whole not only, but a poetical whole as well, with claims upon the unscientific attention which no young mind is likely to deny. It is a history apparently made for school-boys to believe. It could not by clever invention have been given superior qualities of adhesion to whatever young brain it touches. The schoolmaster has been obliged, therefore,–such is the sum of the whole matter,–to abandon an old and relatively easy task for a new and partially impossible one.

The result is of the simplest kind. The college teacher of history finds his pupils without real critical knowledge of the history of Rome; and the teacher of the classics finds them quite unable to understand the historical allusions with which their authors abound, as much alienated from Virgil and Horace as from Livy. This leaves the college to repeat the experiment of the school: to reinculcate the conclusions of modern critical investigation and surmise, and to patch together anew the bits of story which for so many centuries have served literature in the stead of history.

The thing needed is, a more natural division of labor. Let the schools teach the history which Livy believed, the colleges that which modern scholars believe. Let the candidate for entrance into college be examined on the *story* of Rome, the candidate for graduation on her history.

There is, of course, another way out of the difficulty. That is to abandon ancient history as a condition for entrance, and substitute the history of the United States, with or without the addition of the history of England. But that is a step which leads directly away from real literary culture. Roman history as conceived by the Romans is indispensable to the student of thought. Nothing which has entered into the belief and the imagination of every generation of men that has lived from the centuries when history was born down to this present century in which it is grown most critical and self-conscious can be left out of the catalogue of things which every man of education should know, if not well, then as well as may be under existing conditions.

Of course these considerations apply in not a few respects to Greek history no less than to Roman. Greek legendary history is more consistent, less conglomerate than Latin. It is in a sense also more credible. It is easier to perceive its meaning and trace the lines of fact lying at its foundations. Greek history, accordingly, has been less radically reconstructed by modern criticism. It would still present to the Greek eye not a little that was recognizable. But it is crowded with myth, none the less, and needs critical sifting. In its case, as in the case of Roman history, the sifting should be done in college rather than at school, in order that literary culture may be served no less than historical knowledge.

Thus much being said, by way of suggestion, on one head and to one intent, perhaps a single note on another head and to a different intent may be unobtrusively smuggled in at the end. It would seem, to judge by results, that ancient history has lost its hold upon Livy and Herodotus not only, but also upon exact geography. It has not retained the hazy conceptions of history characteristic of the ancient, but it has retained his vague ideas of geographical location. Is it not the experience of college examiners that famous towns and storied rivers are given whole coasts and entire regions as their whereabouts in the understanding of the pupils whom the schools have very carefully instructed in the location of each village in their own State?

W. W.

Printed in the *Wesleyan University Bulletin*, Oct. 15, 1889, pp. 13-15.
[1] Robert Fowler Leighton, *A History of Rome* (New York, 1879 and 1889). [Eds.' note]

To John Franklin Jameson

My dear Jameson, Middletown, 23 Oct., '89

Just a line to say that I have rec'd a card from Pres. Andrews inviting me to stay with him in Providence when I come, and that I have accepted in order to relieve you of the awkward necessity of providing for my lodgment in your boarding place. Thank me by return mail.

Mrs. Wilson presented me last week with another little daughter.[1] Both parties are doing amazingly well, and I am serene.

In haste and affection

Yours as ever, Woodrow Wilson

The Eisenbahnschnellsugverzeichniss rec'd.

ALS (J. F. Jameson Papers, DLC).
[1] Eleanor Randolph, born on October 16, 1889.

From Melville R. Hopewell

Dear Sir, Omaha, Neb, Oct. 25th 1889

I have received from your father certified copy of your mothers will[1] & Probate thereof, and have caused same to be filed for Probate in Burt Co. in accordance with the requirements of our statute. The hearing is set for (I think) the 6th of November. Will notify you as soon as completed,[2] & will close sale to Corbin as soon as it can be done.

There are parties who want to buy, in sections 4 & 9, but they do not offer enough—you or your father may hear from them. In the event you do, I would of course like you to refer them to me, and when they find they can do no better I think they will come to our terms.

I am at Omaha now holding Court, and will be the greater part of the time from this on for the next three months, but will be at home, at Tekamah each Saturday. You can therefore address me there.[3]

Very Truly Yours, M. R. Hopewell

ALS (WP, DLC).
[1] Mrs. Wilson's will, dated July 21, 1884, is recorded in Record Book "S," p. 427, in the Montgomery County, Tennessee, Court House in Clarksville. The will was probated by the County Court on April 26, 1888.

[2] The will was probated by the County Court of Burt County, Nebraska, in Tekamah on November 6, 1889.

[3] This letter marks the end of Woodrow Wilson's long correspondence with Hopewell and others about his mother's lands in Nebraska. Mrs. Wilson had willed her entire estate to Joseph Ruggles Wilson, with a provision for a division among her surviving children if she outlived her husband. Dr. Wilson began to administer the estate as soon as the will was probated in Tekamah.

A News Item

[Oct. 26, 1889]

At a recent college meeting it was decided to add to the number of foot-ball directors [of the Foot-Ball Association] by the appointment of one from the faculty and one from the alumni. Prof. Wilson, and S[eward]. V[incent]. Coffin, '89, were chosen by acclamation.

Printed in the Middletown, Conn., *Wesleyan Argus*, XXIII (Oct. 26, 1889), 14.

From Joseph Ruggles Wilson

My precious son, Clarksville, Tenn., Oct 30, 89

I congratulate dear Ellie and yourself upon the safe advent of babe No. 3. It is always a happy time when, without more than the usual danger to mother and child, there comes to be another addition to an already loving household. The sense of mystery gives place to a sense of relief, and to an emotion of thanksgiving. May God's richest blessing be upon you all! Somehow I had—unreasoningly of course—hoped for a boy—but the divine Father who has events in His own hand, moulds all things for the best. Dode joins me in love-felicitations.

Your affectionate Father.

ALS (WP, DLC), with WWhw figures on env.

To Richard Heath Dabney

My dear Heath, Middletown, Ct., 31 Oct., 1889

Ever since the 10th of June last your letter has lain here on my desk before me; again and again I have been on the point of answering it—all the time I have been wanting, with a sort of longing, to answer it—but could'nt! What could I say? The news had followed all too close upon it that even your little baby had been taken away from you, and that had stunned me. You know of my love and sympathy: what more could I add! But now you are a month advanced in your work at the University[1] and I can write to ask, what cheer, old fellow? Don't you feel as if you had gone back to a *home* which holds out to you a comfort and a shelter? I imagine that the dear old lawns and ranges would have such an effect on me under like terrible circumstances—that the old place would soothe me and in a way carry me *back of my sorrow*, to make a fresh start. And I know you for a man. I know that you will open your mind and heart to such influences and re-new yourself, free from all morbid reaction.

Can't you write to me a full account of what they have given you to do and how you are doing it—with what new methods you are surprising the antique calm of the department of history? I would have an appetite for such a letter—merely as inside University news—as news also of you it will fill my interest to the top. I fancy that the University would seem natural to me, could I happen back and find *you* there. After all, you were a very large part of the great old place for me—and I wish to go back now as I have not often—for fear of finding it changed and strange.

How are ΦΨ and the old Jefferson Society? Do you find anybody there who remembers me?

I asked D. C. Heath to send you a copy of the text-book I have just published, and I hope you will understand my love written on the fly-leaf. A *fact* book is always a plebeian among books, and it is a fact book; but a great deal has gone out of me into it, none the less, and I hope you will receive it kindly on that account.

Perhaps you have seen one of the enclosed circulars[2] and have already pitied me the necessity of doing justice to those abolitionist rascals and the other characters of ante-bellum and postbellum times. And I am afraid I *shall* do them justice! I am getting most unreasonably impartial in this lattitude. But the editor of the series and the publishers both said they wanted that period to go to me *because* I am a Southerner—and I could not resist the subtle compliment.

Mrs. Wilson joins with me, my dear fellow, in messages of warmest friendship and sympathy, and I am, with all the old-time, and with an added *new*-time, ardor,

Your affectionate friend, Woodrow Wilson

ALS (Wilson-Dabney Correspondence, ViU).

1 Dabney had just gone to the University of Virginia as Adjunct Professor of History.

2 About *Division and Reunion*. This enclosure is missing.

From John Franklin Jameson

My dear Wilson: [Providence] November 1, 1889.

Yesterday came a copy of The State, in eminently satisfactory binding. Thank you for it. I am in the height of my busiest time, and have been able to spend only time enough to look it over a little, so I will only say now that I like and admire it, so far as examined, and sincerely congratulate you and Mrs. Wilson on its achievement. In much haste, but with the kindest regards to both, I am Sincerely yours, J. F. Jameson.

ALS (WP, DLC) with WWhw notation on env.: "Ans. Nov. 4/89."

A News Item

[Nov. 4, 1889]

Prof. Woodrow Wilson lectured in the chapel of the Methodist church to a select and cultured audience, on Oct. 15. The lecture, "A Literary Politician," namely, Mr. Edward Bagehot, was pronounced exceedingly fine by all who heard it. It is to be hoped that Professor Wilson will give us frequent opportunities to hear him.

Printed in the Middletown, Conn., *Wesleyan Argus,* XXIII (Nov. 4, 1889), 24.

From Robert Bridges

Dear Tommy: [New York] Nov 5–89

Thank you very much for the copy of "The State" which arrived while Chang was visiting me. By a curious coincidence I had that morning purchased a copy which Lee immediately took off my hands—so that you are indebted to William for one copyright. So far I have only gone over the bones of the book, and find it a skeleton of many ribs. By-and-by I shall hope to read it, and think of the writer on every page.

I hear a great deal about the Princeton professorship. Cleve Dodge told me "confidentialy" the other day that you had been agreed upon. As a matter of fact he knew nothing about it. However, you only have to say so to get it, in my opinion. Sloane came to see me the other day, evidently in the dark about the whole thing. Patton had apparently said nothing to him of your interview. His visit was for pumping purposes. I think I gave complete satisfaction by my apparent frankness and volubility.

I told him one or two things which it seemed to me would be advisable—1) That you would not accept a chair of Economics. 2) That you were really anxious to be associated with Princeton (of which he seemed to have doubt.) 3. That your aptitude and inclinations led you irresistibly toward the study of law and institutions. I think it was wise to do so, because he showed evidences of some feeling, as though your friends were perhaps working in the dark, against him—or rather without his assistance.

I have also arrived at some of the arguments which certain of the Philistines have seen fit to whisper behind their hands: 1) Prof. Wilson is no doubt a fine scholar, but he comes from the South and we want to know more about his patriotism and general views on national topics. 2.) He is, we hear, a little heterodox (shades of Calvin and Witherspoon protect us). 3. He is too learned and deep to interest his students. 4.) We are fearful of his strong affection for English institutions.

These things are "chaff" which intelligent men laugh at, but we know that there is an element at Princeton which is hardly reasonably intelligent.

I mention these things because I know you are too strong to be annoyed by them, and that you may put live coals instead of Chestnuts on any cat's-paws that may be extended to you.

Sloane wants you at Princeton, I am convinced. He is overworked at present, and showed more irritation than I have known him to reveal in his placid countenance. He intimated in one quarter that he should resign if he were not soon relieved of his extra work. (This is very confidential.)

And so the world goes on, each with his little woe and pleasure, and you and I serene in friendship

Yours affectionately Robert Bridges

ALS (WP, DLC) with WWhw notation on env.: "Ans. 6 Nov./89."

To Robert Bridges

My dear Bobby, Middletown, Ct., 6 Nov., '89

Your letter of yesterday has just reached me, containing the first word I have heard about the Princeton matter (except from newspaper notes from the colleges) since my interview with Patton. I have once or twice been on the point of writing to ask whether you had heard anything, but have each time refrained because of a disinclination to worry you about it unnecessarily.

The newspaper paragraphs I have seen have been the cause of some chagrin to me. They have put me in the light of an active candidate for the chair Johnston left vacant, and have made me anxious about the result because non-election would involve the mortification of defeat, in the eyes of the college world—wh. is professionally my world. Nor have the papers so much as contained a rumour as to the establishment of an additional chair, such as Patton's conversation with me almost exclusively concerned. I have had not a word from Princeton, but have remained since July as completely in the dark as if I had personally nothing to do with the affair at all—have been left to speculate about the foundation or significance of the various rumours like any other outsider. The situation is beyond example extraordinary, and has brought me into quite "a state of mind"!

The Trustees, I understand, are to meet to-morrow, so that the matter ought soon to be settled one way or the other. Is Cyrus McCormick in the East, do you know, to attend? I wish he might be at the meeting in order to give me the benefit of some one who knew and understood me. I a little bit wish that I might see and talk with him. Although I am still profoundly averse from assuming the attitude of a candidate, I should not at all hesitate to say anything not undignified that would secure me an election I so much desire. I should even be willing to take the work in economics temporarily, if assurances should be forthcoming that I would *soon* be transferred to a chair of 'public law.'

At the same time, you were perfectly right in the course you took in your interview with Sloane—and I thank you heartily for it. Both in knowledge of me and in knowledge of what is wise you are perfectly qualified to be my full proxy. Surely the course Patton is pursuing is a very extraordinary one, unless we suppose him to be hampered or embarrassed in some way invisible to us. To keep Sloane so in the dark with reference to his own department shows a lack of confidence or of desire for consent which it is quite impossible for me to explain satisfactorily to my own mind. I don't wonder that Sloane became uneasy and even restive under it.

In a note from Princeton in the *Evening Post* some weeks ago it was said that the "Committee on Curriculum" were considering Scott of Rutgers, Thompson of Pa.,[1] and myself, and that it was understood that I would probably be their choice.[2] This I interpreted to mean that I had been fixed upon by the Committee for the new chair (of which news had not yet gotten abroad), and that Thompson and Scott were the prominent names in connection with the economic chair. Thereupon I bethought myself to write to Patton and commend a friend of mine, Albert Shaw. Patton had asked me that day at the Club to give him the names of all the eligible young economists I knew of, and I had forgotten to mention Shaw. I wrote a long letter, in which I said nothing about myself, but heartily commended Shaw for the work in economics. This was about three weeks ago, and I said that, if he would like to correspond with S., I would ascertain his address,—which I did not then know. But no reply of any sort has he ever made.[3] You can easily see that I have had grounds not a few for uneasiness.

If the meeting of the Trustees does not come to-morrow, as I have supposed, but on the *second* Thursday in November, there is of course still time for me to take any course you suggest. But is there anything that I could do—any word that I could say to secure the appointment? I must confess I see nothing for me but simple patience and trying inaction.

Your letter was just what I needed. The items urged against me are certainly astonishing. I think the one that strikes me nearest to the line between wind and water is that which ascribes to me a learning and depth incompatible with ability to interest the boys. Would I *were* learned! It must surely be the influence of that unfortunate after-dinner prose of mine at the Alumni dinner.[4]

If the election is over before the 19th I have more than half a mind to go down to the Princeton Club dinner on that day

You say nothing about the effects of your vacation trip upon you, but I take it for granted that the last part of it, at any rate, in the hills, was good. My sea-voyage to Boston was pretty rough and I lost interest in my meals to some extent. But I kept my grip very much better than I expected and was not positively sea-sick at all. My cold gradually wore off, and before very long I was feeling bully.

My *big* piece of news is, that three weeks ago another daughter was born to us. Both mother and baby are doing and feeling splendidly. There is now "the baby, the little baby, and the littlest baby of all." With warmest regards from Mrs. Wilson, as ever,

Yours Most Affectionately, Woodrow Wilson

ALS (WC, NjP).

1 Austin Scott, Voorhees Professor of History and Political Science at Rutgers, and Robert Ellis Thompson, Welsh Professor of History and English Literature at the University of Pennsylvania.

[2] The New York *Evening Post*, October 9, 1889, reported that the Curriculum Committee of the Princeton Board of Trustees had taken no action at its October meeting on a replacement for the late Professor Johnston in the chair of Political Economy and Jurisprudence, but that the prominent candidates to be considered at the November meeting were Wilson, Thompson, and Scott. This brief note concluded with the remark, "It is thought that Prof. Wilson will be the choice of the Committee."

[3] Patton's belated reply is printed at Nov. 9, 1889.

[4] Printed at March 23, 1886, Vol. 5.

From Robert Bridges

My dear Tommy: *See postscript* New York Nov 7 1889

I shall write you a short and quick note now, rather than wait till evening—so that you may write Cyrus immediately. Almost at the same time with your letter came one from Wilder telling me that Cyrus would be in N. York from Nov 9th to 12th and 17th to 20th. Cyrus says in his note that he will attend the Trustees meeting on Nov 14th—so that you are in time. His New York address will be #500 Madison Avenue.

I have no doubt that Patton is keeping quiet for a wise purpose —and is probably looking out for your interests.

Might it not be wise, however, for you to run down to Princeton on Saturday the 9th and have a talk with him? Also to stop here on your return and have a talk with *Cyrus*? If there are any misunderstandings abroad you can clear them up effectually in that way.

This is the only thing I can suggest.

My congratulations on the new baby.

Faithfully Yours Robert Bridges

P.S. 1 p.m. Before this letter was out of the mail basket Providence in the form of President Patton appeared at my desk. We have had a long talk on points which were contained in my previous letter. I cannot go over them now—but the upshot of it all is that you *must* come to New York Saturday afternoon, Nov 9th and meet President Patton for a long talk at the Astor House at *8 p.m.* Break a leg to do this, Tommy, several if necessary.

I can only say that President Patton is your friend to the backbone, and his apparent silence has been for the best reasons. He has championed you loyally, frankly, and judiciously. *Telegraph* me your decision on receipt of this.

Yours Faithfully Robert Bridges

ALS (WP, DLC).

From Marion Wilson Kennedy

My darling brother and sister; Batesville [Ark.], Nov. 7th/89.

We heartily congratulate you both on the safe arrival of the little blossom intrusted to your care, and on its Mother's well-doing, as well. I suppose Woodrow has had his way, and the baby is called Ellen. Such a pretty name, and with the sweetest of associations, for him, and for baby herself. I have always thought the child named after a parent must feel specially near to that parent.

We thought the end of all Ross' sufferings had come last Saturday night. He was very ill, and even the doctor thought he was probably going. He has rallied again, however, and we feel selfishly thankful to have him with us at least a short while longer. . . .

Your book came safely, and I do not yet see the dry part of it. It has set me to reading up, and proves a most acceptable diversion. I am so constantly in one room and doing the same things, that I am not always as cheerful a companion for Ross as I should be. I often feel ashamed of my lack of brightness, and failure to keep up cheerful looks and subjects of conversation. Ross is weak enough to be easily depressed or cheered, as the case may be.

Write as often as you can. Your dear words of sympathy are a wonderful help to me. Dear Ellie has her hands too full—just now, at any rate—, to make much writing possible, but I would like, more than I can tell, to have a note from her, occasionally, just because I love her so well.

Ross joins me in warmest love to you both, and kisses for the wee bairnies three.

Lovingly your sister, Marion.

ALS (WP, DLC).

From Annie Wilson Howe

Dearest Brother, Columbia, S. C. Nov. 9th 1889

I intended to write and congratulate you as soon as I heard of the birth of the dear little girl, but have put it off from day to day until I am afraid you think it very strange. We were both so glad to know that it was all over and that Ellie was doing well. I hope she continues well. Give her our warmest love. I suppose you have named the baby Ellen?

Now dear I want to thank you for sending me a copy of your book. I have heard so many complimentary things said about it, and its author, that I feel quite proud of you. Mr. Abney talked in the most extravagant way about it the other night at Harriet English's wedding. He told me he had written to you about it. I have not commenced to read it yet, as the boys want me to read it aloud to them and we have not yet succeeded in finding a convenient time for all of us.

I am anxious to hear what your plans as to building summer homes are. You spoke of something of the kind in your last letter. It would certainly be delightful if we could manage in some way to spend the summers together. Life is so short, and we see so little of one another. Write just as soon as you can. I know you are very busy. Dr. George is so busy these days that I see very little of him. There has been a great deal of sickness in Columbia this fall.

I met Sandy Childs in Bryan's store the other day and he begged me to give you his kind regards. Do you remember him? Dr. Flinn asked me to let him see your book, that he would like to write a notice of it for the News & Courier or the Southern Presbyterian. Goodbye dear, we love your dearly & are very proud of you. Kiss dear Ellie for me and the three little girls also.

Your devoted sister, Annie.

ALS (WP, DLC).

From Francis Landey Patton

My dear Professor Wilson: [Princeton] 9 Nov 89

I thank you for your letter recommending Dr Shaw & I have put it on file for further reference.

I must acknowledge my indebtedness to you also for your inscription in The State a copy of which you kindly sent me. I am reading it with great satisfaction

Very Sincerely Yours Francis L. Patton

ALS (Patton Letterpress Books, University Archives, NjP).

A Newspaper Report of a Lecture at Brown University[1]

[Nov. 12, 1889]

Opening Lecture in the Economic Course by
Prof. Woodrow Wilson.

A large and cultured audience gathered in Manning Hall last evening to listen to the opening lecture in this season's course of the Brown University Historical and Economic Association. The lecturer was Prof. Woodrow Wilson, LL.D., of Wesleyan University and his subject was: "What Ought Government to Do?" The speaker was introduced by Vice President Rathbone Gardner of the association, who said that they very much regretted their newly elected President, William B. Weeden, Esq., was unable to be there and preside. He extended thanks for the interest that was shown in the course last year. They felt that it was entirely satisfactory, and that it did foster a community in feeling between the College and the community, which was so much desired. He expressed a wish for an increase of membership in the association, but said all would be welcome to the lectures whether members or not. The audience were also invited to go into the room below, when the lecture should conclude, and inspect a collection of casts that had recently been brought there. The lectures before the association, he said, would be divided into two series. The first would be on "State and Social Reform." The subject of the first would be: "What Ought Government to Do." He did not think it was necessary for him to introduce the lecturer, who would advance thoughts worth listening to and reflecting upon.

Prof. Wilson was received with great applause. He said that last winter, as their President had said, he twice had the privilege of that hall in lectures upon civil government. Now there were schemes of society, of reform in prison administration, of the economic reconstruction of every society to be considered. Questions were pressing along that line in the modern field of discussion, but the older world made itself strenuous about fundamental principles. In the present age, hot with steam, society had a way of crowding, but in former ages there were large cool spaces between individuals. Now there was friction between the forces which had come into existence. No longer was it the society of the village community, but it was one hot with quickened rela-

[1] There is a WWhw outline of this lecture entitled *"What Things Ought Govts to Undertake?,"* with a complete opening paragraph, in WP, DLC.

tions, and men were getting into a puzzle. Troublesome it was, and we began to fear that repose had fled forever. The train was increasing its speed, and we felt that this involved those considerations which were forcing upon us a reconsideration of our ideas as to the construction of modern society. The old world conceived of the state as an aggregation of more or less connected individuals, an organization where laborers were not brought together, but individuals. We had not only come upon an industrial organization, but upon one under the control of a few men. It was a new political world. It was a safe assertion that 100 years ago the theory of government was one of political reaction. The world was then outgrowing its system of government, outgrowing its garments. This was true of England. History showed that it was a coming into control by the community instead of those who were appointed to be its agents. The spirit was one of restraint of power. From England to the Continental Powers this idea was communicated, and they took more or less rationally England's restrictions. Now that was a different political world from ours. Ours is one of progression, because we have different economical factors to deal with. Politics face the future instead of the idea of restriction, at least this was the universal impression. Was there ever a time when men were to a greater extent following fads, as the English say. A novel published could start political gossip, written by those whose imaginations were received in place of scientific thought. It did not mean that the race was mad, but new questions were arising which people were willing to examine, to play with, as it were, when presented by whosoever made it possible that they be made in intelligible language. It was a time when everybody should take care lest he say things which he could not verify, and hope for things he could not expect. Old society thought old thoughts, new society thought new things. Now for such a society, what were the proper functions of government? He thought it would serve their thought in that matter if they divided the functions of government into two classes: First, the constituent functions; second, the ministrant. Belonging to the first class were such functions as preserving order, governing the relation of parent and child, determining what are crimes and how they shall be punished, guarding the rights of private property. All these belonged to the first class, because they were the fundamentals by which government held together, the force which integrated society and held it together, and the conditions without which they could not have any civilized government indeed. The ministrant functions, on the other hand, were optional, for facilitating the privileges of society, such as laws regulating building and repairing of thoroughfares, weights and measures, system of sanitation, etc.; all those things without which society could hold together but could not be facilitated in the exercise of the functions of every day life. If government did not intervene here, others would have to take and accomplish these things in a less satisfactory manner. It was a rough classification, the speaker admitted, but a distinction of convenience, and also necessary for the consideration of the subject. Mill had said: "It is impossible to bring within a ring fence all the functions of government." Even they could not be justified except upon the ground of convenience.

The attitude of modern society was such that the ministrant functions were called in question. The speaker supposed it was a safe proposition that all uneducated people were opposed to the ministrant functions. He supposed that every American was brought up to look upon Government as a necessary evil. They believe in non-interference in matters of government and legislation and argued for this non-interference, but every legislator voted for thousands of things in which he violated his principles, contrary to his let-alone theory. The speaker had taken only a few examples: Railroad legislation, the granger movement, which he explained as originating in the railroad companies' agreeing with the elevators to load only at certain places and to fix rates of receiving and transporting. Western codes bristled with laws regulating railroad traffic, yet the legislators who enacted them believed in individual liberty. One result of this had been confusion, for they had had to give railroad commissioners wide power so that the railroads themselves would not be fettered. In time of plagues from grasshoppers large loads of seeds had been legislated to farmers. Enormous homestead exceptions had been granted; they all knew what homestead exemptions were. But in the rest of the farmers' property in the West, not only his tools were exempted from attachment for debt, but thousands of other things, so that it often happened that debts could be collected only from the rich farmers. The result was that the whole system of collecting debts was out of gear. Again this tendency to interfere with individual rights was seen in the exacting of the oleomargarine laws, butterine it was called in the West, in deference to demands of the farmers. It was admitted that butterine was not in itself injurious. The end of the law was to have butter spelled with two syllables and not with three. It was a State Administration whose machinery was interfering. Then there were cattle codes in the West in formidable proportions, disclosing constant imperfections by restricting method. These arose not with the idea of co-operation, but at the suggestion of the cattle men themselves. Then lumber regulations were numerous as to measurements; no lumber float went down the river but what had been inspected. Then there were laws regulating tolls at the mills. In Germany these would be called Socialistic laws, but not in the country of let-alone legislators. There were many laws again regulating the liability of employers. They were creeping into systems of education, shown in the West in the maintaining of the university just as the common school is maintained, the equipment of higher intellectual departments by the State. The list might be extended to what American legislators have done. Now the startling fact of this was that these men said in their personal opinions that they believed in letting individuals alone. Just as 100 years ago there was a spirit of restraint of power. Now, he thought, it was a dangerous practice to follow one thing in theory and another in practice. It might be practical sagacity, but how fatal to political thought if the lines of theory are to lie so far outside of the lines of practicability! The minute they find out the rottenness of a part, they will be likely to abandon the whole. The simile of a chain is a favorite one in this country, and is often put in the form of a chain of sand. When they find a single link is false, they may throw the whole away. Seeking the reasons for these things, it would seem as if the fundamentals must be gone over again. Does it not seem better rather than to admit defeat?

Now the thing was to be considered in a conservative spirit. Truth is no invalid, and these things should be examined with fearlessness, and when we come to examine them we find a radical difference between America and England. Europe has not adopted English thought. There were two schools of thought, laissez faire, and that which a friend of his called the other thing.[2] The theory was that the more people were let alone, the better the government, the less government does the better. Everybody who has read this knows the sad mistake government has made. A nation must be out of leading strings as well as a man, and a man is not a man until he is out of them. It is said that government is the wisest and most competent and the best informed of any one,

[2] Wilson picked up this phrase from Jameson's letter to him of Oct. 1, 1888.

and that it should consequently control society. Who could not help feeling that majesty of the old state in the countries of classic antiquity, in which every man was as the servant of the people, sinking his own individuality. It was a noble conception of mutual helpfulness and organic growth. Then the medieval law was that no man was elevated unless those below him were raised too. It was a state in which there was no competition; there was co-operation instead of antagonism. When men look at this through the haze of imagination, it seems beautiful. They cannot see the lower status of society. Such a condition of things now would hedge us around so that we could not extricate ourselves. Looking at society now, a man seems a rival of every other man, planning how he can outstrip his fellow being, and in this race the devil is not far behind. Now it is said that a man cannot get along except by helping himself, and they wish for the co-operation of the Middle Ages. But the trouble is as he had said, this was a new world, and the garments of the Middle Ages would set ill upon the present age. This was a new society, a society in which we must depart from old conceptions. Government is a beneficent and indispensable organ of society. Nowhere but in government is society recognized as an element. Society is an indispensable organ of government. Where should we go? to Socialism? No. He was sorry, he said, that the word had been adopted by those who used it. It was too high and noble a word. He would see every man who believed in the perfectability of society within careful bounds a socialist, who believed in the perfectability of society by slow growth and careful adaptation. It would be a state of mutual helpfulness when everyone should stand shoulder to shoulder. Such would be the golden age of civilization. No man could fail to catch the infection of such an idea. It was possible to restrict the functions of government. The instrumentalities for the perfection of government had the ends of society in view. What are the ends of society? The highest development of the individual to which he can attain. Now that government failed which did not give every opportunity to everybody. There should be an equalization of chance. It should control every natural monopoly. A natural monopoly has been defined by the Vice President of the English Board of Trade, a conservative man, as first, something that produces a necessary to society or a necessary to facilitate a community. Second, it occupies some favored spot of land as a railroad or water works system. Third, it can be usable only in connection with this special instrumentality.

Fourth, its activity may be almost indefinitely extended without extending the cost. You can extend the line and the activity and not the outlay. Fifth, an undertaking in which wide co-operation is necessary, not possible for individuals. Competition for you involves nothing less. It is sometimes said if you don't wish to use an article you need not pay for it. What do you mean by that? Simply that we should be 100 years behind our time; we should be in the Dark Ages. A railroad is as much a necessity to modern life as bread. I cannot live in a house of the time of Elizabeth, but I should be as far back as the people of that time. Now all these things were necessary for individuals, and the speaker said that there could not be that freedom of the individual unless there be government control. The speaker drew a comparison between an administration that was carried on by a levy of taxes and one that must be dependent upon business for its support.

The other necessity was for the equalization of privilege. The speaker drew illustrations of street car companies who had no bowels of compassion, compelling their employes to labor 16 or 17 hours a day, while other horse car companies that had bowels of compassion desired to work their employes but 12 hours a day. But to do this the latter corporation would be obliged to hire more men, and in their competition with the other their profits would be entirely obliterated. So the employes of the company that has bowels of compassion must suffer for lack of equalization of privilege. The same thing might be illustrated in the ventilation of factories, one mill corporation killing its employes by keeping them in close, stuffy rooms, while another was willing to furnish the most modern appliances in ventilation, which nowadays required a great deal of science. But, being unable to do this and compete with their rival, the second company must continue to kill its operatives. The consequence of that government has not hesitated to forbid such abuses, taking more and more radical steps in other directions. Now it is not meant that government is going to be a manufacturer, or is going to manage the railroads. Government is saying that if it is necessary for the country to have equalization, I will build a wall. The speaker said that was not restricting liberty at all. They might call him a utilitarian if they pleased, who favored bringing government and society a little nearer together.

Blindly men say they do not believe in interfering with individual liberty. What were the necessary limitations so as not to interfere with the development of the individual. Well, we could not tell. The age of 21 was generally agreed upon as the time when the man was mature enough to be freed from family control and be given over to the care of the State. But some men are not mature at 91, and others are mature at 11. The function of the family led on to high ideals of duty, and the theory that State action should begin when family action ends, by establishing all the conditions which do not abate the speed in the race the least whit. The limits of State interference are those which are not inconsistent with universal co-operation. To go back to a fundamental, it was possible to argue each case upon its merits. Examples of this were bureaus of agriculture and industrial statistics, and it was becoming more possible for agencies of this kind to operate than ever before. No nation could run around sharp corners and progress by letting go of hands with the ages that had preceded it. It would not do to tear up institutions by the roots, and no institution could grow from a clipping.

At the conclusion of his address, Prof. Wilson was long and loudly applauded.

Printed in the *Providence Journal*, Nov. 12, 1889; one editorial heading omitted.

A Newspaper Report of a Chapel Talk

Prof. Wilson at Brown. [Nov. 13, 1889]

Prof. Woodrow Wilson of Wesleyan, who delivered the first lecture of the Economic Association course, at Brown's University Monday evening, remained in the city Monday night, and yesterday morning addressed the students after chapel exercises. In introducing him President Andrews said: "I know that some of you were present at the lecture last evening, but lest all of you may not have seen his face and heard his voice, I have invited Prof. Wilson to say a few words."

Prof. Wilson is evidently accustomed to speaking, and he is also evidently acquainted with tastes of college students. He said: "I consented to speak to you this morning for various reasons. The first was because your President invited me in such a way that I thought he really expected me to comply. Then again I have that natural American instinct to make remarks whenever there is occasion. But the most important reason is because I always like to face college students. I am not many years from graduation, and I still have an interest in the students. I am interested, too, in college athletics. We think down to Wesleyan that we can beat you in base ball. (Applause.) It is one of my duties also to train the foot ball eleven, and when we win I just call attention to the fact I have a share in the victory. But when we do not win I say, I am a member of the faculty and of course cannot be classed with the students. (Laughter.) All these things make my work interesting. But I wish to impress one point upon you, these things which you learn about Political Economy, my department at Wesleyan, these things are not abstract, but they are things which will be of interest and profit after you get out of college. Another point to remember is this, that the weight of influence is in the West, the vigor is in the West, but responsibility is in the East. Rhode Island, however, thinks she can stand alone. She thinks that her independence is an important part of the United States. Now just remember that there are tremendous sparks of vitality elsewhere. Nevertheless you are part of the force, an important part of it. You will soon take the places of those who control. In fact, some local bosses may sit before me now. You may run a corner, but there are other corners just as important.

["]These have been rambling remarks, but I said, you know, that I only stood up to look at you. If I have said anything helpful to you I am satisfied." Prof. Wilson was loudly applauded at the close. After chapel he attended the recitation of the Senior class in psychology.

Printed in the *Providence Journal*, Nov. 13, 1889; one editorial heading omitted.

From A. Elizabeth Wilson Begges

My dear Nephew Cleveland Nov 13 [1889]

I would have sent my grateful acknowledgements earlier for your very kind remembrance but not knowing your address, was obliged to wait for a reply to a letter from your father informing me. My surprise and delight were great upon receiving your valuable book, and I appreciate highly the kind and loving feeling which prompted the sending it. My husband has been greedily devouring it, and I have already taken in the first pages. I go slowly and carefully, as my mental digestion is weak, and milk is much more suitable than strong meat. As I read a feeling comes over me which causes me to say "Elizabeth I do not wonder that Joseph is proud of his boy." Your other book, too was most interesting & instructive. How hard for me to imagine the little child of two years old as I last saw him, now an author and doing credit to that "land of steady habits" in which he lives. In that far off time, the little Woodrow and my own beloved son, who were nearly the same age, were quite rivals in the regard of friends & neighbors, as to the beauty of each, but I freely yielded the palm to my nephew. Even then I was proud of him, you see, and perhaps saw, with the intuition the lords of creation are pleased to ascribe to our sex, through the intervening years, what your future would be. . . .

I was sorry to learn your father had been ill, but hope it was merely a cold, to which he seems subject. Remember me kindly to your wife, & with love to yourself I am your loving Aunt

A. E. Beggs

ALS (WP, DLC) with WWhw notation on env.: "Ans. 1 Dec./89."

From Thomas Alexander Hoyt

My Dear Woodrow– Phila–Nov. 14th, 1889.

Serious illness has hindered an earlier reply to your letter. I am however, quite recovered, now.

First of all, I send my warm congratulations to you & dear Ellie. I wish it had been a Boy, still, it is a great thing to have the three graces–all in a bunch. I hope mother & child are well.

Next, accept thanks for your Book, which I am reading with much interest, & which I feel sure will widely extend your reputation. It is certainly a work of much erudition & marked ability. In explaining the place held by the Family in the civil & religious organization of society, why did you not refer to the early records of the Bible? Perhaps, I have overlooked it.

I have not seen President Patton yet, but hope to do soon, when, I will talk with him of you.

We expect to get into our house next week, & will hope to see you there, whenever you can come.

Give much love to Ellie & the Babies–also to Stockton & Eddie.

Affectionately Yours Thos. A. Hoyt.

ALS (WP, DLC) with WWhw notation on env.: "Ans. 1/6/90."

From Herbert Baxter Adams

My dear Mr. Wilson: Baltimore, Md. November 14, 1889.

I have delayed thanking you for your valuable book, hoping to get time to read it in detail; but I am ashamed to wait longer and take this occasion to assure you of my hearty appreciation of your good work and thoughtful courtesy. I have several times looked through the work and read here and there upon specific points, always with great profit and delight. The book is a real contribution to the history of politics and will undoubtedly be used by teachers and students for many years to come. I congratulate you heartily upon your deserved success and hope that you will continue to serve your day and generation as a writer and as a teacher.

Will it be possible for you to attend the next meeting of the American Historical Association to be held in Washington D. C. December 28-31? A Harvard man named Freeman Snow, whose book you may have seen,[1] proposes to present a paper on Congressional Government, which, as Hart informs me, takes issue with you on some points. I thought it might be interesting for you and your friends to have a discussion of controverted questions.

There will be a good representation of New England men present and I think you will enjoy making a wider acquaintance.

Possibly a vacation outing in the Federal City might be agreeable to Mrs. Wilson as well as to the Middletown Professor.

Very cordially yours, H. B. Adams

TLS (WP, DLC) with WWhw notation on env.: "Ans. 18 Nov. '89."

[1] Freeman Snow, *A Guide to the Study of the Constitutional & Political History of the United States, 1789-1860* (Cambridge, Mass., 1882-83). Snow's paper, "A Defense of Congressional Government," was printed in American Historical Association, *Papers*, IV (July 1890), 309-28.

A News Item

[Nov. 15, 1889]

HOUSE OF COMMONS.

At the first meeting held for the re-organization of the House of Commons, E. A. Bawden, '90, was elected speaker. At this meeting a number of new members were enrolled, and a committee was appointed to arrange the details of reorganization. . . .

Printed in the Middletown, Conn., *Wesleyan Argus*, XXIII (Nov. 15, 1889), 34.

From John Franklin Jameson

My dear Wilson: Providence, Nov. 18, 1889.

I enclose a check for fourteen dollars, which I suppose pays your fare, and leaves you the paltry sum of ten dollars for your admirable lecture. We remain your debtors, but I hesitate to state how much, less you should draw on me at sight for the balance. That would be disastrous, in the present state of my bank-account (the quarterly pay-day not coming until December 5th). This low state of accounts must account for my delay in sending the check. Even this small sum could not be spared, until our Worthy Grand Treasurer turned over some of his receipts. So please excuse the delay.

Tonight's lecture[1] competes with Salvini;[2] how successfully remains to be seen. I, for my part, should choose Salvini in preference to any known form of lecture, other things equal; but we have the great advantage, as to the impecunious, of offering a "free show."

N. B. Don't you dare to excede, evade, erump from New England without sending back my copy of the German magazine containing the article on "Der Mechanismus des Reichstags," nor yet on the other hand (δὲ) [*sic*] that of Mr. Cable's pamphlet on the nigger question![3]

You will have perceived that, however it was with your lecture, your remarks to the students at chapel were well reported. Kindest regards to Mrs. Wilson. Truly yours J. F. Jameson.

ALS (WP, DLC) with WWhw notation on env.: "Ans. 1/6/90."

1 "A Scheme of Social and Economic Reform; its History and present Application," by the Rev. John G. Brooks, of Brockton, Mass.

2 The Italian actor, Tommaso Salvini, who appeared on November 18 as Othello, one of his most famous roles.

3 See J. F. Jameson to WW, Nov. 20, 1888.

To Robert Bridges

My dear Bobby, Middletown, Conn., 18 November, 1889

Once more I am in a state of mind touching the Princeton matter because of ignorance, and appeal to you for light, if you have any to communicate.

I see by the newspapers that the Trustees postponed the election till February, but I know nothing else and have absolutely no means of judging what the significance of their action is *as regards me.* Dr Patton has not written to me. Have you heard anything definite?

What makes me the more anxious to know what the attitude of the Trustees towards me is, is this, that there is a movement here to endow a similar special chair for me, and I am likely to be pressed to declare whether I would accept it or not. Apparently they will constitute the new chair in any way and in any field I prefer. It's a queer, strained situation, altogether!

In haste and affection,

Yours as ever, Woodrow Wilson

ALS (WC, NjP).

Two Letters from Robert Bridges

Dear Tommy: New York Nov 19 1889

We gave a little dinner to Cyrus last night and I only had chance for a word with him. He said that he had talked with a number of the most influential trustees and all were in favor of your election. Owing to the fact that you could not accept till next fall it was deemed best (at least this is what I surmise) to postpone the election till Feb. I have not full light on the subject yet but will tackle some men at the Princeton Club tonight.

Will let you know the result.

There is a game known as foot-ball which the Middle State Barbarians can teach the Boston Brahmins anyhow![1]

Yours hastily Robert Bridges

ALS (WP, DLC). Encs.: two clippings from *The Princetonian,* Nov. 15, 1889.

[1] The Princeton football team defeated Harvard, 41 to 15, on November 16, 1889.

Dear Tommy: New York Nov 20 1889

I talked to Pyne and James W. Alexander last night about the Trustee meeting. They said that Patton thought it best to postpone the election till Feb. as you could not accept till next Sept. So far as they know there is every probability—amounting to a certainty—of your election. However—you will probably hear directly from Dr. Patton within a few days.

Faithfully your Friend Robert Bridges

ALS (WP, DLC).

Francis Landey Patton to James Waddel Alexander

Dear Mr Alexander: [Princeton, N.J.] 21 Nov [1889]

Thanks for your letters: please find Prof Wilson's enclosed.[1] At the present stage I think I shd say nothing about the matter to Prof Wilson. The trustees must be untrammelled & not embarrassed by my going too far privately with Prof Wilson. My belief, for reasons given you, is that we should elect Wilson; but there will be individual & influential opposition unless this opposition is removed. That I will endeavour to do at my first opportunity.

The case stands thus: Prof. Wilson told me he would not wish to enter upon work if called before the beginning of the next academic year—Sept. There was therefore no need of haste in calling him: & in view of what I know regarding the feelings of some on the Board it was wise I am confident to postpone action.

I should be sorry to lose Prof Wilson: & should be sorry to have him risk the loss of a desirable position in Madison thr any expectation of a place here. But I think there is nothing for us to do.

The most that shd be said to Bridges is that a very considerable portion of the Board are favourable to his election & that it is not improbable that he will be elected in February. Beyond that I do not think it safe or wise to go.

So far as the other matter is concerned, there is no reason for anxiety whatever. Political Economy is not taught according to the new schedule until the second term, & there never has been a moment's doubt in my mind that provision & good provision would be made for it. I have said so to the students & of course am responsible for what I have said. Of course that portion of Johnston's work covered by International Law wh Prof Sloane has preferred to take himself meanwhile, I do not expect to provide for until a Professor is appointed. But Political Economy will be taken care of.

Much obliged to you for all you have said

Yr Sincerely Francis L. Patton

ALS (Patton Letterpress Books, University Archives, NjP).

[1] It is missing.

From Horace Elisha Scudder

My dear Mr Wilson Boston, 25 Novr 1889

Are you likely to be in this part of the country soon? I want to see you. Jameson told me that you were to be in Providence to lecture, but I have lost his list, and do not remember the date.

Yours very truly H. E. Scudder.

ALS (WP, DLC) with WWhw notation on env.: "Ans. Nov. 27/89."

A News Item

[Nov. 26, 1889]

HOUSE OF COMMONS.

The House of Commons, founded at the suggestion and under the direction of Professor Wilson, is now organized for its second year of work. At its last meeting it was decided to change the time of meeting to 8 o'clock on the Saturday evening preceding dagger Monday. The resignation of Prime Minister Goodrich created a vacancy which has been filled by the appointment of Gascoigne, '90. Interesting and profitable meetings are looked for, and all members of the college are cordially invited to become members of the house.

Printed in the Middletown, Conn., *Wesleyan Argus*, XXIII (Nov. 26, 1889), 43.

To Horace Elisha Scudder

My dear Mr. Scudder, Middletown, Conn., 27 Nov./89

My lecture in Providence was delivered the evening of Nov. 11th, and I am not now, I am very sorry to say, within sight of any opportunity of being so near Boston again for some time to come. It is of course quite possible that I *may* be drawn to Boston some time before Christmas, and I hope that I may be. I always value an opportunity to see you, and, since you want to see me, there is an added sanction to my wish to enjoy the pleasure and obtain the suggestions I always derive from a talk with you.

Very sincerely Yours, Woodrow Wilson

ALS (WC, NjP).

From Robert Bridges

My dear Tommy: New York Nov 29 1889

I need not remark that yesterday was a great day for Middle State intellect, and that *it* is now respectfully spoken of as "Princeton University."[1]

Last night at the University Club Mr. J. W. Alexander came to me and said that Patton could not say to you directly and semi-officially what he feels to be a moral certainty—that is, that you will be elected to the Princeton professorship. Patton says that he has no right to speak for the committee, and cannot appear so to do. If, however, the Wesleyan Professorship takes the form of a definite proposition—he thinks that you would be right in asking him (Patton) officially for some definite assurance. He could then with a good reason, ask the curriculum committee for some decision. This is all that I can gather, and I fear there may be some misinterpretation, as it has passed through two mediums.

Mr. Alexander quietly said that Dr. P. rather liked to be dilatory, and that he (Alexander) would (in such a case) settle the matter more expeditiously. There is no doubt of Alexander's opinion in your favor.

I learned incidentally that McCarter's father[2] is the "kicker" on the committee, on "free-trade grounds." I think we nailed him at the Isham dinner.[3]

Yours Faithfully Robert Bridges

ALS (WP, DLC) with WWhw notation on env.: "Ans. 1/6/90," and WWsh notes, probably taken on Dr. Azel Washburn Hazen's sermon in the First Congregational Church on November 30, 1889, a transcript of which follows: "You are poor fishers of men, it has been said of a certain class of preachers, you do not go fishing with a rod and a line and with the patient sagacity of true sportsmen. You use a telegraph pole and a cable: with these you savagely beat the water and bid men bite or be damned. And you expect they will be caught."

1 Princeton defeated Yale in football, 10 to 0, on Thanksgiving Day, November 28, 1889, at the Berkeley Oval in New York.

2 Thomas Nesbit McCarter, Class of 1842, trustee, 1879-1901.

3 About the "Isham dinners," see WW to EAW, May 6, 1886, Vol. 5.

Wilson's Copy for the Wesleyan Catalogue for 1889-90

[c. *Dec. 1, 1889*]

HISTORY AND POLITICAL ECONOMY.

Professor Wilson.

I. HISTORIES OF ENGLAND AND FRANCE. A course of topical lectures in which English and French topics are made to run, as nearly as possible, parallel to each other chronologically, with the double object of affording clues to general European history and of setting the history of the English race in its European connections. Fifteen or sixteen lectures on the Renaissance and Reformation are also included in this course, being introduced when the topics in English and French history have been advanced to the fifteenth century. Required parallel reading is assigned, and frequent recitations are held upon the subject matter of the lectures. *Five times a fortnight.*

Course I. is elective for Juniors, in alternate years, alternating with Course II. It is omitted the present year.

II. HISTORY OF THE UNITED STATES. This course will consist, in the first term, of class drill in the colonial portion of Doyle's History of the United States, in Fiske's Critical Period of American History, in Johnston's History of American Politics, and in collateral authorities; in the second and third terms, of lectures on the history of the sixty years beginning with the administration of Andrew Jackson and closing with the administration of Cleveland and the end of the first century of the Constitution. *Five times a fortnight.*

Course II. is elective for Juniors, in alternate years, alternating with Course I.

III. HISTORY OF INSTITUTIONS. The central aim of this course is to put the development of the political institutions and of the politics of the United States in its true historical setting. It covers such topics as the following: The origin and development of government; ancient political systems; mediæval political organization; the constitutional growth of the leading European states, and the chief features of their constitutions; the governments of England and the United States; the functions and aims of government; the nature and development of law, etc. Wilson's The State is used as a text-book. Parallel readings are assigned and frequent oral and written examinations are held. *Five times a fortnight.*

Course III. is elective for Seniors.

IV. CONSTITUTION OF THE UNITED STATES. Cooley's Principles of Constitutional Law is used as a text-book in the legal aspects of the fundamental law of the Union; but the object of the instruction is to familiarize the class with all the main aspects of our constitution, both state and federal, unwritten developments, practical questions, legislative machinery, etc. For this purpose various commentaries of different grades are more or less used, and supplementary lectures are given. *Five times a fortnight during the second half-year.*

Course IV. is required of Juniors.

V. POLITICAL ECONOMY AND STATISTICS. F. A. Walker's Advanced Political Economy is used as a text-book, and lectures are given on the history of economic thought. The work in political economy is supplemented by a brief course in the general principles of statistics. *Four times a week during the first half-year.*

Course V. is required of Seniors.

VI. ROMAN HISTORY. A required course in the early constitutional history of Rome is given by the Tutor in Latin to Classical and Latin-Scientific Freshmen. Ihne's Early Rome is used as a text-book, and is supplemented by lectures and by discussions of special topics. *Weekly through the first half-year.*

VII. GREEK HISTORY. A brief course of instruction in Greek history is given the Classical Freshmen by the Tutor in Greek.

Printed in *Annual Catalogue of Wesleyan University. 1889-90* (Middletown, Conn., 1889), pp. 34-35.

Marginal Notes

Otto von Sarwey, *Allgemeines Verwaltungsrecht*, in Heinrich Marquardsen (ed.), *Handbuch des Oeffentlichen Rechts der Gegenwart* (4 vols., Freiburg im B. and Tübingen, 1883-1906), I.

Transcripts of WW Shorthand Comments

[c. Dec. 1, 1889-c. March 6, 1891][1]

From "Gesetzgebung und Verwaltung," pp. 9-10:

[1] Wilson probably began his reading of Sarwey early in this period. There are two references to Sarwey in Wilson's notes for lectures on administration at the Johns Hopkins in 1890, printed at Feb. 3, 1890. He continued to make extensive use of Sarwey in subsequent lectures on administration and public law at the Johns Hopkins and Princeton, and it is entirely possible that Wilson wrote some of the marginal comments that follow at a later date than here ascribed.

Der staatsrechtliche Begriff des Gesetzes, d. h. derjenige Begriff, welcher die Grundlage für die Bedingungen der Geltung des Befehls als Gesetz in dem Staate bildet, und einzig und allein die Gesetzgebung mit der erforderlichen Bestimmtheit gegenüber der Verwaltungsthätigkeit abgrenzt, ergibt sich aus der Betrachtung der Willensäusserung vom Standpunkte des Bestimmenden aus. Hiernach ist Gesetz keine Norm, welche zu ihrer rechtsverbindlichen Wirkung einer andern Begründung und Rechtfertigung bedarf, als dass sie der wirkliche Ausdruck des Willens des Bestimmenden ist. Umgekehrt ist jede den Willen des Andern ohne Rücksicht auf seine Zustimmung bestimmende Willensäusserung Gesetz, welche nach dem in einem Staate bestehenden Rechtszustand als Thatsache der Willensäusserung des Bestimmenden ohne Weiteres gegen jeden Widerstand und gegen jeden Widerspruch Geltung beansprucht und der Regel nach nur durch den Bestimmenden selbst aufgehoben oder abgeändert werden kann. Ob sie eine allgemeine Norm oder eine Norm für den einzelnen Fall gibt, ist hierbei ohne Einfluss. Diese an sich schrankenlose Bestimmung Anderer ist thatsächlich nur der höchsten Gewalt im Staate möglich; sie ist der unmittelbare Ausfluss derselben, oder was dasselbe ist, der Wille, welchem diese höchste Gewalt im Staate zusteht, ist die gesetzgebende Gewalt, sein Organ das Organ der Gesetzgebung. Für den Gesetzesbegriff ist es gleichgültig, von wem diese Gewalt und wie sie erworben ist. Sie ist zunächst nur eine Thatsache. Wenn aber diese Thatsache von dem Volke, den im Staate verbundenen Einzelnen anerkannt ist, bildet sie die Grundlage seines Verfassungsrechts. Der Staat ist ohne dieselbe nicht denkbar. In jedem Staate gibt es diese höchste Gewalt und in keinem Staate ist eine Norm Gesetz, welche nicht die Willensäusserung derselben ist. Da diese höchste, die gesetzgebende Gewalt, keinen mit ihr im Widerspruch stehenden Willen duldet, so hat jede von einem andern Organ ausgehende Bestimmung des Willens Anderer ohne deren freie Zustimmung nicht durch die Thatsache der Willensäusserung des Bestimmenden, sondern nur vermöge ihrer

Fit this definition to the legislation of the member-state of the federal state.

Uebereinstimmung mit dem Willen der höchsten Gewalt rechtliche Geltung, d. h. eine rechtsverpflichtende Wirkung, sie ist hiermit von dem Gesetzesbegriff ausgeschieden.[2]

At best, however, this is hardly more than a formal distinction. Suppose that the legislature, becoming meddlesome even beyond wont, should undertake to regulate the details of administration, to issue, in short, all necessary ordinances. These would emanate from the highest power in the state, would receive authority only from its law, etc., etc.: would they therefore be acts of legislation as contradistinguished from acts of administration? They would certainly be acts of administration. For the *essential* difference between legislation and administration it will be necessary to look elsewhere. This essential difference it seems to me Jellinek has laid bare.

From "Rechtsprechung und Verwaltung," p. 13:

Hieraus ergibt sich der begriffliche Unterschied zwischen Verwaltung und Rechtsprechung. Wenn die Verwaltung durch die rechtsverpflichtende Bestimmung des Willens Anderer und nöthigenfalls durch Anwendung der staatlichen Zwangsgewalt ihren Zweck verfolgt, so ist diese Willensäusserung formell dieselbe, wie die Willensäusserung in der Rechtsprechung. Gleichwohl unterscheiden sich beide

1. durch die Verschiedenheit des von dem Handelnden verfolgten Zweckes und des die Thätigkeit bestimmenden geistigen Vorgangs. Das Organ der Rechtsprechung fragt nur, was die Rechtsordnung in ihrer Anwendung auf die einzelne Thatsache fordert und wird durch die Beantwortung dieser Frage allein und ausschliesslich bestimmt. Sie will nur die Rechtsordnung aufrecht erhalten, unbekümmert um jedes andere Interesse. Die Verwaltung verfolgt die materiellen Zwecke, welche ganz ausserhalb der Rechtsordnung liegen können. Zu der Rechtsordnung verhält sich die Verwaltung ebenso, wie der Einzelne, welcher seine Interessen verfolgt. Wenn und soweit ihre Thätigkeit durch die

Adjudication has the maintenance of legal regulation as its sole aim, and without immediate regard to the interests involved; but the administration of legal regulations are means simply: its aim is the realization of the public interest. The one comes into play when the law is broken, the other whenever the public interest demands.

[2] At the end of this passage Wilson wrote in the margin, "See note opposite." The "note," a transcript of which follows, was written on a slip of paper and tipped in between pages 9-10.

Rechtsordnung geregelt ist, befolgt sie dieselbe. Sie benutzt sie für ihre Zwecke, im Uebrigen aber bekümmert sie sich nicht um ihre Aufrechterhaltung. *Der Rechtsprechung ist die Aufrechterhaltung der Rechtsordnung Selbstzweck, der Verwaltung nur Mittel zum Zweck.*

2. Eben desshalb unterscheiden sich beide auch durch die Voraussetzungen ihrer Thätigkeit. Die Rechtsprechung setzt eine wirkliche oder vermeintliche Rechtsverletzung voraus, welche um des Rechts willen, aus dem formalen Grunde der Aufrechterhaltung der Rechtsordnung ohne jede Rücksicht auf das hierdurch sonst beförderte oder verfolgte Interesse aufgehoben wird. Die Verwaltung tritt in Thätigkeit, nicht weil die Rechtsnorm verletzt ist, sondern weil diess das öffentliche Interesse fordert.

From "Das Wesen des Verfassungstaats," p. 19:

Das Streben ist, an die Stelle des Präventivsystems des Polizeistaats das Repressivsystem zu setzen. Durch die Strafandrohung soll einerseits der Einzelne vermöge seiner freien Selbstbestimmung von der Verletzung der öffentlichen Interessen abgehalten oder zur Verwirklichung derselben bestimmt, und andererseits soll durch die nachfolgende Strafe die erfolgte Verletzung des Strafgesetzes wieder aufgehoben werden. Dieses Bestreben hat eine fortgesetzte Vermehrung der Strafandrohungen zur Folge, welche in der Mehrzahl in den Strafgesetzbüchern zusammengestellt sind, sich jedoch zahlreich auch in anderen Gesetzen finden. Es ist bekannt, welche Ausdehnung dieses Strafsystem in England gefunden hat. Gleichwohl kann hiermit die Verwirklichung der öffentlichen Interessen nicht so vollkommen erreicht werden, dass neben den Strafandrohungen die Ausübung der staatlichen Gewalt durch die Verwaltungsorgane entbehrt werden könnte, einmal weil durch die nachfolgende Strafe, wenn die Strafandrohung selbst nicht die Kraft hatte, die Verletzung der öffentlichen Interessen durch den Gebrauch des individuellen Selbstbestimmungsrechts zu verhindern, die Verletzung nicht ungeschehen gemacht ist und daher wenigstens auf vielen Ge-

The repressive system of penal codes, so characteristic of the constitutional states[,] cannot altogether take the place of the preventive system of the police state. Administrative choice of means must have some play.

bieten des Staatslebens eine Kraft zur Verhinderung drohender Verletzungen durch die geeigneten Mittel und zur Beseitigung der schädlichen Folgen der Verletzungen organisirt sein muss, sodann weil der Zweck der Strafgesetze sehr häufig nur erreicht werden kann, wenn den Willensäusserungen der Verwaltungsorgane die Bestimmung dessen, was das öffentliche Interesse fordert, anheimgegeben wird, und wenn diese Bestimmung erfolgt ist.

Neben diese Beschränkung des Anwendungsgebiets der staatlichen Gewalt der Verwaltungsorgane durch die Strafgesetzgebung tritt in dem Verfassungsstaat sodann weiter die jene Gewalt beschränkende allgemeine Forderung der gesetzmässigen Ausübung derselben. Mit der organischen Trennung der Verwaltung von der Gesetzgebung ist in dem Willen des Gesetzgebers ein über ihr stehender Wille, der in dem Gesetze zum Ausdruck gelangt, rechtlich vorhanden, gegen welchen der Wille der Organe der Verwaltung keine Geltung beanspruchen kann und keine Geltung hat. Die Forderung der Gesetzmässigkeit der Verwaltung in dem Verfassungsstaat ist daher hiermit von selbst gestellt; sie ist das selbstverständliche logische Produkt des Gesetzes und der organischen Trennung der Verwaltung von der Gesetzgebung. Die Wirkung dieses formellen Grundsatzes auf die Verwaltungsthätigkeit ist jedoch durch den Inhalt der Gesetzgebung des wirklichen Staats bedingt. Sie lässt sich daher in keine allgemein giltige Formel fassen.

In the constitutional state, however, the administrative power is subject to the laws; its acts must square with the rules laid down by the legislature.

From "Die Lehre von der Theilung der Gewalten. Die Exekutive und die vollziehende Gewalt," p. 20:

Allgemein anerkannt ist, dass die Theorie von der Theilung der Gewalten, welche im Sinne des modernen Staats auf Montesquieu zurückzuführen ist, an wesentlichen Mängeln leidet, wie sie auch zweifellos zu Konsequenzen geführt hat, welche weder mit dem monarchischen Prinzip, noch mit den Forderungen des vernünftigen Individualismus vereinbar sind. Wenn Montesquieu neben der *puissance legislative* die richterliche Gewalt (*la puissance de*

Objections:—
(1) The administration is

juger) als die Gewalt, welche die Verbrechen bestraft und über die Streitigkeiten der Einzelnen entscheidet, der Executivgewalt des Staats (*puissance executrice de l'état*), als der Gewalt, welche über Frieden und Krieg entscheidet, Gesandte empfängt und absendet, die Sicherheit aufrecht erhält und die feindlichen Einfälle abwehrt, gegenüberstellt, so lässt er von vornherein eine grosse Lücke, welche erst die spätere Wissenschaft durch den Begriff der Verwaltung und des Verwaltungsrechts auszufüllen hatte. Da der wirkliche Staat die Zwangsgewalt der Verwaltung nicht entbehren kann, so konnte jene Theorie, in welcher man alle Garantieen der Freiheit gefunden zu haben glaubte, nicht verhindern, dass der Polizeistaat, als der Staat der willkürlichen Beherrschung unter Berufung auf das öffentliche Wohl sich neben dem Konstitutionalismus und geschützt durch diesen an die Stelle des absoluten Staats setzte.

something more and greater than the executive power of Montesquieu

(2) To conceive of these powers as separate acts but not affecting the other organs is to deny the unity of the state, not only, but also to make the actual state impractical.

Summary Interpretation of pp. 21-24:[3]

(1) The executive has something to do besides carry out the legislative will. And yet that it has not would seem to be the fundamental theory of the republican state-idea.

(2) The use of the word "power" is misleading. The administration does, indeed, use the power of the state, but this is only a means to an end; and not every act of the administration involves an exercise of power: e.g., the administration of the property of the state, public instruction, legal business, contracts, etc., etc.

(3) "An executive" presupposes a will to be executed: and that will is either the will of the legislator (in which case the administrator is merely an instrument or agent) or the will of the individual or individuals constituting the executive (in which case the latter is the source of independent rules). It is the object of the constitutional state to define and circumscribe the independent sphere of determination on the part of the administration as narrowly as possible.

(4) Administrative law in its widest sense consists of the "sum of the legal rules which determine the use of sovereignty on the part of the organs of administration, and the prerequisites of that use." "The conception of administrative law widens or is honored in accordance with the historical development of the state and of political science." (23-24)

[3] Tipped in between pages 20-21.

(5) The use of political power by the organs of administration is not all of the administrative activity, but simply one, though the principal, means of that activity. Only in the constitutional state is the administration limited by law and statute; in all others its people has withdrawn this, and it has other legal or statute (that is, other than prevenient) means of caring for the interests of the community.

From "Die Funktionen der gesetzgebenden Organe in dem Verfassungsstaat," pp. 24-25:

In dem Verfassungsstaat ist stets eine Mehrheit von Einzelnen nicht nur zur Berathung der Rechtsnormen, sondern als entscheidender Wille zu der Erlassung des Gesetzes berufen. Dieses Zusammenwirken mehrerer in ihrer Aktion mit gleicher Selbstständigkeit ausgestatteter Willen tritt in der konstitutionellen Monarchie schärfer und bestimmter hervor, als in der Republik. In der konstitutionellen Monarchie bedingen sich das Staatsoberhaupt und die Volksvertretung in der Ausübung der Gesetzgebung gegenseitig. Die letztere beschliesst nicht nur den Rechtssatz, sondern auch die Verkündigung des Rechtssatzes als Befehl durch das Staatsoberhaupt unter der Bedingung, dass das Staatsoberhaupt den Rechtssatz als Befehl verkünden will. Formell ist sonach das Gesetz der Befehl des Staatsoberhaupts, allein sachlich ist die Zustimmung der Volksvertretung nicht allein zu dem Rechtssatz, sondern zu seiner Wirkung als Norm, welche befolgt werden muss, also zu dem Befehl selbst, erforderlich. Mit Recht werden daher das Staatsoberhaupt und die Volksvertretung die gesetzgebenden Faktoren genannt. Das Gesetz ist das Produkt des Willens und der Befehl beider. Nicht die Thatsache, dass die gesetzgebenden Faktoren über einen Rechtssatz einig sind, mit nachfolgendem Befehl des Staatsoberhaupts, macht die Willensäusserung derselben zu einem Gesetz, sondern der Wille beider gesetzgebenden Faktoren muss darauf gerichtet sein, dass ein den Willen der Einzelnen bestimmender Ausspruch, der Rechtssatz, befolgt werde und diese Willensrichtung muss einen äusserlich erkennbaren Ausdruck durch den von dem Staatsoberhaupt im Einverständniss

The legislative act, in the constitutional monarchy, is a cooperative act in every stage,—an act of cooperation between the head of the state and the representative body. It is not legitimate to separate the utterance of the principle from the utterance of the command.

mit der Volksvertretung verkündeten Befehl erhalten haben. Gesetz ist hiernach in der repräsentativen Monarchie jeder von dem Staatsoberhaupte mit Zustimmung der Volksvertretung unter ausdrücklicher Bezugnahme hierauf erlassene, in einem Rechtssatz formulirte Befehl. Nach den meisten Verfassungen ist ausser der Erlassung (Sanktion) des Befehls noch weiter die wirkliche Verkündigung (Publikation, auch Promulgation) zur Perfektion des Gesetzes erforderlich.

From "Gesetz im materiellen und formellen Sinn," p. 26:

Diese sämmtlichen Willensäusserungen sind nun aber, auch wenn sie zu ihrer rechtlichen Gültigkeit der Uebereinstimmung der gesetzlichen Faktoren bedürfen, Verwaltungsakte. Sie sind auch rechtlich als solche zu beurtheilen. Es ist eben desshalb eine Verkündigung derselben in Gesetzesform mit der Formel des Befehls weder vorgeschrieben, noch üblich. Die Thatsache der Uebereinstimmung der gesetzgebenden Faktoren genügt. Wenn jedoch die Willensäusserung der gesetzgebenden Faktoren, welche hiernach an sich ein Verwaltungsakt ist, als übereinstimmender Befehl der gesetzgebenden Faktoren formulirt, in Gesetzesform beschlossen und verkündet wird, verliert dieselbe ihre Natur als Verwaltungsakt. Diese auf dem übereinstimmenden Willen der gesetzgebenden Faktoren beruhenden und in Gesetzesform kundgegebenen Verwaltungsakte werden als die Gesetze im formellen Sinne bezeichnet. Gleichwohl unterscheiden sich diese sogenannten formellen Gesetze nicht allein durch die Form von den nicht in der Form des Gesetzes auf Grund der Uebereinstimmung der gesetzgebenden Faktoren ergangenen Verwaltungsakten, sondern auch durch ihre Wirkung. Sie haben als Ausflüsse der höchsten Gewalt im Staate, gegen welche kein Widerspruch berechtigt ist, unbedingte Geltung. Sie sind eine unbedingt und ohne weitere Prüfung ihrer Uebereinstimmung mit andern Gesetzen, auch von den mit der Rechtsprechung beauftragten Organen des Staats zu befolgende Norm, während die Verwaltungsakte, auch wenn sie das

Laws in the formal sense of the word = Acts in their nature administrative which are nevertheless given full form as enactments and thus made commands of the legislative authorities. They differ also from administrative acts sanctioned by the legislature but not given the form of enactments in this, that they have the full force of enactments and are valid and binding whether in agreement with previously existing law or not.

Ergebniss der übereinstimmenden Willensäusserung der gesetzgebenden Faktoren sind, wenn der übereinstimmende Beschluss nicht als Befehl des Gesetzgebers kundgegeben ist, nicht anders, als jeder sonstige Verwaltungsakt wirken. Hierdurch nehmen die formellen Gesetze wieder die Natur eines materiellen Gesetzes an, da sie den Grund ihrer rechtlichen Wirkung nicht in einer ausser ihnen liegenden Form finden und ihre Wirkung über den Kreis derjenigen hinausgeht, deren Willensäusserung sie sind.

From "Die Verwaltungsfunktionen der gesetzgebenden Organe," p. 27:

Die Unterscheidung zwischen Gesetz im materiellen und formellen Sinne findet sich zuerst bei Mohl. Laband hat sie sodann in einem andern Sinne aufgenommen. Gesetz im materiellen Sinne ist nach ihm *jede rechtsverbindliche Anordnung einer Rechtsregel*, Gesetz im formellen Sinne jeder Akt des Staatswillens, zu welchem die Zustimmung der Volksvertretung erforderlich ist. . . . Ein Gesetz, welches einen Rechtsstreit entscheidet, kann nicht wie ein Urtheil, z. B. mit der Nichtigkeitsklage oder *propter noviter reperta* angefochten werden. Es ist, wie die gesetzliche Rechtsnorm allgemein, auch für den Richter bindend. Ein Gesetz, welches einen Verwaltungsakt enthält, kann nicht mehr auf seine Uebereinstimmung mit andern Gesetzen geprüft werden. Andererseits ist, was bei Laband nicht zum Ausdruck gelangt, nicht jede auf Grund der erklärten Zustimmung der Volksvertretung ergangene Willensäusserung des höchsten Verwaltungsorgans, sondern nur die als Gesetz von der Volksvertretung beschlossene und von dem Staatsoberhaupt als Gesetz sanktionirte Willensäusserung Gesetz. Die Grundsätze über das ständische Budgetrecht, welche als in der deutschen Staatsrechtswissenschaft herrschend, auch von Laband anerkannt sind, entbehren ohne diese Unterscheidung der prinzipiellen rechtlichen Grundlage.

The legal binding enactment of the rule of law.

The essential characteristic of law in the formal sense (in the view of the author) is that, as the will of the highest organ of the state, it is without limitation binding, as no administrative act or judicial judgment can be.

From "Die Gesetzmässigkeit der Verwaltung und die Verwaltungsgesetze," p. 33:

Mit der organischen Trennung der Gesetzgebung von der Verwaltung, dem Ausgangspunkte des Verfassungsstaats, ist hiernach der Keim einer Entwicklung gegeben, deren Produkt die *Verwaltungsgesetze* sind. Diese Entwicklung schreitet nur langsam, aber unaufhaltsam je nach den Bedürfnissen des Lebens fort. Sie lässt aber auch auf den von der Gesetzgebung geordneten Gebieten der in der Verordnung und Verfügung sich äussernden freien Verwaltungsthätigkeit ein weites Feld offen. Diess fordern, wie schon bemerkt, die durch die Verwaltungsgesetzgebung zu ordnenden, zeitlich und lokal verschiedenen Bedürfnisse des wirklichen Staatslebens. Die Organe der Verwaltung suchen sich daher um so nachdrücklicher einen möglichst weiten Raum der freien Bewegung zu erhalten, je ernstlicher und gewissenhafter sie ihre Aufgabe nehmen.

Summary:—

The answer to the question whether administrative power is as wide as the sphere in which it may move without infringing the laws, or is on the contrary only as extensive as specific legislative provision makes it, is to be sought for in each country in the constitutional history of that country. The presumption is in favor of the first view [over] the alternate; but the history of the struggle for guaranteed individual liberty has been in favor of the latter view.

Argument (pp. 34-37):[4]

(In the case of Germany, if not in the case of any other country) The present constitutional state having emerged from the absolutist state of former times, and constitutions having taken the shape of a definite association of representative bodies with the head of the state in legislation, the sphere not assigned this cooperative legislation is left for the occupation of administration. Neither constitutional provision nor statute can exactly prescribe or circumscribe administrative action in detail: much must be left to the choice and discretion of administrative authorities; and it is difficult to deny to them the general duty of caring for the interests of the state even in cases not provided for by law.

To set up the authority of the courts of law as a limitation is nothing more than to set up the authority of laws: for courts can not interpret laws which do not exist or impose any naked restraints.

These arguments are made by Gneist to apply to the case of England,—to exclusion of Jellinek's suggestion of common *public* law there.

Gneist, Sarwey, Meyer, et al. put the administration and its activities upon the footing analogous to that occupied by the in-

[4] Tipped in between pages 36-37.

dividual in relation to the laws: just as there is an individual life outside the laws (flowing, so to speak, out of personalities) so there is an administrative activity outside the laws: in both cases the laws limit but do not fully create or prescribe. The idea seems to be this: the administration personates the state: what the state as such may do that must the administration do, acting upon its own views of public duty and necessity in all cases in which its activities are not prescribed or limited by positive law.

From "Die Verwaltungsgesetzgebung als der Regulator der Verwaltungsthätigkeit," p. 38:

Das höchste Organ der Verwaltung tritt hiernach in ein besonderes Verhältniss zu den vom ihm eingesetzten und berufenen Organen, welche zufolge desselben seine Hilfsorgane, seine Beauftragten sind. Vermöge des durch die Uebernahme des Auftrags, die Annahme des Amtes begründeten Dienstverhältnisses sind diese Organe zu dem Gehorsam gegenüber den Aufträgen und Weisungen der Vorgesetzten, in letzter Linie des höchsten Organes der Verwaltung verpflichtet. Die über die Amtsführung und alle hierauf bezüglichen Verhältnisse von dem höchsten Organe der Verwaltung oder in dessen Auftrage von einem anderen vorgesetzten Organe ergehenden Weisungen an die untergeordneten Organe haben im Prinzip, mögen sie in der Form allgemeiner Vorschriften oder eines für den einzelnen Falls gegebenen Befehls, erlassen werden, dieselbe rechtsverpflichtende Wirkung für die untergeordneten Organe, wie das Gesetz für die in keinem solchen Dienstverhältnisse stehenden Einzelnen. Sie bilden die Instruktion, welche das eigentliche Gebiet der Verordnungsgewalt ist. Aus dem zwischen dem höchsten Organe und den untergeordneten Organen bestehenden Auftragverhältnisse folgt endlich das Recht des ersteren, diese zu beaufsichtigen und durch die vorgesetzten Dienstorgane beaufsichtigen zu lassen, die Ausführung der Instruktion zu überwachen, diese nach den gegebenen Verhältnissen zu ändern, den Auftrag selbst zurückzunehmen und alle Folgen etwaiger Pflichtverletzungen gegen die Beauftragten zur Geltung zu bringen.

Even when these are in contradiction to the laws? Is the responsibility for illegal instructions only with those who issue them and not with those who obey them? See pages 41, 11, 104, 105.

From "Die Verwaltungsgesetzgebung als der Regulator der Verwaltungsthätigkeit," p. 41:

Durch die materiellen Verwaltungsgesetze und die Forderung der Gesetzmässigkeit der Verwaltung ändert sich das Verhältniss der einzelnen Verwaltungsorgane sowohl in Beziehung auf das Prinzip ihrer gegenseitigen Unterordnung und der dienstlichen Pflicht zum Gehorsam, als gegenüber den Einzelnen.

Die materiellen Verwaltungsgesetze binden das höchste Organ der Verwaltung ebenso, wie die demselben untergeordneten Organe. Die Pflicht zum dienstlichen Gehorsam ist hiernach durch die Gesetzmässigkeit der den untergeordneten Organen ertheilten Befehle bedingt. Die untergeordneten Organe hören hiermit auf, als die Beauftragten der höhern Verwaltungsorgane zu unbedingtem dienstlichem Gehorsam verpflichtet zu sein. Sie gewinnen innerhalb des ihnen durch Gesetz oder Verordnung übertragenen Geschäftskreises diejenige Selbstständigkeit, welche erforderlich ist, um gegen die Ausführung eines gesetzwidrigen Befehls der Vorgesetzten die nöthige Garantie zu geben. Den Einzelnen gegenüber wird sodann jedes Verwaltungsorgan für die Gesetzmässigkeit und für die Pflichtmässigkeit seines Verhaltens innerhalb des ihm durch die Verordnung oder durch die Verfügung des vorgesetzten Organes gesetzmässig auferlegten Pflichtenkreises verantwortlich. Der Wille der Verwaltungsorgane hat nicht, wie in dem absoluten Staate, dem Willen der Einzelnen gegenüber unbedingt eine höhere, nöthigenfalls erzwingbare Geltung, sondern nur insoweit, als derselbe mit dem Gesetz und der durch die vorgesetzten Organe im Wege der Verordnung oder Verfügung ertheilten, dem Gesetz nicht widersprechenden Instruktion sich in Uebereinstimmung befindet d. h. nur insoweit, als er gesetz- und rechtmässig ist.

Through legal regulation of administration, not only is the relationship of the administrative organs to the individual changed, but also the relationship of the administrative organs to each other in respect of a subordinate. Even the least of administrative organs is bound to disobey instructions which are illegal or unconstitutional, and is in that respect responsible to the individuals.

Argument, pp. 43-46:[5]

In the administration of civil and criminal law it is necessary (1) that judicial power should be separate from legislative, (2)

[5] Tipped in between pages 46-47.

that adjudication should rest upon positive law (no remedy and "no punishment without a law"), (3) that the judges should be independent of all outside influences,—because the individual must be protected against both uncertain, changeable law, and arbitrary decisions.

In the case of administration, however, the matter stands different, (1) Because breaches of administrative law by public officials are likely to be much less frequent than breaches of private or criminal law, in as much as officials are chosen under cautions as to fitness, and are threatened in many cases with criminal punishment, official discipline, or even removal in case of misconduct. (2) Because there are 2 entirely different kinds of administrative law which may be broken, one affecting the maintenance of the public interest solely, the other the preservation of the law of distinction between the sphere of the state and that of individuals and corporations. Cases under these 2 classes cannot be determined according to the same principles or in the same way.

It is the province of administration to secure the public interest, and it has a range of discretion in this sphere which the courts should not be permitted to limit, to which indeed no exact legal rules can be made to apply. This discretion ("jurisdiction") belongs exclusively to administrative organs as should the application of the rules of law to the courts. The only available guarantee for its right exercise is to be found in the proper modeling of administration, in the introduction of "honor offices," in collegiate organization where necessary of administrative organs and in the right of complaint.

Constitute government how you will, there is always an "administrative jurisdiction" outside of and beyond the *positive-law jurisdiction of* the courts. Whether, alongside of this the courts may extend for the decisions of questions of positive administrative law is another question. The question for the courts is the question of legality; the question for administration is the question of propriety, of suitability, of expedience, of utility.

Scientific Development of Administration (51-56):

(1) The idea of the *Rechtsstaat* (that is, of the state as existing by virtue of concrete law) dominant at the first. Here the central thought was that of a position, a balance, between the government and the people, the rights of the people being given expression through representation; and the 2 sets of principles considered were the personal and public rights granted by the

constitutional provision on the one hand, on the other the subordination of class to class or of individuals to the government derived by regular historical development from feudal times. Face to face stood public rights and the "police" powers of the state.

(2) Came R. v. Mohl with his distinction between constitutional and administrative law. But he still clung to the conception of the state as an institute of law (*Rechtsanstalt*) and therefore was prevented from having a full view of administration in its real and essential character.

(3) Mohl's distinction between constitutional and administrative law was preserved, but only actual German law was classified by means of it, and the essential distinction had not, of course, been worked out in that law. Administrative law received nothing more than differentiation into (α) police (β) financial administration. At the same time political economy received its development as a separate science (absorbing most of the subjects under finance) and administration was summed up in the conception of the *Polizeiwissenschaft*, that is the securing of the safety and welfare of the community.

As a result constitutional law has been made too inclusive, and only arbitrarily chosen parts of the administrative law have been kept apart as a separate science. Constitutional law has been made to include all that portion of law which concerns the natural foundations of the state, as well as legislation and the acquirement and use of the governing authority, that is the head of the state, his personal relations and his political duties and obligations; the constitutional council of the head of the state and the form of its governmental acts; the representation of the people, its formation, composition, summoning, duties, and methods of business, the relations of the representatives of the people to the head of the state and to the organs of state subordinate to him; the representation of the state abroad and military affairs,—even so far as such expressions of the will of the state belonged within the sphere of the interior administration. All these matters, as well as the rights of individual liberty granted by constitutions and the separate rights of the several classes of society derived from the feudal state, have been separated from administrative law and made parts of the *Staats-* or *Verfassungsrecht.* For the rest, discussions in the public law confine themselves to a consideration of the connection between administration and the political economy as a whole, that is, to the most general fundamental principles of the administration of justice, of the interior administration including communal arrangements, and of financial administration.

"Since administrative law and the 2 procedures [civil and criminal][6] have been set apart as separate sciences, public law in the narrower sense (constitutional law) only treats, in detailed manner, of functions of legislation, confining itself to the chief principles only of the functions of administration and of justice, passing over the detail of the special sciences."—*G. Meyer.* "The 2 procedures" include much that is administrative in character, and the principle that whatever is handled by the courts belongs to the separate science of adjudication has still further curtailed administrative science proper.

(p. 63) [60-63]:[7]

The administration of justice (the determination of private law contests and application of criminal justice) has been organically separated from the other branches of administration; military and financial affairs have been brought under special rules and special official organization of their own: what remains of administrative activity, with the still further exception of foreign affairs, constitutes the subject matter of a separate science of administration and the sphere of the police (πολιτεία) powers of the state: the whole care of government for the welfare of the state and its citizens.

Under the old idea of the weal-state (page 60) there was no essential limitation to this sphere: nothing short of arrangements of the modern constitutional state sufficed to delimit it. To say (as the maintainers of the idea of the *Rechtsstaat* said) that the administration had no legitimate sphere save such as was given it by positive law was to set limits realizable in no possible state. In the modern constitutional state *positive* (instead of merely negative) expression is given both to the powers of the state and to the rights of individuals,—it is a state of clear definitions, and clear understandings between power and liberty.

99. "Honour Offices":[8]

1. Originally those which all fully qualified citizens were subject to be called upon to occupy, which needed no special professional training, which would not be depended upon by their incumbents as a means of support, though often salaried offices,

[6] WW's brackets.
[7] Tipped in between pages 62-63.
[8] Tipped in between pages 98-99.

but which would be accepted because of a sense of duty or because of the honor or dignity conferred by them.

2. In the second place, came to signify all non-professional offices, whether filled by appointment or by election, upon the ground of position, of property, of rank, or of personal merit, whether paid or unpaid, if only not depended upon as a means of support by their incumbents.

(100-103):[9]

"Self-Administration,["] its several significances:
1. The execution of the will of the state through representatives of certain professional or local interests, who act for the state, indeed, and under its commission, but who also to a certain extent apply their own views of the interests which they represent.
2. Administration through non-professional offices, by persons not drawn from the professional official class.

The range of independent choice of policy and measures on the part of organs of self-administration is of course a range carefully and narrowly restricted by law: it is only within the laws that the independent will of the officers of this branch of service has free play.

The root of self-administration is to be found in the communes and they are based upon the administration of communal property. It is conceived to be nonetheless *self*-administration when the officers who actually exercise the power of the state (as distinguished from consultative bodies) are appointed by central authorities instead of being elected, even when appointed from the ranks of the professional service. (See fine print, page 103). The electoral feature may be confined to the choice of consultative bodies merely, which stand related to the actual executive officers of the district much as the national public representatives stand related to the monarchy.

From "Die Einheit der Verwaltung," p. 104:

1. Die untergeordneten Organe sind nicht nur zum Gehorsam, sondern auch zu der Beobachtung der Verwaltungsgesetze und des Verwaltungsrechts verpflichtet. Eine von einer höhern Behörde erlassene Verordnung oder Verfügung, welche nicht gesetz- und rechtmässig ist, entbehrt in dem Verfassungsstaat, wie jede solche Verwaltungsverfügung, der rechtlichen Wirksamkeit; sie ist also

Securities for legality of action on the part of the Administration: 1. The right and duty of subordinate officials to judge the legality of their instructions, fortified by their

[9] Tipped in between pages 102-103.

auch für die untergeordneten Organe nicht verpflichtend. Allein wenn die untergeordneten Organe in ihrer dienstlichen Stellung von der freien Entschliessung der höhern und höchsten Organe abhängig wären, so würden sie durch den Widerspruch gegen eine nach ihrer Ansicht rechtswidrige Verfügung und die Verweigerung des Gehorsams ihre dienstliche Stellung gefährden. Sie würden sich der sofortigen Entfernung vom Dienst aussetzen, was für alle diejenigen öffentlichen Diener, welche die Besorgung der öffentlichen Geschäfte zu ihrem Lebensberuf gemacht haben, eine Existenzfrage ist. Die Verwirklichung der Forderung der Gesetz- und Rechtmässigkeit der Verwaltung hat aus diesem Grunde in dem deutschen Staate, in welchem dem Berufsamt die innere Verwaltung in ihrer grössten Ausdehnung überlassen war, zu der Anerkennung eines *Rechts auf das einmal übertragene Amt* gedrängt, d. h. zu der lebenslänglichen Anstellung und zu der Anerkennung des Grundsatzes, dass eine Entfernung vom Amt nur unter gesetzlich bestimmten Voraussetzungen und nur durch ein geordnetes Verfahren statthaft ist.

removability except under strictly prescribed conditions and by a formal legal procedure.

From "Die Einheit der Verwaltung," p. 105:

2. Soweit die Funktionen der innern Verwaltung den Organen der Selbstverwaltung zugewiesen sind, ist prinzipiell das Aufsichtsrecht der staatlichen Verwaltungsorgane auf die Ueberwachung der Gesetz- und Rechtmässigkeit derselben beschränkt. Innerhalb des der Selbstbestimmung der Verwaltungsorgane von dem Gesetz freigelassenen Raums handeln die Organe der Selbstverwaltung nach ihrem eigenen freien Ermessen.

3. In der Erwägung, dass die örtlichen Bedürfnisse richtiger von den Organen der Selbstverwaltung erkannt und gewürdigt, und dass die Verfügungen, welche von diesen aus dem Kreise der unmittelbar Betheiligten hervorgegangenen Organen getroffen werden, von den Betheiligten williger befolgt werden, beruft die Gesetzgebung des Verfassungsstaats diese Organe zu der Ordnung derjenigen Verhältnisse, welche lokaler Natur sind und das Gesetz wegen der Verschiedenheit der örtlichen Ver-

2. 3. The self-determined action of the authorities of local self-administration, and the limitation of oversight of the professional organs to the single question whether or not the officers of self-administration keep within the bounds set them by laws.

hältnisse nicht selbst zu regeln vermag, indem sie die Organe der lokalen Selbstverwaltung zu Erlassung rechtsverbindlicher Normen auf diesem Gebiete ermächtigt.

From "Begriff der Grundrechte," pp. 119-20:

Da dieser Theil der Rechtsordnung seinen Ausgangspunkt in dem Gegensatze des Individualismus, der Ansprüche der Persönlichkeit gegen die in die Rechts- und Willensphäre derselben eingreifende Gewalt der Organe des Staats findet, so war es natürlich, dass er sich der Erkenntniss des Rechts zunächst in der Form von Rechten der Persönlichkeit gegenüber der Staatsgewalt, in der Abgrenzung einer für diese unantastbaren Rechts- und Willensphäre der Einzelnen vermittelt hat, woraus sich nach den hiernach anerkannten einzelnen Rechten der Persönlichkeit der Begriff der sog. Grundrechte von selbst ergab. Dabei ist als richtig zuzugeben, dass die Grundrechte zum Theil einen nur negativen Inhalt haben, die Nichtverletzlichkeit der Persönlichkeit, woraus folgt, dass der positive Inhalt dieses Theiles der Rechtsordnung in den Ausnahmen von der Regel der Nichtverletzbarkeit zu suchen ist, in welchen die obrigkeitlichen Befugnisse der Verwaltungsorgane sich äussern. Allein dass diese Ausnahmen nach den in der Persönlichkeit begriffenen Interessen der Einzelnen, welche insoweit der staatlichen Gewalt gegenüber nach der Rechtsordnung sich nicht behaupten können, dargestellt werden, ist nicht ein blosser Nothbehelf, sondern in der Sache selbst begründet. Das Unrichtige und Falsche an der früher herrschenden Theorie der Grundrechte liegt nur in der Meinung, dass durch einige allgemeine Sätze in Verfassungs-Urkunden das Recht der Persönlichkeit gegen die staatliche Gewalt in einer den Bedürfnissen des wirklichen Staatslebens entsprechenden Weise geschützt werden könne, während man hätte einsehen sollen, dass entweder der hierdurch gewährte Schutz ein ungenügender oder dass die Verwirklichung der öffentlichen Interessen hierdurch beeinträchtigt wird. Die in den Verfassungs-Urkunden enthaltenen allgemeinen Sätze, welche man

Qu. How far does the mere statement or enumeration of individual rights in a constitution fail to make them positive rights?

nach dem Vorgang der deutschen Reichsverfassung von 1849 unter dem Titel "Grundrechte" zusammenfasst, sind theils Verwaltungsrechtsnormen, theils Direktiven für die Gesetzgebung, welche nur durch die Verwaltungsgesetze und durch die Entwicklung ihres Inhalts auf dem Wege der wissenschaftlichen Behandlung ihre Wirkung in dem Rechtsleben haben.

From Joseph Ruggles Wilson

My dearest Woodrow— Clarksville, Tennessee, Decr. 5, '89.

Your letter of Decr 1st came last night. It is pleasant to read what you have to say of your aunt Lizzie.[1] She is one of the best of women, and you would esteem her more if you knew her better. Her troubles have been many, but they have not soured her temper, for her heart has been in God's keeping these many days. She is genuine through and through. So too are her coffle of fine daughters, of whom you would be proud were you as well acquainted with them as I am.

I am sorry that your aunt has alarmed your fears as to my state of health. It is on the whole in as fair a condition as ought to be expected, seeing that years are so rapidly piling their grey honors upon my lonely head. When I wrote to my sister I suppose I was not feeling so well as usual, and may have employed stronger words in telling her of my condition than were altogether of historical accuracy. I have not missed a recitation so far, this session. What is chiefly the matter with me is due to the heavy dullness of the life I am compelled to lead. But filling it as I do with work, I make it as light as circumstances will allow. Thus—"so much for Buckingham."

It is satisfying to learn of dear Ellie's recovered strength—of the babe's cryless life—and of the good upstanding of the older little ones. Home-love, with its various fruits, is the best the heart can taste, when there smiles upon it the still higher love of Heaven.

The cheering outlook, too, which you have in the line of your profession is most gratifying—to me as truly as to yourself. I am sometimes afraid, however, that you are giving your mind too much to do in the way of extra work: especially as it is an honorable ambition with you to do your work well. Still your frequent lecturings, here and there, are perhaps needful to make you better and better known, and thus to give you a larger standing in the world of letters. But see to it, my darling son, that you do not get broken down by your much writing and speaking. I rejoice in your successes, yet these *may* be purchased at too great a cost.

What you tell me of the Princeton prospect is immensely cheering,—particularly when placed alongside of the effort that is making to retain you where you are. How grateful you have reason to feel that, at so early an age, you are permitted to occupy so large a position in the view of thinking men! Were I not sure that your mental balance is most stable, I might tremble for its poise. It will be a decided relief to me when all is fixed as to the chair you are to have—whether at P. or at W. My voice is for P.

I must now close—as it is getting near the hour for bed, and I have yet something else to do before Morpheus takes me to his re*sound*ing embrace—for alas I snore (now and then). Dode joins me in love—and our two loves taken together are, for you all, about the biggest of their kind you ever knew.

Your affectionate Father *and Friend.*

ALS (WP, DLC).

1 A. Elizabeth Wilson Begges.

Two News Items

[Dec. 9, 1889]

On Tuesday evening, Dec. 3d, Prof. Woodrow Wilson delivered a lecture at Russell Library hall, in the Y. M. C. A. course, on "Leaders of Men."[1] He said that the literary man sways the people by his writings, but objects to being paraded on the public platform, while the active leader of men enjoys the chance to address the masses in public.

1 This item reports the first delivery of "Leaders of Men," which, as future documents will reveal, Wilson gave many times afterward. The text is a WWhw and WWT MS. on half sheets in WP, DLC. T. H. Vail Motter (ed.), *Leaders of Men by Woodrow Wilson* (Princeton, N. J., 1952), reproduces this first text. A revised version is printed at June 17, 1890, following an Editorial Note.

◇

CELEBRATING THE VICTORY.

When the first news came by telegraph on Thursday of last week that Wesleyan had been successful against her "old rival,"[1] the joy of the students who were left about college knew no bounds. They managed, however, to bottle up their enthusiasm until evening, when they uncorked it to the great edification of the town at large. A walk-around was indulged in, and in the course of it the professors and a number of prominent citizens were serenaded. Professor Wilson showed his appreciation of the importance of the occasion in a speech that he made to the serenaders, and Professor Van Benschoten and Mr. Parshley[2] gave the visitors the hospitality of the season.

But the great celebration over the victory was on Monday evening, when all the students had returned to town. Everyone in the college turned out at 9 o'clock and joined in the triumphal march through the streets of the city. A drum corps led off, followed by the victorious team in the Wesleyan 'bus. A special guard of honor, uniformed in white, accompanied the 'bus, and behind them came the rest of the students, indulging in tin-horns, fireworks and the yell. By 10 o'clock the procession had returned to college, and a bonfire was started on High street. Boxes, barrels, and whatever else was available to add to the blaze, were utilized. This, with the ringing of the chapel bell and the charming rendering of the yell by the co-eds., finished the evening's entertainment.

Printed in the Middletown, Conn., *Wesleyan Argus*, XXIII (Dec. 9, 1889), 54

[1] The University of Pennsylvania, which Wesleyan defeated 10 to 2 in a football game played in New York on November 28. This victory climaxed one of the most successful football seasons in Wesleyan's history to this date.

[2] Clifford Ives Parshley, '92, half-back, presumably entertained at his parents' home in Middletown.

From Albert Bushnell Hart

My dear Prof. Wilson, Cambridge, Mass., Dec. 14, 1889.

In the vain attempt to do three things at once, an answer to your letter of October 31st seems to have been counted out. I sincerely congratulate you upon the interruption in your college duties and hope that it continues to interest but not to hinder.

I have absorbed your book on "The State" with great interest and have adopted it immediately as a text book in History 14, (constitutional government, advanced course.) The compact descriptions of the German and Swiss governments are precisely what I want in my comparative study of federations. In fact I got two copies and incorporated the whole text on these two countries and the United States into my notes, whence they will doubtless often reappear in future lectures to the astonishment of my own students, who will wonder at the unusual accuracy and brilliancy of my comments.

This afternoon by great effort I have dictated a bibliographic note to the government of Switzerland in which due reference is made to your book. I will send you a copy of the Swiss Constitution as soon as finished.

Have you now in hand your briefer book on governments? For my own part I do not find the larger work too long and of course one has his own ulterior views. One of the Longman's was here a few weeks ago and was much interested in the future of the Epochs. Thwaites is about to send me a copy of his three chapters and I hope he will be out before summer. I expect to follow him in the course of the summer and the expectant public will then demand something from your pen, at the convenience of course of yourself and your daughter.

I hear with regret that you were in Boston not many weeks ago without making me a call. It will give me sincere pleasure to see you whenever you are up this way.

Sincerely yours, Albert Bushnell Hart

TLS (WP, DLC) with WWhw notation on env.: "Ans. 1 Jan'y/90."

A Newspaper Report of an Interview

[Dec. 17, 1889]

WESLEYAN'S GIFT.

The semi-anunal meeting of the trustees of Wesleyan university, which was held at New York on Friday of last week, was the most memorable one in the history of that institution. Only two or three members of the board were in the secret concerning the great event that was to transpire at that conference. One of these gentlemen was the president of the board, Judge George G. Reynolds of Brooklyn, N. Y., and it was his felicitous prerogative to be the spokesman of the occasion. The message which he brought to the conference was one of profound interest to the university, disclosing one of the most liberal benefactions yet contributed to the educational institutions of New England.

Two days prior to the conference Dr. Daniel Ayres of Brooklyn, who has been a generous patron of the university, called on Judge Reynolds, who is one of his intimate personal friends, and placed at his disposal $250,000 in funds as a gift wholly without conditions to the Wesleyan university. The sum consisted of government and railroad bonds amounting to $230,000 and a certified check for $20,000. Dr. Ayres in placing this magnificent donation in the hands of Judge Reynolds remarked that he had contemplated making the provision in his will, but after deliberating the matter, it had appeared best to him to make the gift during his life time. . . .

Owing to the great public interest felt in the gift by the friends of education throughout the country, *The Evening Post* sent a representative to Middletown yesterday afternoon to ascertain from President Raymond and associates with him in advancing the interests of the college the uses to which the fund will be put. The president received the reporter with great cordiality and talked without reserve in regard to the magnificent donation. He said it had grown out of the doctor's own interest in the university and contact with Judge Reynolds of the board of trustees. . . .

Professor Wilson, who is a graduate of Princeton and Johns Hopkins university, holds the professorship of history at Wesleyan and is one of the most progressive men in the faculty. He is a Virginian by birth, the town of Stanton in the Shenandoah being his native place, and out of the religious trend of the college; that is, he is not a member of the Methodist church. He is a keen observer of college interests and regards the scientific impulse in the old centers of education and scholasticism as one of the great forces of the period. He pointed out the scientific spirit at Johns Hopkins, Princeton, Yale and Wesleyan with marked satisfaction. Referring to the gift of Dr. Ayres, he said its great value consisted in the fact that it is not tied up, being devoted to the general endowment. Professor Wilson could see no reason why the college should not grow rapidly under the new conditions. At the last commencement he detected a keen sense of hope among the graduates and an enthusiastic expectation as to the future of the university. Wesleyan is a sort of mother, added the professor, among Methodist colleges. But the college does not put any undue emphasis on the fact that it is a Methodist institution. It is becoming less and less denominational. This means expansion. . . .

Printed in the *Hartford Evening Post*, Dec. 17, 1889; some editorial headings omitted.

From Horace Elisha Scudder

My dear Wilson Cambridge, Mass. 20 December 1889.

Do you remember my speaking to you of our plans at Williams

to enlarge the history department by the addition of a professor on the new foundation created by the gift of Dr. Miller,[1] and known as the Professorship of American History, Literature and Eloquence?[2] We are ready now to act, and I write to ask frankly if you will entertain a proposition to take the chair? Of course I hope you will, but I will not trouble you with details until I know if the way is open. Sincerely yours H. E. Scudder.

ALS (WP, DLC) with WWhw notation on env.: "Ans. Dec. 23/89."

[1] John Leland Miller, M.D., physician and gentleman farmer of Sheffield, Mass.

[2] It was, actually, the J. Leland Miller Professorship of American History, Literature and Eloquence, established in 1888.

From Reuben Gold Thwaites

Dear Sir: Madison, Wis., Dec. 23, 1889.

Prof. Frederick J. Turner, assistant in history at our State university, has frequently told me of meeting you socially last winter, while he was doing post-graduate work at Johns Hopkins. No one here knows Turner but to admire him, and the supposition that he equally impressed you is my sole warrant for asking you, unbeknown to him, to do him a great favor.

The death of Professor Wm. F. Allen[1] leaves the chair of history in our university vacant. Professor Allen trained Turner up from an undergraduate with the avowed hope of making him, in due time, his successor. It was a source of great satisfaction to Allen, that Turner returned to Madison at the beginning of the present college year, and he did not disguise the sentiment, among his intimates, that Turner should be considered as in the line of succession. He considered him in every way deserving of being his successor, though the time came sooner than he thought. The students fairly idolize Turner, his fellows on the faculty have keen admiration for him, and resident historical students have high regard for his scholarship, his mental vigor and his upright character.

One would suppose, from all this, that there should be no question about Turner's succeeding Allen. But the president, Dr. Chamberlin,[2] seems to be casting about for another man. It is probable that he will wish to consult with you about the matter. We are doing our best to induce the regents to appoint Turner, and hope we may count on a friendly word from you. Turner of course, knows nothing about this; he is too modest to lift a hand to shape the result.

If you can consistently say it, a word from you to the president of the Board of Regents, Hon. George H. Paul, Milwaukee, Wis., would certainly have great weight. The board meets to consider the matter, January 2, next.

Very truly yours, Reuben G. Thwaites

TLS (WP, DLC) with WWhw notation on env.: "Ans. 12/26/89."
[1] On Dec. 9, 1889.
[2] Thomas Chrowder Chamberlin, President of the University, 1887-92.

From Joseph Ruggles Wilson

My beloved children— [Clarksville, Tenn.] Dec 23rd [1889]

I wish I could invent something to send you each and both. But you own my heart. Or, if there be any portion of it not yet your own, I hereby make it over to you in fee. If the little ones knew their right hands from their left, *they* might enjoy a nick nack or two—but &c. &c.

I am not in the top of the house at present—but rather in the cellar, or sub-cellar even at times. I so long for you all.

Your affc Father

ALS (WP, DLC).

To Horace Elisha Scudder

My dear Mr. Scudder, Middletown, Ct., 23 Dec. '89

Any proposition coming from you comes with a special claim upon my acceptance because of my esteem for you and of my belief in your interest in my welfare. You are, in a sense, my literary Godfather. But, unhappily,—for a chair of American History has a very strong claim upon my interests and desire—I am in the present case obliged to plead 'a previous engagement.' My strongest interest, as you know, lies on the institutional side of politics, in the history of the political habit and of those legal relations and conceptions which underlie Public Law. Now Princeton is, as you may have seen in the newspapers, about to create a professorship in this very field, and, if she does, I shall feel bound to accept it, if offered me, because of the answers I have made to their overtures to me. Besides, Wesleyan, having just received liberal gifts of money, offers in effect to create such a chair as I want if I will stay here, and, if I did not go to Princeton, I should feel bound on many grounds to accept this offer, which is so generous for a small college with departments as yet but partially differentiated.

I venture to thrust this full confidence upon you because I could not in any other way give you a genuine explanation of the impossibility of my considering a call to Williams, which would, under other circumstances be very attractive to me, despite the existence at Williamstown of a climate such as might give any Southerner pause.

While I must make this answer to your question, however, I feel very keen gratification that I should have been your choice for the chair. I somehow wish that I could accept it for the express purpose of trying to prove worthy of your confidence.

With much regard,

Most sincerely Yours, Woodrow Wilson

TCL (RSB Coll., DLC).

To Reuben Gold Thwaites

My dear Mr. Thwaites, Middletown, Conn., 26 December, 1889.

I am sincerely obliged to you for your letter, which came this morning. I not only admire Mr. Turner; I learned, during the six weeks of my acquaintance with him last winter, to have a positive affection for him; and it is a matter of unalloyed pleasure to me to have so early an opportunity to be of some service to him. I determined before leaving Baltimore that, if ever a chance presented itself for assisting him in any way or degree to professional preferment, I would act with all heartiness in his behalf. In one sense this present is not exactly the sort of opportunity I had hoped to see. I had hoped some day to get him into the same faculty with myself, that I might have the pleasure and profit of having him as a colleague. Lacking that opportunity, I was about to urge him for my place here, in the event of my leaving. Of course, so soon as I heard the sad news of Prof. Allen's death I thought of Turner and of his chances for the succession. I was taking it for granted that he was practically sure of the place, young as he is.

I have written to both Mr. Paul and Dr. Chamberlin. It was somewhat awkward writing to them without knowing either of them personally and without being consulted by either, but I put all the diplomacy and carefulness of approach into my letters of which I was capable, as well as the full warmth of my admiration for Turner. In addressing Dr. Chamberlin I gave this turn to my intervention, after confessing impertinence: "You know Mr. Turner, doubtless, as well as I do; and I take it for granted that there is practically no doubt about his succeeding Prof. Allen, by whom he was so much admired and whose natural successor he would seem to be. Perhaps this letter will serve no further purpose than to express my appreciation of Mr. Turner and my very great interest in his fortunes. . . . I throw myself upon your generosity if my course should seem to you in any degree impertinent. I feel that I am simply performing a plain duty by letting you know in what estimation Mr. Turner is likely to be held by all students of history who are thrown into intimate relations with him. . . . I am writing, I am sure, in the interests of historical scholarship in America in thus insisting upon being allowed to speak in his praise." It may be of service to you to know just what line I took. The omitted portions are in the same sense.

It is very gratifying to me to have had this sort of an introduction to my fellow laborer in the 'Epochs of American History.' I heartily wish that we might have some means of knowing each other some time face to face.

Very sincerely Yours, Woodrow Wilson

WWTLS (CSmH).

A Review

[Dec. 26, 1889]

Wilson's 'The State.'[1]

The somewhat complicated title which Prof. Wilson has chosen for this volume suggests the difficulty in which he has been involved by his plan. There is room for doubt as to the wisdom of attempting to compress into one treatise an account of the political institutions of all times as well as an epitome of political history. The subject is too vast to admit of very thorough treatment within such narrow limits, and where so much must be omitted, there will always be differences of opinion as to what the omissions should be. It is, perhaps, on this account that, as the author observes, he has had no predecessors; that "no text-book of like scope and purpose has hitherto been attempted." As a consequence, the book is inconveniently large for a text-book, while it is not full enough for a book of reference. But, in spite of all difficulties and drawbacks, the work has been very well

[1] The author, David MacGregor Means, sometime fellow of the Johns Hopkins, and after 1881 a lawyer in New York City.

done. The best authorities have been followed, and followed intelligently, and the arrangement of details concerning modern institutions of government has evidently been elaborated with the most careful industry. The style is clear, and there is a certain vivacity in the narrative portions of the text that relieves the dryness of the theme.

The earlier chapters treat of the origin and development of government in general, substantially in accordance with the views of such writers as Maine, Lubbock, Spencer, and Bagehot. The ancient city is described in the spirit of Coulanges's essay, and the political history of the leading Greek states is given with considerable detail, and as it is to be found in the standard histories. On the other hand, the treatment of the political institutions of Rome is exceedingly meagre. Scarcely a dozen pages, or about the space given to that mere archaeological curiosity, the government of Lacedæmon, suffice to bring us down to the period of the Empire. The subsequent changes are described with more fulness; still, to take one instance, it would not be very easy to determine from this account the nature of the administration of a municipality in the provinces at the time of the Teutonic invasion. The discussion of the influence of the Roman law could, perhaps, not very well be omitted in a treatise that is for this period mainly historical; but if positive law is to be described among the institutions of government, it is easy to see that, within such space as is here at command, the description must be inadequate. It would have been probably more effective to give more attention to the administrative methods and achievements of the Romans, and to relinquish their jurisprudence to the care of specialists.

As to the Teutonic peoples, the description is taken in the main from accepted authorities; but the student might get the impression that a true nobility existed among them in primitive times. Here, too, we think that the desire to emphasize contrasts leads the author to overlook the existence of personal allegiance among the Romans. It was undoubtedly more prominent among the Barbarians, but it prevailed necessarily under the Roman system of landed estates, and was conspicuous in many of their intestine broils, to say nothing of the extended relation of patron and client. In the account of the separation of the Papacy from the Empire, it is a rather serious omission to say nothing of the influence of the Lombards, and it is a still more serious error, or cluster of errors, to say that "the Pope, arrogating to himself the prerogatives of king-maker, crowned Charles the Great Emperor of the Holy Roman Empire—'Holy' because created by the authority of mother Church." The Empire did not become "holy" for some centuries, probably, after this event, and the title seems to have been assumed in opposition to the exclusive claims of the Church, which was disposed to look down upon the civil power as earthly and profane. In a work of such extensive range, it is highly dangerous for a compiler to vary in the slightest degree from his authorities, and to yield to the temptation to make his style graphic by adding touches of his own origination, which, however well meant, may mislead the ignorant and arouse distrust among the learned.

As the author approaches modern times he treads upon firmer ground, and his description of the political institutions of the leading European countries is perhaps the most valuable portion of his book, containing a good deal of matter that is not easily accessible. Neither Italy, nor Spain, nor Russia, however, so far as we have observed, receives the slightest mention; nor is there anywhere in the book, we believe, anything more than an allusion to the political institutions of the Asiatic peoples. About one-third of the volume is devoted to the governments of England and the United States, an allowance of space that enables the author to give a comparatively thorough treatment to the complicated political machinery of these countries. But in many instances here he is, in our judgment, carried away by his passion for neat theories and sweeping generalizations. Desiring to make an effective contrast between the civilization of the New England colonies and those of the South, he represents the early settlers of Virginia as spreading far and wide in the pursuit of agriculture, while in New England "every circumstance invited to close settlement and trade, to the intimate relationships of commerce and the adventures of seafaring, rather than to the wide-spreading settlements characteristic of an agricultural population." While it is true that commerce after a time arose, no one who is conversant with the early history of New England would maintain that the primitive settlers were not in the main devoted to agriculture, or characterize their settlements otherwise than as wide-spreading; nor do the circumstances of the "long winters" and "bleak coast winds" seem to invite to "the adventures of seafaring" with irresistible persuasiveness.

The futility of such preconceived theories appears plainly enough when they are applied to the middle colonies, which,

> "though possessed of a rich soil, had also fine seaports which invited to commerce; their climate was neither so harsh as that

> of New England nor so mild and beguiling as that of the Southern colonies. Their people, consequently, built towns and traded, like the people of New England; but also spread abroad over the fertile country and farmed, like the people of Virginia. . . .Townships they had, but counties also; they were simple and democratic, like the New Englanders, and yet they were agricultural also, like the Virginians."

Why a people may not be at the same time simple and democratic as well as agricultural is not explained; but, at all events, the diversity of the political institutions of the early colonies is not to be accounted for by such crude statements as these.

Upon another point in this connection–the process of institutional growth in the early colonies of New England–the author is not less superficial. The impression conveyed is, that the towns were in the first place independent communities, which were gradually brought into some kind of federal union. "The process is obviously federative from the first." "Gradually the towns. . . . drew together into the colonies known to later times." "But at first these larger colonies were scarcely more than town leagues." We do not think that this impression would survive a perusal of the early laws of "The Massachusetts"; but we can do no more here than state that it is not to be accepted as in unquestioned correspondence with fact.

There are some chapters at the close of the book upon Law, and upon the nature, forms, functions, and objects of Government. It is of course impossible to deal fairly with such matters in a few pages, but there is much that is judicious in their treatment. Upon the whole, however, the book is not to be recommended without qualification as a text-book. The basis of scholarship upon which it rests seems to be scarcely broad enough or deep enough, and at the same time there are few teachers who have the scholarship with which to neutralize its mistakes. It is to be feared that a tendency exists among our rising school of historical writers to adopt rather a scientific vocabulary than a scientific method. We hear much talk of society as an organism; of growth and development, of crystallization, and integration, and solidarity. These are convenient expressions, but they may sometimes serve to conceal a lack of thought. It is quite possible to mistake a metaphor for a demonstration, and to deal so nimbly with abstractions as to make them pass for the concrete. It is well for every writer to bear in mind that the success of comparative methods depends upon minute and accurate observation, and that without this fund of knowledge the affectation of broad and sweeping generalizations can impose only upon the vulgar.

Printed in the New York *Nation*, XLIX (Dec. 26, 1889), 523-24.

From Horace Elisha Scudder

My dear Wilson Boston 26 December 1889

I did not know of the Princeton move, though I had heard of the Wesleyan plum. I am sorrier than ever after receiving your letter that we cannot have you, but as your friend, and not as a Williams Trustee, I am afraid I should have to say—don't!

Ever sincerely yours H. E. Scudder.

ALS (WP, DLC).

From Wilson's Confidential Journal

Middletown Dec. 28, 1889

If slow development is an intimation and promise of long life, I may certainly expect length of days sufficient for the accomplishment of all I have planned to do. I have come slowly into possession of such powers as I have, not only, but also into consciousness of them, into the ability to estimate them with just insight. Now that I am getting well into the thirties I begin to see my place in the general order of things.

I used to wonder vaguely that I did not have the same deep-reaching spiritual difficulties that I read of other young men having. I *saw* the intellectual difficulties, but I was not *troubled* by them: they seemed to have no connection with my faith in the essentials of the religion I had been taught. Unorthodox in my reading of the standards of the faith, I am nevertheless orthodox in my faith. I am capable, it would seem, of being satisfied spiritually without being satisfied intellectually. The phrase that Bagehot uses to describe the successful constitutional statesman I might appropriate to describe myself: "a man with common opinions but uncommon ability." I *receive* the opinions of my day, I do not *con*ceive them. But I receive them into a vivid mind, with a quick imaginative realization, and a power to see as a whole the long genesis of the opinions received. I have little impatience with existing conditions; I comprehend too perfectly how they came to exist, how *natural* they are. I have great confidence in progress; I feel the movement that is in affairs and am conscious of a persistent push behind the present order.

It was in keeping with my whole mental make-up, therefore, and in obedience to a true instinct, that I chose to put forth my chief strength in the history and interpretation of institutions, and chose as my chief ambition the historical explanation of the modern democratic state as a basis for the discussion of political progress, political expediency, political morality, political prejudice, practical politics, &c—an analysis of the thought in which our age stands, if it examine itself. It is a task, not of origination, but of interpretation. Interpret the age: i.e. interpret myself. Account for the creed I hold in politics. Institutions have their rootage in the common thought and only those who share the common thought can rightly interpret them. No man can appreciate a parliament who would not make a useful member of it (e.g. Carlyle)[.] No one can give a true account of anything of which he is intolerant. I find myself exceedingly tolerant of all institutions, past and present, by reason of a keen appreciation of their reason for being—*most* tolerant, so to say, of the institutions of my own day which seem to me, in an historical sense, intensely and essentially reasonable, though of course in no sense *final*. Why may not the present age write, through me, its political *autobiography*?

Political Liberty: Dec. 29, 1889

"How false is the conception, how frantic the pursuit, of that treacherous phantom which men call Liberty! There is no such thing in the universe. There can never be. The stars have it not; the earth has it not; the sea has it not; and we men have the mockery and semblance of it only for our heaviest punishment.

"The enthusiast would reply that by Liberty he meant the Law of Liberty. Then why use the single and misunderstood word? If by liberty you mean chastisement of the passions, discipline of the intellect, subjection of the will; if you mean the fear of inflicting, the shame of committing a wrong; if you mean respect for all who are in authority, and consideration for all who are in dependence; veneration for the good, mercy to the evil, sympathy with the weak;—if you mean, in a word, that Service which is defined in the liturgy of the English church to be 'perfect Freedom,' why do you name this by the same word by which the luxurious mean license, and the reckless mean change;—by which the rogue means rapine, and the fool, equality; by which the proud mean anarchy, and the malignant mean violence? Call it by any name rather than this, but its best and truest test is, Obedience." *Ruskin*[1]

These noble words are worthy to be taken as a motto for a systematic work on Political Liberty; for, whether in the sense in which their author meant them or not, they are profoundly true—are a clue of much that is dark in the history of Politics.

Obedience is liberty. Obedience to what? Obedience to the laws of character, to the laws of social development. Thus, liberty can never be had by means of a French Revolution, can never be had by a sudden removal of the bonds, a sudden reversal of the duties within which the particular society concerned has formed itself. Political character rests upon antecedent fact, not upon ideal conception. Logic is no fact: it is thought given straight *air* lines, elevated above fact. Politics is made up of *relationships* and Law is the mirror of those relationships. There can be no liberty which is unrelated; and there can be no liberty which is not of Law. Law changes, and so does liberty. There is one liberty for the child, another for the man, but the liberty of the man is no less of Law than is the liberty of the child. The man is no *less* bound than the child, though he is *differently* bound. And so of the ancient State-child, the mediaeval villein, the modern Democrat.

Entries in notebook described at Oct. 20, 1887, Vol. 5.

[1] From Ruskin's *Seven Lamps of Architecture*, Chap. 7, "The Lamp of Obedience," Sects. 1 and 2.

Marginal Notes

Transcripts of WW Shorthand Comments

[Dec. 28, 1889]

Carl Gareis, *Allgemeines Staatsrecht*, in Heinrich Marquardsen (ed.), *Handbuch des Oeffentlichen Rechts der Gegenwart* (4 vols., Freiburg im B. and Tübingen, 1883-1906), I.

From "Einleitung. Das öffentliche Recht," p. 5:

Ist die Existenz von Gemeinschaften, in denen jene des objectiven Rechts fähigen Wesen zusammenleben, eine der drei Voraussetzungen des Rechtslebens, so ist damit die Bedeutung des Gemeinwesens für das objective Recht noch nicht erschöpft; denn ein Gemeinwesen, wie es die Haus- und Blutsgemeinschaft der Familie oder die wandernde Horde, oder die sesshaftgewordene Gemeinde, oder der Staat im

The community both the source and the object of the law

heutigen Sinne darstellt, kann nicht bloss die passive Grundlage, sondern auch die active Quelle, die Schöpferin des objectiven Rechts sein oder werden; und ebendasselbe Gemeinwesen, die Gemeinschaft, *res publica*, welche hiernach Subject, Factor der Rechtsbildung sein kann, kommt auch in die Lage, Object der Rechtsbildung zu sein, sich selbst und seine Interessen Rechtsnormen unterwerfen zu müssen, sich selbst und seine Interessen unter den Schutz von Rechtsnormen zu stellen.

From "Einleitung. Staatsrecht und Privatrecht," p. 15:

III. Die Interessen des Gemeinwesens sind mannigfaltiger als die der Einzelnen; jene sind national verschieden, diese der wesentlich gleichen Menschennatur nach wesentlich gleich; daher die grössere Monotonie und Gleichförmigkeit der Privatrechte, die grössere Receptionsfähigkeit der Privatrechte, die Verähnlichung der bürgerlichen Gesetzbücher; das Privatrecht eines Staates kann in vielen Beziehungen ohne grosse Störungen in einem anderen Staate eingeführt werden, denn die überall wiederkehrenden einfachen Beziehungen von Personen zu Personen und Sachen im Dienste (Interesse) der Einzelnen leiden eine gleichmässige Normierung; wie aber diese Eigenthümlichkeit des Privatrechts in denjenigen Beziehungen, welche mit nationalen, namentlich national-ethischen Eigenthümlichkeiten (z. B. mit der Auffassung von der Freiheit, von der Ehre, von der Familie) zusammenhängen, bereits durch eine nationalverschiedene Gestaltung auch des Privatrechts durchbrochen wird, so bewirkt der gleiche Grund die grosse Verschiedenheit der öffentlichen Rechte und die Schwierigkeit oder Unmöglichkeit der Uebertragung und Reception der im Einzelnen reich gegliederten und divergierenden Staatsrechte. Dagegen ist innerhalb ein und desselben Staates das Staatsrecht gleichmässiger (—in der Fundierung der Herrschaft sogar nothwendig einheitlich) gestaltet, als das möglicherweise in zahlreichen Local- und Provinzialrechten parzellierte Privatrecht.

Private law tends towards a universal character much more than does public law. Men and their needs are alike; states and their historical conditions are variously different.

From "Einleitung. Quellen des allgemeinen Staatsrechts," p. 21:

III. Die Wissenschaft ist für das Staatsrecht so wenig wie für das Privatrecht eine den beiden erörterten Rechtsquellen coordinierte Rechtsquelle; sie ist überhaupt nicht Quelle neuen Rechts; sie kann nur das in den von der Gesetzgebung oder der Gewohnheit aufgestellten Normen latent enthaltene Recht explicieren (herauswickeln), entweder indem sie aus den aufgestellten Principien Consequenzen zieht, oder aus den gegebenen einzelnen Bestimmungen Principien entwickelt. Die Praxis ist, was die Auffstellung von Rechtssätzen anlangt, entweder wissenschaftliche Thätigkeit, also an das vorhandene Recht gebunden, oder Herkommen, das zum Gewohnheitsrecht führen kann. Die "Natur der Sache" ist nur das Ergebniss einer logischen Interpretation von Thatsachen oder Normen, nicht aber Rechtsquelle.

Why, then, are not magisterial decisions also sources of law, inasmuch as they fulfill this very function of interpretation?

From "Die Herrschaft des Staates," p. 37:

Das Wort Republik ist hierbei für eine Staatsform zu gebrauchen, in welcher alle Executiv-Organe des Staates vor der Verfassung–mithin auch das gleichviel aus wie vielen physischen Personen bestehende Staatshaupt–verantwortlich, und zwar persönlich, nicht bloss an Gewissenspflichten und an nichtexiquierbare Rechtspflichten gebunden, sondern rechtlich und persönlich dem Gesetze unterworfen sind.

Republic = Direct personal responsibility of the head of the state, together with complete subordination to the laws.

A Pocket Diary

[Dec. 28, 1889–Nov. 12, 1891]

Inscribed (WWhw) on flyleaf: "Woodrow Wilson Dec. 28, 1889," and on title page: "Woodrow Wilson PUBLIC LAW."

Contents:

(a) WWhw translations of the table of contents and short sections from Carl Gareis, *Allgemeines Staatsrecht.*

(b) WWhw translations of the table of contents and short passages from Johann K. Bluntschli, *Allgemeine Statslehre*, and a summary of and comment on Bluntschli's objections to constitutional interpretation by regular courts.

(c) Two WWhw and WWsh plans for lectures in public law at Princeton, 1890-91.

(d) WWhw diagrams of private and public law and their subdivisions.

(e) WWhw memoranda of courses proposed, 1892-96; WWhw record of courses, 1890-91.

(f) Two WWhw plans for a School of Law at Princeton, the second of which is printed in the Editorial Note, "Wilson's Plans for a School of Law at Princeton," Vol. 7.

(g) WWsh excerpt from a review of James Lorimer, *Studies, National and International*, in *The Juridical Review*, III (1891), 72; transcript printed in the Editorial Note, "Wilson's Plans for a School of Law at Princeton," Vol. 7.

(h) WWhw and WWsh bibliographical and other notes, some on loose sheets, mostly pertaining to public law.

Pocket diary (WP, DLC).

A Pocket Diary

[Dec. 28, 1889–c. Jan. 1, 1902]

Inscribed (WWhw) on flyleaf: "*Woodrow Wilson Aet. 33*"

Contents:

(a) Scattered brief WWhw entries; entries for Jan. 1, Feb. 13, and June 17, 1890, printed at these dates.

(b) Brief WWhw bibliographical and other notes for *A History of the American People*.

(c) WWhw addresses of friends, correspondents, firms, etc., many of which were entered after 1890.

Pocket diary (WP, DLC).

From Reuben Gold Thwaites

My dear Dr. Wilson: Madison, Wis., Dec. 30, 1889.

I have your very kind favor of the 25th December. I confess that I felt somewhat alarmed, after my first letter was sent to you, lest it might be considered unpardonable presumption upon my part, to ask you to write to persons whom you knew not, in behalf of our friend Turner.[1] Nothing but my great anxiety for him, shared by many here, would have prompted me into doing what some may have thought an indiscretion. But you have acted so generously in the matter, and with such tact and grace, that it is a great relief to me to find that I did not err in asking your assistance in our campaign. Your excellent notes to the powers that be, together with other pressure his friends will bring to bear, will, I think, materially help his cause. It would be a great pity, indeed, for the university not to promptly recognize this sterling young worker in American history, especially when there is abundant evidence that it was Professor Allen's heartfelt desire that such recognition should be awarded his gifted associate.

Your kindly "wish that we might have some means of knowing each other face to face" is most heartily reciprocated, I assure you. If the American Historical Association meetings were not held in the midwinter holiday time,—the period when I am up to my eyes in work, preparing for our own annual meeting, the first Thursday in January,—I would have more opportunity than I now enjoy, of meeting my fellow laborers in American history.

Most cordially yours, Reuben G. Thwaites

ALS (WP, DLC).

[1] Thwaites reciprocated by making Wilson a Corresponding Member of the State Historical Society of Wisconsin. See the certificate dated Jan. 2, 1890 (WP, DLC).

From Wilson's Pocket Diary

January, Wednesday 1. 1890.

Spent the day reading Jellinek (Gesetz u. Verordnung),[1] the evening writing letters.

[1] For Wilson's later use of Georg Jellinek, *Gesetz und Verordnung* (Freiburg im B., 1887), and the following memoranda and notes made while reading it, see the lecture notes printed at Feb. 3, 1890.

A Memorandum

[c. Jan. 1, 1890]

Our view compounded of Montesquieu (p. 67, 68) and Rousseau (pp. 69, 70) Contrast Locke (pp. 64-67) and note that the views of the latter only were founded upon fact.

WWhw on recto of loose sheet tucked into Georg Jellinek, *Gesetz und Verordnung*.

A Translation[1]

[c. Jan. 1, 1890]

If a law has as its immediate object to define the sphere of the free activity of personalities towards one another, if it is promulgated for purposes of social delimitation, it contains the ordering of a legal principle, is also, ∴, a law in the material sense, (otherwise, if it have any other object, not)

A material law must establish new right with binding force, i.e. create a right or duty for those subject to the laws not already contained in the existing legal order, or at least give force to existing law, clear up obscure right.

WWhw with one WWsh insertion on verso of loose sheet mentioned above.
[1] Of a portion of Jellinek's *Gesetz und Verordnung*, pp. 240-41.

Marginal Notes

Georg Jellinek, *Gesetz und Verordnung* (Freiburg im B., 1887).

Transcripts of WW Shorthand Comments
[c. Jan. 1, 1890]

P. 73:

Der Einfluss des contrat social auf die Principien der französischen Revolution zeigt sich fast in allen wichtigen Punkten. So auch in der ersten Formulirung des Gesetzesbegriffes durch die Constituante. In der Sitzung vom 17. August 1789 legte Mirabeau als Obmann des Fünfercomités zur Berathung der Erklärung der Menschenrechte einen Entwurf vor, der den Rousseau'schen Gesetzesbegriff seiner Begründung und seinem Inhalt nach adoptirt, indem ausgesprochen wird: "La loi étant l'expression de la volonté générale, doit être générale dans son objet.["] Der auf Antrag Talleyrand's acceptirte Text bringt denselben Gedanken zum Ausdruck, wenn auch in viel weniger präciser Form: "La loi est l'expression de la volonté générale. . . . Elle doit être la même pour tous, soit qu'elle protège, soit qu'elle punisse. Das Gesetz erscheint daher in der Geschichte der französischen Revolution zuerst in seiner Bedeutung als allgemeine Rechtsregel.

How far does this conception have any bearing upon the requirements of American constitutions that laws, at any rate certain laws, should be "uniform"?

P. 87:

So sehr aber die Constituante von abstrakten, dem Wesen des Staates wenig adäquaten Theorien geleitet war, so sehr sie das Wesen der Regierung verkannte, so lebte doch in ihr die Empfindung, dass ausschliesslich mit der blinden Vollziehung des Gesetzeswillens den tausendfältigen gegenseitigen Ansprüchen von Individuen und Staat nicht genügt werden könne. Sie fühlte dunkel, dass es neben der Executive noch etwas geben müsse, das an die Gesetze zwar gebunden, dennoch selbstthätig den wechselnden, aber stets vorhandenen Anforderungen des geistigen und wirthschaftlichen Gemeinlebens Genüge leistet. So kam sie denn zu den Begriffen der "administration générale" und der "administration intérieure," die sie allerdings zu definiren unterlässt. Dieses freithätige Element durfte aber nicht dem König und den von ihm abhängigen Organen zugesprochen werden—aus Misstrauen gegen die Regierung. Es sind vielmehr die Communalverbände und die von der Centralregierung unabhängigen Administrationen der Departements und ihrer Abtheilungen, welchen diese Verwaltungsfunktionen zustehen.

Powers of local authorities rather than real powers. Not unlike attempts in the United States to put the executive power into commission among local authorities.
See pages 89 and 90

Pp. 88-89:

Lebt somit in der "administration" das sich selbstständig entschliessende Moment der Regierungsthätigkeit, welches durch die Durchführung des abstrakten Begriffes des pouvoir exécutif fast gänzlich vernichtet war, wieder auf, so wird das Schwergewicht dieser Administration ausserhalb des Königs und seiner Minister verlegt und damit fällt das nun einmal unentbehrliche Recht inhaltlich freier Verordnungen intra legem in die mit der grössten Selbstständigkeit ausgestatteten niederen und höheren Communalverbände. Dadurch wird faktisch der Zusammenhang zwischen Königthum und Verwaltung zerschnitten. Dass damit zugleich ein Schnitt gegen die Staatseinheit geführt wurde, dass der bisher streng centralisirte Staat in eine Unzahl von locker zusammenhängenden Communen auseinanderfiel, dass damit die völlige Anarchie verfassungsmässig sanktionirt wurde, das haben die Wirkungen dieser Verfassungsexperimente gezeigt. Mit dem willenlosen Königthum hatte man einen willenlosen Staat geschaffen.

How far would this apply to our own system of local government? See page 90 second paragraph.

To Albert Bushnell Hart

My dear Prof. Hart, Middletown, Conn., 1 January, 1890

I am not a little appalled to learn that you and Mr. Thwaites will be ready for publication by the summer. My thoughts are fast taking shape upon my period, my material slowly, my statement of facts and conclusions most slowly of all. Indeed I can hardly say that I have begun to write at all, so little have I formulated. I dare not promise anything except that I will follow you as soon as a diligent use of meagre opportunities for consecutive writing and a careful regard for my health will permit. I have perfectly loyal purposes; but purposes and performances do not always tally.

I am sincerely gratified to know that my text-book in politics is proving of some service to you. It was an experiment, and must prove to be at all points improvable.

I am sorry that you should have reason to suppose that I was in Boston without calling upon you. I was there in the early part of September for about twenty-four hours in order to consult the publisher of my text-book on certain details of business which consumed much time; I was obliged to leave without longer stay; and I was sure that you were not at home. You may be sure that I will not neglect any opportunity to call upon you that really is an opportunity.

With sincere regard,

Yours very truly, Woodrow Wilson

TCL (RSB Coll., DLC).

From Bradford Paul Raymond

My dear Prof. Wilson: Middletown, Conn., Jan 2 1889 [1890]

Enclosed find receipt for quarter's rent. When do you close up your work in Political Economy with seniors? I suppose you leave for Baltimore a little before mid-year examinations, & I wish to get a little extra work out of the class, before that time.

Sincerely yours, B. P. Raymond.

ALS (WP, DLC). Enc.: receipt for $112.50, "for rent, Oct-Dec-1889," dated Jan. 2, 1890.

From M. Florence Taft

Dear Mr. Wilson: Middletown, Ct., Jan. 4th/89[90].

I thank you very much for your letter. Such words of appreciation are worth far more to me than the enclosed check, and give me renewed courage and inspiration for my daily work.

With kindest regards to Mrs. Wilson, believe me

Very sincerely yours M. Florence Taft

ALS (WP, DLC). Enc.: receipted bill for $37 dated Jan. 1, 1890.

To John Franklin Jameson

My dear Jameson, Middletown, Conn., 6 January, 1890

You may recollect that so long ago as Nov. 18, 1889, you wrote me an epistle in which was enclosed a check for fourteen dollars, payment in full for a valuable lecture on the functions of government, and in which were written certain moving lines touching the danger of my decamping from New England with "Der Mechanismus des Reichstags" and the "nigger question." Heaven forbid that I should surrepticiously bear either of these latter about me, and that I should forever neglect to acknowledge the receipt of the money (for the said check was immediately tested and 'availed of' by being turned into cash and enjoyed.) This is to certify that it was good and that the papers shall be returned, so help me Loisette!

See how I can jest in the very presence of the *Nation's* review of "Wilson's 'The State,' "[1]–and by way of reaction from a much more real and trying reality. Mrs. Wilson, the other day, being in the kitchen to instruct a green cook, accidentally spilled a mass of boiling lard on her feet and was terribly burned–not 'seriously' from the doctor's point of view, but so savagely as to have suffered a great deal, and to be still, after the lapse of a week, unable to walk. She is enough better now, however, to make us hope that she will soon be about again as usual.

What about Hart's dinner 'and sech'?[2] I hope he is not fixin' to have it while I am away in Baltimore.

I know nothing more about the Princeton matter. I don't know whether they mean to elect me or not.

As ever, Sincerely Yours, Woodrow Wilson

ALS (J. F. Jameson Papers, DLC).

[1] See the review printed at Dec. 26, 1889.

[2] Hart was apparently scheduled to serve as the host for a meeting of the historians of southern New England.

To Robert Bridges

My dear Bobby, Middletown, Conn., 6 January, 1890

I should have written long ago to thank you for the photograph, had it not been for a painful accident. A week ago Mrs. Wilson, being in the kitchen instructing a green cook, upset some boiling lard on her feet and was most painfully burned. Ever since the accident, of course, every minute of time I could spare from my tasks has been devoted to helping her in various ways. Now at last she is beginning to feel better.

The photograph is exceedingly good and was immensely welcome. It's a solid comfort to have it looking constantly out at me from inside my roll-top desk, at which all my work is done. It ought to keep a fellow strong to be thus always face to face during work hours with a friend like you.

'Vacation' is always my busiest time. The last two weeks have been devoted to preparation for my course of lectures in Baltimore, which come next month.

I am just now suffering rather acutely because of the *Nation's* stinging review of my text-book—'suffering' because the reviewer seems to me profoundly unjust. Convicting me of no error of importance except errors of inexpert statement, he yet throws suspicion on the whole book, and seems at the close to class me with those who "impose only on the vulgar." I try to comfort myself with the knowledge that the book is being gladly used (from Harvard down) as a text-book, and that I am privately assured of its excellence by most competent scholars; but the fine class of readers who take the *Nation* don't know these things, and to them I am misrepresented as a superficial pretender. It may quite conceivably affect very injuriously my chances at Princeton. I should be too proud to write these things to any one but you! I am now convinced that reviews ought to be signed.

I have for some time had a new photo. of myself ready to send you: under provocation from you I shall now send it. Oddly enough (Pach being photographer here) it was taken by the same man who took us at Princeton just ten years before, almost to the month.

Of course you have seen in the papers notices of the recent gifts to Wesleyan. They make certain the division of my chair here—if I stay, its division to suit myself as to subjects. Not only so, but, if I am to stay, I can almost certainly nominate my colleague: an eminently agreeable program.

I have examined with interest the prospectus of the *Magazine* for 1890 and of course my eye rested chiefly upon the 'Citizen's Rights.'[1] Is this series substituted for the one of local govt., etc. which you had in mind in the summer, or is the latter held in reserve? How would a series on the great Legislative Assemblies of the world do for another year? The German Reichstag, the Italian Parliament, the French Chamber, the English Commons, and our own Congress would supply not a little material for effective sketches of debate, of men, of affairs, and not a few uncommon illustrations, which would contain as much entertainment and instruction as a visit to the several bodies while in session would afford. No charge for the suggestion. Doubtless it will seem to you good enough for Harpers, but not good enough for Scribner's. It might, however, if prepared by men like McCarthy or Bryce, be made to convey much dignified and vivid education.

How goes the French class: how enticing, how elevating, is "l'esprit de M. Moliére"? Perhaps you get your enticement and elevation from the company, from the concomitants. You can get a fine training in the gallantry which is as important for your visit to France as the language. I wish we could start off some summer together. You could run the language racket while I absorbed the vacation.[2]

Have you had "la grippe"? The worst thing about the vile thing, it seems to me, is its name: it sounds for all the world like the name of some venereal disease: it is short and significant of hidden things, like 'clap.'

But I must stop this. Mrs. Wilson, who is quite well, except for her feet, joins me in sending warmest regards; and I am, as ever, Your affectionate friend, Woodrow Wilson

ALS (WC, NjP).

[1] Frederick W. Whitridge, "The Rights of the Citizen. I. As a Householder," *Scribner's Magazine*, VII (April 1890), 417-24; Francis Lynde Stetson, "The Rights of the Citizen. II. As a User of the Public Streets," *ibid.*, May 1890, pp. 625-31; Seth Low, "The Rights of the Citizen. III. As a User of Public Conveyances," *ibid.*, June 1890, pp. 771-74; E. L. Godkin, "The Rights of the Citizen. IV. To His Own Reputation," *ibid.*, VIII (July 1890), 58-67; James S. Norton, "The Rights of the Citizen. V. To His Own Property," *ibid.*, Sept. 1890, pp. 307-12.

[2] Wilson had spent the night of December 31, 1889, with Bridges in New York and was referring to subjects of their conversation on that occasion.

From Albert Bushnell Hart

My dear Prof. Wilson, Cambridge, Mass., Jan. 7, 1890.

Yours of January 1st is at hand. I hope you did not take my letter as a suggestion that you were in any way derelict or behind. The Longmans understand perfectly well that you are to have a sufficient time; and though of course they would like your volume at any time, they will wait patiently upon your convenience. I should think that you would find an Epoch a light performance after the vast labor put upon "The State." I find that book very suggestive and exceedingly useful. It is the scope of the book that makes it naturally a text book for the course in comparative constitutions.

Will you accept the article[1] which I send, containing some reflections upon American cities.

Sincerely yours, Albert Bushnell Hart

TLS (WP, DLC).

[1] Hart's "The Rise of American Cities," *Quarterly Journal of Economics,* IV (Jan. 1890), 129-57, sent under separate cover.

From Joseph Ruggles Wilson

My precious son— Clarksville, Jan. 13, 1890.

By way of Batesville in Arkansas, I have been grieved to learn that dear Ellie has met with an accident. If it were anything *very* serious, you would, no doubt, have written about it to me whom you probably continue to recollect with a degree of interest. I do hope, however, that she has by this date recovered, and is fairly upon her feet again. Meanwhile you must have had a bad time of it, nursing being added to your many public engagements. I therefore offer both to yourself and to her my heartfelt sympathies.

As to home (?) news, there is little or nothing to tell. Josie is still unprovided for. I have tried amongst all my "friends," with no result. As to myself there is only monotony, varied with occasional descents to the sub-cellars of heavy thoughts. Teaching has become a tax upon my nerves, especially as stupidity is the pupil. What a prospect has the Christian pulpit, with so many of the lame and the halt (mentally) for its main dependence in the near future! But then, in this profession, (as perhaps in some others) it is the small potato that is preferred by those whom it is appointed to serve. "God moves in a mysterious way His wonders to perform." Do not think that I am becoming more and more cynical: a patent fault of advancing age in instances not a few. Only I look upon the Church as a miracle of endurance, with such ministers of her mysteries as she is compelled to put up with, and almost always has been. What a wonder of vitality is hers, seeing that the utmost "foolishness of preaching" is forever feeding her with the husks and bran of truth! Surely if she had not a divine indweller, she must long ago have gone under. Perhaps, though, if her theological schools were truer to her hopes, her blood would not be so thin or her pulse so slow.

Has any thing new turned up in view of the Princeton professorship? When is it that you are again expected at the Johns Hopkins? I see that a considerable pecuniary donation has been made to Wesleyan—does this have any bearing upon *your* probable future?

It was my intention to send to you both some Christmas token —but nothing suitable presented itself in the meagre stores of this humble town—and besides during all that season my health was poor, and my thought was crippled. Josie and I talked and talked about it, but nothing came of it all save empty breath, as you have known.

I would throw this poor letter aside, and try to compose a better and brighter one were I in the least sure that I could. Anyhow my love is unabated—and my prayers for your welfare are as constant as the hours.

Present me in all affection to my dear Ellie.

Your affectionate Father.

ALS (WP, DLC) with WWhw notation on env.: "Ans. 1/19/90."

From Marion Wilson Kennedy

My very dear brother, Batesville [Ark.], Jan'y 13/90.

We were much distressed and concerned by the news of dear Ellie's accident. How exceedingly painful it must have been. . . .

Ross continues to be about the same,—better at some times than at others—, but on the whole there seems no material change. The doctor wants him to try to regain sufficient strength for traveling, and then wants him to go to San Antonio for the rest of the winter. I do not believe he will ever gain enough strength for that, but there is no telling. He has some fever every day, but not any very high. . . .

Dr. Allen was speaking in highly approving terms of an article of yours he saw copied into the "South Western Presbyterian."[1] I am going to get that from him. But I must stop for dinner. Ross joins me in much love to yourself, dear Ellie and the babies three. Jessie, the only one of our children who is not in school this session, says that I must give her love to "Uncle Woodrow and Aunt Ellie, and kiss those dear little girlies for her." Write when you can, to Your loving sister, Marion.

ALS (WP, DLC).

[1] She referred to a two-paragraph extract from "Character of Democracy in the United States" in the New Orleans *Southwestern Presbyterian*, Dec. 26, 1889.

Two News Items

[Jan. 18, 1890]

Prof. Wilson has announced as collateral reading in Senior History, parts of Bryce's "American Commonwealth."

◇

In the Political Economy class special reports have been made upon the following topics: "Exchange," . . . "The Counting House," . . . "Taxation," . . . "Socialism."

Printed in the Middletown, Conn., *Wesleyan Argus*, XXIII (Jan. 18, 1890), 73.

From Annie Wilson Howe

My dearest Brother, Columbia, S. C. Jan. 20th, 1890

We were all so grieved to hear of dear Ellie's painful accident. I am so glad all the sick are on the mend. Give my love to Ellie, and tell her she has my warmest sympathy.

I have not forgotten the letter you wrote, about the summer home in the mountains. I think it would be a delightful plan. I am not sure that you have selected the best place, however. Cashiers Valley [North Carolina] is so far away from the railroad, at least twenty-five miles, that Dr. George could never be with us at all. What do you think of Saluda [South Carolina]? A great many nice people are buying homes in, and around, Saluda. The climate is said to be "perfect," and building would be cheaper. It is on the railroad, which is a very important thing for *us*. I will write you all that I can find out about both places, in a few days.

Now I want to ask you about a matter that has worried me a good deal. Don't you think there ought to be a tombstone over dear Mother's grave? I spoke to Father about it once, and he said, "No, your Mother and I agreed perfectly as to that—we both disliked tombstones." I do not want anything showy, but think there certainly should be *something*. I have the money for the piano on hand and want Father to let me use a part of it for that purpose. Suppose you write to him, and speak of putting up a tombstone as a matter of course, and then I will write, and propose to use some of the money I mentioned. I am afraid if I write first he will say no. Not that he is unwilling to spend the money, but he thinks such things unnecessary. Let me hear from you soon, please. I know how busy you are.

With warmest love for you both from us *all*—and kisses for the dear children Your devoted sister Annie.
Remember me to Stockton.

ALS (WP, DLC).

From Frederick Jackson Turner

Dear Dr. Wilson: Madison Wis Jan 23, 1890.

I wrote to you early last term replying to your kind letter and to your request for material on the development of the "self-consciousness of the West." The student—a bright young man—whom I put at the work reports that for *1830-1850* there is not very much material, or evidence of importance, but he has not yet presented to the class his final report and for a couple of weeks he has been laid up by illness. As soon as I get his results I will send them to you, and will try to add to his work myself. I am surprised that he has not found more evidence of Western self consciousness than he did—but of that more later.

Mr Thwaites has informed me of your more than kind letters in regard to the succession to Prof Allen's chair. I know how to value such an endorsement. The matter has been very perplexing to me. I have sufficient respect for the learning and the personality of Prof. Allen to feel a decided modesty in urging any claims of mine to succeed him. The knowledge that this was his own wish, however, and that such men as yourself[,] Dr Adams, and Mr Thwaites, as well as other "lay" friends think me worthy of this place, is chiefly what permitted me to allow my name to be used. When I came to my present position last year I discovered that Pres Chamberlin, for some reason other than my work—for of this he could know almost nothing—was very reticent to make any tangible arrangement with me, until practically forced by Prof Allen's wishes and my decision that I would wait no longer. When Prof Allen died, he came to me after a week, to inquire who would make a good successor to him, and particularly what young men had distinguished themselves. I mentioned as the only men who would fully satisfy his requirements, yourself particularly, and Dr Emerton[1] of Harvard. He consulted me about a number of men of whom I had not before heard, and left me with the impression that he desired to select a new man for the head of the department, and that I was not on his list of candidates. But after his visit to Washington at the meeting of the Am. Hist. Association, he decided to recall Mr Spencer[2] to take the classes I had taken, and to give me Prof Allen's work for the year. In his conversations with me he has steadily avoided any distinct statement of his plans for next year. Matters are simply in *statu quo*. Mr. Spencers engagement is distinctly for one year. The board of regents at their January meeting have just ratified this situation of affairs.

Thus I am left to await the Spring market, and in the mean time to be tested I suppose. I am not entirely pleased with the arrangement, for Pres Chamberlin's actions will be entirely impossible of prediction, and in the mean time I am kept like Mohammed's coffin. Still I am trying to possess my soul in patience, spite of the fact that I begin to grow weary of having to keep one eye off my work in order to look out for my official head!

My work itself is pleasant. I am developing my course in Cons. and Political History of the United States along some new lines, and I am getting no little interest and hard work from my students, chiefly from original authorities.

If I were here next year I should try to find a place for your *The State*, with which I am much pleased. I am—(especially since I left the ranks of bachelors)—growing anxious for the income and dignities of the head of a department, but I am sincere in wishing that you might be here to teach this yourself, for I could gladly accept a place in your *comitatus*. I suppose, though, that you are to go to Princeton. I hope that you will go some where where you can follow the lines of work you wish to, for I believe you have a great service to perform for this country by impressing your ideal of Politics upon its young men.

Pardon this so long letter, and its, perhaps, uncalled-for confidences. Very truly yours Frederick J Turner

ALS (WP, DLC) with WWhw notation on env.: "Ans. 1/27/90."

[1] Ephraim Emerton, Professor of Ecclesiastical History at Harvard.

[2] David Ellsworth Spencer.

Two Letters from Robert Bridges

Dear Tommy: New York Jan 23 1890

I have been looking for that portrait which has not yet turned up. I hope it has not been lost.

We expect a great time at the dinner tonight[1]

Yours faithfully Robert Bridges

[1] The annual dinner of the Princeton Alumni Association of New York, held at the Café Savarin. The affair was devoted largely to honoring the championship football team of 1889.

Dear Tommy: New York Jan 24 1890

I have just a minute to write you a line.

The dinner was a great success, and brought me some news of significance to you.

1) Patton sought a few minutes with me, and assured me that he felt morally certain of your election at the Feb. meeting, and that he would so recommend. I judge that the "chaff" has been dispersed by a steady wind—no small part of it being an excellent letter which Ed. Sheldon wrote to a prominent trustee (and I think member of the [Curriculum] Committee) after a long consultation with me at the Club. Sheldon is a quiet, undemonstrative man, but he has proved himself a staunch friend to you and me. His letter was of the kind to do good in the highest quarters.

2). "In the strictest confidence" I was told by [T. N.] McCarter (who sat on my left) that he believed the Committee would undoubtedly recommend your election. I judge that Bob[1] has given the old gentleman some useful points.

3.) Prof. Sloane has just been here to see me. The following dialogue took place:

S. "I came in to see what you knew about Wilson's probable election?"

B. "So far as I can discover his election is reasonably assured."

S. "He *will* be elected—I feel confident of that. I hope Wilson does not think that there has been an unseemly delay?"

B. "I think Wilson believes that the election was postponed entirely for his best interests."

Sl. "I am heartily glad of that."

Now, Tommy, I am in the position of having assured Patton and others, time and again, that you really wanted the Princeton professorship, and would go there with delight. If developments at Wesleyan have changed your attitude, I think it would be wise to write Patton immediately. I hope that you have not changed your point-of-view.

If this letter is not clear, please ask me for information. I am in a great hurry. Your friend Robert Bridges

ALS (WP, DLC) with WWhw notation "Ans." on envs. of both letters.

[1] His son and Wilson's classmate, Robert Harris McCarter, '79.

To Robert Bridges

My dear Bobby, Middletown, Conn., 27 January, 1890

Your letter written after the dinner reached me after I had

sealed my note about the photo. and about spending the night of the 31st with you.

You are the most extraordinary proxy I ever heard of: you act and converse for me better than I can act and talk for myself. The contents of your letter has greatly reassured me. To have a friend like you—and, in this instance, like Ed. Sheldon—might almost tempt a fellow to do nothing for himself. I am honestly at a loss to understand how I ever won such esteem and friendship,—but I am none the less grateful on that account. What Patton said to you seems to me specially significant and conclusive, for, after what I said to him at the Astor House, he must have meant it to be conveyed direct to me. I told him that you were my other self plenipotentiary, and he must have known that anything said to you was virtually said to me.

You need not be uneasy on the score of your assurances that I would gladly accept an appointment at Princeton. That is still strictly true, notwithstanding the new opportunities here. Though this is in truth a delightful place to work, it is not a sufficiently *stimulating* place—largely because the class of students here is very inferior in point of preparatory culture—comes from a parentage, for the most part, of narrow circumstances and of correspondingly narrow thought. The New England men among them, besides, have an added New Eng. narrowness in political study. The only possible doubt, therefore, about my going to Princeton is connected with the question of salary. I shall have to buy a new equipment of books in changing my line of work, besides providing for other expenses now beginning to press, and unless they offer me a full professor's salary at once I shall be obliged to hesitate about moving just a[t] present. But I take it for granted that they will offer me the full $3500. There's no other element of doubt about my willingness to go.

Mrs. Wilson progresses slowly towards recovery from the effects of her accident, but is otherwise quite well. I shall leave a competent nurse with her.

I read about the dinner. What a capital speech Alexander made![1] Hoping to see you before the end of the week. As ever

Yours affectionately, Woodrow Wilson

ALS (WC, NjP).

[1] James Waddel Alexander, '60, president of the New York alumni group, introduced the team with a rousing speech. He said, for example, "One reason you won was because you deserved to win. You won by the honest, earnest application of right athletic principles. Another reason was that the ghost of Poe's [Edgar Allan Poe, '91, captain of the team] great uncle's raven was sitting on the bust of Patton. . . . And that raven still is sitting, still is sitting and must leave us nevermore." *New-York Tribune*, Jan. 24, 1890.

From Robert Bridges

New York, Jan 27 1890

I shall surely expect you Friday [January 31]. Tell me what time you will be at my room, so that I can meet you.

R Bridges

APS (WP, DLC).

To Robert Bridges

Dear Bobby, Middletown, 28 January, '90

Thank you for your postal. I shall expect to reach N. Y. at 3.30 P.M. on Friday, and can probably get to your room by 4. But don't put yourself out to meet me. Just tell 'Winterbottom' that I'm coming and I'll wait for you till you are ready to come up as usual

In haste Yours faithfully Woodrow Wilson

ALS (WC, NjP).

A News Item

[Feb. 1, 1890]

Prof. Woodrow Wilson left for Baltimore Friday [January 31] to deliver his annual course of lectures on the History of Constitutions.

Printed in the Middletown, Conn., *Wesleyan Argus*, XXIII (Feb. 1, 1890), 89.

EDITORIAL NOTE

WILSON'S LECTURES ON ADMINISTRATION AT THE JOHNS HOPKINS, 1890

Wilson's completion of his third series of lectures on administration at the Johns Hopkins in 1890 marked the end of one period in his scholarly career and also signaled the beginning of an even more important stage in his growth as a scholar and teacher.

The publication of "The Study of Administration" in 1887[1] had immediately established Wilson's reputation in the subject of his essay and, along with his other talents and achievements, had led President Gilman and Professor Adams to offer Wilson a three-year appointment as Lecturer on Administration at the Hopkins.

Wilson had attended Richard T. Ely's very short series of lectures on administration at the Hopkins in 1884-85,[2] and he had done some

[1] Printed at Nov. 1, 1886, Vol. 5.

[2] See the lecture notes described in Vol. 3, p. 345.

writing on the subject[3] before composing his famous article, "The Study of Administration." Even so, by the autumn of 1887 he had done little more than explore the field and adumbrate the subject in its most important political aspects from the American point of view. Wilson's main task during the next three years was to define administration as a field of study in light of his own historical and political perspectives. German political scientists—for example, Gneist and Bluntschli—had already begun to demarcate the boundaries of the field, and Wilson followed their guidelines to a large degree.

Wilson achieved his first definition in his lectures at the Hopkins in 1888 and 1889, and this definition he embodied *en passant* in *The State*. While he followed guidelines laid down by German authorities, and while his general work on European systems was largely synthetic, Wilson expanded what were then the frontiers of his discipline. Perhaps it would be more accurate to say that he redrew the boundaries of the field to include the hitherto uncharted terrain of administration in the United States.[4]

The result was a very considerable hodgepodge, not only because the discipline of administration was still quite inchoate, but also because Wilson was intent upon putting administration squarely and fully in the context of the entire field of government and of democratic government in particular. Not only this, but Wilson, like other writers at this time, thought that administration could best be defined after empirical investigation into the machinery and operation of government on various levels.[5] The best insight, he thought, for example, could be obtained by studying the making of budgets.[6] In brief, the study of administration, as Wilson first defined it, should include comparative studies of national and local governments and of the functions of government, in addition to technical problems of administration in cities, states, and nations.

Wilson himself realized and said in his lectures in 1890, not only that he had staked out too extensive boundaries, but also that the boundaries themselves were not properly descriptive of the field. He had hoped to derive the substance of the subject from the form, that is, from government in operation. But he did not find the substance for which he was searching until he read three great works on public law in preparation for his lectures at the Hopkins in 1890—Gareis's *Allgemeines Staatsrecht*, Jellinek's *Gesetz und Verordnung*, and Sarwey's *Allgemeines Verwaltungsrecht*. For the first time, it seems, Wil-

[3] See the Editorial Note, "Wilson's First Writings on Administration," Vol. 5, and Wilson's "Courtesy of the Senate," "Notes on Administration," and "The Art of Governing," all printed at Nov. 15, 1885, Vol. 5.

[4] Leonard D. White, *The Republican Era: 1869-1901, A Study in Administrative History* (New York, 1958), p. 46, has noted: "It was not until 1887 that Woodrow Wilson introduced the country to the idea of administration." Professor White of course did not know about Wilson's subsequent work in the field, as all his writings and notes, except "The Study of Administration," have been heretofore unpublished and ignored by Wilsonian scholars. Another American pioneer in the field, Frank Johnson Goodnow, did not publish his first major work, *Comparative Administrative Law*, until 1893.

[5] See, e.g., "Wilson Launches His Lectures on Administration at the Johns Hopkins," printed at Feb. 17, 1888, Vol. 5.

[6] See the lecture notes printed at Feb. 24 and 25, 1888, Vol. 5.

son came to see administration as being mainly a branch of public law. His definition of administration in his "Résumé," in the body of lecture notes printed at February 3, 1890, comes from these authorities and stands in sharp contrast to the one in *The State* and to the one suggested by his notes for lectures in 1888.

Wilson's second three-year cycle of lectures on administration at the Johns Hopkins, to be printed in the following volumes, will show how well Wilson succeeded in redefining the subject, and how he related it to his larger and growing interest in the field of public law.

In presenting the following notes for lectures on administration at The Johns Hopkins University in 1890, the Editors have followed their usual practice of reproducing documents in a text and form as close to the original as it is possible to achieve. Hence Wilson's abbreviations and misspellings have been reproduced without editorial emendation except when absolutely necessary for clarity.

Wilson of course did not write these notes for publication, and the Editors have had to resort to a few devices in order to put the lectures into printed form. Wilson wrote his footnotes on the versos of his pages and identified them by his own symbols. Since these symbols are in any event very difficult to reproduce typographically, Wilson's notes have been numbered consecutively, along with editorial notes, and printed at the bottom of the page. It was also unfeasible to reproduce exactly the diagram of the structure of local government in Prussia that appears in Part II of the "Résumé." Thirdly, the Editors have eliminated unnecessary dashes and in a few cases have silently changed Wilson's square brackets to parentheses in order to avoid confusion between Wilson's brackets and the Editors'. Finally, the Editors have omitted the following typed addition at the end of Part X, "Central Control: Administrative Integration," which Wilson added in 1893 or later:

Three Points emphasised in these lectures:—

(1) That the City has a characteristic life of its own; but that its functions are, nevertheless, chiefly, if not exclusively, administrative in character;
(2) The Integration of that government;
(3) The integration also of the State government & the exercise of a central *administrative* control, to get rid of our present pernicious system of *legislative* interference.

The reader should bear in mind that Wilson used the following sixteen parts for about twenty-five lectures, and that each part does not necessarily constitute the material for a single lecture.

Notes for Lectures on Administration

[Feb. 3–March 10, 1890]

Introduction

I began this course on Administration two years ago with the promise that it should advance *"from form to meaning"*—from a description of the existing organs and machinery of Administration to a discussion of its standing problems, its general tests of efficiency, its essential principles.

Although I have pursued the plan thus indicated with some diligence, however, I *still*, at the beginning of the third year of the course, find myself *in the region of description*. There is much to discuss, but there is more to describe. Discussion must, moreover, be to a large extent mingled with description: they are without significance when divorced.

I have found myself, besides, driven to a certain amount of *repetition*. The class to which this course is delivered not being the same class from year to year, but largely changing in its membership, it is impossible,—it would be a mere affectation,—to assume each year a familiarity with the topics of the year preceding. I have always, therefore, to begin, as I am now about to begin, with a somewhat explicit *resumé* of the portions of the course already delivered.

Resumé

I. In order to an adequate view of the subject matter of Administration, a consideration, chiefly historical, of
The Functions of Government
The substance of this now in print—need not be resumed.

II. By way of general groundwork,
The Nature, Field, and Method of Study
By *nature*, a subject in *Public Law*, of wh. this *analysis* may be made:

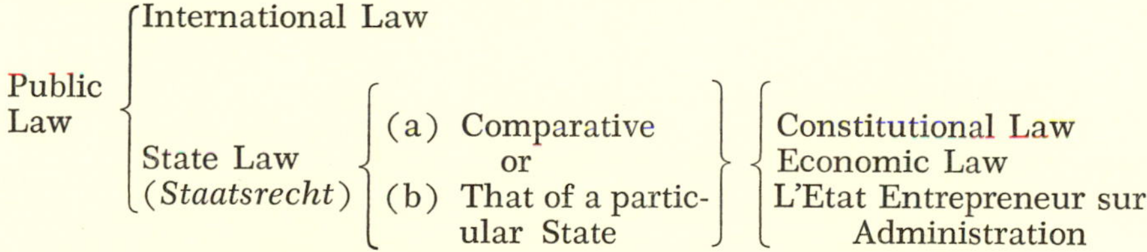

(Gareis, K. *Allgemeines Staatsrecht*, [Heinrich] Marquardsen, [*Handbuch des Oeffentlichen Rechts*] I, pp. 8-10, § 1, 2.)

Administration is *itself a source of Law* (Ordinance) i.e. of the *detail* of law.

Distinction bet. *Legislation*—Independence of will; and *Administration*—Subordination of will.

(Sarwey, O. von, "Allgemeines Verwaltungsrecht," Marquardsen, II, ii, p. 5 *et seq.*)

Its field, that of *organization*, of *effective means*

Should answer the qu. *'What is feasible?'*

Besides, there is an organization that vitalizes and an organization that kills.

Its qus. run in each State along the line which divides Interference (State function) from *Laissez faire. A study of adjustments*—of adjustment to historical conditions, to liberty

Stands near, ∴, to the most vital and pressing qus, both social and political, of the present day.

Its method, of course, *comparative*.
Here arises most prominently the qu. of *nationality*. It should be national *in aim*

III. By way of preliminary chart
General Questions and Principles based upon the *distinction* between *Central Government and Local Government*
This distinction modern:
(a) Greece and Rome
(b) Middle Ages
(c) Modern Times (α) France, as type
(β) England.
(γ) U. S.
Govt. reintegrated.
What division of functions shall be made?
As against
Advantages of central regulation, viz
Certainty, Uniformity, Despatch, Efficiency, set the
Disadvantages: *Too great* uniformity, too absolute despatch, too inexorable certainty and efficiency.
Principles suggested:
(1) *Law* central, uniform,
Ordinance local, adapted.
(2) Knowledge (system?) central (Mill);
Power local
(3) System good, life better
Liberty exists *only when there is life.*

II

Resumé (cont'd)

IV. Somewhat detailed description of *Central* and *Local* Government in France, *Prussia*, *England*, *Switzerland*, *U. S.*, and the *German Empire* (central govt. only)
This now, most of it, in print, and need not, ∴, be resumed.
General Features:
1. Among central govts of the unitary type (France, Prussia, England)[.] Chiefly *differences of legislative responsibility only* discernible. General family likeness in ministerial structure.
Differences also of *administrative oversight* and *financial audit.* (See 'The State,' chap. XII).
2. Among federal States differences of importance in the matter (α) of *central legislative action* and (β) *execution of laws*
(a) *Germany* having virtually complete legislative powers but acting in execution of the greater part of imperial law thr. State officials.
(b.) *The U. S. and Switzerland*, executing their own laws thr. federal officials, but having a narrower legislative competence: that of the U. S. being more strictly limited than that of Switzerland.

3. *In Local Govt.* the differences are *diffs. of centralization*, the types being
   (a) *France* (Prefect and appointed Council) representing centralization.
   (b) *Prussia*, representing indirect, distant local oversight and administration. (See diagram)

The People	Cities (of less than 25 thousand inhabitants) acting thr. councils or (*if in groups*) through electors Unions of landowners Rural Communes in groups through electors
Elect Circle Diet	Nominates *Landrath* and Reeve (*Amtsvorsteher*) Elects Prov. *Landtag* (in conjunction with *other* Diets) *and* Circle Committee (whole)
[Prov. *Landtag*]	Elects *Landeshauptmann and* Prov. Committee
[Prov. Committee]	Elects *Provinzialrath* (5 out of 7) *and* District Committee (4 out of 6).

   (c) England representing legal control with some oversight (Local Govt. Board, loans, etc.)
   (d) U. S. commonwealth govts. Legal control with practically no oversight–control by statute

Place of Municipal Government in Administration

Municipal govt. evidently *a division of Local Govt,*–but there are municipalities and municipalities.

Worth while noting a wide significance given to the words '*Municipal Law*' ("That which pertains solely to the citizens and inhabitants of a state, and is thus distinguished from political law [?], commercial law, and the law of nations.

"It is now, however, more usually applied to the customary laws that obtain in any particular city or province, and which have no authority in neighboring places"–Law Lexicon of J. J. S. Wharton)[1] –National as opposed to International.

A '*Municipality*,' what? (An incorporated body exercising public functions)

Grades of municipalities:

Townships–Counties–Villages–Boroughs–Cities–(The State Itself).

Manifestly *no common footing* for these–no common qus. of organization. *They differ*, not only in degree but *in kind* also.

The contrast as old as Teutonic history: *The Rural Commune* with its free (or vassal) landowning membership and its *solely economic* interests and functions strongly contrasts with the *mediaeval City* with its *all-inclusive interests* and functions ([J. C.] *Bluntschli:* [*Allgemeines*] *Staatsrecht*, Book VIII, Ch. I.)

[1] *Law Lexicon, or Dictionary of Jurisprudence* (Philadelphia, 1860), p. 507. [Eds.' note]

The *only qus. which press* concern the *modern Industrial City.*

(a) *The ancient city* was not industrial, in our sense of the word, but *political.*

(b) *The mediaeval city* had an organization of its own wh. *we could not reproduce.*

(c) *The modern industrial city* is of recent and sudden growth—has an unanalyzed character, an undetermined function, an undiscovered organization.

Rise of the Modern Industrial City:

Has arisen

Bost. Phila Balto London

(a) *By superimposition* of the modern industrial feature upon cities already *politically* made, or made (at least located) by nature.

(b) *By R. R. or canal creation.* This method seen chiefly in *America*

(c) By the attraction of localities possessing extraordinary nat. resources for manufacturing industry

To be noted, that this growth of old and rise of new cities has been not only

Rapid and therefore without equable and adequate adjustment, but also

Artificial in a great degree, not by forces natural either physically or politically.

The Industrial City *has outstripped*, in its growth, the hitherto *possible speed of political development.*

III.

Make-up and Interests of the Modern Industrial City.

A. *The City Elements:*

I. Analysis:

(1) *The Commercial Element*, composed generally of *alert* citizens, *not* necessarily brought under wide and *complex organization*, but both retail and wholesale, *various, informed*, wishing to see the City grow, *jealous of hindrance* or restriction.

(2) *The Manufacturing Element*, representing *Capital* for the most part *immobile*, and liable in large parts to loss from *mistakes* as to a market composed, not of the City, but of the world. For this capital *the city* is *a mere local habitation.* There is *no necessary identification* between business and city save that of *convenience* in commanding labor, transportation, &c.

The Entrepreneur class controlling, *with* an almost unlimited *dominance over the economic status* of the laboring factory class. *The laboring class itself*, living at city disadvantages, having to live *under conditions wh. constantly threaten health and independence*, but over which they have no control because of the collective, inevitable city pressure. ("*The manufacturing cities*, even the smaller ones, are *more closely peopled* than those whose greater interest is commerce"—Hart, p. 136.[2] *This because* commerce does not necessitate the same massing of a laboring population comparatively poor?)

II. Analysis: (concerning chiefly America)

(1) *Natives* in the Cities

(a) Natives of the Cities themselves

(b) " " " country to which the cities belong. The *interests* of both of these elements of the population will probably be *harmonious* with a normal *political* development: they will know what they want and in what way to get it.[3]

(2) *Foreigners* (a) by birth, (b) by descent.[4]

This element, if in the city from the first, will *tend* to make the city *unlike the rest of the country* socially and politically.

Geographical Distribution of Cities: what parts of the country most affected?

New England[5]—the *middle States*—the great *lake region*. This is, however, *being modified* by industrial development. *Washington*, with its population of *political, leisured, literary*, and *scientific classes* attracted by no industrial causes, *quite anomalous*.

B. *The City Duties:*

It cannot

(a) *Regulate economic or political relations* of classes. That function belongs to *the State*.

(b) It cannot *encourage*, by general legislative policy, *manufactures* or *commerce*. That also *the State's*.

It must undertake

(1) *Discipline*—police.

(2) *Sanitation*, including *parks, housing* of the poor (?) or of the working classes.

(3) *Education, including Art, Music, Museums* and the like. *Technical education*?

(4) *Facilitation of its characteristic life*. Includes *paving, lighting, locomotion, preparing of districts for occupation*, &c.

(5) *Guardianship* of *destitute and helpless* classes, ruined by the pressure of city disadvantages.

[2] Albert Bushnell Hart, "The Rise of American Cities," *Quarterly Journal of Economics*, IV (Jan. 1890). [Eds.' note]

[3] Although *Boston* has 34% of her population foreign born, she *retains her old-time individuality* as few of our cities retain theirs[.] Prof. *Hart* declares that her public spirit is due to the fact that she has *old, attached, influential families* identified with her interests. A more *personal*, self-conscious city than others [WW's note]

[4] *Foreign-born*. Cities of U. S., wh. contain 1/4 of the pop., had 1/2 the foreign born (27% of their pop. in medium cities) *Boston* 34%, *N. Y.* 40%, some *factory towns* 48%, *Holyoke and Fall River* 50%, *Chicago* over 50%. Hart, pp. 149, 150. [WW's note]

[5] *New England* possesses 1/12 of the *total population* of the country, 1/4 *of the cities*, 1/7 *of the city population*.—Hart, p. 145. [WW's note]

How Does Influence of the several Classes tell upon the performance of these Duties?

The leading classes will *insist* upon (1) *Police*, but will *not* be inclined to *insist* upon thoroughness in *Sanitation* of parts of the city they do not occupy, *or* upon *Education* which they can provide for themselves; and will be *apt* to make their *wealth tell corruptly* upon (4), especially if (4) be left to *private enterprise.*

A power but not a co-operative power.

The selfish interests of the wealthy city classes *cannot be relied* on to promote the delicate and difficult tasks wh. come from the masses of men *economically dependent.* The *only wholesome power* is the *general interest.*

As regards these people, the efforts of the wealthy classes too apt to avoid part in any philanthropy

How Get and Hold the Attention of all classes of Citizens?

Easily enough *get* it by a long course of *outrageous corruption. Expensive method.*

Hold it only by

(1) *Important, independent*, wide-reaching, conspicuous *functions.* A body politic and generally an imperative duty.

(2) *Organization open*, simple in principle, *accessible, respected; how* to *get this* to be our problem. (I do not pretend to have a pill for the earthquakes.)

What, then, is the Modern Industrial City?

I. *An economic corporation*, in which the chief stock-holders ought to control expenditure? *Or*

II. *A political society*, a delegate plenipotentiary of the State's in all local matters?

Temptation to regard it as both.[6]

It is neither: but *a humane economic society.*

Bluntschli's answer: *A personality.* Therefore a moral person

The corporation idea barren.

[6] "The *department of public works*," says Sterne, "except so much of the activity of that department as may be connected with the care of docks, water fronts and the removal of encroachments from the public highways, is *mainly occupied* with this general coöperative work *for the real-estate owners* in the city" Lalor, I, p. 464. [Simon Sterne, "Administration of American Cities," John J. Lalor (ed.), *Cyclopaedia of Political Science* (3 vols., Chicago, 1881-84)]. "The mayor, when he signs an ordinance for the grading and regulating of the street *between certain avenues*, involving the payment by the owners of property on such street of assessments covering the expense thereof, is *a mere instrument* to make and enforce a contract between property owners for mutual convenience as to such regulation of a street, which by reason of diversity of interests and the perversity of some exceptionally ill-conditioned human beings, it is *inexpedient to leave* entirely *in the hands of individual property owners.*" Id., pp. 463-4. "And *thus with paving, sewering*, and other matters *strictly pertaining to the management of real estate*, as contradistinguished from governmental functions." Id. p. 464.

If there be no reason for these functions but the failure of individuals to agree, what principle of law or justice warrants the making of the contract by an outside instrument. [WW's note]

IV.

Organs of the Industrial City
The Ordinance-making Body.

Analogy usually observed, both in theory and in practice, *between City and State* in organization *most conspicuous* and practically important *in the U. S.*–and yet *least justified there*, and perhaps *most mischievous*.

Return to *former point*: minute *legislative regulation* of local govt. *coupled with* exclusively *local executive action.* The *City*, with us, a thoroughly subordinated *organ of the State*

And yet–and here *lies the difference*, and the excuse for confusion–it is *an organ whose chief duties concern*, not the State, but *itself*.

Reason for the Analogy partly historical, partly theoretical:

(1) *Historical*: city organization *was*, in ancient and mediaeval times, State organization.

(2) *Theoretical*: the long argument (historically enforced and illustrated) about *the division of powers*, wh. has given us the whole idea of the necessity–*throughout govt.*–of *checks and balances*,–of the *separation of origination and execution.* All *our thinking* about executive action and law-making has been *of a piece*.

The Common Council

How far a *law-making* body?

In dealing with its two classes (commercial, industrial) *what can it do*? Keep order, preserve health, educate, facilitate in life and locomotion, care for in distress.

This is not law-making, but administration.

The Common Council is, not a law-making, but *an ordinance-making body–and an ordinance-making body is an administrative body.*

An ordinance lies closer to fact, to practical conditions and detail, *than* does *a law*. Its *test* must be *feasilibity*, administrative experiment[.] *It would follow* that the *Council must be*, not separated from, but *closely associated with, administration Such, under most systems, is the arrangement.*

E.G. *In Germany* (Prussia): Councilmen, Aldermen, Select Citizens, and the *joint committee system.*

In France the municipal council is not a legislature but an administrative council *associated with the mayor.*

In England, mayor, aldermen, and councillors *one body*, in no respect differentiated either in function or in responsibility, and acting thr. *standing committees*[7] (Comp[are]. [Albert] Shaw [*Political Science Quarterly*, IV], June '89, pp. 215-218)

What, then, *becomes of the bi-cameral system* and *all the doctrine* therefrom dependent?[8]

[7] *Standing Committees* are not open to the objection of irresponsibility *when known* as authoritative *and made executive of their own policy*. [WW's note]

[8] In *St. Louis* there was a singular *oscillation* bet. a *one-chambered* and a *two-chambered constitution* for the City Council, ending with the adoption of

It *becomes ridiculous*. Are you to have *checks and balances in administration*, instead of efficiency and clear indubitable responsibility? *Even if you do*, is a body fitted for detecting mistakes or jobs or haste or defects because it is elected from *larger districts simply* or from the city at large?

The single body sh. originate and apply measures. The business is administration.

See what we do, on the contrary: We have

A mayor to nominate and control all administrative machinery

We make this mayor *member of several* executive *boards*.[9]

A Finance Board to spend (approve) the money

A Council (often *checked within* by the bi-cameral system and checked *without* by the mayor's veto) *to ordain* the administration of which it knows nothing, and vote the moneys wh. it is not suffered to apportion (i.e. specifically appropriate).

Finally, sometimes a *State-made* and controlled *police force*.

All this to secure efficiency and responsibility!

These qus. being regarded as settled, we ask next:

What the *system and principle of representation* is to be.

Is the basis to be *Taxes*[10]*—groups of interests*[11]*—localities—individuals*?

Objections to ward representation: there is *no* ground for *real differences of character or interest*: and there is sure to arise *the pest of residence* wh. we owe to forgotten Gov. Phipp.

Chief *advantages* (a) *Simplification of ticket*, and (b) *minority representation*[12]

General ticket emphasizes the whole membership and gives unity.

A City is not a group of localities, nor an aggregation of interests, nor an improving (public-works) corporation, *but an organism*, whole and *vital only when whole and conscious* of its wholeness and identity.

---

the bi-cameral in *conscious assimilation to* the structure of a *state legislature*. Noteworthy that *no foreign* city has a *bi-cameral council*.

Although the analogy of the state const. has controlled the *development* of the city organs, *their origin* was not in all cases so determined. *In Boston and New Haven*, e.g., the Council was consciously substituted for *Town* Meeting. The *township organs* are, however, manifestly *not at all adapted* to the needs of *the industrial city* where skilled *govt.*, not universal *consultation*, is necessary. [WW's note]

9 Prof. Marshall *Snow praises* the city *charter of St. Louis* because "the important offices filled by the Mayor's appointment *are not vacant until the beginning of the third year of his* (four-year) *term of office*, so that as rewards of political work done during a heated campaign they are too far in the dim distance," &c! (Fifth Series, 173) [Marshall S. Snow, *The City Government of Saint Louis*, Johns Hopkins University Studies in Historical and Political Science, 5th Series (Baltimore, 1887)]. [WW's note]

10 *Prussian* and apparently *favored by Bluntschli* [WW's note]

11 *Mediaeval* (guild) system. [WW's note]

12 But *under our system* of unemphasized responsibility, the *minority can only kick or trade*—and *trading* is *more effective* than kicking. [WW's note]

V.

Organs of the Industrial City
The Executive.

The Mayor:
Eccentric history of 'The Executive' in the U. S.

1. *Same theory throughout*, and same *misinterpretation of English experience*, derived fr. *Montesquieu.*
   Influence of our experience with *colonial governors* who represented an *outside power.*
   Influence of *constitution-making–formulation* of institutions, compelling *logical distinctions* and a *scheme of thought.*
2. *Variety* in *practical development*
   The President represents the rigid and courageous application of the theory. He is a real separate Executive, as much coördinated as possible.
   The State Governor has none but a clerical separateness and independence, except as regards his veto power. Executive power dispersed among local authorities.
   The Mayor is approximated to the President.
   Noteworthy that we do not assign a similar organization to *any other local area* e.g., not to *county* or to *township.* This points to recognition of the *complete individuality of the City*, as complete as the State's, possessed, indeed, of a more State-like organization.

A. *The Foreign Mayor.*

1. The *French* Mayor, separate, not as independent and himself constituting the Executive, but as an *instrument of* the supreme *central Authority.* As such has extraordinary powers. May be *suspended* (Prefect, Min. of Int.), *over-ridden* (do. do.), *removed* (President).
2. The *Prussian* Mayor yoked with the Aldermen, being president of the Board of Mayor and Aldermen merely. The *Magistracy collegiate*, and *it* makes all appointments.
   This magistracy an *instrument of the central govt.* in finance, police, and military affs.[13]
3. The *English* Mayor, not even president of a separate executive board, but *presiding* officer of the *board of Aldermen and Councillors, plus* Justice of the Peace. The administration more unified than in either of the other countries mentioned–*all* executive–*all* ordinance-making.

B. *Our own Mayor*: a creation, developed, indeed, but *developed fr. theory.* An effort to reproduce the English Executive,–a *shadow king.*
   Historical development:[14]

[13] Still *further fusion* (negation of separateness) of (α) Magistracy with Council, and of (β) Magistracy and Council with burgesses by the system of *Joint Committees.* [WW's note]

[14] "The government of the City of New York is a growth and not a creation. In the early charters of the City the Mayor was the chief executive officer, having the control of the police, and was himself a Police Magistrate holding

[1.] Beginnings *in Boston*: (α) *Proposals* of a committee of citizens (1822) (β) *Charter* of 1822, substantially in accord with these propositions: Mayor and 8 aldermen—upper branch of Council and having about the *powers of former Board of Selectmen*; & Common Council of 48, possessing "all the *powers* formerly exercised by the inhabitants in *town-meeting*." (Bugbee, p. 25).[15]

2. *In New Haven* at first: Mayor chosen by freemen to hold at pleasure of Legislature (till 1826)—only 4 mayors 1784-1826, 2 dying in office—*assisted in judicial functions* by 4 Aldermen, 2 sitting with him. *Associated with* Aldermen and Councillors in Court of the Common Council.[16]

3. *In Philadelphia* Mayor, elected by Aldermen fr. their own number, sat with Aldermen, Recorder, and councilmen as the city Council (but in order to make an ordinance valid it was necessary that the aff. vote sh. include Mayor or Recorder, a majority of the Aldermen, and a majority of the councilmen.)

4. *In St. Louis*, no charter till 1822, ∴ comparatively recent organization. Still "administration vested in a Mayor and Board of Aldermen (not unlike Prussia.) *No 'second chamber'* ("Board of Delegates") till 1839.

Subsequent changes: e.g. *in New Haven*: 1826 democratic revolution, mayor elected for one year by ballot. 1842 deprived of judicial functions, being replaced by a Recorder.

In Philadelphia "elected first by the Aldermen from their own number, then by councils from the Aldermen, next by councils from the body of the freeholders, and in 1839 by the people from the people."

Everywhere in U. S., the mayor separate, president-like, making appointments, checked by Council, and in his turn checking it. *Coördinated with him* various independently elected officers and commissions.

Tendencies of Present-day Reform in our Industrial Cities well-known. They are to magnify the office of mayor, to make of the mayor a dictator.

---

daily court. The Common Council was a *legislative body*, acting as a check upon the Mayor, in the matter of appointment, and *framing* such *ordinances* as the good govt. of the city might require. The municipality was *always subject to the control of the Legislature*," &c.—A. S. Hewitt, Message, Jan'y 17, 1888. *Illustrates the usual reasoning.* [WW's note]

[15] James M. Bugbee, *The City Government of Boston*, Johns Hopkins University Studies in Historical and Political Science, 5th Series (Baltimore, 1887). [Eds.' note]

[16] Note the survival of the Town and many of its functions inside New Haven. The Town Agent administers Poor Relief.

1. *Executive Board* of 7 persons to be called "*Selectmen*"—amended (in Meeting) "*Aldermen*."
2. One chief executive chosen by Selectmen and called "*Intendant*"—amended "*Mayor*."
3. "A body with mixed legislative and executive powers" called "*Board of Assistants*"—amended "*Common Council*." [WW's note]

Noteworthy that *in no other country* in the world, (Germania or other) is the mayor thus made boss *without being connected with* and subordinated to *the Central Govt.*

Based upon *a radically false theory*—false in two aspects

(1) Concentration of the public gaze and, ∴, of administrative responsibility. In this there is a double danger (*a*) Public inattentive to the ordinary course of administration and spasmodic arousal to occasional official misbehavior, and (b) a complete upheaval of administration, by official removal &c., upon a change of mayors.

(2) No mayor can cover the whole field of administration in a modern industrial city. It can be well done only when the detail of it is of daily interest (and daily or at any rate frequent) obviousness to a large body of the people. General, continuous interest, a sense of solidarity, pride, the organization, not of an army, but of a coöperative society with expert guidance, what is needed.

VI.

Organs of the Industrial City
The Executive (continued).

Departments and Commissions.

Case of Philadelphia aptly illustrates the growth of such instrumentalities:

4 Phases

(1) *Mediaeval Close Corporation*, with judicial and governing powers, but without taxing power.

(2) Close corporation *supplemented by Commissions* (e.g. Street Commission, City Wardens [police], etc.) erected by the Legislature and authorized to tax.

(3) After the more modern governmental conditions had been established, *govt. by boards*, under the *direction of Council Committees*, after a brief trial of appointment by the Mayor.

(4) *In 1887* much executive work put under the charge of *single officers app. by the Mayor*, with the advice and consent of Select Councils, *or* elected by the people: in short, govt. by Standing Committee abolished.

Usual Commissions: e.g.

Board of Public Improvements Board of Police Commissioners Board of Fire Commissioners Board of Assessors Board of Commissioners of Finance.	May be elected by Council or by people. In either case responsibility is made indirect.

In either case the *result* is *disintegration*

Abolition of Boards and appointment of single officers by the Mayor is *no remedy*, because

(1) There is *still disintegration*, intercommunication, investigation, instead of consultation, coöperation.

(2) *The Mayor cannot possibly control* and oversee all Depts. A Dept. is none the less separate and none the less organized for a special service because presided over by a single 'responsible' head. *The Depts. need an integration* wh. they do not receive from the authority of the mayor.

Depts. overlap: e.g. Police and Health; Health and Streets; Streets and Public Works; Fire and Police; Fire and Inspection of Buildings

Judicial functions may be separately, independently erected, *but not administrative Depts.* E.g. The office of Comptroller, and the office of City Treasurer may fairly be called judicial, rather than admin., offices—the former especially. There is advantage in giving these a footing of independence.

The Idea of checks and balances wholly out of place in administration. Its most extreme application, and its most absurd, found in the so-called *non-partisan Boards*, in wh. the political parties are recognized by equal representation. This introduces a balance into the bosom of the Board, with well-known and appreciated results.

Minute legislative prescription as to composition and detailed duties of Boards, as to salaries, as to funds, as to every point of action, *carries the disintegration still further.*

It leads also to the most unfortunate policy of *legislative interference*. "The employees of the City are encouraged and have repeatedly gone to the Legislature to procure the enactment of laws compelling the City to raise their salaries" (Hewitt, Jan'y 10, '88.)

Unless the work and plans of all Depts. meet in the Council itself, and unless that be recognized and compelled to act as an administrative body, it is as if *horizontal lines* were *drawn across* the *administration* of the City.[17]

The evil sought to be remedied is, incompetence or dishonesty on part of Council. *The remedy* is depriving the Council of all real power and multiplying the chances of *incompetency* (*a*) in the Council, wh., after all, is the source of vitality, (*b*) among the separated Depts. wh. depend either upon statute or upon ordinance of Council for their functions and means.

Proper point of view gotten only when the government of a city is regarded as *a whole*—not a thing administrative, a thing legislative, a thing judicial, but *a single administrative whole*—of which the *Council* ought to be *the central administrative body*. The problem is not to create checks and balances but *communal feeling and energy*. Not delegation and machinery, but *duty*.

[17] *Same qus. involved* here that were discussed when speaking of the relations of the administration as a whole to the ministers as a body, of the French *Council of Ministers*, the Prussian *Staatsministerium*, &c. [WW's note]

Singular how successful the govt. of any city having self-conscious identity (personality) and solidarity is, no matter what the *form* of govt.

E.g. The Nashville Experiment: a governing board of three commissioners holding for five (5) years at a first-class salary, and known as the *Board of Government and Public Works* (or something equivalent), overshadowing Council and Mayor, possessing most of the patronage, etc.

Result admirable, because public opinion was awake and the composition of the Board Excellent.

Nevertheless the *principle* was *radically wrong*—the results might have been exceedingly bad. *Keeping an eye on officials is not self-govt.* and watch-keeping affords the least efficient incentives to keeping awake *when nothing is going on.*

Berlin Joint Committees (Describe general structure of Berlin govt.) Types—

(1) *Poor Relief*: Overseen by commission composed of an Alderman as chairman, 8 other Ald. (among them 1 legal adviser, the Treasurer, 1 school commissioner), 17 Councillors, 10 select citizens; staff of clerks and servants. Poor Commission in each ward (*total* of *1,594* citizens—fr. 4-12 in a ward) presided over by citizen chairman, who must be in his office, etc.

(2) *Income taxes*, both state and city, assessed by committees of citizens sitting under official presidency (total of *3,396 citizens*)
At top of the system a *Citizen Court of Revision* under the presidency of a state commissioner.

(3) *Citizens assist* to *draw up jury lists*
serve in *summary trials*
" " trials of *mercantile cases*
act as *permanent arbitrators* in the wards.

(4) *Elementary Education*: Central Board with large no. of citizens, and ward attendance committees (*Total, 1,258*).[18]
Result: more than 10,000 of the wealthier middle class take part in govt. of the city.

Proposal of the Balto. commission (Repub., Dem., Prohibitionist) to put *citizen committees* at head of several depts., e.g. *Fire Dept.*[19]

VII.

Organs of the Industrial City
The Executive (continued)

Police: *Comprises* all those authorities and public servants whose duty it is to defend the *lives, health, and freedom* of all within

[18] *Results: education expenses increased* fr. 9¾ to 19¾ *per cent.* of municipal expenditures—*but poor relief expenses decreased* fr. 18 to 14½ *per cent.* [WW's note]

[19] See also Hewitt's message of Jan'y 17, '88, p. 27. [WW's note]

the community against danger, and to further their *bodily, economic, and spiritual welfare, by limiting* (if necessary, by the use of force) the *freedom of action of individuals* in every respect in which it interferes with or threatens these common interests. (See O. v. Sarwey, §17, p. 64)[20]

This of course *suggests a wide range of duties.* More important still, it emphasizes, when examined, *the solidarity of the community.*

Police Duties

(1) *For the State,* the police must act as the agents of the State in the enforcement of criminal law–and here they stand related to the States-attorney.[21]

(2) *For the City–*

(a) Suppression of *disorder* and (city ordinances).

(b) Arrests for breach of *ordinances against vice.* In these things they act for the city attorney and the city courts.

(c) Prevention of *obstruction of the streets,* in the interests of the Street Cleaning Dept.

(d) Abatement of *nuisances,* in aid of the Health Dept.

(e) Enforcement of *license laws* in behalf of the Excise Dept. *The police* are manifestly, thus, *agents,* directly or indirectly *of almost every branch* of the city government. *No Dept. less suited* than the police, ∴, *to be separately administered;* none better illustrates the needed integration of administration which can be effected only at *a common council-board.*

Dependence of the Police

(1) *On other Depts.* E.g. if Health Board will not push prosecution for nuisances, or the Street Cleaning Dept. prosecutions for obstruction.

(2) *On the Courts.* Here the experience of *New York* instructive and conclusive. (See Mayor *Hewitt's Message* of Jan'y 17, 1888 p. 7 *et seq*)

The *General judicial dependence of a City* and its special disadvantages if its judges be locally elective

Police Discipline. Here *military methods* and *concentration of authority* are quite indispensable. Here again emerges the *absurdity of 'non-partisan' boards* of police commissioners,[22] and the probable *advantage of* steadying police administration to be anticipated from *common council.*

[20] *Distinguished by Sarwey from judicial authorities,* i.e. "those whose official duty is the maintenance and execution of criminal law, the execution of private law through judicial decision, and the precautionary regulation of the interests of individuals in their opposing legal relations." *Our use of the term* includes the ministerial side of this judicial function: e.g. arrests for crime, etc. [O. von Sarwey, *Allgemeines Verwaltungsrecht,* in H. Marquardsen, *Handbuch des Oeffentlichen Rechts,* II.] [WW's note]

[21] For the service and enforcement of *civil process,* the state courts generally have their own *bailiffs.* [WW's note]

[22] Read Hewitt, Message Jan'y 17, '88, p. 15. [WW's note]

Public Works: The question of public works evidently *central to the subject of city govt.* It looks back to the qu., What is the character of the City? The character of public works (their object) and the extent to which the city may undertake them depends upon the degree in which the City partakes of the character & shares the functions of the State—*the degree in which it possesses the character of a body politic.* (The idea of an economic corporation—Sterne—is barren of any extensive sanction of public works).

Classification of undertakings:

(1) *Grading*, *paving*, (and *widening*) of *streets.* An analogy in this to *the road-making functions* of rural authorities. To be noted that there is in the latter case an appearance of mere coöperation to facilitate the use of real estate (compulsory road service).

(2) *Supplying of light and water.* Evidently this is a public function, even *when entrusted to private companies*: for the grant of the privilege to these companies is in reality (and also in form) *a contract*, by which the companies are bound *to the performance of a function of general convenience or necessity.*

(3) *Sanitation*—one of the most imperative functions for making city life possible.

(4) *Trade facilities* (e.g. docks and a cleared water front.) Although it is universally acknowledged, it is difficult to make this function fit any theory of mere private function. It is, moreover, *a function shared with the State* (Board of Trade in Eng., Internal improvements in U. S.—etc.).

(5) *Transit. Not fully recognized in this country*, but evidently of a piece with many that are recognized. *Analogous*, e.g., *with (4).* The life of the city cannot go on without it, and it will be supplied by private companies only where it will yield a profit. *A close analogy* furnished by *the postal service* of the general govt., wh. is conducted at a loss in the South and West.[23]

(6) *Extension (annexation). Even less recognized* than (5), but, like (5) *pressing itself forward* for recognition, and equally entitled to it. Extension cannot be left to haphazard private action—for it must include the poor as well as the rich.

This enumeration evidently *includes the bulk of city functions*; and emphasize *the administrative character* of city govt, taken as a whole.

Note that *these functions have*, however, *come but slowly*, by a growth of experience (yet, perhaps, to bear its fruit of political theory) *within the province of public*, communal *function.*

[23] This matter of transit connects itself with the *right of eminent domain,* wh. cannot be permanently parted with, nor parted with wholly even temporarily. [WW's note]

Old Idea of Self-help, as illustrated by the mediaeval city *trainbands, hautboys*, private *street lamps*, &c.—the absence of police, communal sanitation, etc. *The city* was then *a place rather than a person*—a locality of trades organized for some common purposes—but not a body politic. *A charter of liberties vs. a constitution of duties.*

The scope of public works is, when properly conceived as wide as *the scope of the communal life.*

Limitations imposed from without (particularly as to cost) i.e. *by the State*, as the creator and superior of the municipality, to be discussed later. Suffice it to say here that *the principle* of interference *must be admitted*, but that *the ideal* (could the municipality be but stirred to an active conscience and a vital sense of duty) would be *perfect freedom* of discretion.

VIII

Finances of the Modern Industrial City

The City Budget, a mirror of the city functions (See Mayor Hewitt's Message of Jan'y 10, 1888, pp. 17 *et seq.*)

State control: "The State taxes, the interest on the City debt, the amount to be raised for the payment of principal, *the salaries* of the Police, of the Fire Department, and of the Board of Education, and to a very considerable extent of the other Departments of the public service, *are fixed by statute.* Many of the expenditures for *new improvements are mandatory* upon the City; so that out of the total amount of $37,051,053.93, only $14,689,117.16 is subject to revision by the Board of Estimate and Apportionment." (Message, p. 30).

Note the *N. Y. Assessment Bonds* (pp. 31 *et seq* of Message) as illustrative of the results of *the idea* that street and other improvements, when 'local' within the city, are but a part *of real-estate administration.*

For *analysis of the character of the N. Y. city debt*, see—this same message, Appendix, p. 44 *et seq.*

Limitation of the right of *taxation by statute*[24] + *prescription of expenses by state* means administration of the city; not by the executive authorities of the State, but by the Legislature, *administration by statute—negation of* the (useful and even indispensable) *distinction* between *law* and *ordinance.* Points towards a *radical defect in State government.*

Under such an arrangement, *how can responsibility be fixed*, and how can that *local interest* be *aroused and kept* upon wh. health of the municipality and its efficiency depend? *Interest comes only with a sense of control.*

This state of affairs due, in part, to the fact that *the city is in many*

[24] In Eng. law *all local-govt. corporations* possessed inherently and *by common law the right of taxation* for local purposes. *Our written-const. evolution* has confined us to the thought of *granted powers only* and has thus *deprived local govts.* of their *common-law powers.* (See Hannis Taylor [*The Origin and Growth of the English Constitution*], I, pp. 41-43). [WW's note]

things, and is properly, a mere agent of the State. E.G., in judicial action the city is *merely a local area of State administration.*

In that case *payment for judges' salaries* and most other judicial expenses *sh. come from the State Treasury.* In nothing is *integration* more necessary than in the administration of justice, and integration there is hardly possible without *centralization.*

Possible exception (as regards salaries &c.) in case of *Police* and other *city courts.*

Who shall control taxation and expenditure in the City?

A New York Commission appointed in *1876* proposed for N.Y. City a *Board of Finance* to be elected by "payers of upward of $250 *rent* a year, or owners of $500 of *property* on which taxes were "paid" to have a *veto on proposed expenditure*, and a *confirming power* of the appointment of *Corporation Counsal* and *Comptroller.*

How far is the principle proposed in this suggestion *valid?* Only so far as the theory of coöperative real-estate administration is admitted as the basis of municipal function.

In a rural community in wh. improvements are of hardly more than private use and importance such a theory (and such a Board) might have *some colour of justification.* But *with the wide social function* of the industrial *city*, wh. must act in so many things involving the very heaviest expenditures, not for property owners, but *for the working* and (economically) dependent *classes*, it would be *impossible to justify* principle or practice. *Selfish interests are not cooperative.*

Who, then, ought to control?

Again

It is a qu

(*a*) *of objects* of expenditure; this ought to be determined by Common Council

(b) *of administrative efficiency*—requiring the cooperation of Depts. *General policy* of expenditure sh. be determined *by the* (representative) *general voice*, saddled with full choice and, ∴, full responsibility. *Estimate and apportionment* by *coöperative action of executive Depts*, acting, not as given final power, but *as committees of* Common *Council.*

IX.

The Modern Industrial City
Reorganization

What Shall Be the Principles of Reorganization in City Government?

(1) The *Administration* should be *One Body*, at any rate *in* all *Counsel and Origination.*

Administration and executive action are not one and the same thing. *Administration* is a thing of plans: *execution* is the carrying out of plans. *Those who* actually *carry out plans* ought to act with *individual freedom* and *individual responsibility*, but they ought to execute plans made in counsel, in *common* counsel, so far as all greater features are concerned.

There may be a separate executive board, but it should not be separate in major actions.

(2) *A minority of experienced* or *trained officials* in the governing board. The *Eng.* system of *Aldermen* elected by the Council, but given a longer tenure, would serve as a good model, if it could be *prescribed* that this minority shall have *technical experience or training. Where–how–get that?*

(3) *Only one act of election* on the part of the voter, that, namely, of the *members of the Council.* Let Aldermen, mayor,–all others proceed forth from the Council, directly or indirectly. *'Civil Service' rules* could of course be prescribed and enforced.

A single act of election of itself *simplifies and points responsibility.* A multiplicity of acts of election means obscured responsibility and fatigued interest, flagging attention.

(4) *A widening* and *concentration of city functions. City charities,* e.g., should be taken from private sphere of voluntary organization and endeavour and *made* the *imperative legal duty* of the *Whole.* This as much a public function as Education. Private charities need not be prohibited: they would be absorbed and destroyed by competition.

But this would *not* be wise *without*

(5) *The enforcement of* wide *compulsory citizen duties* in *poor relief, tax assessment, mercantile arbitration, orphan apprenticeship, education,* &c., by a *system of committees,* both *local and central. Self-government must not remain a mere privilege, but must become a duty.* On no other terms can we attain the object set before us, viz. to get and hold the attention of the community for the tasks of govt.

(6) *Central Control: Administrative Integration.* On this a *separate lecture.*

(7) *Separation of judicial from city organization–except,* perhaps, *police courts,* trying breaches of city ordinances, etc.

X

Central Control: Administrative Integration

The Theory of central control of municipal corporations is *fully recognized in our law.* The "charter" of an American city is no longer *a charter* in any proper sense of the word. It is *no longer a grant of privileges* wh. is *of the nature of a contract.* An American city is the creature of the Legislature, to be made, altered, unmade at pleasure.

The Central Control we have adopted, i.e., is *legislative* control, and we have adopted it without limitation or reservation.

The Objections to such control are obvious:

(1) It represents, *not control,* systematic, pliable, selective, discretionary, *but* simply *outside interference,* occasional, arbitrary,

haphazard, and yet minute and, in result rigid—for it must be statutory—specifically formulated and final.

(2) *No one is responsible for it*—not only because the legislature is numerous and the origin of measures hard to trace, their passage hard to follow, but—even more—*because there is no plan of interference*, but one city at a time is tinkered with—and *a single city cannot resist or fix responsibility* through the franchise, even were it of a mind to do so.

Illustration: the *police* of *Boston and Baltimore*, appointment of commissioners by the Governor. There is here *no system of central control*, like that of a *Minister of the Interior* or a *Home Office*, but only a hand of interference thrust into the affairs of *a particular city*,—appointment, merely, not control.

There is *something* (much) *to be said for a uniform police system* controlled from the centre, organic integration of police administration coupled with public responsibility for a well understood and complete function;[25] but *nothing for* these *isolated acts of interference*

The Several Foreign Systems of central control:

In most, if not in all, foreign countries *system* is *displacing charters*—system by means of wh. municipal govt. is being made part, simply, of general schemes of local govt.—and local govt. linked into a centred net-work: a net-work of nerves centring in the central brain, the central govt.

In France: Mayor + one or more assistants: the mayor chief, however, not head of a board, his assistants being, not colleagues, but subordinates[.] *Direct responsibility*, as we have seen, *to Prefect, Minister of Int.*, and *President*

Police appointed by the mayor, but his appointments need the confirmation of the Prefect; in *communes having over 40,000 inhabitants*, ratification by decree.

In Prussia. Election of mayors of the larger cities subject to *confirmation by the Crown* (usually matter of course). In *finance*, *police*, and *military* administration—as we have seen—there is direct control from Berlin. *Towns* have *a double character*: they are at one and the same time representative of the authorities at the capital and of the citizens at home—and they have *a corresponding double responsibility.*

In England the centring of govt., the system, appears in the superintending functions of the Home Office and the Local Govt. Board.

The Home Office superintends the *constabulary*, oversees, to a limited extent, the *local magistracy* and the administration of the *prisons*, and is the instrument of Parl. in carrying out certain statutes restricting in some respects the *employment of labour.*

The Local Govt. Board is, in effect, the Eng. *Dept. of the Interior.* It is charged with the admin. by local authorities "of the laws relating to the public *health*, the relief of the *poor*, and

[25] And this we shall find in foreign systems. [WW's note]

local govt."—duties more important to the daily good govt. of the country than those of any other Dept.

(1) *Police* oversight of the *Home Office*. The uniform, semi-military discipline and organization maintained, aids from the Treasury, &c.

(2) *Financial and sanitary oversight* of the *Local Govt. Board*:

(α) *Financial*: "In each instance, when *a loan* is required by a municipal corporation, the controlling authority (the Local Govt. Board) is to be applied to for its *consent. A local inquiry*, after due notice, is then held, and if the loan is approved, *a term of years* over which the *repayment* is to extend is fixed by the central authority" (Bunce)[26]

(β) *Sanitary*: Power of compelling proper action of local sanitary officers. There is also *centralization of knowledge* in the appointment of a central commissioner with certain powers of oversight.

The Board of Trade, also, controls *harbours, lighthouses*, etc.

Judicial Control: "The English 'Municipal Corporations Act' of 1882 provides that *an order of a borough-council for the payment of money* may be taken to the *High Court of Justice* by writ of *certiorari*, and may there be wholly or partly *disallowed or confirmed*, with or without costs, as pleases the court." *Levermore*—in connexion with the fact that, under the *first charter of New Haven*, 1784, "*any by-law* of the city might be *repealed* within six months after enactment *by any Superior Court* holden in New Haven County, if the said Superior Court judged the by-law to be *unreasonable* or *unjust*" (p. 12, and note).[27]

Reasons for a local government board with more or less extensive and imperative powers.

The State must be accorded the right to see to it that i[t]s local organs are

(a) *Healthy*.

(b) *Observe certain accepted lines of* (e.g. financial) *policy*.

Here arises the qu. *How far may City Councils properly and safely be left to independent origination*? Just as far as city problems are *local and peculiar. The peculiar and self-centred character of city life must never be lost sight of for a moment.* Very great independence of action and *a very absolute dependence on its own* social, political, and pecuniary *resources* indispensable to health and vigor in the complex and perplexed Industrial City.

No reorganization in the direction of central control possible for us *until we re-make our State govts*. The radical administrative weakness of these: *Characteristics*—

A general scheme of law, but *no organic integration*—and a

[26] J. Thackeray Bunce, "Municipal Boroughs and Urban Districts," in J. W. Probyn (ed.), *Local Government and Taxation* (London, 1882). [Eds.' note]

[27] Charles H. Levermore, *The Town and City Government of New Haven*, Johns Hopkins Studies in Historical and Political Science, 4th Series (Baltimore, 1886). [Eds.' note]

scheme of law is necessarily inflexible. Control by general enactment, e.g. % of taxation % of indebtedness.

Through legislation (general or special) and the courts, our State govts. touch their local systems of course, at every point. But *thr. administration* they touch them *scarcely at all.*

State *boards of equalization* and State general *superintendence of education types* of almost the only sort of administration our States undertake.

Our state officers are, so to say, local officers acting at the capital in superintendence of the central conduct of the central machinery of the common govt. *The administration of the laws outside the capital* is controlled entirely by local officials, locally elected, and whose *responsibility* is only *to* their *constituents*, not to any central authorities.

City Govt., ∴, *when viewed in its broadest aspects, as a whole, widens into qus. of State reorganization and general administrative re-integration.*

Law and Ordinance

I.

Development of Theory

Introduction: (*References to Jellinek*)[28]

General Significance of the Discussion

(1) It *creates Administration* a separate science inasmuch as it differentiates its sphere from that of legislation and in doing so *must argue* directly *its character.*

(2) The *basis of constitutional government*, whose most marked characteristic is that it (a) analyzes sovereignty, (b) apportions function, (c) fixes responsibility.[29]

Significance of the Development of Theory: Theory here, as elsewhere within the sphere of conduct, is a mirror, a reflexion, and *a conclusion from practice.* Furnishes, ∴, *a basis for the history of Administration* as a possible, separable science. *Theory an abstract anatomy of institutions.* This will appear.

Ancient theories: These can be inteligently comprehended only after an examination of *the Ancient State.* W. C.[30]

(1) *The Greek State*: A unit, representing the highest possible degree of integration: *but observant of* specific and clearly defined and regulated *forms* of action,—and *in this contrasted with the Roman State* (post.) Take *Athens, for example.* The

28 Georg Jellinek, *Gesetz und Verordnung* (Freiburg, 1887). [Eds.' note]

29 *The Prince Consort* reported to have said on one occasion that *"representative institutions are on trial."* It would be truer to say that they are necessarily *awaiting the more perfect development of the distinction* between the spheres of law-making and of administration. *General law* must in any case rest upon general consent, tacit or explicit; and it will be most vital when it proceeds from the general judgment. *Administration,* however, can never have such an origin; and the only vital ground of objection to popular govt. lies on the side of administrative interference. *The interference of the popular authority* in administration can never be anything but *maladroit.* [WW's note]

30 Wilson's abbreviation for "wherein consider." [Eds.' note]

central body in the govt. of Athens was a *sovereign Council* (The Council of Four (Five) Hundred)[.] In the earlier days entrusted with the decision of all but the very weightiest matters without consulting the Popular Assembly. In later times keeping the *initiative* in all things and retaining administrative control of *finance*, the *navy*, and the *army*. It *prepared all the business of the Popular Assembly* in the form of provisional resolutions (προβουλεύματα). With reference to all matters save legislation proper, *the procedure* was: προβούλευμα (amendatory *motions* permissible) ψήφισμα.

Legislation: Procedure: (προβούλευμα?) (*a*) in 1st. pop. Ass. of the year, *the qu. put*: Shall motions be allowed looking towards the extension or alteration of existing laws? If 'yes,' such motions must be carefully made public. (b) Third Ass. of the year arranged for the constitution of *a legislative committee*, known as *Nomothetae*. (c) All motions considered and dealt with by this committee, special counsel being appointed to defend the existing laws. (No. of the Committee probably about one thousand.)[31]

(2) *The Roman State*: The same unity and (ideal) integration, but *much less symmetry* and logical analysis *of method*. No special procedure imperative for legislation. *Any law passed by the people* (whether the *comitia tributa* or the *concilia plebis* tributa) *upon the initiative of a magistrate* was a a [*sic*] formal law, *whether its purpose was* the alteration or extension of existing *law* or merely some *administrative adjustment* or *judicial determination*.

The *formal sanction* of the *Senate* was at first necessary *before* a magistrate could submit a law (or bill) to the people; *and for long* the *subsequent assent* of the Senate *to all measures* passed; but finally the *practical outcome* was the *self-sufficiency* of the *plebiscita*.

The Theorists and the Theories: This *superior logical analysis of the governmental actions* of the ruling body in Athens, as well as, of course, the more penetrative philosophical power of the Greek mind, *gave to Greece*, what was withheld from Rome in *the theory of law*.

Aristotle.–Recognized law as *a universal abstract rule* enacted by the highest power in the State. But he saw that such general laws cannot possibly provide for all individual cases,–that *good* government must provide *suitable exceptional adjustments*. And this distinction he found *recognized* in the *actual constitutional arrangements* of Athens–in the difference between the νόμος, enacted "by the cooperation of the Council, the Assembly, and the *Nomothetae*," and the ψήφισμα, a mere popular resolution. (Jellinek, pp. 38, 39).[32]

[31] The[re] were *strictly prescribed forms*, too, *for all other business*, such as the examination and discipline of *magistrates, judicial determinations, ostracism*, etc., etc. [WW's note]

[32] *This distinction* was *not concealed from Aristotle*, or even obscured for him, *because both* the νόμος and the ψήφισμα proceeded *from* the sovereign will of *one and the same Body*, namely, the Assembly: the *distinction of functions* was *quite clear*, though the need for a *corresponding distinction of organs* seemed

The Roman Jurists, having no object-lesson of concrete constitutional provision before them, and making no thorough analysis of law, entertained *a wholly formal conception* of law. In their usage *lex* and *jus* practically synonymous. *Law=general rule issuing from the law-making body or person.* In other words, *its formal element its distinguishing element.* Of course *in the imperial period* lex, senatus consultum, magisterial edict were made practically indistinguishable. *Unsuitability* of law to particular cases to be *cured by law*, though even Roman logic admitted that a *jus singulare* was not law in the proper sense of the word.

Cicero[33] *derived from the Greeks* his perception of the fact that generality was essential to law in its true and strict sense and that not all Roman State acts were laws; *but this was borrowed* thought and *had no important influence* upon the *practices* or the *conceptions* of Roman jurisprudence.

Theories of the Middle Ages: Same principle of examination must be adopted here: *What was the constitution of govt.* in the Middle Ages, the formal origin of law, etc? While the characteristic constitutional arrangements of the *Feudal System show us Estates* associated with princes in law-making, *the "great historical fact"* of the Middle Ages is "the more and more concentrated *power of the Prince.*" It is not long before the Prince becomes law-giver.

The qu. of mediaeval theory, ∴, is, "Whether and *how far he who possesses the power of the State* is or may be *bound by the laws*" (57)[34] Is the Prince the *sole source of law*, and himself placed above the laws, *or* is he, while *singulis major, universis minor, possessing a power* from the beginning *limited* by "fundamental agreement" between him and his people?[35]

Bodin[36] answers this qu. partly in accordance with the *theory of Aristotle*, partly in accordance with *the fact of his time*: Law is an "*inflexibilis norma*"; it of necessity *proceeds from the sovereign power* of the State; but *a particular determination* of the Sovereign is *not a law*, because not general, *nor a judgment*, unless it inhere in law, *but a decree.* (44). It is only in the power of the Magistrate, the ruler, that law lives. *"The power of law resides in him who has the power of command"* (i.e. in the Prince.)

---

to him *neither a logical nor a practical necessity.* (More of the qu. how far it is a necessity hereafter). [WW's note]

33 "*De legibus.*" [WW's note]

34 All such page numbers in parentheses refer to Jellinek, cited above. [Eds.' note]

35 It is evident that *this qu. is central* and fundamental *to the determination of the distinction* bet. Law and Ordinance. *In Athens* there was no distinction possible except *a distinction of procedure.* In the Middle Ages, however, the Prince arose as the great, dominating organ of the State. Was he its only organ, its sovereign self? *Here the qu. is, Who is subordinate to law* (the Athenian Assembly was subordinate to law—to law enacted by itself + several organs of its own constitution—in the making of ψηφισματα)[.] *Ordinance is legal regulation made in subordination to law. Determine who* among the Representatives of the State *are subordinate* to the law and yet have the right to issue binding commands, *and you have determined the ordinance-making authority.* [WW's note]

36 "*De republica*" [WW's note]

Emergence of the modern constitutional state—each stage marked by theory. *Concrete phenomena* of the development *in England. "In England,* where since the 15th century the distinction between statute and ordinance or proclamation has received clear recognition and the boundaries of both have been the subject of scientific political inquiry, there *was constructed,* in the course of the 17th century, *the first general theory of the Ordinance Right."* (62). The *great debate concerning* the royal *Prerogative* between *Filmer* on the one side and *Sidney* and *Locke* on the other was nothing else than a contest touching *the fundamental distinction* between *law and ordinance*

Filmer[37] maintained, on the one hand, that *law* was, in its last analysis *nothing other than the will of the king.* A command of the king's, even though in contravention of a statute, must receive the obedience of the subject. *The king* is, in this view, of course *not bound by the law,* can suspend, annul, override it; is superior to this law *because the source of it.*

Sidney[38] maintained, on the other hand, both *on historical grounds* and *on grounds of reason,* that the *law-making power* rested with *the people alone,* acting thr. their Parl.; that the ordinances of the king could have no authority to set aside law or to create it. "They are to be considered only so far as they are conformable to the law, from which they derive all the strength that is in them, and can confer none upon it." *When the king transgresses the law he is no more king*; and his extra-legal commands are not binding upon the subject. In brief, his commands can never have the force of law. (63, 64).

Locke[39] ("His doctrine of the character and range of the Ordinance Right is undoubtedly the most important that the constitutional theory in general has produced"—Jellinek, 64.) He *distinguished 3 powers* in govt.: viz. (a) the *law-making* power (2) the *executive* power (3) the *'federative'* or treaty-making power. The (1) should be exercised by a separate organ from that wh. is entrusted with the others; the (2) and (3) though logically and even essentially distinguishable, may be and should be lodged in the same hands. Now, of course *in authority the (1) is sovereign,* supreme, *the others subordinate*; and yet, in an important sense, the authority of him (or those) who exercise (2) and (3) is the dominant authority of the State. (3) *cannot,* except in a very general way and to a very limited extent, *be circumscribed by law*: it is determinable only by international circumstance and by considerations touching the national welfare. Within (2) the *Executive must be vouchsafed the freedom of Prerogative,* wh. must include the power of supplementing as well as of shaping the law to

[37] "*Patriarcha*" [*or the Natural Power of Kings* by Sir Robert Filmer (1680)] [WW's note]

[38] "Discourses on Government" (1683) [WW's note]

[39] "Essays on Civil Government" "Two Treatises on Government" [WW's note]

fit cases, "*adjuvare, corrigere, supplere Acts of Parliament.*"[40] The *history of Prerogative* has been a history of abrieviation, *curtailment.* Whereas govt. was *at first*, so to say, *all Prerogative*, it is *now* almost *all Law.* But *never*, under any really efficient govt., *can Prerogative be abolished.* It is *the field of administrative discretion*—and administrative discretion is indispensable to good govt. Locke sought to secure the independence of the Executive by what is, in effect *the American principle*, viz. that the possessors of *executive* power are "*subject to the authority, not of the law-making body, but of the Law.*" (65).

Montesquieu,[41] it is noteworthy, made *a radical departure from* the constitutional doctrine of *Locke*, substituting for generalizations extracted directly from Eng. history and existing institutional circumstance *a formal theory* not corresponding to the facts of constitutional history. *Locke*, tho'. he recognized a certain notable independence on the part of the Executive, *accepted*, nevertheless, the logic and fact of *its subordination to the law-making power; Montesquieu*, on the other hand, *maintains the equality of the several powers*, gives them equal weight and rank, and *conceives the idea of a balance*, each power restraining the others from excess or error. *And yet* the independence of the Executive *consists simply* in its *exterior separation* from the Legislature. For the rest, it is the instrument of the Legislature. *The Prerogative consists*, in his view only only [*sic*] in the relations of the monarch to the Houses, in his summoning, proroguing, dissolving, vetoing privileges —*not* in any amending, fitting, or extension of Law. (67, 68)

Rousseau[42] *denied all independence to the executive* power. He deemed it *the mere tool of the Law*, supplying the act wh. was to answer to its Will. It was merely to effectuate the laws, and *could have no independent sphere* of determination, no choice of courses, of its own. He even *imagined the suspension*, the virtual abolution *of the executive power* upon the assembling of the sovereign people—its suspension so long as that assembly sh. sit. He *denied the possibility of a division of powers* upon the ground of the essential unity of Sovereignty. *And yet* Rousseau was *the first to lay a distinct theoretical foundation for the distinction between law and ordinance*, between legislation and administration. The People is sovereign; law is the common will, and it must have a general object, establishing an abstract rule, not making an application of it to any special or individual case. *An individual determination is not a law*,

[40] "Since in some governments *the law-making power is not always in being*, and is usually *too numerous* and *too slow* for the *dispatch* requisite to execution; and because also it is *impossible to foresee*, and so by laws to provide for, all accidents and necessities that may concern the publick, to make such laws as will do no harm, if they are executed with an inflexible rigor on all occasions and upon all persons that may come in their way; *therefore* there is *a latitude left to the executive* power, to do many things of choice which the laws do not prescribe." (on Civil Govt. § 160.) [WW's note]

[41] "*L'Esprit des Lois*" [WW's note]

[42] "Contrat Social." [WW's note]

even though it be made by the sovereign People. And in each such special act the People is bound by general law, is playing the part of an official[.] *The Executive is an element of the indivisible sovereign power*, with distinguishable functions, but no independent standing. There is *no theoretical necessity for the separation of the executive and legislative functions*—and they are not separable in authority. But there is the sharpest possible *essential contrast between the law* as such (*loi*) *and the administrative application of it* (*décret*).

Conclusion: It has been *impossible to get beyond Aristotle except by the aid of the constitutional theory* derived from Eng. constitutional experience.[43] (51-54, 69, 70)

Law and Ordinance

II.

Practical Development of the Distinction in English Constitutional History.

I. *The Several Stages of Development.*

(1) *Dating from the Conquest* and continuing throughout the period during wh. parliamentary control was first asserted. During this time *all law=ordinance*, whether issued upon the sole authority of the king, with the concurrence of the permanent council, or with the assent of the Great Council. The *assent of the Estates* to the Norman legislation was doubtless in most cases *little more than a form*, though the tendency was to give to the laws which had rec'd such solemn, formal sanction the distinguishing name of *Assizes*.[44] Note that *even Magna Carta* was, in form, a mere *royal ordinance*.

(2) *Period of petition based upon* the right of controlling *taxation*. (*a*) *Parl. organization* effected *temp. Edward I* gave to the representatives of the several orders *control of taxation*, although not until the end of that reign can this right be regarded as established. (*b*) *This power* of controlling the supplies *used to give* imperative *force to petitions*. *Procedure*: petitions, with replies thereto, put upon the parl. rolls—and from these parl. rolls a derivative roll of statutes made up. (advice of the judges, etc). *Abuses*: unsatisfactory answers given—statutes not in conformity with petitions and replies promulgated, or statutes withheld.

[43] This *will become evident by means of* a careful examination (1) of *English history* on these points and (2) of *French revolutionary experience* in trying to arrive at a quite incompatible result. [WW's note]

[44] "*From the time of the Conquest down to the establishment of the estate system* in the reign of Edward I., all *the great acts of government*, whether administrative, legislative, judicial, political, or fiscal *enamated from the person of the king*, acting through his inner council, composed of the great officers of state and the household; or from (?) that larger body known as the *Great Council*, composed of those tenants-in-chief who won for themselves the right to be personally summoned, and in whom that right became hereditary." Hannis Taylor, I, 492. [WW's note]

This *a transitional period*, the greater number of *statutes* being (*throughout the 14th cen'ty*) enacted *in answer to petitions*, but important *laws being also made without suggestion from*, or participation by, *Parl. "The initiative determined* whether a jurisdiction hitherto unregulated should be regulated by statute or by ordinance" (Gneist, quoted 22)

(3) *Period of parliamentary initiative* in legislation. *By reign of Edward II.* it had become the established rule that all legislation, to be valid, must receive the assent of the commonalty of the realm. Then came *the final step–temp. Hen VI-Edward IV* –petition gave way to *Bill*, the statute was formulated in the request for it, and *no one could alter the form of a Bill save Parl.* only: the king must grant it or refuse it as presented. *The form to the present day* is enactment by the king on the advice of the Houses.

II. *English Definitions of Law:*

Blackstone: "A rule of civil conduct prescribed by the supreme power in a state, commanding what is right and prohibiting what is wrong." "The making of laws is *entirely the work of* a distinct part, *the legislative branch*, of the sovereign power."

Coke: "*Whatsoever passeth in parliament* by this threefold consent, hath the force of an act of parliament."

Kent: "Municipal law is composed of written and unwritten or statute and common law. *Statute law* is *the express will of the legislature* rendered authentic by certain prescribed forms and solemnities

Stubbs: attempts a formulation of the *distinction between statute and ordinance: "The statute* is a law, or an amendment of law, *enacted by the king in parliament, and enrolled in the statute roll*, not to be altered, repealed, or suspended without the authority of parliament, and valid in all particulars until it has been so revoked; *the ordinance* is *a regulation made by the king*, by himself, or in his council, or with the advice of his council, *promulgated in letters patent or in charter*, and liable to be recalled by the same authority. Moreover, *the statute claims perpetuity. . . . The ordinance is rather a tentative act* which, if it be insufficient to secure its object, or if it operate mischievously, may be easily recalled, and, if it be successful, *may*, by a subsequent act, *be made a statute*."–Stubbs,[45] II, 585, 586. Last clause shows that the essential matter is missed, *the formal element put forward*, tho' glimpses of the true distinction appear.

III. *Examination of the varied matters enacted by Parl. in the form of Statutes.*

(1) *Public Laws.* These have usually the characteristic *universality* of laws, though even they sometimes concern mere administrative adjustments. "*Le roy le veult*," the form of royal sanction. It is characteristic of Public or general Statutes, moreover, that they *originate upon the initiative of Parliament*.[46]

[45] William Stubbs, *The Constitutional History of England.* [Eds.' note]

[46] This *initiative no less that of Parl. because most public acts are introduced*

(2) *Private Bills.*[47] These *originate only in petitions*, not upon any initiative exercised within Parl.,—are assented to thus: *Soit fait comme il est desiré*,—and were not printed until 1815. Moreover, although the courts take knowledge of public acts as of course, *private acts have to be 'proved'* in actions brought before them.[48] Interesting to see in what way *Blackstone* tries to give to private legislation the character of law. He *admits* that *an act directed against a single individual* "is *rather a sentence than a law*," but urges that such an act as that offenses such as a particular person is charged with shall be considered of such and such a rank, has "*permanency, uniformity, and universality*, and *therefore is properly a rule*." *Roman method over again.*

(3) *Money Bills. Grants* given, (by Commons, for historical, not abstract, reasons) *upon petition of the Crown*, the *Commons not* being privileged *to give more* than the Crown asks. (The character of this legislation to be more fully considered hereafter).

IV. *The Common Law must be provided with a place within* the general category, *Law, in English legal history*. Common law=custom accepted by the courts. Part of the general "law of the realm." *A central qu. in Eng. constitutional history* must be, *Is there a Common Public Law*, or is Common Law confined within the field of Private Law? In other words, *Is there custom binding upon the action of the Sovereign*? The answer to this qu. vital under the next head of inquiry, viz.

V. *Prerogative. Appears after the establishment of the control of Parl.* over all legislation, and is involved in the answer to the qu. what governmental acts are beyond the control of Parl. *Definition* of Locke:[49] The power "*to act according to discretion, for the publick good*, without the prescription of the law, and sometimes *even against it*." "Prerogative is nothing but *the power of doing public good without a rule*."

Limitation: Coke: "Proclamations are of great force which are *grounded upon the laws of the realme*." *Blackstone*: "Procla-

---

by the ministers. For, in the exercise of this function, *the ministers* are not to be confounded with the formal executive (i.e. the King). They *introduce bills as members of Parl.* No one not a member can introduce a Bill. [WW's note]

[47] *Parl. formerly* in *the habit of passing all kinds of private bills*, relieving of pains and penalties, *naturalizing*, granting *divorce*, suspending marriage prohibitions in particular cases, &c. &c. [WW's note]

[48] *A petition* for a private act *may be examined by any outsider interested. He may oppose* the granting of the Petition. *A contested bill is debated*—supported —and opposed—by counsel representing the parties in interest *before a committee of "Examiners of Petitions for Private Bills,"* which reports its decision to the House. *The Bill is then introduced by a member* and put thr. *the usual forms of passage*, like other Bills. [WW's note]

[49] *Other definitions: Blackstone*: "That special pre-eminence which the King hath, over and above all other persons, and out of the ordinary course of the common law, in right of his royal dignity." *Coke*: "All powers, pre-eminences and privileges which the law giveth to the crowne[.]" *Cox* confines it to 'all public powers wh. are not conferred upon the Crown by statute" (22). [WW's note]

mations are binding upon the subject, where they do not either contradict the old laws or tend to establish new ones; but *only enforce the execution of such laws as are already in being*, in such manner as the king shall judge necessary." "Yet the manner, time, and circumstances of putting those laws in execution must frequently be left to the discretion of the executive magistrate."[50] *The crucial qu.*—Is the Prerogative *simply limited by law or* is it *derived from it? Gneist maintains* that the Prerogative is not determined by law but *only limited by law* (24). *Coke* says, "*grounded upon the laws* of the realme." *Jellinek* steps in with *the suggestion* (in keeping with the apparent interior meaning of the authoritative Eng. writers from the first) "*In England*, which does not possess a written constitution, *the legal position of the* immediate organs of the State—the *King* and both Houses of Parliament—*rests upon the common law*."(24)[51]

(1) *Ordinances by virtue of the Prerogative*: usually take the form of Orders in Council. Include (*a*) *Treaties*, which need no statute; (*b*) *Suspensions of law*, covered by subsequent *Bills of Indemnity*[52] (*c*) *Calling*, proroguing, and dissolution *of Parl.*, together with the *power to create Peers*; (*d*) *Nominating power*, including Cabinet (?) and Privy Council; (*e*) Granting of *pardons*. (*f*) *Military power*, commander-in-chief, etc.[53] The "*King in Council*" is, nowadays, it is to be noted, only *the King in Cabinet*; and this undoubtedly has a tendency to minimize the independent importance of the Prerogative.

(2) *Prerogative by virtue of the "empowering clauses"* of parliamentary statute. A statute may not only *confer large powers of discretion* upon the executive, but may *also*, "by express words, be *operative until annulled by royal proclamation*." It may also await royal proclamation to come into operation.[54]

(3) It may be proper to *add*, as *a third class*, the *bye-law-making power of local authorities*, wh. they possess by delegation, and *the power of courts to make their own rules* and give to them the penal force of law.

VI. *Prerogative in the U. S.: The President of the U. S.* has been fitted out with portions of Eng. Prerogative in his occasional right of

[50] *Locke again: "to act according to discretion, . . .* without the prescription of the law, and sometimes *even against it.*" [WW's note]

[51] *Suggests also* (25) *that out of the principle* that no contribution shall be levied upon the subject without the sanction of law (*no freedom be abridged save in accordance with the law of the land*) the *principle has sprung* "that *new right* and therewith *new duty cannot be established by ordinance.*" [WW's note]

[52] Noteworthy *instances: Opening Irish ports* to the importation of grain, 1846; *suspension of specie payments.* [WW's note]

[53] Note the very significant *abolition of the system of purchase in the Eng. army* by an *Order in Council*, 1871. [WW's note]

[54] *A case in point* here is the *act passed by the 50th Congress empowering the President to stop*, when he saw fit, *the shipment of goods thr. the U. S. to Canada* in bond, etc. [WW's note]

Proclamation (?); in his powers as *commander-in-chief* of the army and navy; in his powers ('federative') of *dealing with foreign states* (tho.' this is only an initiative); in his *nominating power*; in the *pardoning power*. In our const., however, the continental *theory of Montesquieu*, rather than the Eng. theory of Locke, reigns and obscures.

VII. *Conclusion:* The *English* have manifestly *mixed administrative with law-making powers in Parliament*, with the result that *their conception of Law* is *formal* ("enacted by the King in Parliament") rather than essential. *We*, by the adoption of *the idea of checks and balances*, have still further *obscured the essential outlines of Prerogative*, by mixing the discretion of the Senate with the discretion of the President, *alike in* the exclusively executive *function of appointment*, and in the *'federative' functions of foreign relations.*

Law and Ordinance.

III

Practical Development of the Distinction On the Continent.

I. *In France: Nothing to our present purpose* to be found in the history of France *before 1789*. Down to that year France remained *a Bodin State*—an absolute monarchy derived from mediaeval materials. *Nothing to be added to Bodin's analysis.*

(1) *The Influence of Rousseau at the Revolution.* The *earliest constitutions of the revolutionary period* were made to *carry the formulae of the Contrat Social.* E.G. It was proposed in the *Constituent Assembly* to *define law*, after Rousseau, thus: "Law is *the expression of the general will* and ought to be *general in its object.*" This was *amended* to read, "Law is the *expression of the general will. . . .* It ought to be *the same for all*, whether it protect or punish."[55] This is law in its general, theoretical aspect. *The executive also* bears the imprint of the Rousseau analysis. The distinction between *'loi'* and *'décret,'* recognized by Rousseau, is *accepted, but the law-making* body, which is declared to be permanent, is *declared the source of all conceivable regulations*, in whatever sphere of governmental action, the *King* to be *the 'minister'* only, *the 'clerk'* of the general will. *"Le peuple veut, le roi fait."* There is no rule, administrative or other, which the King can originate of his own pleasure.[56]

[55] There is of course a very *close resemblance* between *this statement* and *the prescription* so usual *in our own written constitutions* to the effect that *laws must be equal and uniform.* It *does not follow*, however, that there is, *because a likeness, therefore a kinship* in the case, powerful as the influence of Rousseau unquestionably was in our revolutionary and constitution-making period. [WW's note]

[56] At the same time it is true that *this first const. recognizes* the further principle of Rousseau (and Aristotle) *that in performing administrative acts the legislative body must obey 'law.' Law*, in the shape of the const., *may command it in the imperative.* Nevertheless in the (12 articled) enumeration of the powers of the Legislative there is not a little mixture of law and decree. [WW's note]

(2) *The Stages of Practical Development*: It was easy to lay down the Rousseau doctrines, but *practical exigencies* presently hastened French constitutional development away from them. Examine the *development by constitutions:*

1. Under *the Constitution framed by the Constituent Assembly* (the, so to say, *Rousseau Constitution*) jealousy of the King's prerogative–even of the phraseology of prerogative –led to an open neglect, if not rejection, of the Rousseau analysis. *The Assembly freely made decrees* on all subjects from the first, to wh., in the beginning, *the King assented in the old variety of forms*, promulgating them in letters patent, in royal decrees, ordinances, etc., accepting the will of the Ass. as his will. *In order to uniformity* in such cases, and in order *to emphasize the sovereignty of the Legislature, the formal conception of law was adopted* and it was enacted that the decrees of the national Ass. "sanctioned by the King should bear *the name and title of laws*."[57] Such decrees were *to be abolished or modified*, moreover, *only in the same way* in which they had been adopted.[58]

(2) *The Jacobinic Constitution* of the Year I (24 June, 1793). Necessary to mention this const., but it does *not*, of course, constitute *a link of practical development* because it never came into operation. Significant because it sought to reestablish *the ideal of Rousseau.* Distinguished bet. *'loi'* and *décret*, tho' not exactly along the same lines with Rousseau; ordained that all *'lois'* should be *submitted to popular vote* (Referendum), while all *other regulations* (décrets) should be established *by* mere *legislative vote*; and that the executive (a Council of 24) should simply superintend, etc.

After the futile passage of the Jacobinic Const., came the *Committee of Public Safety* and the Reign of Terror, when *govt. in France* may be said to have been *all executive, law* being practically *suspended.*

[57] *The veto of the King* was only *suspensive* (delaying the passage of a measure for two legislative terms). There was, ∴, added to the list of decrees wh. were to have the force and title of laws, besides those sanctioned by the King, those passed by three consecutive legislatures: "*Les décrets sanctionnés par le Roi*, et *ceux* qui lui auront été *présenté par trois législatures consécutives* ont force de loi, et portent le nom et l'intitulé de lois." (quoted, 76) [WW's note]

[58] *Reminds of Stubbs'* formal conception: (See notes, red page 11): ["]*not to be altered, repealed, or suspended without the authority of parliament*, and valid in all particulars until it has been so revoked."

Finding it *necessary to deposit genuine executive discretion and power somewhere*, these Rousseau-ridden constitution-makers *committed it to the Commons* and to the new-made *Depts.* This *included* the widest power of public ordinance, oversight of the execution of the laws, *the whole sphere of administrative energy and choice of means.* The Executive was 'put into Commission.' Even the Jacobinic Const. made the *municipalities the organs of the State* for the "application of the revolutionary laws and of the measures of general security and of public safety. Note *our own analogous practices. Jellinek* pronounces the result *'anarchy.'* "With a will-less Kingship there had been created a will-less State" (89). [WW's note]

(3). *The Constitution of the Year III* (The Directory of 5 persons, Council of Elders, and Council of 500–1795) distinguished between *'laws'* and *'legislative acts.'* This distinction does not follow quite the line drawn by Rousseau bet. *loi* and *décret*, but 'legislative acts' are, speaking generally, distinctively administrative in character[.] *The centre of authority* is still *the Legislature* but *the Executive is beginning to revive*, esp. in the military and foreign depts. The *local authorities* are *knit together* thr. local agents of the Directory, the latter is given the position of the *Sept. King*, for the most part, but a power of administrative ordinance is added such as the King did not possess.

(4) In *the Consular Constitution* the *Rousseau analysis* is altogether *abandoned* and the *centre of gravity* radically *shifted*. The law is no longer described as "the general will," but *the formal conception adopted in toto*, that "whatever is determined by the legislative power is law" (80). *All initiative* is suddenly *shifted* to the *Executive*; it is *given* as *free* a *field of administrative origination and action* as could well be conceived: it may even, by the authorization of that singular document itself, *suspend the Constitution* by a *'Nothverordnung'* (urgency-ordinance). The Empire was the speedy and logical result. *"The synthesis of the Revolution,"* thinks *Jellinek*, may be summed up in the statement that *"Ordinance absorbed legislation."*[59]

(5) *Since the Consular Constitution* there have been *few distinct steps* of formulation, either on the side of law or of ordinance. *The formal conception* of law has, for the most part served all constitutional purposes. The history of the interval has been a history of the *re-establishment of legislative control*–but legislation has not absorbed ordinance. The most important fact touching Prerogative arose out of the *attempt of Chas. X.* to suspend, even radically change, the Const. under cover of the clause wh. gave to the Exect. the right to make ["]règlements et ordonnances pour l'exécution des lois *et la sûreté de l'État*." This led to the statement in the *Charter of Louis Phil.* (to the same effect as *in England in 1688*) that the ordinance power sh. not include either the power to suspend the laws themselves or to dispense with their execution.

(6) *At present*: govt. by the Chambers. *French jurisprudence* while recognizing the fact of a more formal conception of law in consts., *distinguishes law proper from administrative acts*, wh. are none the less such because performed by the law-making body. With regard to the Executive, it *distinguishes* bet. (*a*) the *'Gouvernement,'* wh. may be summarily described as *the guiding political power*, with

[59] "As, before the Revolution, the centre of gravity of directive activity lay in the *conseil du roi*, so in the consular and imperial period it lay in the newly-made *conseil d'État*, whose province it was *de rédiger les projets de lois* et les règlements d'administration publique." (93, 94) [WW's note]

respect to both internal and foreign affs. *Analogous to the Eng. prerogative.* Sphere of the *Cabinet* as contradistinguished from the *Council* of Ministers. (b) The '*Administration*,' whose function it is *to give effect to the laws.* (Capped by the *Council of State*). The powers of *local authorities* are in *part subordinate* to the Administration and *in part*, in a sense *coördinate* with it, being in one sphere deputies, in another independent bodies with a movement and ordaining energy of their own.

Law and Ordinance

IV

The Budget

Introduction:

Importance of the subject, because it is a sort of *middle ground* bet. law-making proper and administrative regulation. *It is the support of institutions*—which are of the central substance of law. Topic *best approached through*

Procedure: W. C.

I. *In England: Committee of Supply*—the *Estimates* (submitted early in each annual session). Votes (resolutions) upon each item. *Committee of Ways and Means*—the *Budget.* (1) Votes of the Committee of Supply made up into one resolution wh. is presently made *a Bill*, etc. (2) Alterations in taxation embodied in distinct resolutions, wh. become *Bills*, etc. *Difference of responsibility of ministers on Supply and Taxation*—the first being administrative, the second legislative. All this annual; but there are *Permanent Acts* covering 3/5 of the whole annual expenditure (*Interest* of the debt, sums for the *civil list*—historical reasons—*annuities, pensions, expenses of the courts* of Justice).

II. *In the United States: The 'Letter'* of the Sec'y of the T. to Congress (Dec.)—*the Committee on Appropriations*, and others—resulting Appropriation Bills (Formerly a general "Act making Appropriations for the Support of the Govt.") The *House and* the *Senate. Habit of under-appropriation* and resulting *Deficiency Bills* (*semi*-annual appropriations). "*Permanent Appropriations*" (interest on pub. debt, sinking fund, int. on Pac. R. R. bonds; militia service, collection of customs rev., int. on bequest to Smith. Inst.) amounting sometimes to about 2/3 of the annual expenditures. Note—*Permanent pension bills* and civil list and *yet annual apps.* for satisfying them. *Separation of Executive from* the business of *supply*, with which in Eng. their responsibility is most closely associated.

Committee of Ways and Means; guided in some measure by the 'Reports' of the Sec'y of the T. (wh. exhibit state of industry, etc.). *Duties*, not annual, but *occasional. Revenue* is, with us, *disassociated from administration* thus quite sharply. (See Analysis, *post.*)

III. *In France*: The rôle of the omnipotent *Budget Committee* (33 members), in the matter of credits, principally; but also, to some extent, in the matter of taxation.

Analysis. Throughout *the force of Statute*; but not always the substance of law. (a) *Taxation* the field of law proper—the all-important field of the economic function of the State; (b) *Appropriation* the field of administration, of ordinance. *Anomalous position of our Committee on Rivers and Harbours.* The *imperative character of the Budget*, both on the side of Appropriation and on the side of Taxation: imperative (1) because of *constitutional* provisions, (2) because of *statutory* provisions. *The field of choice*=the field (a) of dispensable insts (b) of administrative efficiency. *Suppose no appropriations are voted*(?) A nice test qu.

Historical view: Development of the modern budget-supported State out of the early self-supported State. *Development* of *control*, and of *procedure.*

Constitutional view (written const. or no written const.)

Support of insts., how far imperative. *How far are insts independent of const. provision?*

Failure of the Budget: a series of causes, bona fide, mala fide[60]

Remedies

Responsibilities.

Field of administrative activity in the light of this discussion—discretionary effectiveness of institutions, *the field, not of law, but of legalized function.*

Law and Ordinance

V.

Conclusion.

What, then, *is law*, in the strict sense of the word? It is the will of the State touching the civic conduct of those under its authority. *It is that expression of the will of the State which has for its object the creation, or the clearer definition and development, of some right or duty on the part of the citizen; as contradistinguished from every expression of the will of the State which has for its object the creation of new undertakings for the State (within the range of old functions), the imposition of new, or the extension of old, duties on the part of public servants.* Nothing wh. merely adds to the items of legal activity on the part of the State is law, but only that which effects some change in the legal privileges or obligations of the citizen.[61]

[60] *Here comes in the qu.*: How far has the budget-controlling authority the right to command, by means of this power the exercise of functions otherwise constitutionally separated from its field of control, e.g. *the treaty-making power*? [WW's note]

[61] Examples: (1) On the side of law: Public authority, citizen subordination and duty, state function, individual right (in so far as this is not merely *in thesi* but provided with legal force, sanction).—even codification, enactment of customary law, etc., usually. (2) On the side of governmental action merely: contracting a loan, sale of public property, foundation of a University, grant

Stated again, it is the delimitation of the sphere of free personal action in society. (240-241)

The characteristic of universality, attributed since Aristotle, is an an attribute of law, but *not its essential characteristic*. Its heart-test lies, not in its abstract width of applicability, but in its object,—in *what it proposes to do*. Law is *the characteristic act of govt.*, for govt. alone can create or modify social rights and duties.

It is *not essential that law should be permanent*; it may be merely transitory, if it do, for the time being, the characteristic thing. And its *universality may be only potential*: it may apply only to a limited number of specified cases, only under certain exceptional circumstances.

The two provinces often overlap: certain expressions of the will of the State may lie partly in the field of law proper, partly within the field of mere govt. activity. E.G. *The Budget: Taxation*, when imposed merely for the sake of revenue, has for its object the support of insts., the support of administration, but it *creates also duties* on the part of the citizen. This still more the case, of course, if taxation have also for its object the direction of the economic life of the people: it then creates rights. *Appropriations*, on the other hand, *create neither rights nor duties*. (Other examples)

Inferences: Field of administrative activity=the field of the discretionary effectiveness of insts.,—the *field, not of Law, but of the exercise* (realization) *of legalized function.*

Qu. of political organization: Does it follow that the law-making body should confine itself to the making of law proper? By no means: there are many questions of giving effectiveness to insts., many choices of means, wh. ought to be settled by the common voice. *But it does follow* that in this latter field the representative body sh. have the guidance of the administrative body. Moreover, inasmuch as action within the field of law-making proper is best done only when done under the guidance of men trained in the observance of political fact and force, *the heads of administration are the most convenient leaders*, the most likely and most available, *in that function also*. Besides, leadership in the second sort strengthens and informs leadership in the first.

Administrative Justice

Basis of the distinction bet Administrative and ordinary Courts, either (a) French, or (b) arbitrary.

(a) *The French* are very decisive and logical in their insistance on on a complete separation of powers. *The administration cannot be subject to the Judiciary, ergo* it must decide the legality of its own acts or that legality must go without decision (the idea of *Andrew Jackson*)

(b) *In other European countries* the distinction *arbitrary* springing

---

of aid to the population of an inundated district of country, bounty to a victorious army, naturalization of a foreigner, giving permission for the erection of a trust (Jellinek), creation of a corporation, etc., etc. Organization belongs to (2), but function to (1) [WW's note] out of "an incomplete political development" and 'destined in the course of time to disappear' (Sarwey). *The only idea*, besides one of convenience, at the bottom of it is that *the exercise of sovereignty* must be adjudicated apart from individual claims of right. For this is the usually accepted distinction,

The Distinction between cases arising out of the exercise of governmental functions (in the field of Public Law) and *cases arising* out of the legal relationships or antagonisms of *individuals* (in the field of Private Law).[62]

Still this *distinction is not strictly observed*, the administrative jurisdiction being *generally defined by enumeration* (as in case of inferior U. S. courts).

The *distinction in its most general form* may be identified with that bet. *law and ordinance*—but with careful distinctions.

In England and the U. S. practically *no such distinction* is observed. There are certain processes, (*mandamous, quo warranto, habeas corpus*, etc.) by wh. *ministerial action* may be either *restrained* or *commanded.* Otherwise the process is simply civil or criminal as against a non-official person (*the idea being*: an officer acting outside the warrant of the law, no officer).

European methods

(1) *Complaint*, to superior officer, whole Board, or what not,—a higher ruling authority in the instance. *Result*, correction or non-correction of the abuse.

(2) *Charge, judicial process*: Regular judicial forms of trial. *Difference* bet. this and ordinary trial is in its *thoroughness.* The administrative *court* does not satisfy itself with examining & deciding the mere qu. of law at issue but *looks into the whole legal relationship*—the entire legal situation involved—*and settles that*,—affords substantial redress, not mere legal certainty as to point involved. *No suit* is permissible merely *in these*, for the court is *not a court of law*, but a court to protect concrete individual interests wh. have been invaded. The *court cannot be invoked to limit* administrative *discretion. Nor* will the court *enforce a public function* by whose intermission an individual thinks his interests affected.

The Presumption is *in favour of the ordinary* civil *jurisdiction*; the other is in fact exceptional.

Organization: Here *the qu.* is shall contests touching the legality of actions of the administration be decided by the immediate administrative authorities themselves, or by bodies secured in judicial separateness and independence?

Two ways of answering: two types

(1) *The French* (a) The Prefectural Council[.] Prefect and 3 or 4 other members appointed and removable by the President

[62] *Stein* established "the principle that cases arising out of the exercise of *the state's sovereignty* should be separated in adjudication from cases between private individuals and be allotted to special courts" (The State §500) "Where the use of the state's sovereignty (*Hoheitsrechte*) begins, there begins the competence of the administrative courts" ([Hermann] *Schulze*, p. 160) ["Das Staatsrecht des Königreichs Preussen," in H. Marquardsen, *Handbuch des Oeffentlichen Rechts*, II]. [WW's note]

(Minister of the Int.) *Qualifications*: 25 yrs. of age, degree of licentiate in law, or 10 yrs. service in admin. of justice, in a Council General, or the mayor's Council. This Council is an ordinary administrative body. (b) The *Council of State* also an ordinary admin. body composed of the ministers and various permanent high officials of the ordinary service. *The French administration is a judge in its own cases.*

(2) *The Prussian*: (1) *The Circle*[63] or the City *Committee* (latter consisting of Burgomaster + 4 members, qualified for high judicial or the highest admin. office) elected by the magistracy of the City for 6 yrs. (2) *District Committee* (3) *Superior Administrative Court* (in Berlin), app. by King as other judges (same footing as members of the *Reichsgericht*) *for life*. Here is *independence of origin and authority* + *official guidance*, for the matters dealt with administrative.

Court of Conflicts: Here again the *diff. bet. France and Prussia* is pointed (See '*The State*' §§ 357-502).

In Italy there are *no special* administrative *courts*, but *a special class of* administrative *cases* is recognized and is given a specially facilitated and speeded process *in the ordinary courts*.

Argument for special administrative courts

(1) Simplicity and *speed* of trial

(2) Completeness of *remedy*

(3) Special *skill* of the Court.

Levermore suggests such a city court as check on the now fashionable Seth Low *mayor*.

WWhw and WWT lecture notes with a few WWsh outlines (WP, DLC).

[63] See diagrammatic scheme. [WW's note]

From Frederick Jackson Turner

Dear Dr Wilson: Madison Wis., Feb. 5, 1890

I need hardly say that I appreciate the cordiality in your letter received a few days ago.

As the situation now appears to me, Pres Chamberlin delayed action on the permanent appointment of a successor to Prof. Allen on two grounds; first, his cautiousness and his desire of taking the initiative, as you say; and second, because he desires to keep the door open in the hope of finding some man with a *reputation* such that he would lift the institution into prominence, ready to take the chair next Spring. I think if such a man does not appear, there is no question of my securing the place. I do not think it will be easy for Dr Chamberlin to find a man who is conversant with Northwestern history, has taught a considerable time, has a reputation, and possesses the other ideal qualifications that he would wish for the chair. But while I feel reasonably confident that my appointment will be made, and while I think, as do you, that if I can succeed Prof Allen, I ought to do so, and while I think I have the good opinion of faculty and students,–yet I feel that no one can be sure of Pres. Chamberlin. He is a psychological puzzle to me!

Under these circumstances, all I can say is that I would feel entirely free to entertain a proposition from Weslayan. If I do not receive reasonable assurance of succeeding Prof. Allen, I would feel more satisfaction and pride in going to Weslayan than elsewhere. I have not the data regarding expenses, relative salaries etc. to enable me to give an intelligent reply to your query as to salary, yet. If matters progress to this point, I should hope to answer a proposition upon the matter.

My teaching began in 1885, spring term, when I took a couple of Prof Allen's classes while he was in Europe. 1885-6 I taught rhetoric and oratory. 1886-7 and 1887-8, I assisted Prof. Allen, in history–general and United States, and also held the instructorship in the branches just named. 1888-9 was spent at JHU., and in 1889-90 I have had nothing but history, succeeding in the winter term to Prof. Allen's classes, and the conduct of the department. The courses include French Revolution, Ancient Society, General History, Political and Constitutional History of United States, Northwestern History, and (Spring) Nineteenth Century. But my work is chiefly along the lines of modern and American history.

I have had occasion to consider recently some of the less pleasant aspects of *State* Universities, but I know you will agree with me in setting down as one of their *good* qualities their ignorance on the subject of the instructor's religion. Of course, however, I have no hesitancy in giving you my attitude in this respect, while I think I can see you smile as you read it. I am a Unitarian, and my creed is summed up in the commandment which enjoins love to God, and to man. But I am not a proselyter, and my ambition would be satisfied in this regard, if my religion found expression in conduct such as is fitting to a man.

I am very happy in my home life. We have just gone to housekeeping in a modest little house, and "happiness and strength," have, indeed, been added to me. Mrs. Turner desires me to say that she considers your letter to me a most pleasant introduction, and that we both have the hope that sometime you may come West, and that if you can visit Madison, *and we are here*, we shall be most happy to welcome you and Mrs. Wilson to our cosiest corner. Very truly yours Fredk J Turner

ALS (WP, DLC).

From the Minutes of the Johns Hopkins Seminary of Political and Historical Science

February 7th 1890.

Seminary met at 8.08 P. M., Prof Adams in the chair. The minutes of the last meeting were read by Mr. Haskins. . . .

The paper for the evening was on "The Agrarian Laws of Rome during the Republic" and was by Mr. Stephenson.[1] . . .

The paper was then discussed by Prof. Adams and Messrs. Vincent, Haskins, and Steiner.[2]

Prof. Ely spoke of the destructive character of the Roman land law and suggested the profitableness of a comparative study of Greek and Roman Law from an economic standpoint.

Prof. Wilson said the fault was not so much that of the law at Rome as of its administration.

Mr. Vincent compared the Frankish land system with that of Rome. The Romans had a feeling for law; the Franks were more individual. Under Charles the Great there were three kinds of landed property 1) private, 2) royal demesne, 3) feldmark. The latter two were the ager publicus and were obtained in slightly different ways; the last by silent assent to possession; the former by possession and symbolical ceremony.

Seminary adjourned. Bernard C. Steiner.

Hw entry (MdBJ).

1 Andrew Stephenson, who later published his study as *Public Lands and Agrarian Laws of the Roman Republic*, Johns Hopkins University Studies in History and Political Science, 9th Series (Baltimore, 1891).

2 Bernard Christian Steiner, then completing his work on the Ph.D. in history. He was later head of the Enoch Pratt Free Library of Baltimore and a prolific chronicler of Maryland's history.

From Wilson's Pocket Diary

February, Thursday 13. 1890.

Elected to chair of Jurisprudence and Political Economy, Princeton, Salary, $3,000. Promise that within 2 yrs. Political Economy be erected into separate chair and I be left with *Public Law* only.

Entry in pocket diary described at Jan. 1, 1890.

To Robert Bridges

My dear Bobby, Balto., Md., Feby 13, '90

A telegram from M. Taylor Pyne[1] received about an hour ago says, "We elected you full professor to-day. Trust you will accept[.]" I suppose this means a full professor's salary, and that the only thing to be negotiated is the continuation of my present arrangement with Johns Hopkins, which is of so great advantage to me that I shall be very loath to give it up.

I am profoundly gratified by this election, and I feel, Bobby, that it is due in large part, if not altogether, to you—to your incomparable friendship. I don't need to tell you what I think about it—and about you—I shrink from trying lest it should seem formal: it would necessarily lack the true, warm colour of my thought. But you know my sentiments, Bobby, and the genuineness of my appreciation.

I am kept desperately hard at work here. I hardly have time for so much as a leisurely wink, my lecture-preparing has to go so steadily and rapidly forward; but I still retain the warmth I got from you and Sheldon during my few hours in N. Y. I have time to remain consciously

Your affectionate friend Woodrow Wilson

ALS (Meyer Coll., DLC).
[1] It is missing.

From Abram Woodruff Halsey

My dear Wilson, New York, Feb 14th 1890

The morning paper informs me that you have been called to the vacant chair of "Jurisprudence and Political Economy" at Princeton. Please accept my hearty congratulations: '79 is proud of you, may the honors you have so deservedly won be but the beginning of a long and useful career. I trust you will see your way clear to accept the honor, and that one more 79 man will be added to the Professorial Roll at Princeton *macte virtute*.

Cordially, A. W. Halsey.

ALS (WP, DLC).

From Albert Bushnell Hart

My dear Prof. Wilson: Cambridge, Mass. Feb. 14, 1890

Most heartily do I congratulate you on your election to the Princeton professorship. The opportunity is an unusual one. The College has the authority of age and the vigor of activity. Prof. Johnston had begun to stamp himself upon the community, the college, and the country; his successor will affect the political method of thought of the most influential class in the next generation

With sincerest pleasure in your prospects, I am

Yours very truly, Albert Bushnell Hart

ALS (WP, DLC).

Two News Items

[Feb. 15, 1890]

TO GO TO PRINCETON.

Prof. Woodrow Wilson has been elected Professor of Jurisprudence and Political Economy at Princeton, to enter upon his duties next year. His loss will be severely felt here.

◊

Special reports have been made in the Political Economy class upon these subjects: "An Honest Dollar," . . . "The Industrial Transition in Japan," . . . "The Growth of Cities," . . . "Distribution of Foreigners throughout the Country, and their Concentration in Cities."

Printed in the Middletown, Conn., *Wesleyan Argus*, XXIII (Feb. 15, 1890), 98.

From Charles Andrew Talcott

My dear 'Doctor': Utica Feby 17, 1890.

I saw in today's N. Y. Tribune that you had been called to Princeton. I can not tell you how glad I am to learn it: glad for Princeton's sake and yours. Ever since you assumed the title 'professor,' I have thought a Chair at Princeton yours by right. You are needed there now and I believe you will do much to hasten the attainment of standard, reputation, and spirit which I am sure the future has in store for Princeton. I quite envy you too; for there is no place to which my thoughts turn so often as to the Princeton which we knew together; and in the most pleasant of the pictures that arise unbidden, you are most often the central figure. You being there will add to the thought of the place a sort of home feeling.

Affectionately Yours C. A. Talcott

ALS (WP, DLC).

From Elijah Richardson Craven[1]

My Dear Sir: Philadelphia Feb 17th, 1890.

It gives me great pleasure to inform you that at the meeting of the Trustees of the College of New Jersey, on the 13th inst., you were unanimously elected Professor of "Jurisprudence & Political Economy."

The salary attached to the chair is Three Thousand Dollars *per annum.*

Trusting that I may soon receive an official notification of your acceptance of the position in your Alma Mater thus cordially tendered you, I remain,

Yours, very respectfully, E. R. Craven.

ALS (WP, DLC).

[1] Princeton, '42, Secretary of the Board of Publication and Sabbath Social Work of the Presbyterian Church in the U.S.A. and Clerk of the Board of Trustees of the College of New Jersey.

From James McCosh

My Dear Sir Princeton, N. J. Feb 17 1890

I am glad they are bringing you back to your old college. You will receive a welcome here and will have a wide field of usefulness. You will enter in and possess it. I am

Yours truly James McCosh

ALS (WP, DLC).

From Francis Landey Patton

My Dear Sir: [Princeton, N. J.] Feb 18 '90

At the meeting of the Trustees on Thursday, you were unanimously elected to the Chair of Political Economy & Jurisprudence, at the annual salary of Three thousand dollars.

I hope that you will see the way clear to an acceptance of this position & that we may have you with us at the beginning of our next academic year.

The Re[d] Dr Craven will communicate to you officially this action of the Board.

Had I seen you during the past month or two I should have taken the liberty to tell you of one or two criticisms that I have heard regarding your work on the State.

I did not think it necessary to mention these criticisms to the

Board nor even to the Committee on the Curriculum, though I did speak of them to Dr. Green.[1] It seemed to me that they were not of sufficient moment after my later conversation with you[2] & after what I had heard about you from your friends to make it nice to embarrass the question of your election by referring to them.

And yet now that you have been chosen by the unanimous vote of the Board I think I ought to speak of them & I feel that you can without any sacrifice of academic independence give them such weight as they may deserve in your consideration of the question before you.

My attention has been called—this is the criticism I refer to—by two or three parties—to the fact that in your discussion of the origin of the State you minimise the supernatural, & make such unqualified application of the doctrine of naturalistic evolution & the genesis of the State as to leave the reader of your pages in a state of uncertainty as to your own position & the place you give to Divine Providence. More particularly have I been reminded of the fact that while you have devoted inordinate space to Roman law & while you credit Roman law with its full share of influence upon the regeneration of modern society, you are silent with respect to the forming & reforming influences of Christianity.

I do not mention these matters as expressing my own judgments: but I think that I ought to say what I am sure you already know[,] that the Trustees of the College mean to keep this College on the old ground of loyalty to the Christian religion: that they expect the high topics pertaining to your chair & that of the chairs contiguous to that one you are chosen to fill to be dealt with under theistic and Christian presuppositions: & they would not regard with favour such a conception of academic freedom or teaching as would leave in doubt the very direct bearing of historical Christianity as a revealed religion upon the great problems of civilization. I feel that entire frankness in this matter is demanded of me as the head of the College and I am sure that you will so far appreciate the [–] responsibility that rests upon my shoulders as to pardon my freedom and put the proper interpretation upon my motive.

Again affirming the great pleasure I have in hoping that you may be a co[-]labourer with us in the next year: & congratulating you on the honour that your Alma Mater has bestowed upon you.

I am very sincerely Francis L. Patton

ALS (Patton Letterpress Books, University Archives, NjP).

[1] The Rev. Dr. William Henry Green, Professor of Oriental and Old Testament

Literature at Princeton Theological Seminary; member of the Board of Trustees of the College of New Jersey; and, as the *Dictionary of American Biography* puts it, "the scholarly leader in America of the ultraconservative school of Biblical criticism."

2 Probably at the Astor House in New York on December 31, 1889. See WW to R. Bridges, Jan. 27, 1890.

To Robert Bridges

My dear Bobby, Balto, Md., 18 February, 1890

May I trouble you once more for advice about Princeton? Dr Patton is here (for the Princeton dinner to-night) and I have had an interview with him which puts me in full view of the situation as a whole. They offer me $3,000. It seems that that was the amount of Johnston's salary; that all but the older Profs. (who get $3,400—$400 being regarded as a 'house allowance') receive $3,000 or less—Hunt,[1] e. g., and Ormond[2] and West[3]—and might—such is Dr P's argument—be jealous of any one who should be given more than that; and that—most important of all—the interest available on investments being on the decrease, large blocks of the college funds which have been yielding 7% are now falling in and will have to be re-invested at 4%. In short, it is claimed that economy dictates and recent precedent sanctions the offer to a 'full' professor of $3,000 rather than the formerly more usual $3,400.

As to the work, the chair is *not* to be divided as yet. I should have to take the whole of Johnston's work for one year, perhaps for two years (*probably* for two, I gather), but 'certainly for not more than two.' After that—'so soon, indeed, as the proper man is found'—political economy would be separated and public law alone left to me, thus giving me 'not more than four hours a week' and 'as leisurely a chair as any.' In brief the salary would be no more than I am making now; for the first two years at any rate, there would be no less work than at Wesleyan—the number of hours being about the same and the classes much larger. Under such circumstances there is but one argument for Princeton, namely, that it *is* Princeton—a big institution of the first class, with superior facilities for work, with the best class of students, and affording a member of its faculty a certain academic standing. All this *unless* I be allowed to continue my present plan of a six weeks' course here at the Hopkins. Concerning the possibility of that Dr Patton seems to hesitate—personally inclined to favour it, but afraid of the Trustees and the faculty—of jealousy on their part—for Princeton, for themselves.

I am inclined to make an *ultimatum* either of the continuance of the Hopkins arrangement or of a greater salary—of the former rather than of the latter; but I don't want to do so without consulting you, upon whom I feel all the dependence of closest friendship and completest trust. Wont you think it over and tell me your candid thought? I should be sacrificing much more than what I receive in money from the Hopkins if I were to break with it—should be giving myself to Princeton very cheap indeed.

With fullest gratitude & affection, as ever

Your sincere friend, Woodrow Wilson

ALS (Meyer Coll., DLC).

[1] Theodore Whitefield Hunt, born Metuchen, N.J., Feb. 19, 1844. A.B., College of New Jersey, 1865; graduated from Princeton Theological Seminary, 1869; ordained to Presbyterian ministry, 1878. Taught throughout his academic career at Princeton as tutor in English, 1868-71; Adjunct Professor of English, 1873-81; and Professor of English Language and Literature, 1881-1918. Honorary Ph.D., Lafayette College, 1880; Litt.D., Rutgers College, 1890. Died April 12, 1930.

[2] Alexander Thomas Ormond, born Punxsutawney, Pa., April 26, 1847. A.B., College of New Jersey, 1877; Ph.D., same institution, 1880. After teaching at the University of Minnesota, he came to Princeton as Professor of Mental Science and Logic in 1883 and served as McCosh Professor of Philosophy, 1898-1913. President, Grove City College, 1913-15. Died Dec. 18, 1915.

[3] Andrew Fleming West, born Allegheny, Pa., May 17, 1853. A.B., College of New Jersey, 1874; Ph.D., same institution, 1883. Professor of Latin, 1883-1928, and Dean of the Graduate School, 1901-28, at Princeton. Scholar and epigrammatist. LL.D., Lafayette College, 1897; D.Litt., Oxford University, 1902. Died Dec. 27, 1943.

From Robert Bridges

My dear Tommy: New York Feb 20 1890

I know you will pardon me for writing less in detail than I should if I could find a quiet hour at the Club. Rather than delay I take this opportunity.

Preliminary. Cyrus [McCormick] could not get to the trustee meeting; so I frankly wrote Patton that "I was in position to state" that you were receiving something more than $3000. (all told) and would expect a full professor's salary of $3500. This he has probably told you. I could not do more without seeming officious.

The Main Question:

1) That you should be at Princeton and have a chair of your own creating, with four hours a week (assured you positively in two years) seems to me the paramount consideration. As I look at it, you want position and opportunity to carry out (with least friction) your life-work which you have definitely planned. If this scheme does not offer it in the near future it should be abandoned.

2) (Interrogative?) Could two years at Wesleyan, no matter how adjusted to your wishes, bring you the same opportunity?

3) If not, then two years at Princeton at the same salary and with similar work are to be preferred, because they will bring you to what you want.

4.) As to the Johns Hopkins lectureship—It is certainly a desirable thing to retain it—whether it is so essential as to be made an ultimatum is, of course, only to be seen clearly by you—for the conditions are entirely personal. Could you not arrange a compromise? That you be allowed two or three weeks in February after the mid-year examinations at Princeton, and that the rest of your course be delivered on Fridays or Saturdays at J.H.U.? This would not push you physically as the journey is a short one.

This is all the light I see on the subject—I have put it didactically merely for purposes of clearness. I hate the "cock-sureness" of that form of statement for it merely represents a point-of-view, and is open to all sorts of modifications and answers.

Whatever the solution I hope that it will somehow land you at Princeton. Faithfully Yours Robert Bridges

ALS (WP, DLC).

To Ellen Axson Wilson

My own darling, Baltimore, Md., 20 Feby., '90.

It is odd how often I am obliged to write you a love letter, pure and simple: I say 'obliged' because it happens to me again and again that when I sit down to write to you all thoughts save those of a passionate lover are driven out of my head—and I have nothing but love to speak of. The minute I begin to think about you your sweet image and all your sweet ways rise up to dominate my whole mind,—and straightway I fall down and adore you, never recovering my equilibrium till I find myself at the end of my sheet and obliged to sign myself your own Woodrow. I realize you in my mind's eye, realize you,

"A Spirit, yet a Woman too!
Her household motions light and free,
And steps of virgin liberty;
A countenance in which do meet
Sweet records, promises as sweet;
A Creature not too bright or good
For human nature's daily food;

For transient sorrows, simple wiles,
Praise, blame, love, kisses, tears, and smiles.

"And now I see with eye serene
The very pulse of the machine;
A Being breathing thoughtful breath;
A Traveller between life and death;
The reason firm, the temperate will,
Endurance, foresight, strength, and skill;
A perfect Woman, nobly planned,
To warm, to comfort, and command;
And yet a Spirit still, and bright
With something of an angel light."[1]

As I read these lines last night, darling, my pulses quickened as if I had suddenly come upon a picture of you. I adopt the whole of it, and shall go to it always in your absence to satisfy my heart with a description of you! And yet you don't deserve such constant—such deliberate and explicit love-making as I ply you with because of any example you set me. You deserve it all for what you *are*, but not for what you do, my beauty. Once and again, when you are angry with some one whom you suspect of not appreciating me, you burst into a passion of love-making which makes my heart leap all day with uncontrollable joy—with a sort of mad joy which you would wish to produce often, I am sure, if you could but see its effects upon me. You *have* seen it, darling, when you have had me with you and have let your love speak without restraint by means of every sweet jesture and passionate embrace. Oh, Eileen, you will love me so when I come back to you, wont you—and you will promise it once and again, wont you, in your letters by giving free vent to your love for

Your own Woodrow

ALS (WP, DLC).

[1] From Wordsworth's "She Was a Phantom of Delight."

From Marion Wilson Kennedy

My dearest Woodrow: Batesville [Ark.], Feb. 20th, 1890.

I hope I will be one of the first to congratulate you on your new position. Ross says he was expecting it, but I must confess, I had not thought of it as likely that such a young chap as you are, would be elected professor to fill that chair at Princeton. Surely, it is quite an honor, and will make a very pleasant change in your life, I should think. If the society of Princeton is anything like as intellectual as I have always understood Ellie will be pleased too. When you can, write and tell us all about your plans, Woodrow. . . .

Father writes rather discouragingly of himself, doesn't he? Have you any idea as to his plans?

Let us hear from you as soon as convenient. With lots of love from Ross,—who is not as well as usual—, and myself to yourself, Ellie and the bairnies three,

Your loving sister, Marion.

ALS (WP, DLC).

From Bradford Paul Raymond

My dear Prof. Wilson: Middletown, Conn., Feb. 25th, 1890.

We regret very much the prospect of your leaving us. I wish we could make the field so attractive that there could be no temptations from without. Nevertheless, I know that Princeton has attractions that we cannot offer. And now when the decision is reached, what about a successor? Will you give us the names of some of the men in the field, and your opinion in regard to them. It appears to me that the most feasible plan for us is to put some man into the field, who will carry all the work for two or three years, but who has a decided preference for either political economy and sociological questions, or for history. In the mean time we can either find or fit some young man to take part of the work.

With this plan in mind I wish you would give me your opinion of young Davenport, of the class of '89. In many respects he seems to me to be a promising man. He is teaching classics, it is true but that is because a good place opened to him, and he had to do something. He told me when I was at Wyoming Seminary a few weeks ago that his elective work was not done along that line, and that his preference was for history. I think he did elective work in that line did he not?

Prof. Van Vleck has spoken of the plan of employing two young men. Have you the men in mind? The department would suffer unless one of them was made Professor, & we are hardly ready for two men in the field. Any suggestions you may give me will be highly appreciated. I shall not be able to see [you in] Baltimore while you are there.

Sincerely yours, B. P. Raymond.

ALS (WP, DLC).

From Edward Webster Bemis

Vanderbilt University
Dear Sir: Nashville, Tenn Feb. 26 1890

Permit me to congratulate you on your call to Princeton, and to express my great appreciation of your last book which I shall soon review for a local journal of some standing. Will send you a copy.[1]

On the supposition that you would accept the call to Princeton a friend of mine in New England who may have a little influence at Wesleyan asks if I would permit my name to be used for the vacancy. I feel undecided and write you as a friend. Any inquiry however would be needless if you think some decision in favor of another has already been reached.

Supposing the position still open, may I ask in confidence of the extent to which the faculty welcome a young instructor and how pleasant you have found the work and environment? Is the chair one of history or of history and economics as I would prefer?

I like my work here exceedingly, but in default of further endowment from the Vanderbilts which seems improbable the University cannot pay large salaries. It has spread over too much ground to support the various departments well, especially the new ones. I receive $1800.

I am sorry thus to bother you for you must be very busy, but you may not object to replying briefly.

Very sincerely yours Edward W. Bemis
Adjunct professor, in charge of history and economics.

ALS (WP, DLC).
[1] It is printed at March 15, 1890.

From the Minutes of the Johns Hopkins Seminary of Historical and Political Science

Bluntschli Library Feb. 28th 1890.

The Seminary was called to order at 8 P.M. Dr Adams in the chair. Minutes of the previous meeting were read by W. I. Hull and approved.

The President with a few remarks introduced the speaker of the evening Gen. Bradley T. Johnson[1] who read a paper on the ["]Federal Constitution of 1787 and the Confederate Constitution of 1861."

The design of the paper as a study in comparative politics was to present the author's views of the development of our constitutional government from 1775 to 1865.

The lecturer had had full opportunities of knowing the opinions and feelings of the southern people, and, in regard to the Civil War, could speak from personal observation. As he had been acquainted with all the leading actors, both in the field and in the Cabinet he could speak with assurance on the attitude of the South towards the Constitution.

During the War of Independence the bond of Union was the common cause. The Articles of Confederation formed a loose compact, in which the individual sovereignty of the states was unimpaired. The Constitution was framed to form a more perfect union. It was an expansion of the Articles of Confederation as the Bill of Rights was an expansion of Magna Charta. As the states separately signed the treaty of alliance with France during the progress of the war, and the treaty of peace with Great Britain at its close, so the Constitution was ratified by the states separately and in the original draft they were severally named in the preamble, and that their names are not found therein to-day is due to the stylist to whom the Constitution was submitted for polishing.

The true causes of the Civil War were sought in the hereditary and conservative character of the Southern people. Their institutions had the sanction of antiquity; not a civilized people in history but had maintained the institution of slavery, basing it upon natural and moral grounds, and preserving it as an industrial and social necessity.

Slavery, however, is not to be considered the cause of the war. That was but a single issue, one point of conflict between the two peoples. The Sothrons, a conservative people, jealous of their rights and liberties, cherished the institutions inherited through a line of twenty generations from their Teutonic ancestors. They cherished and were ready to fight in defense of those monuments of freedom forced from unwilling kings of England. They were true descendents of those English yeomen who wrung from the traitor John the Magna Charta; more immediate descendents of the revolutionists of 1688 whose achievement for freedom was the Bill of Rights, and loyal sons were they of the heroes of the War of Independence.

Now it was to preserve these institutions and to defend these liberties that they took up arms in a second War of Indepen[den]ce.

At the North on the other hand there was a heterogeneous people, rendered so by the large influx of foreigners. Consequently an altogether different conception of the constitution prevailed. There the rallying cry was, "Away with slavery, Constitution or no Constitution." In this the South saw the culmination of that tendency towards federal absolutism which she had vainly fought against since the adoption of the Constitution. The southern states therefore began to secede. A Congress was held a[t] Montgomery and a Confederacy formed.

Thus far they had proceeded peaceably and it was hoped that war might be averted. The federal Constitution was so amended as to render it, they believed, adapted to meet the exigencies of the time, and form a more perfect union. It was thought that all of the United States would come to recognize the superior excellence of the amended Constitution and so join the Confederacy. To bring about this end a body of commissioners were sent to Washington to negotiate with the federal authorities. Nothing, as the world knows was accomplished, and the inevitable came to pass.

The lecturer cited certain constitutional amendments made by this Congress, and commented on their merits.

For convenience of comparison he had copied the two Constitutions, the Federal Constitution of 1787 and the Confederate Constitution of 1861, in parallel columns with corresponding clauses adjacent.

The reading of the paper ended, invitation was extended by the President to any who wished to question the lecturer on the subject of his address.

To the question, whether it was a constitutional struggle, Gen. Johnson replied that it was not entirely so. There were different views held of the constitution, the limits & extent of the powers it granted to the Federal Government. Difference of construction of the phrase "we the people" prevailed. Hamilton was quoted as interpreting it to mean the people in their capacity of citizens of their respective states. As to how far the people of the South grasped the constitutional issue of the conflict the speaker said they were sensible of the invasion of their rights and awake to the fact of federal encroachment. The flame of passion was kindled by President Lincoln's unjustifiable conduct in calling for troops.

The character of the Negro was commented on and his conduct during and after the war contrasted. Slavery it was said had done more for the Negro in two hundred and fifty years than

African freedom had done since the building of the pyramids. His two present needs were,—1) a disposition to work, and a knowledge of agriculture. 2) Moral Culture.

Dr. Woodrow Wilson explained the war as the clashing of two facts. At the South one view of the Constitution had grown up and become dominant, while at the North a totally different view was held. These diverse and opposed interpretations by the people at large were the real facts of the Constitution, and it was between these that the conflict was for the mastery. It was further pointed out that a fundamental contrast existed between the manner of viewing national questions before the war and the manner after the war. The constitutionality of a measure was formerly the first consideration, while now that matter is often disregarded. . . .

Unsigned hw entry (MdBJ).

[1] Johnson, a former Confederate brigadier and prominent Maryland and Virginia lawyer and politician, was at this time practicing law in Baltimore.

From Richard Heath Dabney[1]

My dear Woodrow: University of Virginia March 1st, 1890.

I was sorry that you were unable to run down to Washington to the meeting of the Historical Association, but I don't wonder that you didn't have time to do so. It is, in fact, amazing to me how you manage to do so much work. . . .

Let me congratulate you most warmly upon two things, upon the great success already achieved by your valuable work on "The State," and upon your recent election to the Chair of Political Economy & Jurisprudence at Princeton. If "The State" is necessarily in large measure a "fact book," as you say, the facts are at all events very important, and the work contains a great deal besides facts. There is a great deal of *you* in it, and that is equivalent to saying that it is a good book—"illimitable idiot" though you be. May you realize from it not only reputation but also a goodly pile of ducats. And I will say the same in advance of your expected work on "Division & Reunion." I have expected for some time that you would be elected to the Princeton chair & was therefore not surprised at the news. As Princeton is one of your *almae matres*, you doubtless feel great satisfaction at the prospect of going there to live. As Princeton is nearer Virginia than Middletown is, I feel that I, too, am to be congratulated; for I hope that we may be able to see each other every now & then.

You are right in supposing that, now that I have had to take up the burden of life anew and to fight the battle alone, I am glad to be once more in this dear old place. To have returned to Indiana would have been intolerable. But here, while the burden of sorrow is heavy indeed, I still have the comfort of feeling that I am again upon the soil of that dear old commonwealth which gave birth to my beloved, at a place where her feet have trod, and among men whom I trust and respect. The pleasant memories connected with this beautiful spot do soothe me, as you say, in some measure. I dearly love Old Virginia and the South, and the most sustaining and comforting thought to me now is that I have the opportunity here to be of some benefit in an humble way to this sunny land of ours for which our fathers fought & bled and suffered and died. This thought that I have a duty to perform to my own people helps me to forget myself and my sorrows. . . .

With kindest regards to Mrs. Wilson & thanks for her message, I remain, as ever,

Your affectionate friend R. H. Dabney.

ALS (WP, DLC).

1 Wilson wrote at the top of this letter: "Ask Heath about the Southern Soc'y, its library etc for Jameson."

From Bradford Paul Raymond

Middletown, Conn.

My dear Professor Wilson: March 3rd 1890

I leave for Chicago tomorrow morning and wish to submit a question before I go. Can we not emphasize the doubt, by dividing your work & giving you just the line of work you wish to carry? I should be glad to hear from you when I return.

Sincerely yours, B. P. Raymond

ALS (WP, DLC).

From Annie Wilson Howe

My darling Brother, Columbia, S. C. Mar. 3d, 1890

Ever since I saw the notice of your election to a professorship at Princeton, I have intended to write and congratulate you. The notices we see in the papers are very pleasant to read, especially as we know that you *deserve* every word of them. There is no flattery in them. Have you decided whether you will accept or not? . . .

You have not answered my last letter. I suppose you are so busy that you find it almost impossible to write. . . . Have you said anything to Father about the tombstone? I want to write after you do.

Isn't it dreadful to think of Marion having to support her family. She is a brave little woman. Her life is about as sad a one as I can imagine. Josie will soon be old enough to help her, I should think. Some one is coming in so I will say goodbye. George joins me in warmest love to Ellie and your dear self. Kiss the dear children for me. Your devoted sister, Annie.

ALS (WP, DLC).

To Mary Gresham Machen[1]

My dear Mrs. Machen, [Baltimore, c. March 3, 1890]

It is nothing short of a trial to have to decline your kind invitation for Thursday next; but I am under bonds to my doctor,[2] and dare not disobey him just now. He has forbidden me to accept social engagements of any kind for the present,—particularly on days when I must lecture; but he has not forbidden me short calls, and just so soon as I feel a little more like myself (I am over my attack, but still nervous after the writing I am obliged to do every morning) I am promising myself a cosey talk with you.

I am fairly ashamed to be taking such care, such ridiculous care of myself; but the doctor insists it is not foolish, and I must submit with such grace as I can command. I know, at any rate, that you will understand and sympathise,—and forgive; and will believe me, with affectionate regards,

Most gratefully Yours, Woodrow Wilson

ALS (in possession of Arthur W. Machen, Jr.).

[1] Mary, or Minnie, Gresham (Mrs. Arthur Webster) Machen, whom Wilson had known since his graduate school days. Mrs. Machen's father, Judge John B. Gresham of Macon, Ga., was an old friend of Joseph Ruggles Wilson.

[2] As WW to JRW, March 20, 1890, and other letters reveal, Wilson had a severe attack of the "grippe" during the latter part of his stay in Baltimore.

From Ellen Axson Wilson

My own darling, Tuesday [March 4, 1890].

I am afraid I must begin with business tonight and disagreeable business at that;—too bad with such a glorious letter as this one in my lap waiting to be answered. But I have found long ago that if I begin with such a subject as that—or as *you* yourself—I am sure to end with it also, and this business has been neglected a month already. I allude to Camp's bill. It came just after you left and was for *two* months $70.26 (!), and I have been intending ever since to ask you if that was correct–if the "bill rendered" before was really unpaid. Now it has come again today –for 3 mos. & has grown to $104, and I suppose it ought to be attended to. Is there enough money in bank for such a huge bill though? I have drawn $60.00,–$20.00 for you and the rest chiefly for wages since you left.

Here is another puzzle too. Jessie's cloak is so *entirely* worn out and *dirty* that it is simply *impossible* for her to go on the street at all,–I havn't let her do so since you went away. I can't shop to get either the cloak or the materials to make one–& I couldn't get them here if I were well. I was counting on attending to it in New York, though it has been very inconvenient to wait so long. But now that I can't go to meet you I am at my wits end. Do you think you could attend to it either in Balt. Phila or N. Y., or shall I write to Aunt Saidie[1] to do it & let you bring it home. I am rather afraid to trust her or Allie,[2] they might be extravagant. The nicest way would be for you to get her to go down with you to select it. At this season, as I know by experience one can sometimes get a cloak made up actually *cheaper* than the materials; and of course I should be particularly glad to do so now, for cloak-making, with its heavy pressing, fine tailor-like stitching, &c. is rather troublesome work for a lame girl. Those cloaks that I got before at Wanamaker's were $3.00 & $6.00. They were much reduced. As the garment must be larger now I suppose it must also cost more, but not much. Of course it must be for Margaret & Jessie will have hers. Get it for five years old, *rather* light weight, of any colour that suits your taste. Unless it had some colour in it like the enclosed plush (which isn't likely) you will have to get the plush &c. for me to make a cap to match; & the old cap can be put away for baby with the plush cloak for which it was made. The enclosed slip will tell you how much material to get for the cap. The ribbon is 2 inches wide. I am so sorry to give you all this trouble but "what can't be cured must be endured,"– burnt feet for instance, with their consequences. As I was saying today my foot seems to me about as bad now as an ordinary hot water scald, when fresh. I am afraid you will find me just where you left me sitting by the window with my foot in a chair and an old sock on it! There is one comfort anyhow, I am getting the good of that *odd slipper*!–whose mate you know came to pieces when comparatively new! You know how I grieved over losing the wear of the good one. I experience a sense of solid satisfaction every morning when I put that slipper on! But it is after nine and I won't make a poor pretence of answering that sweet love-letter now, but keep it for a more fitting occasion. Such subjects show to better advantage when not too closely crowded by bills.

Jessie seems perfectly well and there is no mark of any sort on her back. I suppose there is nothing to worry about. Good-night my own love, my whole heart is yours in its every throb, my whole life is yours in its every breath, I am altogether

Your own Eileen.

If you think you can get the cloak for me in Phila there are one or two other things I would like you to bring me from Wanamaker's. If not I will send for them. You spoke in your last as if you would go straight through to Princeton. But while it made my heart leap to think of seeing you a few days earlier than I expected, I still hope you will make your visits, & so get a longer rest.

ALS (WP, DLC).

[1] Mrs. Thomas A. Hoyt.

[2] Alice Hoyt Truehart.

From Azel Washburn Hazen

My dear Friend: Middletown, Conn. 4th March 1890.

For some days it has been in my mind and heart to send you a line. First of all, I want to congratulate you upon the invitation from Princeton. It is a most pleasant thing to receive such tokens of esteem—an experience which everybody anticipated for you. We here wish, with all our souls, that you might see the way open to decline the flattering proposal of your Alma Mater. Can we do anything to *open* it? Pres Raymond assured me yesterday that the authorities here would grant you almost any request, if you could be induced to prolong your stay here for a time. And I must gratify myself, though I cannot hope to influence you, by saying that I should be a sincere mourner, if you were to leave this city.

Mrs Hazen has seen Mrs Wilson several times in your absence, and I am anticipating a call upon her myself this week.

With cordial esteem and warm affection,

Very truly yours A. W. Hazen

ALS (WP, DLC).

From Eugene Schuyler[1]

Dear Professor Wilson, Cairo. March 4, 1890.

Allow me to congratulate you on your election to a professorship at Princeton. Our ideas are so nearly alike on so many subjects, that I feel as if your promotion were a personal matter to me. I have not yet seen your book on the *State*,—indeed since the season has begun here I have been too busy to read anything—but I have no doubt that I shall agree with you in the main.

Your *Congressional Government* of course I have or had; but as I had to lend it about to Laveleye,[2] Geffcken,[3] Lord Acton & others, I am not sure of its present habitat. I know only that it is doing good work somewhere. I have an idea that the new Rules of Congress (H. R.)[4] are the outcome of it, but I have not yet seen them.

Pray believe me always

Yours most sincerely Eugene Schuyler

ALS (WP, DLC).

[1] Diplomat, author, Russian scholar, university lecturer, and, in 1890, American Consul General in Cairo. Schuyler had lectured at the Johns Hopkins in March 1885 and had come to know Wilson on this occasion. See WW to ELA, March 2, 1885, Vol. 4.

[2] Émile Louis Victor de Laveleye, Professor of Political Economy at the University of Liège.

[3] Friedrich Heinrich Geffcken, former diplomat and Professor of International Law at the University of Strasbourg.

[4] The new rules adopted on February 14, 1890, by the House of Representatives under the leadership of Speaker Thomas B. Reed of Maine, to prevent obstruction of business by the minority.

From Ellen Axson Wilson

My own darling, [Middletown, Conn.] Wed. Mar. 5/90

Your "scolding" (!) letter[1] came to hand this afternoon; and I would "give a pretty," dear, if I could only speak to you and so reassure you at once, and not wait on the slow movements of the mail to accomplish it. I do assure you, dear, I have *never* tired myself sewing except that once;—and I didn't say I had done an enormous quantity of sewing, but that I had an enormous deal *to do*,—a very different thing, unfortunately. What I have done has been of the pleasantest, easiest sort,—dresses for the children, —I have enjoyed every stitch of it; and it has really been a great resource. I should have been very lonely and blue during these weeks of your absence if I had not been busy in that way. As it was I have kept constantly bright and cheerful. And in considering the way I "work," dear, I think you don't take enough into account the difference between the nature of your work & mine. Of course it would tire anyone to do brainwork very long. But the day isnt long enough to tire a perfectly *well* person with manual work when it requires no muscular exertion. There is a great deal in disposition too & that ought to be taken into account, sir;—it is my *nature* to work steadily and continuously at every task & *therefore* it doesn't weary me to do so. It does tire me,—nay more it *torments* me—*not* to work that way;—to do things by snatches, and go from one to another in a miscellaneous unsystematic fashion. Oh dear! It never occurs to me that I ought to have been a man except when I think how much positive suffering I have endured because of that *passion* for concentration, so misplaced in a "house-mother" & yet so valuable to a man in any calling. But enough of this, I only want to persuade you to put yourself in her place, for I am sure that if you did so you would see this whole question of work quite differently. And I do promise you that I *will* and assure you that I *do* take good care of myself,—just as good as you could, my darling.

I enclose a pathetic letter from Mr. Dabney.[2] Poor fellow! I am *so* sorry for him. Surely there must have been more in that little woman than appeared if he could love her so for ten years.

But I was delayed in my writing until late by the boys &c., and have had to scribble very hurriedly, and must now close. But I love you my own darling, as much as if I had time & space to tell you so all over a dozen pages. I *will* do *anything* you wish to prove it[—]even that hardest of all things,—nothing at all!

Your little wife Eileen.

ALS (WC, NjP).

[1] It is missing.

[2] R. H. Dabney to WW, March 1, 1890.

From Francis Landey Patton

My dear Professor Wilson: Princeton, March 5 1890

I thank you for writing to me so frankly as you did in your letter of Feb 21st. I understand very fully the anxiety you feel in regard to the pecuniary side of our invitation to you to become a Professor here. As I said to you I should have been glad had the way seemed clear for us to offer you $3,400—the maximum salary. But in view of the fact that so many—your seniors in office here—are now receiving only $3,000, & in view of the further fact that we must face the prospect of a diminished income from vested funds it did not seem to me wise to recommend that the salary be made more than $3,000.

I have thought over your questions respecting the continuance of your relations to Johns Hopkins should you come to Princeton. As I said to you in conversation the authority to make this arrangement lies with the Trustees & with them alone. I hardly think that you would wish a meeting of the Trustees called to consider the question. It would be better not to do so I think. My own opinion is that you ought under the circumstances referred to in your letter to be allowed to continue your work at Johns Hopkins, and that we should be as indulgent in this respect as the authorities at Wesleyan have been. I do not think that there will be any difficulty in regard to this matter.

I should say that you might safely accept our chair & feel confident that for the present at least you would be unhindered in the prosecution of your work at Johns Hopkins, it being understood that your lectures in the future would consume no more of your time than they now do & that if it ever proved to be feasible that time might be reduced. After a little you may find that other literary avenues may open. With diminished classroom work will probably come new literary leisure & more opportunity to earn an income by your pen. And after a few years it may seem best to the Trustees that your academic relationships should be limited to Princeton. I can hardly say that I think the Trustees would be willing to stipulate for an indefinite that is to say for a permanent extension of your lectureship at Johns Hopkins. But I feel quite confident that you need give yourself no great anxiety about that for the present; and you may count upon me always as your advocate & friend so far as it shall ever be in my power to make your life in Princeton happy & useful.

I am most faithfully Francis L. Patton Prs

ALS (WP, DLC).

From Ellen Axson Wilson

My own darling, [Middletown, Conn.] Friday, Mar. 7/90

I enclose in this a couple of letters, though with some little doubt as to whether I am wise in so doing. But I suppose this is certain to reach you by Tuesday at any rate. And just to think that this is the very last letter this time! One would think I found it a species of torture to write you, I am so overjoyed at that reflection. Oh my darling, my Woodrow, my own love I will one week from tonight, be the happiest woman in all the world,—God willing. My heart leaps within me and then beats almost to suffocation at the mere *thought* of it. What then will the reality be? The rapture of such meetings *almost* compensates for the pain of parting. Even my present feeling is far from unenviable though the joys of anticipation are mingled with the uneasiness of intense longing, for the joy predominates, and there is something very exhilerating in the excitement of happy expectation if the longed-for moment is not *too* far in the future.

You percieve that I won't let myself expect you positively on Friday night, for I want you to feel at liberty to spend your free week in any desirable way, & to change your plans at the last moment even without fear of disappointing me too much. So I shan't really *count* on you until Saturday, that is I won't let my mind *dwell* too much on the hope of an earlier meeting. If I knew your address in N. Y. I would write you there. I wonder if it would do to direct to Mr. Bridges'. You won't get this in time to answer. I think I will try a short note at any rate. Alas, just after writing that it occurred to me that I had forgotten *his* address,—I *always* forget *all* addresses,—and five minutes pondering fails to recall it. So unless you write,—no, I have it now, I will write to Princeton, care Prof. Sloane.

We are having a perfect carnival of sleighing here, the fine moon-light nights invite them to keep it up quite late. Some boys have just come for Stock but he was at Prof. Winchesters. Alexander[1] took him sleighing this afternoon & they were out for hours. Am so glad he had such a good taste of it this winter. I went yesterday chiefly on his account but of course today was much better for him.

Day before yesterday one of the boys, Day, was terribly hurt by Pullman with a snow shovel, as they were playing together.[2] It happened just across the street and he is now at the Alpha Delta house. He will be badly disfigured, they say, but his eyes fortunately escaped. The Dr. says he don't see how such wounds *could* be inflicted with such an instrument. His face was "cut to pieces," he had to put in twenty-one stitches.

I had the Dr. called in today, when he was across the way, to look at my foot again, as you seemed to wish it. He says its appearance is satisfactory & I was right to leave off the poultice when I did;—says I can walk a little, but the less the better. I had a pleasant visit from Dr. Hazen yesterday & went down stairs to see him.

Some photographs of your have come & there are only eleven; how is that? But it is time to stop writing to you & to begin *dreaming* of you instead,—so good-night & pleasant dreams to my darling from His little wife Eileen.

All send love & the children, who constantly speak of you, send kisses. They are all perfectly well.

When in Phila. please be sure to mention *incidentally* that we have almost decided to send Ed to Mr. Johnston in April so that if Uncle T.—or rather if Aunt Saidie wishes[3]—he can renew the invitation given last summer to stay with them & so save his board.[4]

ALS (WC, NjP).

1 Either Howard Townsend Alexander, '90, or William Wellington Alexander, '90.

2 Walter Burrows Day, '91, and John Stephenson Pullman, '92.

3 The Rev. Dr. and Mrs. Thomas Alexander Hoyt.

4 This referred to her brother Edward Axson, who was to go to Philadelphia to Mr. Johnston, a speech therapist, for help in curing Edward's stuttering.

To Azel Washburn Hazen

My dear Dr Hazen, Baltimore, Md., 8 March, 1890.

Your kind letter of March 4th warmed my heart as it has not been warmed in a long while. I do not know, I am sure, how I have deserved the affectionate friendship you have offered me and I have so eagerly accepted; but I do know that that friendship has itself done not a little towards rendering me worthy of it, so much have I been stirred and benefited by it. Mrs. Wilson and I have regarded our relationship with you and Mrs. Hazen as one of the chief advantages and pleasures of our life in Middletown; and I sincerely wish that I might say that there was a prospect of our continuing to enjoy it. But I have virtually committed myself to the Princeton authorities, and must accept their call. My only demand was that I be allowed to continue my connection with the Johns Hopkins, and to that they have very generously consented. I shall leave Wesleyan with genuine and profound regret; but with many most valuable additions to the roll of my indulgent friends. Expecting and hoping to see you very soon again, and with warmest regards both to Mrs. Hazen and yourself,

Cordially, affectionately Yours, Woodrow Wilson

ALS (photostat, RSB Coll., DLC).

To Robert Bridges

My dear Bobby, Baltimore, Md., 8 March, 1890

I thank you sincerely for your prompt, and wise, answer to my letter asking for your advice. It helped me to make up my mind to go to Princeton in any event; but, happily, it has not been necessary for me to carry out that resolution, for Dr Patton now assures me that I may accept in full confidence that the Trustees will consent to my continuing my engagement here at the Hopkins. I shall send my formal acceptance to Dr. Craven, the Clerk of the Board, as soon as I can consistently with courtesy to the Wesleyan people.

I am to dine with Sheldon at the Univ. Club next Thursday evening (the 13th) and if you are not going to be able to be there I am to be counted on to look you up during the few hours which will be mine outside the hours of the engagement. Till then, goodbye.

As ever Your sincere friend, Woodrow Wilson.

P.S. I leave Balto. Tuesday morning, and stop in Phila. and Princeton (to look up a house) on my way home. W.

ALS (WC, NjP).

From John Franklin Jameson

My dear Wilson: Providence, March 9, 1890.

I have so long delayed writing to you that now I am uncertain whether you are at Baltimore or whether you have returned to your "respective home." I'll address to the latter at a venture; and hope you have had a prosperous session at the former. I have heard from Mrs. Carey that you were ill during a part of the time, but hope that that is now far back in the past. I hope, too, that Mrs. Wilson has fully recovered from the accident, of which I was extremely sorry to hear. While you were in Baltimore I got some news of you and others in a pleasant letter from Adams. He was, as usual, in a high state of satisfaction with the progress of the Association, but I, for my part, have my doubts about some of its developments,—and made free to tell him so. It seems to me to be giving more and more weight to those members who are simply "prominent citizens," presidents of local historical societies and that class of person, distinguished for being distinguished, and to be injuring its scientific value by striving to achieve popular distinction and prestige. But I may be wrong; I was unable to be present at this last meeting.

I am using your book, and at present enjoying the use of it, though, if you will not exclaim with Canning,

> "But, of all plagues, kind Heaven, thy wrath can send,
> Save, save, oh save me from the candid friend!"

I will say that I think the chapter on Germany, which we have just traversed, includes too many details. I did not think so until I came to use that chapter with a class; but they found it very hard. I am noting misprints, as well as a few things which seem to me to be errors, in order some time to send them to you, and chasten, what must needs be chastened in every man, your pride as a proof-reader.

I do not know that there is any valuable historical news to be forwarded hence, save that Weeden's Economic History of New England[1] is nearly through the press. I am convinced that it will be thought a highly important and valuable contribution, as well as a very laborious piece of truly original research. Our lecture-course was exceedingly successful. During our first course our hall was full every night, crowded sometimes; and even in the second, with less popular topics, we had larger audiences than last year. The Boston Herald had an editorial commending the movement as a new move of the Andrews administration,[2] quite oblivious of the three mighty men who last year fought their way through to the remote wells of Middletown and elsewhere, and brought thence refreshment for our thirsty college and its friends. But we don't mind that, for really we are delighted at the success with which Andrews is urging the college forward and at the favorable turn which public opinion respecting it is taking. . . . I hear nothing from Hart, and hardly like to poke him up. It is not impossible that Mrs. Hart may be in a state which makes them unwilling to entertain. In that case, would you like to have them (i.e. the men) come to Middletown? If you would, I can use that on Hart, delicately, so as to make him show his hand. Morse[3] is ill, and probably cannot ask us. Write me soon about this.

I suppose one may properly congratulate you, if what I hear is true; you will enjoy your life there, but I shall be sorry to have you and Mrs. Wilson leave New England. I suppose Turner is booked for Allen's place. Is there a better man in the country to take yours than Levermore? I know he would go there, and, with your consent and in support of your efforts if they tend that way,

I should be glad to write to Raymond on his behalf, for I have great respect for his abilities & acquirements. Please give my kindest regards and best wishes to Mrs. Wilson.

Sincerely yours, J. F. Jameson.

ALS (WP, DLC) with WWhw notation on env.: "Ans. 3/20/90."

[1] William B. Weeden, *Economic and Social History of New England, 1620-1789* (2 vols., Boston and New York, 1890).

[2] *Boston Herald*, Nov. 12, 1889. This editorial also warmly commended Wilson's speech at Brown University on November 11, 1889, for showing that the eager hopes of socialists were impossible of realization except through the natural movement of institutions.

[3] Probably Anson Daniel Morse, Professor of History at Amherst.

To Ellen Axson Wilson

My own darling, Baltimore, Md., 10 March [1890]

I simply can't write to you to-night. *To-morrow* morning I start *towards* you and that blessed fact makes me so impatient of pen and ink that I am simply too nervous to use them. I am coming, darling, I am coming! and I'm the happiest man in the world. I can think of nothing but you, my blessed little wife, and the kisses and caresses there are in store for me. I am coming and, oh, I am so happy that I am Your own Woodrow

ALS (WP, DLC).

From Ellen Axson Wilson

My own darling, [Middletown] Mon. Mar. 10/90

According to promise I write a few lines to send to Princeton. I wish though I had said I would direct to "Princeton" merely, for you could have gotten it from the office & so perhaps been saved trouble. Yet I suppose you *must* see Prof. Sloane. I fear this will find you engaged in a discouraging business, house-*hunting* but not house-*finding*. How *can* we pay rent on two houses for two months and *such* high rent too on both! It seems *impossible*—with the moving and all. Suppose we try "light housekeeping" for a year. I throw this out of course as the merest suggestion but I really think it worth inquiring into. Did you not tell me that the hotel there,—University Hall?—is used as an apartment house? We might get four rooms there (or elsewhere) and have them serve our dinner while we prepared the other meals on an oil stove. We would keep one good servant,—Mary, if possible, who would sleep in a corner of the room in which we did our light cooking, with a screen partition. The sitting-room would also be the dining-room and we could wheel some of the cribs in it at night. Your study would be in another part of the house. Uncle Tom lived that way when they first went to Phila. & they were quite comfortable. We would do all the simple cooking for the children's early dinner & order dinner for *two* persons only if Ed was away at school, for three if he was with us. Of course if he were there another room would be needed. You know how anxious I am for him to go off to school, but I am afraid if he has to go to Phila. it will be impossible because of that expense. I sent Uncle R. a long letter on the subject. But stay! A sudden idea strikes me; if we should try the "light house-keeping" it would be cheaper for *us* to board him in a Southern school than with us! Really this plan grows in favour with me as I write of it! I hope you will make careful inquiries about it. We must if possible, by one means or another, "live cheap" next year. In the houses you examine please notice the *wall-papers* very carefully & if they are dingy, or ugly & unsuitable insist upon having them changed in the principal rooms.

This was a good day, darling, a very good day indeed for your little wife, for it brought me two *such* lovely letters from you.[1] Really, dear, I think you must have made up your mind to turn my head entirely; do you suppose, sir, that *any* feminine head is strong enough to stand such deep draughts of mingled love and praise as you have been administering to me of late? I assure you if you do you are badly mistaken. As for me those maddening draught's have had such an effect that I am kept in an almost constant state of intoxication.

> "Kings may be blest but [she][2] was glorious.
> O'er all the ills o life victorious."

I am fairly "beside myself"; and yet I think I have a remarkably steady head not to show it more than I do. The rest of the family don't seem to suspect that I have "had more than was good for me" anymore than they suspect what an extraordinary woman I am—how very superior to the rest of my sex. In fact Mary the nurse was the only member of the domestic circle besides yourself who appreciated me; she percieved my superiority to the rest of the family! You percieve that I am giving practical proof of my determination to "accept" your praises.

But oh dear! I had best close this for I *can't* write to you now,—not a *love*-letter I mean,—for as the time for dispensing with the make-shift of letters drawers nearer I become more and more impatient of writing them, more and more dissatisfied with the inadequacy of what I *have* written. My very pulses which throb so & my nerves which quiver at the thought of your speedy coming rebel against any further thralldom to pen and ink. He is coming, my darling is coming! Only four days more,—and "days are short this time of year"! Ah dearest, if you can read the language of love and understand its meaning—its *full* meaning—you will indeed have no reason to complain of the welcome given you by

Your little Wife.

ALS (WC, NjP).

[1] These are missing, as are most of the letters between Woodrow and Ellen during the period of Wilson's stay in Baltimore in 1890.

[2] EAW's brackets. The lines are from Burns's "Tam o' Shanter."

Edward Webster Bemis's Review of *The State*

[March 15, 1890]

"The State," by Woodrow Wilson.

Such is the title of the most valuable work on the history of government and the best brief account of the present political institutions of Europe and America that has appeared. In a compact, well-written volume of nearly seven hundred pages, from the press of D. C. Heath & Co., of Boston, Prof. Wilson, of Wesleyan University, now called to succeed Alexander Johnston, at Princeton, and well-known as the author of "Congressional Government," has summarized the results of recent scholarship relative to the origin and growth of government. Its origin was the family under the absolute control, tempered by custom, of the patriarch. The distinctive features of Greek, Roman, and feudal institutions, and the rise of Teutonic representative government are well portrayed. But that part which will most interest the average reader and which is least known is the full account of the present constitutions of France, Germany, Switzerland, Austro-Hungary, and Sweden-Norway. Hitherto that part of government has been most studied which concerns us least. What goes on in Washington really affects us far less, whether it be tariff or pensions, unless we get one, than the proceedings of our State legislators on local taxation and a score of other topics, or the means taken by our city council to assure us good and cheap gas, and well-paved dustless streets. Recent investigation has turned to these latter points and Prof. Wilson, a native, we believe, of

South Carolina, has well, though briefly, sketched the local institutions of this country, both North and South, and enables us to compare them with these in Europe. The secret of the instability of the republican government in France is readily understood when it is shown how, until recently, and still in a measure, all local officers such as governors of provinces and mayors of cities, and even local legislative bodies have been appointed and controlled from Paris by the central government. Under such a system of centralization, training in republican self-government, which must be largely local government, has been impossible. The French are becoming aware of this grave defect and are gradually decentralizing, while England, once as fully possessed of independent township and county government as ourselves, and indeed the source and model of our forefathers in that regard, is also returning to these local institutions which had gradually fallen into desuetude since the time of the Stuarts. The book under review closes with a study of the functions of government as shown rather in practice than in any theories of what the State ought or ought not to do. A few sentences will illustrate the treatment of this much mooted point. The contrasts between ancient and modern States "are contrasts of policy not of power. . . . If the ancient State was regarded as the ultimate owner, the modern State is regarded as the ultimate heir of all estates. Failing other claimants, property escheats to the State. If the modern State does not assume, like the ancient, to administer their property upon occasion for competent adults, it does administer their property upon occasion for lunatics and minors. The ancient State controlled slaves and slavery[;] the modern State has been quite as absolute, it has abolished slavery." The modern State, however, as he says, deems it wise to leave the individual free in many ways to develop himself as he may choose. One more quotation must suffice: "What is society? It is an organic association of individuals for mutual aid. Mutual aid to what? To self-development. . . . The individual must be assured the best means, the best and fullest opportunities, for complete self-development; in no other way can society itself gain variety and strength. But one of the most indispensable conditions of opportunity for self-development, government alone, society's controlling organ can supply. All combination which necessarily creates monopoly, which necessarily puts and keeps indispensable means of industrial or social development in the hands of a few, and those few not the few selected by society itself but the few selected by arbitrary fortunes, must be under the direct or the indirect control of society. To society alone can the power of dominating combination belong, and society can not suffer any of its members to enjoy such a power for their own private gain independently of its own strict regulation or oversight."

EDWARD W. BEMIS.

Printed in the Nashville *Round Table*, I (March 15, 1890), 14-15.

From Charles William Kent[1]

My dear Wilson, Knoxville, Tenn., March 19th 1890

The estrangement, which has no further cause than a mere separation by space and perchance a slight difference in interests, is yet sufficient to render a letter, after a long silence, more strained and less spontaneous than would be a personal greeting and an old-time clasp of hands. How I wish I could substitute these for this note and live over with you in rapid sketch but with most ardent interest, our experiences since the days of our warm hearted and loyal intercourse. You may not recall now, as you must have recognized then and as I am only too glad to acknowledge at all times, that your friendship, being that of an older and more experienced student was directly beneficial and encouraging. How often I have wished that I might fall in with you again, perhaps be thrown near enough together in space, to allow us to come very much nearer in renewed interests and revived expressions of the friendship which I am certain, still lives unhurt by lapse of time. And may not an occasion of our meeting be at hand? You have under consideration, I hope with all your desires linked with our petition, our invitation to deliver an address before our University at its commencement exercises.[2] It would not be hard for you to conjecture that the first suggestion of that request came from me, but it would not be a part of your conjecture that your name is so well known with us through your own work and through the able service of your honored father at our last commencement,[3] that it met with most cordial recognition and hearty approval. I wish to add to your deliberations the small weight of my own personal desire and to turn by this small weight the balance in our favor. I trust it will be convenient for you to come and that we can have several long talks.

I congratulate you upon your election to the chair at Princeton and yet I am almost sorry to have you go there, because with a number of your friends I wish to see you at the University of Va, and I am afraid it would be difficult to entice you to leave Princeton after you had once settled there.

Enjoying the anticipation of hearing from you and the hope of seeing you I am

Faithfully & fraternally Charles W. Kent.

ALS (WP, DLC) with WWhw notation on env.: "Ans. Mar. 26/90."

1 Kent was at this time Professor of English and Modern Languages at the University of Tennessee.

2 This invitation is missing, but see WW to C. W. Kent, March 26, 1890.

3 See JRW to WW, May 9, 1889.

From Edward Ireland Renick

My dear Wilson, Washington, D. C., March 20, 1890.

I have been intending to write to you ever since I heard of your call to Princeton, in order to extend my cordial congratulations; now that you have, as it were, stepped into my room—for, as Mrs. Mayrant[1] used to say, "it [the photograph][2] is the living, breathing image of the man"—I must put aside all else, even Government claims, to say first "Thank you," and second—"Hurrah for Wilson." I do most sincerely—all of us do most sincerely—glory in you. And your new book? That—though some critics carp at its size and scope—is sure to redound to your credit, and to serve a good purpose. An appreciative notice of it is to be found, by the way, in the last number of "The Round Table," a new literary venture of Nashville, which you may have seen. Will you take your new chair next session? What change, if any, will be made in your course of lectures? I imagine that they will take on more of a legal coloring. Is it not so? We are now organizing a society here in the Treasury for the thorough study of the origin and developement of the Executive Departments, the various services under them, and the administrative law bearing upon them. I sent yesterday to the Political Science Quarterly an article on "The Comptrollers and the Courts"[3] which, if it ever sees the light, will give you an idea of the nature of our (the new Society's) investigations. We have some men here who could vastly improve our machinery, if they could get together and succeed in securing a hearing. All are well & join in kind regards to you & your little band.

As ever, E. I. Renick

ALS (WP, DLC). On env.: WWhw notation, "Ans. April 28/90," and WWhw sums and memorandum about clothing purchased.

1 Of Aiken, S. C., mother of Kate Drayton Mayrant and an acquaintance of Wilson and Renick during their Atlanta days.

2 Renick's brackets.

3 E. I. Renick, "The Comptrollers and the Courts," *Political Science Quarterly*, v (June 1890), 214-23.

To Joseph Ruggles Wilson

My precious father, Middletown, Conn., 20 March, 1890.

Everything seems to resist a swift progress for our correspondence. During my last weeks in Baltimore I had the "grippe," in a mild form, but severely enough to make lecturing a torture: and yet I was obliged to lecture, in order to get through in the time allotted me. The lectures had to be prepared, too, from day to day: —altogether I was a very wretched individual; and, when I reached home last Friday, a very much used-up one. I am better now, and I am sure that it will not take long for home influences to make me perfectly well again.

I stopped at Princeton on my way home, to look for a house,— by no means an easy thing to find there. I have not yet formally accepted the call to P., but I have accepted it in all except form, for Dr Patton has assured me that I may accept in full assurance that the Trustees will consent to my continuing my present arrangement with the Johns Hopkins. That concession will certainly be sufficiently liberal, and I have every reason to be satisfied.

This is the only news. Of course our plans as to moving etc. are not yet matured.

I find that everybody regards my election to P. as a sort of crowning success: congratulations pour in from all sides: evidently I am 'writ down' in the category of 'successful men.' I suppose I ought to feel an immense accession of personal satisfaction,—of pride; but somehow I can't manage it. I feel grateful and full of courage at the prospect of having an opportunity to do just the studying and writing I want to do under the most favourable circumstances; but, so far as personal gratification is concerned, I would infinitely rather know that I was going to have a chance to be cured of the heart-sickness from which I suffer because of my separation from you and 'Dode.' My *mind* can't give me gratification: I know it too well,—and know it a poor thing: I have to rely on my *heart* as the sole source of contentment and happiness, and that craves, oh *so* fiercely, the companionship of those I love. It seems to me that the older I get the more I need you: for the older I get the more I appreciate the debt I owe you, and the more I long to increase it. It seems to me that my separation from you, instead of becoming a thing of wont, becomes more and more unendurable. Are you *quite* well, now? Please, Sir, let me know as early as possible your plans for the summer —how soon they include us. I suppose dear 'Dode' will come

North too *this* summer. I keep his picture on my desk all the time, and all the time long to see him.

Dear Ellie is much better, though her foot is still far from being well. She pretends to love you and 'Dode' as much as I do: but that is impossible. Your devoted son Woodrow

ALS (de Coppet Coll., NjP).

To John Franklin Jameson

My dear Jameson, Middletown, Conn., 20 March, 1890.

I don't often ask a friend to endure a machine-made letter, such a letter seeming impersonal in its make and therefore not sufficiently friendly; but just now I am in such a state of body and hand that I can hardly endure the slow fatigue of a pen, and feel that since I must write to you at once I must write in this way, with the aid of this old copier of mine.

The fact of the matter is that that monster "La Grippe," which I escaped so long as I remained at home, got hold of me in Baltimore; I struggled through with my lectures notwithstanding him; and the result is that I am left limp and worthless, *getting* well but by no means well or in working trim. The mere effects of the grippe, however, would not keep me from adopting with pleasure your suggestion about entertaining the history professors were Mrs. Wilson fit to undertake the necessary preparations; but her foot, so terribly burned during the Christmas holidays, (did I tell you of the accident?) is still so far from being well that she can only hobble about and can attend to none of her ordinary household duties. It would be out of the question to invite the men to partake of a Middletown hotel or caterer's dinner: their maledictions would follow me the rest of my days. Inasmuch as I am about to leave New England I should particularly like to do this entertaining just now; but unhappily it is out of the question. It is very odd that Hart should have said nothing about his promise and the non-fulfilment of it. The explanation you suggest is the only likely one,—sufficient and yet awkward to mention.

I noticed the article in the Boston *Herald* which gave Andrews the credit for what you had yourself accomplished at Brown, and my heart entertained much indignation thereat. You are very generous and disinterested not to care.

As for Levermore and the succession to the history chair here, I am quite of your mind, that he is the man for the place, if the chair is to remain undivided particularly; and I know that they have been considering his name among others. The great obstacle,—the obstacle which may prove insurmountable,—is his previous connection (?) with the chair. The only serious governmental crisis in the history of the college grew out of, or at any rate was connected with, the rejection by the Trustees of the Faculty's nomination of Levermore for the instructorship in history,—or, rather, the smuggling in by the president of another man, a candidate of his own.[1] There are still influential men among the Trustees who are sore about the final defeat and rejection of the said president, which grew out of the quarrel, though most of the Trustees regretted their own action in the Levermore case almost as soon as it was taken. The president really deceived them, and they acted in the dark, not meaning to antagonize the Faculty by departing from the immemorial precedent of accepting Faculty nominations. It would be an act of poetical justice to put Levermore into the full chair now, and I should heartily like to see it done; but what a timid, or, rather, cautious, set of men will do must until the final action is taken remain in doubt. The doubt is rendered none the less by the rather large number of available and desirable men in sight. I wish you would let Levermore know what my attitude in the matter is. If it were the selection of an assistant or colleague in my Department, my advice would, I am confident, be conclusive; but whether I shall be able to determine who my successor shall be is another question.

No, I am not satisfied with the House of Commons plan,[2] tho.' I still think that it contains more that is helpful and promising than any other plan of legislative imitation. Besides, I do not believe that the scheme has yet been tried under favourable conditions. At the Hopkins there were scattered city residence and the allurements and distractions of city life to rob it of vitality. Here the House is kept moribund by the vitality of the fraternities. These things, added to the "*esprit frondeur*" to which you allude, have robbed the House of the predominant and permanent attractiveness, the regular, matter of course interest, which would be needed to put it on the best footing.[3] The tendency to too rapid changes of ministry is as pronounced as in France.[4] But, on the whole, despite these serious limitations, I believe the plan better, because more interesting, than others.

I am sincerely obliged for your criticisms on the 'State' and hope that you will make them as numerous and as definite as you can. Is the excess of detail in the chapter on Germany in the large or in the fine print, do you think, or is no such distinction observable in the matter? I have myself been conscious of the same thing in my class use of the book; but I have not yet seen my way clear towards correcting the difficulty. The Prussian system, particularly, is essentially complex, and could hardly be more simply described; and it has been my idea all through that it was only by running the details of such systems through the minds of the student that he could be made to retain the general features. I do not hold my classes responsible for the details on examination, but only in recitation.

I shall be unaffectedly sorry to leave Wesleyan; but I shall be glad to go to Princeton, not only because it is my *alma mater* (that I believe to be no special advantage), but because I shall, in the course of two years at the outside be given the opportunity there to confine my teaching to the special lines in which I most want to study and write. We shall move, probably, about July or August in order to get settled before the opening of the college year. I hope we shall have a chance of seeing you before we leave.

Mrs. Wilson joins me in warmest regards.

Faithfully Yours, Woodrow Wilson

WWTLS (J. F. Jameson Papers, DLC).

[1] The Levermore affair was apparently closely connected with a more important episode in the history of Wesleyan University—the removal of the Reverend John Wesley Beach from the presidency of the university in 1885.

The faculty, on May 20, 1885, nominated Levermore as Instructor in History and Political Economy to replace the ailing Hedding Professor of History and Political Economy, George L. Westgate. The Middletown, Conn., *College Argus*, XVIII (June 12, 1885), 188, in fact announced that Levermore would take Westgate's place during the next academic year.

However, President Beach ignored the faculty's recommendation and persuaded the Board of Trustees, at its meeting on June 23, 1885, to appoint Abraham Winegardner Harris, Wesleyan '80, as Instructor in History and Political Economy, a post which he held until 1888.

This action caused great furor among the faculty and students and seems to have precipitated a showdown which resulted in the Board's action on June 27, 1885, declaring the presidency vacant and appointing Professor Van Vleck as Acting President. Beach, who had become president in 1880, had long since lost the confidence of "all elements of the college community—students, faculty, alumni, trustees." (John W. Spaeth, Jr., Archivist of Wesleyan University, to A. S. Link, April 20, 1967.)

[2] Wilson was replying to an inquiry about the Wesleyan House of Commons in a missing letter or postcard from Jameson.

[3] That the organization had languished since the preceding autumn is attested to by the fact that the college journal, the *Wesleyan Argus*, had printed only one news item about it since November 26, 1889—a report in the January 18, 1890, issue about the fall of the Gascoigne ministry!

[4] "The following fall [of 1889] the House of Commons began anew under the direction of the young professor [Wilson]. But the game of turning out a Ministry became too tempting a diversion for the boys, and the whole affair degenerated almost to a farce." Carl F. Price, "When Woodrow Wilson Was at Wesleyan, II," New York *Christian Advocate*, XCIV (Aug. 14, 1919), 1030-31.

From John Hanson Kennard, Jr.

My dear friend, New Orleans. Mch. 22d 1890

Out of the profoundest depths of the consideration of the extent to which the holder "of a bill is permitted to profit by an accidental payment, tho' the drawer's name be forged" I am lifted by the arrival of y'r photograph in the hands of my office boy just returned from the afternoon's mail. Many thanks for the kind remembrance. The photograph is the embodyment to me of so much that I like to look back upon in the past, that you put me under much obligation to you in sending it. I like it greatly, and hope it may not be many days before I see the original. Your charming wife and your warm and cordial hospitality to us are among our pleasantest remembrances and Mrs Kennard and I have the hope that you will give us the pleasure of having you at our home one of these days. . . .

As for my own self I have been busy getting together the *necessary* both in the law and on the outside, and cannot complain half as much of past results as of future prospects.

Come, write me a good long letter, full of news of yourself[,] your wife and babies—and I won't bother you again for twelve months.

Very truly, Y'r friend, John Hanson Kennard.

ALS (WP, DLC) with WWhw notation on env.: "Ans. April 1/90."

To Charles Dexter Allen

My dear Sir, Middletown, Conn., 26 March, 1890

I wish to express, through you, my sincere pleasure at the kind resolution of congratulation upon my election to a chair at Princeton passed by the Owl Club and sent me accompanied by your gratifying letter of March 19.[1] It is matter of very sincere gratification to me to have won the friendship of the Owl Club, an honorary place in its membership, and its interest in my work. It is no slight stimulation to be so believed in and generously supported; and I beg that you will convey to the Club my very hearty thanks and greetings.

For yourself, please accept assurances of my warm regard

Sincerely Yours, Woodrow Wilson

ALS (WC, NjP).

[1] It is missing.

To Charles William Kent

My dear Kent, Middletown, Conn., 26 March, 1890.

It was a sincere pleasure to receive your letter of the 19th. I have thought of you I can't tell you how often; have asked about you as often as possible from common friends like Dabney and Trent (how many of us have become professors—Dabney, Trent, and I all in the same lines, though T. is in part with you); and have wished most sincerely that I might see and know you as of old. I have just accepted the kind invitation of your Faculty for the next Commencement, and the desire to see you was no small part of my motive in doing so. It will be my first venture in the direction of Commencement addresses, and I shall make it with a good deal of trepidation: I shall rely upon the one or two friends I know in the audience for a consciousness of support, and so shall try to keep in countenance.

I hope that you like your position in the University of Tennessee,—that the work is congenial in kind and not too taxing in amount. I think that these are the elements of happiness for a college professor: the right kind of work and not too much of it. I am about to make the change to Princeton largely because the work I shall have there will be strictly within the lines in which I most wish to study and write, and moderate in amount. My position here has been in every way delightful and profitable, except that I have had to devote a great deal of time and energy to teaching things that I did not care to teach "es a constancy" (as they say in the "Great Smoky" mountains). As soon as possible—within two years at the outside—they will secure a special professor of Economics at Princeton, (such is the definite promise made to me) and leave me only four hours a week in my own favourite lines, of Public Law.

I note what you say about the University of Va. with surprise: I did not know that I had been in anyone's eye in connection with the Faculty of the grand old place. If I were to be offered a chair there in such a way as not to interfere in any degree with Dabney's prospects of promotion to full title and salary, it would be a sore temptation to me, such are my love and reverence for the University; but of course I would not put myself, even indirectly, into rivalry with Heath.

I have a family of three little daughters now (the youngest just five months old) and am beginning to feel very sedate, very patriarchal. Work and paternity are 'calculated' to sober a fellow!

And yet I feel, at the same time, a great deal of the boy revived in me by the companionship of my little ones.

Looking forward with genuine pleasure to seeing you again,

Affectionately Yours, Woodrow Wilson

ALS (Tucker-Harrison-Smith Coll., ViU).

To Herbert Baxter Adams

My dear Dr. Adams, Middletown, Conn., 27 March, 1890.

I have been somewhat surprised and distressed by the character of Iyenaga'a[1] examination paper in Administration. It shows what seems to me a very meagre knowledge of the subject indeed. I should say, however, that, reckoning it numerically, he might fairly be credited with answering fifty *per cent.* of the questions. If that entitles him to a certificate from me, you may file the enclosed to his credit; if it does not, why of course the matter must be reconsidered. I suppose that it is only fair to take his present over-worked condition into account and his comparative inability to express himself fully and exactly in English. I have taken these things into account in making out the certificate. I would not have given it on this paper to an American student.

I am hard at work here again, and fairly recovered from the grippe. With warmest regard,

Faithfully Yours, Woodrow Wilson

WWTLS (H. B. Adams Papers, MdBJ).

[1] Iyenaga received his Ph.D. from the Johns Hopkins in 1890.

From Joseph Ruggles Wilson

My precious son, Clarksville, Tennessee, Mar 27/90

It is always good—most good—to get a letter from you; and if I should receive very many of them in quick succession, devouring each as ravenously as the few angel-resembling ones are hurried to their destination, a sort of dyspepsia might ensue! But do not feel solicitous—one meal of this rich food every month or so will not damage my digestive powers: you need not therefore be any more careful in ministering to my hunger than you now are! Ah, yes—*hunger* is the word. I am however kept from actual downright starvation, by the pleasing thoughts it is permitted me to have with respect to one who is dearer to my heart than all else: I include in this beloved unit the dear Ellie, for both of you constitute a single object—only I have known you longer!

Right sorry I am that you have been afflicted with that huzzy among the diseases, La Grippe. It must have required not a little pluck to go on lecturing with her a-tugging at the "innards." But thus some have fought her off: by just not yielding to her rough importunities. The other sex can tolerate anything except neglect, and this kills.

It satisfies me, dearest one, to know that you have concluded to accept the Princeton offer, and done so upon your own terms. I was anxious touching the matter, lest some hitch might occur. It is hardly possible for me to tell of the gratification to my paternal pride your whole course has been so far. Somehow, though, I cannot get up any feeling of surprise. It is altogether what was to have been expected, in view of your fine accomplishments taken in connection with your manly modesties and noble industries. Yet, even with all these, it is not often that success like yours has been achieved, for such rapidity of movement towards the higher places of your profession is seldom marked with so much that has deserved an honorable distinction. And that the great position you have gained does not render you vain, is only another proof of this desert. God has signally favored you, my darling son, but in nothing so much as in enabling you to experience that true solidity of character which is evinced by your being so little elated: and I am more thankful for this than for all else. Your continued child-love for me fills my heart with gladness as, whilst I write, it suffuses my eyes with tears. That this affection is abundantly reciprocated may go without the saying. Never was son dearer to father—for never was son so lovely. As to securing a house for your residence at Princeton, I have thought that it might be possible for us to *buy* or *build* one. You know that it cannot be long until I shall need a home, and I have been dreaming of the possibility of having this with you and Ellie, if it could be so managed as that I might not be an encumbrance: and I know of no better way than to have a room or two (for a "den") that I should myself *own*, in the way of a wing, perhaps, to the house which should otherwise be all yours. I would get together a few thousand dollars to be devoted to such a purpose. What do you think? Are houses too costly in P. to justify so fond a dream? It may indeed be, that, owing to certain physical disabilities, I shall be compelled to leave here before another year is over. If, therefore, we may not buy or build, I should like you to look out a *big* house for renting—big enough to stow me away without in the least interfering with the comfort of the family—I paying the additional rent, and more.

Dode joins me in large love to dearest Ellie and yourself.

Your loving & grateful Father.

ALS (WP, DLC) with WWhw notation on env.: "Ans. 31 Mar., 1890."

EDITORIAL NOTE

WILSON'S WORKING BIBLIOGRAPHY, 1883-90

Although Wilson had early developed the habit of jotting down bibliographical citations in notebooks and on slips of paper and the backs of envelopes, the bibliography printed below represents his first attempt to compile a systematic and well-arranged card file of works and sources in the fields of his major interests. He probably began putting this bibliography together in the autumn of 1883, soon after commencing graduate study at the Johns Hopkins. That this is true is evidenced by the fact that Wilson copied some of the titles from his classroom notebooks in Herbert Baxter Adams's courses in history and Richard T. Ely's in political economy. The text illustration on page 443 of Volume 2 gives graphic evidence of Wilson's method. Wilson continued to add to his bibliography after leaving the Hopkins, and internal evidence indicates that he made the largest additions while in Baltimore in February and March of 1889. The last entry was a brief review clipped from the New York *Nation* of March 27, 1890, hence the terminal date assigned to the bibliography. There are descriptive comments and analyses, some in shorthand, on many of the cards, and some of these Wilson copied from his classroom notebooks. Other such comments were Wilson's, some of which—for example, the biographical outline on Sir Henry Maine—he added after writing up the card with Maine's titles. Transcripts of the shorthand comments are printed without special identification.

A study of this bibliography in conjunction with materials in this and preceding volumes back to 1883 will make the significance of the bibliography at once clear. Wilson obviously included some (for him) esoteric topics and titles which he did not use extensively, if at all. However, the main body of the bibliography constitutes the core and also reflects the range of Wilson's scholarly reading and research for the period 1883-90. The list of authors and titles, moreover, reveals his increasing dependence upon the works of European, particularly German, scholars. It should be added, perhaps somewhat emphatically, that Wilson did not prepare this bibliography for work on *The State*, although, to be sure, in that book he cited many titles that he had included in his working bibliography.

The Editors found Wilson's file cards for the bibliography printed below in the Wilson Papers, Library of Congress, tied in bundles, and it was impossible to determine whether the cards were then in their original order. For the convenience of the reader, the Editors have arranged all of Wilson's cards (for both topics and authors) alphabetically and have assigned numbers in square brackets to each card for purposes of editorial cross-referencing. In addition, Wilson's abbreviated and incomplete references have been filled out, *in situ*, where possible, or in supplementary citations. In a few cases it was impossible to provide bibliographical information.

Wilson later—in early 1893—compiled a new bibliography on legal studies. Printed in the Editorial Note, "Wilson's Working Bibliography on Law," Volume 8, it is revealing about the range and emphasis of his scholarly work between 1890 and 1893.

A Working Bibliography

[c. Oct. 1, 1883–c. March 27, 1890]

[1] *Administration*:

Bulletin de la Société de législation comparee [71 vols. (Paris, 1869-1948)].

"[Traité des] Jurisdictions administratives et particulièrement des Conseils de Prefecture" by [Adrien Arnauld] *De Praneuf* [Paris, 1868].

[2] *Administration*:

"Conférences sur l'administration et le droit administratif,["] by [Léon] *Aucoc* [3 vols., Paris, 1869-76].

"Lehrbuch des deutschen Verwaltungsrecht," by [Edgar] *Loening* [Leipzig, 1884].

[3] *Administration*:

"Cours de Droit Administratif," by [Théophile] *Ducrocq* (Welter 12 f[rancs]) [Paris, 1862].

"Droit Administratif," by *Boeuf*.

[François Boeuf, *Résumé de répétitions écrites sur le droit administratif* (Paris, 1886).]

[4] *Administration*

"Encyclopädie der Rechtswissenschaft," (v. Holtzendorff?) Title 'Verwaltungslehre' (ed. 1882 $6.25).

Important to get last edition[.] Treats of the reforms[.] Gneist in Prussian administration—a notable instance of what one man can do in such matters.

[Franz von Holtzendorff, ed., *Encyklopädie der Rechtswissenschaft in systematischer und alphabetischer Bearbeitung* (5 vols., Leipzig, 1880-82).]

[5] *Administration.*

"English Administrative Law of the Present in Comparison with German Administrative Systems," by *R. Gneist*[.] See *Gneist*

[6] *Administration,*

1. "Études administrative," by [Alexandre François Auguste] *Vivien* [2 vols., Paris, 1859].

2. "Droit administratif," by *Boeuf* [*see* No. 3].

[7] *Administration*

"Handbuch der politische Oekonomie" ([Gustav von] Schönberg)

Title "Verwaltungslehre' [3 vols., Tübingen, 1885-86]

I. Statistics–history and theory.
II Organization of administrative authority–the hierarchy.
III Sanitary administration and Police
IV Police of Forests
V. Care of the Poor[.] Police having control of this
VI The administration of morality.

[8] *Administration*
"Handbuch der Verwaltungslehre" with comparison of the literature and legislation of France, England, Germany and Austria, by L[orenz Jacob] v. Stein.
[*Handbuch der Verwaltungslehre, mit Vergleichung der Literatur und Gesetzgebung von Frankreich, England, Deutschland und Oesterreich* (Stuttgart, 1876).]

[9] *Administration*
"History of English Administration" by *R. Gneist*[.] See *Gneist.*

[10] *Administration*
"Lehre vom modernen Sta[a]t," III, 465-469, by J[ohann]. C[aspar]. Bluntschli [3 vols., Stuttgart, 1875-76].

[11] *Administration*
"Polizeiwissenschaft," by *R*[obert]. *v. Mohl*
[*Die Polizeiwissenschaft nach den Grundsätzen des Rechtsstaats* (3 vols., Tübingen, 1866).]

[12] *Administration*
"Précis de drois administratif," by *Pradier Foderé.* 7 editions.
[Paul Louis Ernest Pradier-Fodéré, *Précis de droit administratif* (Paris, 1853-72).]

[13] *Administration*
"Self-government in England" by *R. Gneist.* See *Gneist*

[14] *Administration*
"Verwaltungslehre" by L. v. Stein. 10 parts pub. 1865-'85.

I. The government and constitutional law of government with special reference to England, France and Germany.
II Self-government and its legal system
III System of association and laws governing this system
IV Population and administrative law relative thereto
V. Sanitary administration
VI. Education, schools. Schools of antiquity; schools of modern times.
VII Police guardianship
VIII General education and principles. Immorality, games of hazard and prostitution
IX. Dissolution of feudal rules, opposition thereto, and conditions imposed upon feudal tenants; expropriation in general.

[*Die Verwaltungslehre* (8 vols. in 4, Stuttgart, 1865-84).]

[15] *Administration,–Berlin*
"The Government of Berlin," by Dr. *Rudolph Gneist* (*Contemporary Review*, 46 [Dec. 1884]: 769)

[16] *Administration–English.*
"Institutions of the English Govt., Legislative, Judicial, Administrative["] by *Cox.* "Only Gneist's work can be compared with it"–C. K. Adams.
[Homersham Cox, *The Institutions of the English Government; being an Account of the Constitution, Powers, and Procedure, of the Legislative, Judicial and Administrative Departments* (London, 1863).]

[17] *Administration*: *European.*
"Institutions municipales et provinciales comparées (Organization locale en France et dans les autres pays de l'Europe; Comparaison; Influence des institutions locales sur les qualités politique d'un peuple et sur le gouvernement parlementaire; Reformes)" by H[enri]. de Ferron. Paris: Felix Alcan, 1884

[18] *Administration–France*
"Le Justice administratif en France" by *R*[odolphe]. *Darest*[e] [de la Chavanne] (Paris 1862).

[19] *Administration–France* and *England.*
"Administration locale en France et en Angleterre" by [Paul] *Leroy-Beaulieu* [Paris, 1872].

[20] *Administration* (French)
"Theorie des französischen Verwaltungsrechts," by O[tto]. Mayer [Strassburg, 1886].

[21] *Administration–German*
"Deutche Staatsrecht," by *Schülze.*
"Deutche Staatsrecht," by v. Rönne.
[Hermann Johann Friedrich Schulze, *System des deutschen Staatsrechts*, I (Leipzig, 1865); Ludwig von Rönne, *Das Staatsrecht der deutschen Reiches* (Leipzig, 1876).]

[22] *Administration–Prussian*
"Der Staatsdienst in Preussen" (treats only administration) by *Perthes*
"History of the Prussian Civil-Service," by *Isaacsohn.*
[Clemens Theodor Perthes, *Der Staatsdienst in Preussen, ein Beitrag zum deutschen Staatsrecht* (Hamburg, 1838); Siegfried Isaacsohn, *Geschichte des preussischen Beamtenthums vom Anfang des 15 Jahrhunderts bis auf die Gegenwart* (3 vols., Berlin, 1874-84).]

[23] *Administration–Prussian*
"Preuschische Staatsrecht," by *v. Rönne.* (4 vols.–3 and 4 relate to administration. "A work to be consulted rather than read.")
[L. von Rönne, *Das Staatsrecht der preussischen Monarchie* (4 vols. in 2, Leipzig, 1864).]

[24] *Administration–Prussian*
"Preuschische Staatsrecht," by *Schülze* (2 vols., [Leipzig] 1872-'77).

[H. J. F. Schulze, *Das preussische Staatsrecht auf Grundlage des deutschen Staatsrechts dargestellt*].

[25] *Administration–Roman Provinces.*
"Roman Provincial Administration to the Accession of Constantine the Great," *W. T. Arnold*[.] Macmillan, 1879[.] pp. 240.
[William Thomas Arnold, *The Roman System of Provincial Administration to the Accession of Constantine the Great* (London, 1879).]

[26] *Administrative Courts*
"Traité de la Juridiction administrative et des recours contentieux," by *E. Laferrière.* (See *Laferrière.*) Tome I: *Notions générales et legislation comparée. Histroire, organization, compétence de la juridiction administrative.* Paris: Berger, Levrault, et Cie, 1887. Tome II *announced.*

[27] *America–Discoveries*:
Collections of Me. Hist. Soc., Vol. I.
"Pre-Columbian Discov. of Am." *De Costa.*
"America Not Disc. by Columbus," *Anderson.*
"Life of the So-Called Christopher Columbus," *Goodrich.*
[Maine Historical Society, *Collections*, I (Portland, 1865); Benjamin Franklin De Costa, *The Pre-Columbian Discovery of America by the Northmen* (Albany, N. Y., 1868); Rasmus Björn Anderson, *America Not Discovered by Columbus. An Historical Sketch of the Discovery of America by the Norsemen, in the Tenth Century* (Chicago, 1874); Aaron Goodrich, *A History of the Character and Achievements of the So-Called Christopher Columbus* (New York, 1874).]

[28] *America–Discoveries*:
"Earliest Discovery of America," *Stevens*
"The Cabots"
"*Antiquitates Americanae*" (Hist. Soc., 1837) *Rafn*
"How America Came To Be Discovered" *Fiske*, Jno. (Harper's Mag., Dec. 1882)
[Henry Stevens, *Historical and Geographical Notes on the Earliest Discoveries in America, 1453-1530* (New Haven, Conn., 1869); H. Stevens, *Sebastian Cabot–John Cabot=O* (Boston, 1870); Carl Christian Rafn (ed.), *Antiquitates Americanae; sive, Scriptures septentrionale, rerum anti-columbianarum in America* (Hafniae, Denmark, 1837); John Fiske, "How America Came to be Discovered," *Harper's New Monthly Magazine*, LXIV (Dec. 1881), 111-19.]

[29] *America–Discoveries*:
"Exploration of the World" (N. Y. 1879) *Verne*, Jules.
"Submerged Continent" *Dunnally*, Ignatius.
"The Rise of Our Constitution," Lieber in 2nd Vol. of Misc. Writings.
[Ignatius Donnelly, *Atlantis: The Antediluvian World* (New York, 1882); "The Rise of Our Constitution and Its National Features," *The Miscellaneous Writings of Francis Lieber* (2 vols., Philadelphia, 1881), II, 17-85.]

[30] *America–Discoveries*:
Voyages of Marco Paulo (Ed. Col. Yule)
Hakluyt volume on Cathay
" Society: Voyages of the Zeni.
"Voyages of Northmen to America."
[Henry Yule (transl.), *The Book of Ser Marco Polo, the Venetian, Concerning the Kingdoms and Marvels of the East* (2 vols., London, 1871); H. Yule (ed. and transl.), *Cathay and the Way Thither; being a Collection of Medieval Notices of China* (Hakluyt Society, *Works*, XXXVI-XXXVII, London, 1886); *The Voyages of . . . Nicolo and Antonio Zeno to the Northern Seas, in the XIV Century* (Hakluyt Society, *Works*, L, London, 1873); Edmund Farwell Slafter (ed.), *Voyages of the Northmen to America* (Boston, 1877).]

[31] *America–State Law*
"American Statute Law" by F[rederic]. J[esup]. Stimson (Bost. C. C. Soule $6.50).
[*American Statute Law, An Analytical and Compared Digest* (2 vols., Boston, 1886-92).]

[32] *American* Constitutions
v. Holst on–see "Constitutions modern"
Precautions in Studying Constitutions[,] see "Constitutions."

[33] *Amos*, Sheldon
"The History and Principles of the Civil Law of Rome" (Lond. Kegan Paul, Trench, & Co., 1883)

[34] *Anderson*
"America Not Discovered by Columbus" [*see* No. 27].

[35] *Arnold*, [Wilhelm]
"Kultur und Recht der Römer." ([Berlin] 1868).

[36] *Arnold*, Wilhelm
"Recht und Culturleben"
"Recht und Wirthschaft."
[*Cultur und Rechtsleben* (Berlin, 1865); *Recht und Wirtschaft nach geschichtlicher Ansicht* (Basel, 1863).]

[37] *Arnold–W. T.*
"Roman Provincial Administration to the Accession of Constantine the Great." pp. 240[.] Macmillan, 1879 [*see* No. 25].

[38] *Aucoc*,
"Conférences sur l'administration et le droit administratif" [*see* No. 2].

[39] *Bachhoven*
"China."

[40] *Beaune*, [Henri]
"Introduction à l'étude historique du droit coutumier" (1880).
[*Introduction à l'étude historique du droit coutumier français jusqu'à la redaction officielle des coutumes* (Lyon, 1880).]

[41] *Behaim*, Martin
"Martin Behaim," *Morris* (Pubs. Md. Hist. Soc.)
[John Gottlieb Morris, *Martin Behaim, the German Astronomer and Cosmographer of the Times of Columbus* (Maryland Historical Society Publications, III, Baltimore, 1855).]

[42] *Belgium*, Administrative Law of
"Le droit administratif de la Belgique" by [Alfred] *Giron* [(3 vols., Brussels, 1885)]

[43] *Berlin*—Govt. of,
"The Government of Berlin," by Dr *Rudolph Gneist*. (*Contemporary Review*, 46 [Dec. 1884]: 769.)

[44] *v. Bethmann-Hollweg* [Moritz August].
"Der Römische Civilprozess." (3 vols., 1864-'66).
[*Der Civilprozess des gemeinen Rechts in geschichtlicher Entwicklung* (6 vols., Bonn, 1864-74); Vols. I-III subtitled *Der römische Civilprozess* (1864-66).]

[45] *Biddle* [Richard].
"Memoir of Sebastian Cabot, with a Review of the Hist. of Maritime Discovery" [London, 1831].

[46] *Biedermann* [Karl]
"Ueber den Merkantilisme" [Innsbruck, 1870].

[47] *Bisset* [Andrew]
"[A Short] History of the English Parliament" [I] pp. 189 (Lond., 1882) (2nd vol. 1883, pp. 132)
"[The History of] The Struggle for Parliamentary Government in England" (2 vols., London, 1877)

[48] *Blanqui* [Jérôme Adolphe]
"History of Political Economy in Europe" [translated by Emily J. Leonard (London and New York, 1880)].

[49] *Blumer*, *J*[ohann]. *J*[acob].
"Handbuch des Schweizerischen Bundesstaatsrechts" [2 vols., Schaffhausen, 1863-64].

[50] *Bluntschli*, J. C.
"Lehre vom modernen Stat." 'Verwaltung,' III, 465-469 [*see* No. 10].

[51] *Bluntschli*: J. C.
"Staats und Rechtsgeschichte von Zürich."
"Geschichte der Republik Zürich" (3 vols. [Zürich, 1847-57]).
["] " des Sweitzerischen Bundesrechts."
[*Staats- und Rechtsgeschichte der Stadt und Landschaft Zürich* (2 vols., Zürich, 1838-39); *Geschichte des schweizerischen Bundesrechts von den ersten ewigen Bünden bis auf die Gegenwart* (2 vols., Zürich, 1849-52).]

[52] *Boeckh* [August]
"The Public Economy of Athens" (trans.) [by George Cornewall Lewis (2 vols., London, 1828)]

[53] *Boeuf*,
"Droit administratif" (1886) [*see* No. 3].

[54] *Bonar* [James].
"Malthus and His Work" [London, 1885] (See *Nation* [No.] 1060) [reviewed in New York *Nation*, XLI (Oct. 22, 1885), 345-46].

[55] *Bourinot*, [John George]
"Parliamentary Procedure and Practice in the Dominion of Canada." [*Parliamentary Procedure and Practice; with an Introductory Account of the Origin and Growth of Parliamentary Institutions in the Dominion of Canada* (Montreal, 1884).]

[56] *Boutmy*, [Émile]
"Études de droit constitutionnel" [Paris, 1885].

[57] *Boutmy*–
["]Precautions in studying constitutions," see "Constitutions" [No. 93].

[58] *Brownson, Dr. O*[restes]. *A*[ugustus].
"The American Republic: Its Constitution, Tendencies, and Destiny" (New ed. '86–N. Y. P. O'Shea).

[59] *Brunner, H*[einrich].
"Geschichte und Quellen des Deutchen Rechtes," (1870 in v. Holtzendorff's *Encyclopädie der Rechtswissenschaft*,–4 ed. 1882) [*see* No. 4].

[60] *Bruns, C*[arl]. *G*[eorg]. (editor)
"Fontes juris romani antiqui." (4 ed., [Tübingen] 1879.)

[61] *Bryce* [James]
"Holy Roman Empire" [London and New York, 1887].

[62] *Büdinger*, Max.
"Vorlesungen über Englische Verfassungsgeschichte" (Wien, 1880) pp. 341.

[63] *Burchardi*, [Georg Christian]
"Lehrbuch des Römischen Rechts" (3 v., [Stuttgart] 1841-'46).

[64] *Cabots*:
Stevens.
"The Period of Great Discoveries," *Peschel.*
Enc'ly. Brit.
"Memoir of Sebastian Cabot, with a Review of the Hist. of Maritime Discov." *Biddle*
"Life of Cabot" (1869) reviewed in pamphlet by Stevens. *Nicholls.*
"American Biography" (Sparks) Art. by *Heywood.*
[For Stevens, *see* No. 28; Oscar Ferdinand Peschel, *Geschichte des Zeitalters der Entdeckungen* (Stuttgart and Augsburg, 1858); "Sebastian Cabot," *Encyclopaedia Britannica*, 9th edn., IV, 622-23; for Biddle, *see* No. 45; James Fawckner Nicholls, *The Remarkable Life, Adventures and Discoveries of Sebastian Cabot . . .* (London, 1869); Charles Hayward, "Sebastian Cabot," Jared Sparks (ed.), *Library of American Biography*, 1st Ser., IX (New York, 1856).]

[65] Canada, Constitution of,
"The Constitution of Canada" by J[oseph]. E[dwin]. C[rawford]. *Munro.* Demy 8vo. $2.50 Camb. Univ. Press [1889].

[66] *Capes*:
"Early Empire." (Epochs of [Ancient] History.)
[William Wolfe Capes, *Roman History. The Early Empire, from the Assassination of Julius Caesar to that of Domitian* (London, 1876).]

[67] *Carlyle* [Thomas]
"Frederic the Great" [6 vols., London, 1858-65].

[68] *Carter*, Calvin H.
"Connecticut Boroughs," (New Haven Hist. Soc'y, Vol. IV).
[New Haven Colony Historical Society, *Papers*, IV (New Haven, 1888), 139-83.]

[69] *Celtic Britain*—(Series on *Early Britain*)
"Celtic Britain" ([London] 1882) J[ohn]. *Rhys.*

[70] *Celtic History*
"Origines Celticae" E[dwin]. Guest, L.L.D. (McM, & Co., 1883—ed. by W. Stubbs, C. Deedes) [2 vols., London, 1883].

[71] *Chancery*—Hist. of the Court of
"History of the High Court of Chancery and other Institutions of England, from the time of Caius Julius Caesar intil the Accession of Wm and Mary," Conway *Robinson* (Richm., Balto., Phila., Bost., 1882).

[72] *Cherbuliez*:
"Swiss Democracy."
[Antoine Élysée Cherbuliez, *De la démocratie en Suisse* (2 vols., Paris, 1843).]

[73] *China.*
"The Middle Kingdom" *Williams.*
"Chinese Classics" *Legge* (Ed. in one vol. by *Loomis.*)
"Chinese Commission" (Govt. Rept.)
"Diary of a Chinese Ambassador" (*Littel*, Nov. 1880: from *Nineteenth Century*)
[Samuel Wells Williams, *The Middle Kingdom: A Survey of the Geography, Government, Literature, Social Life, Arts, and History of the Chinese Empire and Its Inhabitants* (2 vols., New York, 1883); James Legge (ed. and transl.), *The Chinese Classics* (5 vols., Hongkong and London, 1861-72); Augustus Ward Loomis (ed.), *Confucius and the Chinese Classics; or, Readings in Chinese Literature* (San Francisco and New York, 1867); F. S. A. Bourne (transl.), "Diary of Liu Ta-Jen's Mission to England," *Littell's Living Age*, CXLVII (Nov. 6, 1880), 344-50, reprinted from *Nineteenth Century*, VIII (Oct. 1880), 612-21.]

[74] *China*—History
"The Middle Kingdom"—*Williams*
"Staatsworterbuch" (Bluntschli)
Ency. Brit.—Titles 'China' (Douglas) 'Confucius' (Legge)

[For Williams, *see* No. 73; J. C. Bluntschli, *Staatswörterbuch* (3 vols., Zürich, 1869-72); Robert Kennaway Douglas, "China," *Encyclopaedia Britannica*, 9th edn., v, 626-72; James Legge, "Confucius," *ibid.*, vi, 258-65.]

[75] *China*–Literature
"Chinese Classics"–*Legge* ed. [*see* No. 73]

[76] *China*–Modern
"The Chinese"–Martin (President, American College in Peking)
"China"–*Gray* (Kulturgeschichte) Lond. '78.
"China"–*Bachhoven.*
[William Alexander Parsons Martin, *The Chinese: Their Education, Philosophy, and Letters* (New York, 1881); John Henry Gray, *China: A History of the Laws, Manners, and Customs of the People* (2 vols., London, 1878).]

[77] *China*–Religion
"The Religions of China"–[James] *Legge* ([New York] Scribners, 1881)

[78] *Chroniclers*, of Europe and Eng., The Early,
"Early Chroniclers of Europe and England" Jas. *Gairdner* (Pub. under the direction of the Soc. for Promoting Christian Knowledge) [London, 1879]

[79] *Chronicles*
Matthew Paris's (Bohn's Antiq. Lib., 3 vols.)
[J. A. Giles (transl.), *Matthew Paris's English History. From the Year 1235 to 1273* (3 vols., London, 1852-54).]

[80] *City*–The Ancient.
"The Ancient City" [Numa Denis] *Fustel de Coulanges* [Boston, 1874]

[81] *City Government* (Roman Empire)
"Verfassung der Städte des römischen Reichs" by *Emil Kuhn*[.] 8vo. Leip., 1874.
[Emil Kuhn, *Die städtische und bürgerliche Verfassung des römischen Reichs bis auf die Zeiten Justinians* (2 parts, Leipzig, 1864-65).]

[82] *Civilization.*
"The Origin of Semitic Civilization," [Archibald Henry] *Sayce.*
[Probably *Lectures on the Origin and Growth of Religion as Illustrated by the Religion of the Ancient Babylonians* (London, 1887).]

[83] *Clement*, Pierre
"Histroire de Colbert et de son Mercantile System."
[Pierre Clément, *Histoire de Colbert et de son administration* (2 vols., Paris, 1874).]

[84] *Clodd* [Edward]
"The Childhood of Religions" [London, 1875].

[85] *Confucius*:

"Confucius and the Chinese Classics"–*Loomis* (Phila., 1867).

"Digest of Confucius"–*Faber*.

"The Mind of Mencius"–"

"Confucianism"–Douglas (condensation of above works) Lond. '79.

[For Loomis, *see* No. 73; Ernst Faber, *A Systematical Digest of the Doctrines of Confucius,* translated by P. G. von Moellendorff (Hongkong, 1875); E. Faber, *The Mind of Mencius; or, Political Economy Founded upon Moral Philosophy. A Systematic Digest of the Doctrines of the Chinese Philosopher Mencius, B. C.* 325, translated by Arthur B. Hutchinson (London, 1882); R. Douglas, *Confucianism and Taouism* (London, 1879).]

[86] *Confucius*:

Ency. Brit. Title 'Confucius' (Legge)

"Chinese Classics" *Legge* ed. 7 vols. [*see* Nos. 73 and 74]

[87] *Connecticut: Local Govt. in*

"Connecticut Boroughs," by *Calvin H. Carter* (New Haven Hist. Soc'y, Vol. IV) [*see* No. 68].

[88] *Constitutional* History–America:

"Rise of the Constitution," *Lieber* (miscellaneous works)

["] " " " Republic," *Frothingham*

"History of the U. S." (from 1763, 2 vols. N. H., 1828) *Pitkin*

["] " " " " of Am." (3 vols.) *Neumann*

[For Lieber, *see* No. 29; Richard Frothingham, *The Rise of the Republic of the United States* (Boston, 1881); Timothy Pitkin, *A Political and Civil History of the United States of America, from the Year 1763 to the Close of the Administration of President Washington* (2 vols., New Haven, 1828); Karl Friedrich Neumann, *Geschichte der Vereinigten Staaten von Amerika* (3 vols., Berlin and New York, 1863-66).]

[89] *Constitutional Law.*

"Das ungarisch-osterreichische Staatsrecht," by [Wenzel] *Lustkandl* [Vienna, 1863].

[90] *Constitutional Law*

"Études de droit constitutionnel," by *Boutmy* [*see* No. 56].

[91] *Constitutional Law.*

"Lehrbuch des deutschen Staatsrechts," by *G*[eorg]. *Meyer* [Leipzig, 1878].

"Grundsätze des gemeinen deutschen Staatsrechts" by [Heinrich Matthias] Zöpfl [2 vols., Leipzig, 1863].

[92] Constitutional Law (Germany)

"Die deutschen Verfassungsgesetze der Gegenwart," by *H*[einrich]. *A*[lbert]. *Zachariae* [Göttingen, 1855].

[93] *Constitutions*

Precautions in Studying Constitutions (treats principally of American Consts.) by [Émile] Boutmy[.] Revue Politique et Literaire[,] 7 & 21 June & 7 July 1884.

["Droit public comparé: Des précautions à prendre dans l'étude des constitutions étrangères," *Revue Politique et Littéraire* (*Revue Bleue*), 3rd Ser., XXXIII (June 7 and 21, 1884), 705-11, 773-78; XXXIV (June 12, 1884), 33-40.]

[94] *Constitutions: Greek*
'Handbuch der griechischen Staatsallerthümer.' 2 vols. *Gustav Gilbert* [Leipzig, 1881].

[95] *Constitutions: modern*
"Handbuch des Oeffentlichen Rechts der Gegenwart, in Monographien." Herausgegeben von Dr. Heinrich Marquardsen, Professor in Erlangen. In Half-volumes. First 2 (vol. I) of a general nature; next 4 (vols. II, III) devoted to the Germ. States; Vol. IV to the consts. of other countries. Of these, vol. II complete + first ½ vol. I & second ½ vol. III. Of vol. IV. only "America" by v. Holst and Austria, by Albrich, with G. Britain and dependencies, by Marquardsen. "America" = 3rd. Abtheilung of first ½ vol. of vol. IV (189 pp.) Freiburg i. B.: J. E. [C.] B. Mohr [4 vols., Freiburg and Tübingen, 1883-1906].

[96] *Constitutions of Europe*
"Constitutions Europeenes," G. Demombynes.
"Europaische Verfassungen," Poelitz. (From 1790 down)
"Constitutions" de la Croix.
"Verfassungs Urkunden," Schubert.
[Gabriel Demombynes, *Constitutions européenes* . . . (2 vols., Paris, 1883); Carl Heinrich Ludwig Poelitz, *Die Europäischen Verfassungen seit dem Jahre 1789 bis auf die neueste Zeit* (3 vols., Leipzig, 1832-33); Jacques Vincent Delacroix, *Constitutions des principaux états de l'Europe et des États-Unis de l'Amérique* (3 vols., Paris, 1791); Friedrich Wilhelm Schubert, *Die Verfassungsurkunden und Grundgesetze der Staaten Europa's, der nordamerikanischen Freistaaten und Brasiliens* (2 vols., Königsberg, 1848-50).]

[97] *Contzen*, [Heinrich C. W.]
"Geschichte der Volkwirthschaftlehre Literatur im["]
[*Geschichte der volkswirthschaftlichen Literatur im Mittelalter* (Berlin, 1872).]

[98] *Cossa*–[Luigi]
"Guide to the Study of Political Economy" [London, 1880].

[99] *Cox*,
"Institutions of the English Govt., Legislative, Judicial, Administrative." "Only Gneist's work can be compared with it"–C. K. Adams [*see* No. 16].

[100] *Cox, S*[amuel]. *S*[ullivan].
"Union–Disunion–Reunion. Three Decades of Federal Legislation, 1855 to 1885; memories of Events preceding, during, and since the American Civil War." Providence, R. I., 1885, 1. 8°.

[101] *Creighton*, M [andell].
"The Age of Elizabeth" (Epochs of Mod. Hist.) [London, 1876]

[102] *Croix*, de la
"Constitutions" [*see* No. 96].

[103] *Crump*, Arthur.
"A short Inquiry into the Formation of Political Opinion from the Reign of the Great Families to the Advent of Democracy." Lond., 1885. 8°.

[104] *Curtius*
"History of Greece" (5 v. Scribners)
[Ernst Curtius, *The History of Greece*, translated by Adolphus William Ward (5 vols., New York, 1870-74).]

[105] *Daire*
"Collections of the Principal Economists" (contains writings of the Physiocrats)
[Eugène Daire, *Physiocrates* (Paris, 1846).]

[106] *Darest, R.*
"Le Justice administratif en France," by *R. Darest* (Paris, 1862) [*see* No. 18].

[107] *De Costa*:
"Pre-Columbian Discoveries of America" [*see* No. 27].

[108] *Democracy*
"La Democratie Autoritaire." By A. Gigot. N. Y., 1885 (Christern)
[Albert Gigot, *La démocratie autoritaire aux Etats-Unis. Le général André Jackson* (Paris, 1885).]

[109] *Democracy*,
"La Democratie en [et] Ses Conditions Morale[s]," by *Le Vte Philibert D'Ussel*[.] Paris 1884–E. Plon, Nourrit et Cie[,] Rue Garancière.

[110] *Democracy*:
"The Great Political Superstition" (the divine right of Parliaments) by *Herbert Spencer* (*Contemporary Review*, 46 [July 1884]: 24).

[111] *Democracy* (American)
"The American Republic: Its Constitution, Tendencies, and Destiny," by Dr. O. *A. Brownson* (N. Y. 1886 ed. P. O'Shea)

[112] *Democracy: (Swiss)*
"Democracy in Switzerland." Art. N. Y. *Nation*, 43:410[.] No. 1116, Nov. 18, 1886.

[113] *Demombynes*, G.
"Constitutions Européenes" [*see* No. 96].

[114] *Departments of Govt.*
"Zur Geschichte des Doctrin von den drei Staatsgewalten" by *v. Ranke*.

[115] *Diocesan Histories.*
(Soc. for Promoting Xn Knowl.)
"Canterbury,"–R[obert]. C[harles]. *Jenkins*, M.A. [London, 1880]
"Chichester,"–W[illiam]. R[ichard]. W[ood]. *Stephens* [*The South*

Saxon Diocese, Selsey–Chichester (London, 1881)].
"Durham,"–J[ohn]. L[ow]. *Low*, M.A. [London, 1881]
"Peterborough,"–G[eorge]. Ayliffe *Poole*, M.A. [London, 1881]
"Salisbury,"–W[illiam]. H[enry]. *Jones*, M.A., F.S.A. [London, 1880]

[116] *Discoveries, Early*
"The Period of Great Discoveries[.]" "The best thing on the connection between discovery and old world history." *Peschel* [*see* No. 64].
"The Rise of Our Constitution" *Lieber* Misc. Vol. 2 [*see* No. 29].
"The Life of Prince Henry of Portugal" [Richard Henry] *Major* [London, 1868].
"Life of Martin Frobisher." *Jones*, Rev. F[rank]. [London, 1878]

[117] *Douglas*
"Confucianism" Lond. 1879. (A condensation of Faber's two works, "Digest of Confucius" and "Mind of Mencius") [*see* No. 85].
"China" (Ency. Brit.) [*see* No. 74]

[118] *Droysen* [Johann Gustav]
"History of Prussian Politics."
[*Geschichte der preussischen politik* (5 vols. in 14, Leipzig, 1868-86).]

[119] *Droysen* [J. G.]
"Manual for Writing History." "One of the most suggestive studies known, containing more practical suggestions and more philosophy in 50 pages than contained in any book." Adams.
[*Grundriss der Historik* (Jena, 1858).]

[120] *Dubs, J*[acob].
"Das oeffentliche Recht der Schweizerischen Eidgenossenschaft" [2 vols., Zurich, 1877-78].

[121] *Ducrocq.*
"Cours de droit administratif" [*see* No. 3].

[122] *Dühring*
"Critical History of Political Economy and Socialism."
[Eugen Carl Dühring, *Kritische Geschichte der Nationalökonomie und des Socialismus* (Berlin, 1875).]

[123] *Du Mesnil-Marigny*
"Histroire d'Economie Politique des anciens peoples de l'Inde, de l'Egypt, de la Judée, et de la Gréce."
[Jules du Mesnil-Marigny, *Histoire de l'économie politique des anciens peuples* . . . (2 vols., Paris, 1872).]

[124] *Duncker*, Max [Wolfgang].
"History of Antiquity" (Trans. 1879; 3 vols. Lond.) "The very best modern authority on ancient history."
[Translated by Evelyn Abbott (6 vols., London, 1877-82).]

[125] *Dunnally*, Ignatius
"Submerged Continent" [*see* No. 29].

[126] *Early Empire*
"Early Empire" (Epochs of History) *Capes* [*see* No. 66]

[127] *Edwards* [Edward]
"Life of Raleigh."
[*The Life of Sir Walter Ralegh . . . Together with His Letters; now First Collected* (2 vols., London, 1868).]

[128] *Ehrenberg* [Victor]
"Commendation und Huldigung [nach fränkischem Recht]." ([Weimar] 1877)

[129] *Eichhorn. K*[arl]. *Fr*[iedrich].
"Deutche Staats- und Rechtsgeschichte." (1808–5 ed. 1843.) [4 vols., Göttingen, 1843-44]

[130] *England,–Political Opinion in*
"A short Inquiry into the Formation of Political Opinion from the Reign of the Great Families to the Advent of Democracy" by *Arthur Crump*[.] Lond., 1885, 8°.

[131] *England,–Thought in*
"History of English Thought in the Eighteenth Century," by *Leslie Stephen* (Portions on Burke, Hobbes, Locke, &c.) [2 vols., London, 1876].

[132] *English Constitution*
"The Crown and Its Advisers, or[,] Queen, Ministers, Lords, and Commons." pp. 222 (Ed[inburgh]. and Lond., 1870) *A*[lexander]. *C*[harles]. *Ewald* (Record Office)

[133] *English Constitution*
"The Government of England,["] by W[illiam]. E[dward]. *Hearn* ([London and New York] 2 ed. 1887).

[134] *English Constitution*–History.
"Constitutional History of England from 1760-1860" Chas. Duke *Yonge* (London, 1882)

[135] *English Constitution*–History.
"English Constitutional History" ([London and Boston] Houghton, M., & Co., 1881) pp. 766 [Thomas Pitt] *Taswell-Langmead*

[136] *English Constitution.*–History.
"History of the English Parliament" pp. 189. (Lond., 1882) *Bisset.* 2nd vol. 1883, pp. 132 [*see* No. 47].

[137] *English Constitution*–History
"Vorlesungen über Englische Verfassungsgeschichte" von *Max Büdinger* (Wien, 1880) pp. 341.

[138] *English History*
"History of England from the Conclusion of the Great War of 1815" Spencer *Walpole* ([London] Longmans, 1879[-80], 3 vols)

[139] *English History* (see also "*Epochs of Mod. History*")
"The Duke of Buckingham and Chas. I., 1624-'28" ([2 vols., London] 1875)

"The Personal Government of Chas. I., 1628-'37" ([London] 1877) (2 vols.)

"The Fall of the Monarchy of Chas. I., 1637-'49." ([London] 1882 (2 vols[.)]

(Longmans) S[amuel]. R[awson]. *Gardiner*

[140] *Epitome of the Synthetic Philosophy*. By F. Howard Collins. With a preface by Herbert Spencer. D. Appleton & Co. 1889.

["]A more admirably executed second-hand synopsis of a system of philosophy never was. Considered simply as an index to Spencer's systematic works, this 'Epitome' is invaluable; and to persons who read and reread those thick volumes, not because they believe in them, but only because they want to know what it is that so many others believe, and to whom the writings of the dreariest scholastic doctor are less heartbreakingly tedious, this one volume of 500 pages in place of a library of 5,000 pages is like balm of Gilead. Would it only embraced an introduction boiling the whole thing down to 50 pages! It is printed uniformly with Spencer's works, upon agreeable paper with clear type, and published by the same eminent firm which, by the dissemination of those writings, has contributed so much to the culture and thought of our people.["]

[Clipping from the New York *Nation*, L (March 27, 1890), 265.]

[141] *Epochs of Modern History* (Longmans and Scribners)

"The Age of Elizabeth"	*Creighton*
"Lancaster and York,"	*Gairdner*
"The Puritan Revolution, 1603-'60"	"
"The Fall of the Stuarts,"	E. *Hale*.
"The Age of Anne,["]	E. E. *Morris*
"The Era of the Protestant Revolution,"	*Seebohm*.

[For Creighton, *see* No. 101; James Gairdner, *The Houses of Lancaster and York, with the Conquest and Loss of France* (London, 1874); S. R. Gardiner, *The First Two Stuarts and the Puritan Revolution, 1603-1660* (London, 1874); Edward Hale, *The Fall of the Stuarts and Western Europe from 1678 to 1697* (London, 1874); Edward Ellis Morris, *The Age of Anne* (London, 1877); Frederic Seebohm, *The Era of the Protestant Revolution* (London, 1877).]

[142] *Epochs of Modern History* (Longmans and Scribners)

"The Early Plantagenets," [William] *Stubbs* [London, 1876].

"Edward the Third," W[illiam Parsons] *Warburton* [London, 1874].

"The Epoch of Reform [1830-1850]," [Justin] *McCarthy* [London, 1874]

[143] *Ewald*, A. C.

"The Crown and Its Advisors, or[,] Queen, Ministers, Lords, and Commons" pp. 222 (Ed[inburgh]. and London, 1870)

[144] *Faber*

"Digest of Confucius" [*see* No. 85]

"The Mind of Mencius: Political Economy Founded on Moral Philosophy" (H., M., & Co., Boston) See *Douglas*

[145] *Factory System*:
"Introduction to a History of the Factory System" by *E.* [R.] *Whately Cooke Taylor*. Lond: Rich. Bentley and Sons, 1886[.] 8vo. pp. 441.

[146] *Family*–History of
"League of the Iroquois"–L. H. *Morgan*
"Systems of Affinity and Consanguinity in the Human Family"–L. H. *Morgan* (Sm. Inst.)
"Ancient Society,"–L. H. *Morgan*
"Studies in Ancient History"–*McLennan*.
[Lewis Henry Morgan, *League of the Ho-dé-no-sau-nee, or Iroquois* (Rochester and New York, 1851); L. H. Morgan, *Systems of Consanguinity and Affinity of the Human Family* (Smithsonian Contributions to Knowledge, XVII, No. 218; Washington, 1871); L. H. Morgan, *Ancient Society; or, Researches in the Lines of Human Progress from Savagery, through Barbarism to Civilization* (New York, 1877); John Ferguson McLennan, *Studies in Ancient History: Comprising a Reprint of Primitive Marriage* (London and New York, 1886).]

[147] *Family*–History of.
"Principles of Sociology," Vol. I, Part III–[Herbert] *Spencer* [3 vols., London, 1876-86].
"Early Law and Custom," Chap. III–*Maine*
"Aryan Household"–*Hearn*
[Henry James Sumner Maine, *Dissertations on Early Law and Custom* (London, 1883); William Edward Hearn, *The Aryan Household, Its Structure and Its Development: An Introduction to Comparative Jurisprudence* (London, 1879).]

[148] *Family*–History of.
Studies of the Family Relations of the Omaha Indians (Am. Soc. Sci. Proceedings, 1882) A[lice]. C[unningham]. *Fletcher*
"Early History of the Family" (Contemp. Rev., [XLIV] Sept. 1883 [406-22].) A[ndrew]. *Lang*

[149] *Family*–History of.
"The Ancient City" *Fustel de Coulanges* [*see* No. 80]

[150] *Ferron*, H[enri]. de
"Institutions municipales et provinciales comparées (Organization locale en France et dans les autres pays de l'Europe; Comparaison; Influence des institutions locales sur les qualités politique d'un peuple et sur le gouvernement parlementaire; Reformes)["] Paris, Felix Alcan, 1884.

[151] *Feudalism*:
1. "Geschichte des Beneficialwesens" (Erlangen 1850) by [Paul R. von] *Roth*
2. "Feudalität u. Unterthanenverband" ([Weimar] 1863) *by same*
3. "Commendation u. Huldigung" by *Ehrenberg* (1877) [*see* No. 128]

[152] *Fisheries*, Their History.
"Relation of the Fisheries to the Discovery and Settlement of N.

America." *Woodberry.* (1880)

Govt. Report of the Am. Fisheries[.] *Sabine.*

"A Review of the F. Industries of the U. S. and of the Work of the F. Commission." *Goode*

[Lorenzo Sabine, "Report on the Principal Fisheries of the American Seas," United States Treasury Department, *Annual Report of the Secretary . . . on the State of the Finances, 1851-52* (Washington, 1853), pp. 131-493; George Brown Goode, *A Review of the Fishery Industries of the United States and the Work of the U. S. Fish Commission* (London, 1883).]

[153] *Fiske,* Jno.

"How America Came To Be Discovered" (Harpers Mag., Dec., 1882) [*see* No. 28]

[154] *Flanders: Legal History of.*

"Flandrische Staats- u. Rechtsgeschichte bis zum Jahre 1305" by [Leopold August] *Warnkönig* (4 v. [3 vols., Tübingen], 1835-'42).

[155] *Fletcher,* A. C.

Studies of the Family Relations of the Omaha Indians (Am. Soc. Sci. Proceedings, 1882) [*see* No. 148]

[156] *Flint,* Robt.

"Philosophy of History [in France and Germany]" [Edinburgh and London, 1874].

[157] *Florida*–History. J. H. Kennard

B. R. French: "Hist. Collections of La. and Fla."

R. Hakluyt: "Coll. of Voyages" vol. III, pp. 364-433 [*see* No. 159].

W. Hilton: "Rel. of a Discov. made on the Coast of Fla."

T. Irving: "Conquest of Florida."

W. Irving: "Life of Columbus," vol. V. See Ponce de Leon (Companions of Columbus)

[Benjamin Franklin French, *Historical Collections of Louisiana and Florida* (New York, 1875); William Hilton, *A Relation of a Discovery Lately Made on the Coast of Florida . . .* (London, 1664); Theodore Irving, *The Conquest of Florida, under Hernando de Soto* (2 vols., London, 1835); Washington Irving, *The Life and Voyages of Christopher Columbus; to which are added those of his companions* (3 vols., New York, 1849.]

[158] *Florida*–History. J. H. Kennard

D. G. Brinton: "Notes on the Floridian Peninsulas."

Encyclopaedia Britannica: Art. "Florida."

G. R. Fairbanks: "History of Florida."

P. Force: "Hist. Tracts," vol. IV (1836-46) papers by B. R. French and R. Hakluyt.

[Daniel Garrison Brinton, *Notes on the Floridian Peninsula, Its Literary History, Indian Tribes and Antiquities* (Philadelphia, 1859); S. A. Drake, "Florida," *Encyclopaedia Britannica*, 9th edn., IX, 338-41; George Rainsford Fairbanks, *History of Florida from Its Discovery by Ponce de Leon, in 1512, to the Close of the Florida War, in 1842*

(Philadelphia and Jacksonville, 1871); Peter Force (comp.), *Tracts and Other Papers Relating Principally to the Origin, Settlement, and Progress of the Colonies in North America, from the Discovery of the Country to the Year 1776* (4 vols., Washington, 1836-46).]

[159] *Florida*—History. J. H. Kennard

R. Kerr: "Coll. of Voyages" vol. V. 1824. Discovery of Florida by the Spaniards, chap. V [X].

J. H. McCulloh, jr.: "Aboriginal America."

F. Parkman: "Pioneers of France in the New World."

F. de Soto: "Discovery of Florida."

H. de Soto: "Letter on the Conquest of Florida."

[Robert Kerr, *A General History and Collection of Voyages and Travels* (18 vols., Edinburgh, 1824); James Haines McCulloh, Jr., *Researches, Philosophical and Antiquarian, Concerning the Aboriginal History of America* (Baltimore, 1829); Francis Parkman, *Pioneers of France in the New World* (Boston, 1865); *The Discovery and Conquest of Terra Florida by Don Ferdinando de Soto . . . Written by a Gentleman of Elvas*, translated by Richard Hakluyt, edited by William B. Rye (London, 1851); Hernando de Soto, *Letter of Hernando de Soto . . .* (Washington, 1854).]

[160] *Foderé*, Pradier.

"Précis de drois administratif." 7 editions [*see* No. 12].

[161] *Folk Moots*

"Primitive Folk-moots" by Geo. Laurence Gomme (London [1880)]

[162] *France: Early Constitutional History.*

"Die fränkische Reichs- u. Gerichtsverfassung," by *R*[udolf]. *Sohm* [Weimar] 1871.

[163] *France*—History.

"Lectures on the History of France." Sir *James Stephen* 2 vols. 8vo. Lond. 1857.

[164] *France: Legal History of.*

1. "Französische Staats- u. Rechtsgeschichte," by [Leopold August] *Warnkönig* & [L. J. von] *Stein* (3 v. [Basel] 1846-'8)

2. "Geschichte der Rechtsverfassung Frankreichs" by [Wilhelm] *Schäffner* (4 v. [Frankfurt a. M.] '45-'50) Last volume treats legal history of revolution.

3. "Histroire de droit français" by [Firmin Julien] *Laferrière* (6 v. [Paris] '52-'58) First 3 volumes treat Roman, Gaulish, and Frankish law; last 3 customs.

[165] *France*: *Legal History of*,

4. "Histroire du droit français" by *A*[lfred]. *Gautier*, (1, v., 1881)

5. "Introduction à l'étude historique du droit coutumier" by *Beaune* (1880)

[A. Gautier, *Précis de l'histoire du droit français* (2 vols., Paris, 1882); for Beaune, *see* No. 40.]

[166] *France–Literature.*
S[t]e Beuve.
Lotheissen, 17th Cent. (4 vols. 1877)
Hettner, 18th "
Nisard } *General Sketches.*
Villemain }

[Charles Augustin Sainte-Beuve, *Portraits littéraires* (3 vols., Paris, 1862-64); Ferdinand Lotheissen, *Geschichte der französischen Literatur im XVII. Jahrhundert* (4 vols., Vienna, 1877-84); Hermann Julius Theodor Hettner, *Literaturgeschichte des achtzehnten Jahrhunderts* (6 vols., Braunschweig, 1872); Désiré Nisard, *Histoire de la littérature française* (4 vols., Paris, 1844-61); Abel Francis Villemain, *Cours de littérature française* (4 vols., Paris, 1847).]

[167] *France*: Local Government.
"Institutions municipales et provinciales comparées" by H. de Ferron, q. v. Paris: Felix Alcan, 1884 [*see* No. 150].

[168] *France: The Revolution*
"A History of the French Revolution" by H[enry]. Morse Stephens. Vol. I, 1886[.] Lond: Rivingtons[.] N. Y: Scribners.

[169] *France: The States-General*
"Histroire des Etats Généraux" by *M.* [Edmé Jacques B.] *Rathery.* Paris, 1845.

[170] *Franks*, Laws of the,
"Fränkische Reichs- und Gerichtsverfassung" by *Sohm* [*see* No. 162].

[171] *Freeman*, E[dward]. A[ugustus].
"Growth of the English Constitution." Opening on the Swiss Federation
"Federal Government"
"Comparative Politics."
"Historical Essays." 3 Series.

[*The Growth of the English Constitution from the Earliest Times* (London, 1872); *History of Federal Government, from the Foundation of the Achaian League to the Disruption of the United States*, I. *General Introduction–History of the Greek Federations* (London and Cambridge, 1863); *Comparative Politics* (London, 1874); *Historical Essays* (London, 1871), 2nd Ser. (London and New York, 1873), 3rd Ser. (London, 1879).]

[172] *Frobisher*, Martin,
"Life of Martin Frobisher," Rev. F. *Jones* [*see* No. 116].

[173] *Frothingham* [Richard].
Concerning local govt. in New England, Am. Antiquarian Soc's. Proceedings, Oct., 1870 (answer to Joel Parker, q.v. [No. 280]).
["Report of the Council of the American Antiquarian Society," American Antiquarian Society, *Proceedings* (October 1870), pp. 15-38.]

[174] *Frothingham*
"The Rise of the Republic" [*see* No. 88].

[175] *Fustel de Coulanges, N. D.*
"The Ancient City" [*see* No. 80]
"Recherches sur quelques problemes d'histroire" *Contents*: Le colonat romain.—Du régime des terres en Germanie.—De la marche germanique.—L'organization judiciaire dans le royaume des francs. Paris, 1885. 8°.

[176] *Gairdner*, Jas.
"Early Chroniclers of Europe and England" (Soc. for Promoting Xn Knowl.) [*see* No. 78].
"Lancaster and York" (Epochs of Mod. Hist.) [*see* No. 141]

[177] *Gardiner*, [Samuel Rawson]
"Case Against Sir Walter Raleigh." Fortn. Rev., Vol. 7 ([May 1,] 1867) [pp. 602-14].

[178] *Gardiner*, S. R.,
"The Puritan Revolution, 1603-1660" (Epochs of Mod. Hist.)
"The Duke of Buckingham and Chas. I., 1624-'28" (1875)
"The Personal Government of Chas. I., 1628-'37" (1877) (2 vols.)
"The Fall of the Monarchy of Chas. I., 1637-'49." (1882) (2 vols.)
} (Longm
[*See* Nos. 139 and 141.]

[179] *Gautier, A.*
"Histroire du droit français" (1 v., 1881) [*see* No. 165].

[180] *Geib*, [Carl Gustav]
"Geschichte des Römischen Kriminalprozess" ([Leipzig] 1842).

[181] *Geography—Earliest:*
Strabo, 1:65
"Ferdinand and Isabella" II:11-18. *Prescott*
[Strabo, *Geography*, Book 1 (WW's "65" refers to one of a series of numbers appended to the extant manuscript copies of the *Geography* and reproduced in many printed editions); William Hickling Prescott, *History of the Reign of Ferdinand and Isabella, the Catholic* (3 vols., Boston, 1838).]

[182] *Geography—Earliest*:
[George A. Jackson] "The Beginnings of the Science of Geography." (Pop. Sci. Monthly, [XVI] Dec., 1879 [236-47].)
"Submerged Continent," *Dunnally*, Ignatius [*see* No. 29].
"Medea" Act. II *Seneca*

[183] *German Const. Law*
"Grundsätze des gemeinen deutschen Staatsrechts" by *Zöpfl* [*see* No. 91]

[184] *German Empire* (Judicial Jurisdiction 15th Cent'y)
"Die höchste Gerichtsbarkeit des deutschen Königs und Reiches im XV Jahrhundert," by *J*[ohann]. *A*[dolf]. Tomaschek [Vienna, 1865].

[185] *Germany: Constitutional History.*
"Deutche Verfassungsgeschichte" by G[eorg]. *Waitz.* (1844–2 vol. 3 ed. '82; 3 v. 2 ed. '83; 4 v., 1860)

[186] *Germany* (Const. laws of)
"Die deutschen Verfassungsgesetze der Gegenwart" by *H. A. Zachariae* [*see* No. 92].

[187] *Germany: Early Constitutional History.*
"Die fränkische Reichs- u. Gerichtsverfassung" by *R. Sohm* 1871 [*see* No. 162].

[188] *Germany–Govt. of the Empire.*
"Handbuch der Verfassung und Verwaltung in Preussen und dem deutchen Reiche." Von Graf Hue de Grais. See "Prussia–Admin. and Const." [No. 375].

[189] *Germany–Public Law of*
"Einleitung in das deutsche Staatsrecht," by *Otto Mejer.* (*very valuable*) J. C. B. Mohr (P. Siebeck) 1 vol. '85 (8m.[)]

[190] *Germany: The Empire.*
"Geschichte der Deutschen Kaiserzeit." Wilhelm v. Gies[e]brecht [2 vols., Braunschweig, 1855-58].

[191] *Germany: The Old Empire.*
1. "Deutche Staats- u. Rechtsgeschichte" by *K. Fr. Eichhorn.* (1808–5 ed. 1843) [*see* No. 129].
2. "Deutche Rechtsgeschichte" by *H*[einrich Matthias] *Zöpfl.* (1841 –4 ed. [3 vols., Braunschweig] 1871)
3. "Deutche Rechtsgeschichte," by *Ferd. Walter* ([2 vols., Bonn] 1852-7.)

[192] *Germany: The Old Empire*
4. "Lehrbuch der Deutche Staats- u. Rechtsgeschichte," by *J*[ohann]. *Fr*[iedrich]. *v. Schulte* ([Stuttgart] 1861–5 ed. 1881)
5. "Geschichte u. Quellen des Deutchen Rechtes" by *H. Brunner* (1870 in v. Holtzendorff's *Encyclopädie der Rechtswissenschaft,*–4 ed. 1882[)]. [*see* Nos. 4 and 59]

[193] *Gervinus.*
"Fundament[al] Principles of Writing History."
[Georg Gottfried Gervinus, *Grundzüge der Historik* (Leipzig, 1837).]

[194] *Gierke* [Otto Friedrich von]
["]Johannes Althusius und die Entwickelung der naturrechtlichen Staatstheoren" [Berlin, 1881].

[195] *Gies[e]brecht,* Wilhelm v.
"Geschichte der Deutschen Kaiserzeit" [*see* No. 190].

[196] *Gigot,* A.
"La Democratie Autoritaire.["] N. Y., 1885 (Christern) [*see* No. 108]

[197] *Gilbert*, Gustav.
'Handbuch der griechischen Staatsalterthümer.' Vol. I 'Der Staat der Lakedaimonier und der Athener.' Vol II Other States [*see* No. 94].

[198] *Giron*
"Le droit administratif de la Belgique" [*see* No. 42].

[199] *Gneist, Dr Rudolf*
1. "Englische Verfassungsgeschichte" (B[erlin] '82).
2. "Das englische Verwaltungsrecht der Gegenwart" (3 ed., 2 vols., Berlin 1883, 1884).
3. "Selfgovernment, Communalverfassung, u. Verwaltungsgerichte" (3 ed., B. 1871).

[200] *Gneist, Dr. Rudolph.*
1. "Self-government in England["] (3 edition [Berlin] 1871)
2. "The English Administrative Law of the Present in comparison with German Administrative Systems.["] (3 vols.—third not published 1885) '83. '84—2 vols., 3rd edition.
First edition published under title "History and Form of Offices in England" (1857).
Second edition (1867) "English Constitutional Law, Including the Army, the Courts and the Church."
1863 First edition "Self-government in England" considered first part of another work.
1881 Separate historical part of treatise under title "History of English Administration."
(There are 3 works of this man's, therefore, noted specialist.) See next card

[201] *Gneist, Dr. Rudolph.*
"The Government of Berlin" (*Contemporary Review*, 46:769) [*see* No. 15].

[202] *Gomme*, Geo. Laurence
"Primitive Folk-Moots" (London[)] [*see* No. 161].

[203] *Goode*, Prof. G. B.
"A Review of the Fishery Industries of the U. S. and of the Work of the Fisheries Commission" (Read in Eng. before International Congress Concerning Fishery Industries) [*see* No. 152]

[204] *Goodrich*
"Life of the So-Called Christopher Columbus" [*see* No. 27].

[205] *Government*:
"Primitive Folk Moots" by Geo. Laurence Gomme (London[)] [*see* No. 161].

[206] *Government*:
"The Limits of Individual Liberty[.]" An essay by *Francis C. Montague*[.] Lond: Rivingtons, Waterloo Pl., 1885. Most highly commended by *Westm*[*inster*] *Rev*[*iew*], [LXVII] Apr. 1885 [539-42]—Takes the large state-function view.

[207] *Grais, Hue de.*
"Handbuch der Verfassung und Verwaltung in Preussen und dem deutchen Reiche." See "Prussia–Admin. & Const." [No. 375].

[208] *Gray*
"China" Lond. 1878 (Hist. of laws, manners, and customs of the people) [*see* No. 76].

[209] *Greece*–History.
"Universal History: The Oldest Group of Nations and the Greeks" *L*[eopold]. *v*[on]. *Ranke* (trans. G. Prothero) (N. Y., Harpers, 1885)

[210] *Greece–Institutions.*
Handbuch der griechischen Staatsallerthümer. 2 vols. *Gustav Gilbert* [*see* No. 94].

[211] *Greek Ethnology*:
"The Dorians"–*Müller*
"History of Greece"–*Curtius*[.] Indicate chapters (most modern view)
[Karl Otfried Müller, *The History and Antiquities of the Doric Race*, translated by Henry Tufnell and G. C. Lewis (2 vols., Oxford, 1830); for Curtius, *see* No. 104.]

[212] *Greek Institutions*:
"Antiquities of Greece"–*Schömann.*
"Federal Government"–*Freeman.*
"Comparative Politics"– "
[Georg Friedrich Schömann, *The Antiquities of Greece*, translated by E. G. Hardy (London, 1880); for Freeman, *see* No. 171.]

[213] *Greek Law*, History of
"Gräco-italische Rechtsgeschichte" by [Burkard Wilhelm] *Leist* [Jena, 1884].

[214] *Guest*, E., L.L.D.
"Origines Celticae," (McM, & Co., 1883; 2 vols., ed. by W. Stubbs, C. Deedes) [*see* No. 70].

[215] *Hahn*, [Friedrich von]
"Die materielle Uebereinstimmung der Römischen und Germanischen Rechtsprinzipien" ([Jena] 1856)

[216] *Hakluyt*, Richard,
"The Principal Navigations, Voyages, and Discoveries of the Eng. Nation" ([London] 1589). An enlargement of this work, in 3 volumes, appeared in 1598 [3 vols. in 2, London, 1598-1600]. It has been called "The Prose Epic of the English Nation."
"Virginia Richly Illustrated" (1609) An advertisement for colonization.
[Richard Hakluyt (transl.), *Virginia richly valued, by the description of the main land of Florida, her next neighbour: Out of the foure yeeres continuall travell and discoverie . . . of Don Ferdinando de Soto. . . . Written by a Portugall gentleman of Elvas* (London, 1609).]

[217] *Hakluyt*, Richard (1553-1616)
"Introduction" of *Niell's* "Earliest Eng. Discoveries of America."
Doyle's Eng. Colonies in America, 1:106-9, 397.
[Edward Duffield Neill, *English Colonization of America* (London, 1871); John Andrew Doyle, *English Colonies in America* (5 vols., London, 1882-1907).]

[218] *Hakluyt Society*:
"Search for El Dorado" 1560-1.
"Voyages of the Zeni."
" " towards the North-west."
"First Voyage Around the World–Magellan."
[P. Simon, *The Expedition of Pedro de Ursua and Lope de Aguirre in Search of El Dorado and Omague in 1560-61* (Hakluyt Society, *Works*, XXVIII, London, 1861); for "Voyages of the Zeni," *see* No. 30; T. Rundall (ed.), *Narratives of Voyages toward the North-west . . . 1496-1631* (Hakluyt Society, *Works*, V, London, 1849); H. E. J. Stanley of Alderley (ed. and transl.), *The First Voyage Around the World, by Magellan* (Hakluyt Society, *Works*, LII, London, 1874).]

[219] *Hale*, E.
"The Fall of the Stuarts" (Ep'chs of Mod. Hist.) [*see* No. 141].

[220] *Hare*, Prof. [John Innes Clark]
"The Law of Contracts[.]" Valuable statement and comparison of development and peculiarities of Roman and English law of contract, and procedure thereupon. Boston: Little Brown, & Co., 1887.

[221] *Hearn.*
"The Aryan Household" [*see* No. 147].

[222] *Hearn, Wm. E.*,
"The Government of England" (2nd ed., Longmans, Green, & Co., Lond., 1887) [*see* No. 133].

[223] *Heeren* (Götingen)
"Hist. Researches into the Politics, Intercourse, and Trade of the Nations of Antiquity."
3 vols. on the Asiatic States (Oxford 1833)
2 " " " African Nations (" 1832)
"The only books that take up the *economics* of the oriental nations."
[Arnold Hermann Ludwig Heeren, *Historical Researches into the Politics, Intercourse, and Trade of the Principal Nations of Antiquity* (6 vols., Oxford, 1833-34).]

[224] *Heeren* (Götingen)
"Manual of Ancient History" (Oxford 1840) contains a summary of his larger work. Heeren and Ukert *series*

[225] *Hegel*
"Philosophy of History."
"Philosophie des Rechts."
[*Lectures on the Philosophy of History*, translated by J. Sibree (London, 1861); *Naturrecht und Staatswissenschaft im Grundrisse; Grundlinien der Philosophie des Rechts* (Berlin, 1820).]

[226] *Held* [Adolf]
"Carey's Socialwissenschaft und das Merkantil-System" ([Würzburg] 1866).

[227] *Hermann, Karl Fried.*
"Gesetz, Gesetzgebung, und gesetzgebende Gewalt im griechischen Alterthume."

[228] *Hildenbrand* [Karl]
"Geschichte und System der Rechts- und Staatsphilosophie" [*Das klassische Alterthum* (Leipzig, 1869)].

[229] *History*–Philosophy of.
"Philosophy of History"–*Flint.*
" " " –*Hegel*
" " " –*Schlegel*
"Scheme for a Theory of History"–*Wachsmuth* (1820).
"On the Task of the Historian"–von *Humboldt.*
"Fundamental Principles of Writing History"–*Gervinus.*
"Manual for Writing History"–*Droysen.*
[For Flint, *see* No. 156; for Hegel, *see* No. 225; Karl Wilhelm Friedrich von Schlegel, *The Philosophy of History*, translated by James Burton Robertson (2 vols., London, 1835); Ernst Wilhelm Gottlieb Wachsmuth, *Entwurf einer Theorie der Geschichte* (Halle, 1820); Wilhelm von Humboldt, "Ueber die Aufgabe des Geschichtschreibers," *Gesammelte Werke* (7 vols., Berlin, 1841-52), I, 1-25; for Gervinus, *see* No. 193; for Droysen, *see* No. 119.]

[230] *Holst*[,] v.
On Constitution of U. S.–See "Constitutions modern" [No. 95].

[231] *House of Commons, Procedure of*
"The Procedure of the House of Commons." *J*[ames]. *E. T*[horold]. *Rogers.* Contemporary Review [XLI], March 1882 [503-18].

[232] *Hugo,* [Gustav]
"Lehrbuch der Geschichte des Römischen Rechts bis Justinian" ([Berlin] 11 eds., 1790-1832).
"Geschichte des Römischen Rechts seit Justinian" ([Berlin] 3 ed., 1830).

[233] von *Humboldt.*
"On the Task of the Historian" [*see* No. 229].

[234] *Huschke,* [Philipp Eduard] (editor)
"Jurisprudentiae antejustinianae quae supersunt." (4 ed. [Leipzig], 1879.)

[235] *Ihering, R*[udolf] *v.*
"Geist des römischen Rechts" [*see* No. 236].
["]This is the most suggestive, and in my opinion, the soundest, book ever written on the subject. It is primarily a discussion of old Roman law, but is really a work on the evolution of law in general."–M. Smith [to WW, Feb. 19, 1887, vol. 5].
French trans: 'Esprit du droit Romain' [translated by O. Meulenaere (4 vols., Paris, 1877-78)].

[236] *Ihering*, [R. von]
"Geist des Römischen Rechts auf den verschiedenen Stufen seiner Entwicklung." ([Leipzig] since 1852 vols. 1-3).

[237] *Ihering*, v., *Dr. Rudolph*
"The Struggle for Law" (*trans.* [by John J. Lalor]) Chicago, Callighan & Co., 1879.

[238] *India*
"India and What It Can Teach Us" [Friedrich] *Max Müller* ("Standard Lib.") [London, 1883].
"[The History of] British India" *Jas. Mill* [3 vols., London, 1817].
"Vedic and Brahminic India." *Wheeler.*
[James Talboys Wheeler, *The History of India from the Earliest Ages* (4 vols. in 5, London, 1867-81).]

[239] *Isaacsohn*,
"History of the Prussian Civil-Service" [*see* No. 22].

[240] *Jackson*, Andrew
"La Democratie Autoritaire,["] By A. Gigot. N. Y., 1885 (Christern) [*see* No. 108]

[241] *Jones*, Rev. F.
"Life of Martin Frobisher" [*see* No. 116].

[242] *Judicial System* (of the Franks)
"Fränkische Reichs- und Gerichtsverfassung" by *Sohm* [*see* No. 162].

[243] *Jurisdiction*, Judicial.
"Die höchste Gerichtsbarkeit des deutschen Königs und Reiches im XV Jahrhundert," by *J. A. Tomaschek* [*see* No. 184].

[244] *Jurisprudence*
"Essays on Jurisprudence & Ethics," by F[rederick]. *Pollock* [London, 1882].

[245] *Karlowa* [Otto]
"Römische Rechtsgeschichte" [2 vols., Leipzig, 1885-1901].

[246] *Kautz.*
"Theory and History of Political Economy"
[Gyula Kautz, *Theorie und Geschichte der National-Oekonomik* (2 vols., Vienna, 1858-60).]

[247] *Keller* [Ferdinand]
"Lake Dwellings" "One of the very best books on the Stone Age." [*The Lake Dwellings of Switzerland and Other Parts of Europe*, translated by John Edward Lee (2 vols., London, 1878).]

[248] *Keller*, [Friedrich Ludwig von]
"Der Römische Civilprozess" (5 ed., [revised] by *Wach*, [Leipzig] 1876).

[249] *Kingsley*, Ch[arles].
Article on Sir Walter Raleigh, Littel's Living Age, Vol. 9 (1855). ["Life of Sir Walter Raleigh," *Littell's Living Age*, XLV (June 9, 1855), 579-614.]

[250] *Knies* [Karl Gustav Adolf]
"Political Economy from the Standpoint of the Historical Method." [*Die politische Oekonomie vom Standpunkte der geschichtlichen Methode* (Braunschweig, 1883).]

[251] *Kuhn*, Emil
"Verfassung der Städte des römischen Reichs" 8vo. Leip., 1874.

[252] *Kuntze*, [Johannes Emil]
"Institutionen und Geschichte des Römischen Rechts." (2 vols., 2 ed. 1879, 1880.)

[253] *Laferrière*,
"Histroire du droit français." (6 v., 1852-'8) First 3 volumes treat Roman, Gaulish, and Frankish law; last 3 customs [*see* No. 164].

[254] *Laferrière*, *E*[douard Louis Julien]. (Vice-Pres. Council of State)
"Traité de la Juridiction administrative et des recours contentieux."
Tome I *Notions générales et legislation comparée. Histroire, organization, compétence de la juridiction administrative.* XVIII, 670 pp.—1887
Tome II (*announced*) to be on "the limits of the administrative power" and "the exact competence and jurisdiction of the various administrative courts" of France. (See F. J. Goodnow, rev. *Pol. Sci. Quarterly* [II], Dec. 1887 [709-12].)
Paris: Berger, Levrault et Cie. [2 vols., Paris, 1887-88]

[255] *Lang*, A.
"The Early History of the Family," Contemp. Rev., Sept. 1883 [*see* No. 148].

[256] *Laurent*, [François]
"History of International Law and International Relations" (18 vols).
[*Histoire du droit des gens et des relations internationales* (18 vols., Paris, 1855-70).]

[257] *Lavergne* [Léonce Guilhaud de]
"French Economists of the 18th Century"
[*Les Économistes français du XVIII siècle* (Paris, 1870).]

[258] *Law, American Statute*,
"American Statute Law" by F. J. *Stimson* (Bost.—C. C. Soule $6.50) [*see* No. 31]

[259] *Law, Greek*
"Gesetz, Gesetzgebung, und gesetzgebende Gewalt in griechischen Alterthume," by Karl Fried. Hermann.

[260] *Law*, History of,
"Gräco-italische Rechtsgeschichte" by *Leist* [*see* No. 213].

[261] *Law*, Philosophy of,
"Geschichte und System der Rechts- und Staatsphilosophie" by *Hildebrand* [*see* No. 228]

[262] *Law*, Philosophy of,
"Philosophie des Rechts," by *Stahl.*
[Friedrich Julius Stahl, *Die Philosophie des Rechts nach geschichtlicher Ansicht* (2 vols. in 3, Heidelberg, 1830-37).]

[263] *Law, Public*
"Das ungarisch-osterreichische Staatsrecht," by *Lustkandl* [*see* No. 89].

[264] *Law, Public* (German)
"Lehrbuch des deutschen Staatsrechts," by *G. Meyer.*
"Grundsätze des gemeinen deutschen Staatsrechts," by *Zöpfl.*
[*See* No. 91.]

[265] *Law*, Roman
"Römische Rechtsgeschichte" by *Karlowa* [*see* No. 245]

[266] *Law*: the History of
"Beruf unserer Zeit für Gesetzgebung und Rechtswissenschaft," by [Friedrich Karl von] *Savigny* [Heidelberg, 1815]
French trans: [not found]
Eng. " : [*Of the Vocation of Our Age for Legislation and Jurisprudence*, translated by Abraham Hayward (London, 1831)]
"Contains chapters on the evolution of law which are to this day unsurpassed["]–Monroe Smith [to WW, Feb. 19, 1887, vol. 5].

[267] *Law: the History of,*
"Geist des römischen Rechts" by *R. v. Ihering*
French trans: "Esprit du droit romain."
["]This is the most suggestive, and in my opinion, the soundest, book ever written on the subject. It is primarily a discussion of old Roman law, but is really a work on the evolution of law in general"–Monroe Sm[ith] [*see* Nos. 235 and 236].

[268] *Law* and Society
"Recht und Culturleben" by Wm Arnold
"Recht und Wirthschaft" " " "
[*See* No. 36.]

[269] *Legge*
"Chinese Classics"* (7 vols.)
"Sacred Books of the East."
"The Religions of China."
"Confucius" (Ency. Brit.)
*Ed in one volume by Loomis
[For "Chinese Classics," *see* No. 73; James Legge (transl.), *The Sacred Books of China: The Texts of Confucianism* (4 vols.), *The Sacred Books of China: The Texts of Tâoism* (2 vols.), Vols. III, XVI, XXVII, XXVIII, XXXIX, and XL of Friedrich Max Müller (ed.), *The Sacred Books of the East* (50 vols., Oxford, 1879-1910); for "The Religions of China," *see* No. 77; for "Confucius," *see* No. 74; for Loomis, *see* No. 73.]

[270] *Leist*
"Gräco-italische Rechtsgeschichte" [*see* No. 213]

[271] *Lenorment.*
"Introduction to the History of Western Asia."
"History of Occidental Asia." Germ of–
"Manual of Ancient History."
[The first two titles apparently both refer to Charles Lenormant, *Cours d'histoire ancienne. . . . Introduction à l'histoire de l'Asie occidentale* (Paris, 1838); the third title probably refers to François Lenormant and E. Chevallier, *A Manual of the Ancient History of the East to the Commencement of the Median Wars* (2 vols., London, 1869-70).]

[272] *Leroy-Beaulieu,*
"Administration locale en France et en Angleterre" [*see* No. 19].

[273] *Liberalism,*
"Liberty and Liberalism," by [Arthur] *Bruce Smith* (Lond: *Longmans*, 1887).

[274] *Liberty*
"Liberty and Liberalism," by *Bruce Smith* (Lond: Longmans, 1887).

[275] *Lieber*
"The Rise of the Constitution" (incomplete essay in his miscellaneous works, edited by Gilman and Adams) [*see* No. 29].

[276] *Livy* (criticism)
"Essai sur Tite Live" by *H*[ippolyte Adolphe] *Taine* (12mo. Paris, 1856)

[277] *Local Government and Taxation*
[J. W. Probyn, ed.] "Local Government and Taxation in the United Kingdom" (Great Britain) (Series of Essays by *Cobden Club*, [London] Cassell, Petter, Galpin, & Co., 1882).

[278] *Local Government: U. S.*
"Connecticut Boroughs" by *Calvin H. Carter* (New Haven Hist. Soc'y., Vol. IV) [*see* No. 68].
"Local Government in Wisconsin" by *David* [E.] *Spencer* (Wis. Hist. Soc'y Collections, Vol. 11 [Madison, Wis., 1888, pp. 502-11]).

[279] *Local Government* (U. S.)
'Jaffrey Address' by *Joel Parker*, 1873.
[Anthony Van Wyck] "Shires and Shire Towns in the South" Lippincott's Mag. [xxx] Aug. 1882 [200-205].
[J. Parker, *An Address Delivered at the Centennial Celebration, in Jaffrey, August 20, 1873* (Winchendon, Mass., 1873).]

[280] *Local Government* (U. S.)
"Origin, Organization, and Influence of the Towns of New England," by *Joel Parker* (Proceedings Mass. Hist. Soc., June 1866 [Boston, 1867, pp. 14-65].

Am. Antiquarian Soc's Proceedings, Oct. 1870 by *Frothingham* [*see* No. 173]

[281] *Loening,*
"Lehrbuch des deutschen Verwaltungsrecht" [*see* No. 2].

[282] *Loomis*
"Confucius and Chinese Classics" (Phila[.] 1867) [*see* No. 73]

[283] *Lustkandl,*
"Das ungarisch-osterreichische Staatsrecht" [*see* No. 89].

[284] *Lyall,* Sir A[lfred Comyns]
"Asiatic Studies" [London, 1882]

[285] *McCarthy,*
"The Epoch of Reform" (1830-50) (Epochs of Mod. Hist.) [*see* No. 142]

[286] *McLennan*
"Primitive Marriage," which is included in his "Studies in Ancient History" [*see* No. 146].

[287] *Madvig,* [Johan Nikolai]
"Die Verfassung und Verwaltung des Römischen Staates." (1 vol., [Leipzig] 1881).

[288] *Maine,* Sir H. S.
"Early Law and Custom" [*see* No. 147]
"Ancient Law" [London, 1861].
"Early History of Institutions" [London, 1875]
"Village Communities and Miscellanies" [London, 1876].
Chief dates of Maine's Life:

Born	1822
B.A. Degree	1844
Regius Prof. C. L. (Camb.)	1847
Called to Bar	1850
"Ancient Law"	1861
Legal memb. Gov. Genl's. Council (India)	1862
Corpus Prof. Jurisp. (Oxford)	1869.
Memb. of Ind. (Secy of State's) Council	1871
Master Trinity Hall	1877
Whewell Prof. Intern. Law	1887
Died, (Feby. 3)	1888.

[289] *Major,* R. H.
"The Life of Prince Henry of Portugal" [*see* No. 116].

[290] *Mallock, W*[illiam]. *H*[urrell].
"The New Republic" N. Y. 1878–Scribner & Welford.

[291] *Malthus*:
"Malthus and His Work" by Bonar [*see* No. 54].
"Die Stellung der Sozialisten zur Malthus'schen Bevölkerungslehre" by Dr. Heinrich Soetbeer (Berlin 1886).

[292] *Manning*, (Cardinal)
"No Commonwealth without God"–Contemporary Rev., [XLIV] July, 1883 [19-31].

[293] *Marco Paulo*:
Voyages edited by Col. Yule [*see* No. 30].

[294] *Marquardsen*, Heinrich.
"Handbuch des Oeffentlichen Rechts der Gegenwart, in Monographien." See "Constitutions Mod." [No. 95]

[295] *Marquardt*, [Karl] *J*[oachim].
"Römische Staatsverwaltung." (3 vols., 1873-'78; 2 ed. of vol. 1, 1881.)
[Vols. IV-VI of K. J. Marquardt and T. Mommsen, *Handbuch der römischen Alterthümer* (7 vols., Leipzig, 1871-88).]

[296] *Martin* (President, American College in Peking)
"The Chinese" [*see* No. 76]

[297] *Massachusetts and Plymouth Union*
Lowell Institute Lectures: Mr. *Brigham*, 1883.
[William Brigham, *The Colony of New Plymouth, and Its Relations to Massachusetts: A Lecture of a Course by Members of the Massachusetts Historical Society, Delivered Before the Lowell Institute, Jan. 19, 1869* (Boston, 1869).]

[298] *Mayer*, O.
"Theorie des französischen Verwaltungsrechts" [*see* No. 20].

[299] *Mediaeval History*
"Studies in Mediaeval History" C[harles]. J[aneway]. Stillé, D.D. [LL.D.], ([Philadelphia] Lippincott, 1882)

[300] *Mejer, Otto*
"Einleitung in das deutsche Staatsrecht." (*very valuable*) J. C. B. Mohr. (P. Siebeck) 1 vol. '85 (*8m*[.)] [*see* No. 189]

[301] *Mencius* (Pupil of Confucius)
"The Mind of Mencius: Political Economy founded on Moral Philosophy"–*Faber* (Bost., H., M., & Co.) [*see* No. 85]

[302] *Meyer*
"Handlexikon."

[303] *Meyer*, G.
"Lehrbuch des deutschen Staatsrechts" [*see* No. 91].

[304] *Mill*, James
"British India" [*see* No. 238].

[305] von *Mohl*, [Robert]
"History and Literature of Politico-Economic Science" (3 vols) (in monographs)
[*Die Geschichte und Literatur der Staatswissenschaften. In Monographieen* (3 vols., Erlangen, 1855-58).]

[306] *Mohl*[,] R. v.
"Polizeiwissenschaft" (1866–3rd edition in 3 vols.) [*see* No. 11].

[307] *Mommsen, Theodor,*
"Römisches Staatsrecht." (2 vols., 2 ed. 1876, 1877).
[*Römisches Staatsrecht* (3 vols., Leipzig, 1871-88). Vols. I-III of K. J. Marquardt and T. Mommsen, *Handbuch der römischen Alterthümer* (7 vols., Leipzig, 1871-88).]

[308] *Montague, Francis C.* (Fellow, Oriel Col., Oxford, & Univ. Col., Lond.)
"The Limits of Individual Liberty" An Essay. See 'The State, Functions of.' Lond: Rivingtons, Waterloo Pl., 1885 [*see also* No. 206].

[309] *Morey, Wm. C.* (Prof. Hist & Pol. Sci. Rochester Univ. & Ph.D.)
"Outlines of Roman Law: comprising its Historical Growth and General Principles." $1.75. G. P. Putnam's Sons, 1884[.] See 'Roman Law' [No. 404].

[310] *Morgan*, L. H.
"The League of the Iroquois"
"Systems of Affinity and Consanguinity in the Human Family" (Smithsonian Contributions, Vol. 13.)
"Ancient Society"
[*See* No. 146.]

[311] *Morris.*
"Martin Behaim" (Md. Hist. Soc. Pubs.) [*see* No. 41]

[312] *Morris*, E. E.
"The Age of Anne" (Epochs of Mod. Hist.) [*see* No. 141]

[313] *Moser*, J[ohann]. J[acob].
"Von der Landeshoheit in Regierungssachen" [Frankfurt and Leipzig, 1772]

[314] *Muirhead*, Dr. [James]
"Historical Introduction to the Private Law of Rome." ["]In point of interest and of a clear presentation of the topic, such as to meet the wants of the general student, and in particular, of careful students of our own law, we have met no book in our language so satisfactory as this." [New York] Nation [XLIV] Feb. 24, '87 [170-71.] Edinb: Adam & Chas. Black, 1886.

[315] *Mulford*, Elisha,
"The Nation: The Foundations of Civil Order and Political Life in the United States." (Boston, H. M., & Co., 1882, 1 vol., pp. 418–$2.50.)

[316] *Müller* [Karl]
"The Dorians" [*see* No. 211].

[317] *Müller*, Max.
"India and What It Can Teach Us" ("Standard Library") [*see* No. 238].

[318] *Müller*, [Wilhelm]
"Political History of Recent Times." (translation).
[*Political History of Recent Times, 1816-1875, with Special Reference to Germany*, translated with an appendix covering the period from 1876-1881 by John P. Peters (New York, 1882).]

[319] *Municipal Government*
"De L'Organization Communale et Municipale en Europe[,] aux États-Unis et en France" *Henri Pascaud*[.] Full for *France*—poor for rest. Paris 1877[.] pamphlet pp. 288.

[320] *Municipal Govt.* (Roman Empire)
"Verfassung der Städte des römischen Reichs" by *Emil Kuhn*, 8vo. Leip., 1874 [*see* No. 81].

[321] *Nation*, The
"The Nation: The Foundations of Civil Order and Political Life in the United States." Elisha *Mulford*, L.L.D. (Boston, H., M., & Co., 1882, 1 vol., pp. 418.—$2.50.)

[322] *Nature*, Law of,
"Johannes Althusius und die Entwickelung der naturrechtlichen Staatstheoren," by *Gierke* [*see* No. 194].

[323] *Nature, Law of,*
"Lehrbuch des Vernunftrechts und der Staatswissenschaften" by [Karl Wenzeslaus Rodecker von] *Rotteck* [(4 vols., Stuttgart, 1829-35)].

[324] *Neumann*:
"History of the United States of America" (3 vols.) [*see* No. 88].

[325] *New England Confederacy*
"Acts of Commissioners" (vols. 9 and 10 Plymouth Colony Records)
"Mass. Hist. Soc." (vol. 9, 3rd series)
Pitkin
Lieber
[United Colonies of New England, *Acts of the Commissioners of the United Colonies of New England* (2 vols., Boston, 1859), Vols. IX and X of New Plymouth Colony, *Records of the Colony of New Plymouth, in New England*, edited by Nathaniel B. Shurtleff and David Pulsifer (12 vols., Boston, 1855-61); John Quincy Adams, "The New England Confederacy of 1643," Massachusetts Historical Society, *Collections*, 3rd Ser., IX (Boston, 1846), 189-223; for Pitkin, *see* No. 88; for Lieber, *see* No. 29.]

[326] *Nicholls,*
"Life of Cabot." (Reviewed in pamphlet by Stevens) [*see* Nos. 28 and 64].

[327] *Oncken* [Wilhelm]
"Die Staatslehre des Aristoteles" [2 vols. in 1, Leipzig, 1870-75].

[328] *Oriental History.*
"Hist. Researches into the Politics, Intercourse, and Trade of the Principal Nations of Antiquity" *Heeren* [*see* No. 223].

"The [Five] Great Monarchies of the Ancient Eastern World" (Scribners) [George] *Rawlinson* [(4 vols., London, 1862-67)].

[329] *Oriental History*
"History of Antiquity" *Max Duncker* (Trans. 1879, 3 vols. Lond.) "The very best modern authority on ancient history" [*see* No. 124].

[330] *Oriental History.*
"Introduction to the History of Western Asia" [*see* No. 271].
"History of Occidental Asia." *Lenorment* [*see* No. 271].
"Manual of Ancient History" [*see* No. 271].
"History of International Law and Int. Relations." (18 vols: vol. I, "The Orient") *Laurent* [*see* No. 256].

[331] *Oriental History*
"Universal History: The Oldest Group of Nations and the Greeks." *L. v. Ranke* (trans. G. Prothero) (N. Y., Harpers, 1885) [*see* No. 209].

[332] *Paris*, Matthew
"Chronicle" (Bohn's Antiq. Lib., 3 vols.) [*see* No. 79]

[333] *Parker, Joel*
"Origin, Organization, & Influence of the Towns of New England" (Mass. Hist. Soc's. Proc., June 1866[)] [*see* No. 280].
'Jaffrey Address,' 1873 [*see* No. 279].

[334] *Parliamentary Law*
"Parliamentary Procedure and Practice in the Dominion of Canada," by *Bourinot* [*see* No. 55].

[335] *Pascaud*, Henri.
"De L'Organization Communale et Municipale en Europe[,] aux États-Unis et en France." Paris 1877[.] pamphlet pp. 288 [*see* No. 319].

[336] *Perthes*
"Der Staatsdienst in Preussen" (treats early administration) [*see* No. 22]

[337] *Peschel*
"The Period of Great Discoveries" "The best thing on the connection between discovery and old world history" [*see* No. 64].

[338] *Pessimism*
"The World as Will and Idea," by *Arthur Schopenhauer*. Translated from the German by R. B. Haldane and J. Kemp. ([3 vols.,] Lond: Trübner & Co., [18]83-'86.[)] "The translators' work has been admirably done . . . the inexhaustible stores of wit and wisdom stored up in these volumes."–N. Y. *Nation* [XLII] June 17, '86 [510]

[339] *Peter*
"Staatslexikon" (Excellent reference book for anything on English institutions)

[340] *Phear*, Sir J[ohn Budd]
"Aryan Village in India and Ceylon" [London, 1880].

[341] *Philosophy*–German.
"The World as Will and Idea," by *Arthur Schopenhauer*. See '*Pessimism*' [No. 338]

[342] *Philosophy of the State* and of Law
"Geschichte und System der Rechts- und Staatsphilosophie" by *Hildebrand* [*see* No. 228]

[343] *Pitkin*
"History of the United States" (from 1763, 2 vols., New Haven, 1828) [*see* No. 88].

[344] *Poelitz*
"Europaische Verfassungen" (from 1790 down) [*see* No. 96]

[345] *Political Economy*
"Ansichten der Volkswirthschaft aus dem politischen standpunkt" (2 vols., [Leipzig] 1878). *Röscher* [Wilhelm Georg Friedrich Roscher]

[346] *Political Economy*
"Ansichten der Volkswirthschaft" [Carl David Heinrich] *Rau* [*Ansichten der Volkswirthschaft mit besonderer Beziehung auf Deutschland* (Leipzig, 1821).]

[347] *Political Economy*
"Collections of the Principal Economists" (containing the writings of the Physiocrats) *Daire* [*see* No. 105].

[348] *Political Economy*
"Principles of Political Economy" (2 vols., [New York and Chicago, 1878] transl. by [John J.] Lalor). *Röscher* [W. G. F. Roscher]

[349] *Political Economy*
"System der Volkswirthschaft" (3 vols. Stutt[gart], 1880 [1879-82]). *Röscher* [W. G. F. Roscher]

[350] *Political Economy*
"Tableau Economique" [François] *Quesnay*
["Analyse du tableau économique," *Oeuvres économiques et philosophiques de F. Quesnay*, edited by Auguste Oncken (Frankfurt and Paris, 1888).]

[351] *Political Economy*–History.
"Carey's Socialwissenschaft und das Merkantil-System" (1866) *Ad. Held* [*see* No. 226]

[352] *Political Economy*–History.
"Critical History of Political Economy and Socialism" *Dühring* [*see* No. 122].

[353] *Political Economy*–History.
"Die Staatslehre des Aristoteles" *Oncken* [*see* No. 327].

[354] *Political Economy*–History.
"French Economists of the 18th Century." *Lavergne* [*see* No. 257].

[355] *Political Economy*–History.
"Gechichte der Volkwirthschaftlehre Literatur im [Mittelalter"] *Contzen* [*see* No. 97]

[356] *Political Economy*–History
"Guide to the Study of Political Economy" *Cossa* [*see* No. 98]

[357] *Political Economy*–History
"History and Literature of Politico-Economic Science" (3 vols–monographs) von *Mohl* [*see* No. 305].

[358] *Political Economy*–History.
"History of German Trades in the 19th Century" *Schmöller* [Gustav Friedrich von Schmoller, *Zur Geschichte der deutschen Kleingewerbe im 19 Jahrhundert. Statistische und nationalökonomische Untersuchungen* (Halle, 1870).]

[359] *Political Economy*–History.
"History of Political Economy in Europe" *Blanqui* [*see* No. 48]

[360] *Political Economy*–History
"History of Political Economy in Germany" [W. G. F.] *Röscher* "Geschichte der national-oekonomik in Deutschland" [(Munich, 1874)].

[361] *Political Economy*–History.
"Histroire de Colbert et de son Mercantile System" *Pierre Clement* [*see* No. 83].

[362] *Political Economy*–History.
"Histroire d'Economie Politique des anciens peoples de l'Inde, de l'Egypt, de la Judée, et de la Gréce" *Du Mesnil-Marigny* [*see* No. 123],

[363] *Political Economy*–History.
"Political Economy from the Standpoint of the Historical Method" –*Knies* [*see* No. 250]

[364] *Political Economy*–History
"Political Economy of the Present and Future" [Bruno] *Hildebrande* [*Die National-ökonomie der Gegenwart und Zukunft* (Frankfurt am Main, 1848).]

[365] *Political Economy*–History.
"The Introduction of Protection into the United States" [William Graham] *Sumner*.
[*Lectures on the History of Protection in the United States* (New York, 1877).]

[366] *Political Economy*–History.
"The Public Economy of Athens" (trans.) *Boeckh* [*see* No. 52]

[367] *Political Economy*–History.
"Theory and History of Political Economy" *Kautz* [*see* No. 246].

[368] *Political Economy*–History
"Ueber den Merkantilisme" *Biedermann* [*see* No. 46]

[369] *Political Economy*–History.
"View of the Progress of Political Economy in Europe Since the 16th Century" (1845) [Travers] *Twiss* [London, 1847]

[370] *Politics: Pol. Opinion in Eng.*
"A short Inquiry into the Formation of Political Opinion from the Reign of the Great Families to the Advent of Democracy," by *Arthur Crump*[.] Lond., 1885, 8°.

[371] *Pollock, F.*
"Essays on Jurisprudence and Ethics" [*see* No. 244]

[372] *Praneuf, de*
"Jurisdictions administratives et particulièrement des Conseils de Prefecture" [*see* No. 1].

[373] *Primitive Society.*
"Aryan Village in India and Ceylon" Sir J. *Phear* [*see* No. 340].

[374] *Procedure* of the *House of Commons*
"The Procedure of the House of Commons" *J. E. T. Rogers*[.] Contemporary Review, March 1882 [*see* No. 231].

[375] *Prussia–Administration* and *Constit'ion.*
"Handbuch der Verfassung und Verwaltung in Preussen und dem deutchen Reiche," Von [Robert Achill Friedrich Hermann,] Graf Hue de Grais. Berlin: Julius Springer. 5th ed. 1886 (*yrly eds.*[)]
"The best, in fact the only adequate, exposition, of the Prussian and German Govts. which exists in a comparatively condensed form." N. Y. *Nation* [XLIII], July 8, 1886 [40-41].

[376] *Prussia*–(Constitutional)
"Introduction to German Const. Law." *Schultze*
"Prussian Constitutional Law" (1872 Leipsic, 2 vols) (Historical, while *present* is treated of by [Rönne] in his book on the law) *Schultze.*
"The Story of Prussian Const. Law." *Rönne* (Leip '71)
S's "Introduction" most convenient summary for the constitutional law of all Germany.
[H. J. F. Schulze, *System des deutschen Staatsrechts*, I (Leipzig, 1865); for "Prussian Constitutional Law," *see* No. 24; L. von Rönne, *Das Staats-Recht der preussischen Monarchie* (2 vols., Leipzig, 1870-72).]

[377] *Prussia General History*
Harpers *Mag.* Apr. 1883: "The Hohenzollerns"
"Twelve Books of Prussian Hist," 1848 and '74, *Ranke*
"History of Prussian Politics," *Droysen.*
" " " Prussia," *Tuttle* [4 vols., Boston, 1884-96].
"Holy Roman Empire" (Supplementary chapter) *Bryce.*
"Frederic the Great," *Carlyle.*
[Herbert Tuttle, "The Hohenzollerns," *Harper's New Monthly Magazine*, LXVIII (April 1884), 689-705; L. von Ranke, *Neun Bücher Preussischer Geschichte* (3 vols., Berlin, 1847-48), and *Zwölf Bücher Preussischer Geschichte* (5 vols., Leipzig, 1874); for Droysen, *see* No. 118; for Bryce, *see* No. 61; for Carlyle, *see* No. 67.]

[378] *Public Law.*
"Handbuch des Oeffentlichen Rechts der Gegenwart, in Monographien." Herausgegeben von Dr. Heinrich Marquardsen. See "*Constitutions*," modern [No. 95]

[379] *Public Law–German.*
"Einleitung in das deutsche Staatsrecht" by *Otto Mejer. Very valuable*[.] J. C. B. Mohr (Paul Siebeck) 1 vol. '85 (8*m*.[)] [*see* No. 189]

[380] *Puchta,* [Georg Friedrich]
"Kursus der Institutionen" (9 ed., [edited] by [Paul] Krüger, 2 v., [Leipzig] 1881)

[381] *Quesnay*
"Tableau Economique" [*see* No. 350].

[382] *Rafn*:
"*Antiquitates Americanae*" (Hist. Soc., 1837) [*see* No. 28].

[383] *Raleigh*, Sir Walter.
"Case Against Sir W. Raleigh" Fort. Rev. Vol 7 (1867) *Gardiner. Bancroft*, Vol. I.
"Collier[,] Archaelogia," Vol. V. (1853)
Littel's Living Age, Vol. 9 (1855) Ch. *Kingsley*
[For Gardiner, *see* No. 177; George Bancroft, *A History of the United States, from the Discovery of the Continent* (6 vols., Boston, 1876); John Payne Collier, Letters on Sir Walter Raleigh, Society of Antiquaries of London, *Archaeologia; or, Miscellaneous Tracts Relating to Antiquity*, XXXIV (London, 1852), 137-70; XXXV (London, 1853), 213-22, 368-78; for Kingsley, *see* No. 249.]

[384] *Raleigh*, Sir Walter.
"Life of Raleigh" *Edwards* [*see* No. 127].
"Charters and Constitutions" 2:1379-82, for R's first Charter.
[Benjamin Perley Poore (compiler), *The Federal and State Constitutions, Colonial Charters, and Other Organic Laws of the United States* (2 vols., Washington, 1877).]

[385] *Ranke*
"Twelve Books of Prussian History," 1848 and '74 [*see* No. 377].
"Universal History: The Oldest Group of Nations and the Greeks" (trans. G. Prothero) [*see* No. 209].

[386] *Ranke*, v.
"Zur Geschichte der Doctrin von den drei Staatsgewalten."

[387] *Ransome*, Cyril.
"Rise of Constitutional Government in England," pp. 259. [London] Rivington's, 1883.

[388] *Rathery, M.*
"Histroire des Etats Généraux" Paris, 1845 [*see* No. 169]

[389] *Rau*
"Ansichten der Volkswirthschaft" [*see* No. 346].

[390] *Rawlinson.*
"Great Monarchies of the Ancient Eastern World" (Scribners) [*see* No. 328].

[391] *Reference Books*—History
"Staatslexikon"—*Peter* (anything in English institutions)
"Handlexikon"—*Meyer*

[392] *Rein.* [Wilhelm]
"Kriminalrecht der Römer (von Romulus bis auf Justinianus]" ([Leipzig] 1844).
"Das Privatrecht und der Civilprozess der Römer von dem alteste Zeit bis auf Justinian" (2 ed., [Leipzig] 1858).

[393] *Religions.*
"The Childhood of Religions" Clodd (Humboldt Lib.) [*see* No. 84]

[394] *Rhys.* J.
"Celtic Britain," (Series on *Early Britain*) 1882 [*see* No. 69].

[395] *Robinson,* Conway
"History of the High Court of Chancery and other Institutions of England, from the time of Caius Julius Caesar until the Accession of William and Mary (in 1688-9) (Richm., Balto., Phila., Boston, 1882)

[396] *Rogers,* J. E. Thorold,
"The Procedure of the House of Commons," Contemporary Review, March 1882 [*see* No. 231].

[397] *Roman History*
"Roman Imperialism and Other Lectures and Essays," J[ohn]. R[obert]. *Seeley* ([Boston] Robert Bros., 1871)

[398] *Roman Imperialism*
"Roman Imperialism, and Other Lectures and Essays," pp. 335 (Boston, 1871) *J. R. Seeley*

[399] *Roman Law and English Law.*
"Influence of the Roman Law on the Law of England," by Thomas Edward *Scrutton.* Cambridge Univ. Press, 1885.

[400] *Roman Law, and English Law*
"The Institutes of Justinian illustrated by English Law," by *James Williams,* B.C.L.[,] M.A., Barrister. (1 vol., London, 1883. Wm Clowes & Son.)

[401] *Roman Law (character)*
1. "Geist des Röm[ischen] Rechts" (1852–; 3 v.). *Ihering.*
2. "Der prinzipielle Unterschied zw. d. Römischen u. Germanischen Rechte" ('53) *Schmidt.*
3. "Die materielle Uebereinstimmung der Römischen u. Germanischen Rechtsprinzipien" ('56). *Hahn.*
[For Ihering, *see* No. 236; Carl Adolf Schmidt, *Der principielle Unterschied zwischen dem römischen und germanischen Rechte.* Vol. 1: *Die Verschiedenheit der Grundbegriffe und des Privatrechts* (Rostock, 1853); for Hahn, *see* No. 215.]

[402] *Roman Law (character)*
4. "Kultur und Recht der Römer" ('68) *Arnold* [*see* No. 35].

[403] *Roman Law (character)*
"Geist des römischen Rechts," by *R. v. Ihering*[.] French trans: 'Esprit du droit Romain' [*see* Nos. 235 and 236].

[404] *Roman Law*: Civil
"Outlines of Roman Law: comprising its Historical Growth and General Principles" by W[illia]m. C[arey]. Morey, Ph.D. $1.75. [New York and London] G. P. Putnam's Sons, 1884.

"We do not hesitate to say that a fairly wide and very accurate acquaintance with Roman Law can be got from this little book, and a more special study of any particular branch will be immensely facilitated by the useful list of references at the end of each chapter, and at the end of the book." *Westm*[inster] *Rev*[iew, New Series, LXVII], Apr., 1885 [549].

[405] *Roman Law*–Civil.
"The History and Principles of the Civil Law of Rome," *Sheldon Amos.* (Kegan Paul, Trench, & Co., Lond. 1883.)

[406] *Roman Law.* (Criminal)
1. "Kriminalrecht d. Römer ('44) *Rein* [*see* No. 392].
2. "Das Kriminalrecht d. Röm. Republik" (2 v. '65, '68). A. W. Zumpt.

[August Wilhelm Zumpt, *Das Criminalrecht der Römischen Republik* (2 vols. in 4, Berlin, 1865-69.]

[407] *Roman Law* (History)
"Römische Rechtsgeschichte" by *Karlowa* [*see* No. 245].

[408] *Roman Law* (private) *History.*
1. "Geschichte des Röm. Rechts seit Justinian." (3 ed., 1830) by *Hugo.*
2. "Vom Beruf unserer Zeit zur Gesetzgebung und Rechtswissenschaft." (1814) *Savigny.*
3. "Lehrbuch d. Geschichte d. Röm. Rechts bis Justinian" (11 ed., 1790-1832) by *Hugo.*

[For the two works by Hugo, *see* No. 232; for Savigny, *see* No. 266.]

[409] *Roman Law* (private) *History.*
4. "Kursus der Institutionen" (9 ed. by Krüger, 2 v., 1881) *Puchta.*
5. "Lehrb. d. Röm. Rechts." (3 v. '41-'46) by *Burchardi.*
6. "Das Privatrecht u. der Civilprozess d. Römer v. d. altesten Zeit bis auf Justinian," *Rein* (2 ed. 1858.)

[For Puchta, *see* No. 380; for Burchardi, *see* No. 63; for Rein, *see* No. 392.]

[410] *Roman Law* (private) *History.*
7. "Institutionen u. Geschichte des Röm. Rechts" (2 v., 2 ed '79, '80). *Kuntze* [*see* No. 252].
8. "Geschichte des Röm. Rechts." (3 eds., [Bonn] '40-60) [Ferdinand] *Walter.*

[411] *Roman Law* (private) *History*

"Historical Introduction to the Private Law of Rome" by Dr. Muirhead (University of Edinburgh) Edinb: Adam & Chas. Black 1886

"In point of interest and of a clear presentation of the topic, such as to meet the wants of the general student and, in particular, of careful students of our own law, we have met no book in our own language so satisfactory as this." Nation, Feb. 24, '87 [*see* No. 314].

[412] *Roman Law (procedure)*

1. "Der Röm. Civilprozess." [5 ed (*Wach*) '76] *Keller*.
2. "Der Röm. Civilprozess" (3 v., '64-'66) *v. Bethmann-Hollweg*.
3. ["]Gesch. d. Röm. Kriminalprozess." (1842) *Geib*.
4. ["]Der K-prozess d. Röm. Republik." ('71) *A. W. Zumpt*.

[For Keller, *see* No. 248; for Bethmann-Hollweg, *see* No. 44; for Geib, *see* No. 180; August Wilhelm Zumpt, *Der Criminalprocess der Römischen Republik* (Leipzig, 1871).]

[413] *Roman Law*, (public)

1. "Römisches Staatsrecht." (2 v., 2 ed. '76, '77.) *Th. Mommsen* [*see* No. 307].
2. "Röm. Staatsverwaltung." (3 v., '73-'78; 2 ed. v. 1, '81) *J. Marquardt* [*see* No. 295]
3. "Die Verfassung u. Verwaltung d. Röm. Staates." (1 v. 1881) *Madvig* [*see* No. 287].

[414] *Roman Law, Sources*.

1. "Fontes juris Romani antiqui" (4 ed., 1879) ed. *C. G. Bruns* [*see* No. 60].
2. "Jurisprudentiae antejustinianae quae supersunt," (4 ed. '79) by *Huschke* [*see* No. 234].

[415] *Roman Provincial Administration*

"Roman Provincial Administration to the Accession of Constantine the Great," by *W. T. Arnold*[.] Macmillan 1879. pp. 240 [*see* No. 25].

[416] *Rome*, Early History of,

"Essai sur Tite Live" by *H. Taine*. 12mo. Paris, 1856 [*see* No. 276].

[417] *Rönne*

"The Story of Prussian Constitutional Law" (Leip., 1871). Treats present [*see* No. 376]

[418] *Rönne*[,] v.

"Preuschische Staatsrecht" (4 vols.–3 and 4 relate to administration). A book of reference only [*see* No. 23].

"Deutche Staatsrecht" [*see* No. 21].

[419] *Röscher*

"Ansichten der Volkswirthschaft aus dem politischen standpunkt" 2 vols. (1878) [*see* No. 345].

[420] *Röscher* [W. G. F.]

"Die Grundlagender Nationalökonomie (Stutt., 1857)

[*Die Grundlinien der Nationalökonomie* (Stuttgart, 1857).]

[421] *Röscher*
"History of Political Economy in Germany." "Geschichte der national-oekonomik in Deutschland" (1874) [*see* No. 360]

[422] *Röscher*
"Principles of Political Economy" (transl. by J. J. Lalor, 2 vols., '78) [*see* No. 348]

[423] *Röscher*
"System der Volkswirthschaft" (3 vols., Stutt., 1880) [*see* No. 349].

[424] *Roth,*
"Geschichte des Beneficialwesens" (Erlangen, 1850) [*see* No. 151]
"Feudalität und Unterthanenband" (1863) [*see* No. 151].

[425] *Rotteck*
"Lehrbuch des Vernunftrechts und der Staatswissenschaften" [*see* No. 323].

[426] *Ruttimann* [Johann Jacob]:
"Das Nordamericanische Bundesstaatsrecht verglichen mit den politischen Hinrichtungen [Einrichtungen] der Schweiz" [Zurich, 1867].

[427] *Sabine*
["]Govt. Report on American Fisheries" [*see* No. 152].

[428] *Sarwey,* O[tto]. *von,*
"Das öffentliche Recht und die Verwaltungsrechtspflege." [Tübingen] 1880.

[429] *Savigny*
"Beruf unserer Zeit für Gesetzgebung und Rechtswissenschaft"
Eng. trans:
French trans:
"Contains chapters on the evolution of law which are to this day unsurpassed[."] Monroe Smith [*see* No. 267]

[430] *Savigny,*
"Vom Beruf unserer Zeit zur Gesetzgebung und Rechtswissenschaft["] (1814) [*see* No. 267].

[431] *Sayce.*
"The Origin of Semitic Civilization" [*see* No. 82].

[432] *Schäffner,*
"Geschichte der Rechtsverfassung Frankreichs" (4 v., 1845-'50) Last volume treats legal history of revolution [*see* No. 164].

[433] *Schlegel* (1772-1829) A romantic and dreamer
"Philosophy of History" [*see* No. 229].

[434] *Schmidt,*
"Der prinzipielle Unterschied zwischen den Römischen und Germanischen Rechte" (1853) [*see* No. 401].

[435] *Schmoller*
"History of German Trades in the 19th Century" [*see* No. 358]

[436] *Schömann*:
"Antiquities of Greece" [*see* No. 212]

[437] *Schopenhauer, Arthur.*
"The World as Will and Idea" Translated from the German by R. B. Haldane, M.A. and J. Kemp, M.A. 3 vols. Lond: Trübner & Co. '83-'86. See '*Pessimism*' [No. 338]

[438] *Schouler, James.*
"History of the United States of America under the Constitution." Vols. I. and II (1789-1817) Wash. '80, '82.

[439] *Schubert.*
"Verfassungs Urkunden" [*see* No. 96].

[440] *Schulte, J. Fr. v.*
"Lehrbuch der Deutche Staats- und Richtsgeschichte" (1861–5 ed. 1881) [*see* No. 192].

[441] *Schultze*
"Introduction to German Constitutional Law." Most convenient summary of constitutional law of all Germany.
"Prussian Constitutional Law" (Leip., 1872[,] 2 vols.) Historical. [*See* No. 376.]

[442] *Schülze*
"Preuschische Staatsrecht" (2 vols., 1872-'77).
"Deutche Staatsrecht."
[*See* No. 376.]

[443] *Scrutton, Thomas Edward.*
"Influence of the Roman Law on the Law of England." Cambridge Univ. Press, 1885.

[444] *Seebohm*,
"The Era of the Protestant Revolution" (Epochs of Mod. Hist.) [*see* No. 141]

[445] *Seeley*, J. R.
"Roman Imperialism and Other Lectures and Essays" (Roberts Bros., 1871) [*see* No. 397].

[446] *Semitic Civilization.*
"The Origin of Semitic Civilization." *Sayce* [*see* No. 82].

[447] *Separation of govt'mental Functions*
"Zur Geschichte der Doctrin von den drei Staatsgewalten" by *v. Ranke.*

[448] *Smith, Bruce*:
"Liberty and Liberalism," (Lond: Longmans 1887) [*see* No. 273].

[449] *Smith–John*
"True Travels, Adventures, and Observations of Capt. Jno. Smith" (Richm, 1819)
"A True Relation of Virginia" (1608)
"History of Virginia Combined with the Hist. of New Eng. down to 1626" (Not all by Smith himself)
[*The True Travels, Adventures and Observations of Captaine John Smith, in Europe, Asia, Africke, and America: beginning about the yeere 1593, and continued to this present 1629* (2 vols., Richmond, Va., 1819); *A True Relation of Such Occurences and Accidents of Noate as hath happened in Virginia since the first planting of that colony* (London, 1608); *The Generall Historie of Virginia, New-England, and the Summer Isles . . . from their first beginning, ano. 1584 to this present 1626. . .* (2 vols., Richmond, Va., 1819).]

[450] *Society*–History of.
"The Ancient City" *Fustel de Coulanges* [*see* No. 80]

[451] *Soetbeer, Dr. Heinrich,*
"Die Stellung der Sozialisten zur Malthus'schen Bevolkerungslehre." (Wm Godwin, Thompson (Owenite), Fourier, Blanc, Proudhon, the German Socialists, and Henry George.) (Berlin, 1886) See [New York] *Nation* [XLIII, No.] 1114 [Nov. 4, 1886], p. 375.

[452] *Sohm*, R.
"Die fränkische Reichs- u. Gerichtsverfassung" (1871) [*see* No. 162].

[453] *Sovereignty, Territorial*
"Von der Landeshoheit in Regierungssachen," by J. J. *Moser* [*see* No. 313].

[454] *Spencer, David,*
"Local Government in Wisconsin" (Wis. Hist. Soc'y's Collections, Vol. 11) [*see* No. 278]

[455] *Spencer*, H.
"Principles of Sociology" [*see* No. 147]

[456] *Spencer, Herbert.*
"The Great Political Superstition" ('the divine right of Parliaments') (*Contemporary Review*, 46:24) [*see* No. 110].

[457] *Stahl*, [F. J.]
"Philosophie des Rechts" [*see* No. 262].
"Staatslehre" [Heidelberg, 1856].

[458] *State, Functions of the*
"The Limits of Individual Liberty," An Essay by *Francis C. Montague*[.] Most highly commended in *Westm. Rev.*, Apr., 1885.–Takes a large state-function view. Lond: Rivingtons, Waterloo Pl., 1885

[459] *State*, Philosophy of the,
"Geschichte und System der Rechts- und Staatsphilosophie," by *Hildebrand* [*see* No. 228].

[460] *State*, Theory of the,
"Staatslehre" by *Stahl* [*see* No. 457].

[461] *State* and *Religion*
"No Commonwealth without God[.]" Cardinal *Manning* in Contemporary Rev., July, 1883. ("Authority, obedience, brotherhood") [*see* No. 292].

[462] *State Law* (U. S.)
"American Statute Law," by F. J. Stimson (Bost. C. C. Soule $6.50) [*see* No. 31].

[463] *States-General, The, of France.*
"Histroire des Etats-Généraux," by *M. Rathery*[.] Paris, 1845 [*see* No. 169].

[464] *Statistics*,
"Almanac de Gotha" (published for 115 years–most scholarly of all Almanacs)
"Statesman's Year-Book"–*Martin.*
"Reports U. S. Bureau of Statistics"
" " " Nav. do.
"Journal of the Prussian Statistical Bureau"
[*Almanach de Gotha: Annuaire généalogique, diplomatique et statistique* (179 vols., Gotha, Germany, 1763-1942); *The Statesman's Year-Book: Statistical and Historical Annual of the States of the World*, edited by Frederick Martin, 1864-82, (London, 1864–); U. S. Bureau of Statistics (Dept. of Agriculture), *Report of the Statistician*, New Series, Nos. 1-156 (Oct., 1883-April 1899).]

[465] *Statistics.*
"Dictionary of Statistics"–*Mulhall* (especially valuable for commercial studies)
Yearly publication of commercial statistics by *Neumann-Spallert.*
[Michael George Mulhall, *Mulhall's Dictionary of Statistics* (London and New York, 1886); Franz Xavier von Neumann-Spellart (ed.), *Uebersichten über Produktion, Verkehr und Handel in der Weltwirthschaft* (3 vols., Stuttgart, 1878-80).]

[466] *Stein.*
"Französosche Staats- u. Richtsgeschichte" with *Warnkönig* (3 v. 1846-'8) [*see* No. 164].

[467] *Stein*, L. v.
"Verwaltungslehre" (see Administration) [*see* No. 14]
"Handbuch der Verwaltungslehre" [*see* No. 8].

[468] *Stephen, Leslie.*
"History of English Thought in the Eighteenth Century" (Mostly *religious* thought, but chapters on political thought also) [*see* No. 131].

[469] *Stephen, Leslie.*
"The Science of Ethics" [London, 1882].

[470] *Stephen*, Sir James,
"Lectures on the History of France." 2 vols. 8vo., Lond. 1857.

[471] *Stephens*, H. Morse (Balliol Col., Oxford)
"A History of the French Revolution" Vol. I 1886. Lond: Rivingtons[.] N. Y. Scribners [*see* No. 168].

[472] *Stevens*:
"Earliest Discovery of America"
"The Cabots."
[*See* No. 28.]

[473] Stillé, C. J., D.D.,
"Studies in Mediaeval History" (Lippincott, 1882) [*see* No. 299]

[474] *Stimson*, F. J.
"American Statute Law" (Boston: C. C. Soule) $6.50 [*see* No. 31].

[475] *Stone Age*
"Lake Dwellings" *Keller* [*see* No. 248]

[476] *Strikes*:
"Annual Report of the Sect. of Internal Affairs (Pa.) Part III: Industrial Statistics–1876-7." pp. 33-57 Article "Strikes."

[477] *Stubbs*,
"The Early Plantagenets" (Epochs of Mod. Hist.) [*see* No. 142]

[478] *Sumner*–Prof.
"The Introduction of Protection into the United States" [*see* No. 365].

[479[*Swiss Confederation*:
"Das Nordamericanische Bundesstaatsrecht verglichen mit den politischen Hinrichtungen der Schweiz," *Ruttimann* [*see* No. 426]
"Swiss Democracy" *Cherbuliez* [*see* No. 72].
"Growth of the Eng. Const." (opening chapter) *Freeman* [*see* No. 171].

[480] *Swiss Confederations*: Randall
Edinburgh Review, 129:127
Fortnightly " , 2:533
British Quarterly Review, 57:305.
Atlantic Monthly, March 1861.
["The Legend of Tell and Rutli," *Edinburgh Review*, CXXIX (Jan. 1869), 65-79; Edward A. Freeman, "The Proposed Revision of the Swiss Federal Constitution," *Fortnightly Review*, II (Oct. 1865), 533-48; "Swiss Federal Reform," *British Quarterly Review*, LVII (April 1873), 165-84; "The Men of Schwyz," *Atlantic Monthly*, VII (March 1861), 334-46.]

[481] *Swiss Confederations* Randall
History of Switzerland–*Zschokka*
" " " –*Wilson* (Cabinet Cyclop.)
" " Helvetic Confederation by *Planta*
Defense of the Constitution–*Adams*
Lectures (VIIIth) *Smyth*

[Heinrich Zschokke, *The History of Switzerland, for the Swiss People*, translated by Francis George Shaw (New York and London, 1855); John Wilson, *History of Switzerland* ("The Cabinet Cyclopaedia," edited by Dionysius Lardner; London, 1832); Joseph Planta, *The History of the Helvetic Confederacy* (2 vols., London, 1800); John Adams, *A Defence of the Constitutions of Government of the United States of America* (3 vols., London, 1787-88); William Smyth, *Lectures on Modern History; from the Irruption of the Northern Nations to the Close of the American Revolution* (Cambridge, 1840).]

[482] *Switzerland.*
"Democracy in Switzerland" Art. N. Y. *Nation*, 43:410[,] No. 1116, Nov. 18, 1886.

[483] *Switzerland:*
"Staats und Rechtsgeschichte von Zürich"
"Geschichte der Republik Zürich" (3 vols.)
" des Sweitzerischen Bundesrechts"
J. C. *Bluntschli* [*see* No. 51]

[484] *Switzerland,* (Government).
1. "Handbuch des Schweizerishen Bundesstaatsrechts," by J. J. *Blumer* [*see* No. 49].
2. "Das oeffentliche Recht der Schweizerischen Eidgenossenschaft," by J. *Dubs* [*see* No. 120].

[485] *Taine,* H
"Essai sur Tite Live" 12mo., Paris, 1856 [*see* No. 276].

[486] *Taswell-Langmead*
"English Constitutional History" (Houghton, M., & Co., 1881) pp. 766 [*see* No. 135]

[487] *Taylor, E. Whately Cooke.*
"Introduction to a History of the Factory System." Lond, Rich. Bentley & Sons, 1886[.] 8vo. pp. 441 [*see* No. 145].

[488] *Tomaschek,* J. A.
"Die höchste Gerichtsbarkeit des deutschen Königs und Reiches im XV Jahrhundert" [*see* No. 184].

[489] *Tuttle*
"History of Prussia" down to Frederick the Great [*see* No. 377].

[490] *Twiss*–Travers
"View of the Progress of Political Economy in Europe Since the 16th Century" ('45) [*see* No. 369].

[491] *United States: Constitutional History.*
"Union–Disunion–Reunion. Three Decades of Federal Legislation, 1855 to 1885; Memories of Events preceding, during, and since the American Civil War," by *S. S. Cox*[.] Providence, R. I., 1885. 1. 8° [*see* No. 100].

[492] *United States–History*
"History of the United States of America under the Constitution" by *James Schouler* Vols. I. and II (1789-1817) Wash. '80, '82 [*see* No. 438].

[493] *United States,–Politics*
"The American Republic: Its Constitution, Tendencies, and Destiny," by O[restes]. *A*[ugustus]. *Brownson* (N. Y. P. O'Shea, ed. 1886).

[494] *Ussel,* D', *Le Vte Philibert.*
"La Démocratie en Ses Conditions Morale" Paris 1884–E. Plon, Nourrit et Cie[,] Rue Garancière [*see* No. 109].

[495] *Verne,* Jules.
"Exploration of the World" (N. Y. 1879)

[496] *Vivien,*
"Études administrative" [*see* No. 6].

[497] *Wachsmuth.*
"Scheme for a Theory of History" [*see* No. 229].

[498] *Waitz,* G.
"Deutche Verfassungsgeschichte" (1844; 2 vol., 3 ed. '82; 3 v. 2 ed. '83; 4 v., 1860) [*see* No. 185]

[499] *Walpole,* Spencer
"History of England from the Conclusion of the Great War of 1815" (3 vols, Longmans, 1879) [*see* No. 138]

[500] *Walter,*
"Geschichte des Römischen Rechts" (3 eds., 1840-'60) [*see* No. 410].

[501] *Walter,* Ferd.
"Deutche Rechtsgeschichte" (1852-7) [*see* No. 191].

[502] *Warburton,* W.
"Edward the Third" (Epochs of Mod. Hist.) [*see* No. 142].

[503] *Warnkönig,*
"Flandrische Staats- u. Rechtsgeschichte bis zum Jahre 1305" (4 v. 1835-'42) [*see* No. 154].
"Französosche Staats- u. Rechtsgeschichte" with *Stein* (3 v. 1846-'8) [*see* No. 164].

[504] *Wheeler*
"Vedic and Brahminic India" [*see* No. 238].

[505] *Williams*
"The Middle Kingdom" [*see* No. 73].

[506] *Williams, James,* B.C.L., M.A., Barrister.
"The Institutes of Justinian illustrated by English Law." (1 vol., London, 1883, Wm Clowes & Son.)

[507] *Wisconsin, Local Govt. in,*
"Local Government in Wisconsin," by David Spencer, (Wis. Hist. Soc'y's Collections, Vol. 11) [*see* No. 278].

[508] *Woodberry*
"Relation of the Fisheries to the Discovery and Settlement of N. America" [*see* No. 152].

[509] *Yonge*, Chas. Duke,
"Constitutional History of England from 1760-1860" (Lond., 1882).

[510] *Zachariae*, H. A.
"Die deutschen Verfassungsgesetz der Gegenwart" [*see* No. 92].

[511] *Zeni*, The
"Voyages of the Zeni" (Hakluyt Society)
Article by Capt. *Zahrtman*, Journals R. G. S., Vol. V (1836).
Review of same, No. Am. Rev., July 1838.
" " Antiquitates Americanae," No. Am. Rev., Jan. 1838.
[For "Voyages of the Zeni," *see* No. 30; C. C. Zahrtmann, "Remarks on the Voyages to the Northern Hemisphere Ascribed to the Zeni of Venice," Royal Geographical Society of London, *Journal*, V (1835), 102-28; "Voyages of the Zeni," *North American Review*, XLVII (July 1838), 177-206; "The Discovery of America by the Northmen," *North American Review*, XLVI (Jan. 1838), 161-203.]

[512] Zöpfl,
"Grundsätze des gemeinen deutschen Staatsrechts" [*see* No. 91].

[513] *Zöpfl, H*
"Deutche Rechtsgeschichte" (1841–4 ed. 1871) [*see* No. 191].

[514] *Zumpt, A. W.*
1. "Das Kriminalrecht der Römischen Republik" (2 v., 1865, 1868) [*see* No. 406].
2. "Der Kriminalprozess der Römischen Republik["] (1871) [*see* No. 412].

From George Howe, Jr.

Dear Woodrow, Columbia, S. C., Apl 2 1890

I am very sorry that Ellie continues to suffer from that scalding. I supposed she was well of it ere this.

You are well aware that any prescription of mine is as it were in the dark, but you have given such a good account of the condition of the foot that I do not feel altogether *in the dark*.

1st Cleanse the foot or feet thoroughly with (castile) soap & water then rinse it off with a solution of Bichloride of Mercury 1 part to 2000 of water

2d Dust the parts, especially any raw surface with Sub-Nitrate of Bismuth. (dry)

3d envelop the foot in a layer of white cotton wadding, or better in sheet absorbent cotton.

4th Apply a cotton bandage 2½ inches wide & 6 or 9 ft long, evenly, snugly from the toes up, as far as the calf of the leg or a little above.

This 4th item I suppose you are familiar with, as you mention the use of the bandage. But the smoothness of the application is *very* important. It should press equally in all parts. It should fit snugly but not press sufficiently to interfere with the circulation.

No. 1 should be repeated every morning if there is any discharge[.] If there is no discharge, repeat on alternate days. The same holds for 2 & 3. No 4 should be repeated every day & if the bandage slips or becomes loose it should be reapplied every night & morning. Do not attempt to force off scabs, but let them fall off, unless there is considerable discharge.

There will be some red spots for some time after it is all well[.] But they will gradually assume the natural color of the skin. Until all raw surfaces are healed over, the feet should be kept elevated. Ellie should not let her feet hang down while sitting, nor should she walk upon them, except for a few steps at a time. After everything is healed, the bandage should be worn for a week or more. This course of treatment I feel quite sure will cure her.

We are just recovering from the effects of La Grippe, still feeling some of the weakening results

If Annie were at hand she would send all sorts of loving messages, in which I would most heartily unite

Yrs affly Geo Howe

I enclose prescriptions—1 tablet in 1 quart of water makes 1 to 2000. All this quart need not be used at once. Don't let the children get hold of it

ALS (WP, DLC).

From Bradford Paul Raymond

Dear Sir: Middletown, Conn., April 4, 1890

Your check for $112.50 in payment for rent to April 1, 1890 I acknowledge with thanks.

Yours truly, B. P. Raymond, per C. V. V.

ALS (WP, DLC) with WWhw notation on env.: "House Rent April '90."

A Newspaper Report of a Lecture[1]

[April 8, 1890]

SYSTEMS OF CITY GOVERNMENT.

A lecture was delivered last evening before the Massachusetts Society for Promoting Good Citizenship in the Old South Meeting House. The lecture, second in the series and upon the topic, "Modern Systems of City Government," was given by Prof. Woodrow Wilson of Wesleyan University. Prof. Wilson is the author of the work, "Congressional Government." He has lately been called to a chair in Princeton College. His treatment of the subject in hand was historical, to a great extent, and was not complimentary to the system of city government prevalent in the United States. Here, in fact, according to Prof. Wilson, there is no system of municipal rule at all.

After a brief resume of ancient systems of city government, the professor said that they are now controlled by the state. They are now agents, instead of remaining principals. Self-ruling cities at first represented a form of government; next, in the middle ages, a form of privilege; now a form of duty. Under our modern system of government the charter is belated. It is not now a granting of privileges, but a mere method of incorporation. It has no peculiar feature except that of giving special complexity of duty. People now live in Philadelphia, New York or Boston, not because they wish to perpetuate the privileges handed down to them, but because it suits their convenience. Coming more particularly to methodical systems of city government, Prof. Wilson said that the most logical system is in vogue in France. There a central power exerts its influence. The unit of government is a commune, and every commune has a mayor. There are 36,105 mayors in France. The professor likewise reviewed the Prussian system, which is more irregular than that of France, but in which certain general principles obtain. There is one popular election; namely, that for members of the city council. Aldermen are elected by the council. They are specially trained citizens, and act as a sort of executive board. The mayor also is elected by the council. He is not a dictator, but simply president of the city council.

The lecturer then spoke of English methods, which are looser than those of Prussia, but are still characteristically Germanic. When he came, finally, to the United States, Prof. Wilson had little to commend. He said our system is conspicuous chiefly because of its lack of system. In almost all our states we require separate incorporating acts of the Legislature for large towns or cities. Between the federal and the rural governments you will find the municipal governments being squeezed out. We make statutes to run our local governments, and then let our local governments run themselves. Instead of a vital system, we have a statutory system, which leaves localities to govern themselves as best they may.

In conclusion the speaker said that this system may be in harmony with our institutions, but it is capable of reform.

Printed in the *Boston Herald*, April 8, 1890; one editorial heading omitted.

1 This lecture was based in large part upon Wilson's public lecture at the Johns Hopkins, "Systems of Municipal Organization," printed at March 2, 1888, Vol. 5.

From James Woodrow

My dear Woodrow: Columbia, S. C., April 14, 1890

I write to congratulate you, as I do most heartily, on your election to Princeton. I was glad when you were called to Middletown; but there were always the two facts diminishing this gladness—that M. is in New England, and that the University is Wesleyan. Of course other things may have entirely neutralised them; but I am glad you will be where there will be no such needs of neutralisation. Then, besides, it is in many respects an elevation. But I need not compare further—I am *extremely* glad of the change.

Let me thank you for the excellent likeness of yourself you sent me recently. It is very good.

It has gratified me highly to see a number of complimentary notices of The State—the longest in the new journal at Nashville.[1]

I hope you and dear Ella and the babies are all well and happy.

Your affectionate uncle, James Woodrow.

ALS (WP, DLC).

1 It is printed at March 15, 1890.

To Eugene Schuyler

My dear Mr. Schuyler, Middletown, Conn., 14 April, 1890

By reason of some extraordinary stupidity at the Princeton P. O., your kind and cordial letter of March 4th reached me only this morning.

Let me thank you most heartily for its contents. It heartens and encourages me immensely to receive such assurances of friendship from men like yourself, whose opinions I so much value[.] To say the plain truth, I much prefer the backing of men of scholarship *and affairs* to the backing of any person whatever not connected with public life. Politics seems to me one of the things whose study cannot be put "upon a scientific basis," in the sense of being made a thing only for scholars, without being robbed of use and significance.

I go to Princeton with very high hopes of opportunity for effective work. My teaching will lie exclusively within the particular fields in which I most want to study and write: and those are of course ideal conditions for one in my profession. I shall not assume the duties of the chair till next Sept.; meantime I am finishing out my year's work here at Wesleyan.

Thanking you again most heartily for your kind letter,

Most sincerely Yours, Woodrow Wilson

ALS (WC, NjP).

From Henry Randall Waite

American Institute of Civics, New York

Dear Sir: [c. April 22, 1890].

Your remittance of three dollars, membership fee for one year, from July 1st, 1889, to July 1st, 1890, has been received and placed to your credit.

Thanking you on behalf of the Institute and its work, and personally, for the encouragement afforded by your cordial cooperation,

I have the honor to be,

Very truly yours, H. R. Waite President.

TLS (WP, DLC).

From Theodore L. Flood[1]

My Dear Sir: Meadville, Pa. April 25, 1890.

Permit me to call your attention to *The Chautauquan*, sample copies of which I send you, and to the work of The Chautauqua Literary and Scientific Circle. You will see from the enclosed circular[2] the plan of the organization and from the magazine which I send, you will see that we publish over one-half of the reading required of the members of the Circle. Our next course for next year is to be mainly on English History and Literature. I want to publish in the Magazine about twelve thousand words on the English Constitution. My plan is to have a popular and simple story on where England got her Constitution and what it is. As these articles are to be used in connection with the text book on English History,[3] you will see, I think, that the space given to them is not so narrow as it might first seem to you. I am very anxious to secure you to prepare me this paper; I should want copy of the first three thousand words by the first of August and the remainder of the instalments at intervals of thirty days. I should be glad to give you for the twelve thousand words, $120. I hope that you will be willing to undertake the work. I am sure that you will find our Chautauquan readers earnest and appreciative. Kindly let me hear from you at your earliest convenience.[4]

Very Truly Yours, T. L. Flood T.

Dictated by I. M. T.

TLS (WP, DLC) with WWhw notation on env.: "Ans. April 28/90 $150.00."

[1] Editor of *The Chautauquan*, 1880-99.

[2] The enclosure is missing.

[3] James Richard Joy, *An Outline History of England* (New York, 1890).

[4] Wilson's articles, published under the title, "The English Constitution," are printed at Oct. 1, 1890, Vol. 7.

From Joseph R. Wilson, Jr.

My dearest brother: Clarksville, Tenn. April 25th 1890

You will be somewhat surprised, probably, to learn that I am now engaged in reporting for a daily newspaper.[1] I commenced work this morning, and am getting on very well so far. My main object in taking the position is to be able to secure certain advantages in studying Phonography &c. which I have decided to take up. I hope after a while to go into the tobacco business, and an able shorthand writer will be able to command a much better salary, probably, than any other class of employee. Mr. Boyd, the local editor of the "Progress," gives me daily lessons in short hand, to which he will add lessons on the type writer. A knowledge of these two things will enable me to always find employment, no matter what happens. You know the demand for this work is increasing largely from time to time even in our small Southern towns, and good Phonographers command good salaries. I will report my progress *on* the "Progress' " staff, at a later date.

Father is pretty well now, I think, comparatively speaking. He went to Presbytery at Shelbyville, Tenn., last week and returned on Monday night. He reported a pleasant but rather tiresome time. He goes to the Assembly about the middle of May you know, at Ashville N. C.[2] I am well with the exception of a cold which troubles me somewhat.

Father joins me in a great deal of love to you all.

Your loving bro. Joseph.

ALS (WP, DLC).

[1] The Clarksville *Daily Progress.*

[2] The General Assembly of the southern Presbyterian Church met in the First Presbyterian Church of Asheville, May 15-24, 1890.

To Albert Shaw

My dear Shaw, Middletown, Conn., 29 April, 1890.

I have been very anxious ever since you got back from Europe either to see you or hear from you; I have been intending all the time, too, to write to you, "but have been let hitherto." I was not without the hope, the almost expectation, that you would on your homeward way drop in on a fellow, or at least tell him where he could catch you *en route* and so refresh a friendship which he would not for the world have grow rusty or dim. And yet now, when the first opportunity that *is* an opportunity offers for a word to you it must be a semi-business word. The people here want you very much in the chair which I am about to vacate, and they are willing to make it a more comfortable chair than it has been for me; and, although I am very anxious to see you at Princeton, in the new chair of Economics which is to be established there in the very near future, I entertain so great, so affectionate, a regard for the people and the college here that I am disposed to help them all I can.

To say the truth without exaggeration, this is as pleasant, and academically as free, a place as a fellow could wish to be. The men in the faculty are most of them cultured and progressive, the people of the town are also cultured and attractive, the college is unquestionably, as it seems to me, at the opening of a period of very liberal development. One of the first chairs they mean to develop, now that money is coming in to them, and promises to come in with increasing bulk, is the department of History and Political Economy. The near future, I should judge, will see two full professors in it. If they can get you, they would be willing, I feel confident, to put in an assistant at once, such a man as would take the drill work off your hands and leave you free to develop lecture courses pretty much as your interests led you to do on either side of the work. If you want a satisfactory berth, it would be unwise to let this one go by unconsidered.

Our President, I know, has also written to you. The time is so short before the end of the college year that I feel like asking [you] to *telegraph* us, at our expense, if you think that you cannot consider the matter favourably at all.

In any case, please write me a long letter, of the old-time kind. I am hungry for some word from you, for I am whole-heartedly Your sincere friend, Woodrow Wilson

WWTLS (Shaw Coll., NjP).

From Theodore L. Flood

My Dear Prof. Wilson: Meadville, Pa. April 30, 1890.

I am very much pleased that you are willing to undertake the scheme for the articles which I proposed. I shall be glad to make the pay what you suggest, that is, $150 for the twelve thousand words. May I look for the first installment by August first? Very Sincerely Yours, T. L. Flood T.

P.S. omitted. TLS (WP, DLC) with WWhw notation on env.: "Ans. May 6/90."

From John Franklin Jameson

My dear Wilson: Providence, April 30 [1890].

Unless the penalties for writing threatening letters are very severe in Connecticut, I have a mind to ask if you know any reason why I should not come over to see you and your family at the end of next week, spending Saturday and Sunday. I ask for various reasons:

a. Because I suppose you can hardly come over here for two or three days, (though if you can I hereby cordially invite you); and yet

b. I want to see you before you leave New England, and should like to see Mrs. Wilson also;

c. I have no classes on Saturday or on Monday at present, and no engagement on that Saturday evening;

d. Grub that is good enough for you is good enough, perhaps even too good, for me, and I feel so far a friend that my coming need not impose any care on Mrs. Wilson, as the entertainment of a number of men would;

e. I don't see that we shall meet at ary professorial dinner;

f. My mother says I can come if you urge me.

But I can well conceive that, however cogent these reasons may seem, it may be inconvenient to receive me on a given day. If so, by all means say so. And if at any time you can come over here for any time, by all means do so.

I hope Mrs. Wilson is better; if not, consider this unwritten.

Sincerely yours, J. F. Jameson

ALS (WP, DLC) with WWhw notation on env.: "Ans. 2 May/90."

Two Field Examinations at the Johns Hopkins

(May, 1890.

Degree Examination in Administration (Minor)[1]

1. Show, by analysis, the place of Administration as a branch of Public Law, and set forth the grounds of distinction between Legislation and Administration.

2. Describe carefully the differences (a) in administrative integration and oversight, (b) in central financial audit, and (c) in financial control of local government, existing between the governments of England, Prussia, France, and the States of our Union. (See also question 4).

3. Outline the development of the English Treasury Department, and discuss its present organization and Cabinet influence as a means of central administrative integration in England.

4. Show (more fully than under question 2) the absence of administrative integration in the administrative arrangements of our States.

5. What were the local government reforms of 1888 in England, and what reasons existed for undertaking them?

6. Describe "The Administration" in Prussian local government.

7. What contrasts of administrative organization exist between European cities and our own, and what reasons are there for such contrasts in the different principles and analogies of development followed here and there?

[1] As Wilson's notation on the verso reveals, this was his part of the general doctoral examination for Westel Woodbury Willoughby, William Howe Tolman, and Robert Johnston Finley.

(May, '90

Examination in Administration.

Henry B. Gardner.

1. "Liberty depends incomparably more upon administration than upon constitution"—Niebuhr. "For Forms of Government let fools contest; whate'er is best administered is best"—Pope. Criticise the above for the purpose of determining the distinction and the relationship between constitutional questions and administrative questions.
2. What are the functions of government? How far is this an administrative question?
3. Describe the organization of central government in England. Contrast it with the organization of the central government in France, and give reasons for the contrast.
4. What were the processes of centralization in France?
5. Outline the organization of local government in France and point out the principles which characterize it.
6. What part did Stein have in the reform of administration in Prussia, central and local?
7. What differences are there between the executive organization of our federal government and the executive organization of our States?

WWT MSS. (WP, DLC) with WWhw notations and reading lists on versos.

From Albert Shaw

My Dear Wilson: Minneapolis, Minn. May 2. 1890.

Your good letter came last night, and it was as welcome as this beautiful May weather after our long Northwestern winter. I have thought of you often and followed your work with the pride and satisfaction of a friend, even though we haven't had time to exchange many letters. The suggestion that I may be wanted to fill your Middletown place comes, of course, very unexpectedly. But I shall not pass it by without consideration. I like my newspaper work,[1] but it allows me no time for study and careful writing. For the sake of leisure and better opportunities to do good work, I am seriously thinking of leaving the editorial desk. Several things have been offered or half-offered of late, but I do not want to make a change unless I get something very much more to my taste than my present work (which in many ways is highly congenial). I want your perfectly candid advice as to the Middletown chair. You are kind enough to suggest that you would like to see me in the Chair of Pol. Econ. at Princeton. When is that chair to be established, and do you suppose there is a fair probability of my name being favorably considered for it? Some months ago President Patton wrote asking me if I was in a position to consider an invitation to take temporary charge (for the current half year) of the Economics at Princeton. But of course I couldn't consider that. Is Professor Sloane still at Princeton? I have some reason to think that he has a kindly side for me. I found last summer, to my surprise, that he had recommended me in a most influential way, for a certain New York newspaper position of high responsibility that I happened to think not suited to me. I had met him at Mr. Bryce's in London.

You will of course enjoy your work at Princeton. It brings you back to your old college home. For my part I am a confirmed Westerner; and it would give me sharp pangs to leave Minneapolis,—a beautiful city with a bright future, in which my hopes and affections seem to be peculiarly centered. But we cannot always live just where we would like best to be; and it may be my duty to go East.

That European sojourn of mine was full of pleasure and instruction, and was also a rest to me. But I have been grubbing away so busily since I came home last summer that it already seems like ancient history or a lovely dream to me. I must buckle on the harness and go at my day's work. Hoping to hear from you again soon, I am as ever

Sincerely Yours: Albert Shaw

ALS (WP, DLC) with WWhw notation on env.: "Ans. 5/5/90."

[1] Shaw was now associate editor of the Minneapolis *Tribune*.

To John Franklin Jameson

My dear Jameson, Middletown, Conn., 2 May, 1890

I have waited twenty-four hours to answer your welcome letter in order that I might know how to answer it. I need not say how delighted both Mrs. Wilson and I were at the thought of having you with us again: and I need hardly add our determination, that *it must be*, and that as soon as possible. It would be a sore disappointment to us to miss a visit from you, and we don't mean to, if we can help it.

But somehow there's an inevitable 'if' to every plan or wish that we form nowadays. Mrs. Wilson's foot is almost entirely well at last; but she is now in bed with an attack of acute tonsillitis, which the doctor says she may get over in two or three days, or may not get over for a week, and which [is] accompanied by a wearing fever. Our second child (she of the rotund body) is just recovering from a similar attack, and it was no doubt the fatigue of nursing her, added to the weakness and susceptibility to cold naturally induced by her long confinement to the house necessitated by the accident to her feet, that made Mrs. Wilson take the disease and then proceed, as she has done, to develop a much more serious case of it than Jessie's. This is a tale of woe: but Mrs. Wilson earnestly wishes me to say (and "Barkis is a-villin") that you must come as *per* programme unless in the meantime I write you that she is obliged to confess that she is not strong enough to see *any*one. But, even in that case, you must understand, there is to be a postponement only, not an abandonment, of the visit. We can't give it up. Our domestic plans have had all sorts of ups and downs; but they must not cheat us of seeing you before we leave New England. We pretty confidently hope that all will be well with us by next Saturday.

In haste, but with warmest regards from us both,

Your sincere friend, Woodrow Wilson

ALS (J. F. Jameson Papers, DLC).

From John Franklin Jameson

My dear Wilson: Providence, May 4, 1890.

I have received your letter, and thank you for so cordially seconding my nomination. I am very sorry to hear of Mrs. Wilson's illness. I hope indeed that it may prove brief. But if a man is friend enough to invite himself, he is surely friend enough to be told that you will see him later. And so, as I can come just as well on the 23d as on the 9th, I shall hope that, out of regard for all three persons concerned, you will send me word if a postponement will be better for you-all. A notice which should reach me on Friday morning would arrive quite in season. If I should receive none, I should leave here on the train arriving in Middletown next before six that afternoon. Or,–no, to allow for your having hospitably parvified the disability, perhaps, I should be more considerate to assume a postponement unless the contrary is heard, and will do so,–the more as I can come also on the 17th (Saturday afternoon) though not on the 16th, Friday. But that would be the train.

I will leave all news till I see you, for very late hours during the continuance of the Convention of the Psi Upsilon Fraternity, *quorum* Jameson, have left me passing somnolent this Sabbath evening. Please give Mrs. Wilson my heartiest assurances of sympathy, and my best wishes.

Sincerely yours, J. F. Jameson.

ALS (WP, DLC).

To Albert Shaw

My dear Shaw: Middletown, Conn. 5 May, 1890.

I am going to answer at once your letter which came this morning, and I trust that you will excuse a machine-made letter. It seems more friendly to put one's own 'fist' into a letter to a friend; but it is not so as a fact in my case. I use the machine because so out with a new pen as to have my ideas and affections positively checked by it.

Being an ardent friend of Wesleyan and yet at the same time very earnestly wanting to see you at Princeton, whose future is necessarily so much bigger than Wesleyan's, where the very best cultured class of students go, and where your companionship would be invaluable to me, to say nothing of its value to the college, I am "in a strait betwixt two." I will divide my discourse into two parts, a Princeton part and a Wesleyan part. Of the latter first.

My candid opinion is that, the size of the college being considered, the conditions of work at Wesleyan are thoroughly satisfactory. The faculty and trustees are liberal and progressive in all matters of college policy; the desire is to develop, and to develop each department in accordance with the advice of the man at the head of it; money is coming in and development consequently seems reasonably assured. Middletown is a manufacturing town, but more prominently a residence town with a large number of cultured, established families in it which furnish a man with very satisfactory society. I have found that neither Boston nor New York is far away, and that there is not the least jealousy on the part of the authorities of the college of a man's going off to lecture or on business (or on pleasure, for that matter) within any reasonable limits. The salary of a full professor, the rank which would of course be offered to you, is $2,500. and each man's work averages about eight or eight and a half hours a week of class room work. If one's class work lies within the field in which one wants to write, original work for publication is not at all difficult, and I believe it would be less difficult for you than it has been for me. Each professor is allowed very great freedom in mapping out his courses, but of course the greater part of my work has necessarily lain in the lines of history, in which I do not care to publish. As I understand Dr. Raymond with reference to the plans for next year, it would be quite possible to give you an assistant who would take off your hands much of the routine work (class drill in texts, etc.) and not a little of the drudgery of reading examination papers. In a small college a man has one very distinct advantage, namely small classes, and I feel that the work must be very much less absorbing here than at Princeton. I am distinctly of the opinion that the chair here is one of the most desirable of its scope in the country. The scope of the assistance to be given you you could of course arrange with the authorities before coming. I very much hope for Wesleyan's sake that you will give the matter very serious consideration, and I shall as your friend hope that you will take so comfortable a place.

And now as to Princeton. The new chair in Political Economy will be erected just so soon as they can find the man they want to put into it. I believe that they do not think their finances quite in shape for the creation of the chair for the next academic year; but the year after next they will assuredly be ready. I carry the course in Economics in the mean time. The average salary at Princeton is $3,000. If Dr. Patton were not the worst correspondent in the United States, I could probably say something definite about the likelihood of your name being considered favourably for the place. As it is, I can give you only my impressions. Sloane is still at Princeton and is a very hearty friend indeed when once his friendship is enlisted. I should judge from what you say about his connection with the New York newspaper appointment that he could certainly be counted on. Before my own election to Princeton I wrote Dr. Patton a letter about you in which I did the best commendatory writing that I know how to do, telling him very plainly that you were the man for the appointment in Economics. Again, about two weeks ago I wrote him another, a short, letter, in which I told him that I had heard that you were to be called for next year to Cornell, and that I was not willing to sit still and see Princeton miss getting you through any fault of mine.[1] He is a 'powerfull' cautious man, committing himself to no opinions till he has thoroughly canvassed the field, and the trustees and friends of the college. To neither letter, therefore, have I received any definite reply. But my impression is, on the whole, that you would stand an extremely good chance of getting elected, if your friends had your permission to push you for all their influence is worth. As for the advantages of Princeton, I really think them greater than those of any other college in the East. It has size and progressiveness without the unbearable and dwarfing academic Pharisaism of Harvard or the narrow college pride of Yale; without the crude miscellaneous student body of Cornell, Philistine to the core, or the too pronounced political connections and dependencies of Michigan. There is as much culture and withal as much earnestness and high-bred enthusiasm in Princeton, I venture to say, as you will find anywhere, unless the character of the place has very much changed since I was there. The student body is representative of the earnest classes all over the country, and the faculty has of late years received an infusion of young blood which promises very distinct advances in method and result. The President is a thoroughly wide-awake and delightful man.

But of course I prefer Princeton.

I wish I had time to write more, but I have written out my time as it is. It was a genuine pleasure to see your handwriting once more; to be associated with you in college work would be strength and delight.

Please write soon again, and I will do the same.

Cordially and faithfully yours, Woodrow Wilson

TCL (in possession of Virginia Shaw English).

[1] Both of Wilson's letters to President Patton are missing. For Patton's replies, see F. L. Patton to WW, Nov. 9, 1889, and May 13, 1890.

To John Franklin Jameson

My dear Jameson, Middletown, Conn., 8 May, 1890

Alas, my dear fellow, it is as I feared, not as I hoped. Mrs. Wilson and the (rotund) little girl are better, but the other (oval faced) little maiden is under now! It is a deep disappointment to us both. Please give us either the 17th or the 24th as you prefer; but choose, if you please, the time when you can come earliest and make the longest stay. For we are determined not to be disappointed in amount, even though we must be in time, unless it be absolutely unavoidable.

Mrs. Wilson joins me in the most cordial regards and regrets.

Affectionately Yours, Woodrow Wilson

ALS (J. F. Jameson Papers, DLC).

From John Franklin Jameson

My dear Wilson: Providence, May 10, 1890.

I am very sorry that the little girl is ill. But for me it is, I find, quite as well that I should be here on Monday morning, and as for you, those of you who are not actually ill will be feeling a great deal better, I hope, two weeks from now. Therefore, *au revoir* on the 23d; I can't so well be absent on the 17th. A House of Commons is at work here, with some difficulties to contend against, but with some prospect of success, and much present interest. With the best wishes for the little girl, and with kind regards to Mrs. Wilson,

Sincerely yours, J. F. Jameson.

P.S. Feel perfectly free to postpone again on the 22d if there should be need.

ALS (WP, DLC).

From Marion Wilson Kennedy

My own dear brother: Batesville [Ark.], May 11th/90.

How glad I was to receive your loving letter, and how ashamed it made me feel that I had so long neglected relieving your *pressing* anxiety. Now, we have just passed through another such experience, with this difference,–it leaves Ross much more prostrated than the former attack left him. His temperature has been down as low as 94½° more than once this week, and then he has nearly constant fever. If we did not feel sure that it was all for some good purpose, and that Ross himself will be blessed by means of it, I do not see how we could live through these dreadful periods. Ross is certainly doing most effective preaching, as he lies here so uncomplainingly month after month. Everyone comments on the cheerfulness which lights up his face all the time. That is now interfered with by his extreme weakness of both body and mind. His seasons of prostration are rendered all the more trying because they are also seasons of mental aberration, and he dreads them so much. He never says anything but good things, though, and is oftenest explaining some passage of Scripture, or some doctrine, always in a delightfully practical strain. He always imagines himself in serious trouble, however, and is perfectly miserable. He even went through the agony of dying and finding himself forever lost once. You can judge the trial this is to us all, when we can't convince him it is imaginary!

Don't be too unhappy for us, my brother and sister. We are far from comfortless, and our Elder Brother seems constantly nearer and more dear to us than ever before. So we are spared the misery of doubts. We do not know how near or how far off is the end. Desolate as it will leave me, I have not the heart to pray for its delay. I only pray that Ross may meet death with an unclouded mind, and with as little suffering as possible. . . .

Write when you can, dear. Though you are not demonstrative, I have always,–judging you by myself–, felt sure of your hearty sympathy, my brother, and also sure of that of dear Ellie. Kiss my dear sister and the bairnies, for

Your loving sister, Marion.

ALS (WP, DLC).

From Hiram Woods, Jr.

My dear Tommy: Baltimore, May 12, 1890.

My friend Fay,[1] whom you met at the Princeton dinner, called to see me this afternoon, and asked me to get from you some information. Fay gets a Ph.D. from Hopkins this year. He has been pursuing a classical course and is best up on "Sanskrit"– an eminently practical thing for a fellow to be able to teach. Fay is an able fellow, and has won the praise of all the men at the University who have taught him. He is also full of ambition and poverty. So much by way of introduction. He has been offered a place in Texas to teach primary Latin and Greek. The pay, I believe, is fairly attractive, but Fay says it will be burying himself to go there. He has heard rumors of Wesleyan's desiring a man to teach Sanskrit. I was told myself during the Winter that Bloomfield had written to Wesleyan recommending Fay for the place. Of the truth of this I know nothing. Fay, however, is anxious to get to some "live" place where he can work and progress. If there is a chance at Wesleyan he wants to know, and work it for all there's in it. He has asked me to get this information for him from you. I am personally fond of Fay, and hope to see him get a good place.

I was sorry I did not see more of you when you were here. Your visit caught me at the time when I had most to keep me busy during the whole Winter. Shall hope for better luck next time. My Wife sends her regards to Mrs Wilson and yourself.

As ever your Friend, Hiram Woods, Jr

ALS (WP, DLC).

[1] Edwin Whitfield Fay, who found a position teaching Sanskrit at the University of Michigan for the academic year 1890-91 and was later Professor of Latin at the University of Texas and Washington and Lee University.

From Thomas Dixon, Jr.

My Dear Wilson: [New York] *May 12, '90.*

I congratulate you on the success of the year—your entrance into Princeton, where you will take your place as one of the leaders of economic thought in America. *Come to see me when you come to New York.*[1] I enclose you report of our years work from a late paper.[2] Fraternally, Thos. Dixon jr.

ALS (WP, DLC).

[1] Dixon was at this time pastor of the 23d Street Baptist Church in New York.

[2] The enclosure is missing.

From Francis Landey Patton

My dear Professor Wilson Princeton, 13 May [1890]

I was glad to get your letter & sympathize fully with you regarding Mr Shaw[.] I wrote Prof Shaw during the winter & wished him to come here & lecture; my object being to get acquainted with him.

I am confident that our Trustees would not elect a man so little known to a position so important & while I should be sorry to have Cornell run off with the prize I do not see that we can help it. Besides, I wish to get an endowment for your chair, & I think the wise course will be to make effort to secure it before dividing the work & calling another Professor.

I am very sincerely Francis L. Patton

ALS (WP, DLC).

To John Franklin Jameson

My dear Jameson, Middletown, Conn., 20 May, 1890

This is to remind you that we are looking forward with not a little enthusiasm to your coming next Friday, the 23rd. We are actually all well again, and, unless the present dreadful weather wrecks some one of us again, you may expect to see us as radiant as Nature alloweth. With cordial beckonings from us both,

Faithfully Yours, Woodrow Wilson

ALS (J. F. Jameson Papers, DLC).

From Marion Wilson Kennedy

Dear W.: Batesville [Ark.], May 20th [1890].

R. was taken from his sufferings last night at 10.30 o'clock. His end was very peaceful, and we grieve only for our loss, which is assuredly his great gain.

I will write in a few days, giving particulars. Please write when you can. Your sister, *M.*

API (WP, DLC).

From John Franklin Jameson

My dear Wilson: Providence, May 22, 1890.

I received your kind letter yesterday, and thank you, and am glad you are all well. I may be expected to arrive in Middletown at 8.05 tomorrow evening; and, by the way, I shall have had my three meals for the day. I shall need to return at 8.53 on Monday morning. A brass band to meet me at the station will not be necessary; Providence is full of brass bands, and we hear them every day. Indeed, it is probable that their instigation is at the bottom of the enormous frequency of processions here. Please give my kindest regards to Mrs. Wilson, and believe me

Sincerely yours, J. F. Jameson.

ALS (WP, DLC).

From Charles Homer Haskins

My dear Dr. Wilson: Baltimore, Md. May 25, 1890.

Now that my examinations are over and I at last am free, I want to ask you about two or three matters. First, as to my thesis. After two months of the hardest work that I ever did I succeeded in getting it in by the last of April, but it is not yet in shape to print.[1] I have exhausted all the material accessible in Baltimore and Washington and think I ought to visit Georgia before closing the account. I am told that Julius Brown of Atlanta, son of Senator Brown, has a collection of pamphlets bearing directly on the Yazoo land companies. Do you know whether I could probably get access to this collection? If you think I can, how would I best go about it? I think he must have some things of moment and am very anxious to get at them. If I go to Atlanta, I want to use the legislative records also.[2]

Would I have any difficulty in using the library of the State historical society? It is at Savannah, is it not? The subject has proved of more general interest than I expected. It has led me in some detail into the politics of Jefferson's first administration and into the history of the Supreme Court. I have tried to prove that the principle of the irrevocability of public contracts originated in Fletcher vs. Peck (1810) rather than in the Dartmouth College case. This may occasion some discussion.

May I ask you the address of the Leipsic book dealer of whom you spoke? Hendrickson[3] recommends Calvary of Berlin. Do you know anything about him? You mentioned a cheap reprint of standard German works on politics. Where can I get an announcement of it?

The historical department sends up eight men for the degree this year. Woodburn,[4] Iyenaga, McPherson,[5] and I have finished. Stephenson,[6] Gardner,[7] Vincent, and Turner are still on the books. The number of openings is surprisingly small. I cannot complain however. I have been offered the chair of history and politics in the University of South Dakota at a salary of $1500 and expect to hear of my election very soon, although I have not accepted the President's offer as yet. Chamberlin of Wisconsin has been lazily coquetting with me for some time, wavering between Spencer,[8] Mills[9] of Cornell, and me. He doesn't want to pay more than $1000. Mills will go for that and I won't. He (Chamberlin) seems to have awakened a little since the Dakota offer and may come down to something definite. Turner has been pushing me well but is uncertain of his own position. He will be on this week. I had in view something better than either, but it has collapsed.

Matters here are still chaotic. The students, graduate and undergraduate, are much dissatisfied. The graduates think that most of the year's work has been pretty thin. They feel it especially as there have been no graduate lectures except Dr. Ely's since you left, and Dr. Ely's illness cut his short. Dr. Adams has been working hard at Jared Sparks and the men resent it. After four or five weeks on the colonies the American history course was turned over to Woodburn, McPherson, Willoughby,[10] and Steiner. Some of their quizzes I hear were good, some I know were not. Of course there has been no unity.

The undergraduates complain of Smith[11] more than ever.

The worst thing about the situation is the prospect that next year will be like this. There seems to be no chance of getting

Jameson or anyone else—money, of course. I am quite sure that Dr. Adams doesn't realize how the students look at it. Nothing will be done until President Gilman's return in July;[12] probably nothing then. I am told by both Smith and Dr. Adams that Smith will keep up his work here. My work will probably be divided, Vincent taking the Greek and Roman history and the Latin reverting to the classical department. I know nothing about the American history. In all likelihood it will be as it was this year. I have been told that I could stay and continue the same work. Possibly (a mere conjecture) I could get the American history, but that would be gratuitous. At the most there is only $525 in the whole thing.

Have you heard of Dr. Ely's illness? He has had a bad time with typhoid fever, which, although the worst is over, has left him very weak. His absence next year would make matters worse.

Willoughby himself has become dissatisfied with his "Notes." The latest is that his study of the Supreme Court will be out this summer as an extra volume of the Studies![13] I tremble for it.

I hope you will pardon me all this stuff. I thought you might be interested in hearing how the students regard things and what the prospects are for next year. It is hard to say anything in a letter; I wish I could have a talk with you. Of course this is all *inter nos*.

The Phi Psis here are trying to secure a chapter-house for next year. They think they can pay the rent if they can collect enough from the alumni to furnish the house. I promised them to ask you for a subscription. I think they need advice quite as much. They would be glad to receive any suggestions on the subject.

Hoping that I am not troubling you too much with my questions, I remain Yours very truly, Charles H. Haskins.

ALS (WP, DLC) with WWhw notation on env.: "Ans. May 27/90."

1 Published as "The Yazoo Land Companies," *Papers of the American Historical Association*, v (Oct. 1891), 395-437.

2 Wilson answers these and other questions in his reply printed below.

3 Probably George Lincoln Hendrickson, a fellow-student of Haskins' at the Johns Hopkins, 1886-88, who had studied at the Universities of Bonn and Berlin in 1888-89 and was at this time teaching at Colorado College.

4 James Albert Woodburn.

5 John Hanson Thomas McPherson.

6 Andrew Stephenson.

7 Henry Brayton Gardner, then teaching at Brown University.

8 David Ellsworth Spencer.

9 Herbert Elmer Mills, then Instructor in Ancient History, Cornell University.

10 W. W. Willoughby.

11 Charles Lee Smith, who had taken his Ph.D. at the Johns Hopkins in 1889 and was an instructor in history at this time.

12 President Gilman was on leave during the academic year 1889-90 in Egypt, Syria, Greece, and other Mediterranean countries.

[13] W. W. Willoughby, *The Supreme Court of the United States: Its History and Influence in our Constitutional System* (Johns Hopkins University Studies in Historical and Political Science, Extra Vol. VII, Baltimore, 1890).

To Charles Homer Haskins

My dear Haskins, Middletown, Conn., 27 May, 1890.

It was a real pleasure to receive your letter this morning, and I am going to answer it at once. As it happens, I sent you the circular about those German reprints yesterday. The book-dealer from whom I get German works is Th. Stauffer, Universitätstrasse 24, Leipsig. I find him honest, prompt, and very reasonable in his charges. The best man I know of from whom to get French books is H. Welter, 59 Rue Bonaparte, Paris. I do'nt know anything about Calvary of Berlin, whom you mention. He may be just as good as Stauffer: I doubt if he can be better.

But to turn to the more important things in your letter. I very much fear that I cannot be of any assistance to you in the Georgia matter. I know of Julius Brown, who is a son of the notorious Jos. E. Brown, but I do not know him personally and cannot say what his disposition would be about letting a stranger make use of his library. I cannot conceive of his being so ungentlemanly as to refuse, and yet I must record the fact that gentlemanliness is not a characteristic of the Brown family, and that when I lived in Atlanta the said Julius had the reputation of being of a very ugly selfish temper. I can do this. My wife's brother, Mr. Stockton Axson, is with us and he knows very intimately a friend of Julius Brown's to whom he will cheerfully write, if you wish and will tell him at what time you contemplate being in Atlanta, asking him to see that you get the right sort of introduction to Mr. Brown. This friend is Mr. Albert Howell, son of the principal editor of the Atlanta Constitution, a splendid young fellow who would take genuine pleasure in showing you any attention.

The State legislative records I have no doubt are accessible, and I am sure that there would be no trouble at all about using the collections of the Historical Society's Lobrary [Library] in Savannah. It is open to all, and the librarian, I understand, is an unusually courteous and helpful gentleman.

I am glad the subject has grown and widened so on your hands, and I feel very confident that you will make a capital thing out of it. I shall await its appearance in print with real interest.

Your account of the conditions of work at present in the department is indeed gloomy, and has quite given me the blues. I wish I knew of some way in which I could, without either betraying your confidence or myself seeming officious, make Dr. Adams understand how serious the situation is for the future of the University. The bottom will drop out of the History Department visibly to the world if things are not soon amended. But apparently something direful must happen before the eyes of the authorities will be opened. I am glad you wrote me as you did: I may think of something feasible to be done or said.

The account you give of your own professional prospects interests me deeply. I wish you could go to Wisconsin and be with Turner[1] rather than to that uttermost part of the earth, South Dakota; but I do not believe that you will be buried, wherever you may go.

The affairs in the history department here are still quite undecided. We do not yet know what will be done. I worked for Turner with great enthusiasm and made, I am sure, a good deal of impression on the authorities. But they are very shy of making so young a man full professor (the more blind they!), and, finding that they were not likely to offer T. anything better than he now has (whatever might be the difference in prospects), I felt that the truest friendship for him would be shown by letting his case drop, and letting him abide by the chances in a section where he belongs by reason of his characteristics and chosen work rather than in a section where living is much more expensive and where he could do none of the work he prefers at all. Not knowing finally as yet what will be done, I have not written to him, to give an account of my stewardship of his interests here; but I have done for him just what I should have wished to have done for myself under like circumstances. If this letter reaches you while he is in Baltimore, please give him my love and promise him a letter from me at an early date.

I must not write more this afternoon. Let me hear from you as often and at as great length as may be, and beli[e]ve me,

Cordially and faithfully Yours, Woodrow Wilson

P.S. Please give my cordial regards to Miss Ashton and Miss Hannah also, and tell the former that my little girls have greatly enjoyed and appreciated the cards and picture she was kind enough to send.

Yours, W.W.

I have just been bled for my own chapter of $\phi\psi$ (Va. Alpha) and am afraid I cannot bleed again for the Hopkins chapter. Am sincerely yours. But moving is expensive. W.W.

WWTLS (C. H. Haskins Papers, NjP).

[1] Haskins did go to Wisconsin, as his letter to Wilson of July 2, 1890, reveals.

An Examination in American History

May 28/90

Junior History (3 hours

1. Indicate the main points of contrast between the Colonial history of Mass. and the Colonial history of Va.
2. How were the fate and character of the treaty of peace of 1783 bound up with European, and especially with English, politics?
3. Reproduce the substance of Fiske's chapter on the Constitutional Convention of 1787 and its work.
4. Sketch our party history from 1787 to the inauguration of Jackson, describing in some detail the decline and fall of the Federalist party.
5. Trace the European antecedents
   (a) of the War of 1812
   (b) of the Monroe Doctrine.

WWhw MS. (WP, DLC).

From John Franklin Jameson

My dear Wilson: Providence, May 28, 1890.

I have been paying for my outing, and for another one I mean to take, by being very busy. But you will have anticipated this, and will not be surprised that I have not written. You can't easily imagine what a world of good it did me to have those delightful two or three days of visit with you and Mrs. Wilson and the lovely little girls. I have been a better boy ever since! I join you all, you see, not flattering *you* individually. I love to be the friend of a man, especially of an able man of similar pursuits; but I also greatly love to be the friend of a family, and it does me good. Be sure I shall leave no effort unmade to find a place where we can together recumb beneath the patulous fage and meditate the Muse on the slender ō' mē' of the summer hotel.

Speaking of family ties, what do you suppose is the last caper of our sprightly faculty? An invitation was sent us, to send a delegate to the 25th anniversary of Vassar. Two or three of the older men, being suggested, said they had engagements that day. Some one jocosely suggested that we ought to send an unmarried member. Another replied that such were scarce in this faculty, and, looking around, they discovered only me, and at once elected me unanimously. I suppose I shall go, though I don't greatly want to. They said, "Don't dare to come back alone!" "I hardly dare to *go* alone," said I. Thus are the weightiest issues decided with irresponsible levity.

I meant to ask you Sunday whether Professor Van Vleck came to call on me that Saturday morning, or called on you and found me there. If the former, I'm sorry I didn't go to call on him, and beg you to make any explanation you think most fit.

In spite of our forty-eight hours of conversation I did not, as I meant to do, ask you concerning the Southern Society, of New York. I wish that, when you write, you would tell me what you can of the present state and future prospects of its library, how far useful to me.

Gardner has come back from Baltimore successful, though he professes himself dissatisfied with his performance. Didn't feel well while there. Probably also his project of matrimonial alliance has had a disturbing effect on his studies. You have probably received cards for the wedding, on the ninth. I wish you could both come over. Ely has the typhoid fever. Gardner was examined in political economy by Franklin and Emmott,[1] therefore.

I shall be absent on the 10th, 11th, and 12th, and leave here about the 21st. (This, as to your examination papers).[2]

I thank you most warmly for your hospitality. Give my kindest regards to Mrs. Wilson and Mr. Axson, please, and my love to the little girls. Sincerely yours, J. F. Jameson.

ALS (WP, DLC) with WWhw notation on env.: "Ans. June 6/90."

1 Fabian Franklin, then Associate Professor of Mathematics, and George Henry Emmott, Associate Professor of Logic and Ethics and Lecturer in Roman Law at the Johns Hopkins.

2 Jameson had promised Wilson that he would read the papers for the Harrington Prize, awarded annually to the senior who excelled in history. Wilson had announced in the Wesleyan catalogue for 1889-90 that the prize would go in 1890 to the senior writing the best paper in a special examination on the history of institutions. The examination is printed at June 9, 1890.

From Marion Wilson Kennedy

My very dear brother; Batesville [Ark.], May 29th 1890.

Your comforting letter came today, and I feel that it will be easier to answer it now than at any other time, though it has always seemed quite natural to express my thoughts and feelings to you, dear Woodrow.

Though the months of suffering Ross had to experience have, in some respects, added to this trial, in some others, they have made the final blow less hard to bear. Can't you see how *even I* would be *glad* to know that these sufferings, which increased greatly towards the last–, are finally ended and exchanged for heaven? Truly, Woodrow, though I daily realize a little more of my loss, that is as nothing beside his infinite gain, even now, when I am just *widowed*. . . .

Please write again whenever you can, and ask dear Ellie,—the unseen sister I love so well—, to write also. With unbounded love to you all, Lovingly your sister, Marion.

P.S. omitted. ALS (WP, DLC).

From Charles Homer Haskins

My dear Dr. Wilson: Baltimore. May 29, 1890.

Many thanks for your kind letter. I enclose Mohr's prospectus.[1] I shall be glad to take advantage of Mr. Axson's kindness. As things look now, I hope to be in Atlanta about June 20. The time depends somewhat on my arrangements for next year. The Secretary of State[2] informs me that I can have ready access to the papers in his office.

The bottom has dropped out of my South Dakota offer. Monday morning a note came from the President informing me that he found on his return that the Trustees had made arrangements for the temporary filling of the chair of history. Which is a peculiar way of doing business. Just now my stock consists of chances at Hopkins and Wisconsin, and neither of them makes me enthusiastic. However, McPherson and Stephenson haven't even that much, nor do the men in other departments find anything. Will the call of Smith[3] from Bowdoin to Yale move things around much?

Turner will be here to-morrow to stay until Tuesday at least.

Yours very sincerely, Charles H. Haskins.

P.S. If possible, I am anxious to learn of my probable success with Mr. Brown before I go.

ALS (WP, DLC) with WWhw notation on env.: "Haskins."

1 Of the publishing firm of J. C. B. Mohr of Freiburg and Tübingen. This enclosure is missing.

2 Nathan C. Barnett, Secretary of State of Georgia.

3 Charles Henry Smith.

To Albert Shaw

My dear Shaw: Middletown, Conn. 30 May, 1890.

The President has received your telegram and letter: we have just had a faculty consultation and he is going to telegraph you a formal offer at once, which I sincerely hope to see draw from you an acceptance. I am afraid that Dr. Raymond is not very clear in his putting of things. He certainly meant to make you a virtual offer of the chair. For fear he miscarries again, this time in his attempt to explain why we must be in desperate haste about obtaining a definite answer, I am going to give a volunteered and unofficial explanation of my own. The fact is that the end not only of our own but of all other college years is so close at hand that unless this matter may be brought to a settlement very soon, it may fail of settlement altogether. If we can't get you, we must try for some other man; the other man must be someone now in college work; and we must ask him while there still remains time enough for his college to make arrangements to fill his place, should he determine to come here.

I write hastily, in order that this may get off as soon as possible; but I want to add a very sincere hope that you will come. The conditions of your work here will be as favourable as they have the means to make them; and the men you will work with are scholars and white men. I fear that the Princeton matter must wait a year or so, from what Dr. Patton tells me; but you won't escape college observation or be out of the bidding should you accept this thoroughly desirable place. No college position is without drudgery and drawback; but a college position is the one for original work, and this is, I am convinced, among the most comfortable and most advantageous.

With affectionate regards,

Faithfully yours, Woodrow Wilson

TCL (in possession of Virginia Shaw English).

From Charles William Kent

My dear Wilson, Knoxville, Tenn., May 30th 1890

I am holding an examination. This is a scene too suggestive of hard toil and the drudgery of life to have been chosen by preference as a time to write to you, but, as a matter of fact I am a little too much hurried just now to consider preference at all.

I am just getting ready to do some very uncongenial work for the University of Tenn. but work which I have persuaded myself it is my duty to do viz: visit the high schools of the state in order to try to infuse a little more life into some of them, to find out what others are doing, and try to get in closer sympathy with them all. To this end I leave Knoxville this afternoon and shall be gone about two weeks. I expect, however, to be back several days before our final exercises and to be on hand to give you a whole-souled welcome and to enjoy your company and your address. I can not tell you how much pleasure I anticipate from both, and how much delight it is going to give me to live over with you some of our past experiences.

I have much to tell you of my own work since we last met but more to ask you about your own, much to tell you about my own past discouragements and my plans, and more to gain from some account of your experiences. In a word I don't know of any of my old friends and companions, whom I would rather see now than you.

You will have a good audience of average intelligence to hear you and one that will be very kindly disposed, so you may speak with confidence in its sympathy and faith in its capacity to appreciate your words. Our U of Va. Alumni Association here had a very delightful reunion recently and among others entertained Mr Thornton,[1] who gave us much gratifying information about the present prosperity of our Alma Mater. His modesty did not allow him to appropriate any of the credit of this success but those who know his energy and devotion willingly concede it.

Pardon the abruptness. I am called off to another professorial duty, so I must close. We shall have a chance to pick up the threads of this scrappy note.

Affly yr. friend Charles W. Kent.

ALS (WP, DLC).

1 William Mynn Thornton, Professor of Applied Mathematics and Civil Engineering, University of Virginia.

Wilson Reviews His Lectures at the Johns Hopkins

[*c. June 1, 1890*]

Dr. Woodrow Wilson gave twenty-five lectures on Administration. The course consisted of two distinct parts. About one half of the lectures concerned the history, principles, and organization of cities, particularly the rise, functions, and organization of modern industrial cities. The method of presentation in this part of the course was largely descriptive and comparative of American with foreign systems of municipal government; but the purpose of both description and comparison was the elucidation of the administrative character of city government, and the discovery of the best division of functions in municipal administration. The second part of the course was devoted to a discussion of the distinction between law and ordinance, with a view to discerning the true line of division between administration and the other activities of government. It included a sketch of the history of theory in these lines, a discussion of budget legislation as a test of theory, and a general statement of conclusions. The course ended with a brief discussion of administrative courts and administrative justice.

Printed in the *Fifteenth Annual Report of the President of The Johns Hopkins University,* 1890 (Baltimore, 1890), p. 56.

From Herbert Baxter Adams

My dear Mr. Wilson: Baltimore, Md., June 4, 1890.

I am requested by Acting President [Ira] Remsen to inform you that yesterday the Trustees voted to re-engage you as Reader upon Administration for a period of three years on the same terms as before. It seemed best to the Trustees to settle academic matters before the return of President Gilman. Having received your programme for next year and your assurance that re-engagement would be agreeable to you, even under your new professorial conditions at Princeton, I trust that you will regard the matter as definitely settled, and tell me so by letter. Here is an advanced copy of our programme for next year, but we hope still to improve it by certain additions in the shape of short lecture courses. Very cordially yours, H. B. Adams

TLS (WP, DLC) with WWhw notation on env.: "Ans. 6 June '90."

To John Franklin Jameson

My dear Jameson, Middletown, Conn., 6 June, 1890.

You need not think that you are the only one who enjoyed your recent visit to this borough and household. We enjoyed it not a whit less than you did yourself: there being more of us to do the enjoying, we doubtless enjoyed it more than you did.

We regard your visit to Vassar with profound solicitude. What may come of it we dare not think. That your bachelor calm should be subjected to so great and so sudden a storm of disturbing influences must make all your friends withhold prophecy as to your future.

That examination in "The State"[1] is to be held Monday afternoon next, June 9. I shall mail the papers so that they may reach you on the 13th., after your return from the absence of the 10th.-12th.

I am sorry and a bit ashamed to say that I know next to nothing about the Southern Society. I know a man[2] who probably can find out all about it for us, and I will mention it to him when I write next and report results to you.[3]

Mrs. Wilson and her brother join me in warmest regards

Affectionately Yours, Woodrow Wilson

WWTLS (J. F. Jameson Papers, DLC).

[1] For the Harrington Prize.

[2] Richard Heath Dabney.

[3] See Wilson's note on R. H. Dabney to WW, March 1, 1890.

From Albert Shaw

My Dear Wilson: [Minneapolis] Friday, June 6. 1890.

It seems to me best, upon the whole, not to accept the invitation to go to the Wesleyan. I reach this conclusion with sincere reluctance, for the position has many attractions that appeal to me. You have known, I think, of certain possibilities for me at Cornell. While nothing has been finally arranged for me there, President Adams now writes that within a year he thinks that certain contemplated changes will be made, and that I shall be called to a chair for which the University Senate has already formally recommended me. I had heard of this by rumor, but did not know of it otherwise until three or four days ago. The Cornell place would be much more *special* as I understand it than the one at Wesleyan. Moreover, a very strong consideration,—the strongest, in fact,—that moves me toward Cornell, is the circumstance that my mother who has always lived with me but who is now an invalid living with my sister in western New York misses me greatly and longs to have me near her. At Cornell I should be in easy reach of her and my sister's family; and on that account I should deem it a filial duty to go to Ithaca if a place were made for me. But if I have this in mind, it would not be fair to the Wesleyan to accept a place there. Perhaps I shall be very sorry a year hence that I have cut off this excellent chance for a professorship; for there is no certainty about the Cornell place,—only a fair probability. But I must take the chances. On very many accounts I should like Princeton better than Cornell; and if the gates of Ithaca are closed against me I may be tempted to seek your kind offices with respect to that situation. But at any rate I cannot quite see my way clear to go to Connecticut, and it would be unjust to all concerned for me to go there regarding the place as a makeshift or a temporary stepping-stone. I have a high opinion of the Wesleyan, and the warmest feeling of gratitude for the kindness that it has shown me. For your own generous and brotherly treatment of me, I can only say that I appreciate it deeply. If you wish you may show this to the President, or tell him the essential parts. Of course I write him also.

Faithfully Yours, Albert Shaw.

ALS (WP, DLC).

From Marsh and Wright

Dear Sir: Princeton, N. J., June 9, 1890

Your favor of the 1st inst. duly received.[1] I have waited to answer after seeing different parties. There is no guarantee of the Beekman house by Sept. 1st. Now, I have had Dr. McGill here, and he is willing to remove the shelves from present library, and he is still better willing to carry the heat to the second story in all the rooms, paint, paper &c, wherever needed & put the house[2] in first-class condition. So I have closed the renting today for you at $500. He wants to retain one room on the 3d floor if possible. I don't suppose you will need it. Will you be down to chose paper &c. Will you want to use any of the furniture? There is an excellent silver burglar & fire proof safe & side board you can use if desired, please let me hear from you soon & oblige

Yours truly Crowell Marsh W. M. Wright

ALS (WP, DLC).

[1] This was the last of several letters from Marsh and Wright, realtors and insurance brokers, concerning a house in Princeton for the Wilsons. Earlier letters in the Wilson Papers, DLC, are dated April 30 and May 2, 15, and 29, 1890.

[2] A large frame house at 48 Steadman Street (now 72 Library Place), built by Charles Steadman and owned in 1890 by Dr. John Dale McGill of Jersey City, son of the former owner, the Rev. Dr. Alexander Taggart McGill of the Princeton Theological Seminary, who had died in 1889.

A Prize Examination

9 June, '90.)

Senior Prize Examination (on the *State*)

History.

1. In what points of structure was Roman government like Teutonic; in what points unlike?

2. Give the characteristic features of English local government from the fourteenth century to the nineteenth (down to reforms of 1888), and contrast with the history of local government in France.
3. Trace the development (1) of the offices of the five Principal Secretaries of State, and (2) of the Treasury Dept. in England as typical of English administrative development, and discuss the present organization and Cabinet position of the Treasury Dept. as a means of central administrative integration in England.
4. Describe carefully the difference (1) in administrative integration and oversight, (2) in central financial audit, and (3) in financial control of local government between the governments of England, France and Prussia.
5. Outline the organization of local government in France and point out the principles which distinguish it (1) in respect of central control and (2) in respect of administrative action from local government in Prussia.
6. Compare the organization and functions of the French Department (1) with those of the Prussian Province and (2) with those of the Prussian Government District.
7. In what respects of structure and principles do dual governments like those of Austria-Hungary and Sweden-Norway differ from federal governments of the modern type, like those of Switzerland, Germany, and the United States?
8. Characterize and distinguish the relations of the executive ministry to the Legislature in the following countries: England, France, Germany, Switzerland, Austria-Hungary (the common government).
9. Why is government by the Chambers, that is by a popular representative body, more dangerous in France than in England?

WWT MS. (WP, DLC).

From Henry Nevius Van Dyke

Dear Sir— Princeton, June 10, '90.

In a package of letters sent me yesterday by President Patton I find yours written to him June 6th. I suppose therefore that your acceptance sent to Dr. Craven through him was duly received. Dr. Patton sent with your letter no instructions concerning reply. He is unable at present to write personally.

Yours very truly H. N. Van Dyke, President's Secr.

ALS (WP, DLC).

An Examination in American History

12 June, 1890.

1. Give fully and carefully reasons for regarding 1828 and the accession of Jackson as a turning point in our national history,

discussing for the purpose the state of parties during the administrations of Monroe and J. Q. Adams, and showing what questions arose or took new shape during Jackson's terms of office.

2. Discuss the question of the United States Bank; the origin and progress of Jackson's hostility towards it; the means of its overthrow; and the fiscal instrumentalities substituted for it.
3. Trace the history of the slavery question through its several stages from the Missouri Compromise to Secession.
4. How has the question of Secession been from the first connected with the territories of the United States? What events were the immediate occasion of the secession of the Southern States in 1860 and 1861? How did they secede, and what were their first purposes in seceding?

WWT MS. (WP, DLC) with hw notation on verso: "Dr. Mulford will call on the afternoon of the 28 inst if he does not hear from you before"

From John Franklin Jameson

My dear Wilson: Providence, June 15, 1890.

Your examination is a corker, Herr Geheimoberregierungsrath, and I am glad I do not have to pass such, having now no more examinations to pass, I trust, until one hales me before Rhadamanthus, Aeacus and Minos. But your students do passing well; I wish mine could make as good a showing. I will send the papers to you tomorrow. My report is in favor of "Victim."[1] I will give you the percentages. It was necessary to estimate them on per cents., question by question, for they were too near together to distinguish off-hand. Viz.: (on severe marking).

"Victim," 80.
"Sam," 79.
"McGinty," 74.
"Grotius," 71.
"No. 247," 69.
"Jack," 69.

I enclose a letter received from the manager of the Manomet.[2] I do not remember anything about the rooms mentioned, but doubtless they are good. The charges are quite a bit more than I said. Meanwhile, I have another suggestion to offer. Mrs. Carey, it seems, has been persuaded by my cousins in Washington to go where they go year after year, to Kennebunkport, Maine, a very nice place, everyone says. She and Estelle are to have a room there for $12 a week, & to be there, probably, all July. I may add that my cousins, the Chickerings, are one of the most entertaining families I know. I mean to go there for a week or two, myself. Now why won't it be a good plan for you to go there? Equally easy and cheap of access, within a few cts. My only hesitation is from not remembering whether you wanted especially warm water. It isn't as cold at K. as in most of Maine, and Mrs. C. and Estelle found it not too cold in August, at least. Tell me what you think. Mrs. Carey will arrive in Boston Sunday with them, & I will have inquiries of price made. Kindest regards to Mrs. Wilson, Mr Axson, & the minors.

Trly yrs. J. F. J

ALI (WP, DLC). Enc.: P. A. Roberts to J. F. Jameson, June 9, 1890.

[1] "Victim" was Martha Josephine Beach of Middletown.

[2] The Manomet House, Manomet, Mass.

From Wilson's Pocket Diary

June, Tuesday 17. 1890.

Commencement address ("Leaders of Men") University of Tennessee, Knoxville. (Staubs Opera House)

Entry in pocket diary described at Jan. 1, 1890.

EDITORIAL NOTE

"LEADERS OF MEN"

After Wilson had accepted the invitation of the faculty of the University of Tennessee to deliver an address during the commencement exercises of 1890, he wrote to his old friend, Charles William Kent, then a professor at that institution, that the occasion would be his "first venture in the direction of Commencement addresses," and that he would undertake it with "a good deal of trepidation."[1] There seems to have been no ground for such fear, for the Knoxville newspaper reported on the morning after Wilson's speech that "a representative Knoxville audience had the pleasure of listening to a most excellent address. . . . For over an hour and a half [the speaker] held his audience entranced."[2]

The address that Wilson delivered in Staub's Opera House on the evening of June 17, 1890, was a slight revision of the lecture, "Leaders of Men," that he had first delivered in Middletown on December 3, 1889.[3] "Leaders of Men" was one of Wilson's most

[1] WW to C. W. Kent, March 26, 1890. Actually, as the program in the University of Tennessee Archives reveals, Wilson delivered "Leaders of Men" as the "Annual Address before the Faculty and Students of the University," not as the commencement address. Commencement itself, in which Wilson took no part, came on the next day, June 18. However, Wilson had presented the medals of the Chi-Delta Literary Society on June 16. This ceremonial duty, according to the student journal, he discharged "in the most graceful manner." Knoxville *Tennessee University Student*, May [June], 1890.

[2] *Knoxville Journal*, June 18, 1890.

[3] See the news item printed at Dec. 9, 1889.

notable addresses, yet there is no documentary record concerning its composition. No specific allusions to it appear in surviving correspondence. No indications of advance work on it or of the writing process are to be found.

Wilson typed the text of what might be called the Tennessee version, reproduced below, on his Caligraph directly from his handwritten Middletown copy, making a number of minor changes as he went—for example, taking note of Browning's recent death. In addition, either at this time or before later deliveries, he made a number of handwritten emendations, polishing and compacting the style. A few errors of 1889 were corrected in 1890; a few were carried forward, one being the repetition of the mistake of calling Henry Addington "John" Addington. Wilson made a few new errors in the Tennessee text, such as misspelling Disraeli's name. There was only one substantive addition of any significance to the Tennessee draft—the two paragraphs on compromise which are indicated by the twelfth footnote to the text.

The version printed below is, the Editors believe, substantially the one that Wilson used at Tennessee. Insofar as is known, he delivered "Leaders of Men" only four times following its delivery at Knoxville: before the Kent Club of the Yale Law School on March 18, 1891; at the Oberlin College commencement on June 19, 1895; at a benefit for a church in Princeton on January 20, 1898; and at a boys' school in Bridgeport, Connecticut, on May 24, 1898. Footnotes to the text printed below indicate the few changes that Wilson made to bring the lecture up to date upon these occasions.

In form, "Leaders of Men" is loose and free-flowing. In substance and style, it is poetic, emotional, and prophetic. It may have been the product of a flash of insight in which, in the relative euphoria that came from the growing success of 1889, Wilson's accumulated ideas and experiences became, as it were, fused. "Leaders of Men" is a far cry from "that laboured composition,"[4] *The State*, completed only six months before the delivery of the Wesleyan version. Yet the lecture is clearly kin to everything that Wilson had written in the field of politics. In his essay on Gladstone, composed at the University of Virginia in 1880, he had stated, for example: "Great statesmen seem to direct and rule by a sort of power to put themselves in the place of the nation over whom they are set, and may thus be said to possess the souls of poets at the same time that they display the coarser sense and the more vulgar sagacity of practical men of business."[5] This rather matter-of-fact description of the leader as the thinking man in action was translated in 1889 into words of deep feeling, which in application extended far beyond the character of a single man. Of course this process of accretion and expansion did not end in 1889 or 1890. To cite only one example, Wilson in 1891 incorporated the gist of "Leaders of Men" in another and broader gauged lecture entitled "Democracy."[6] Interestingly, "Democracy,"

[4] WW to J. F. Jameson, Oct. 5, 1889.
[5] Vol. 1, p. 628.
[6] Printed at Dec. 5, 1891, Vol. 7.

like "Leaders of Men," was first delivered in the Russell Hall Library in Middletown.

"Leaders of Men" was a highly personal statement. Wilson long had struggled to reconcile the sometimes conflicting attributes and purposes of the thinker and doer, and doubts as to how well he was using his powers persisted even as he moved from Bryn Mawr to Wesleyan. Writing "Leaders of Men," Wilson reviewed his long inner debate and, at least for a time, resolved the conflict between thinking and doing. When he had finished the lecture, he wrote in his Confidential Journal: "Interpret myself. Account for the creed I hold in politics. Institutions have their rootage in the common thought and only those who share the common thought can rightly interpret them. . . . Why may not the present age write, through me, its political *autobiography?*"[7] This objective, it might be added, Wilson achieved more definitively in "Democracy" than in "Leaders of Men."

Less striking than the elements of self-revelation in "Leaders of Men," but no less important to an understanding of it, are two features which might be briefly noted. The first is the lecture's remarkable reflection of Victorian faith in the almost inevitable working out of the law of political progress. Secondly, in "Leaders of Men" Wilson used the language of the King James Version for the first time in his political writing and, more important, expressed, again for the first time, the conviction that the Christian law of love was the only force that could unite societies and provide the proper motivation for political leaders. This, certainly, was not a new conviction on his part. However, it seems highly probable that the warm, evangelical preaching of his pastor at Middletown, Dr. Azel W. Hazen, had already begun to catalyze Wilson's political as well as theological thought. That this was true is dramatically revealed by Wilson's use of a passage from Dr. Hazen's sermon on November 30, 1889, in "Leaders of Men."[8] Further testimony to the minister's influence will be found in Wilson's letter to Hazen of July 1, 1891, printed in Volume 7.

[7] Entry for Dec. 28, 1889.
[8] See n. 11 to the text printed below.

An Address

Leaders of Men.

[June 17, 1890]

Only those are 'leaders of men,' in the general eye, who lead in action. The title belongs, if the whole field of the world be justly viewed, no more rightfully to the men who lead in action than to those who lead in silent thought. A book is often quite as quickening a trumpet as any made of brass and sounded in the field. But it is the estimate of the world that bestows their meaning upon words: and that estimate is not often very far from the fact. The men who act stand nearer to the mass of men than do the men who write; and it is at their hands that new thought gets its translation into the crude language of deeds. The very crudity of that language of deeds exasperates the sensibilities of the author; and his exasperation proves the world's point. He may be *back* of the leaders, but he is not the leader. In his thought there is due and studied proportion; all limiting considerations are set in their right places, as guards to ward off misapprehension. Every cadence of right utterance is made to sound in the careful phrases, in the perfect adjustments of sense. Translate the thought into action and all its shadings disappear. It stands out a naked, lusty thing, sure to rasp the sensibilities of every man of fastidious taste. Stripped for action, a thought must always shock those who cultivate the nice fashions of literary dress, as authors do. But it is only when thought does thus stand forth in unabashed force that it can perform deeds of strength in the arena round about which the great public sit as spectators, awarding the prizes by the suffrage of their applause.

Here, unquestionably, we come upon the heart of the perennial misunderstanding between the men who write and the men who act. The men who write love proportion; the men who act must strike out practicable lines of action, and neglect proportion. This would seem to explain the well-nigh universal repugnance felt by literary men towards Democracy. The arguments which induce popular action must always be broad and obvious arguments. Only a very gross substance of concrete conception can make any impression on the minds of the masses; they must get their ideas very absolutely put, and are much readier to receive a half truth which they can promptly understand than a whole truth which has too many sides to be seen all at once. How can any man whose method is the method of artistic completeness of thought and expression, whose mood is the mood of contemplation, for a moment understand or tolerate 'the majority,' whose purpose and practice it is to strike out broad, rough-hewn *policies*, whose mood is the mood of action? The great stream of freedom which

"broadens down
from precedent to precedent,"[1]

is not a clear mountain current such as the fastidious man of chastened taste likes to drink from: it is polluted with not a few of the coarse elements of the gross world on its banks; it is heavy with the drainage of a very material universe.

[1] From Tennyson's "You Ask Me Why." [All notes Eds.']

One of the nicest *tests* of the repugnance felt by the literary nature for the sort of leadership and action which commends itself to the world of common men you may yourself apply. Ask some author of careful, discriminative thought to utter his ideas to a *mass-meeting*, from a platform occupied by 'representative citizens.' He will shrink from it as he would shrink from being publicly dissected! Even to hear *some one else*, who is given to apt public speech, re-render his thoughts in oratorical phrase and make them acceptable to a miscellaneous audience, is often a mild, sometimes an accute, form of torture for him. If the world would really know his thoughts for what they are, let them go to his written words, con his phrases, join paragraph with paragraph, chapter with chapter: then, the whole form and fashion of his conceptions impressed upon their minds, they will know him as no platform speaker can ever make him known. Of course such preferences greatly limit his audience. Not many out of the multitudes who crowd about him buy his books. But, if the few who can understand read and are convinced, will not his thoughts finally leaven the mass?

The true leader of men, it is plain, is equipped by lacking such sensibilities, which the literary man, when analyzed, is found to possess as a chief part of his make-up. He lacks that subtle power of sympathy which enables the men who write the great works of the imagination to put their minds under the spell of a thousand individual motives not their own but the living force in the several characters they interpret. No popular leader could write fiction. He could not conceive the 'Ring and the Book,' the impersonation of a half-score points of view. An imaginative realization of other natures and minds than his own is as impossible for him, as his own commanding, dominating frame of mind and character is impossible for the sensitive seer whose imagination can give life to a thousand separate characters. Mr. Browning could no more have been a statesman—if statesmen are to be popular leaders also—than Mr. Disreali could write a novel. Mr. Browning could see from every individual's point of view—no intellectual sympathy came amiss to him. Mr. Disreali could see from no point of view but his own,—and the characters which he put into those works of his which were *meant* to be novels move as mere puppets to his will,—as the men he governed did. They are his mouthpieces simply, and are as little like themselves as were the Tory squires in the Commons like themselves after they became his chess-men.

One of the most interesting and suggestive criticisms made upon Mr. Gladstone's leadership during the life of his ministries was that he was not decisive in the House of Commons as Palmerston and Peel had been before him. He could not help seeing two sides of a question: the force of objections evidently told upon him. His conclusions seemed the nice result of a balancing of considerations, not the commands of an unhesitating conviction. A party likes to be led by very absolute opinions: it chills it to hear it admitted that there is some reason on the other side. *Mr. Peel* saw both sides of many questions; but he never saw both sides at once. He saw now one, and afterwards, by slow and honest conversion, the other. While he is in opposition,[2] Mr. Gladstone's transparent honesty adds to his moral weight with the people: for in opposition only the whole attitude is significant. But it was different when he was in power. For a governing party *particulars* of posture and policy tell. For them the consistency of unhesitating opinion counts heavily as an element of success and prestige.

That the leader of men must have such sympathetic and penetrative insight as shall enable him to discern quite unerringly the motives which move other men *in the mass* is of course self-evident; but the insight which he must have is not the Shaksperian insight. It need not pierce the particular secrets of *individual* men: it need only know what it is that lies waiting to be stirred in the minds and purposes of groups and masses of men. Besides, it is not a sympathy that serves, but a sympathy whose power is to command, to command by knowing its instrument. The seer, whose function is imaginative interpretation, is the man of science; the leader is the mechanic. The chemist knows his materials interpretatively: he can make subtlest analysis of all their affinities, of all their antipathies; can give you the point of view of every gas or metal or liquid with regard to every other liquid or gas or metal; he can marry, he can divorce, he can destroy them. He could suppose fictitious cases with regard to the conduct of the 'elements' which would appear most clever and probable to other chemists: which would appear witty and credible, doubtless, to the 'elements' themselves, could they know. But the mining-engineer's point of view is very different. He, too, must know chemical properties, but only in order that he may *use* them—only in order to have the right sort

[2] In editing the MS for future lecture uses, Wilson altered verbs from present to past tense to make his references to Gladstone and Home Rule consistent with Gladstone's return to the office of Prime Minister on August 15, 1892.

of explosion at the right place. So, too, the mechanic's point of view must be quite different from that of the physicist. He must know what his tools can do and what they will stand; but he must be something more than interpreter of their qualities,—and something quite different. "It is the general opinion of locomotive superintendents that it is not essential that the men who run locomotives should be good mechanics. Brunel, the distinguished civil engineer, said that he never would trust himself to run a locomotive because he was sure to think of some problem relating to his profession which would distract his attention from the engine. It is probably a similar reason which unfits good mechanics for being good locomotive runners."[3]

Imagine Thackeray leading the House of Commons, or Mr. Lowell on the stump. How comically would their very genius defeat them. The special gift of these two men is a *critical* understanding of other men, their fallible fellow-creatures. How could their keen humourous sense of what was transpiring in the breasts of their followers and fellow-partisans be held back from banter? How could they take the mass seriously—themselves refrain from laughter and also from the temptation of provoking it? Thackeray argue patiently and respectfully with a dense country member, equipped with nothing but diverting scruples and laughable prejudices? Impossible. As well ask a biologist to treat a cat or a rabbit as if it were *a pet* with no admirable machinery inside to tempt the dissecting knife.

The competent leader of men cares little for the interior niceties of other people's characters: he cares much—everything for the external uses to which they may be put. His will seeks the lines of least resistance; but the whole question with him is a question *of the application of force*. There are men to be moved: how shall he move them? He supplies the power; others supply only the materials upon which that power operates. The power will fail if it be misapplied; it will be misapplied if it be not suitable both in kind and method to the nature of the materials upon which it is spent; but that nature is, after all, only its means. It is the *power* which dictates, dominates: the materials yield. Men are as clay in the hands of the consummate leader.

It often happens that the leader displays a sagacity and an insight in the handling of men in the mass which quite baffle the wits of the shrewdest analyst of *individual* character. Men

[3] M. N. Forney, "American Locomotives and Cars," *Scribner's Magazine,* IV (Aug. 1888), 192.

in the mass differ from men as individuals. A man who knows, and keenly knows, every man in town may yet fail to understand a mob or a mass-meeting of his fellow-townsmen. Just as the whole tone and method suitable for a public speech are foreign to the tone and method proper in individual, face to face dealings with separate men, so is the art of leading different from the art of writing novels.

Some of the gifts and qualities which most commend the literary man to success would inevitably doom the would-be leader to failure. One could wish for no better proof and example of this than is furnished by the career of that most notable of great Irishmen, Edmund Burke. Everyone knows that Burke's life was spent in Parliament, and everyone knows that the eloquence he poured forth there is as deathless as our literature; and yet everyone is left to wonder in presence of the indubitable fact that he was of so little consequence in the actual direction of affairs. How noble a figure in the history of English politics: how large a man; how commanding a mind; and yet how ineffectual in the work of bringing men to turn their faces as he would have them, towards the high purposes he had ever in view! We hear with astonishment that after the delivery of that consummate speech on the Nabob of Arcot's debts, which everybody has read, Pitt and Grenville easily agreed that they need not trouble themselves to make any reply! His speech on conciliation with America is not only wise beyond precedent in the annals of debate, but marches also with a force of phrase which, it would seem, must have been irresistable;—and yet we know that it emptied the House of all audience! You remember what Goldsmith playfully suggested for Burke's epitaph:

> "Here lies our good Edmund, whose genius was such,
> We scarcely can praise it, or blame it too much;
> Who, too deep for his hearers, still went on refining,
> And thought of convincing while they thought of dining:
> Though equal for[4] all things, for all things unfit,
> Too nice for a statesman, too proud for a wit;
> For a patriot too cool, for a drudge disobedient,
> And too fond of the right to pursue the expedient.
> In short, 'twas his fate, unemployed or in place, sir,
> To eat mutton cold, and cut blocks with a razor."

[4] A copying error, for the MS of 1889 correctly has "to." The lines are from Oliver Goldsmith's "Retaliation" as they are abridged in an edition of Ward's *English Poets.*

Certainly this is much too small a measure for so big a man, as Goldsmith himself would probably have been the first to admit; but the description is *almost* as true as it is clever. It is better to read Burke than to have heard him. The thoughts which miscarried in the parliaments of George III have had their triumphs in parliaments of a later day,—have established themselves at the heart of such policies as are to-day liberalizing the world. His power is literary, not forensic. He was no leader of men. He was an organizer of thought, but not of party victories. "Burke is a wise man," said Fox, "but he is wise too soon." He was wise also too much. He went on from the wisdom of to-day to the wisdom of to-morrow,—to the wisdom which is for all time. It was impossible he should be followed so far. Men want the wisdom which they are expected to apply to be obvious, and to be conveniently limited in amount. They want a thoroughly trustworthy article, with very simple adjustments and manifest present uses. Elaborate it, increase the expenditure of thought necessary to obtain it, and they will decline to listen. You must keep it in stock for the use of the next generation.

Men are not led by being told what they do not know. *Persuasion* is a force, *but not information*; and persuasion is accomplished by creeping into the confidence of those you would lead. Their confidence is not gained by preaching new thoughts to them. It is gained by qualities which they can recognize at first sight, by arguments which they can assimilate at once: by the things which find easy and immediate entrance into their minds, and which are easily transmitted to the palms of their hands or to the ends of their walking-sticks in the shape of applause. Burke's thoughts penetrate the mind and possess the heart of the quiet student. His style of saying things fills the attention as if it were finest music. But his are not thoughts to be shouted over; his is not a style to ravish the ear of the voter at the hustings. If you would be a leader of men, you must lead your own generation, not the next. Your playing must be good *now*, while the play is on the boards and the audience in the seats: it will not get you the repute of a great actor to have excellencies discovered in you afterwards. Burke's genius, besides, made conservative men uneasy. How *could* a man be *safe* who had so many ideas?

Englishmen of the present generation wonder that England should ever have been ruled by John Addington, a man about whom nothing was accentuated but his dullness; by Mr. Perceval, a sort of Tory squire without the usual rich blood and diverting irregularities of his kind; by Lord Castlereagh, whose speaking was so bad as to drive his hearers to assume that there *must* be some great purpose lurking behind its amorphous masses *somewhere*, simply because it was inconceivable that there should be in it so little purpose as it revealed. Accustomed to the aggressive and persistent power of Gladstone, the epigrammatic variety of Disreali, the piquant indiscretions of Salisbury, they naturally marvel that they could have been *interested* enough in such men to follow or in any wise heed them. But, after all, the Englishman has not changed. He still has a sneaking liking for prosy men with a solemn practical air and a sneaking distrust of successful men of thought like Mr. John Morley. An Englishman is made as uncomfortable and as indignant now by the vagaries of a man like[5] Lord Randolph Churchill as he formerly was, in times he has forgotten, by the equally bumptious young Disreali. The story is told of a thorough-going old country Tory of the time when Pitt was displaced by Addington that, going to tell a friend of the formation of a new ministry by that excellent mediocrity, he repeated with unction the whole list of common-place men who were to constitute the new Government, and then, rubbing his hands in demonstrative satisfaction, exclaimed, "Well, thank God, we have at last got a ministry without one of those confounded men of genius in it!" Cobden was doubtless right when he said that "the only way in which the soul of a great nation can be stirred, is by appealing to its sympathies with a true principle in its unalloyed simplicity," and that it was "necessary for the concentration of a people's mind that an individual should become the incarnation of a principle"; but the emphasis should be laid on the "unalloyed simplicity" of the principle. It will not do to incarnate too many ideas at a time if you are to be universally understood and numerously followed.

Cobden himself is an excellent case in point. Embodying a true principle of unhampered commerce in its "unalloyed simplicity," he became a power in England second to none. Never did England so steadily yield to argument, so steadily thaw under persuasion, as while Cobden occupied the platform. Cobden was singularly equipped for leadership,—especially for leadership of this practical, businesslike kind. He had in him nothing of the literary mind, which conceives images and is dominated by asso-

[5] Wilson inserted "the late" here presumably for the delivery of this address at Oberlin College on June 19, 1895, some six months after Churchill's death.

ciations: he conceived only facts, and was dominated by programs of reform. Going to Greece, he found Issus [Ilissus] and Cephisus [Cephissus], the famed streams of Attica, ridiculous rivulets and wondered that the world should pause so often to study such Lilliputian states as classical Hellas contained when there were the politics of the United States and the vast rivers and mountains of the new continents to think about. "What famous puffers those old Greeks were!" he exclaims. He journeyed to Egypt and sat beside Mehemet Ali, one of the fiercest warriors and most accomplished tyrants of our century, with a practical eye open to the fact that the royal viceroy was a somewhat fat personage who fell into blunders when he boasted of the cotton crops of the land he had under his heel, and a shrewd perception that his conductor and introducer, Col. C., had hit upon the wrong resource in beginning the conversation by a reference to the excellent weather in a latitude "where unlimited sunshine prevails for seven years together."[6] He keeps the world of practical details under constant cross-examination. And when, in later days, the great anti-corn law League is in the heat of its task of reforming the English tariff, how seriously this earnest man takes the vast fairs, the colossal bazaars, and all the other homely, bourgeois machinery by means of which the League keeps itself supplied at once with funds for its work and with that large measure of popular attention necessary to its success. This is the organizer, who is incapable of being fatigued by the commonplace—or amused by it—and who is thoroughly in love with working at a single idea.

Mark the simplicity and directness of the arguments and ideas of such men. The motives which they urge are elemental; the morality which they seek to enforce is large and obvious; the policy they emphasize purged of all subtlety. They give you the fine gold of truth in the nugget, not cunningly beaten into elaborate shapes and chased with intricate patterns. "If oratory were a business and not an art," says Mr. Justin McCarthy, "then it might be contended reasonably enough that Mr. Cobden was one of the greatest orators England has ever known. Nothing could exceed the persuasiveness of his style. His manner was

[6] The quotation is from a letter written by Cobden, December 20, 1836, as quoted in John Morley, *The Life of Richard Cobden* (2 vols., London, 1881), I, 61. Morley, on page 56, identifies "Col. C." only as the English Consul at Cairo, "a martinet taken from the regimental mess." This passage evidently gave Wilson trouble in the copying and rewriting. His final revision was re-typed on a slip of paper and pasted over eight lines eliminated from the version of 1889.

simple, sweet, and earnest. It persuaded by convincing. It was transparently sincere."[7] But we see the same things in the oratory of Bright, with whom oratory was not a business but an art. Hear him appeal to his constituents in Birmingham, that capital of the spirit of gain, touching what he deemed an iniquitous foreign policy; "I believe," he exclaims, "there is no permanent greatness in a nation except it be based upon morality. I do not care for military greatness or military renown. I care for the condition of the people among whom I live. There is no man in England who is less likely to speak irreverently of the Crown and Monarchy of England than I am; but crowns, coronets, mitres, military display, the pomp of war, wide colonies, and a huge empire, are, in my view, all trifles light as air, and not worth considering, unless *with* them you can have a fair share of comfort, contentment, and happiness among the great body of the people. Palaces, baronial castles, great halls, stately mansions, do not make a nation. The nation in every country dwells in the cottage; and unless the light of your constitution can shine *there*, unless the beauty of your legislation and the excellence of your statesmanship are impressed there on the feelings and conditions of the people, rely upon it you have yet to *learn* the duties of government.

"May I ask you, then, to believe, as I do most devoutly believe, that the moral law was not written for men alone in their individual character, but that it was written as well for nations, and for nations great as this of which we are citizens. If nations reject and deride that moral law, there is a penalty which will inevitably follow. It may not come at once, it may not come in our lifetime; but, rely upon it, the great Italian poet is not a poet only, but a prophet, when he says,—

> 'The sword of heaven is not in haste to smite,
> Nor yet doth linger.'

We have experience, we have beacons, we have landmarks enough. We know what the past has cost us, we know how much and how far we have wandered, but we are not left without a guide. It is true we have not, as an ancient people had, Urim and Thummim—those oraculous gems on Aaron's breast—from which to take counsel, but we have the unchangeable and eternal principles of the moral law to guide us, and only so far as we

[7] Justin McCarthy, *A History of Our Own Times* (2 vols., New York, n. d.), I, 216.

walk by that guidance can we be permanently a great nation, or our people a happy people."[8]

How simple, how evident it all is,–how commonplace the motives appealed to,–how old the moral maxim–how obvious every consideration urged. And yet how effective such a passage is,–how it carries,–what a thrill of life and of power there is in it. As simple as the quiet argument of Cobden, it is yet alight with passionate feeling. As direct and unpretentious as a bit of conversation, though elevated above the level of conversation by a sweep of accumulating phrase such as may be made effectual for the throwing down of strongholds.

Style has of course a great deal to do with such effects in popular oratory. Armies have not won battles by sword-fencing, but by the fierce cut of the sabre, the direct volley of musketry, the straightforward argument of artillery, the impetuous dash of cavalry. And it is in the same way that oratorical battles are won: not by the nice refinements of statement, the deft sword-play of dialectic fence, but by the straight and speedy thrusts of speech sent through and through the gross and obvious frame of a subject. It must be clear and always clear what the sentences would be about. They must be advanced with the firm tread of diciplined march. Their meaning must ring clear and loud.

There is also much in physical gifts, as everybody knows. The popular leader should be satisfying to the eye and to the ear: broad, sturdy, clear-eyed, musically voiced, like John Bright; built with the statu[r]e and mien of a Norse god, like Webster; towering, imperious, persuading by voice and carriage, like Clay; or vast, rugged, fulminating, like Daniel O'Connell, fit for a Celtic Olympus. It is easy to call a man like Daniel O'Connell a demagogue, but it is juster to see in him a born leader of men. We remember him as the agitator, simply, loud, incessant, a bit turbulent, not a little coarse also, full of flouts and jibes, bitter and abusive, in headlong pursuit of the aims of Irish liberty. We ought to remember him as the ardent supporter of every policy that made for English and for human liberty also, a friend of reform when reform was unpopular, a champion of oppressed classes who had almost no one else to speak for them, a battler for what was liberal and enlightened and against what was unfair and prujudiced, all along the line. He was no courter of popularity: but his heart was the heart of his people: their

[8] From a speech delivered by John Bright at Birmingham on October 29, 1858. A text is in *Great Orations*, with an introduction by Thomas B. Reed (New York, 1899), p. 298.

cause and their hopes were his. He was not their slave, nor were they his dupes. He was their mouth-piece. And *what* a mouth-piece! Nature seems to have planned him for utterance. His figure and influence loom truly grand as we look back to him standing, as he so often did, before concourses mustered, scores of thousands strong, upon the open heath to hear and to protest of Ireland's wrongs.

> "His Titan strength must touch what gave it birth;
> Hear him to mobs and on his mother earth."

Here is the testimony of one who saw one of those immeasurable assemblies stand round about the giant Celt and saw the Master wield his spell:

> "Methought no clarion could have sent its sound
> Even to the centre of the hosts around;
> And, as I thought, rose the sonorous swell,
> As from some church-tower swings the silvery bell.
> Aloft and clear, from airy tide to tide,
> It glided, easy as a bird may glide;
> To the last verge of that vast audience sent,
> It played with each wild passion as it went;
> Now stirred the uproar, now the murmur still'd
> And sobs or laughter answer'd as it will'd.
> Then did I know what spells of infinite choice,
> To rouse or lull, has the sweet human voice;
> Then did I seem to seize the sudden clue
> To the grand troublous Life Antique—to view
> Under the rock-stand of Demosthenes,
> Mutable Athens heave her noisy seas."[9]

This huge organization, this thrilling voice, ringing out clear and effectual over vast multitudes were, it would seem, too big, too voluminous for Parliament. There were no channels offered there which were broad and free enough to give effective course to the crude force of the man. The gross and obvious vigour of him shocked sensitive, slow, and decorous men, not accustomed to have sense served up to them with a shout. The open heath was needed to contain O'Connell. But even in Parliament where the decorum and reserve of debate offered him no effective play, his honesty, his ardour for liberty, his good homour, his

[9] From Edward Bulwer's *St. Stephen's, A Poem,* Part III.

transparent genuineness won for him at last almost his due meed of respect.

The whole question of leadership receives sharp practical test in a popular legislative assembly. The revolutions which have changed the whole principle and method of government within the last hundred years have created a new kind of leadership in legislation: a leadership which is not yet, perhaps, fully understood. It used to be thought that legislation was an affair proper to be conducted only by the few who were instructed, for the benefit of the many who were uninstructed: that statesmanship was a function of origination for which only trained and instructed men were fit. Those who actually conducted legislation and undertook affairs were rather whimsically chosen by Fortune to illustrate this theory, but such was the ruling thought in politics. The Sovereignty of the People, however, that great modern dogma of politics, has erected a different conception—or, if so be that, in the slowness of our thought, we adhere to the old *conception*, has at least created a very different *practice*. When we are angry with public men nowadays we charge them with *subserving* instead of forming and directing public opinion. It is to be suspected that when we make such charges we are suffering our standards of judgment to lag behind our politics. When an Englishman declares that Mr. Gladstone is truckling to public opinion in his Irish policy, he surely cannot expect us to despise Mr. Gladstone on that account, even if the declaration be true, inasmuch as it is now quite indisputably the last part of the Nineteenth Century, and the nineteenth is a century, we know, which has established the principle that public opinion *must* be truckled to (if you *will* use a disagreeable word) in the conduct of government. A man, surely, would not fish for votes, (if that be what Mr. Gladstone is doing) among the minority—particularly if he be in his eightieth year and in need of getting the votes at once if he is to get them at all. He must *believe*, at any rate, that he is throwing his bait among the *majority*. And it is a dignified proposition with us—is it not?—that as is the majority, so ought the government to be.

Pray do not misunderstand me. I am not radical. I would not for the world be instrumental in discrediting the ancient and honorable pastime of abusing demagogues. Demagogues were quite evidently, it seems to me, meant for abuse, if we are to argue by exclusion: for assuredly they were never known to serve any other useful purpose. I will follow the hounds any day in pursuit of one of the wily, doubling rascals, however rough the country to be ridden over. But you must allow me to make my condemnations tally with my theory of government. Is Irish opinion ripe for Home rule, as the Liberals claim? Very well then: let it have Home Rule. Every community, says my political philosophy, should be governed for its own interests, as it understands them, and not for the satisfaction of any other community.

Still I seem radical, without in reality being so. I advance my explanation, therefore, another step. Society is not a crowd, but an organism; and, like every organism, it must grow as a whole or else be deformed. The world is agreed, too, that it is an organism also in this, that it will die unless it be vital in every part. That is the only line of reasoning by which we can really establish the majority in legitimate authority. This organic whole, Society, is made up, obviously, for the most part, of the majority. It grows by the development of its aptitudes and desires, and under their guidance. The evolution of its institutions must take place by slow modification and nice all-around adjustment. And all this is but a careful and abstract way of saying that no reform may succeed for which the major thought of the nation is not prepared: that the instructed few may not be safe leaders except in so far as they have communicated their instruction to the many—except in so far as they have transmuted their thought into a common, a popular thought.

Let us fairly distinguish, therfore, the peculiar and delicate duties of the popular leader from the not very peculiar or delicate misdemeanors of the demagogue. Leadership, for the statesman, is *interpretation*. He must read the common thought: he must test and calculate very circumspectly the *preparation* of the nation for the next move in the progress of politics. If he fairly hit the popular thought, when we have missed it, are we to say that he is a demagogue? The nice point is to distinguish the firm and progressive popular *thought* from the momentary and whimsical popular *mood*, the transitory or mistaken popular passion. But it is fatally easy to blame or misunderstand the statesman.

Our temperament is one of logic, let us say. We hold that one and one make two and we see no salvation for the people except they receive the truth. The statesman is of another opinion. 'One and one doubtless make two,' he is ready to admit, 'but the people think that one and one make more than two and until they see otherwise we shall have to legislate on that supposition.' This is not to talk nonsense. The Roman augurs very soon discovered that sacred fowls drank water and pecked grain with no sage intent of prophecy, but from motives quite mundane and simple. But it would have been a revolution to say so in the face of a people who believed otherwise, and executive policy had to proceed on the theory of a divine method of fowl appetite and digestion. The divinity that once did hedge a king, grows not now very high about the latest Hohenzollern;[10] but who that prefers growth to revolution would propose that legislation in Germany proceed independently of this accident of hereditary succession?

In no case may we safely hurry the organism away from its habit: for it is held together by that habit, and by it is enabled to perform its functions completely. The constituent habit of a people inheres in its thought, and to that thought legislation,—even the legislation that advances and modifies habit,—must keep very near. The ear of the leader must ring with the voices of the people. He cannot be of the school of the prophets; he must be of the number of those who studiously serve the slow-paced daily demand.

In what, then, does political leadership consist? It is leadership in *conduct*, and leadership in conduct must discern and strengthen the tendencies that make for development. The legislative leader must perceive the direction of the nation's permanent forces, and must feel the speed of their operation. There is initiative here, but not novelty. There are old *thoughts*, but a progressive *application* of them.

There is such initiative as we may conceive the man part of the mythical *centaur* to have exercised. Doubtless the centaur acted, not as a man, but as a horse, would act, the head conceiving only such things as were possible for the performance of its lower and nether equine parts. He never dared to climb where hoofs could gain no sure foothold: and we may be confident that he knew that there were four feet, not two, to be provided with standing-room. There must have been the caper of the beast in all his schemes. He would have had as much respect, we may suppose, for a blacksmith as for a haberdasher. He must have had the standards of the stable rather than the standards of the drawing-room. The headship of the mind over

[10] Wilhelm II, who had acceded to the throne on June 15, 1888, and had dismissed Bismarck on March 18, 1890.

the body is a like headship for all of us: it is observant of possibility and of physical environment.

The inventing mind is impatient of such restraints: the aspiring soul has at all times longed to be loosed from the body. But such are the conditions of organic life that if the body is to be put off dissolution must be endured. As the conceiving mind is tenant of the body, so is the conceiving legislator tenant of that greater body, Society. Practical leadership may not beckon to the slow masses of men from beyond some dim unexplored space or some intervening chasm: it must daily feel under its own feet the *road* that leads to the goal proposed, knowing that it is a slow, a very slow, evolution to wings, and that for the present, and for a very long future also, Society must *walk*, dependent upon practicable paths, incapable of scaling sudden, precipitous heights, a road-breaker, not a fowl of the air. In the words of the master, Burke, "to follow, not to force, the public inclination,—to give a direction, a form, a technical dress, and a specific sanction, to the general sense of the community, is the true end of legislation." That general sense of the community may wait to be aroused, and the statesman must arouse it; may be inchoate and vague, and the statesman must formulate and make it explicit. But he cannot and he should not do more. The forces of the public thought may be blind: he must lend them sight; they may blunder: he must set them right. He can do something, indeed, to *create* such forces of opinion; but it is a creation of forms, not of substance:—and without such forces at his back he can do nothing effective.

This function of interpretation, this careful exclusion of individual origination it is that makes it difficult for the impatient original mind to distinguish the popular statesman from the demagogue. *The demagogue* sees and seeks *self-interest* in an acquiescent reading of that part of the public thought upon which he depends for votes; the *statesman*, also reading the common inclination, also, when he reads aright, obtains the votes that keep him in power. But if you will justly observe the two, you will find the one trimming to the inclinations of the moment, the other obedient only to the permanent purposes of the public mind. The one adjusts his sails to the breeze of the day; the other makes his plans to ripen with the slow progress of the years. While the one solicitously watches the capricious changes of the weather, the other diligently sows the grains in their seasons. The one ministers to himself, the other to the race.

To the literary temperament leadership in both kinds is impossible. The literary mind conceives images, images rounded, perfect, ideal; unlimited and unvaried by accident. It craves outlooks. It handles such stuff as dreams are made of. It is not guided by principles, as statesmen conceive principles, but by conceptions. Principles, as statesmen conceive them, are threads to the labyrinth of circumstances; principles, as the literary mind holds them, are unities, instrumental to nothing, sufficient unto themselves. Throw the conceiving mind, habituated to contemplating wholes, into the arena of politics, and it seems to itself to be standing upon shifting sands, where no sure foothold and no upright posture are possible. Its ideals are to it more real and more solid than any actuality of the world in which men are managed.

The late Mr. Matthew Arnold was wont now and again to furnish excellent illustration of these points. In the presence of the acute political crisis in Ireland, he urged that no radical remedy be undertaken,–except the *very* radical remedy of changing the character of the English people. What was needed was not home rule for Ireland but a sounder home conscience and less Philistinism in England. 'Wait,' he said, in effect, 'don't legislate. Let me talk to these middle classes a little more, and then, without radical measures of relief, they will treat Ireland in the true human spirit.' Doubtless he was right. When America was discontented, and, because England resisted home *rule*, began to clamour for home *sovereignty*, peradventure the truest remedy would have been, not revolution, but the enlightenment of the English people. But the process of enlightenment was slow; while the injustice was pressing: and revolution came on apace. Unquestionably culture is the best cure for anarchy; but anarchy is swifter than her adversary. Culture lags behind the practicable remedy.

There is a familiar anecdote that belongs just here. The captain of a Mississippi steamboat had made fast to the shore because of a thick fog lying upon the river. The fog lay low and dense upon the surface of the water, but overhead all was clear. A cloudless sky showed a thousand points of starry light. An impatient passenger inquired the cause of the delay. "We can't see to steer," said the captain. "But all's clear overhead," suggested the passenger, "you can see the North star." "Yes," replied the officer, "but we are not going that way." Politics must follow the actual windings of the channel: if it steer by the stars it will run aground.

You may say that if all this be truth: if practical political thought may not run in straight lines, but must twist and turn through all the sinuous paths of various circumstance, then compromise is the true gospel of politics. I cannot wholly gainsay the proposition. But it depends almost altogether upon how you conceive and define compromise whether it seem hateful or not, —whether it *be* hateful or not. I understand the biologists to say that all *growth* is a process of compromise: a compromise of the vital forces within the organism with the physical forces without, which constitute the environment. Yet growth is not dishonest. Neither need compromise in politics be dishonest,—if only it be progressive. Is not compromise the law of society in all things? Do we not in all dealings adjust views, compound differences, placate antagonisms? Uncompromising thought is the luxury of the closeted recluse. Untrammelled reasoning is the indulgence of the philosopher, of the dreamer of sweet dreams. We make always a sharp distinction between the literature of conduct and the literature of the imagination. 'Poetic justice' we recognize as being quite out of the common run of experience.

Nevertheless, leadership does not always wear the harness of compromise. Once and again one of those great Influences which we call a *Cause* arises in the midst of a nation. Men of strenuous minds and high ideals come forward, with a sort of gentle majesty, as champions of a political or moral principle. They wear no armour; they bestride no chargers; they only speak their thought, in season and out of season. But the attacks they sustain are more cruel than the collisions of arms. Their souls are pierced with a thousand keen arrows of obloquy. Friends desert and despise them. They stand alone: and oftentimes are made bitter by their isolation. They are doing nothing less than defy public opinion, and shall they convert it by blows? Yes. Presently the forces of the popular thought hesitate, waver, seem to doubt their power to subdue a half score stubborn minds. Again a little while and those forces have actually yielded. Masses come over to the side of the reform. Resistance is left to the minority, and such as will not be convinced are crushed.

What has happened? Has it been given to a handful of men to revolutionize by the foolishness of preaching the whole thought of a nation and of an epoch? By no means. None but Christian doctrine was ever permitted to dig entirely new channels for human thought, and turn that thought rapidly about from its old courses: and even Christianity came only in "the fulness of time," and has had a triumph as slow-paced as history itself. No cause is born out of time. Every successful reform movement has had as its efficient cry some principle of equity or morality already *accepted* well-nigh universally, but not yet universally applied in the affairs of life. Every such movement has been the awakening of a people to see a new field for old principles. These men who stood alone at the inception of the movement and whose voices then seemed as it were the voices of men crying in the wilderness, have in reality been simply the more sensitive organs of Society—the parts first awakened to consciousness of a situation. With the start and irritation of a rude and sudden summons from sleep, Society at first resents the disturbance of its restful unconsciousness, and for a moment racks itself with hasty passion. But, once completely aroused, it will sanely meet the necessities of conduct revealed by the hour of its awakening.

Great reformers do not indeed *observe* times and circumstances. Theirs is not a service of opportunity. They have no thought for occasion, no capacity for compromise. But they are none the less *produced* by occasions. They are early vehicles of the Spirit of the Age. They are born of the very times that oppose them: their success is the acknowledgement of their legitimacy. For how many centuries had the world heard single, isolated voices summoning it to religious toleration before that toleration became inevitable, because not to have had it would have been an anomaly, an anachronism. It was postponed until it should fit into the world's whole system,—and only in this latter time did its advocates become leaders. Did not Protestantism come first to Germany, which had already unconsciously drifted very far away from Rome? Did not parliamentary reform come in England only as the tardy completion of tendencies long established and long drilled for success? Were not the Corn Laws repealed because they were a belated remnant of an effete system of economy and politics? Did not the abolition of slavery come just in the nick of time to restore to a system already sorely deranged the symmetry and wholeness of its original plan? Take what example you please, and in every case what took place was the destruction of an anomaly, the wiping out of an anachronism. Does not every historian of insight perceive the *timeliness* of these reforms? Is it not the judgement of history that they were the products of a period, that there was laid upon their originators, not the gift of creation, but in a superior degree the gift of insight, the spirit of the age? It was theirs to hear the inarticulate voices that stir in the night-watches, apprising the lonely sentinal of what the day will bring forth.

Turn to religious leaders, and similar principles will be found to govern their rise and influence. Of course among religious leaders there is one type which stands out above all the rest, catching the eye of the world. This is the type to which Bernard of Clairvaux, Calvin, and Savonarola belong. Of course Bernard was no Protestant reformer, as Calvin was, and Savonarola played the part towards the Church neither of Calvin nor of Bernard. But I do not now speak of ecclesiastical reform; I speak simply of leadership. There is one transcendent feature in which these three men are alike. Each spoke to his generation of righteousness and judgment to come. Each withstood men because of their sins, and each himself dominated because of eloquence and purity and personal force.

Perhaps there is no beauty in any career that may justly be preferred to the beauty which was wrought into the life of the saintly abbott of Clairvaux, the man who, without self-assertion, was yet raised to rule, first over his fellows in the church, afterwards once and again over kings and in the affairs of nations, because he feared God but not man, because he loved righteousness and hated the wrong. When caught in the entanglements of fierce international disputes, men called to quiet Clairvaux for help, and there came out of the cloister a man simple in mien and habit, simple also in life and purpose, but bearing upon his sweet, grave face a stamp of godly courage that sent to the heart of the haughtiest men a thrill of awe; a man regarding his fellowmen with a calm gaze that nevertheless glowed with such a clear perception of the truth as held the proudest men in check. Pride and Self-will broke against the spirit of this quiet man as if they were the mist and he the rock. He stood in the midst of his generation a master, a living rebuke to sin, a lively inspiration to good.

There is much less of grace, but there is no less of power in the figure of Savonarola, the pale, burning man who substituted a pulpit for the throne of the Medici, who made the dimly lighted church, where were to be heard the oracles of God, the only centre of power. How excellent, and how terrible, is the force of the man, *lashing* Florence into obedience with the quick whips of his almost inspired utterences. And then there is Calvin, ruler and priest of Geneva:—how singular and how elevated is the place such men hold among the greater figures and forces of history. Theirs, it would seem, was a leadership of rebuke. With how stern a menace did they apprise men of their sins and constrain them to their duty. Their sceptre was a scourge of small whips; their words purified as with flame; they were supreme by reason of the spirit that was in them.

And yet it does not seem to me that even these men escape from the analysis which must be made of all leadership. I have said that no man thinking thoughts born out of time can succeed in leading his generation, and that successful leadership is a product of sympathy, not of antagonism. I do not believe that any man can lead who does not act, whether it be consciously or unconsciously, under the impulse of a profound *sympathy* with those whom he leads,—a sympathy which is insight,—an insight which is of the heart rather than of the intellect. The law unto every such leader as these whom we now have in mind is the law of love. In the face of Savonarola, marked and hollowed as it is by the fierce flames of his nature, solemn, sombre, cast in the mould of anxious fear rather than in the mould of hope, is nevertheless to be seen but a close mask for an inward beauty of tenderness. The sensitiveness of a woman lurks in the stern features, not to be identified with any one of them, and yet not to be overlooked. In Calvin, too, love is the sanction of justice. And in Bernard it is love that reigns, not enmity towards his fellowmen. Such men incarnate the consciences of the men whom they rule. They compel obedience, not so much by reason of fear as by reason of their infallible analysis of character. Men *know* that they speak justice, and obey by instinct. By methods which would infallibly alienate *individuals* they master multitudes, and that is their indisputable title to be named leaders of men.

It is a long cry from Savonarola and Calvin to Voltaire, but it is to Voltaire that I at this point find it convenient to resort for illustration and comment. The transition is the more abrupt because I cannot claim leadership for Voltaire in any of the senses to which I have limited the word. But there are literary men, nevertheless, who fail of being leaders only for lack of initiative in action; who have the thought, but not the executive parts of leaders; whose minds, if we may put it so, contain all the materials for leadership, but whose wills spend their force, not upon men, but upon paper. Standing as they do, half way between the men who act and the men who merely think and imagine, they may very neatly serve our present purpose, of differentiating leaders from the quieter race of those who content themselves with thought. And of this class Voltaire was a perfect type.

Our slow world spends its time catching up with the ideas of its best minds. It would seem that in almost every generation men are born who embody the *projected* consciousness of their time and people. Their thought runs forward apace into the regions whither the race *is advancing*, but where it will not for many a weary day *arrive*. A few generations, and that point, thus early descried, is passed; the new thoughts of one age are the commonplaces of the next. Such is the literary function: it reads the present fragments of thought as completed wholes, and thus enables the fragments, no doubt, in due time to achieve their completion. There are, on the other hand, again, other periods which we call periods of critical thought, and these do not project their ideas as wholes, but speak them incomplete, as parts. Whoever can hit the latent conceptions of such a period will receive *immediate* recognition: he is simply the articulate utterance of itself.

Such a man, of such fortune, was Voltaire. No important distinction can be drawn between his mind and the mind of France in the period in which he lived,–except, no doubt, that the mind of France was diffused, Voltaire's concentrated. It was an Englishman, doubtless who said that he would like to slap Voltaire's face, for then he could feel that he had given France the affront direct. I suppose we cannot imagine how happy it must have made a Frenchman of the last century to laugh with Voltaire. His hits are indeed palpable: no literary swordsman but must applaud them. The speed of his style, too, and the swift critical destructiveness of it are in the highest degree exhilerating and admirable. It is capital sport to ride atilt with him against some belated superstition, to see him unseat priest and courtier alike in his dashing overthrow of shams. But for us it is not vital sport. The things that he killed are now *long* dead; the things he found it *impossible* to slay, *still triumph* over all opponents,–are grown old in conquest. But for a Frenchman of the last century the thing was *being done*. To read Voltaire must have made him feel that he was reading his own thoughts; laughing his own laugh; speaking his own scorn; speeding his own present impulses. Voltaire shocked political and ecclesiastical magnates, but he rejoiced the general mind of France. The men whom he attacked felt at once and instinctively that this was not the mere premonitary flash from a distant storm, but a bolt from short range; that the danger was immediate, the need for some shelter of authority an instantaneous need. No wonder the people of Paris took the horses from Voltaire's coach and themselves dragged him through the streets. The load ought to have been light, as light as the carriage, for they were pulling themselves. The old man inside the coach was presently to die and carry away with him the spirit of the eighteenth century. If Voltaire seriously doubted the existence of a future life, we can have no just ground for wonder. It *is* hard to think of *him* in any world but this. It is awkward to conceive the eighteenth century given a place in either of the realms of eternity. It would chill the one; it would surely liberalize the other. That singular century does not seem to belong in the line of succession to *any* immortality.

Men who hit the critical, floating thought of their age, seem to me leaders in all but initiative. *They* are not ahead of their age. They do not conceive thoughts in future wholes. They gather to a head each characteristic sentiment of their day. They are at once listened to; they would be followed, if they would but lead.

There are some qualities of the mind of Thomas Carlyle which seem to place *him* in this class. To speak of him is to go a good part of our way back to the great *preachers* of whom I have spoken. Carlyle was the apostle of a vague sort of lay religion, as *imperative* as Calvinism, though less provocative of *organization*,—a religion with a sanction, but without a hierarchy. He was not all preacher, however; and while he was something less than a prophet, he was also something more than a Jeremiah. He throbbed, as much as a Scotch peasant could, with the pulses of the nineteenth century. He was hotly moved by its forces; he felt with a ke[e]nness which reached the pitch of suffering the puissant influences abroad in his day. He withstood them, it is true; he would have beaten many of them back with denunciations; but there is a deep significance in his fierce longing for action, in his keen desire to be a leader. It is noteworthy that there is no wholeness in his thought, either, as in most products of the purely literary mind there would be. Its parts are *disjecta membra.* His ideas are flashes struck out by hot contact with the forces of thought active about him. With almost inarticulate fervour, he seems once and again to break forth with the very spirit of our century upon his lips. It would of course be absurd to compare Carlyle with Voltaire, the spiritual man with the intellectual; and yet it seems to me that Carlyle is as representative of the spiritual aspects of our century as Voltaire was of all the mental aspects of his own very different age. Incoherent and impossible in his proposition of measures, sadly in need of interpretation to the common mind even in his utterance of the thoughts brought to him out of his century, eager often to revert to old standards of action, a figure rugged, amorphous, needing to be explained, Carlyle was yet the very voice of his own age, not a prophet of the next. In his writings are thrown up, as if by a convulsion of nature, the hidden things of the modern mind. Those who lead may well look and learn. His mind is a sub-soil plow and in its furrows may crops be sown.

If there were no other quality which marked the absence of any *practical* gift of leadership in Carlyle, his fierce *impatience* would be sufficient evidence. The dynamics of leadership lie in persuasion, and persuasion is never impatient. 'You are poor fishers of men,' it has been said of a certain class of preachers; 'you do not go fishing with a rod and a line, and with the patient sagacity of the true sportsman. You use a telegraph pole and a cable: with these you savagely beat the water, and bid men bite or be damned. And you expect they will be caught!'[11]

A wide sympathy and tolerance is needed in dealing with men, and uncompromising men cannot lead.[12] We are sometimes struck in a rather unpleasant way by the apparent pliancy of public men, their apparent laxness as towards the principles they profess. We are inclined to exact of a public character, not only that he incarnate a principle "in its unalloyed simplicity," to use Cobden's phrase again, but also that he incarnate it in active and continuous antagonism to all other principles and *their* incarnations. It is a bit disconcerting to learn that men who sit and debate on opposite sides of the Senate or the House afterwards go off to lunch together between sessions and are always great cronies in private. It throws us out of all our political reckonings to hear that the Irish members of the House of Commons are received into hale fellowship in the smoking-room of the House by the very men who habitually vote for coercion measures when the House is sitting. How can the Irishmen themselves consent thus to smoke and joke with those who are abusing and injuring Ireland every day; and how can obstructionists be acceptable company for Tory ministerialists? We have an uncomfo[r]table impression that these men must surely hold their political principles only in a Pickwickian sense; that their public motives and their private characters are somehow separable; that it is quite unbearable from a moral point of view that the incarnation of one principle should smoke and chat and hobnob with the incarnation of an opposite principle. And in conversation with public men we have received the same disquieting impressions. They are so unstrenuous in it all! They have such an easy, unimpressed way of talking about influences which they

11 For the probable origin of this quotation, see R. Bridges to WW, Nov. 29, 1889, transcript of shorthand in location-description line.

12 Wilson added this and the next paragraph, which have no counterparts in the MS. of 1889.

are supposed to be combating with might and main. Surely they are like lawyers, engaging their *minds* in certain causes, but not *themselves,* as easily to be obtained by one side as by the other.

And yet it seems to me that these phenomena of conduct which so disturb us are but further illustrations of the principles of leadership upon which I have most insisted. There is and must be in politics a sort of pervasive sense of compromise, an abiding consciousness of the fact that there is in the general growth and progress of affairs no absolute initiative for any one man, but that each must both give and take. If I am so strenuous in every point of belief and conduct that I cannot meet those of opposite opinions in good fellowship wherever and whenever conduct does not tell immediately upon the action of the state, you may be sure that when you examine my schemes you will find them impracticable,—impracticable, that is, to be *voted* upon. You may be sure that I am a man who must have his own way wholly or not at all. Of course there is much in mere everyday association. Men of opposite parties, seeing each other every day, are enabled to discover that there are no more tails and cloven hoofs on one side in politics than on the other. But it is not all the effect of use and companionship. More than that, it is the effect of openness of mind to impressions of the general opinion, to the influences of the whole situation as to character and strategy. Now and again their [there] arises the figure of a leader silent, reserved, intense, uncompanionable, shut in upon his own thoughts and plans; and such a man will oftentimes prove a great force; but you will find him generally useful for the advancement of but a single cause. He holds a narrow commission, and his work is soon finished. He may count himself happy if he escape the misfortune of being esteemed a fanatic.

What a lesson it is in the organic wholeness of Society, this study of leadership! How subtle and delicate is the growth of the organism, and how difficult initiative in it! Where is rashness? It is excluded. And raw invention? It is discredited. How, as we look about us into the great maze of Society, see its solidarity, its complexity, its restless forces surging amidst its delicate tissues, its hazards and its exalted hopes,—how can we but be filled with awe! Many are the functions that enter into its quick, unresting life. There is the lonely seer, seeking the truths that shall stand permanent and endure; the poet, tracing all perfected lines of beauty, sounding full-voiced all notes of love or hope, of duty or gladness; the toilers in the world's massy stuffs, moulders of metals, forgers of steel, refiners of gold; there are the winds of commerce; the errors and despairs of war; the old things and the new; the vast things that dominate and the small things that constitute the world; passions of men, loves of women; the things that are visible and which pass away and the things that are invisible and eternal. And in the midst of all stands the leader, gathering, as best he can, the thoughts that are completed, that are perceived, that have told upon the common mind; judging also of the work that is now at length ready to be completed; reckoning the gathered gain; perceiving the fruits of toil and of war,—and combining all these into words of progress, into acts of recognition and completion. Who shall say that this is not an exalted function? Who shall doubt or dispraise the titles of leadership?

Shall we wonder, either, if the leader be a man open at all points to all men, ready to break into coarse laughter with the Rabelaisian vulgar; ready also to prose with the moralist and the reformer; with an eye of tolerance and shrewd appreciation for life of every mode and degree; a sort of sensitive dial registering all the forces that move upon the face of Society? I do not conceive the leader a *trimmer*, weak to yield what clamour claims, but the deeply human man, quick to know and to do the things that the hour and his people need.

"How beautiful to see
Once more a shepherd of mankind indeed,
Who loves his charge, and ever loves to lead;
One whose meek flock the people joy to be,
Not lured by any cheat of birth,
But by his clear-grained human worth,
And brave old wisdom of sincerity!
They know that outward grace is dust;
They cannot choose but trust
In that sure-footed mind's unfaltering skill,
And supple-tempered will
That bends like perfect steel to spring again and thrust.
His is no [lonely] mountain-peak of mind,
Thrusting to thin air o'er our cloudy bars,
A sea-mark now, now lost in vapours blind;
Broad prairie rather, genial, level-lined,
Fruitful and friendly for all human kind,
Yet also nigh to heaven and loved of loftiest stars."[13]

WWT MS. (WP, DLC) with WWhw and EAWhw markings and emendations.

13 From James Russell Lowell's "Ode Recited at the Harvard Commemoration," with Lowell's verbs changed to the present tense.

From Ellen Axson Wilson

My own darling, Middletown June 17 [1890].

This is a strictly *business* epistle. It has occurred to me that as we had no opportunity before you left to discuss the important subjects of paper and paint perhaps I had better write and give you a few of my ideas.[1] The parlour paper I think should be just what it is now, blue and bronze. I send you a sample of the right tone of blue, but I should like the woodwork best without blue,—all "old ivory," almost buff, about the shade, tell them, of the *marked spot* on the enclosed sample; *all* the ceilings in the house the same. I think as regards the painting we had better keep our scheme of colour as simple as possible because we will no[t] be there to match shades. I would have all the bedrooms, halls &c the same "old ivory," the study and dining room a rich walnut, not to[o] dark; but if the woodwork is *already* dark of course it would take too many thick coats of paint to make it all light again. In that case it might be *all* walnut, except the parlour which *must* be light. I should like the paper in the big double bed-room downstairs a good warm colour as much as possible like that in our guest room;—I send sample. In the guest room there, one golden olive in tone—not dark though[,] with yellowish pink flowers. I send sample of the *border* in our Bryn Mawr dining room because you remember the golden brown of it[s] ground was what we liked best for the *dining-room.* I really don't know what I want for the hall so I leave it entirely to your judgment,—and I will also have the good grace to let you choose the paper for your *own* room—only I wouldn't have it as it is now. I think it too *brick-dusty.* Will you please look at the bath-tub particularly and if it is a horrible black thing like this, which *no* scrubbing can improve, insist upon having it renovated. A boarding house tub could not be more uninviting than this!

When your are in New York don't you want to be on the lookout for little screens and if you see on[e] of reasonable price buy it for me to paint those birds on? The size of the picture is 12 1/2 inches horizontally by 9 ins the other way, and the opening would have to be somewhere near that size, the wood-work at the top completing the square. It must be mounted in canvas,—the back might be old gold or copper coloured satteen something like the breast of the bird. I don't think I should like a *red* screen but almost anything else would do, bronze, gilt, black, imitation bamboo.* Don't get anything expensive, and don't bother about it at all if you are pressed for time.

Your telegram was most welcome;[2] how I wish I had a private line and could hear from you every hour while you are away,—could know what you are doing and how you feel at that very time and not how you *felt* two or three days before when the poky letter which brings the report was written. But I know that when you receive this neither time nor place will serve for the perusal of love letters, so I will restrain myself and indulge in no *effusion*. But all the same *I love you*, dearest, from the bottom of my heart. As ever Your little Wife.

We are all quite well.

*One of some cheap wood *bronzed* I think would be especially pretty.

ALS (WC, NjP) with WWhw notes on verso of letter: "Inside shutter in present study. Wood-work up-stairs all white and new[.] Outside paint? Shelf in front parlour."

[1] Ellen and Woodrow had obviously gone to Princeton to look at the McGill house after renting it, and Ellen now gives Woodrow certain instructions about its decoration to convey to the real estate agents when he stopped in Princeton on his return from Knoxville.

[2] It is missing.

From John Franklin Jameson

My dear Wilson: Providence, June 21 [1890].

I have just received your dispatch, and have telegraphed back my award to "Victim."[1] I can see that it must have been very inconvenient to you that my letter did not reach you, and do not understand it at all. There seems no chance that it did not get properly mailed, because I made a special journey to the Post-Office on Monday morning before breakfast, with it and it alone, in order to catch the 8.30 mail to Middletown.[2]

I am sorry that I cannot now reproduce the percentages by which I marked the various candidates; I remember that it was impossible to decide between them otherwise than by careful marking on per cents, and that "Victim" led by but a little. I also remember that it was a corker of an examination, and that I was glad I didn't have to try to pass it; but they did *very* well with it.

At the same time I enclosed you a letter from the new proprietor of the Manomet House. The sense of it was that he could give you two satisfactory rooms for your "party" for $36 a week, and for the boy of fourteen would charge $8. Meanwhile, Mrs. Carey has decided, at the instance of my cousins the Chickerings of Washington, to go to a place which they much frequent and like, the Beach House at Kennebunk, Maine. I have written to the proprietor thereof to know what he can do for you. The prices are less than at the Manomet, where I think they must have risen a little. It is said to be a pretty place. The expense of reaching it is but a few cents more than in the case of the Manomet. The water will not be so warm. You must let me know if that is a crucial point. If it isn't, I hope you will go there. My cousins are, I may say, a very entertaining family. I shall go up there for a week or two in July. I will have Mrs. Carey spy out the land for you, if you desire. She is on her way to Boston now.

My kindest regards to Mrs. Wilson, Mr. Axson, and the damosels. I hope we may manage to be together somewhat. Sorry about the mischance respecting the award.

Sincerely yours, J. F. Jameson.

ALS (WP, DLC).

[1] This telegraphic exchange is missing.

[2] Jameson's letter of June 15 is postmarked "Providence, R. I. Jun 16 9 AM 90." WW to J. F. Jameson, June 27, 1890, clears up the mystery.

From Joseph Ruggles Wilson

Dearest Woodrow N. York, Monday, June 23 [1890]

I am expecting to leave for Saratoga to-morrow; and after remaining there a little while, to make for Middletown to stay a few days if it will be perfectly convenient for dear Ellie.

Address me at Drs. Strong, Saratoga Springs.

Affectionately as always Your loving Father

P.S. I would go at once to M. were this not commencement week when your house will be full I dare say.

ALS (WP, DLC).

Remarks at Class Day Exercises at the Worcester Polytechnic Institute

[June 26. 1890]

CLASS DAY AT THE TECH.

Fair skies and a cooling breeze awaited the members of the class of '90 of the Polytechnic Institute as they assembled on the campus for their class day exercises yesterday. . . .

Prof. Wilson, the commencement orator, was next introduced. He said he had left Middletown to escape a similar banquet where he would be expected to speak, and had been taken in here in Worcester. "I was a stranger and you have taken me in," is the version that applies to my case. He then made a witty address, and, closing in a serious vein, he said he was very glad to hear that the course in physical and political economy was to be instituted. Formerly political economy was contained within the text books, but now it has been loosed. It was demented; now it is becoming sane, and he hoped that the school might realize the connection between school affairs and political economy. . . .

Printed in the *Worcester* [Mass.] *Daily Spy*, June 26, 1890; some editorial headings omitted.

A Report of a Commencement Address

[June 27, 1890]

COMMENCEMENT AT THE POLYTECHNIC INSTITUTE.

Yesterday was the 20th annual commencement of the Polytechnic Institute, and all day the members of the faculty and the graduating class were kept busy. . . .

Departing from the usual custom of holding the commencement exercises in Mechanics Hall, the graduation took place last evening in Association Hall. A fair sized audience was gathered to listen to the various numbers arranged, but not so large an assembly as the principal speaker deserved. . . .

After prayer by Dr. Mears, Hon. P. Emory Aldrich, the president of the board of trustees . . . introduced Prof. Wilson of Princeton College, who spoke substantially as follows:

When I was first invited to speak here by Dr. Smith I promptly replied that I would do so, choosing a semi-literary subject, which I thought the proper thing. I received in return a very diplomatic letter that ended by suggesting that a better subject would be something in reference to city governments, which I was only too glad to do, for I am loaded to the muzzle on municipal reform. But I am happy to find that an audience would rather listen to an address on municipal reform from anybody than a talk on a semi-literary subject from somebody. There is hard work in reform and very little entertainment.

The subject is so large that there is not allowed to any one the gift of covering the whole field in the time allotted to me. I can simply make a framework of the matter and furnish possible food for reflection. In the older world, that went without steam or electricity, the[n] men busied themselves with the essentials of liberty. We, however, look more to the details of organization and mutual aid. The future has in store a greater compacting of the population than now, and an endeavor to avoid the evils of social friction—socialism.

The cities for which we arrange a system of government are not like those of the ancient world, for being almost like separate states it was with them only a question of politics. Our questions are purely those that have come up in this century. Cities in our time have not grown slowly; they have no musty charters in their archives. The history of old Boston has nothing to do with the records of the present city after going back a few decades. For the true city we must look to some younger place, like Minneapolis, for instance, that has sprung up and grown rapidly.

The old city was an aggregation of men for commercial purposes, while now it is more especially for manufacturing allied with commerce. Formerly the city was placed where nature pointed because of advantages to be gained from the country, such as water power. Now we place our finger upon the map and say we will have a city there, and thus make other things conform to our wishes. The new agencies of steam and electricity make this possible. The modern city can exist anywhere that a railroad can reach, little reference being paid to water or sanitary conveniences. The growth of the modern city is artificial.

Manifestly these are new phenomena. Look now at the make-up of the modern city. We have no old political class, but instead an economic class. The rest of the people are divided into two classes, the commercial and the manufacturing, both differing very radically. The commercial class are better informed in nine cases out of ten, are more alert and public spirited, for they are dependent upon the growth of the city. The men who compose this class are dependent upon the prosperity of the people about them. Men no longer manufacture upon orders, but upon speculation concerning the needs of the communities, so they must look out for over-production. There is, therefore, a radical difference between the two classes, and it may be carried still farther by noting the differences in the manner of living. The first class is composed largely of men whose salaries are such that they can afford to live in the better parts of the city, while the others must live nearer their work without regard to what the locality may be. From this arises the need for artisans' dwellings that may be kept neat and clean. Rapid transit becomes therefore a pressing need in order that the poor may be enabled to live in healthful quarters.

It is said that the men who make the laws ought to be especially educated for that purpose, but the rule is that they are generally taken from the wealthier class, without particular reference to fitness. Such men have the interest of the city partially at heart, but not wholly. In the modern city also cannot be given encouragement to manufacturers such as is given by the protective tariff, which is the choice of the country and not the city. But it is the duty of the city to look after the police and sanitary arrangements and provide for schools, to facilitate commercial and manufacturing life, the citizens must pave the streets, provide rapid transit and fix up outlying districts so as to enable the people to live there, and finally they must provide for the poor. You visit New York and you will not find it very clean, nor yet conspicuously dirty. Upper Broadway and Fifth avenue, the residences of the wealthy, are clean because the people pay to have them kept clean. The education of others than themselves does not occur to them. This class, as is generally known, only touch things to corrupt them. They get a charter for a street railway and then run the road to line their pockets, without reference to the public.

A city has been defined as an economic corporation. The big avenues belong to the public, highways they are called. The side streets are known as private property and owned by those who live upon the street, they agreeing to keep it in repair, and if a difficulty arises a third party comes in to settle the trouble. We have to get the attention of the community to begin any reform. But there is one way to do, and that is to let corruption run on until it becomes scandal, when the matter is looked after at once. It causes a small revolution every time, but there seems to be no other way.

A familiar way of organizing a city is to give a charter, but this is a relic of by gone days, of the middle ages, when men fought for what they got and felt proud of their rights. This system of charters is not now in vogue in England, France or Germany, but all have a form which is the same for each city, a blank being left for the name and the number of wards. Taking Berlin as a type of such a city as all ought to be, and also because there is more self-government there than anywhere else, we notice several curious things. Each voter has only a single act to perform, for he votes only for one councilor. The councilors meet to elect the aldermen, who afterwards elect the mayor, subject to the nominal approval of the crown. Committees are chosen to look after various affairs, consisting of an alderman as chairman, with a greater number of councilors, and a still larger number of citizens. In each ward there are also a series of committees, a councilor at the head. In each ward there is a committee of ladies, who look after waifs. Thus it comes about that there are not less than 10,000 persons connected with the government. If a man does not accept the position his taxes are raised from one-sixth to one-third. In England there is much the same arrangement, though the committees differ slightly.

We have gone to work upon a wrong basis in organizing our cities. We speak of the executive and legislative departments, but by having these we cannot place responsibility just where it belongs. It should be a question of administration, not of checks and balances. We mistake in calling the work of the city council legislative, for it is two-thirds administrative. Systems must supersede separate charges. Suppose Worcester needs legislation from the state. Other cities are not concerned, and are willing to see it pass, if enough lobbying is done. If there was a system, all the other cities would be interested in the change. Everybody recognizes the state government as being squeezed in between the city and national governments.

In a very brief way, I have tried to sketch some features of the modern city governments, which, however, has been done at express train rate, with only a stop at the principal points. It is a vast subject to cover, but a most entertaining one in many respects.

Printed in the *Worcester Daily Spy*, June 27, 1890.

To John Franklin Jameson

My dear Jameson, Middletown, Conn., 27 June, 1890

Your letter had come after all, and I beg your pardon for troubling you with the telegram! It fell out in this wise. I was away from home almost all of last week—in Tennessee—and when I got back at the close of the week I asked if you had been heard from about the prize. Mrs. Wilson said 'No: the papers had been returned, but no letter,'—and she showed me the drawer full of mail which had come in my absence: papers and letters, but nothing from you. I waited a mail or two and then telegraphed.

The very evening I did so—while my young brother was down street sending the message indeed—I opened one of the newspapers which had been sent me, and *out fell your letter*, which had all the while been hidden in its folds! It's too bad—I apologize! Since then I've been off to Worcester to lecture and have had not not [*sic*] a minute to write your honour an explanation.

And now let me thank you very heartily for your kindness in adjudging the prize. 'Victim' was Miss M. J. Beach, the only woman in the class, but a host in herself. I have not the slightest doubt that she deserved the rank you gave her in the examination, and I'm glad she got the prize.

Of course the Manomet letter was in the lost-found epistle, and we are much obliged to you for sending it. I don't believe that we care to go there if you and the Careys are not going. It was the prospect of such company that constituted the inducement for us. And I fear—very much against my inclination—that Maine is too far from our base of operations in the matter of moving to be seriously thought of. It's hard luck: we are heartily sorry, disappointed.

I send this to Providence because I don't know your address. Let me know what your addresses are to be and I will try to fire another epistle at you.

Is there anything in the report which I heard at Worcester that H. B. Adams is a likely candidate for the Amherst presidency?

Mrs. Wilson sends her most cordial regards,

Affectionately Yours, Woodrow Wilson

ALS (J. F. Jameson Papers, DLC).

From Joseph Ruggles Wilson

My precious son, Saratoga Springs, N.Y. June 27 1890.

I hardly know what to decide upon in the matter of a visit to Middletown. I wrote you from N. York last week, stating that my plan was to come here for a few days—until your commencement fussifications were over—and then, if Ellie should find it perfectly convenient, to go over to M. for a brief stay. Having heard nothing I *ought* to assume that the way is clear—as a matter of course—and will do so should I hear nothing from you. I expect to go over about Tuesday or Wednesday 1st or 2nd July.

Love to all Your affc Father

ALS (WP, DLC).

An Editorial from the *Wesleyan Argus*

[June 28, 1890]

Several changes in the faculty are made this year. Professor Woodrow Wilson leaves us to accept the chair of Jurisprudence, made vacant by the death of Professor Alexander Johnston, in Princeton college, his alma mater. During his two years' occupancy of the chair of History and Political Economy, Professor Wilson has won the cordial esteem of the entire body of undergraduates, both by his work in the class-room and his active support of all the athletic interests of the college. As an instructor, Professor Wilson does much more than impart knowledge; he has clearly defined opinions concerning the lessons taught by the history of the past, and their bearing upon the future, and while never unduly obtruding those opinions upon his students, he does not fail, as the occasions present themselves, to inculcate those practical lessons of political duty which the patriot can never learn too well. His work has been an inspiration to the students who have sat under his instruction.

Printed in the Middletown, Conn., *Wesleyan Argus,* XXIII (June 28, 1890), 173-74.

From John Franklin Jameson

My dear Wilson: Winchester, Mass., July 1, 1890.

Your letter is received. No apologies needed as to the letter, surely; but I am sorry it did not get to you seasonably. I supposed from the handwriting that "Victim" was a woman, but was uninfluenced thereby.

But my dear man, you *are* going to Maine; indeed you are. I will not have it otherwise. Do not be led astray by what the late Lord Verulam called *idola fori.* In name, Maine may seem more remote than Plymouth. In fact, the Wentworth House, Kennebunk Beach, is not so remote as the Manomet. It is more so in miles, but it is easier of access. . . .

Now, then, ὤγαθε, show cause, if any you have, why you should not at once resolve to go up to this paradise. I suppose I shall go up, for a week or two, on or about July 12, next week Saturday, i.e. I shall be much disappointed if you and Mrs. Wilson and the little girls do not join us. Pray do come! It will do you all good, and me a great deal. We should all be delighted if you chose to break your journey by coming up from Middletown in the afternoon (arr. Boston 6.50), spending the night with us, and proceeding to the shore next day.

I have heard Adams' name mentioned among those of candidates for the presidency of Amherst, but he is not the leading candidate, and I doubt if he could be elected.

The kindest regards to Mrs. Wilson and the family generally. My family send regards, and join in my invitation.

Sincerely yours, J. F. Jameson.

ALS (WP, DLC). Enc.: printed advertisement for the Wentworth House, Kennebunk Beach, Maine, April 1890.

From Charles Homer Haskins

My dear Dr. Wilson: Meadville, Pa., July 2, 1890.

I was obliged to postpone my trip to Georgia, chiefly on account of the hot weather. I hope it may not be necessary for me to go; if it is, I must wait. I should like to have some correspondence with Mr. Brown about his collection. Possibly a word through Mr. Howell might help me in that.

I suppose you have heard that I am going to Madison next year. Notice of my election came Saturday. They give me $1200 next year. Turner and I will each have 13 hours a week.

I have been shut out from academic news since I left Baltimore two weeks ago. Dr. Adams told me then that he had recommended Stephenson and Woodford for Wesleyan! It seemed probable that McPherson would get a cheap instructorship at Michigan. Woodburn returns to Indiana as Professor of American History.

The outlook for the department is no brighter so far as I can see. I had a good chance to tell Dr. Adams of the dissatisfaction with the American history course, but the only result was a resolve to do less John Smith and Plymouth Rock and, I inferred, to give it over more completely to the fellows—Willoughby and Steiner. I rather think Vincent will have the undergraduate work after next year. He will have next year the part that I have had. He is good so far as he goes, but they need another Jameson—if there were another. The B. and O. deal may help.

Laughlin's appointment[1] at Cornell was a great surprise to me. Does it mean that "socialism" is becoming an issue?

Very sincerely yours, Charles H. Haskins.

ALS (WP, DLC) with WWhw sums on env.

[1] James Laurence Laughlin, just appointed Professor of Political Economy and Finance at Cornell University.

To Azel Washburn Hazen

My dear Dr. Hazen, Middletown, 5 July, 1890

I want to express to you again my gratitude for the valuable present of Elliot's Debates[1] which your generosity prompted you to make me yesterday, and my gratification that books I shall have so many occasions to use, and use familiarly, should come to me from you. They will be companions of my working hours and will seem something more than authorities, and something better because they represent a valued and refreshing friendship. In short, their value will be not a little enhanced in my view because they were given to me by you. Certainly, too, you knew the appropriate day on which to make such a present!

Sincerely, affectionately Yours, Woodrow Wilson

ALS (photostat, RSB Coll., DLC).

[1] Jonathan Elliot (ed.), *The Debates in the Several State Conventions on the Adoption of the Federal Constitution* . . . (5 vols., Washington, 1836-45). The first volume of this set, still in the Wilson Library in the Library of Congress, is inscribed "Dr. Woodrow Wilson With the affectionate esteem of A. W. H. Middletown, Conn. Independence Day 1890."

To John Franklin Jameson

My dear Jameson, Middletown, Conn., 9 July, 1890.

Alas, my dear fellow, your own letter, much as it adds to our desire to be with you and the Careys this vacation, adds another reason why we cannot: you are going to be at the seaside in July, while we cannot go till the second or third week in August. The fates are much agin us truly, for is not my own sister probably coming to be with us part of the time, coming all the way from South Carolina, if we can find a place within reach, and would she not regard Maine as equivalent to the North Pole?

I cannot tell you how much we appreciate your kindness and that of your family in extending to us so cordial an invitation to stop at Winchester. We shall not give over hoping that Mrs Wilson may have a chance to find you in your home as I did; but apparently it must not be this Summer.

Of course I am going to write to you again before long; but this sitting is after bedtime, and I must do little more than send you our love, and our warm regards to your family.

Faithfully and affectionately, Woodrow Wilson

WWTLS (J. F. Jameson Papers, DLC).

From Adrian Hoffman Joline[1]

My Dear Sir: New York, July 9, 1890.

On my return to the city, I find your letter of the 7th inst. for which I thank you. I am very sincerely pleased that you approve of the little prize.[2] I think five years will suffice to show whether it is of any real service. If it should prove attractive, I hope—if I live—to then endow it permanently.[3] You have, of course, hit upon my idea exactly. I have made our political history a pet study for thirty years—beginning as a boy—and it seemed to me that the period 1789-1820, as the formative one—and as requiring real study to comprehend—was an appropriate one. No newspaper perusal can fit a man to understand it—and it antedates the parties of to-day—though I cannot altogether rid myself of the idea that those who call themselves "Republicans" are the legitimate discendants of Hamilton, while the "Democrats" are (perhaps slightly degenerate) offspring of Jefferson. Still, to trace the descent, requires familiarity with history and knowledge of facts not popularly known.

While I agree with you that teachers may be prejudiced in favor of attractive pupils, I am not sure that, after all, they do not make the best judges—I will defer entirely to your judgment in the matter. I confess I should be gratified if I could myself have some share in the award—not to make the decision, but to act in an advisory way. Don't you think that if you could let me read the essays and tell you what I think of them, you could decide yourself.[4] It seems hardly worth while to put the award in commission, as it were. However, it is for you to determine—I leave it to you entirely.

I am glad to know that you are at work on "1829-89" for the Epoch series. It is indeed a delicate task—but a fascinating one. It is not easy to steer a steady course through such a sea. I have no doubt that it will be well done.

I have under my control Martin Van Buren's Autobiography and his private letters—letters *to* him from Jackson, Wright, et al—and my partner, Mr Wm Allen Butler, in whose hands they have been left, has been talking with me about editing them. There is a good deal in them never yet made public. They are a little *dry* for the general public, but quite a mine for the historian. If I could snatch a little time from bread-winning, I should like to bring them out. Perhaps some day we may be able to do something with them. Old Jackson's letters are particularly good—

I wish you could see them. They give the lie to those who accused him of illiteracy.

Pardon me for the length of this. My pen runs on when I get on my hobby. I hope sincerely that the prize may attract bright fellows to look into the story of their own country.

Ever yrs faithfully Adrian H Joline

ALS (WP, DLC) with WWhw sums on env.

1 Born at Ossining, N. Y., June 30, 1850. A.B., College of New Jersey, 1870; A.M., same institution, 1873; LL.B., Columbia Law School, 1872. Practiced law in New York, specializing in trusts, mortgages, and the legal affairs of railroads. Collected autographs and rare books and published several books on collecting. Unsuccessful candidate for election to Princeton Board of Trustees in 1910. Died on Oct. 15, 1912.

2 Joline had informed the Board of Trustees of the College of New Jersey on June 30, 1890, that he was giving $250 to establish the C. O. Joline Prize in American Political History for a five-year period. This prize of $50, to be given both for the best paper in an examination in American political history, 1789-1820, and for the best thesis on some topic connected with this period, was founded in memory of Joline's father, Charles Oliver Joline, '34.

3 He did so endow it. The Joline Prize is now awarded to the Princeton senior submitting the best thesis in American history.

4 In his missing letter to Joline of July 7, Wilson must have suggested the wisdom of having an outside committee to award the prize.

From John Franklin Jameson

My dear Wilson: Winchester, July 11, 1890.

I'm very sorry too. I had thought it was in July that you were going somewhere. About the second or third week in August our family are going to some place in southern New England together, probably Monument Beach, at the head of Buzzard's Bay, within the reach of a two-and-a-quarter round-trip from Boston. My sisters probably go there August 1st, and will report. I also recommend the Manomet, where I know some pleasant people are to be at the beginning of August. I go up to K. B. tomorrow, and, I repeat, am sorry you can't. Give my love to Mrs Wilson, please, and believe me

Affectionately yours, J. F. Jameson.

P.S. I haven't heard the result as to your successor.

ALS (WP, DLC).

From Joseph Ruggles Wilson

Dearest Woodrow N. York July 21/90

I write a line to say that when I last wrote I forgot to let you know that Westerman[1] did not have the book about which I was to enquire: "Universitäts-Kalendar.["] I called at his place the day after my return to N. York, when I was told that he could get me a copy in about 4 to 6 week. I of course did not order it, as you had requested—but I ought to have communicated the fact of failure to you.

What a curious place you have found for a few week's sojourn (curious as to *name* certainly).[2] I doubt whether it will be possible for me to go there (or anywhere in the North) after Aug 12 —for my present purpose is to get to Tennessee by that date. I do hope that you will all have a good time nevertheless. I am pretty well—and am getting quite tired of my vacation!

Congratulating you upon this "cool wave" and with much love to dear Ellie, I am as ever Your affc Father

ALS (WP, DLC).

1 Bernard Westermann, books, 838 Broadway.

2 Sagaponack, near Bridgehampton, Long Island, where the Woodrow Wilsons planned to vacation at a Mrs. Sidney S. Topping's in mid-August.

From George Howe, Jr., and Annie Wilson Howe

Dear Woodrow Columbia, S. C., July 22 1890

I have delayed writing to you, hoping to be able to say to you that I had persuaded Annie to join you and Ellie on the coast. She claims that she has stood the Summer so well up to this date, that she ought not to go away until she finds her health demands it. She has gotten along so much better than usual in the hot weather, and so much better than I expected her to do, that I cannot insist up[on] her going. If I find August is proving too much for her, I will pack her up and send her to you, either on the coast, or at Princeton. Wilson [Howe] leaves next week for the mountains with a party in private conveyances to be gone a month. The rest of us propose to sit it out here. I hope Ellie's leg is better before this.

Annie is out or she would send a message to you.

Love to Ellie and the little folks.

Yrs affly Geo Howe

I have just come in, and must add a word for myself. George does not say how anxious I am to go to see you and Ellie. I would give *anything* to be with you, but feel that as I do not *need* the change, it would not be right for me to take such an expensive trip. With warmest love for you both & kisses for the babies,

Your devoted sister, A.

I cannot tell you what a temptation it is for me to go. I want to see your babies *so badly.*

ALS (WP, DLC).

From Joseph R. Wilson, Jr.

My dearest Brother: Clarksville, Tenn. July 27th 1890

It seems a shame, does it not, that we have not exchanged a single letter this summer? I hardly know where to address this, supposing that you must be either moving to Princeton or already moved. If I send to Middletown, however, it will be forwarded if you have left Yankey land.

I am still a poor news paper reporter, but I see some chance of an early promotion to editorship (local), which will pay me about $75.00 probably, per month. This will be a very respectable salary for a young man. . . .

I have been rather lonely and a little homesick during the last two weeks or so. Father is away, you know, and Kate is away also, so I am left completely alone. By the way, I never have told you anything about Miss Kate and myself, have I? You remember my telling you of the Opera I took part in last winter? Well, we were both in this Opera and a very firm *friendship* grew up between us then. She was just the friend to me that I have so long thought would exactly suit me. You remember Miss Kate Wilson, dont you? She is the leading singer in our choir—the youngest of the three Wilson girls who are in the choir. She is just as sweet and pretty, and as fine a little woman as ever was. Funny to say, father took quite a fancy to her last winter, and said he was not surprised at my liking her so much. Well, we seemed to be so well suited to each other, our dispositions seemed to fit in so nicely together, that we became constant companions. There is no use telling any more—except that I think it possible the day may come when she will change her station in life from "single blessedness to double cussedness," without the usual change of name.[1] I hope, then, that she will remain Kate Wilson all her life. Father, I think, is very well satisfied with the idea, so I am content. This matter is only to be known by you and sister Ellie and the other sisters, remember, so *mum* is the word which is not to be broken. I know you would like Kate if you could know her. I hope some day you will learn to love her, brother, for her own dear sake as well as mine, for I would be unhappy to think that those who are nearest and dearest to me could not dearly love the one whom I choose as my wife. I hope, within the next two or three years at least to have a happy home of my own, presided over by one whom I love with all my heart. It is one of my most pleasant dreams to think of having a home to which I can invite my brother & sisters. With what pride and joy I could welcome them. Oh! if our precious mother could have seen me in my own home before leaving us, how glad I would be, and I pray that our dear and noble father may be able to bless *my* household before he is taken from us. I was twenty three last Sunday, today one week, and I feel that I should think about these things.

My health is pretty good now although I am very thin for me. With unbounded love to you, sister Ellie and the dear children,

Your aff. bro. Joseph.

Please write to me soon.

It seems a little queer that Kate and I were in the choir together for about two or three years before we ever went together at all, does it not?

ALS (WP, DLC).

[1] They were married in 1892.

From Daniel Collamore Heath

Dear Prof. Wilson: Boston, Mass. July 30, 1890.

Yours of the 29th received. If Mr. Dole's book[1] is likely to conflict with yours[2] to any great extent, we better publish it if we are to publish yours, because you will save competition, where it would surely come, if another publisher were to take it and push it for all it is worth. It would interfere much more with yours than if we had them both on our list. It would make no difference to us which we sold, as we should make as much money on one as on the other, and we should push them both for all they are worth. You will remember that Ginn & Co. have six Latin Lessons on their list and two or three books of a kind on other subjects. Such is the case with other publishers. We are going to bring out two series of Arithmetics at the same time, but they will differ just enough to to [*sic*] allow us to put in one series where the other couldn't possibly go, or, in many cases this will be true.

We should like to publish Dale's book, for we think it is a good book, but we are even more anxious to publish yours. Dale's doesn't seem to us a book that will conflict with yours. It is rather for private schools, Sunday schools, girls' schools and Reading Circles than for a regular text-book in grammar Schools and high schools, such as yours will be. There are already a dozen good books of this kind and to this dozen, his is sure to be added.

We believe his will stand less in the way of the sale of yours with us than with another House.

It will be some time before yours will be ready, and we shall have had such an experience with Dale's as will be valuable to you in the making of yours. If you will write us that you will still give us your book, provided we conclude to publish his, we shall decide to take it and we want to take it very much. We believe that for its purpose it is a good book and we should hate to see it go to another House.

Truly yours, D. C. Heath & Co.

TL (WP, DLC) with WWhw notation on env.: "Ans. 5 Aug. '90."

1 Charles Fletcher Dole, *The American Citizen*, which Heath published in 1891.

2 That is, Wilson's projected high school text in American government.

From Augustus N. Sampson

Dear Sir: Boston, August 4, 1890.

Your favor of the 30th of July to the Edison Elec. Mfg., Co., has been referred to us for reply. We desire to say that we control the New England territory for phonographs,[1] and we should like a little more definite information from you as regards the purpose you desire to use this phonograph for, and where you are to take it. You say in your letter that "you are to leave home in about two weeks, and want to obtain a phonograph before you leave." Now we should like to know something more definite than this before we can give you the information you desire. We lease phonographs for $40.00 a year, payable in advance, cylinders $2.00 a dozen and packing, battery and the necessary motor to run it will cost you $15.00 to $20.00 according to the kind you selected.

Please write a little more definitely and we will try to meet your wants. We are,

Yours truly, Aug. N. Sampson General Manager,
New England Phonograph Company.

TLS (WP, DLC) with WWhw notation on env.: "Ans. 5 Aug. '90."

1 An early dictating machine.

From Albert Bushnell Hart

Dear Prof Wilson: Cambridge, August 9, 1890.

The first volume of the Epoch series is now in press.[1] Would it be asking too much of you, if I should send the proofs for your suggestion? You need, of course, pay no attention to typographical or grammatical errors, which the author and proof-reader will pick up. I ask that you will note errors of fact, redundancies and omissions, in text or bibliographies

I am very anxious to make this first volume successful. I understand that Scribners have a similar scheme; but a good volume coming out before them would give us the prestige

Shall you not be in this vicinity during the summer? I shall be away for the four weeks after Aug 23d, but shall be here the rest of the time

Sincerely yours, Albert Bushnell Hart

ALS (WP, DLC) with WWhw notation on env.: "Ans."

[1] Reuben G. Thwaites, *The Colonies, 1492-1750* ("Epochs of American History," Vol. I, New York and London, 1891).

Two Letters from Joseph Ruggles Wilson

Precious Son— Saratoga Springs, N. Y. Aug 14 1890

I am here for a few days, hoping for benefit to a somewhat disordered body. But now my mind is depressed by reason of news from Batesville. Josie telegraphs me that our darling Marion is seriously—if not fatally—ill. He has gone to her. So I believe has Annie. It was simply impossible for me to take such a journey in my present condition of health. So I must wait in anxiety. Neither can it be possible for *you* to go to Batesville at this time. I thought it right, however, to let you know the state of the fact so far as I know the same myself. I expect to go down to N. York (if the "strike" will permit) on Saturday next, or Monday. And then to start at once for Tennessee where I shall be *nearer* to Marion than I now am—which will be a little comfort.

Not having your last letter at hand, I cannot recall the name of your L. Island P. O. So I send this to Middletown for being forwarded.

Love to dear Ellie, and for yourself all that can be expressed.

In haste your Most affc Father

Dearest Woodrow— Saratoga Springs, N. Y. Aug. 16 1890

I wrote you as to our beloved Marion's illness. It turned out to be far more serious than I had dreamed of. Josie telegraphs me that *she died* on the 14th and was buried on the 15th (yesterday!)[.] Oh is not this a bereavement, indeed? Not indeed for her, the now sainted darling, but for us who survive! I dare not trust myself to write much about it. The children, what shall become of them.[1] Dr & Mrs. Long[2] will of course do what is possible in the premises—and I shall hurry home to confer with Josie who knows the situation. I shall require your counsel, my loved one, in this emergency.

I again direct to Middletown hoping the letter will be promptly forwarded.

Love to dear daughter Ellie.

Your loving loving Father

ALS (WP, DLC).

[1] Joseph Leland, William Blake, Wilson Woodrow, and Jessie Kennedy (identified more fully in WW to EAW, Aug. 13, 1886, n. 1, Vol. 5).

[2] The Rev. Dr. Isaac Jasper Long and Callie Kennedy Long. Dr. Long was president of Arkansas College in Batesville. Mrs. Long was A. Ross Kennedy's sister.

ADDENDA

A Private Notebook

[c. Sept. 1, 1873-June 22, 1875]

Inscribed on back flyleaf (WWhw):

"T. W. Wilson Private"

Contents: (all WWhw except for a few WWsh additions):

(a) Notes taken in second semester of Prof. Charles Phillips's course at Davidson College in algebra and geometry.

(b) Synopsis of sermon by Prof. James F. Latimer, April 26, 1874, printed below.

(c) "Journal. May 3rd 1874," printed below.

(d) "Notes on a sermon by Revd. Professor [J. Monroe] Anderson May 10th [1874]." Page blank except for heading.

(e) Greek exercises written c. Dec. 11, 1874-c. Feb. 1, 1875.

(f) Excerpt from "The Prayer," printed in full in Vol. 1, pp. 33-35.

(g) Latin exercises, written May 13-June 22, 1875.

(WC, NjP).

Excerpts from a Private Notebook

April 26th '74.

The Rev. Prof Latimer[1] preached a sermon this morning that makes me think all the trouble is within.

Synopsis of the Sermon.

Micah 6th Chapter 8 verse, especially these clauses: "He hath showed thee, O man, . . . what the Lord requireth of thee . . . to walk humbly with thy God."

1st The contrast between the service imposed on the offending Jew and that required of the children of God. The Jew required to do outward service. No outward service will avail for the man of God or sinner now, only heart service can avail with God. What is it to walk with God? (Cruden's[2] deffinition quoted) 1st It is a living in sweet communion with God. This communion was lost by Adam's fall. And, as it w'd have been more than presumption for Adam to attempt the tree of communion, wh. God had so strictly gaurded by angels and the flaming sword of fire on every side, so it is more than presumption for us to try to walk with God until our sins are expiated and our peace made with him. By Christ alone are we required to walk with God.

2nd Walking with God is the *result* of expiated sin and *not* the means thereto.

3rd God requires us to walk humbly. Humility is the sine qua non of religion. A man must feel that he is nothing in himself, that he has nothing that can recommend him to God. He requires that they come with nothing in their hands, to humble themselves before his throne and take Christ as their portion. Rock of Ages quoted. Not only must the sinner but the Christian be humble. It is true that the Xians' reward is in proportion to their faithfulness but it is all of grace. He must feel that his righteousness is only imputed to him by Christ. They must be humble 1st because they are proud. And pride deprives the Xian of his peace & makes him trust in himself more than in Christ. 2nd Because he trusts in his own strength not in Christ. God looks tenderly upon the sins of his Saints but it is only because they ask forgiveness in X name. The Xian feels sorrow for his sins because he knows he is proud. Christ is alone his plea. They must remember that their strength is only weakness. "I am the vine[;] ye are the branches &c. . . , without me ye can do nothing," but "I can do all things through X wh. strengtheneth me."

If Xians would humble themselves & walk with God, what a triumph would the Gospel have. The success of the Church. The difficulties of those who do not believe that the gospel can be spread over the world are because they do not trust God's strength. All the sources of Heaven are pledged in the strugle. Xians are weak because they do not want to believe what they cannot understand. "God works in a misterious way" &c[.] As the children of Israel when persued by Pharaoh were ordered to go forward when they could see no way for them to go and God opened the Red Sea, So we must not stumble at difficulties. The Xian is lead to humble himself when he considers the misterious providences of God. He takes whole families within the fold & rejects whole families. He takes an outcast of a family & leaves a darling &c &c &c. Grace is generally most abundant to the temporally poor. The transcendental doctrines, The doctrine of X the Son of God, of the trinity &c are the stumbling stones to those who require reason for every-thing. Because we cannot see these doctrines it is no want of reason to humble ourselves and walk with God where reason can't walk. We should not make reason all but at times trust without sight. How much fear we would spare ourselves if we were to humble ourselves and trust all to God. Though the way be dark & we see nothing, understand nothing, we should put our hands in His and and [*sic*] trusting in Him walk with with [*sic*] him. We ought to humble ourselves because he humbled himself and commanded us to take his yoke upon us &c.

[1] The Rev. James F. Latimer, Professor of Psychology, Logic, and Ethics at Davidson College.

[2] Alexander Cruden (1701-1770), whose *A Complete Concordance to the Holy Scriptures of the Old and New Testament . . .* (London, 1738) was reprinted into the twentieth century.

◇

Journal. May 3rd 1874

"For in that he himself hath suffered being tempted, he is able to succour them that are tempted." Heb. 2.18.

I am now in my seventeenth year and it is sad, when looking over my past life to see how few of those seventeen years I have spent in the fear of God, and how much time I have spent in the service of the Devil. Although having professed Christ's name some time ago,[1] I have increased very little in grace and have done almost nothing for the Savior's Cause here below. O, how hard it is to do that which ought to be my greatest delight! *If God will give me the grace I will try to serve him from this time on, and will endevour to attain nearer and nearer to perfection.* The following is a copy of Dr. Cabbots [Cabot's] letter in "Stepping Heavenward,"[2] parts of it, at least; "Make your complaint, tell him how obscure everything still looks to you, and beg Him to complete your cure. He may see fit to try your faith and patience by delaying this completion; but meanwhile you are safe in his presence, and while led by his hand, he will excuse the mistakes you make, and pity your faults. He has a reason for everything he does. Having been pardoned by your God and Savior, the next thing you have to do is to show your gratitude for this infinite favor by consecrating yourself entirely to him, body, soul, and spirit. It is true that such an act of consecration on your part may involve no little future discipline and correction. As soon as you become the Lord's by your own deliberate and conscious act, he will begin that process of sanctification which is to make you as holy as He is holy, perfect as He is perfect. He becomes at once your Physician as well as your dearest and best friend, but he will use no painful remedy that can be avoided. Remember that it is his *will* that you should be sanctified, and that the work of making you holy is his not yours. If you find, in the course of daily events, that your self-consecration is not perfect—that is, that your will revolts at his will—do not be discouraged, but fly to your Savior and stay in his presence till you obtain the spirit in which he cried in his hour of anguish, 'Father, if Thou be willing, remove this cup from me; nevertheless, not my will but thine be done.['] Every time you do this it will be easier to do it. Just think of honor and the joy of having your will one with the Divine will, and so becoming changed into Christ image from glory to glory! In reading the bible I advise you to choose detached passages, or even one verse a day rather than whole chapters. *Study* every word, ponder and pray over it till you have got out of it all the truth it contains. As to the other devotional reading, it is better to settle down on a few favorite authors, and read their works over, and over, and over until you have digested their thoughts and made them your own.

["]You can will to choose for your associates those who are most devout and holy.

["]You can will to read books that will stimulate you in your Christian life rather than those that merely amuse.

["]You can will to spend much time in prayer, *without regard to your frame at the moment.*

["]You can will to prefer a religion of principle to one of mere feeling; in other words to obey the will of God when no comfortable glow of emotion accompanies your obedience.

["]You cannot will to possess the spirit of Christ; that must come as his gift, but you can choose to study his life and imitate it. If the thought of such self-denial is repugnant to you, remember that it is enough for the disciple to be as his Lord. And let me assure you that as you penetrate the labyrinth of life in pursuit of Christian duty, you will often be surprized and charmed by meeting your Master himself amid its windings and turnings, and receive his soul-inspiring smile. Or, I should rather say, you will always meet him, wherever you go.["]

1 See the extract from the Minutes of the Session of the First Presbyterian Church of Columbia, S. C., July 5, 1873, Vol. 1, pp. 22-23.

2 Wilson is quoting from Elizabeth Payson Prentiss, *Stepping Heavenward* (New York, 1869), pp. 100-106.

From Janet Woodrow Wilson

April [May] 26th [1874] Columbia S. C.

My darling Boy, Tuesday morning.

Lucinda, the house girl, has been sick for several days, so that I have no one to stay in the house with me at night, and I have been spending the nights over at Dr. Howe's,[1] and the days at home. Dr. G. takes us[2] back and forth in his buggy night and morning–they G. & A. are just as sweet and nice as can be, and it is very pleasant to be so much with them, but it cuts up my time so that I accomplish nothing. Especially does it make it impossible for me to get my letters written, which has been my chief regret in the arrangement. I expected confidently to send you a letter before this and now I must be satisfied to send you a poor little note for this time. I hope to write you again very shortly however.

I sent you $5. the other day–in my last letter. Did you get it dear? I feel a little uneasy about it, as I had to send the letter to the P. O. by Hardy, the old gardener, and he did not seem to understand very well what he was about. I hope it reached you safely however.

I had a note from your dear father yesterday.[3] I am sorry to hear that there is still a possibility that the Ass. may refuse to let him off from here. He heard that the Committee on Seminary matters were going to report to the Ass. *against* the acceptance of the resignation. I feel *very* anxious to hear the result.[4] But we must be happy, dear, whatever is decided, though it will be a great trial now to be forced to stay, after coming around to the belief that it is right & best to go to W. We must leave the matter with God, dear, as your father has been enabled to do. If we can only know what is *right* we can easily submit.

My dear boy, I *am* anxious about your cold. If your cough continues, you will have to come home. I feel miserably anxious about these constant colds. What can be the reason for your taking cold so frequently? Write again at once, please, if only half a dozen lines, and let me know how you are.

Good bye my sweet boy. I love you with my whole heart, and long to see your dear face again. Josie joins me in warmest love to dearest brother. Your own Mother

ALS (WP, DLC) with WWhw notation on env.: "Rec'd. May 28th/74." This letter is postmarked May 27.

[1] George Howe, Jr., M.D., who had married Annie Wilson in 1873. The date of their marriage given in n. 1, p. 4, Vol. 1, as 1876 is incorrect.

[2] That is, Mrs. Wilson and her son, Joseph R., Jr., referred to later in this letter as "Josie."

[3] Dr. Wilson was attending the General Assembly of the southern Presbyterian Church in Columbus, Mississippi.

[4] Dr. Wilson was eager to resign his professorship at the Columbia Theological Seminary in order to accept a call from the First Presbyterian Church of Wilmington, North Carolina. In fact, the General Assembly did accept Dr. Wilson's resignation from the seminary. See JWW to WW, May 20, 1874, n. 1, p. 50, Vol. 1, and WW to EAW, Oct. 12, 1884, n. 2, p. 350, Vol. 3.

From Janet Woodrow Wilson[1]

Arden Park [N. C.] Hotel,
My darling Son, Wednesday night Sep. 19, '83.

The enclosed came today.[2] I cannot send it to you without enclosing a line, to tell you that I was very, very glad, to hear the good news contained in your note written in the cars.[3] I was not very much surprised, for I thought I could discern that she cared for you–when she was here. She seemed to me so sweet, so modest, so bright and intelligent, that it was impossible not to love her–and now that she is my precious boy's promised wife, I shall love her very dearly. And now your heart is at rest, you will be able to give yourself to the work before you, with all your heart–and I have no fears for the result.

Your father's letter from B[altimore]. received tells me that he found the St James hotel closed, & went to the Mt. Vernon, where you found him if you reached B. in time. For fear you have missed him, I will quote part of his letter received today: "I have seen Leighton Wilson, and also–accompanied by Dr. W[ilson].–Prof. Gildersleeve of the University here. They will both take a special interest in W.–the former for many reasons–the latter because he and James Woodrow were classmates, and are friends, and because of *me*, he was kind enough to say–and, as Leighton Wilson added, "You will, sir, also because of the young man himself, who is an exceptional student." ["]There will be no difficulty about his getting good plain board at $25 or $30 dollars a month."

If I were you, dear, I would go to Dr Leighton at once, and he will be able & willing to help you look for a boarding place–if, that is, your father did not engage it for you. . . .

Lovingly your own Mother

ALS (WP, DLC).

1 This recently discovered letter is the enclosure mentioned as missing in WW to ELA, Sept. 22, 1883, Vol. 2, pp. 437-38.

2 Wilson identifies this in the letter just cited.

3 That is, that Ellen and Woodrow had become engaged just before Wilson left Asheville.

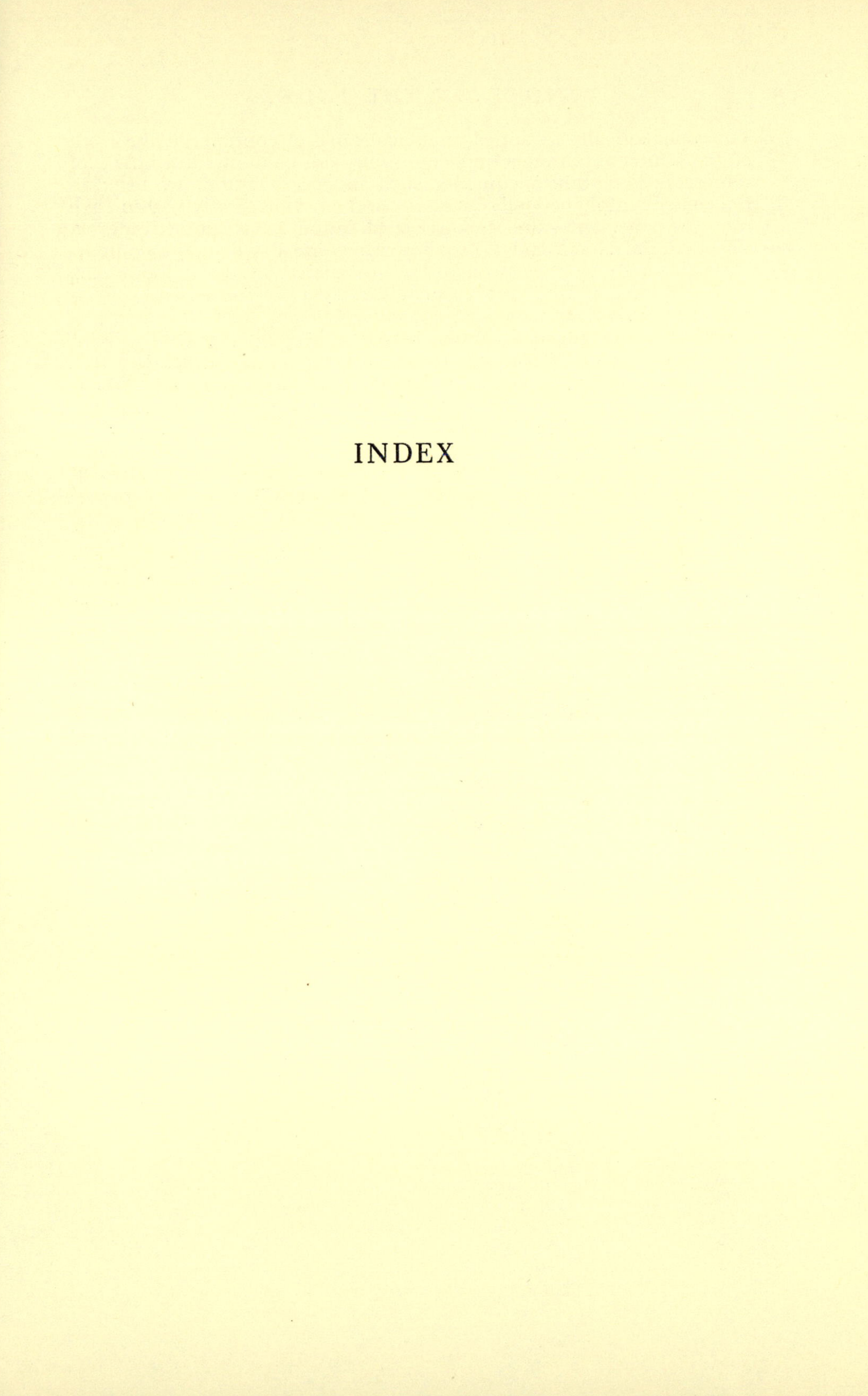

INDEX

NOTE ON THE INDEX

THE alphabetically arranged analytical table of contents at the front of the volume eliminates duplication, in both contents and index, of references to certain documents, such as letters. Letters are listed in the contents alphabetically by name, and chronologically within each name by page. The subject matter of all letters is, of course, indexed. The Editorial Notes and Wilson's writings are listed in the contents chronologically by page. In addition, the subject matter of both categories is indexed. The index covers all references to books and articles mentioned in text or notes. Footnotes are indexed. Page references to footnotes which place a comma between the page number and "n" cite both text and footnote, thus: "624,n3." On the other hand, absence of the comma indicates reference to the footnote only, thus: "55n2"—the page number denoting where the footnote appears. The letter "n" without a following digit signifies an unnumbered descriptive-location note.

An asterisk before an index reference designates identification or other particular information. Re-identification and repetitive annotation have been minimized to encourage use of these starred references. Where the identification appears in an earlier volume, it is indicated thus: "*1:212,n3." Therefore a page reference standing without a preceding volume number is invariably a reference to the present volume. The index supplies the fullest known forms of names, and, for the Wilson and Axson families, relationships as far down as cousins. Persons referred to in the text by nicknames or shortened forms of names can be identified by reference to entries for these forms of the names.

A sampling of the opinions and comments of Wilson and Ellen Axson Wilson covers their more personal views, while broad, general headings in the main body of the index cover impersonal subjects. Occasionally opinions expressed by a correspondent are indexed where these appear to supplement or to reflect views expressed by Wilson or by Ellen Axson Wilson in documents which are missing.

INDEX